P9-APA-035

THE COMPLETE ARBITRAGE DESKBOOK

Other Titles in the Irwin Library of Investment and Finance

Quantitative Business Valuation
by Jay B. Abrams

High-Yield Bonds
by Theodore Barnhill, William Maxwell, and Mark Shenkman

Pricing and Managing Exotic and Hybrid Options
By Vineer Bhansali

Convertible Securities
by John P. Calamos

Risk Management and Financial Derivatives
by Satyajit Das

The Handbook of Credit Derivatives
by Jack Clark Francis, Joyce Frost, and J. Gregg Whittaker

Asset Allocation, 2nd edition
by Roger Gibson

Active Portfolio Management, 2nd edition
by Richard Grinold and Ronald Kahn

Equity Management
by Bruce Jacobs and Kenneth Levy

The Hedge Fund Handbook
by Stefano Lavinio

Implementing Credit Derivatives
by Israel Nelken

Pricing, Hedging, and Trading Exotic Options
by Israel Nelken

Valuing a Business, 4th edition
by Shannon Pratt, Robert Reilly, and Robert P. Schweihs

Valuing Small Business and Professional Practices, 3rd edition
by Shannon Pratt, Robert Reilly, and Robert P. Schweihs

The Handbook of Advanced Business Valuation
by Robert F. Reilly and Robert P. Schweihs

Valuing Intangible Assets
by Robert F. Reilly and Robert P. Schweihs

Managing Financial Risk
by Charles W. Smithson

Global Investment Risk Management
By Ezra Zask

THE COMPLETE ARBITRAGE DESKBOOK

STEPHANE REVERRE

New York Chicago San Francisco Lisbon London Madrid
Mexico City Milan New Delhi San Juan Seoul Singapore
Sydney Toronto

Library of Congress Cataloging-in-Publication Data
Reverre, Stephane.
The complete arbitrage deskbook / by Stephane Reverre.
p. cm.
ISBN 0-07-135995-8
1. Arbitrage. I. Title.

HG4521 .R48 2001
332.64′5—dc21 00-048945

McGraw-Hill
A Division of The ***McGraw-Hill*** *Companies*

1 2 3 4 5 6 7 8 9 0 DOC/DOC 0 9 8 7 6 5 4 3 2 1

ISBN 0-07-135995-8

This book was set in 10.5pt/13pt PalmSprings by Keyword Typesetting Services Ltd, Wallington, Surrey.

Printed and bound by R. R. Donnelley & Sons Company.

This book is printed on recycled, acid-free paper containing a minimum of 50% recycled, de-inked fiber.

To Francoise and Ulysse
for their patience and support.

To my parents and family
for all they taught me.

CONTENTS

PREFACE

The first and foremost question to ask about a new book, and one that I have been asked repeatedly, is "Who is the target reader?" In the particular case at hand, the answer is relatively easy: Considering its heavy algebraic content, this book is written for junior professionals on capital markets, or nonprofessionals with a serious interest in Wall Street. Both groups will find here the basic knowledge necessary to make informed arbitrage decisions, at least in the world of equities.

This precise focus does not mean that another public could not find attractive substance in these lines. There is a lot to deal with, sometimes with painful details, and a weakly motivated reader would probably see less value overall. I have tried, however, to address this concern by keeping some parts entirely algebra-free, for example, Part I. Meant to introduce the subject and the products, it could very well be seen as sufficient for anybody interested in getting a thorough introduction. Along the same lines, Part III is essentially a qualitative description of well-known arbitrage situations and could also be considered educational in its own right.

In short, even if the mathematical treatment was a necessity to achieve the goal of a rigorous coverage, I hope to have done an adequate job at laying down much more than that, enough to keep even a mildly technical reader interested.

This hope is in fact rooted in what I believe makes this book unique. I am not the first one to write about equity products or arbitrage techniques. Indeed, arbitrage is the abc of modern trading, and as such is present in one form or another in virtually all books on financial markets. The originality here is the fact that the present work is *entirely* dedicated to arbitrage, precisely *equity* arbitrage. If I have found countless descriptions more or less theoretical of arbitrage on fixed-income instruments, I have found very little on the equity side. If there is an abundant literature on relative-value trading, notably risk arbitrage, I found very little on index arbitrage, and very little trying to tie together the many strategies practiced throughout the marketplace. Therefore to the best of my knowledge, there is no precedent in offering a comprehensive view of equity arbitrage, including a theoretical presentation as well as a detailed mathematical development.

In addition, the treatment of such-and-such technique is generally focused on a single market, typically the United States. Naturally for many this is a natural consequence of the size and maturity of the U.S. financial markets, but this is hardly a satisfactory justification because foreign markets, albeit smaller in size, would be far more interesting if they were indeed less mature specifically because trading would yield higher margins. Alternatively, one could argue that there is no need to expand a given idea to foreign markets because if it works in one place it probably works in others. Unfortunately this is not necessarily true. I have had the chance in my professional experience to be exposed to several of the largest markets, always in the context of an arbitrage activity. I found the differences between these markets fascinating, and I realized progressively that even if the tools were essentially the same, local particularities were a defining factor in the existence and shape of trading opportunities. For example, in European markets, fiscal arbitrage has traditionally been the bread and butter of index arbitrageurs, whereas opportunities of that type are almost unknown in Japan or the United States. Hence the second differentiating factor of this book: its international scope. The point is naturally not to propose enough details to enable the reader to trade indifferently in any of the markets covered, but rather to offer insights from diverse backgrounds as a way to uncover the universe of what is possible. For example, a situation in which interest rates diverge by up to 0.50 percent between domestic and off-shore institutions is extremely counterintuitive; still, this is exactly what happened in Japan repeatedly because of its domestic liquidity crisis.

Finally I believe that the last important aspect of this work is an attempt to unify miscellaneous techniques under a generic umbrella. An arbitrage is a convergence, and that simple fact dictates the entire framework in which an opportunity should be evaluated and managed. I tried my best to develop that concept and the surrounding framework. And, as before, the purpose is not to answer all the questions, just the most important ones. The goal is to "educate" in the traditional sense: In the end, the reader should be able to ask more questions than those presented here and have a fair sense of where to look for the answers.

Note, however, that if I tried to include as much substance as possible, there are many things that this book is not. For one, it is not a trader's user's manual. In other words, nobody will gain from these lines a precious knowledge that could be turned into an immediate profit. The trading ideas exposed are always well known and practiced actively. As I mention on many occasions, experience is the best predictor of success on a trading floor, and you cannot learn about that in a book. Another important point is that this book is far from exhaustive, even in its mathematical presentation. In the interest of space and time I have left out numerous instruments, such as equity-linked swaps. Along the same lines there are many variations and flavors of arbitrage that I don't mention, and certainly some that I don't even know about. Again the idea is to present an introduction solid enough that readers will be able to form their own judgments in due course. Finally, I am not even sure this work can be considered a "reference." Despite the many concepts that have a general application, the vocabulary or specific treatment of certain ideas may differ, for example, from a highly specialized hedge fund with only a few traders to a huge trading floor in New York. After all, nobody has ever been able to tell what the fair price of a stock should be at a given time, so don't expect too many absolute truths on Wall Street in general.

Given the objective of a broad-yet-rigorous presentation of equity arbitrage for a potential future practitioner, it was necessary to start from the very beginning on many fronts. Naturally, the notion of arbitrage is defined and discussed in detail, but financial instruments used in the implementation of a position are "dissected" as well, even those traditionally considered simple, like stocks. The reason for that choice is based on my experience as a junior trader. Everybody knows what a stock is, but few people really understand the intricacies of fiscal arbitrage, which is nothing more than a simple stock loan if you think about it. It took me a few months to get a sense of what my job would be as an arbitrageur, and years to painfully master the zillions of small details. My intention is to bring to light enough of these details that a reader will save considerable time in climbing the experience curve.

Part II of the book is built around the same idea. Valuation and risk analysis are absolutely critical in the life and success of a professional trader. Too often are these performed by a beginner without a clear overview of the purpose they serve and of their underlying principles. The emphasis here, therefore, is on those goals and principles, with the development of the algebra as an application exercise. Finally Part III is meant to bring all the concepts together. Through the examination of actual examples and practical situations, the goal is to achieve an integrated view of arbitrage opportunities, precisely as a trader would see them.

PART I
THEORY AND TOOLS

1

INTRODUCTION

WHAT IS ARBITRAGE?

Arbitrage is "the simultaneous purchase and sale of the same, or essentially similar, security in two different markets for advantageously different prices."[1] The word should be read in a very general sense because both legs of the arbitrage can be a number of securities or derivatives.

The definition essentially underlines two structural features of these transactions. First, the operations on the different instruments must be simultaneous. This characteristic is a direct consequence of the fact that arbitrage opportunities must be risk-free and are consequently short-lived. Secondly, the securities should be the same or essentially similar. If we broadened the scope, we would include securities that are not actually similar but are believed to behave in a very similar way. This similarity in essence is an insurance contract, and by construction, it eliminates all and every risk beyond immediate execution. This idea is commonly described as the *law of one price*, and it is

---

[1] Zivi Bodie, Alex Kane, and Alan J. Marcus, *Investments*, 4th ed. (New York: Irwin/McGraw-Hill, 1999), p. 307. The common term *arbitrage* is in fact used in many more situations. See, for example, Jochen E. M. Wilhelm, *Arbitrage Theory* (New York: Springer-Verlag, 1985), which makes a distinction between *arbitration* ("the search for the lowest cost in achieving a certain intended financial position"), *spreads* (simultaneous sale and purchase, i.e., *our* arbitrage), and *free lunches* ("turning from one combination of assets to another one which is equivalent but has a lower market price"). In this terminology, we are primarily concerned with spreads.

used extensively in the context of derivative pricing: If two portfolios have the same payoff at maturity, their price should be equal today, and if they are not, they can be expected to converge back toward equality.

Therefore, a close examination of arbitrage should focus primarily on these two aspects, execution and convergence. Understanding how we can execute requires an examination of why opportunities appear in the first place. In the context of mature financial markets, efficiency is a given, and conventional wisdom states explicitly that arbitrage opportunities should not exist. Naturally markets would not be efficient without arbitrageurs to make them efficient, but we need to understand specifically how discrepancies occur. In addition, the convergence issue requires us to examine the notion of maturity: If the securities are actually fairly priced and similar, we should be able to exit from the arbitrage at some point in the future. This may be a known—for example, the expiry of a futures—or unknown date, but at that time both legs should come together. In some cases the convergence is embedded in the system—a futures contract, for example—but in many instances it is more assumed than it is certain. The remote chance that it does not materialize is by far the biggest risk faced by all arbitrageurs. Finally, we need to consider the implications of safely carrying this position for a period of time that is typically uncertain. In some instances we know an upper bound for the time to exit—derivative expiry, merger effective date—but we do not know if an opportunity will not allow us, or an unexpected event force us, to exit before.

In fact, the convergence problem entirely dictates the appropriate methodology to evaluate and manage arbitrage positions, and that is precisely what we will try to demonstrate. All risks are subordinated to it, and by nature this is the only one we cannot and do not want to hedge. For example, consider the case of index arbitrage: The convergence could not be more certain, and the arbitrageur's risk management is then focused on "secondary" risks—typically interest rates, dividends, and so on. At the other end of the spectrum, a pair trader takes a position on stocks under a fairly optimistic assumption that their prices will remain highly correlated in the future. In that case interest rates and dividends do not matter much; profit and losses have to be conservatively evaluated based on market prices as opposed to a theoretical relationship, and the primary measure of risk is the behavior of the spread between the companies considered.

Consequently the natural path to follow is to start with a closer examination of the convergence issue. From there we will examine the hypothesis of market efficiency and its implications, and we will propose a certain number of necessary conclusions about valuation and risk, developed in Part 2.

CONTEXT

Money Managers versus Proprietary Traders

An essential prerequisite for this discussion is that it occur within the context of professional trading. We want to take the perspective of a proprietary trader in a large financial institution, typically the trading subsidiary of a large bank.[2] We cannot emphasize this particularity enough because it has fundamental implications in several respects: incentives and performance evaluation, information flows, capital availability, and financing costs.

Proprietary traders are entrusted with money from their employer and allowed to take defined risks in order to generate as much profit as possible. Their compensation packages are generally indexed very directly to their performance, usually after costs. The fact that the capital used is proprietary means that this money is not an investment from a set of investors looking for the best use of their excess resources. It is borrowed by the trader using the balance sheet of the institution. To understand the implications of this situation, consider in contrast a typical investment manager at a mutual fund, insurance company, or pension fund. The fund is an investment vehicle with a clear strategy. Investors hope for and expect a return, but these expectations do not have any cost per se. Obviously, poor performance will make it harder to attract new clients and may eventually decrease assets under management, but the manager does not have to actually pay to attract funds—leaving marketing costs aside. A proprietary trader, on the other hand, incurs financing charges as a true cost. If both the trader and fund manager buy a stock, hold it for six months and sell it at a

[2] In the United States, until recently, the 1933 Glass-Steagall Act strictly restricted the type of activities that banks, securities firms, and insurance companies might engage in. As a result, banks used to set up subsidiaries to engage in trading activities. Over the past few years, however, legislators have significantly weakened the act's original provisions. See, Bernard Shull, "The Separation of Banking and Commerce in the United States: An Examination of Principal Issues," for example, *Financial Markets, Institutions and Instruments*, vol. 8, no. 3, New York University Salomon Center, 1999. A similar regulation exists in Japan due to the heavy influence of the post–World War II U.S. regulators, but there is not one in Europe.

price equal to the entry price, the manager exhibits only a mediocre performance—"not my fault because the market did not move"—while the trader would show an actual loss equal to the financing cost over six months.

In fact, the cost is higher because the financial institution carrying the borrowing on its balance sheet puts a fraction of its capital at risk. International regulations and banking practices require banks to match part of their risky assets with equity to protect creditors, that is, depositors. For every $1 borrowed, the bank has to allocate, for example, $0.10 of its tier-one capital, which will not be available to back any other opportunity. As a result of this commitment, the bank will ask the trader for a compensation commensurate with the risk taken and with its cost of equity. Say that this return is 15 percent. Then $0.10 of capital must return $0.015 to pay for the capital consumption, in addition to the financing charge. Overall, the interest rate will be increased by 1.5 percent on the original $1. This is a complex description of a very intuitive fact: As a risk taker, the trader is required to generate returns above the risk-free rate.[3] By contrast, investment companies are also required to maintain a capital base, but the protection against market movement is not a concern anymore because investors are using such vehicles explicitly for the purpose of accessing the market.[4]

One of the most fundamental differences between traders and money managers is in fact that managers are usually benchmarked. Consider again that both of them buy and hold a stock for six months. At this point they sell it at a loss, say, 5 percent. If the broader market lost 5 percent over the same period, the fund manager has fared honorably—"not my fault, in line with the market." On the other side, the trader shows a loss of 5 percent, no matter what. Schematically, because they are benchmarked, money managers do not have any exposure to broad market movements. Naturally this is a very shortsighted view because it does not apply to all fund managers; neither does the opposite describe all traders. Hedge funds specifically are notable exceptions: Because of their particular nature, most are only remotely benchmarked and thus carry a full market risk. However, for

[3] This discussion is an introduction to the notion of cost of capital and solvency ratios. Both will be discussed in more detail in Part 2.

[4] Indeed, for investment companies the concerns are of two types: disclosure, to ensure that fund managers are following their mandate and maintaining appropriate risk levels, and protection of assets, against fraudulent activity and misappropriation.

the purpose of our introduction, this schematic description captures the essence of the issues at hand.

An interesting corollary of this difference is the fact that traders are usually marked to market systematically every day, while money managers may not be subject to such stringent reporting requirements. Of course, virtually all fund managers compute and publish a net asset value every day, but full disclosure to investors in most cases is required only periodically—for example, every quarter for mutual funds. By contrast, trading positions are reviewed much more frequently by risk managers and head traders, with the consequence that a particular strategy has to be justified sooner if it takes too long to turn a profit. In addition, because in many cases marketing material for money managers is based on month-end data, it is easier for them to use window dressing to improve performance on paper.[5]

The second set of structural differences materializes with regard to information flows. For obvious reasons, professional traders have better access to research and real-time data than most investors, and that applies to some extent to institutional investors as well. For them, the costs related to information systems are directly charged against a fund's return. By contrast, on a trading floor, it is much easier for traders to get sophisticated information because of economies of scale in disseminating this information throughout the entire firm. For example, all major players maintain a quantitative and research department whose sole function is to crunch numbers continuously with a decent amount of brain—and computing—power. These resources are naturally very expensive and not available to all.[6]

Finally, probably the most important structural difference is the availability of capital and its cost. As we will see, it is not uncommon for arbitrage positions, particularly index arbitrage, to reach several billion dollars in nominal. These amounts can be borrowed in minutes at consistent rates—typically the LIBOR[7] with no difficulty whatsoever for a trader in a large bank. This flexibility is critical in scaling positions and risks in relation to market opportunities, and it is available only to the largest names and the most creditworthy institutions.

---

[5] *Window dressing* refers to artificial trading activity designed to move prices of certain securities ahead of a particularly important date, typically month end or year end.

[6] Naturally this presentation is a simplification. Large institutional investors have adequate resources to compete with large trading firms, but it remains true that the underlying economic model and the ability to absorb costs are not the same.

[7] London Interbank Offered Rate. See Chapter 4 for a complete description.

For all these reasons, arbitrage tends to be practiced on a large scale by a few qualified professionals, typically hedge fund managers and proprietary traders. It is generally beyond the scope of most other institutional investors, and even if it were not, the structural features we listed above would virtually prevent them from competing with more specialized players. We do not mean to imply that it is the secret garden of a select few, but that only a limited number of people in the broad population of investors have the resources to aggressively and systematically pursue arbitrage opportunities.[8] Index arbitrage is a typical example: Optimistically, there are no more than a dozen traders actively involved in it on any major market.

Arbitrage and Competitive Advantage

If indeed arbitrageurs are relatively few in number with unlimited access to capital, we need to ask what type of competitive advantage is needed to succeed.

The first one to spot an opportunity is probably the only one to profit significantly from it; therefore, *competitive advantage* here means primarily being the fastest to push the button. Consider, for example, that all arbitrageurs agree on what is an opportunity and what is not, as would—almost—be the case for an index arbitrage or risk arbitrage situation. Would all of them rush to trade at the same time? In an ideal world where taxes and credit risks do not exist, the answer to this question is most probably yes. In reality, because of differences in tax treatment or costs related to poor credit ratings, some arbitrageurs appear to enjoy structural advantages. For example, taxes would change the amount of expected net dividends over a future period, and credit ratings would change the financing rate until the next futures expiry, both of them affecting the fair value of an index arbitrageur. The example of taxes is in fact very meaningful because it is truly discriminative among market participants. In Japan, for example, domestic and offshore entities have different transaction and

---

[8] Indeed, it *was* for a long time truly performed by a select few, and thus it was a well-kept secret. See, for example, the description of arbitrageurs in *Risk Arbitrage II* from Guy P. Waser-Pratte (Salomon Brothers Center for the Study of Financial Institutions, Graduate School of Business Administration, New York University, 1982): a "cliquish band of specialists." The 1987 crash and the resulting bad press for proprietary traders in general forced numerous institutions out of these strategies. In addition, the reporting requirements instituted afterward called for much more transparency and eventually brought to light what had been thus far a restricted gentlemen's club.

dividend taxes, which introduces a structural bias in trading parameters.

However, structural differences of this nature are usually fairly easy to bypass because large institutions have the financial and operational ability to converge toward the optimal structure—legal and otherwise—to take advantage of market opportunities. Thus arbitrageurs in our context usually stand on common ground, and these biases become minor. In addition, most of the time such differences are actual impediments to trading—transaction or financing costs, for example. Therefore, their net effect is to eliminate players from the field while those remaining do not have any long-standing competitive advantage relative to their peers.

If we assume then that structural differences cannot protect an arbitrageur's competitive advantage for long, it is natural to ask if it can be based on superior information. If, for example, dividend estimates are diverging between two firms—even if their tax treatment is similar—their respective index fair values will diverge, in turn affecting their trading strategies on index arbitrage. From there one firm could possibly realize a higher return because it is consistently right about its dividends expectations. However, although theoretically possible, this phenomenon is short-lived because it is mean reverting. Assuming, for example, one index arbitrageur adopts an extreme stance and sets dividend expectations to zero, he or she will compute a future fair value much higher than that of the market. As a result, he or she will see the future's price being much too low in the market compared to his or her model, and he or she will be liquidating his or her position as fast as possible.[9] In front of such an apparent mispricing, any rational person would spot an anomaly and review the underlying trading assumptions, with the probable result of questioning dividend assumptions and revising them upward. In the reverse case where dividends would have been too high, the exact opposite effect would have been triggered, and the same trader would not have been able to buy stocks fast enough.

The result of this short discussion is to complete our profile of typical arbitrageurs. Not only is this group small and highly specialized, it is also somewhat undifferentiated with regard to market opportunities and critical parameters. For example, if a large institution

---

[9] Index arbitrageurs buy futures and sell stocks when the index future is priced too low in the market compared to its theoretical value. More details on that in the last part of this chapter. The future's fair value is the difference between the future's theoretical price and the price of its underlying index.

decided to start an arbitrage activity in Japan, one of its first steps would probably be to open a local subsidiary to circumvent the taxation issue, and it would engage rapidly in peripheral activities to guarantee its arbitrage desk an adequate support. At this point it would place itself only on equal footing with other players. Therefore, differentiation—and competitive advantage—on an arbitrage desk resides primarily in execution skills, at least when the convergence is fairly certain.[10] This does not mean that arbitrageurs *always* intervene at the same time and for the same typical profit. For example, position limits, by placing constraints unrelated to the market, may have the effect of restraining a particular trader when all the others are as aggressive as ever. Nevertheless, in general, arbitrageurs tend to intervene at the same time, and for probably the same expected profit, reinforcing the need for better execution.

Arbitrageurs versus Investors

There is one more important piece that needs to be incorporated in this preliminary discussion. Arbitrageurs have their own agenda, and in many cases their incentives are not aligned to those of the investor community at large. We will argue later that the presence of arbitrageurs is usually a good sign for investors because it indicates that market institutions—in terms of execution, settlement, and liquidity—are functioning properly. However, this does not mean that investors necessarily consider it a blessing in and of itself.

It is true that arbitrageurs bring prices closer to efficiency, but that is a byproduct of their activity, not an overt goal. Consider, for example, the case of risk arbitrage in which the divergence of interest is unambiguous. Arbitrageurs do not care about shareholder value created by a proposed transaction. Indeed, were a given transaction to destroy value, they could not care less. Their only concern is to see the transaction effected, if and only if they carry a position.[11] In addition, their risk is limited to the effective date of the merger, meaning that if its implementation turns out to be a disaster, they are not affected in any way.

---

[10] Execution skills have to be considered from a broad perspective. For example, the ability to carry more risk—because of better systems—or to borrow or lend stocks more aggressively—because of better relationships throughout the marketplace—also translates into improved execution capabilities because the arbitrageur will trade more often compared to his or her peers.

[11] The case of *reverse arbitrage*, in which a trader bets on a deal being called off, happens as well, albeit very infrequently.

Other examples of such conflicts of interest include the replacement of a constituent of an index.[12] Arbitrageurs want, above all, predictability in execution, even if that implies a relative loss of liquidity. This, in turn, translates into a need for an all-electronic marketplace where reporting is instantaneous and screen prices accurate, which effectively makes dealer markets undesirable. On the other side, investors interested in small- or micro-capitalization companies have a stronger interest in dealer markets because market makers are usually required to quote continuously, even for small sizes, effectively providing liquidity of last resort.

These important differences should not be overlooked. Combined with the fact that arbitrageurs in general are a small—but financially active—community partly explains why arbitrage has been under more and more scrutiny over the years and as a result, has become more and more regulated in some countries.[13]

DIFFERENT TYPES OF CONVERGENCE

Absolute (Index Arbitrage)

Index arbitrage provides the perfect example of an absolute convergence. By definition, a futures expires on a price set to equal that of its underlying cash. The only possible reason that this would not occur would be the exchange's closure or failure. The probability of this happening is fairly low considering all the precautions taken on margin deposits by futures exchanges worldwide. However, it should not be considered impossible, as was sadly shown by the unexpected failure of the Russian Exchange in 1998. Consider also the collapse of Barings in 1995 that turned out to be fairly innocuous but sent shock waves throughout the world financial markets and was dangerously close to a general debacle. Again safety nets in place at all levels of modern

---

[12] If the effective date for a change is after the announcement date, the stock "coming in" tends to be bid up before it enters the index, while the one being replaced is usually performing poorly while it is still included. The index return does not benefit from the "spike up" and reflects the "spike down." In that case index arbitrageurs are naturally hedged, and investors in index funds are forced to take an opportunity loss.

[13] See, for example, Craig W. Holden, "Current Issues: Index Arbitrage," *Financial Analysts Journal*, 1991, pp. 8–9, for a brief examination of the bad press resulting from the October 1989 minicrash.

financial markets reduce this risk to a comfortable level, but it should not be ignored entirely.

An absolute convergence has two types of attributes: economic and temporal. The common price is unknown but realizable; that is, all market participants have access to its definition and can theoretically execute on it if necessary. The timing of this convergence is also known with certainty.

In practice, the fact that futures settlement values are realizable does not eliminate execution risks. For example, on exchanges where the final value is an average over a period of time—typically European exchanges—the chances of trading at the exact expiry price are virtually nil. On the other hand, the official definition is crystal clear, and under normal circumstances market participants can get fairly close to the final settlement price. The question of labeling this difference is somewhat artificial: If we know we will not be able to execute at this price, we could fairly say that the whole convergence hypothesis fails. It is clearer, in fact, to segregate the issues and to consider that the convergence still occurs and the risk gets translated to executing on it.

As a general rule, absolute convergence is a comfortable situation in which we can be confident that the difference in price captured now, if properly managed, is secured once and for all.[14] These are in fact the only positions that can be labeled "arbitrage" because for the most part, once the convergence is established, all other risks can be dealt with and kept under control. This is as close as it gets to risk-free trading.

Opportunities are profitable if transaction costs and hedging costs are lower than price discrepancies in the market. In the case of index arbitrage, surprisingly enough, all the markets we consider satisfy this condition and support profitable arbitrageurs. Still, opportunities of that nature do not abound. An absolute convergence in the way we define it is not accidental; it must be written in stone, which means that the only situations in which it develops recurrently are between derivative products and their underlying reference.

Note, however, that *derivative product* here is used in a very broad sense. The Nikkei 225 future contract listed on the Chicago Mercantile Exchange (CME), for example, can be considered a derivative of the Nikkei 225 future listed on the Osaka Stock Exchange (OSE). The same characterization applies also to the Singapore Monetary Exchange

---

[14] Note, however, that the realization of this profit comes with the convergence. Unless we find some opportunity to reverse a position before expiry, only at that time will we explicitly realize the profit traded today.

(SIMEX) Nikkei 225. The three of them do not have the same trading characteristics, but they expire on the same day, at the same price. Because the OSE contract carries the largest liquidity, it is fair to say that it constitutes the underlying reference. The other two are priced according to their specifics,[15] but it is possible to build an arbitrage position between the three because of the fundamental convergence.[16]

Index arbitrage is the best example of an absolute convergence because it involves numerous execution difficulties and a wide range of risk management techniques. We will use it extensively throughout this book and give a detailed presentation of it in the last chapter.

Explicit (Risk Arbitrage)

In a risk arbitrage situation a position is taken on the announcement of a merger or acquisition (MOE) between two corporate entities. Schematically, if company *A* decides to merge with company *B*, it offers to buy or exchange *B* stocks against cash or its own shares. For example, in the case of Citibank and Travelers, Travelers offered to exchange each Citibank share for 2.5 of its own shares.

There may be numerous variations of this situation. The offer may be a combination of both equity and cash, and there may be provisions to alter the exchange ratio if one of the stocks—typically the acquirer's—exits from a preset price range. The reasoning is that below a certain price, shareholders of *B* do not get a fair deal anymore and the ratio should be revised upward. At the other extreme, if the price of *A* is high, shareholders may consider the transaction too expensive and the ratio should go down. In general, revisions are infrequent because preset price ranges are fairly wide.

We term this type of convergence *explicit*.[17] In general, mergers and acquisitions involve high-level negotiations between all parties, which result in strong commitments. Even if the industrial logic or the strategic value is questioned by market participants and analysts, which can lead to a fall in share prices after the announcement, such decisions are meant to be final. Therefore, there is more than pure speculation in the relationship between the two share prices once the merge decision

---

[15] Notably, the CME contract is settled in U.S. dollars, not Japanese yen.

[16] In practice, the CME contract trades on Chicago time, when both the SIMEX and OSE are closed, which effectively forbids such positions. However, arbitrage between SIMEX and OSE is possible.

[17] The term *explicit* is not market practice, and it refers to the fact that in a risk arbitrage situation, for example, the convergence has been explicitly defined by the terms of the transaction.

has been made public. Problems do occur regularly, however, for diverse reasons. Antitrust issues are getting more and more common as a result of a decade of M&A activity, culminating in a $115 billion bid from MCI WorldCom for Sprint in October 1999. Beyond legal concerns there may be more pragmatic reasons that these deals fail from time to time, related to the so-called agency problem. All proposed transactions do not necessarily target shareholder value as a paramount goal, and managers often tend to have their own agenda.[18] Numerous hostile takeover attempts fail, and even friendly weddings may turn sour before the ceremony. The tentative merger of MCI with British Telecom in 1997 is a perfect example, and it will serve as a numerical example of what losses amount to when convergence fails to materialize despite a strong conviction as to the contrary. Therefore, our definition of *explicit convergence* may look like this: "fairly certain, but not quite."

In these situations, judgment is the ultimate risk management tool. A sound analysis of the industrial project and a careful assessment of the shareholders' respective positions and of the regulatory environment certainly help, but they are not sufficient. The vast majority of risk arbitrageurs still lost a great deal of money on British Telecom (BT) versus MCI Communications (MCI).

Just as we proposed earlier that there are natural consequences to draw from a situation of absolute convergence, there are also straightforward implications of the intrinsic uncertainty of risk arbitrage. In fact, the actual market prices reveal much more about true market expectations and effectively price the risk of nonconvergence. Therefore, they cannot and should not be ignored. Exposure on dividends or interest rates, while still critical to assess profitability, has little impact on the overall level of risk of a particular transaction.

BT/MCI is a good case study of the risks, and we will extensively review this case, as well as that of Staples (SPLS) and Office Depot (ODP), another example of a failed transaction. More generally, however, mergers and acquisitions deals tend to proceed smoothly when the underlying strategy is sound and when regulatory issues are not a threat. To get a sense of a typical deal, we will look at Citibank (CCI)

---

[18] See, for example, Randall Morck, Andrei Shleifer, and Robert W. Vishny, "Do Managerial Objectives Drive Bad Acquisition?" *Journal of Finance*, 45, 1990, pp. 31–48.

and Travelers (TRV), and Credit Commercial de France (CCF) and Hong Kong and Shangai Bank (HSBC), which happened to be mergers of substantial size.

Hypothetical (Pair Trading)

Pair trading is a popular strategy that appeared initially in the 1980s, and it consists of matching stocks with similar behavior—that is, high correlation—and trading on their divergence.[19] It has been refined over the years and nowadays typically involves stocks with somewhat identical business models from identical industry groups.

Because these positions involve a divergence-convergence process, they are abusively labeled "arbitrage" although there is no fundamental reason in general that a convergence should materialize after a divergence has occurred. Indeed, these positions are driven by statistical analyses and can be characterized as small regular gainers and big one-time losers. For some time an arbitrageur will capture small recurrent profits, but at the first blowup the loss may be such as to engulf those profits and more. The reason is that exceptional events or announcements—earnings related, for example—tend to widen the spread instantaneously, even if the companies have similar profiles. By contrast, except for a merger announcement, it is difficult to conceive of new information that would induce the two prices to converge that fast. Only in the medium to long term does the market adjust prices to account for underlying similarities. This strategy therefore is generally quite fragile and exposed to price shocks.

We term this type of position *speculative arbitrage*, which is—intentionally—somewhat of a contradiction. Even more than risk arbitrage, convergence is here the most risky side of the strategy, and success is usually subordinated to a rigorous discipline in cutting losses for failed bets. The opportunities of that type tend to live longer than others because the broader market does not recognize the price difference as an anomaly. In essence, the convergence is "proprietary" in nature because only a small number of players truly believe it is justified.

Now we do not mean that these strategies are doomed to fail. Indeed, there has been some evidence that they can be quite profitable

---

[19] For a complete description and study of pairs trading, see Evan G. Gatev, William N. Goetzmann, and K. Geert Rouwenhorst, "Pairs Trading: Performance of a Relative Value Arbitrage Rule," National Bureau of Economic Research, Working Paper 7032, www.nber.org.

when executed properly. Also, it is possible to identify pairs that have structural characteristics, ensuring that convergence is not left entirely to chance. Therefore, discrepancies of that sort may be profitably exploited, but there must be rigorous analysis, tight management, and diversification—that is, a large number of pairs—to offset inherent weaknesses in the underlying model.

To study further this type of position, we will perform a simple statistical exercise with the stocks of the Dow Jones index. Extracting pairs from simple regression techniques, we will examine if these pairs exhibit a profitable pattern. We will also consider Royal Dutch Petroleum (RD) and Shell Transport and Trading (SC). These companies have shares listed in the United States and in Europe, and they are two faces of the same coin: RD holds 60 percent of the group Royal Dutch/Shell, and SC holds the remaining 40 percent. In both cases the companies are "shells" deriving their income from their participation only. Therefore, they have equity claims on the same asset base, and their market prices should follow a predictable relationship based on the 40/60 partition of these assets.

Leap of Faith (Technical Trading)

The final category we explore is technical trading. *Technical trading* can be defined as any trading strategy based entirely on statistical analysis and/or charting analysis, in which a position is taken on the belief that an identified "pattern" will repeat itself in a predictable manner. The same causes will bring the same effects, allowing an investor to anticipate and take the appropriate position, which is not even necessarily hedged. Strictly speaking these strategies do not fit our definition of arbitrage, but they constitute an extension of it because the underlying reasoning is that of a relative value analysis, not against another security but against the same one taken in another time frame.

Our interest in these positions is double: On one side it is interesting to investigate what type of strategy may fit into this category, out of curiosity and to establish a contrast to the three previous categories we described. At the same time, the very existence of profitable technical trading rules has been consistently denied by numerous academics, because like arbitrage, these positions violate an underlying fundamental principle in that they indicate stock prices may indeed be *predictable*. Numerous practitioners, on the other hand, will testify that technical trading can actually be profitable if only because it has a self-fulfilling characteristic.[20]

Therefore, our analysis will be short and focused on these two points. We will present two rules and limit the analysis to an explanation of the underlying principle and testing results. These rules are similar and derived from the idea that stock prices tend to exhibit a mean-reversion property in the very short term. In particular, we will examine how it is possible to generate profits by taking a position against an unexpected significant move in the market.

Arbitrage and Oscillators

In physics oscillators are phenomena that repeat themselves periodically and vary around an average value. This is intuitively very close to the idea of a recurring convergence, and we want to explore here to what extent we can extend the parallel.

Consider a random variable X—a stock price or any other variable related to market prices. Without knowing its distribution, we draw a value X_t at regular intervals and compute an average $E_T(X)$ over a large period of time T:

$$E_T(X) = \frac{1}{T} \sum_{t=t_0}^{t=t_0+T} X_t$$

We do not impose any particular condition on X, and intuitively we say that X is an oscillator if $E_T(X) \to 0$ when $T \to \infty$. In other words, if we wait long enough, X is equal to zero on average.

This formalism is very simple and has the advantage of applying directly to many financial concepts. For example, numerous technical indicators are oscillators, meaning that their expected value over a long period of time is known and usually 0, and any significant deviation from that value is interpreted in a specific way.

Clearly, an arbitrage is always based on an oscillator, by nature. Regardless of its value now, the relative mispricing is expected to average 0 over time, and that is precisely what we presented as convergence. Therefore it may be interesting to apply tools traditionally

[20] The moving average crossover rule is a classic example. Supposedly when two moving averages of different periodicity cross over, the underlying security is likely to start a short-term trend. If a lot of investors believe in this rule, regardless of its theoretical value, the effect of their aggregate trading will be observable in the market, effectively realizing the original prediction.

dedicated to cyclical phenomena to arbitrage situations and to try to extract a better analytical understanding of the cycle involved, notably in terms of expected periodicity. Typically, for example, Fourier analysis is frequently used to decompose periodical functions into elementary components, and it has many applications in the world of financial oscillators.

However, the most interesting advantage of oscillators lies in the exploration of the opposite relationship: Is every oscillator associated with an arbitrage opportunity? The answer to this question is unfortunately no, but clearly every oscillating indicator should nevertheless be considered as a potential candidate and examined accordingly. The careful design and exploration of financial oscillators probably constitutes one of the best ways to systematically come up with new ideas and new opportunities. Typically this approach is very useful for statistical arbitrage, which tries to establish and test relationships based on perceived recurrent patterns.

To illustrate the point, consider a popular trading strategy called *mean reversal*. It is based on the assumption that when a stock gets too far from a short-term moving average, it tends to come back at some point, and the strategy is to try to capture this move back. Consider, for example, the chart in Figure 1-1.

It shows the normalized deviation between the General Electric (GE) closing price and its 10-day moving average over a period of one year.[21] The deviation oscillates around zero, and it seems to be relatively symmetrical. This suggests that if we sell GE at a peak or buy it at a bottom, we can probably lock the move back to the 0.

Unfortunately this simple operating procedure does not really work because we cannot "trade" the moving average. Therefore, we have to take a position exclusively on GE, which may or may not move in the right direction. Consider the two examples in Tables 1-1 and 1-2.

In the first case we decide to take a long because the difference between GE and its 10-day moving average has crossed the −1.5 standard deviation threshold and we expect it to come back to zero.[22] We

---

[21] The normalized deviation is obtained by taking the difference between GE and its 10-day moving average, minus the average of this difference and divided by the standard deviation of the difference. This transformation is called a Z transform, and it is used to allow a rapid comparison to a normal distribution.

[22] For a normal distribution, a realization of 1.5 standard deviation corresponds to a probability of 13 percent. In other words, a deviation of 1.5 standard deviation from the moving average has 13 percent chances of occurring. Naturally, the underlying

TABLE 1-1

Date	GE Closing Price	10-Day MA	Norm. Deviation
Nov. 27, 1998	$92 5/16	$92.00	−0.83
Nov. 30, 1998	$90 3/8	$92.22	−1.85
Dec. 1, 1998	$91 1/8	$92.29	−1.32

take a long position on November 30 at $90 3/8, and as early as December 1 the position is showing a profit of $0.75, that is, 0.83 percent.

By contrast in the second situation the outcome is not a profit. Based on the same criteria, we would go short on December 18 at $96 7/8. Unfortunately the price of GE does not come back, and indeed, if we were to cut the next day we would lose $1.50. Assuming we want to wait for the normalized deviation to come back below 1.5 1/2, we would indeed keep the position until December 24, at which time the total loss is $4.06, that is, 4.2 percent. Clearly the strategy does not work in that case.

This simple example shows that even in the presence of a clear-cut oscillator, profitable arbitrage is far from assured. We could naturally work further with this model, for example, in trying to hedge each position against a future. Overall there is no doubt that the opportunity is worth exploring, but it is far from certain that we will be able to transform it into a money machine. More generally

TABLE 1-2

Date	GE Closing Price	10-Day MA	Norm. Deviation
Dec. 17, 1998	$94 5/16	$90.51	1.38
Dec. 18, 1998	$96 7/8	$91.19	1.92
Dec. 21, 1998	$98 3/8	$91.94	1.94
Dec. 22, 1998	$99 1/16	$92.81	1.76
Dec. 23, 1998	$101 3/8	$93.94	1.89
Dec. 24, 1998	$100 15/16	$95.19	1.28

(Footnote continued)
assumption is that the distribution of the deviation is normal, which is a convenient approximation but an approximation nevertheless. We could have chosen any other threshold than 1.5, as long as the resulting probability clearly indicated the event is infrequent enough to be remarkable. The figure 13 percent is as good a number as any for the purpose of our discussion. If we were to actually trade this strategy, it would be critical to test different values and choose accordingly.

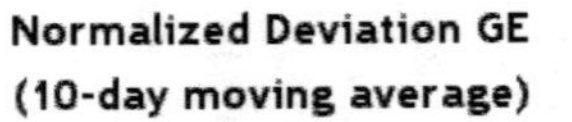

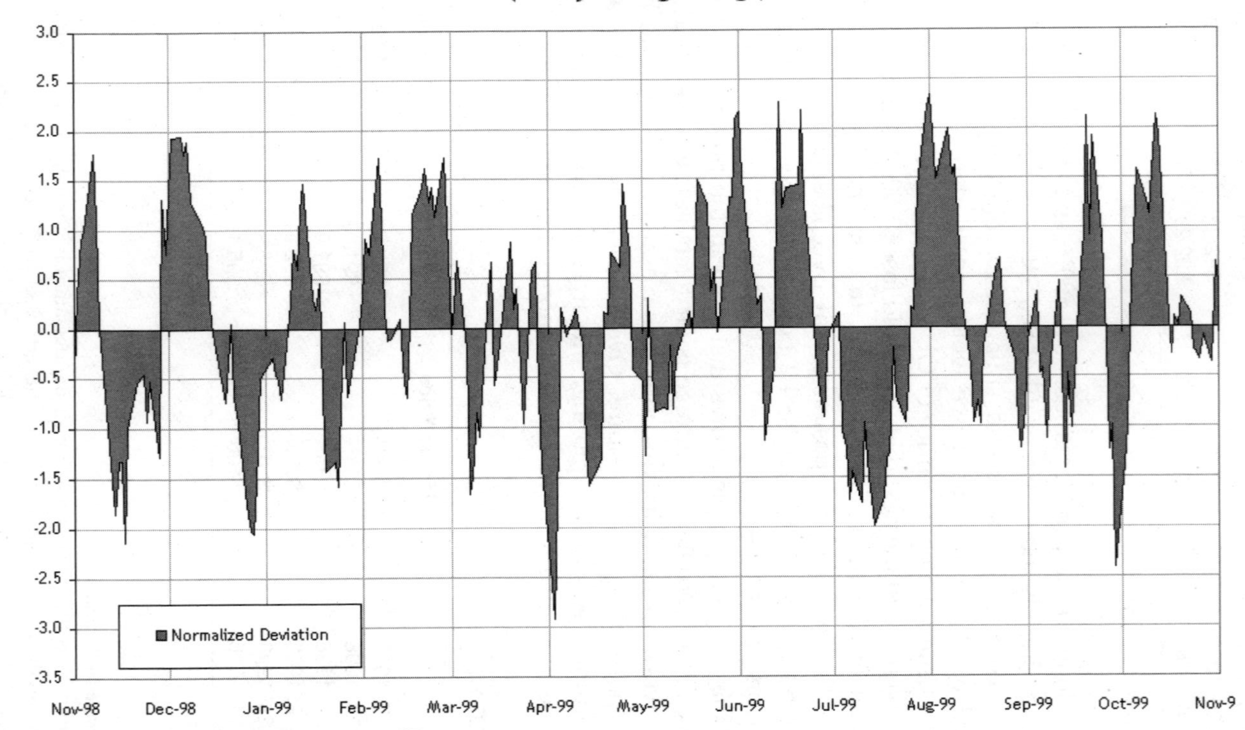

Figure 1-1 Normalized Deviation GE
(*Source*: Compiled by author from Datastream data.)

the same thing is true of all sorts of oscillators: They are well worth exploring, but success is hypothetical. Still the concept gives an entry point in the quest for opportunities.[23]

ARBITRAGE AND PRICING

Market Efficiency

The *efficient market hypothesis* states that "prices of securities fully reflect available information."[24] It basically comes in three flavors depending on the strength of the underlying assumptions about information dissemination. The weak form asserts that stock prices already reflect all information contained in the history of past prices. The semistrong form asserts that stock prices already reflect all publicly available information. The strong form, which has been made illegal in some countries by laws against insider trading, states that stock prices reflect all relevant information including insider information.

The most important consequence of an efficient market is that most securities are, by definition, fairly priced by the market. There may be issues about liquidity to weaken this general statement, but certainly there cannot be any gross mispricing in an efficient market. In other words, arbitrage opportunities cannot exist. If they do, they may be the result of an optical illusion—typically nonsimultaneous prices—or their magnitude is such that they do not create profitable opportunities when transaction costs are included—for example, the put-call parity on listed European options.

For the most part all these arguments hold in the marketplace. However, there are still numerous opportunities that support profitable dedicated traders. For example, the three categories we introduced before—index and risk arbitrage and pair trading—are actively and profitably traded in the world's largest markets. This apparent paradox has been studied extensively in the academic sphere.[25] The resolution of the conflict comes from two different arguments.

---

[23] Note, however, that such opportunities are necessarily speculative in nature because if the convergence were absolute or explicit, we would presumably know about it beforehand.

[24] Cited in Bodie, Kane, and Marcus, *Investments*, p. 933.

[25] See, for example, Craig W. Holden, "Index Arbitrage as Cross-Sectional Market Making," *Journal of Futures Markets*, 15, 1995, pp. 423–455, for a general discussion of market efficiency and index arbitrage.

On one side, the theory states that because arbitrageurs usually do not carry any inventory, they should not be able to realize a profit—this would be a risk-free profit.[26] However, we can argue that the zero inventory is not a rigorous assessment because the execution of arbitrage transactions involves two legs, and execution risk exists on each of them. Carrying this execution risk, even for a short period of time, justifies the return earned. In addition, arbitrageurs transfer liquidity between markets, which can be considered market making to a certain extent, and also justifies returns.

A second argument, much more practical and quite trivial, is that market efficiency is a *consequence* of arbitrageurs' activity. Markets become efficient because a lot of independent players explicitly or implicitly behave in a way that is consistent with that hypothesis. Nobody is in a position to extract large profits from arbitrage-driven strategies, but everyone benefits from them. It can be argued that the convergent forces that bring an efficient equilibrium almost always result in profits being extracted from the market, but in general these are spread out widely across participants in such a way that everyone sees them as negligible.

In essence, the first argument relates to structural characteristics of different instruments and markets. The second argument, on the other hand, is seemingly in contradiction with an earlier statement, that arbitrageurs were few and highly specialized. The necessary distinction here is the notion of *explicit* versus *implicit* arbitrage. There are relatively few participants involved in explicit arbitrage—that is, an aggressive quest of opportunities—because of all the reasons exposed earlier. However, virtually everybody is doing passive or implicit arbitrage. Think about a merger situation: If you need to go long on any of the stocks involved in the merger, you will probably buy the acquired company because target companies tend to trade at a discount compared to their fair value in the proposed deal. Beyond the case of a merger, if you need to go long of the market, as a general rule you will probably buy the futures if it is at a discount to its fair value, provided that you are legally in a position to trade indifferently cash or futures. Therefore, in both instances your behavior is consistent with an efficient market, and your trade will push the market toward full efficiency. You can

[26] *Inventory* in that context refers to a net position at risk. The term is also used to describe, for example, the residual position that specialists on the NYSE or NASDAQ market makers carry on an ongoing basis as a result of their duties to quote prices and provide liquidity.

hardly be described as an arbitrageur, yet you take advantage of a discount and therefore extract a small profit from a situation in which prices did not reflect fair values. As opposed to a professional arbitrageur, you only *modified* your behavior as a result of a perceived opportunity but did not *initiate* a trade following that perception. Because your intervention is conditional to other parameters, it is clearly less effective in bringing the prices back to their fair values. Depending on the opportunity, the relative proportion of explicit versus implicit arbitrageurs changes considerably, and the profits generated by bringing the market back online accrue to a concentrated set of specialists, or broadly to all participants, in which case each individual has the perception that the market is indeed efficient.

The Clientele Effect

Let us take the reasoning in a slightly different direction and introduce the notion of clientele effect. Different instruments attract different trading populations, and these populations interact with the market in specific ways driving prices, liquidity, and volatility. The idea of distinct trading populations is very clearly illustrated by the fact that most index derivatives in the world are not listed on the same exchange as their underlying references.[27] Historical as well as technical reasons explain this situation,[28] but it is clear that derivatives were created to address specific problems that stocks and "cash" securities were unable to solve—hence, the different exchanges and trading populations. At the extreme are mutual funds, which by and large are explicitly forbidden to trade derivatives. When a derivative product is involved in the arbitrage, it is therefore not surprising to witness distinct, and unaligned, investor groups. In the case of risk arbitrage, the two products are similar in

---

[27] Note the following examples: the New York Stock Exchange for S&P 500 index; the Chicago Mercantile Exchange for S&P 500 futures; the Tokyo Stock Exchange for the Nikkei 225 index; the Osaka Stock Exchange for the Nikkei 225 futures and options; the London Stock Exchange for the FTSE 100; the London International Future Exchange for FTSE 100 futures; and the Bourse de Paris for the CAC 40 and the Matif for CAC futures. There are counterexamples: TOPIX (Tokyo Stock Exchange) has its future listed on TSE as well.

[28] For example, the need existed for a central clearinghouse to handle margin requirements for derivative transactions in order to eliminate counterpart risks.

nature and are usually listed on the same exchange, but in fact the clientele effect still holds, at a micro level.

If in practice it is naturally impossible to identify any set of investors following a particular security, it is important to realize that the investor population is always fragmented in a multitude of smaller groups with distinct interests and expectations.

Equities versus Other Securities

Traditionally equities have not been the preferred instruments of arbitrage. Fixed-income securities and foreign exchange markets have attracted much more attention and activity in that regard. The reasons for this are very natural: These securities exhibit a strong and predictable relationship to macroeconomic aggregates; therefore, a solid understanding of economic theory leads to fairly adequate prediction of probable future moves. By contrast, equity valuation is a much more subtle exercise.

For instance, it is difficult to envision a country eradicating its inflation overnight, but countless companies have taken financial markets by surprise with bad earnings virtually from one quarter to the next. Therefore, macroeconomic aggregates exhibit consistent stability over time, which is critical because it gives plenty of time to revisit basic assumptions and adjust positions if necessary. Obviously the Asian crisis has demonstrated that things can go *very* bad *very* quickly, but in general volatility on country macroeconomics is relatively low. Equally important is predictability. Considering that modern and developed governments in general have similar goals and tools, it is not extremely difficult to preempt future moves meant to address known problems. Again, there may be many variants, but it is not unreasonable to expect, for example, tighter monetary policy against inflationary pressure as a general remedy. Trading based on such reasoning is usually termed *macro trading*, and it is generally like arbitrage in nature because it is based on an expected convergence.

However, these same reasons that make fixed income and foreign exchange so attractive also tend to be drawbacks in practice. If macroeconomic aggregates take time to adjust, arbitrageurs may have to carry their position for quite a while, and things may get much worse before they get better. Also if price discrepancies are so large and fundamental criteria so compelling, chances are good that participants have spotted the same opportunities. Altogether this means that macro arbitrage is not necessarily simpler even if the context is somewhat more attractive.[29]

We would argue that equities in general present a very favorable terrain to arbitrage as well, even for macro arbitrage, although arbitrageurs have to have different goals and methods to be successful. Whereas there are only a few dozen currencies traded worldwide and as many governments susceptible to issue sovereign bonds, several thousand stocks are listed and trade with a decent level of liquidity in the United States alone. Macro arbitrage targets large profits from infrequent trading and bold mispricings, and these mispricings, as infrequent as they are, can also be exploited from equity positions chosen wisely. Furthermore, equities offer the additional opportunity for high-volume–low-profit strategies expected to produce results through the accumulation of small successful trades. This is generally the basic premise behind strategies like pair trading or statistical arbitrage.

Consider, for example, the two charts in Figures 1-2 and 1-3 as an illustration of macro arbitrage in the context of an equity strategy. Both charts present opportunities resulting from the Asian crisis, respectively in the banking and retailing sectors. The first case is based on the observation that French banks had a considerably higher exposure to Asia than German banks. After hedging the spread in local markets—respectively versus the CAC and DAX indices—the relative difference between French and German banks exhibits a striking widening spread with French banks outperforming, which can be viewed as an anomaly.[30] The second situation is also built on the same type of hypothesis—that is, the relative exposure to Asia from two French retailers, Promodes and Carrefour.[31] The arbitrage is less obvious and based on the trend of the Asia ex-Japan index; if it is identified early, it is possible to speculate that Carrefour/Promodes will follow a similar path and enter the relative spread accordingly.

Overall arbitrage in these two situations is entirely based on a perceived mispricing, and the execution is subject to an additional

---

[29] For a complete discussion of these strategies and numerous illustrations, see, for example, Gabriel Brustein, *Macro Trading and Investment Strategies: Macroeconomic Arbitrage in Global Markets* (New York: John Wiley & Sons, 1999).

[30] For clarification, the trade implied by the chart is the following: short a portfolio composed of a spread between French bank hedged against the CAC versus long another portfolio of German banks hedged against the DAX.

[31] Note that the hedge of local market risk is not necessary because both companies are French and traded in Paris.

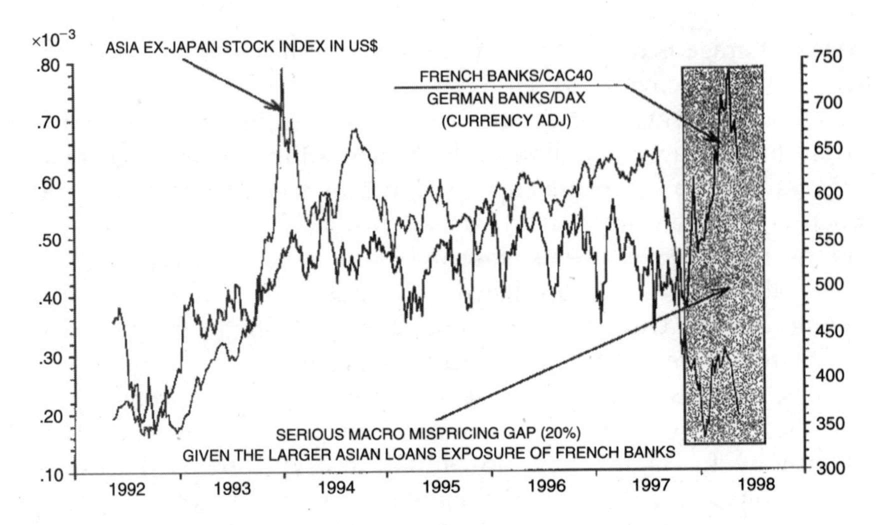

Figure 1-2 Macro Arbitrage, French Banks versus German Banks
(*Source*: Gabriel Burstein, *Macro Trading and Investment Strategies: Macroeconomic Arbitrage in Global Markets*. Copyright © John Wiley & Sons, 1999. Reprinted by permission of John Wiley & Sons, Inc.)

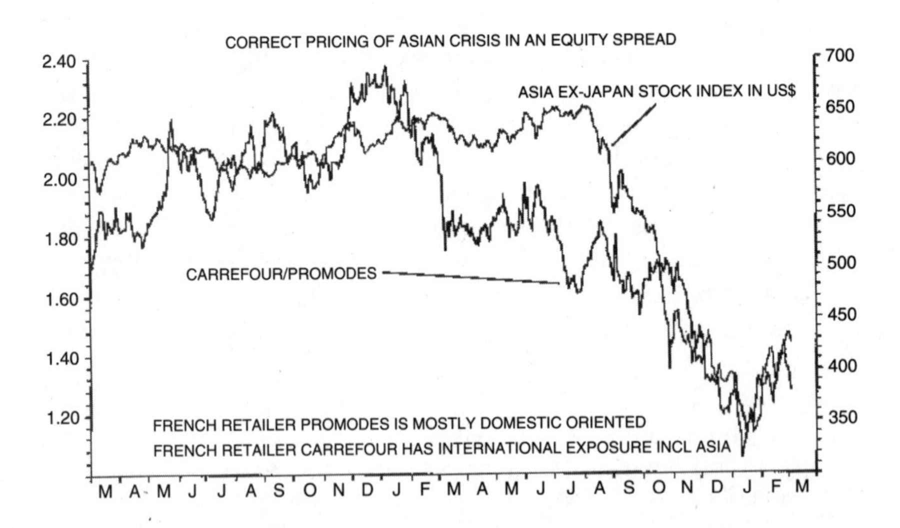

Figure 1-3 Macro Arbitrage, Carrefour/Promodes
(*Source*: Gabriel Burstein, *Macro Trading and Investment Strategies: Macroeconomic Arbitrage in Global Markets*. Copyright © John Wiley & Sons, 1999. Reprinted by permission of John Wiley & Sons, Inc.)

uncertainty because the specific stocks chosen also present idiosyncratic risk related to their general business. In addition, it can be argued that the Asian crisis was certainly an exceptional event and that opportunities of that type would not necessarily abound under normal market circumstances. Nevertheless, these are two examples of astute arbitrage in which equities have been used as proxies for larger macroeconomic factors, clearly an indication that opportunities exist.

VALUATIONS: MARK TO MARKET VERSUS THEORETICAL

An arbitrage position is built on convergence expectations. It relies entirely on the comparison between observed—that is, traded—prices and a theoretical relationship we believe should prevail in the long run. Therefore, it can always be evaluated at any time from any of these two angles.

A sure convergence can always be used as a foundation for valuation, because whatever the market prices are, we know we can show a profit if we fully execute each leg at the time of trading. At the other extreme, in the case of speculative arbitrage, we have to use market prices because of the inherent uncertainty, and we may have to show a loss, possibly large, if the original divergence widens.

Consider, for example, the case of a risk arbitrage situation: Company *A* is acquiring company *B* through a 2-for-1 stock swap. Table 1-3 presents their hypothetical prices over a few days. On Day 1, we enter a position by buying 2 shares of *B* and selling one share of *A* (we neglect all transaction costs). At the end of the day, the theoretical valuation is \$1: the theoretical spread is 0—because one share of *A* should be equal exactly to 2 shares of *B*—and we realized a spread of +1 in the market ($\$1 = 100 - 2 \times 49\frac{1}{2}$). However, the mark-to-market valuation is 0 because the spread we realized is no better than the spread at the close of the market. On Day 2 as a result of usual market volatility, *A* and *B* close with a spread somewhat smaller than the previous day. The theoretical valuation is unchanged by definition, while the mark-to-market shows a profit of +½.

On Day 3, the spread comes back to its previous level. Again the theoretical valuation does not move while the mark-to-market valuation is losing what it had just made on Day 2,−½, for a cumulative figure back to 0.

TABLE 1-3

Day	*A*	*B*	Theoretical Evaluation (Cumul.)	Mark-to-Market Evaluation (Cumul.)
1	$100	$49½	+1	+0
2	$97	$48 8⁄14	+1	+½
3	$98	$48½	+1	+0
4	$95	$46	+1	−2
5	$92	$43½	+1	−4

On Days 4 and 5 some bad news accumulates on *A* and *B*, altering significantly the perspective of the acquisition. Naturally the market reacts by selling both stocks, and the spread widens significantly because the acquisition is not certain anymore. At the extreme, on Day 5, the market simply does not price any convergence anymore. The mark to market turns largely negative, and the theoretical is unchanged.

This simple simulation shows that theoretical and mark-to-market valuations capture different aspects of the position. Whereas one captures the entire profit immediately and with 100 percent certainty, the other tracks the actual occurrence of the convergence in the marketplace. Therefore, consistency requires the choice of the valuation method be primarily dictated by the nature of the position.

Traders in general focus more on the theoretical part because it unambiguously shows an expected profit as if it were realized. Risk managers,[32] on the other hand, tend to focus more on mark to market because these figures are unquestionably a reflection of what is happening in the market. The difference in methodology can be a source of misunderstanding, both ways. For example, for index arbitrage where the convergence is certain, virtually all traders value their position on theoretical grounds. When the futures closes far from its theoretical value, mark-to-market valuation shows huge differences compared to results declared by front-office valuations. Support for the theoretical figures is not difficult to get, but it requires all parties to understand the underlying strategy and its structure. Now consider an analogous situation in which the mark-to-market valuation shows huge losses whereas theoretical still indicates profits, but where the convergence is not certain anymore. Risk managers will naturally be as inquisitive as before,

---

[32] *Risk managers* here denotes financial controllers, internal auditors, and more generally all personnel involved in monitoring risk.

and the same argument can be used to demonstrate that mark to market is temporarily erroneous. But in this situation the demonstration is not logically acceptable because of uncertainties at maturity, and the mark to market is indeed the most accurate valuation. The point in this exercise is to realize that the existence of two different profitability measures for the same position creates the need for a rigorous reconciliation. One of the parties has to give way to the other, for the better or the worst: If the arbitrage argument is used indiscriminately, it may help justify carrying losing positions long after they should have been liquidated or at the very least reconsidered.

This difference between observed and theoretical valuations will become clear as we develop the necessary formalism in the chapter dedicated to valuation techniques. As a safety rule, both should be tracked at all times because they are complementary, but more importantly because the reconciliation process to translate one into the other is generally valuable to all parties involved.

RISK

Risk can be segmented according to different criteria. From an analytical standpoint, traders care about *parametric risks*—that is, risks arising from the randomness of market parameters—and consequently we will have to develop a framework to understand and manage these risks later on. For the purpose of our introductory discussion here, we adopt a different segmentation and consider in turn the issues of execution, carry, and nonconvergence.

Execution

Execution risk covers all risk associated with building and unwinding a position. It would be convenient to associate a high level of confidence regarding the final convergence to a lower execution risk, on the grounds that simultaneous execution on highly correlated instruments seems a comfortable challenge. Paradoxically, in general, the exact opposite is true, and in fact it is legitimate to turn the hypothesis around and state that the execution risk becomes relatively minor for speculative positions.[33] Consider, for example, the extreme situation in which a particular spread is arbitraged only by one player, everybody

[33] At expiry, however, it is true that for an absolute or explicit convergence, execution risk is theoretically nonexistent because of the nature of the position. In practice, it may persist still, for example, if the position involves a future expiring on an average.

else being indifferent to it. This particular player is in no hurry to execute his or her strategy and indeed should take some time to minimize a possible impact he or she may have on the prices of the securities he or she wants to trade. At the other extreme, an index arbitrageur always faces a situation in which the whole market perceives an opportunity at the same time he or she does, and he or she has to compete to be the first to take advantage of it. He or she may very well get "stuck" in the middle of his or her execution because other participants rush to sell the futures when it shows a premium or buy it when it trades at a discount.

This leads us to the notions of timing and hedge in arbitrage trading. Simultaneous trading requires that we carry an equivalent amount of risk on both legs of the arbitrage at all times. Risk here is fairly simply measured by the traded nominal; therefore every dollar executed on the long side should be matched by the appropriate number of dollars of executed short and vice versa.[34] Therefore, from a risk perspective, synchronous execution on both legs is far more important than instantaneous execution of a large nominal, which would be key to capturing an opportunity. This operating procedure, assuming it is feasible, is the only guarantee to minimize execution risk by being perfectly hedged at all time.

It is necessary to realize, however, that it also leads to seemingly lost opportunities. If the market has a tendency to form clear trends, even for short periods of time, a trader might very well implement a strategy of trading on the waves. Nonsimultaneous trading on both legs in that case may result in higher profits. It is fair to say that this is still arbitrage, but it is not risk-free arbitrage anymore. This trader could very well do the exact same thing and capture the same movements using only one of the legs—the most liquid and cheapest to trade, for example. This discussion is less trivial than it seems because nonsimultaneous trading is usually embedded in traders' behavior, and it is very difficult to disentangle. Yet it should be clearly separated: Pure arbitrage requires rigorous simultaneous execution, and if the only way to make money is to skillfully play the short-term waves, then the arbitrage activity should be stopped or reduced and resources refocused on pure speculative trading based on wave recognition.

---

[34] Note that we say the "appropriate number of dollars," not "an equal number of dollars." As we will see shortly, hedging a position may be done in ways other than dollar for dollar.

Hedge Strategies

From a broad perspective we can say that there are two categories of hedge strategies: static and dynamic. These two broad methodologies correspond to different needs and are applicable in specific circumstances. A *static hedge* essentially applies to a position that is considered appropriately hedged once and for all when it is initiated. Conversely, a *dynamically hedged position* needs to be continuously monitored and adjusted.

Static Hedge: Fixed Quantity

A *fixed-quantity hedge* rests on the premise that the two legs of a position are bound by a rigid relationship with respect to their respective size. If the position is an arbitrage, this relationship can be deducted from it, as is the case of an index arbitrage position, for example. The ratio of the appropriate quantities on each leg—the hedge ratio—is measured directly on expiration, and the fixed-quantity approach simply postulates that the same ratio is also valid at any time before. Therefore, once we know the right hedge for a possible transaction, this ratio is kept constant from initiation to expiry, except for minor adjustments warranted by the specifics of the position.[35] In an index arbitrage, for example, arbitrageurs define a strict equation between the number of futures and the stock position they carry, and this equation holds permanently. All executions, including expiry, reflect this ratio. In the case of risk arbitrage, for example, the ratio is part of the terms of the transaction, and once set, it is not expected to change.

In general, an absolute or explicit convergence dictates the adequate ratio to be used, in *absolute* terms. Regardless of who is entering the arbitrage, or at what moment in time, the ratio is consistently equal to an absolute reference available to all. By contrast, an arbitrage on a more speculative convergence may rely on a *relative* ratio—that is, a ratio deducted from a certain number of proprietary hypotheses—for example, the past behavior of securities in the arbitrage.

In that last category, a common hedge ratio derived from portfolio management theory is the relative beta of two portfolios or securities. The definition of beta is that of the capital asset pricing model, but it is adapted to the needs of the situation. Specifically:

---

[35] Among such adjustments is the hedging of financing costs for margin calls on futures positions. See the chapters dedicated to futures and index arbitrage for more details.

$$\beta_{A/B} = \frac{\text{cov}(r_A, r_B)}{\sigma_B^2} = \rho_{A/B} \frac{\sigma_A}{\sigma_B}$$

where $\beta_{A/B}$ is the beta of A versus B, $\text{cov}(r_A, r_B)$ denotes the covariance of returns from A and B over the relevant period of time in the past, $\rho_{A/B}$ their coefficient of correlation, and σ_A^2 and σ_B^2 their respective variances. This ratio captures the relative behavior of A and B: A 1 percent move in the price of B has historically translated into a $\beta_{A/B}$ percentage variation in the price of A. Therefore, each dollar of exposure on A has to be matched with $\beta_{A/B}$ dollars of exposure on B if the position is to be hedged with regard to past returns.[36]

If N_A and N_B stand respectively for nominal exposures, this last condition is equivalent to:

$$N_B = \beta_{A/B} \cdot N_A$$

At all times, the valuation of a spread portfolio between A and B can be expressed as[37]:

$$V = N_A - N_B$$

This is true because an increase in N_A results in a profit, whereas an increase in N_B results in a loss. A variation in V captures an overall profit or loss from the time we take the position to the time we exit. Alternatively, V can be regarded as the total exposure of the portfolio because it gives access to possible losses in the case of unfavorable market moves.

It follows that:

$$V = N_A - N_B = N_A - \beta_{A/B} \cdot N_A$$

Following a market movement, V varies with N_A and N_B according to the following equation:

$$\Delta V = \Delta N_A - \Delta N_B$$

---

[36] It can be shown that this hedge ratio is the one that minimizes the variance of the position's profit and loss. See, for example, John C. Hull, *Introduction to Futures and Options Markets*, 3rd ed. (Englewood Cliffs, N.J.: Prentice Hall, 1998), p. 90.

[37] A spread portfolio is here a portfolio holding a spread position between one or several securities. In the simple case above, we are long A and short B.

where the traditional operator Δ indicates a change in the associated variable.[38] If we define the percentage variations of A and B as $p_A = \Delta N_A / N_A, p_B = \Delta N_B / N_B$, then ΔV becomes:

$$\Delta V = p_A \cdot N_A - p_B \cdot N_B = p_A \cdot N_A - \beta_{A/B} \cdot p_B \cdot N_A =$$
$$(p_A - \beta_{A/B} \cdot p_B) \cdot N_A$$

If A and B behave as they have historically, the definition of $\beta_{A/B}$ implies $p_A = \beta_{A/B} \cdot p_B$, which essentially indicates that $\Delta V = 0$. Therefore, using a beta as a hedge ratio is clearly motivated by an historical perspective, and the whole position is profitable only if A and B break away from the statistical pattern that beta captured.

Beyond the case of a ratio deducted from a convergence—which looks at the future—and that of a beta hedge—which looks at the past—the third option in terms of a fixed-quantity hedge is to consider the current market as the most appropriate source of information and derive a ratio from there. Typically, if $t = 0$ indicates today's date, we fix the ratio as of today, to $(N_A/N_B)_{t=0}$, and the valuation of the portfolio at a later date is then:

$$\Delta V = \Delta N_A - \left(\frac{N_A}{N_B}\right)_{t=0} \cdot \Delta N_B$$

The clear advantage of this solution is its simplicity: We hedge the position today and simply keep it static going forward. This is clearly a choice of default, however. If we knew about a likely relationship between A and B, we would use some type of ratio based on it. In the absence of such a relationship, the next best alternative is to postulate that historical data capture a large part of the information we need. Then if this historical perspective is not considered legitimate for some reason, the only fixed-quantity hedge left is based on today's market.

By nature, all fixed-quantity hedge strategies are static: Once the ratio is set, it is unlikely to change. If it does, this change generates a profit or a loss because the readjustment of the position creates a distortion. This property is convenient in the world of arbitrage because it ensures that the carry of the position is easy to implement: There is simply nothing to do.

[38] Precisely $\Delta V = V_{\text{final}} - V_{\text{initial}}$.

It is also important to note that a fixed-quantity hedge does not usually result in a portfolio being hedged in nominal exposure. For example, the two legs of a portfolio hedged in beta are always of different nominal because $V = N_A - \beta_{A/B} \cdot N_A \neq 0$ unless $\beta_{A/B} = 1$. This is an important consideration because it shows that the notion of hedge is dependent upon the metrics chosen to evaluate risk.

First- and Second-Order Exposure

Reconsider the above portfolio with two securities, A and B, in the general case where we have a generic spread position, which we write $V = N_A - N_B$. Given the conventions we used earlier, we already know that:

$$\Delta V = \Delta N_A - \Delta N_B = p_A \cdot N_A - p_B \cdot N_B$$

If we are hedged in nominal terms, as opposed to hedged in number of units, $N_A = N_B = N$ and $\Delta V = (p_A - p_B) \cdot N$. Therefore, if $p_A = p_B$, the portfolio does not show any profit or loss regardless of the amplitude of the absolute market move. Because the outcome is determined by a performance differential, V is what we call a *second-order exposure*.

Now assume that we carry this position for a while, and at some point $p_A \neq p_B$ resulting in a divergence between N_A and N_B. If we have $N_A \neq N_B$ today with $N_A = N_B + \Delta_N$, the variation in V following a market move becomes:

$$\Delta V = p_A \cdot N_A - p_B \cdot N_B = (p_A - p_B) \cdot N_B + p_A \cdot \Delta_N = (p_A - p_B) \cdot N_A + p_B \cdot \Delta_N$$

The term ΔV is now the sum of two terms, a similar differential component, $(p_A - p_B) \cdot N_B$ or $(p_A - p_B) \cdot N_A$, and a new quantity $p_A \cdot \Delta_N$ or $p_B \cdot \Delta_N$.

The interpretation of these two terms is very straightforward: $(p_A - p_B) \cdot N_B$ is the result of a performance differential, and can be considered a second-order exposure. On the other hand, $p_A \cdot \Delta_N$ is directly dependent on the absolute performance of the first security, and as such it is what we call a *first-order exposure*. Δ_N itself represents the extent to which the two legs of the position are not exposed on the same nominal.

This discussion has the very simple goal of showing that the valuation—and exposure—of a spread portfolio can always be separated in two terms of distinct nature. Whereas this analysis was not relevant to a fixed-quantity hedge—because we knew that we could not expect the two legs of the portfolio to be equal anyway—it is critical to understand a strategy of dynamic hedge.

Dynamic Hedge: Delta

A *delta hedge*[39] is based on the premise that we want to get rid of first-order exposure as often as necessary. Typically we trade away the term Δ_N in the market to ensure that the overall exposure is only differential between A and B.[40]

This hedging procedure is very common on options, from which it derived its name. It is based on the analysis of the delta of the position, which indicates what is the nominal mismatch between the option and the rest of the portfolio. This mismatch is generally systematically traded away by adjusting the composition of the portfolio with respect to the underlying stock.

Delta hedging is very resource intensive in many respects. It requires a lot of analysis time to assess the delta of a portfolio. Furthermore, to be efficient, trading must be continuous, or at least very regular, which may turn out to be costly in the presence of transaction costs. The most important problem with this approach, however, resides in the fact that we are shifting away from true arbitrage, because the position is far from being risk free even after it has been fully executed.

Consider, for example, the common strategy of convertible bond arbitrage. It consists of trading both a convertible bond and its underlying stock, in effect breaking down the bond into a risky straight bond and a warrant with a strike price deducted from the terms of the conversion. It is referred to as *arbitrage* although in practice it does not pass our definition for three reasons. First, the warrant imbedded in the bond is highly dependent on volatility, which is not the case of the stock. In other words the two securities do not have a similar behavior, the volatility exposure remains throughout the life of the position, and even when delta hedged, this is not a risk-free proposition.[41] The second reason is related to the carry of the position—that is,

[39] For an exhaustive and very practical discussion of dynamic hedging, see Nassim Taleb, *Dynamic Hedging: Managing Vanilla and Exotic Options* (New York: John Wiley & Sons, 1997).

[40] The choice of trading A or B to get rid of Δ_N is based on a risk management perspective. If $\Delta_N > 0, N_A > N_B$, and trading A, for example, will reduce N_A to N_B. Conversely, trading B will scale the overall nominal of the position up to N_A.

[41] It is naturally possible to hedge the convertible bond with options and introduce volatility in both legs of the arbitrage. This would solve the first difficulty but not the second because the overall portfolio has to be dynamically hedged anyway.

its behavior through time. Delta hedging the option requires continuous trading and is not risk free because if we leave the position unattended, it is susceptible to developing a significant exposure on the overall market. Finally, the bond portion is exposed to a credit risk that may be significant and for which we do not necessarily have any satisfactory hedging procedure.

Application

It is certainly useful here to consider a numerical application to understand better the differences between the two approaches fixed quality versus delta hedge. Consider two stocks S_1 and S_2 with the price sequence given in Table 1-4. The simplest hedge method here is the fixed-quantity approach. Consider, for example, that the price relationship on January 18, $S_1 = 2 * S_2$, is more than a coincidence and is actually the result of a known merger transaction between the two corporations. If we were to take a position on the spread between S_1 and S_2, we would naturally adopt the same hedge ratio. Table 1-5 summarizes the arbitrage. Assuming all transactions are executed on the close, we originally buy 1 share of S_1 at \$100 and sell 2 shares of S_2 at \$51. On January 18 when the convergence is realized, we buy back S_2 at \$45 and sell S_1 back at \$90. The total profit here is $1 * (\$90 - \$100) - 2 * (\$45 - \$51) = \$2$.

Suppose now that we do not factor in the merger transaction but simply want to benefit from a spread perceived too wide between S_1 and S_2. To do so, we first consider the appropriate hedge ratio as being given by the current market conditions, but we adopt again a fixed quantity. S_1 and S_2 trade respectively at \$100 and \$51; therefore, the appropriate hedge is $\$100/\$51 = 1.961$. Under these assumptions, we would manage the position as in Table 1-6. Here the total profit of the position is $1 * (\$90 - \$100) - 1.961 * (\$45 - \$51) = \$1.765$, slightly inferior to the previous case because we were less short of S_2.

TABLE 1-4

Date	S_1	S_2
Jan. 15	\$100	\$51
Jan. 16	\$105	\$52
Jan. 17	\$98	\$50½
Jan. 18	\$90	\$45

TABLE 1-5

Date	S_1	S_2	Deals S_1	Deals S_2	Pos. 1	Pos. 2	$V = N_1 - h \cdot N_2$ [a]
Jan. 15	\$100	\$51	+1 @ 100	−2 @ \$51	1	−2	−\$2
Jan. 16	\$105	\$52	—	—	1	−2	\$1
Jan. 17	\$98	\$50½	—	—	1	−2	−\$3
Jan. 18	\$90	\$45	−1 @ \$90	+2 @ \$45	—	—	—

[a] h stands for the relevant hedge ratio to compute V. Note that we neglect the time value of money in these calculations for simplicity.

Now consider a small variation of the above scheme in which we adopt the beta of the two stocks as the appropriate ratio. If we want \$100 exposure on S_1—that is, 1 share, we know that we should take an exposure of $\beta_{1/2} * \$100$ for S_2. Assuming, for example, $\beta_{1/2} = 1.3$, we need \$130 of S_2 which turns out to be $\$130/\$51 = 2.549$ shares. In that case, the position evolves as in Table 1-7. The total profit is here even higher, at $1 * (\$90 - \$100) - 2.549 * (\$45 - \$51) = \$5.294$, because the move in S_1 and S_2 from January 15 to 18 was significantly different from the original beta suggested. S_2 lost 11.76 percent [= (\$45 – \$51)/\$51], and consequently, S_1 should have lost 15.3 percent (= 11.76 percent ∗ 1.3) because of the beta of 1.3. Because S_1 lost only 10 percent, we ended up with a significant gain on the long, in comparison to what historical data would have suggested.

It is interesting to note in these three examples that $V \neq 0$, and still we consider the position hedged adequately. This particular point shows that hedging a position in number of units, as we do, does not imply that it is also hedged in nominal terms, something we mentioned earlier.

Finally, assume we want to hedge the position in delta and get rid of excess nominal exposure at the close every day. We start with a ratio similar to that of a previous case and trade from there, as in Table 1-8.

On January 16, the existing position has a nominal valuation of $1 * \$105 - 1.961 * \$52 = \$3.038$, which we have to hedge away, by selling S_1 or buying S_2. We decide for example to sell S_1, to reduce the

TABLE 1-6

Date	S_1	S_2	Deals S_1	Deals S_2	Pos. 1	Pos. 2	$V = N_1 - h \cdot N_2$
Jan. 15	\$100	\$51	1 @ \$100	−1.961 @ \$51	1	−1.961	—
Jan. 16	\$105	\$52	—	—	1	−1.961	\$3.039
Jan. 17	\$98	\$50½	—	—	1	−1.961	− \$1.020
Jan. 18	\$90	\$45	−1 @ \$90	+1.961 @ \$45	—	—	—

TABLE 1-7

Date	S_1	S_2	Deals S_1	Deals S_2	Pos. 1	Pos. 2	$V = N_1 - h \cdot N_2$
Jan. 15	$100	$51	+1 @ $100	−2.549 @ $51	1	−2.549	−$30.00
Jan. 16	$105	$52	—	—	1	−2.549	−$27.55
Jan. 17	$98	$50½	—	—	1	−2.549	−$30.73
Jan. 18	$90	$45	−1 @ $90	+2 .549 @ $45	—	—	—

exposure on each leg, and we have to sell $\$3.038/\$105 = 0.029$ shares. On January 17, the position is unhedged again, and this time we decide to buy back S_2. The total profit is more difficult to compute because of the succession of deals, but it amounts to $0.029 * (\$105 - \$100) + 0.971 * (\$90 - \$100) - 0.076 * (\$50½ - \$51) - 1.884 * (\$45 - \$51) = \$1.788$. Notice also that V is systematically equal to zero, which is the intended effect of the hedging procedure.

The point behind these examples is not to demonstrate that one particular method is better than the others, but to show that they yield different results, indeed different by a wide margin. Each method is the consequence of a number of assumptions and expectations about the securities in the portfolio or in contrast to their observed historical behavior. In any case, the adequate choice depends on the trading strategy implemented.

Arbitrage and Hedging

Static and dynamic hedging are critically different in terms of risk management. In a context of arbitrage, it can be argued that the very nature of the underlying convergence requires some sort of fixed-quantity hedging, for two reasons. The first one has been advanced already and consists of a pure risk assessment. Because delta hedging essentially means that no satisfactory hedge can ever be achieved permanently, it is not well equipped to describe situations in which we expect the hedge to be so perfect that we consider our profit to be locked even before the expiry of the position.

TABLE 1-8

Date	S_1	S_2	Deals S_1	Deals S_2	Pos. 1	Pos. 2	$V = N_1 - h \cdot N_2$
Jan. 15	$100	$51	+1@$100	−1.961@$51	1	−1.961	—
Jan. 16	$105	$52	−0.029@$105	—	0.971	−1.961	—
Jan. 17	$98	$50½	—	+0.076@$50½	0.971	−1.884	—
Jan. 18	$90	$45	−0.971@$90	+1.884@$45	—	—	—

A second set of issues has to deal with information and time consistency. The informational content of an arbitrage position is very high because by postulating a convergence, we actively project what should happen. It is also stable over time because usually the convergence is as certain today as it was yesterday. By contrast, delta hedging is a purely reactive approach, in which the position is managed as a consequence of market behavior. And it is not stable, in the sense that it is as randomly distributed as the underlying market prices. Therefore, we are now in possession of one more test of arbitrage-ness, the hedge ratio. Furthermore, we know why we cannot expect options in general to be ideal candidates to implement arbitrage strategies.[42]

Carry

The *law of one price* requires instruments with similar payoffs to have equal prices today, and more generally everyday until the convergence is "consumed"—that is, one of the legs expires or we decide to exit. Because the relationship supporting the convergence is by nature continuous, the arbitrage once set up should take care of itself, and not require any more intervention. This implies in turn that the hedge ratio be constant and known with relative certainty.

Therefore we can fairly safely make the conclusion that the first-order market risk disappears, but there may be other risks we have to take into consideration. In the case of index arbitrage, for example, financing, or an uncertainty about expected dividends, is particularly important. Even though we can argue that these other risks are indeed of second-order magnitude, there are cases in which they can be serious and even become critical, for example, in the case of a squeeze on the short side of a risk arbitrage position.[43] If suddenly shares of the acquirer company cannot be borrowed anymore, and shares already borrowed get recalled, arbitrageurs may have to unwind their position at a loss. In markets where borrowing secu-

[42] This may again be perceived as a somewhat excessive generalization. For example, a violation of the put-call parity on listed options is certainly an arbitrage, yet it involves options. There are clearly examples of pure arbitrage situations developing with options, but to be really risk free they must consistently exhibit a delta as close to zero as possible. This is the case with a position derived from a violation of the put-call parity.

[43] A squeeze indicates a situation which a scarce resource becomes even scarcer to the point where it cannot be borrowed anymore. This phenomenon may happen with securities that cannot be borrowed anymore, or with cash liquidity that becomes suddenly extremely expensive to borrow. More on this last point in Part 2.

rities is easy and cheap, this risk tends to be small. In the United States, for example, a significant portion of the market capitalization is held by institutional investors with a long-term investment horizon—pension funds typically—and their holdings usually constitute stable sources of shares for this type of situation. In Japan, by contrast, the market for borrowing securities is far less mature, and costs and liquidity are primary concerns.

Therefore, if it is always true that the carry of an arbitrage position should induce only moderate trading, it is not always absolutely risk free. Because we continuously have a short leg, if this leg is not a derivative, we know that we are exposed to a possible squeeze on the securities we borrow. Furthermore, even if the magnitude of a squeeze is highly unpredictable, its consequences are not: Arbitrageurs have to liquidate their full position quite rapidly and at the same time, with the inevitable consequence that all of them realize a significant loss.

Is that the only risk we should care about? Unfortunately the answer is no. Consider again the case of index arbitrage, where supposedly we do not have anything to do after execution until expiration. Say you are long cash and short future, and the market is rallying sharply. If the position is properly hedged, the market movement in and of itself is of no consequence. However, the short future position needs to be financed because the exchange will request margin deposits to cover the losses generated by the up-move. The theory says that if you cannot finance these margin calls at a rate equal to that of the position, you are losing the rate differential. In a stable interest rate environment, this is clearly not a serious concern, but in case of a liquidity squeeze, it may become just that.[44]

This second example confirms that the carry of the position, even in the comfortable situation of an absolute convergence, is not risk free. Interestingly, both examples refer to a *squeeze* as a possible source of losses. When a trader builds a position, he or she intuitively knows the level of noise inherent in all the secondary parameters—interest rates, borrowing costs, dividends—and will trade accordingly. If during the life of the position these parameters exit the confidence interval he or she priced, he or she is most certainly going to lose from these unexpected moves, and these small accumulated losses may significantly damage the original profitability when the arbitrage was locked.

---

[44] Liquidity "squeezes" tend to develop recurrently at the end of calendar years, as we will see when we examine the market for overnight funds.

Naturally this is a dynamic process, and a trader faced with these annoying losses would draw obvious conclusions and adjust. Whatever he or she does, however, there is always a chance that unexpected moves will spoil the party.

Returning to our original question, this means that carrying an arbitrage position is generally risk free, but it requires at least as much attention as initiation and expiry. Furthermore, it is clear from this discussion that arbitrageurs are not indifferent to the uncertainty about the time frame between execution and exit: With equal profitability, opportunities with short and known carry are much more desirable.[45]

Nonconvergence

Nonconvergence refers primarily to a situation at expiry in which both legs of the arbitrage do not come together as expected. In the case of a speculative position there is no real expiry; therefore, an alternative view of the same concern is to acknowledge that the convergence has not materialized after a reasonable amount of time. The magnitude of what is reasonable here is dictated essentially by judgment and supported by historical data or precedents if the strategy has been traded before. In any case, as we said before, every position of that type should have embedded in it a specific time horizon, and success usually depends on how disciplined the traders are in taking losses.

Because the convergence is precisely what drives the position in the first place, it should be the focus point of testing and modeling efforts prior to engaging any capital in trading. In particular, the most important question can be formulated with a simple probabilistic approach. Assuming the execution and carry are flawless, what is the probability of failure and associated loss that make the arbitrage a profitable proposition overall? Consider that historical convergence occurs within a few months with a probability of 80 percent and generates on aggregate a 5 percent return after transaction and financing costs. If P stands for the maximum expected loss in the 20 percent of cases in which convergence fails, it must be such that we still keep a weighted profit:

$$80\% \times 5\% - 20\% \times P \geq 0 \Rightarrow P \leq 20\%$$

Therefore, if we cannot be assured that, on average, losses remain below 20 percent when we are wrong, the whole strategy is question-

[45] See, for example, James Dow and Gary Gordon, "Arbitrage Chains," *Journal of Finance*, 49, *Papers and Proceedings of the Fifty-Fourth Annual Meeting of the American Finance Association*, 1994, pp. 819–849, for a discussion of trading horizon in arbitrage situations.

able. This is a very simplistic approach, but it has an enormous advantage in forcing us to quantify average profits, maximum losses, and success rates in a consistent way.

Incidentally, this simple formalism is powerful enough to handle the case of an absolute convergence. Consider that there is a 0.01 percent chance that a major exchange fails and that a future is not settled on a price equal to that of its underlying index. This corresponds to 1 in every 10,000 days—that is, every 40 years. Applying the above formalism and denoting p the profit associated with an individual transaction of index arbitrage:

$$99.99\% \times p - 0.01\% \times P \geq 0 \Rightarrow P \leq 9999 \times p$$

Based on these assumptions, if we believe that we cannot lose more than $9999p$ even if the exchange fails, index arbitrage is a profitable strategy over the long term. Is that reasonable? Assume that index arbitrage generates a 0.20 percent return.[46] The above condition states that P should be under 20 percent for us to break even on average. Therefore, the ultimate question is: Are we going to lose more than 20 percent of the total nominal of the position if the market breaks down? This is clearly an interesting question, and the answer is most likely yes: In most cases exchange members are directly liable when one of them fails, which would be the most likely cause of a general breakdown. For the whole system to collapse, there would have to be massive losses, and 20 percent is certainly a low estimate as to what would disappear to fill this gap.[47] As becomes evident, this whole exercise opens more doors than we like, and an arbitrageur should practice it actively to make sure he or she has an appropriate grasp of the risk involved.

Leaving aside the problem of expiry, there is another convergence failure that we need to consider to be exhaustive, and that is the effect of a disproportionate divergence after we have taken a position. We said earlier that arbitrageurs should know when to take a loss, and certainly the apparition of an exceptional divergence is one situation in

[46] We will come back to the examination of profitability. The figure 0.20 percent is based on the hypothesis that an arbitrageur captures the whole bid-ask spread on the S&P 500 index, independently of any other profit.

[47] As an interesting exercise, consider that 1929 was the closest we know of to a general market breakdown, and note that it happened once in the century, that is, with a probability of 1 over 25,000 days. The above calculation indicates a 50 percent acceptable loss for a profit of 0.20 percent.

which this skill might be needed. However, this is not the whole story because even in a fairly certain convergence situation, arbitrageurs may be driven to cut their positions even in the face of an extraordinary opportunity. This seemingly contradictory situation is similar to the notorious martingale about the roulette game. If you keep betting on the same color, twice the previous amount after each loss, statistically you have to break even after a finite amount of time. The main reason this does not work in practice is the limited amount of capital most of us have access to. If we keep losing and losing, chances are we will run out of money before we can make everything back.[48] In terms of arbitrage, even if the position is perfectly hedged, a divergence in the market actually costs money, through actual flows—in the case of margin calls, for example. The paper or actual loss may trigger management decisions to cut a position, at the worst time because the opportunity has never been as good, and at a considerable loss.[49] This is in essence what happened to LTCM[50]: The fund literally disappeared as a result of actual flows and paper losses, and it declared bankruptcy when it became apparent that the spreads it carried would not correct in the short run. There is no certainty that the underlying positions were true arbitrage; however it seems that the spreads did actually come back to somewhat normal levels in 1999.

Therefore, the convergence risk can take several forms and be of major importance at any time during the life of the position. As should become more and more apparent, this risk drives the implementation of the strategy and the different tools to evaluate it.

CONVERGENCE CONTINUUM

Although the above presentation looks like a precise segmentation, in practice, things are naturally not that simple. Absolute convergence stands out in the crowd because it is usually easily identified.

---

[48] In addition, to make sure that nobody ever tries his or her statistical chance, most casinos impose restrictions on the size of the bets.

[49] See Andrei Shleifer and Robert W. Vishny, "The Limits of Arbitrage," *The Journal of Finance*, 52, 1997, pp. 35–55, for a complete model of this phenomenon.

[50] LTCM (Long-Term Capital Management) was a very famous hedge fund established in the 1990s by some of the most respected "financial minds." It failed in 1998 as a result of heavy—and naturally unexpected—losses in Russia and other emerging markets. The managers claimed to be doing "arbitrage" all along. For more information on LTCM, see "Hedge Funds, Leverage and the Lessons of Long-Term Capital Management," *Report of the President's Working Group on Financial Markets*, April 1999, USGPO.

Explicit and hypothetical situations are much less apparent. For example, pair trading between similar companies can be managed as preemptive risk arbitrage: If the industry is mature and prone to consolidation, choosing the right pair based on strategic criteria is easier and safer than pure statistical analysis. Furthermore, trading strategies based simply on mean-reversion expectations can be considered akin to arbitrage strategies because of the assumed underlying divergence-convergence pattern, and they are much more developed than our restricted exposé suggests. Indeed, mean reversion in stock prices is a property that has been extensively studied,[51] and many traders or fund managers run sophisticated models to exploit it.

Therefore, our classification is somewhat too restricted to reflect the reality prevalent in the marketplace. Market participants involved in arbitrage, in a very general sense, expect a convergence that can exist in any state from absolute to hypothetical, from public to proprietary, and they can vary significantly over time. To account for this variety, we need to consider a broader scale, tabulated on the level of certainty about the eventual convergence, as in Table 1-9. We will apply this framework in more detail when we examine practical arbitrage situations at the end of this book. What should be clear already is the fact that qualifying a particular trading strategy as an arbitrage has necessary logical implications: valuation, risk analysis, and virtually all important characteristics related to this position are dictated by this qualification.

OTHER EXAMPLES

Cross-Exchange Listings

A *cross-exchange listing* is a classic example of an arbitrage situation because there is no complexity whatsoever in capturing value out of the arbitrage. The only skill required is execution, and the arbitrage can theoretically be handled automatically without any human intervention on hundreds of stocks at the same time if both legs accept electro-

[51] See, for example, Werner F. M. De Bond, and Richard H. Thaler, "Anomalies: A Mean Reverting Walk Down Wall Street," *Journal of Economic Perspectives*, 3, 1, winter 1989, pp. 189–202, and Eugene F. Fama and Kenneth R. French, "Permanent and Temporary Components of Stock Prices," *Journal of Political Economy*, 96, 2, April 1988, pp. 246–273, for early articles on the subject. This is exactly the property we propose to explore later with technical trading rules.

TABLE 1-9

	Absolute ←	**→ Hypothetical**
Valuation	Theoretical	Mark to market
Convergence type	Public	Highly proprietary
Convergence risk	Low to nonexistent	Critical
Execution risk	Critical	Low
Hedge	Fixed quantity	Fixed quantity or delta
Risk of carry	Important	Low
Time horizon	Known or bounded	Unknown
Window of opportunity	Very short	Longer
Profitability[a]	10 × 1	1 × 10
Robustness[b]	Strong	Weak
Implications	Pricing	None (Inefficient market?)

[a] The term 10 × 1 denotes repeated opportunities with relatively low profits. By contrast, 1 × 10 indicates infrequent but highly profitable trades.

[b] By *robustness*, we denote the ability of the position to resist a jump in the price of one or both legs—for example, bad earnings on one of the two securities, or a general and unexpected market movement of significant amplitude.

nic order submission. Obviously, this type of arbitrage requires an efficient access to both markets in terms of transaction costs and information flows.

A slightly more elaborate version of this arbitrage appears when one of the legs is an *American Depository Receipt* (ADR)—that is, the same share listed in domestic currency.[52] The carry of the position may generate a foreign exchange risk that needs to be monitored closely.

Domestically, the equivalent of cross listing is the proliferation of the electronic communications network (ECN), driving trading away from traditional platforms. These networks carry already more than 20 percent of all trading volumes. This fragmentation of exchanges, in sharp contrast to what is happening on the international scene, is the consequence of the current structure of the market, especially that of the NASDAQ. All ECN sponsors believe they can address this problem and propose better and cheaper executions. Whether they can sustain such trading volumes remains to be seen and is mostly dependent on traditional exchanges' competitive response.

In general, because of its simplicity, a strategy based on cross listing is unlikely to generate significant profits either because the price

[52] As we will see later, the abbreviation ADR may also be applied to derivatives—for example, the Nikkei 225 contract listed on the Chicago Mercantile Exchange versus the same contract listed in Osaka.

difference in itself is very small, or because the level of liquidity is relatively low as associated with "abnormal" prices.[53] Nevertheless, it is clear that many traders keep an eye on these opportunities.

Ex-Dividends

Traditional wisdom says that the price of a stock should go down by the amount of the dividend on the day it goes "ex."[54] This hypothesis is institutionalized, for example, by the fact that NYSE open orders are modified by the amount of dividend on an ex-day: The price of a buy limit order is actually reduced in the specialist's book by the amount of dividend.

However, this description is valid only in a world without taxes. In reality, in the United States dividends are taxed as income for most investors—and corporations—and therefore, depending on the specifics of a particular investor's tax status, it may be advantageous to sell the stock just before the ex-date. Because of the multitude of individual particularities, it is therefore virtually impossible to predict by what amount the price of the stock will *actually* fall.

Now consider the situation of a tax-advantaged investor, or trader.[55] He or she enjoys a tax bracket lower than the majority of market participants and could potentially lock an arbitrage by buying the stock on the day before ex-date at close and then selling it back just on open the next day. If the stock falls by less than the dividend, the loss generated by the decline in price is advantageously compensated by the cash dividend. This works because the tax rate embedded in the market price decline is higher than the investor's own rate.[56]

---

[53] As an illustration of this point see K. Kato, S. Linn, and J. Schallheim, "Are There Arbitrage Opportunities in the Market for American Depository Receipts?" *Journal of International Financial Markets, Institutions and Money*, 1, 1992, pp. 73–89.

[54] By definition, an *ex-dividend day* is the first day on which the stock trades without its dividend privilege.

[55] Index arbitrageurs in the United States enjoy such advantages because the tax shield from interest expenses resulting from the carry of the position is more than enough to offset the total amount of dividends paid by the stocks in the position.

[56] A variant of this arbitrage is to trade a derivative of the stock highly dependent on the dividend, like an American call. See, for example, Avner Kalay and Marti G. Subrahmanyam, "The Ex-Dividend Day Behavior of Option Prices," *Journal of Business*, 57, January 1984, pp. 113–128, or Ki-Young Chung and Herb Johnson, "Dividend Spreads," *Journal of Business*, 61, July 1988, pp. 299–319. These articles are not recent, but they describe how ex-day behavior may be taken advantage of with options.

Naturally as it is presented here, the arbitrage is not risk free because if the stock falls by more than the dividend due to a broad market move, the position is losing. One solution is to hedge it—for example, with an index futures. Does this work? In theory yes; in practice it is less certain. After accounting for transaction costs and execution risk, only those stocks with a high dividend yield are possible candidates, and those are precisely the ones that everybody monitors for this exact reason. On the other hand, in countries where the tax code has an intricate treatment of dividends there are real opportunities.[57] What is important here is to recognize that an arbitrage based on dividends is intimately dependent upon the local tax code, and a change in this code may result in more or less opportunities for arbitrageurs.[58]

Closed-End Funds

Introduction

Closed-end funds are investment vehicles that issue only a limited number of shares and, in contrast to open-end funds, shares cannot be issued or redeemed on an ongoing basis. Only at the stated maturity will the fund be opened and all the assets liquidated. Before that date, a majority of shareholders must support the opening for it to happen. In any case the ordinary or extraordinary conditions under which the fund is susceptible to open are stated in the fund's charter.

The shares are usually traded on an exchange, and because their market price may be different from the underlying net asset value (NAV), the funds trade at a discount or premium. Figure 1-4 shows for example the premium of the Japanese Equity Fund (JEQ) from October 1998 to October 1999. This fund is managed by Daiwa International Capital Management, and it invests in nonfinancial stocks listed on the Tokyo Stock Exchange.

---

[57] In particular, the question of tax rebate on dividends is an important driver of dividend-related arbitrages. See the chapter dedicated to stocks for a discussion of issues related to dividends taxation.

[58] See, for example, Ameziane Lasfer, "Ex-Day Behavior: Tax or Short-Term Trading Effects," *Journal of Finance*, 50, *Papers and Proceedings of the Fifty-Fifth Annual Meeting, American Finance Association*, Washington, D.C., January 1995 (July 1995), pp. 875–897, for a discussion of the impact of the 1988 Income and Corporation Taxes Act on ex-day stock price movements, or Ravinder K. Bhardwaj, and LeRoy D. Brooks, "Further Evidence on Dividend Yields and the Ex-Dividend Day Stock Price Effect," *Journal of Financial Research*, 22, winter 1999, pp. 503–514.

In fact, the existence of premiums and discounts on closed-end funds remains to this day one of the biggest mysteries in modern finance. These funds have been traded consistently at a discount over the years, both in the United States and the United Kingdom, as shown in the charts in Figure 1-5[59]:

There is no clear explanation of why this situation exists and persists. Numerous factors have been put forward to account for what appears to be a persistent inefficient market, with some success, but none has provided a definitive answer. Examples of the most common reasons are the following:

- *Unrealized capital appreciation* (–): Investors face built-in capital gains tax liability from a substantial amount of unrealized capital appreciation.
- *Distribution policy* (+/–): This policy has tax implications for investors with regard to current or deferred tax liabilities. In addition, to the extent that a fund is trading at a discount, a partial liquidation of assets in the form of a dividend allows investors to capture part of this discount, making it relatively more attractive.
- *Restricted, or letter, stock* (–): Stocks in the fund carry restrictive clauses and cannot be sold before the end of a stated holding period—for example, unregistered stocks acquired as a result of a private placement.
- *Holdings of foreign stocks* (+/–): Holdings of foreign stocks in countries with different tax treatments or legal environments may be particularly attractive or unattractive, especially if individuals are unable to replicate the same portfolio on their own.
- *Performance* (+/–): This is the most common argument. A fund will command a discount or premium based on the perceived ability of its management team to deliver outstanding results.
- *Turnover* (–): In general, transaction costs, in the form of brokerage fees or bad execution in the market, drive a fund's return down.
- *Management fee* (–): This is equivalent in nature to the previous argument because management fees are charged directly against the fund's return.[60]

---

[59] Therefore, the JEQ is much more an exception than a general case.

[60] Burton G. Malkiel, "The Valuation of Closed-End Investment Company Shares," *Journal of Finance*, 32, June 1977, pp. 847–859. The use of plus or minus signs indicates if the effect acts in the direction of a premium or discount.

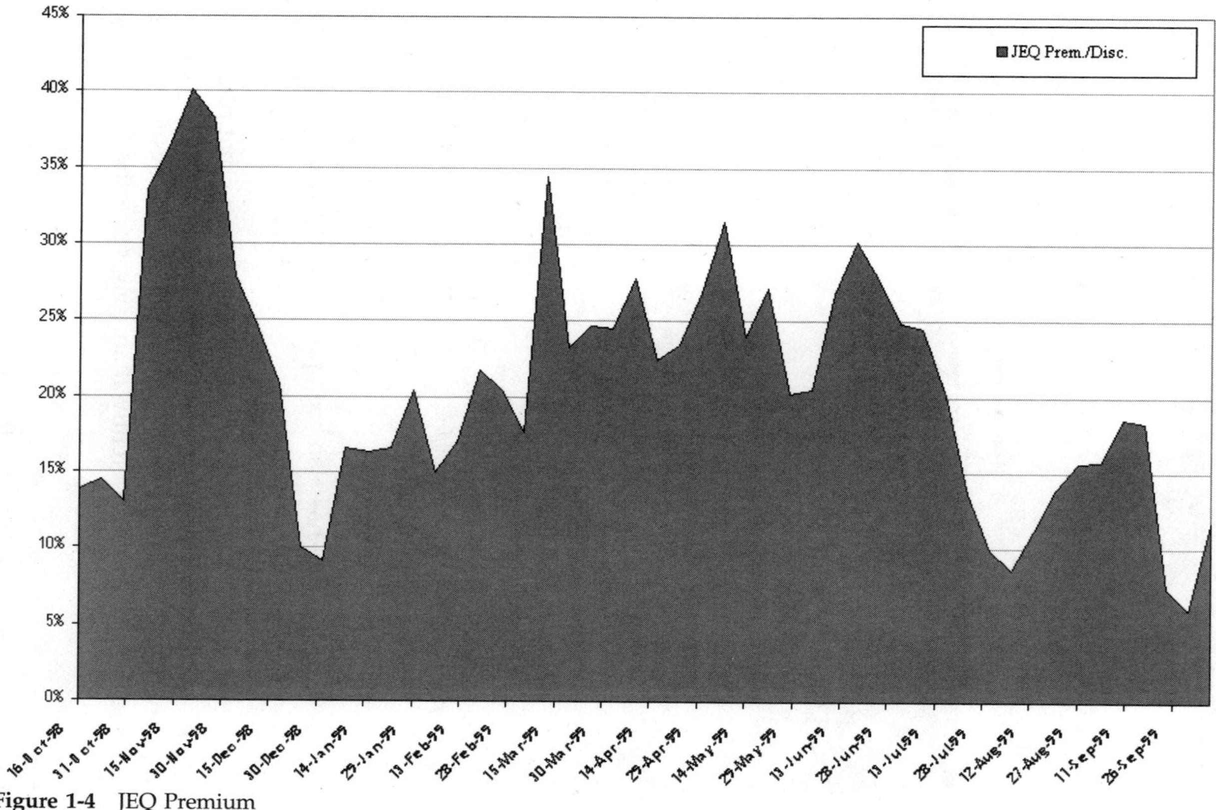

Figure 1-4 JEQ Premium
(*Source*: Compiled by author from Bloomberg data.)

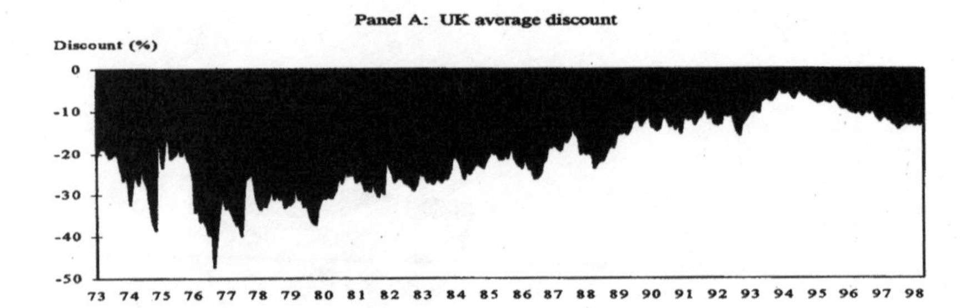

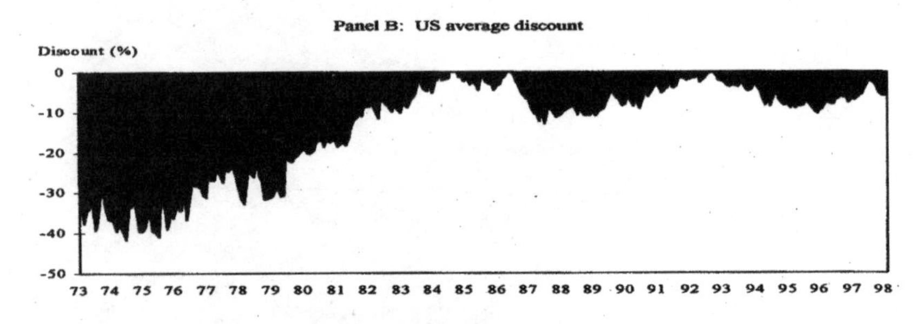

The Closed-End Fund Discount 1970–1998

The average discount is expressed as the logarithm of the unweighted mean ratio of Share Price to NAV. Panel A shows that the average discount of UK closed-end funds widened dramatically during the first half of the 1970s. Since then it has narrowed from almost 50% to around 10% in recent years. For the UK, we consider almost the entire industry, with the exception of funds that invest in unquoted securities (Venture & Development), specialist funds (Commodity & Energy and Property), Emerging Markets and Split Capital Funds. The data source for panel A is Datastream. Panel B shows the average discount of US domestic equity closed-end funds, using data made available by CDA/Wiesenberger.

Figure 1-5 Closed-End Fund Average Premium
(*Source*: Elroy Dimson and Carolina Minio-Kozerski, "Closed-End Funds: A Survey," *Financial Markets, Institutions and Instruments*, vol. 8, The NYU Salomon Center for Research in Financial Institutions and Markets, 1999.)

To this list a last one has also been proposed in the particular case of country funds:

- *Market sentiment*[61] (+/−): Based on the observation that premiums in foreign country funds tend to move together, this hypothesis suggests that U.S. investors in aggregate price the systematic risk attached to a country differently than they price the U.S. market

[61] See, for example, James N. Bodurtha, Jr., Dong-Soon Kim, and Charles M. C. Lee, "Closed-End Country Funds and Market Sentiment," *Review of Financial Studies*, 8, autumn 1995, pp. 879–918, or Charles M. C. Lee, Andrei Schleifer, and Richard H. Thaler, "Investment Sentiment and the Closed-End Fund Puzzle," *Journal of Finance*, 46, March 1991, pp. 75–109.

risk. Discounts or premiums in closed-end funds are one manifestation of this risk perception.

In that context, closed-end funds have been subject to intensive academic study.[62] One particular chapter of this research is of interest to us: the perspective of an arbitrageur confronted to a seemingly inefficient market, in other words a potentially very profitable opportunity.

Arbitrage

As a regulated investment institution, a closed-end fund is required to issue a prospectus regularly, in which it is generally possible to find a detailed list of the assets held and of the general allocation policy. From there arbitrage is a step away: If the fund trades at a discount and if it is possible to replicate its underlying portfolio at a reasonable cost, an arbitrageur would buy the fund, sell the equivalent portfolio and lock the discount until the fund opens upon maturity.

This simple form of arbitrage has many variants. For example, instead of trading the underlying assets, an arbitrageur may want to buy funds at a discount and sell others at a premium. The rationale is that the position would profit from a narrowing of the spread. Because discounts and premiums tend to vary over time in a relatively unpredictable fashion, this strategy may be profitable, but the funds should naturally be chosen carefully. In fact, the most efficient way to arbitrage a closed-end fund is also the most difficult to implement: It consists of purchasing shares just before the fund is about to open.[63] Figure 1-6 for example, shows that funds stated to open come back to their net asset value progressively.[64]

---

[62] In particular, Elroy Dimson and Carolina Minio-Kozerski, "Closed-End Funds: A Survey," *Financial Markets, Institutions and Instruments*, vol. 8, The NYU Salomon Center for Research in Financial Institutions and Markets, 1999, presents a very comprehensive review of the literature and of the issues behind the closed-end fund puzzle.

[63] Indeed, the best way is to force it to open. However, this requires a significant ownership and carries a lot of uncertainties because numerous funds' charters include protective clauses against hostile takeovers.

[64] Note the implications of Figure 1-6. The consistent discount on closed-end funds suggests some inefficiency in the market with regard to their pricing. However, when a fund is scheduled to open, it starts showing a premium compared to its peers, suggesting the discount decreases or disappears and prices return to efficiency. This selective efficiency is an integral part of the closed-end fund puzzle.

Naturally there are numerous difficulties in these simplistic approaches.[65] In a strategy based on the expectations that the fund will open, any news in that direction would provoke the market to react and probably the discount to decrease significantly. Indeed, the more certain the opening, the smaller the discount.

With respect to strategies based on portfolio replication, the first and foremost problem is that the fund's holdings are not constant; therefore a replicating portfolio has to be adjusted regularly. This usually happens much longer after the fund itself has been rebalanced because rebalancings are made public only infrequently—typically quarterly. These adjustments generate transaction costs and slowly dissipate the initial discount.[66] The second most important problem is the maturity of the position. Because there is no certainty that the fund will open anytime soon—except if the arbitrageur is a major shareholder and in a position to make it open—the arbitrage has to be carried until the discount disappears. If the replicating portfolio is not perfect, and in practice it rarely is, correlation with the fund will most likely deteriorate over time. Combined to a discount that may worsen before it improves, the arbitrageur may face situations in which the mark-to-market valuation is simply terrible. At this point is it justified to keep faith, or should the position be cut? A third difficulty occurs if the fund certificate cannot be borrowed; the reverse arbitrage in which the fund is sold to cash, the premium is then impossible, and an arbitrageur *has* to wait for a discount to even take a position. Even if the fund can be short-sold, a squeeze is always apt to appear and force the arbitrageur out at a loss.[67]

For all the reasons above arbitraging a closed-end fund is in general a difficult proposition. However, precisely because of these apparent and real intricacies, and also because there is usually a lot of value to extract—consider the 20 to 30 percent premium of JEQ as an example—it can be very profitable if executed properly.

---

[65] For a more comprehensive discussion about closed-end funds and quantitative results of arbitrage opportunities, see Carolina Minio-Paluello, *The UK Closed-End Fund Discount*, Ph.D. thesis, London Business School, London.

[66] For a discussion about the costs attached to an arbitrage position, see Jeffrey Pontiff, "Costly Arbitrage: Evidence from Closed-End Funds," *Quarterly Journal of Economics*, 111, 1996, pp. 1135–1151.

[67] A squeeze typically happens at the worst moment, for example, after the fund has appreciated sharply. The lender wants to take his or her profit right away and the short seller is forced to buy back the shares when they are at an unusually high price.

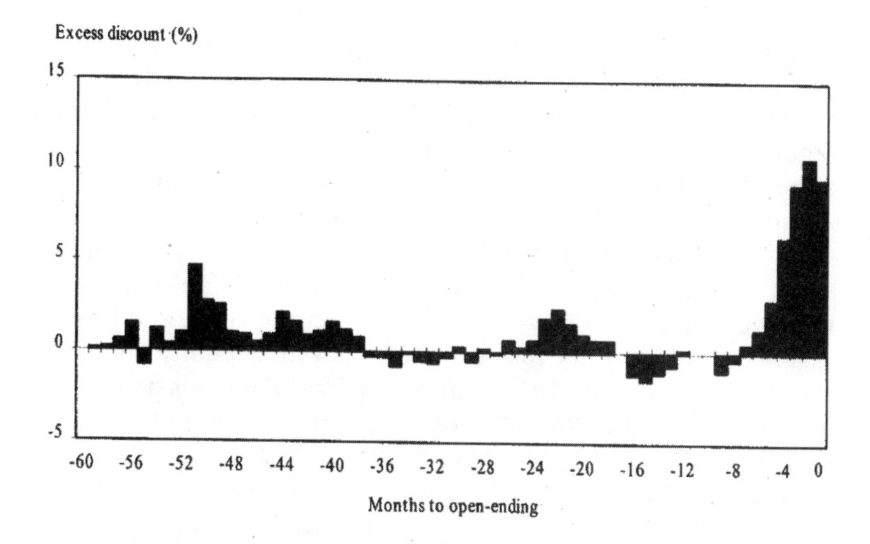

Mean Discount on Funds that Open-End

The average discount during the 60 months preceding open-ending is measured as the logarithm of the average price-to-NAV ratios across the 94 UK closed-end funds that disappeared during the period from January 1980 to December 1996. The figure plots the mean discount of the funds that open-end measured relative to the mean discount of the entire closed-end fund industry.

Figure 1-6 Premium to Maturity
(*Source*: Elroy Dimson and Carolina Minio-Kozerski, "Closed-End Funds: A Survey," *Financial Markets, Institutions and Instruments*, vol. 8, The NYU Salomon Center for Research in Financial Institutions and Markets, 1999.)

Convertible Funds

Convertible funds exhibit features that are a blend of open- and closed-end funds. Usually the fund is offered through an initial funding process during which institutional investors are main contributors. The fund is then listed on an exchange, and redemption or issuance of new shares is allowed upon delivery of physical assets identical to those already held by the fund.

This type of fund has originally been used to track indices. In this case the conversion option is equivalent to receiving or delivering shares of the members of the underlying index in proportion to their weighting. One early example of such a fund is the S&P 500 Standard and Poor's Depository Receipt (SPDR) listed at the beginning of 1993 on the American Exchange (AMEX), or the Nikkei 300 fund listed in 1995 on the Tokyo Stock Exchange and managed by Nomura

Investment Trust and Management. These products are typically targeted at individual investors and allow them to actively trade the index as a common share. The conversion clause specifies a minimum amount to redeem or issue new shares (for example, 50,000 shares for the SPDRs) and the rules to compute the exact number of shares in the delivery process.

In the United States these funds enjoy considerable interest and trading volume. In agreement with the old adage "You don't change a winning team," more have been issued over the years, and it is now possible to trade country funds—known as World Equity Benchmark Shares (WEBS)—or other index funds—such as Diamonds based on the Dow Jones Industrial Average, NASDAQ 100 Tracking Stock or S&P 400 SPDRs.[68] By contrast, the Nikkei 300 Fund has not been a trading success once listed. Indeed, arbitrageurs massively converted the fund into Nikkei 300 shares in the first year, dramatically reducing its trading liquidity. Because of high costs to create new shares, the fund manager was unable to maintain a decent liquidity, and market interest for the fund melted away progressively.

The arbitrage is based on the equivalence between the funds and its underlying assets. Because of the conversion clause, the fund is effectively a closed-end fund that can be opened at will. If its market price is higher than its net asset value, an arbitrageur would buy the underlying assets and sell the fund. In that situation the arbitrageur can always create new shares by delivering the assets, thereby closing the short leg easily. A possibly important question is to determine what is the minimum time to reach the conversion threshold. During the period when conversion is not possible because the minimum size has not been met, the arbitrageur is exposed, particularly if he or she short-sold the fund. If we take the example of S&P 500 SPDRs, this potential concern is in fact negligible because SPDRs rank regularly among the 10 most actively traded issues on the AMEX with volumes of several million shares a day. By contrast, this was not the case with the Nikkei 300 Fund.

In arbitraging convertible funds, the two most critical issues are the fund's distribution policy and the conversion process. Typically, index-tracking funds distribute the largest part of the dividends they receive, but they may be taxed on these. In addition, timing is important because distributions may occur sporadically—for example, every quarter for SPDRs—whereas the universe of underlying stocks, on

[68] See the AMEX Web site for more details.

aggregate, pays dividends virtually every day. Conversion is generally not free, and quantity-rounding problems may generate significant friction costs over several hundred different names.

Therefore, as is true with most other arbitrages, convertible funds are the source of profitable opportunities when handled rigorously. Here more than in any other case, arbitrageurs play an active role in providing trading liquidity.[69] These funds are primarily traded by retail investors for relatively small sizes, and arbitrageurs are apt to bring considerable size to the market, at a "fair price."

Holding Corporations

It is a well-known fact that a lot of holding companies in the 1980s were destroying an immense amount of shareholders' value, and corporate raiders had an easy game buying them and tearing them apart. The parts were often individually valued much higher than the whole, creating huge opportunities for financial engineers and skilled buyout investors. Eventually, the wave of terror that spread through corporate America led to massive divestitures from large corporations improperly diversified, and strategic focus became the credo of the day.[70] Breakup opportunities progressively disappeared, and nowadays the overhanging shadow of that period, combined with an incredible liquidity accessible to private equity funds, act as a powerful reality check on corporate diversification.

Holding companies have not disappeared, however, and surprisingly some of the same pricing anomalies still exist today with respect to the capitalization of the whole compared to that of its parts. Examples are relatively abundant, notably in foreign markets, because these markets have not been through a massive wave of consolidation and buyouts like the United States over the past 10 to 20 years. Even in

---

[69] Obviously this is a mixed blessing. In the case of the Nikkei 300 Fund, arbitrageurs actually drove liquidity away by converting their shares. A combination of high costs and poor market reception kept institutional investors from originating new shares, and arbitrageurs were unable to short-sell the fund in quantities large enough to create some new shares either. Eventually the fund died a slow death. Nevertheless, this is not a general case because SPDRs in the United States have been successful for quite a while without entering the same death spiral.

[70] For a discussion on takeovers and their consequences, see, for example, Michael Jensen, "Takeovers: Their Causes and Consequences," *Journal of Economic Perspectives*, 2, 1988, pp. 21–48 or Gregg Jarrell, James Brickley, and Jeffry Netter, "The Market for Corporate Control: The Empirical Evidence Since 1980," *Journal of Economic Perspectives*, 2, 1988, pp. 49–68.

the United States, however, some arbitrage opportunities are worth exploring, and we illustrate this point with the case of Loews Corporation (LTR).[71]

Loews consists of five subsidiaries, out of which three are listed and two are still private: CNA Financial Corporation (CNA, insurance), Diamond Offshore Drilling (DO, oil drilling contractor), Bulova Corporation (BULV, watches and timepieces), Loews Hotels (hotels), and Lorillard (tobacco products).

As of April 2000, LTR has 99.389m shares outstanding, holds 70.1m shares of DO (51.73 percent of its total capitalization), and 159.457m shares of CNA (87 percent of its capitalization). Bulova is relatively small, around \$100m in capitalization. It only makes the conclusion truer but does not change anything numerically. With market prices of respectively \$51 5/16 (LTR), \$35 9/16 (DO), and \$30 5/8 (CNA) on April 10, LTR is worth \$5.1b, whereas its holdings of DO and CNA amount to \$2.49b and \$4.88b, for a total of \$7.37b. The difference is \$2.27b, not even accounting for Lorillard or Loews Hotels. As it happens, Lorillard is a very profitable and cash-rich business, which only aggravates the mispricing.[72] All together, LTR should be at least \$2.27b higher, which translates into \$22.90 on its share price. The discount is therefore 30.86 percent compared to its minimum fair value based on CNA and DO holdings. The discount has not always been as large, and in fact in the past Loews has also traded at a premium, as shown in Figure 1-7.[73] The reasons for the existence of such a consistent discount are unclear, and the whole situation is not without similarities to the closed-end fund puzzle.[74] Some explanations propose the illiquid nature of LTR's underlying assets as a possible route, or the existence of huge liabilities

---

[71] This particular opportunity was originally mentioned by two friends, Vincent Jacheet and Laurent Saltiel, and I very much appreciate their suggestion.

[72] Recall, for example, the RJR Nabisco buyout by Kolhberg, Kravis, Rogers & Co. (KKR) in 1989. The tobacco industry has some very interesting features, notably the relatively low-tech environment and highly "loyal" customers, which made RJR essentially a cash cow. To some extent, the same thing is true of Lorillard, which manufactures and distributes well-known brands.

[73] Figure 1-7 shows the discount as a positive number. On April 10, for example, the value of 30.9 percent indicates that LTR is too low by 30.9 percent compared to CNA and DO holdings. Note also that what appears to be a premium before may still be an actual discount in reality if LTR is still too low compared to the value of its entire holding portfolio.

[74] In particular, when a holding corporation announces a spinoff or liquidation of some of its assets, its discount disappears very quickly, an effect that has been observed as well on closed-end funds.

hanging over Lorillard due to its tobacco business. In any case, even if the magnitude of the discount remains a mystery, the arbitrage opportunity is probably real. The discount appears to be distributed around 0, which indicates that it may be possible to trade it alternatively on both sides and lock the difference. Indeed, it could be assimilated to an oscillator, except for its sharp increase during the last month of 1999. In addition, the more volatile it is, the better because an arbitrageur will have more opportunities to trade around its local average value. Taking advantage of this opportunity requires a lot of patience, however, because typically there cannot be any certainty about an improvement in the near future. Even if a position turns profitable after a while, the cost of carry may have been significant, possibly lowering the return to unattractive levels.[75]

Historical Performance

For obvious reasons, it is difficult to access data about specific strategies involving arbitrage. The closest we can get to this is to extract data from hedge fund records because there is simply no way to access information about proprietary strategies. Table 1-10 presents the aggregate asset size of different classes of hedge funds, as of November 1999.

The strategies mentioned explicitly refer to arbitrage or relative value, even though it is difficult to know exactly what is behind the label. As we indicated earlier, convertible arbitrage is questionable from an arbitrage perspective if volatility is a large component of the risk of carry, and the same thing is true of option arbitrage.

These funds have posted very decent performances over the years as shown in Figure 1-8 (value of $100 invested on the first year, compounded at the annual rate of return of the fund category). Interestingly enough, market-neutral funds are traceable for 25 years, hold the largest amount of capital by far, and their uninterrupted exponential growth suggests that markets are not necessarily getting more efficient on aggregate.

The chart in Figure 1-9 also gives some interesting insight as to the relative profitability of the different strategies. Except for option arbitrage which seems to stand out from the crowd, all others have similar

---

[75] For another example of a holding corporation trading at a discount, see also "What Is CMGI Worth?" *The Industry Standard*, August 16, 2000, p. 79. The article suggests an aggregate valued of $39 a share, for the underlying portfolio for a traded price of $33.19. For an example of a holding corporation that is also a closed-end fund, see also the MeVC Fund (ticker: MVC) www.mevc.com.

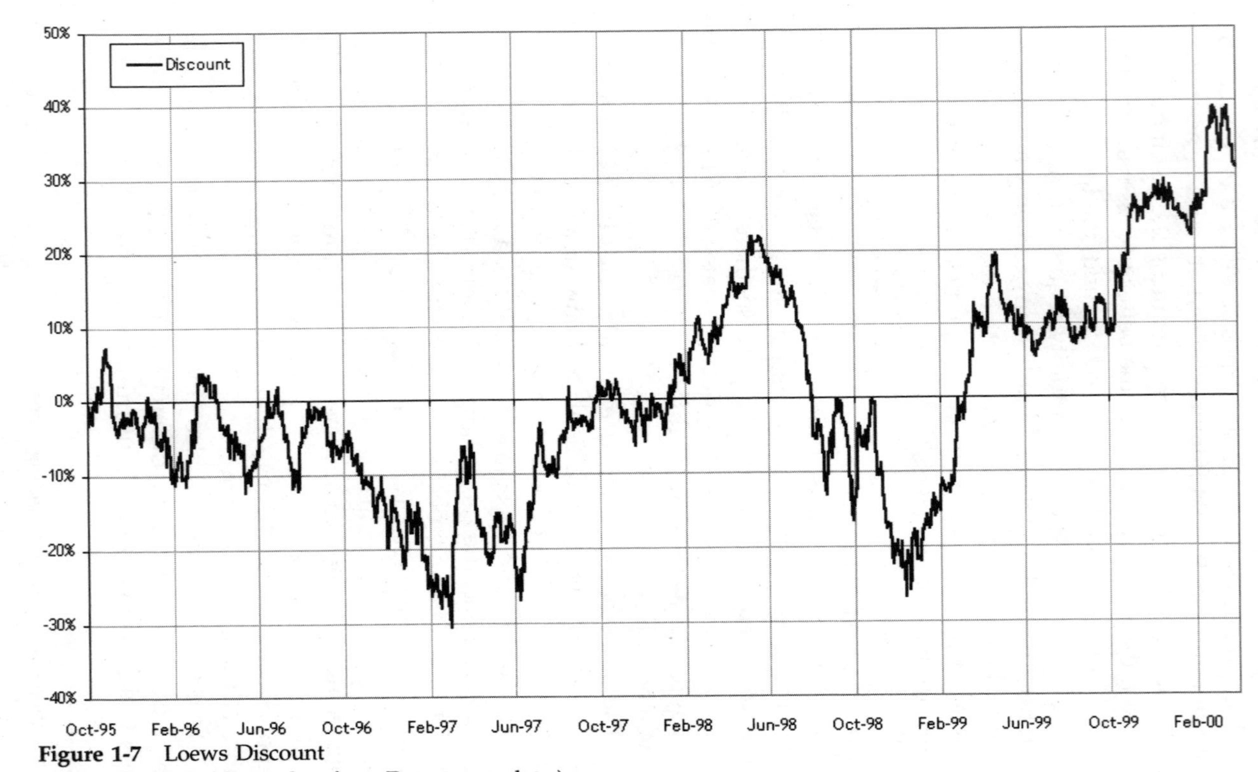

Figure 1-7 Loews Discount
(*Source*: Compiled by author from Datastream data.)

TABLE 1-10

Strategy	Assets ($ millions)	CAGR[a]
Convertible arbitrage	$1,865	14.9% (9)
Fixed-income arbitrage	$1,584	15.5% (18)
Market neutral	$4,165	16.0% (25)
Options arbitrage	$778	28.4% (5)
Risk arbitrage	$3,001	13.2% (9)
Statistical arbitrage	$1,440	19.0% (8)
Other relative value	$2,627	8.2% (5)
Total	**$15,460**	

[a] CAGR: Compounded annual growth rate. The number in parentheses is the number of years of data available.

(*Source*: HedgeFund.net. Reprinted with permission.)

and steady performances. Are these profits a reflection of the level of market inefficiency in the United States? Probably to some extent if we assume that the level of risk associated with these strategies is relatively low, which is far from certain. No similar data are available from other international markets, but it is reasonable to assume that there are at least as many opportunities, leaving aside uncertainties about different regulatory environments.

In any case, $15 billion is certainly not sufficient to arbitrage the U.S. market. These profits, therefore, represent only a tiny fraction of the money extracted by all arbitrageurs together, implicit as well as explicit.

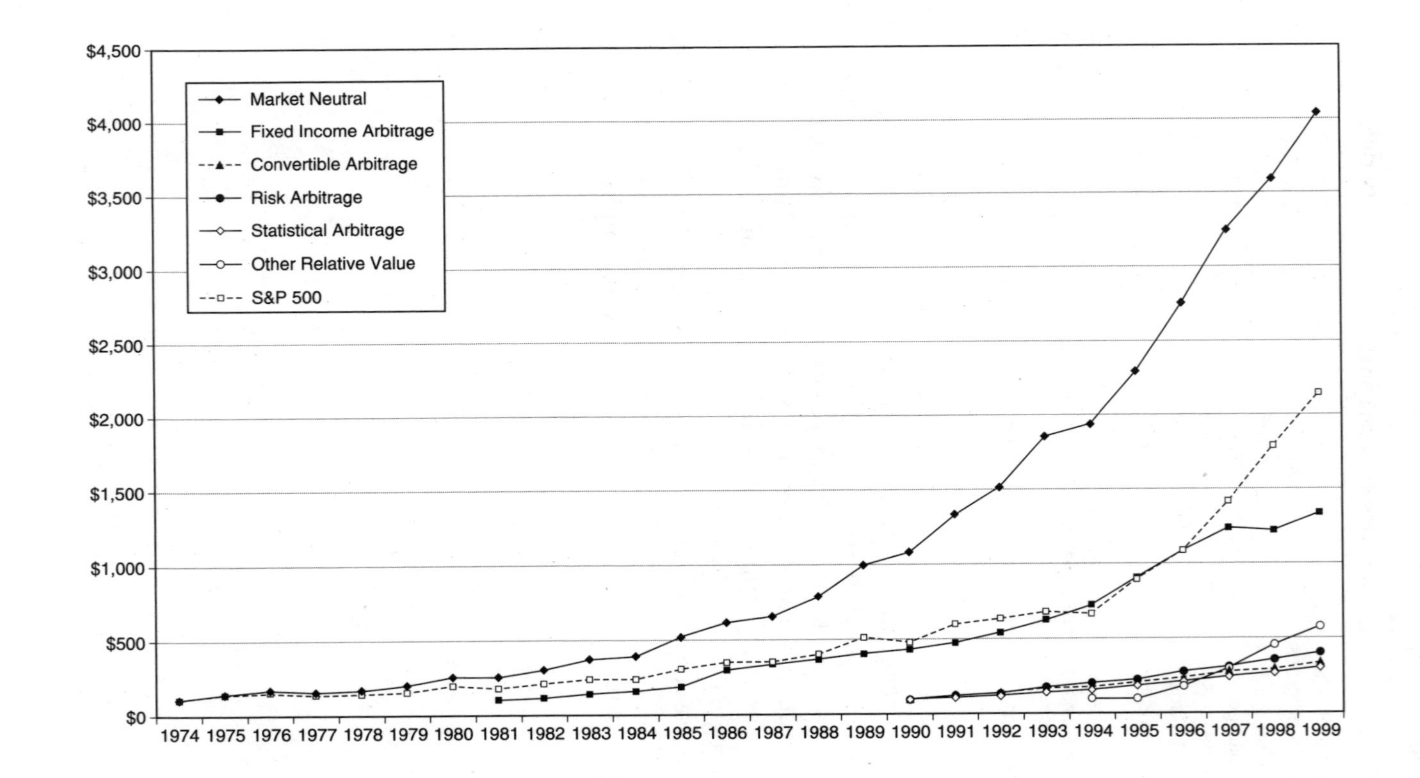

Figure 1-8 Hedge Fund Performance by Strategy
(*Source*: HedgeFund.net. Reprinted with permission.)

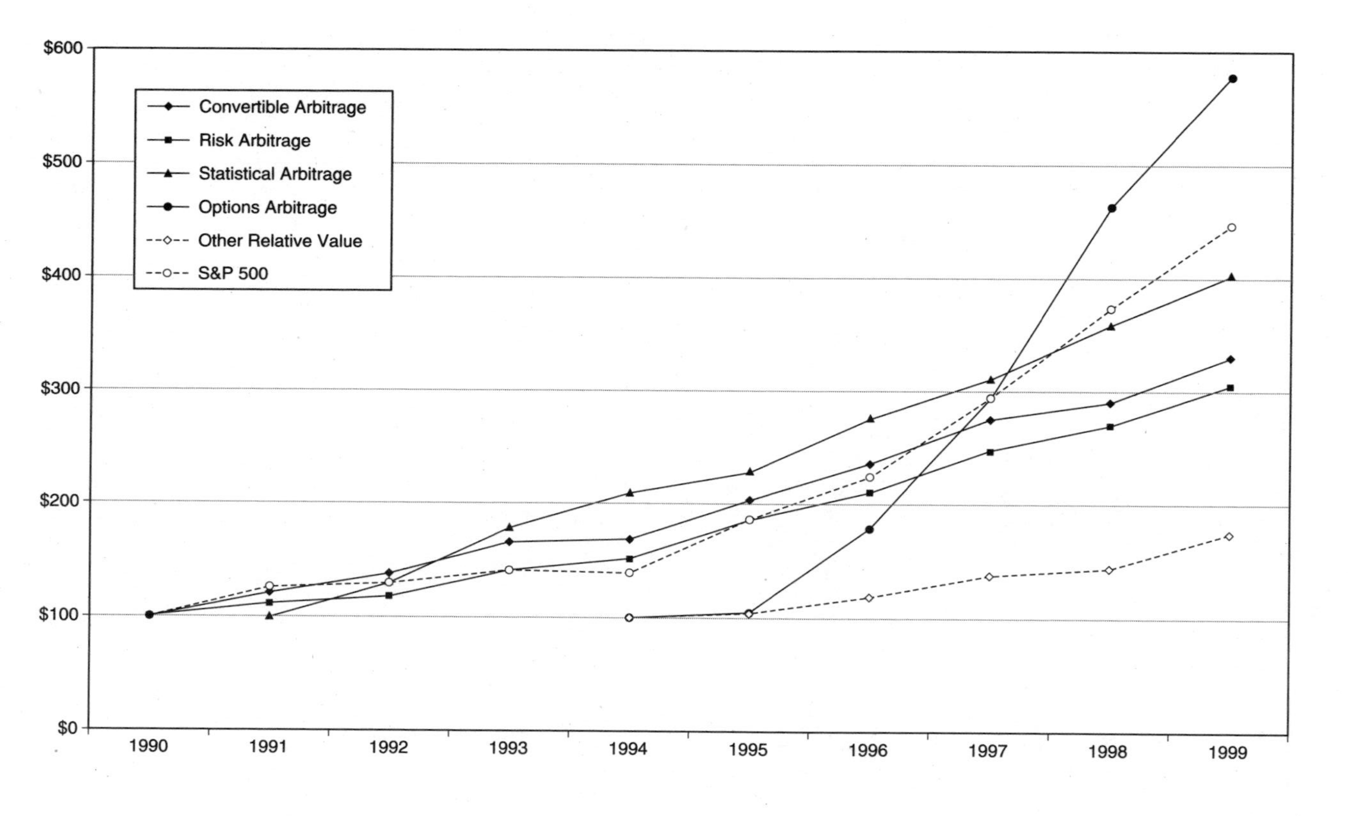

Figure 1-9 Hedge Fund Performance by Strategy
(*Source:* HedgeFund.net. Reprinted with permission.)

2

STOCKS

INTRODUCTION

By way of introduction, Table 2-1, along with Figures 2-1 and 2-2, present the world equity capitalization and the details of the five largest markets.

Considering that the world stock market capitalization was $21,626 trillion in 1997 and $25,683 trillion in 1998, these five combined markets list more than 75 percent of the world equity wealth. This particular percentage has varied significantly over the years and seems to be steadily going up at this time. Figure 2-2 gives an indication about the direction of equity capital allocation throughout the world. After being extremely attractive to foreign investors until 1993 and 1994, "emerging markets"—in a broad sense, any market other than the five largest—have progressively lost ground, presumably as a consequence of the Mexican crisis in 1994. From that time a multiplication of crises in Asia and South America has steadily pushed capital back to more mature markets.

With respect to arbitrage, the overall share of these five markets is undoubtedly much higher than 75 percent. Indeed, outside the markets of continental Europe, North America, and Japan, it is fair to say that arbitrage is hardly more than embryonic because of inadequate trading structures, lack of liquidity, or regulatory restrictions. Therefore, our analysis is indeed inclusive of all the significant markets in the realm of equity arbitrage. It also turns out that they present striking differences in many respects, making their successive examination instructive as well as entertaining. Table 2-2 provides a simplified overview of the major exchanges and some of the issues we will cover.

TABLE 2-1 World Equity Markets

Exchange (Domestic Shares Only)	Capitalization 1997 (US$ Trillions)	Capitalization 1998 (US$ Trillions)	Average Daily Volume (1998, Million Shares)	Average Daily Nominal (1998, US$ billion[a])
New York[b]	10,617	12,800	679.0	26.89 (TSV)
Tokyo	2,161	2,440	492.9	3.00 (TSV)
London	1,996	2,373	1,668.2	4.17 (REV)
Frankfurt	825	1,094	166.8	5.57 (REV)
Paris	676	991	36.5	2.30 (TSV)
				8.05 (REV)
Total	**16,275**	**19,698**		

Notes: *TSV stands for trading system view*: Exchanges count as turnover only those transactions that pass through their trading systems or that take place on the exchange's trading floor. *REV is regulated environment view*: Exchanges include in their turnover figures all transactions subject to supervision by the market authority (transactions by member firms, and sometimes non-members, with no distinction between on and off market, and transactions made into foreign markets reported on the national market).

[a] The nominal data have been calculated using a monthly exchange rate. At year-end 1998, 1USD = 5.8262FRF, 1USD = 112.8JPY, 1USD = 1.6656DEM, 1USD = 0.6011GBP.

[b] Including NYSE and Nasdaq.

(*Source*: Compiled by author from International Federation of Stock Exchanges (FIBV) data, www.fibv.com. Data as of December 31, 1998.)

DEFINITIONS

For the purpose of our discussion, a *stock* is a certificate of ownership issued by a company, entitling its holder to certain *benefits* (such as dividends, capital appreciation, or distribution of new shares), and *rights* (such as voting rights or preferred subscription rights for new issuance).

The definition above is simplified, but it captures the largest part of the information we need:

- As a *partial owner*, the stockholder is not a creditor, as opposed to a bondholder. As such, the failure of the issuing entity is the most critical risk.[1]
- The benefits and rights can usually be expressed in terms of monetary flows—that is, capital gains, regular dividend pay-

[1] This risk is not the only one, however; settlement risk, for example, is important when buying and selling securities. We concentrate in general on market risks because those are the ones over which traders have some control by adjusting the size and composition of their position.

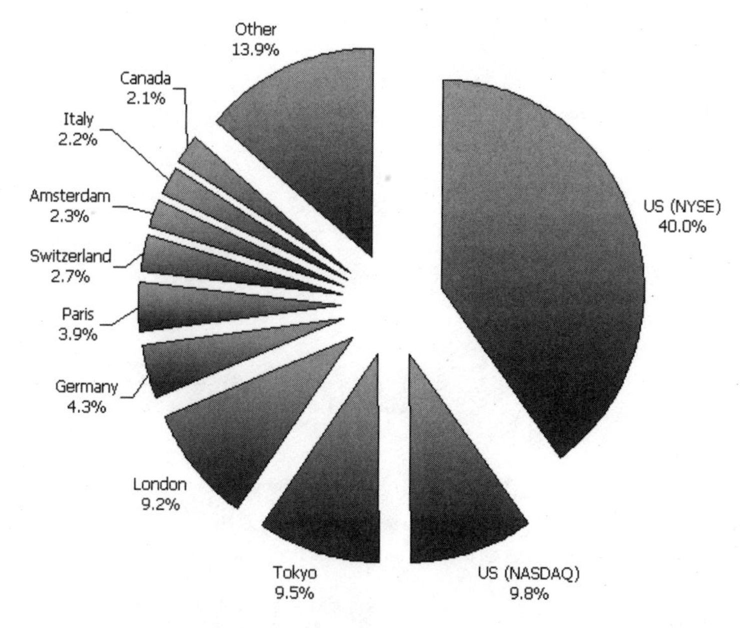

Figure 2-1 World Equity Markets by Capitalization, 1998
(*Source*: Compiled by author from FIBV data.)

ments, or distribution of free shares. The nonmonetary benefits or rights—for example, voting rights—are usually not relevant to arbitrageurs.[2]

- The rights attached to the stock can be extremely diverse. Those of interest to us are mainly affecting either the outstanding number of shares—for example, splits, buybacks, preferred subscriptions to new issues—or the total capitalization of the company—as would be true of a merger or recapitalization.

The types of corporate equity and their characteristics vary considerably from one market to the other. European stocks commonly offer detachable rights that can be traded separately because preferred subscriptions to new issues are fairly common. Germany and the United Kingdom have lots of preferred shares, many included in major indices. In Japan preferred shares and rights are extremely uncommon, limited to banks and other financial

[2] There may be exceptions—for example, if a risk arbitrageur holds a position large enough to influence the final likelihood of a corporate decision or is in a position to force a closed fund to open. In practice, this rarely happens.

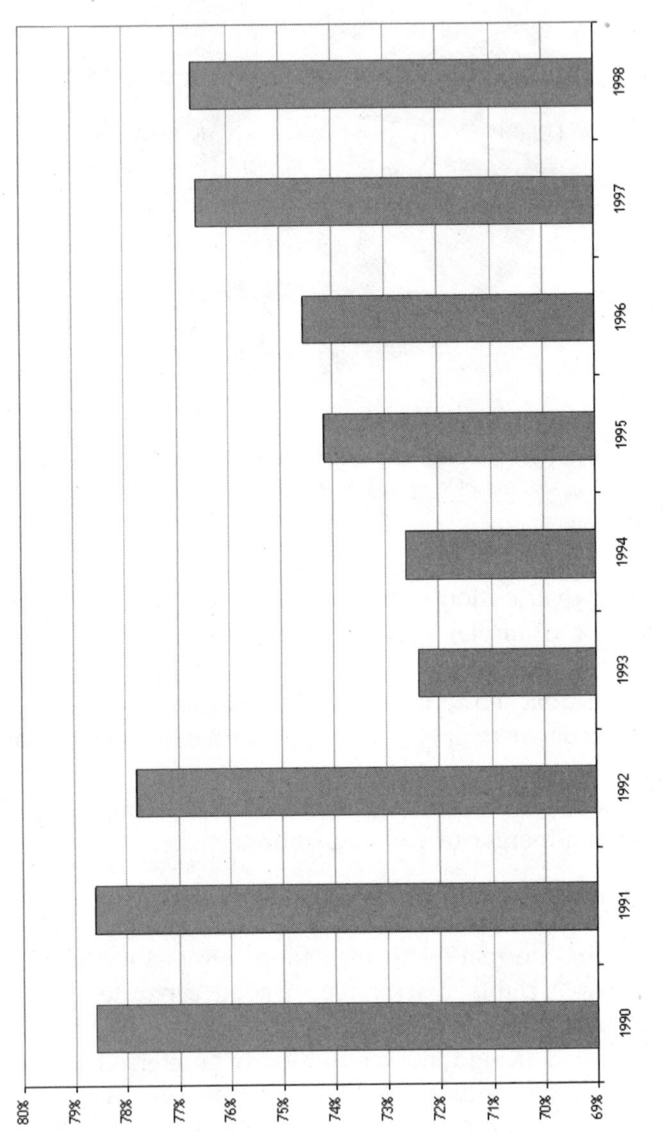

Figure 2-2 Share of World Capitalization: Five Largest Markets
(*Source:* Compiled by author from FIBV data.)

institutions.[3] In the United States, splits, share buybacks, mergers, and spinoffs are more frequent than anywhere else, whereas they are nonexistent in Japan and growing but still limited in Europe.[4]

From an investor's perspective, it is certainly important to clarify a company's capital structure, and therefore its debt and equity characteristics. From an equity arbitrageur's point of view, the important concern is continuity in the *listed* equity capitalization. For example, the issuance of a bond—even a convertible bond—has usually no effect on an arbitrage position and therefore can be regarded as irrelevant.[5] On the other hand, *conversion* of outstanding convertible bonds may affect the outstanding capitalization and therefore should be monitored. In practice, only massive conversions are considered (i.e., redemption at expiry).

In the analysis that follows, a stock will be characterized mostly by its price, dividend stream and capitalization—in the form of its outstanding number of shares.

SETTLEMENT

General Process

Without entering too far into painful details, it is necessary at this point to consider the general settlement procedures for stocks:

- The exchange receives and handles the orders—that is, it matches buyers and sellers, each of them being uniquely identified.

---

[3] In general, preferred shares carry a preferential dividend yield that is generally cumulative; no dividend on common shares is allowed until the preferred have been paid. They also have privileged claims on corporate assets compared to common shares, but these claims are still subordinated to those of debt holders.

[4] For a specific discussion of share buybacks in Europe compared to the United States, see for example, "Charms of Buy-Backs Are Resisted," *Financial Times*, May 11, 2000.

[5] An important distinction here is *price* vs. *structural* impact. The issuance of new preferred equity shares, for example, may be perceived negatively by market participants, driving the price of the common stock down, and the same thing may be true of a bond issuance. However, this would be considered for all practical purposes an exogenous shock. The actual conversion of convertible securities, on the other hand, will generally not affect the price of the stock but rather, require an index arbitrageur, for example, to adjust his or her holdings and buy or sell more of the stock, as a direct result of the change in the *structure* of the listed capitalization. Naturally this is entirely misplaced for strategies based on convertible arbitrage.

TABLE 2-2 Market Information on FIBV Member Exchanges, 1999

Exchange	Types of Securities Traded	Trading System/ Derivatives Market	Trading Hours	Supervisory Body	Clearing and Settlement Organization	Settlement Cycle	CSD	Taxes on Transactions	Taxes on Dividends, Interests
American Stock Exchange	Stocks	Floor trading, PER (for equities) and AMOS (for options) order routing and reporting systems.	9.30–16.00	Securities and Exchange Commission (SEC)	National Securities Clearing Corporation (NSCC) for all securities other than options	$T+3$	Depository Trust Company (DTC)	None	*US Citizens and Residents*: Dividends, interest, and short-term (assets held not more than 18 months) capital gains are taxed as ordinary income (39.6% marginal rate). Long-term capital gains are taxed at a 20% marginal rate. State and local authorities may impose additional income taxes. *Non-Resident Aliens* Dividend and interest income is subject to a 30% withholding tax. This tax may be reduced or eliminated if the nonresident is entitled to the benefit of a tax treaty. Capital gains generally are not subject to income tax.
	Warrants	Auction market with specialists.	9.30–16.00			$T+3$			
	Equity hybrid securities	Electronic limit order books for equities and options.	9.30–16.00			$T+3$			
	Portfolio depositary receipts		9.30–16.15			$T+3$			
Deutsche Börse —Frankfurt SE	Shares Bonds Warrants	Floor trading (BOSS-CUBE) Xetra (screen-based)	8.30–17.00 8.30–17.00	Ministry of Economics of the State of Hesse	Deutsche Börse Clearing AG	$T+2$	Deutsche Börse Clearing AG	None	*Residents*: Depending on total annual income. Max. 53%. *NonResidents*: Dividends: depending on double taxation treaties, average: 15% with possible claim of refund of 10%.
London	FTSE 100	SETS	8.30–16.30	Her Majesty's Treasury (Competent Authority) Financial Services Authority	CREST	$T+5$	CREST	0.5%	Dependent on taxpayer at taxpayer's marginal rate of taxation
	Other UK equities	SEAQ SEATS Plus (inc AIM)							
	International equities	SEAQ International	Variable		Euroclear/Cedel/local systems	As home market			
NASD	Shares	Screen-based quote system with automated execution system. There are 2 systems in Nasdaq: the Small Order Execution System (SOES), for automatic execution of small orders (up to 1,000 shares), and SelectNet for negotiated transactions and electronic executions.	9.30–16.00	Securities and Exchange Commission (SEC)	National Securities Clearing Corporation (NSCC) and Depository Trust Company (DTC)	$T+3$	Depository Trust Company (DTC)	No stamp duty and transfer taxes on transactions	15%–28% (treated as ordinary income)

(continued)

TABLE 2-2 (*continued*)

Exchange	Types of Securities Traded	Trading System/ Derivatives Market	Trading Hours	Supervisory Body	Clearing and Settlement Organization	Settlement Cycle	CSD	Taxes on Transactions	Taxes on Dividends, Interests
New York	Stocks Bonds Warrnts	Floor Trading (SuperDot order routing and reporting system) Auction market with specialists	9.30–16.00	Securities and Exchange Commission (SEC)	National Securities Clearing Corporation (NSCC)	$T + 3$	Depository Trust Company (DTC)	None	15%–28% (treated as ordinary income)
Paris	Equities Bonds	NSC (Nouveau Système de Cotation)	10.00–17.00	CMF/COB	*Clearing-house*: SBF-Bourse de Paris *Settlement*: SICOVAM	$T + 3$ and monthly settlement basis	SICOVAM	Capital gains above 50,000 taxed at 26% Stamp duty on French securities for French individual investors	Dividends and interest are declared as revenue and taxed accordingly. There is a tax credit on dividends ("avoir fiscal")
Tokyo	Shares Stock investment trust certificates	Floor and screen-based trading with CORES (Computer-Assisted Order Routing and Execution System)	9.00–11.00 and 12.30–15.00	Ministry of Finance	TSE, Japan Securities Clearing Corp. (JSCC)	$T + 3$	Japan Securities Depository Center (JASDEC)	0.10%	*Dividends*: *Residents*: Aggregate or separate (35%) *Nonresident*: 20%

(*Source*: Compiled by author from FIBV data.)

- A clearinghouse receives shortly after—usually the next day—an electronic download of these transactions.[6] It allocates these trades among its members, and it informs them of the transactions it knows.
- On settlement day, stocks are received and delivered for payment, and the corresponding entries are recorded in the book of a national depository trust.

Even if each market has its own settlement rule and its particular entities, the value chain is virtually identical. It is imposed by the volume of transactions commonly handled by exchanges around the world and the demand for a safe and reliable settlement environment. Indeed, it is important to emphasize that this apparently complex structure has been designed to reduce a major settlement concern, the risk that a counterpart receives securities and fails to pay for them because it defaults. Institutions with clearly defined roles and a close integration with the Fedwire system—which handles most monetary flows in the United States—intervene to ensure that a delivery does not occur without a corresponding payment. Even with the level of effort applied into the design of an efficient system, the credit risk inherent in the settlement process has not entirely disappeared and remains a real concern even in the United States.[7]

Date Convention

We will refer to the *trade date* (TD) or *operation date* (OD) as the date on which the transaction is actually executed on the exchange, and to *value date* (VD) or *settlement date* (SD) as the date on which the shares are physically received or delivered against full payment. From a risk point of view, market exposure appears on the operation date, not the settlement date.[8]

---

[6] In some countries a single clearinghouse clears all the trades at a national level. In other countries several distinct small clearinghouses exist and manage the clearing process through a set of electronic automated links.

[7] Under some circumstances, a *fail to deliver* may occur even with large names. Under tight borrowing conditions, for example, short sellers of a given security may be punctually unable to fulfill their obligation to deliver. Most day-to-day failures are isolated and corrected rapidly and therefore inconsequential.

[8] Naturally, from a financing perspective, interests on the money received or paid start or stop accruing from the settlement date.

In the United States, the standard value date is three business open days: VD = OD + 3.[9] This holds for all U.S. stocks, regardless of the exchange they are listed on. The exact definition of *business day* is a day on which *U.S. banks are opened for business*—in other words, a day on which monetary transactions can be settled. Some days are banking holidays but not exchange holidays; no stock transaction is settled even though the exchange is open.

In the United Kingdom, stocks settle on OD + 5; in Germany, OD + 2; in Japan, OD + 3. The most interesting example of uncommon settlement is France, which uses a liquidation process for the main section of the Paris Stock Exchange, known as *Règlement Mensuel* (monthly settlement). Transactions are physically settled only on the last open day of each month. Six days before, a general liquidation process is run; the total volume of outstanding buys is matched against the total volume of outstanding sells, stock by stock. Each participant has announced prior to the matching his or her intention to settle his or her position, or, on the contrary, to carry it over into the following month. Accordingly, the liquidation shows an outstanding balance of shares unsettled; an excess of sellers who decide not to deliver will create a borrowing position on the security, and reciprocally. Eventually, each participant with a position carried over receives or is liable for the *cost of carry*, according to the settlement unbalance.[10] To ensure a minimum coverage for the risk outstanding and not settled, the exchange requires a 20 percent deposit on all open positions[11] to be paid on the operation date. This process is similar to the deposit requirement of a futures

---

[9] The United States is currently moving toward a settlement at OD + 1, mandated by the Securities and Exchange Commission for 2002.

[10] The cost of carry can be of two types: If a buying position is unsettled and a long balance of stocks appears as a result of the liquidation, there is a deficit of cash on the market. Many sellers have claimed their proceeds, and too few buyers are paying for their purchases. Accordingly, the necessary injection of money is charged to the buyers, and as a result, their cost of carry is equivalent to a financing cost from this liquidation to the next. The second type of cost is the opposite, and it is less frequent: Sellers are unable to deliver the shares—because there are too many short-selling positions, for example. In that case, they are charged, in essence, a borrowing fee.

[11] The liquidation offers "financing-free trading," to a certain extent. An investor settling his or her trade at the first liquidation after his or her transaction will save the financing cost on 80 percent of his or her position from trade date to liquidation date. However, if he or she carries over, he or she ends up paying a charge equivalent to a full month financing until the next liquidation.

contract. It also implies margin calls when mark-to-market losses exceed the initial deposit.[12]

CROSS-EXCHANGE LISTING

Introduction

Considering the ongoing globalization in the markets for goods and services, it is no surprise that a parallel globalization is occurring in the markets for capital. When corporations that are traditionally established in delimited geographical areas expand to a global scale, it is a legitimate concern for them to reconsider the localization of their investor base. Having listed decades or years earlier their shares in their home market, they face the opportunity to list those shares on foreign exchanges, with distinct benefits and costs.

Cross listing is important from an arbitrageur perspective because it is a very simple and straightforward opportunity, as we mentioned earlier. In addition, it is more and more frequent, therefore it is of interest to our overall target. The following discussion focuses primarily on the rationale for cross listing and details the most important innovation: depository receipts.

International Cross Listing

Rationale

The rationale for a cross-listing initiative can be multifaceted. The most basic motivation is to raise capital from international investors to establish a presence in capital markets untapped before.[13] If raising capital is not needed, listing the stock might attract a wider shareholder base and

[12] At the time of writing, the Règlement Mensuel is still in existence, but its days are numbered. Indeed, the French Stock Exchange has announced that all stocks will follow a regular settlement cycle OD + 3 from September 25, 2000. Individual investors will still have the option to postpone settlement to the end of the month like a monthly settlement, but this service becomes a convenience feature provided by brokers, at a cost.

[13] In the case of non-U.S. companies listing their shares in the United States, evidence suggests that the overall cost of equity goes down subsequent to the listing by more than 1 percent.

diversify control of the company. The reasons for doing that may be diverse, but undoubtedly the growing interrelation of world markets call for a reexamination of corporate control beyond geographical borders.[14] In addition, attracting new investors may improve the overall liquidity of the stock.[15]

Therefore, in a context where the need exists, numerous solutions have been proposed to address it. The simplest form of cross listing, for example, is a direct listing on a domestic exchange of a foreign stock. The company applies for listing directly to the exchange, and it must satisfy all the conditions set forth in the listing agreement,[16] in addition to paying a—usually significant—listing fee. Numerous exchanges have indeed developed "foreign sections" in their effort to attract foreign corporations. However, this process can be long and expensive, and one alternative has been proposed and been very successful over the years: depository receipts.

Depository Receipts

Depository receipts were invented by JP Morgan in the late 1920s. Instead of having a firm apply directly for listing, an American institution—usually a bank—holds some of its shares and issues a depositary receipt in the United States against them.[17] For example, in a 1-to-1 ADR, each depository receipt corresponds to one share of the company. The receipts are then listed in the United States by the issuing institution, and they are traded as if they were actual shares of the

---

[14] For a complete discussion of this phenomenon, see Andrew Karolyi, "Why Do Companies List Share Abroad? A Survey of the Evidence and Its Managerial Implications," *Financial Markets, Institutions and Instruments*, The NYU Salomon Center for Research in Financial Institutions and Markets, 1998.

[15] A subsequent interesting question is whether the overall liquidity aggregates in one particular marketplace. See Melek Pulatkonak and George Sofianos, "The Distribution of Global Trading in NYSE-Listed Non-US Stocks," NYSE Working Paper 99-03, 1999, for a more complete examination of this issue.

[16] Indeed, it must also satisfy the disclosure and accounting requirements in the targeted country. This particular condition is especially constraining for a listing in the United States, which probably has the most stringent accounting standards.

[17] Depository receipts can be American (ADR) when the recipient market is the United States or global (GDR). Originally this structure was used by companies looking to list their stock in the United States; therefore, *ADRs* has become the generic term to describe these papers, and we will follow this convention here.

ADRs can be created and redeemed at will by investors, like open-end funds. The management of these operations is performed by the issuing institution for a fee.

foreign company. The whole process is faster and cheaper than a direct listing.[18] The price of the ADR is directly established by the conversion in dollars of the stock price traded on the primary exchange of the company.[19]

ADRs can be sponsored or unsponsored by the foreign company. The main difference between these two statuses is that the depository of a sponsored ADR is assured of an exclusive agreement and a favorable cost allocation for the expenses related to the daily operations of the ADR. In general, sponsored ADRs tend to offer more transparency to shareholders in terms of corporate activity—board and shareholder meetings and voting rights—because the corporation is explicitly backing the effort to develop a presence in the market where ADRs are listed. ADRs can also be of several types depending on the exchange on which they are listed and the depth of the registration process the issuing corporation has opted for. For example, for an ADR issued to raise capital, the registration process with the Securities and Exchange Commission in the United States is much more stringent than for a receipt listed for trading purposes only.

ADRs have become particularly popular for firms operating in emerging markets because they give access to a shareholder base in a stronger and more mature environment, typically the United States. ADRs from South America and Southeast Asia accounted for a third of the 300 listed ADRs on the NYSE, Nasdaq, and AMEX in 1997.[20]

The Settlement Problem

Generally speaking, a critical difficulty in following ADRs or cross-listed stocks is related to the settlement of the different transactions. The date of delivery of the certificates may be different between two marketplaces, and more importantly the currency used to settle the trades may also be different. In addition, clearing institutions might also be distinct, possibly creating a nonstandard transfer of ownership and delaying settlement beyond the normal period.

---

[18] Notably, the underlying corporation does not have to appoint a custodian for its shares in the market where it wants to be listed. The institution issuing the receipts undertakes this function as part of the overall ADR arrangement.

[19] Because of this particular feature, ADRs can be considered derivative securities for all practical purposes.

[20] Amar Gande, "American Depository Receipts: Overview and Literature Review," *Financial Markets, Institutions and Instruments*, The NYU Salomon Center for Research in Financial Institutions and Markets, 1997.

A mismatch in settlement dates is a minor concern and will create only a financing residual. For example if a purchase is effected on a market where the settlement cycle is long, the amount of money to be delivered will remain longer on the account generating additional interests. This financing residual can be positive or negative depending on the settlement conventions on each leg, on the interest rate differential and naturally on the direction of the trade.

The issue of the currency is slightly trickier. Consider the stock XYZ of a European company listed somewhere in Europe—in euros—and in the United States—in dollars. Assume that the exchange rate is 1 today, that is, $\$1 = €1$, and the price is $P = \$100 = €100$. For simplicity, both markets settle with the same cycle.

If an American investor buys the stock in the United States, he or she delivers \$100 in exchange for the certificates. The same investor wants to sell the certificates a few days later, and at that time the European price is €102, the exchange rate 1.1 ($\$1 = €1.1$). The price in the United States is therefore $P = \$92.73$ ($= 102/1.1$) because any other price would create an arbitrage opportunity.

The resulting situation is somewhat surprising because the stock has appreciated in Europe, from €100 to €102 and yet the investor would realize a loss, from \$100 to \$92.73 if he or she sold his or her share. Maybe the right answer is to sell it in Europe, for €102. However, this transaction would not solve the problem because the investor would receive €102 on settlement day and would have to manage a foreign exchange position from then on. If he or she wanted to get rid of it, he or she could exchange euros for dollars at a rate of 1.1, and then end up with \$92.73 anyway. This simple example shows clearly that the investor carries an exposure to the \$/€ rate, despite the fact that he or she never intended to. The stock appreciated by 2 percent, but the euro depreciated by 10 percent, and because the company is European, the U.S. price adjusted downward with the depreciation of the currency.

In this example, the European price is driven by pure market forces whereas the U.S. price is simply a conversion and is affected primarily by the exchange rate. The reason for this is that we implicitly assumed Europe to be the primary exchange, that is, the main source of liquidity. If the same company had been listed and had been doing business primarily in the United States, the price there would have been subject to market forces whereas the European price would have followed the exchange rate. Incidentally, the same foreign exchange risk exists with respect to dividends if they are declared and paid in a foreign currency.

DIVIDENDS

Definitions and Conventions

A *dividend* is a distribution of accumulated profits from a corporation to its shareholders. It can take two basic forms: a cash payment or a distribution of new shares, both being rarely combined.[21] We will examine here only cash dividends because a share dividend can also be considered a *variable cash payment*.

There are four important dates in the process of dividend payment:

- *Announcement day*: The company, as decided by its executive board, announces when the dividend will be paid and what its amount will be.
- *Last trading day*: This is the last day on which buying the stock entitles the holder to claim the dividend.
- *Ex-date*: The stock trades "ex"—that is, without dividend rights.[22]
- *Payment date*: Payment is effected by the trust bank of the paying corporation.

In the United States, dividend distribution follows a quarterly pattern, and companies usually have a clear policy about disclosing information as early as possible. The actual payment takes place only a few days after the ex-date. By contrast, in Japan the amount of dividend is, before payment, a pure estimation.[23] Companies generally do not disclose any information before the board meeting that actually fixes the amount, and this meeting is usually called between three and four months after the ex-date. Payment itself occurs a few days after. In Europe, most companies disclose their dividends in advance as in the United States, although distributions are made yearly in general.

For medium- or long-term projections, even for companies that have established a track record of early and consistent disclosure, dividends cannot be much more than an educated guess, both in terms of the ex-date and the amount.[24] A very interesting version of this pro-

---

[21] There are many other ways for corporations to channel wealth to their shareholders, share buybacks being probably the most common example.

[22] The *ex-date* is logically the next business day after the last trading date.

[23] Note that this situation creates a significant risk. The stock goes ex by an *estimated* dividend amount, and all trading parameters, like the fair value of a futures, are calibrated on this estimation. If the actual payment is different, the difference between the two generates a profit or a loss.

[24] In that context "medium" or "long term" is anything beyond six months.

blem appears with JP Morgan, for example. The company distributes quarterly dividends with an ex-date around the third Friday of March, June, September, and December. As it turns out, these are expiration dates for the S&P 500 as well as for Dow Jones futures—and other derivatives such as options. Depending on when the stock actually goes ex, the fair value of each index can be significantly affected. The company is usually not in a position to confirm the exact ex-date more than three months in advance, resulting in systematic uncertainties.

No particular registration is necessary to receive payment from a dividend distribution: The depository trust automatically credits its members' accounts according to their balance when payment is made from the company's trust bank. In some rare cases, however, stocks are still materialized, and the presentation of the actual stock certificates to the trust bank is required.[25]

Taxation

Because dividends are cash payments, an additional problem lies in their taxation. In general, tax optimization is beyond the scope of a trader's responsibilities, and it is performed at a much higher level. For dividends, however, the issue is critical and needs to be considered carefully.

Dividends are generally not tax free and are therefore effectively subject to a double taxation. Corporations are taxed a first time on their earnings through corporate tax, and dividends, distributed off net income, are after-tax money re-taxed a second time at the recipient's level. Fiscal authorities throughout the world are well aware of this issue and have decided individually to ignore or correct it.

In the United States, for example, dividends are taxed as regular income, for corporations as well as individuals. In the vast majority of cases, investors cannot claim any tax break or credit to offset the second layer of taxation, making dividend distribution a very tax ineffective way of redistributing corporate wealth.[26] Under certain

---

[25] This is the case in Japan for a handful of securities. In order for the government to monitor the pool of shareholders in industries considered sensitive, some companies require shareholders to register physical certificates. Investors must withdraw these papers from the depository trust and make themselves known. These companies are mostly information networks such as Nippon Television and air carriers such as All Nippon Airways and Japan Airlines.

[26] A notable exception to this rule is the case of a corporation holding a majority equity interest—above 80 percent—in a subsidiary. In this situation, the dividend is received tax-free.

circumstances, however, dividends are shielded from taxation because of other deductions—interest expense, for example. Japan has a different taxation rule, but the result is essentially the same. A fixed withholding tax is applied to all dividend payments, and no credit or tax break is allowed to offset it.

In Europe, the issue of double taxation is considered from a more positive angle by fiscal authorities. Dividends are recognized as regular income and taxed accordingly. However, corporations as well as individuals are allowed to deduct from their payable taxes an exceptional credit—called a *tax rebate*—equal to the amount of taxes "overpaid" through the double taxation.

For example, consider a French corporation receiving a dividend of €15. This income will be taxed at the corporate tax rate, say, 33⅓ percent, generating a tax liability of €5 and net income of €10. According to the fiscal law, the corporation is allowed to recognize a 50 percent tax credit, applicable to net dividends. Therefore, it will deduct 50 percent of €10—that is, €5—from its tax bill, in effect eliminating the original €5 tax liability. This mechanism is designed to make dividends effectively tax free and remove the second layer of taxation.[27]

It is important to realize, however, that there is no reimbursement from fiscal authorities, only a deduction from existing taxes.[28] Therefore:

- It can be claimed only by an entity subject to corporate taxes in the country, such as a domestic corporation, a broker-dealer, or investment fund.
- By nature, it is deductible from a *positive* amount only—that is, the entity must show a profit.
- For the exact same reason, it is capped by the total amount of taxes reported.

The tax rebate is a source of many arbitrage opportunities, as we will see shortly. Its days are numbered, however, because governments throughout Europe are slowly but surely taking it apart. In the United Kingdom, for example, the Labor government had announced

[27] The reality is naturally more complex than that. The French corporate tax rate has been revised several times over the years, and is not at 33⅓ percent anymore. Individuals are also entitled to the full benefit of tax rebates, regardless of their marginal tax rate.

[28] Furthermore, restrictions apply: For example, in Germany this rebate cannot be claimed against an index arbitrage position.

during its campaign a major fiscal reform, and it effectively launched one once in power. The tax rebate was purely and simply abolished, except for some institutions—typically pension funds. In Germany and France, the trend is toward more restrictions and lower credit allowance, and it would not be surprising to see the rebate evaporate progressively.

International versus Domestic Accounts

In fact, the issue of dividend taxation is even more complex because we implicitly focused so far on domestic corporations' paying domestic shareholders, which is somewhat restrictive. Nonresident investors also receive payments and face a complex situation because they are potentially liable for taxes in their home countries in addition to being taxable in the country of the paying corporation.[29] To avoid a possible double taxation, cross-border taxation issues have been negotiated over the years between states and are now often governed by bilateral treaties.

Most of the time, treaties call for mutual recognition and effectively create a single taxation regime. However, the practical realization of this regime is not necessarily straightforward. In many cases, dividends are taxed by the country of the paying corporation, and the recipient is allowed to recognize a corresponding tax credit with regard to domestic taxes. The process does not necessarily ensure that all taxes can be recovered, a point that is essentially dependent on the depth of the mutual recognition agreement.

Therefore, different players located in different countries will not have the same dividend expectations on the same security. For example, a domestic entity may very well benefit from a tax rebate while a nonresident does not, or only partially, depending on the prevalent bilateral agreement with its domestic fiscal authorities. This situation introduces a bias between participants of the same market and paves the way for fiscal arbitrage.

Assume, for example, that a nonresident stockholder is ready to lend his or her portfolio to a domestic participant, in a country where domestic investors receive dividends essentially tax free, while nonresidents do not. If these shares appear on the book of the domestic entity when dividends are paid, and if it has taxable income, chances are it

[29] Incidentally, a similar problem exists for foreign companies listed on domestic exchanges, or for ADRs. Dividends from ADR stocks held by domestic investors are usually taxed differently from domestic corporations' dividends.

will be in a position to claim the tax rebate, on a position that is only temporarily borrowed. At this point it could very well return the stocks and pay the original owner dividends net of taxes because this is what he or she would have received anyway due to its tax status. The operation is risk free for the domestic player, and it results in a profit equal to the amount of the tax rebate. Naturally, in practice, all is not so easy because the original lender would probably claim part of this rebate for the reason that he or she originally permitted the operation by lending his or her portfolio. The domestic entity will "kick back" part of the rebate, and this kickback is usually referred to as *tax rebate pricing*. A tax rebate priced at 20 percent means that the borrower of a security would return 20 percent of the rebate to the lender.[30] The rebate pricing is a market variable: Intuitively there is no reason why it should differ from 50 percent, but in practice, it is influenced, for example, by the supply of stocks to borrow and the competition between potential borrowers and lenders.

This arbitrage effectively transforms the tax rebate into a traded commodity. To benefit from it, however, participants must have a profitable legal representation within countries with a tax-rebate policy, which means essentially Europe. In the context of the professional trading we have in mind, this particular requirement illustrates the "competitive convergence" we mentioned very early on. If trading as a nonresident leads to opportunity losses or lack of competitiveness, major players have the financial strength to take the necessary steps and open a subsidiary wherever it is needed. Eventually, all major market participants end up with a similar structure, a move that effectively eliminates obstacles but does not create any additional advantage for any of them.

Market Rebate

If the tax rebate is a traded commodity, it should be observable directly in the marketplace. Indeed it is, in two ways. On one side, borrowing and lending of securities are transacted under terms that have to include a rebate pricing because they constitute the primary vehicle

[30] A little bit of illustrative arithmetic: If the tax rate is 30 percent, and the rebate priced at 20 percent, net dividends are 70 percent of gross, and the lender of a security would claim 76 percent of gross (70 percent plus 20 percent of 30 percent). By extension, the rebate is sometimes said to trade at 76 percent. Note that the repartition of profits is asymmetric: The nonresident investor receives an additional 6 percent of gross dividends in the arbitrage, while the domestic arbitrageur receives 30 percent and nets 24 percent after paying the 6 percent kickback.

through which this rebate actually changes hands. On the other side, the rebate influences the total amount of dividends receivable from a given security and after aggregation, directly appears in the calculation of the fair value of the future.[31] Therefore, market participants have a straightforward access to the level of market rebate by looking at borrowing and lending transactions, or at the activity of index arbitrageurs.[32]

The Importance of Careful Dividend Management

Most indices throughout the world yield between 2 percent and 4 percent in dividends, even less in some instances. Even if we consider dividend to be taxed at 20 percent for example, the possible tax loss is fairly low, between 0.40 percent and 0.80 percent. For most investors, including fund managers, a loss of that magnitude is certainly not good news, but it is quite negligible in front of capital gains commonly in excess of 20 percent over the past few years. Therefore, it is only legitimate to ask if we really care about dividend taxation at all. The answer to this question is most definitely yes, and the reason is related to the difference we detailed earlier between traders and fund managers.

We said essentially that fund managers were benchmarked and that their performance was directly evaluated with regard to a broad market base. In that context, dividends, and their taxation even more, are relatively unimportant because by definition they are always consistent with the market.[33] From a trading perspective, dividends are purely market parameters. Every decision is made with a set of expected values, and any realization different from this set will generate a profit or a loss.[34] This is all the more true with derivative products, which are extremely dependent on distributed income like dividends and coupons. For example, an unexpected slide of the S&P 500 yield from 1.2 percent to 1.1 percent would result in a loss of $5

[31] We will detail the fair value calculation in the chapter dedicated to index arbitrage. Broadly speaking, the fair value is equal to financing minus dividends. A higher tax rebate means more dividends, which translates into a lower fair value.

[32] In practice, the activity of index arbitrageurs depends on many other parameters, making the impact of the rebate rather difficult to isolate. Borrowing and lending of securities is a much easier way to extract this information.

[33] Again this is intentionally a very broad statement. Managers of income funds are naturally accountable for their decisions with respect to the overall yield of their portfolio.

[34] Note again here the coexistence of theoretical—expected—and mark-to-market—actual—parameters.

million on a $5 billion long position. Positions of that size are fairly common, and their expected profitability is not sufficient to allow for that high a loss.

FUNDAMENTALS

We consider a *fundamental piece of information* to be any data related to the *operating and financial results* of a company: earnings—realized or estimated—cash flows, balance sheet aggregates, and so on. Under that definition, dividends for example, or corporate events—splits, mergers—are not fundamentals because they are the results of a distribution or industrial policy, not of the operating performance of the organization.

Fundamentals have a paradoxical importance in the world of arbitrage. In some cases, financial analysis is the most critical aspect of a trading decision—for example, in the case of some market-neutral hedge funds.[35] At the same time in other situations—index arbitrage notably—they are almost irrelevant if only because arbitrageurs cannot possibly follow several hundred stocks at the same time.

We will take here the relatively extreme position that fundamentals have generally only a minor impact on an arbitrage trading decision.[36] An absolute convergence, for example, does not depend in any way on economic performance. Even an explicit convergence is relatively immune to these considerations because of the short- to medium-term horizon of the underlying position. Only in the case of a speculative position, concentrated on a small number of securities, is there a strong necessity to focus on microeconomic—or macroeconomic—fundamentals.[37]

That said, the economic environment should not be totally ignored. It may not be necessary to follow a particular corporation in detail to trade it, but it is certainly useful to have a fair idea about its operating environment and performance. In addition, com-

---

[35] In a market neutral strategy, funds invest in shorts and longs at the same time in order to keep a relatively low net market exposure.

[36] *Trading decision* refers to the decision process leading to the initial transaction for a reasonable size. It can be argued that fundamentals have much more impact on risk management—that is, the process of adapting the overall size of the position to market opportunities.

[37] This is typically the case of market-neutral hedge funds that tend to carry only few securities in their portfolio. Another example of a strategy highly dependent on fundamental analysis is naturally macro arbitrage.

mon sense usually holds that better information leads to better decisions, and this is most certainly true in times of crisis. If only because of that, a basic understanding of micro- and macroeconomics can be very helpful. In practice, many long-time traders acquire such knowledge over time. This sense of judgment is particularly valuable, and it undoubtedly differentiates an average from an outstanding trader.

BORROWING AND LENDING OF SECURITIES[38]

Securities- and Cash-Driven Transactions

The borrowing and lending of securities can be separated in two broad categories, based on the ultimate purpose of the transaction: securities-driven and cash-driven.[39] *Securities-driven transactions* consist of loans of specified securities for a period of time. The fact that the securities borrowed are clearly identified is important because the purpose of the whole operation is usually to sell them. Borrowing in that case is indeed the only way to acquire the possibility to sell without owning a particular security. The alternative to that would be a sale without any associated delivery, something largely forbidden. In other words, the need to sell is driving the requirement to borrow, which in turn creates an opportunity to lend. There is a small variation in this schematic description in countries where fiscal authorities recognize the existence of tax rebates. There, securities-driven transactions may also be effected to benefit from a cash distribution—typically dividends—through fiscal arbitrage. In that case the securities need to be clearly identified as well. By contrast, a *cash-driven transaction* consists of an exchange of securities against cash, which is essentially a collateralized loan. The particular set of securities included in the collateral is relatively irrelevant, provided that they meet certain requirements, in terms of liquidity, for example.[40]

[38] For a *very* comprehensive description of the market for borrowing and lending of securities throughout the world, see: "Securities Lending Transactions: Market Development and Implications," International Organization of Securities Commissions (IOSCO), July 1999, available online at www.iosco.org. This document considers a range of issues like taxation, accounting, regulation, credit, and counterpart risk management.

[39] This terminology is borrowed from the IOSCO report.

[40] Note that it is perfectly reasonable to conceive a security versus security transaction. Therefore, the distinction between securities-driven and cash-driven is certainly helpful, but other structures do exist.

Security loans are essentially transactions negotiated over the counter. Functionally, one party borrows a security from another, with the legal commitment to return it at a later date. Practically, they may take distinct forms. In a repurchase agreement, the lender agrees to sell some securities and buy them back at a specified price at a later date. The fact that the operation goes through an actual sell ensures that the borrower acquires the legal ownership of the securities. In a security loan, the contract recognizes a loan between the parties, but it is structured in such a way that the borrower acquires ownership anyway; otherwise the transaction is of no interest to him or her. In a sell-buyback, the lender sells and buys its shares back simultaneously, but the settlement of the purchase is deferred.[41] Regardless of the specifics, the lender is entitled to all the economic benefits—monetary and otherwise—attached to the securities that he or she would otherwise enjoy *if he or she held them*.[42] This situation is particularly important in the context of arbitrage where corporate events may have disastrous consequences for the borrower, as we will see.

Our examination of the borrowing and lending market here will be somewhat schematic. Even though it is virtually possible to borrow any type of security, we will consider exclusively equities as we have done consistently before. Also, despite the relative variations in actual structures, we want to concentrate on core issues and build a stylized view of the process as opposed to getting deeply involved in the intricacies of specific markets. Indeed, the subtleties behind a security loan versus a repurchase agreement are not of a particular relevance from a trading perspective.[43]

---

[41] The difference between a repurchase and a sell-buyback lies in the operation date of the purchase. In a repurchase, the lender agrees to buy back but has not done so yet. In a sell-buyback, the purchase has occurred, only its settlement is postponed.

[42] This precision is important: The lender is legitimately in a position to claim something similar to a *replacement* value. For example, if a foreign lender is taxed on dividends at 20 percent, but the borrower enjoys tax-free payments, the lender has no automatic claim on the 20 percent saved taxes. This is the essence of fiscal arbitrage.

[43] The reasoning behind this statement is the following: Most trading organizations have profit centers dedicated to the activities of borrowing and lending securities. These desks naturally have a comprehensive understanding of the types of transactions they effect, and they manage their risks accordingly. From his or her perspective, the arbitrageur is concerned primarily with the cost of borrowing a particular security or the potential revenue generated by lending it. Beyond this quantitative aspect, it is conveniently simple for us to assume that the actual form of the transaction is irrelevant.

Securities-Driven Lending

Lending a stock is equivalent to delivering it to a determined counterpart against payment, with the explicit agreement that this counterpart will deliver it back later in the future, again in exchange for monies.[44] The payments at initiation and expiry need not be exactly known from the very beginning and indeed are usually not. Consider the situation from the lender's perspective: The loan is effected and terminated against payment, which implicitly prices the securities at both ends of the transaction. If all prices were known at initiation of the loan, the lender would actually be hedged against any market movement in the price of the securities for the whole period of the loan. Therefore, the loan would have significant economic consequences beyond a pure temporary transfer of ownership. By contrast, in the absence of a preset price at expiry, the lender is fully exposed to market fluctuations. In order to establish this exposure and restrict the whole operation to a pure loan, the price at expiration is specified with respect to a market reference, typically the closing price on the main exchange of the underlying securities. This procedure also allows a simple calculation of amounts to be settled.

In general, borrowing and lending transactions can be better understood by looking at the monetary flows, so let's consider the position of each party. The lender delivers shares otherwise held idle and receives a cash collateral against them. The transaction is structured in such a way that he or she is assured of all economic benefits attached to the shares, except one, the opportunity to sell them. Therefore, he or she would expect to be compensated for this right through a fee paid periodically by the borrower. Because he or she owes interests on the collateral, *in effect he or she borrowed liquidity at an advantageous rate while getting an additional fee.*[45] The borrower naturally carries an opposite position: He or she receives the shares,

---

[44] Because we do not want to enter technical details here, the expression "delivery versus payment" is actually the best way to describe all transactions alike. The payment may be a regular payment in the case of a repurchase or sell-buyback agreement, or a collateral in a loan.

[45] The rate is advantageous because the transaction is collateralized by the stocks—that is, the credit risk disappears.

Note that if the lender does not have any particular use for the collateral he or she receives, he or she may invest it and receive market rates, used to pay the counterpart. In that case the economic benefit of the stock loan is limited to the fee.

sells them, and delivers the cash as collateral.[46] He or she pays the borrowing fee regularly, which means that he or she does not get the full proceeds of the sale. Essentially *the borrower ends up with a short position for which the proceeds from the sale are delivered as collateral*. In securities-driven loans, the whole purpose of the transaction is in the establishment of this short, as we indicated earlier.

There are several important additional mechanisms involved in stock loan transactions:

- Because the market prices of the securities vary continuously, the amount of collateral needed to guarantee the loan varies as well, creating a need for margin calls. If market prices go up, the borrower needs to deposit more against the shares, and vice versa. These payments occur periodically, typically daily or weekly.
- The borrowing fee is often called the *repo rate*—a contraction of *repurchase rate*. Indeed, common practice is to refer to stock loans as *repo transactions*. The repo rate is usually a percentage of the nominal amount of the transaction and is actually paid regularly, typically weekly.[47] Depending on the liquidity of the market for stock loans, the magnitude of the fee varies wildly. In the United States, the largest and most liquid market, securities under normal market conditions can be borrowed typically for less than 0.30 percent. In Japan, the other extreme, it is not uncommon to borrow securities at more than 1 percent, sometimes much higher. In general, naturally the fee depends dramatically on the number of short sellers. In a situation of risk arbitrage, the repo rate for the acquiring company can go much higher than its usual level because of the particular situation and opportunities related to the arbitrage.
- During the whole period of the loan, the lender is unable to sell the stock. To address a possible difficulty here, most stock loans carry a

---

[46] There is a minor sequencing problem: The shares have to be secured on the account before they can be sold. Therefore, the borrower cannot deliver the proceeds from the sale immediately; he or she has to borrow the collateral for a short period of time during which he or she receives the shares and actually sells them.

[47] Note that if the fee is proportional to the amount, it varies with the market. From the lender's perspective, this variability may represent a risk because the revenue stream is unsecured. From the borrower's perspective, the risk is the opposite because the stream of payments is unsecured. Both may have to hedge it, for example, with a derivative such as a futures.

In certain instances, the contract is established so that the repo is settled through delivery of additional shares instead of cash. This may be advantageous to the borrower who does not want to pay the fee in cash.

recall clause, allowing the lender to recall shares after a predetermined notice—typically five business days. In some—rare—cases, the loan explicitly forbids recalls, in which case the repo is way higher, compensating the lender for a strict impossibility to change his or her mind. The recall clause is clearly another major risk faced by arbitrageurs entering short positions.[48]
- During the period of the loan, all corporate events modify the liability of the borrower. For example, after a split the outstanding position is automatically adjusted by the split ratio.[49]

The business in general is very much driven by client relationships. Traders on stock loan desks tend to be much more salespeople than they are traders per se. In particular, in numerous situations shares availability is critical, and the best names can sometimes find shares that others will not be able to see. Risk arbitrage is, for example, absolutely dependent upon the arbitrageur being able to short-sell the overpriced company. The more profitable the opportunity is, the more difficult it is to get those shares. In that situation, a respected and established loan desk is a particularly valuable asset.

As a general rule, stable lenders tend to be institutional investors who are not in a situation of high turnover. This typically includes pension funds, insurance companies, and similar institutions. The stability of their holdings through time and their huge portfolios make them ideal partners, and a sizable source of short-selling power, particularly in the United States. These institutions are primarily interested in improving the yield on their portfolio, which would remain unproductive otherwise. Borrowers tend to be traders

---

[48] The reasoning was exposed earlier with closed-end funds arbitrage. Typically a lender might want to sell his or her stock after a sharp increase in price, and to that purpose exercise the recall option. A short seller in that situation has to find another lender or buy back the shares at a much higher price than when he or she sold them, realizing a loss. In the case of an arbitrageur, this loss on one leg does not necessarily transform into an overall loss because the spread between the two legs may have moved in the right direction. The problem is that the position may have to be closed regardless of its current profitability. The recall option is therefore a very interesting feature similar to the option to recall embedded in most corporate bond issues. In general, traders on stock loan desks enter "gentlemen's agreements" not to recall unless unexpected circumstances make it absolutely critical. By and large these agreements are respected.

[49] We will examine in more detail how this liability is modified and the risks that are associated with it in the chapter dedicated to corporate events.

with specific strategies, and arbitrage strategies are a large component of that.[50]

Tax-Driven Lending

Consider the situation we introduced earlier: a French corporation paying a dividend of €15, taxed at a 33⅓ percent rate at the recipient's level. The gross dividend of €15 is then divided in two: withheld taxes of €5 and net dividend of €10. We assume that a French shareholder would be in a position to claim a €5 tax rebate from fiscal authorities, in effect making the dividend distribution tax free. At the same time, imagine a foreign investor holding the same security but unable to claim any rebate. If the investor agrees to lend his or her shares to the domestic institution, he or she might expect to receive a regular borrowing fee and part of the €5 rebate.[51]

In order for this structure to work, the domestic investor must be able to claim a rebate from fiscal authorities. As we mentioned before, this means that the organization behind him or her must show a taxable profit; otherwise no deduction is possible. This amount of taxable profit must naturally be commensurate with the expected level of additional rebate acquired through stock loans. Overall, this type of arbitrage requires a strict and rigorous tax management, at the highest corporate level.[52]

In terms of nomenclature, a rebate claim acquired through a stock loan transaction is said to have been purchased. Conversely, when a claim is being transferred away, it has been sold. These appellations reflect the fact that the rebate is a marketable commodity, something we mentioned earlier. Indeed, consider, for example, that a French domestic investor borrows the shares described above with a rebate

---

[50] Arbitrageurs are certainly not responsible for the totality of the short interest in the market. Note, also, that their position must always be relatively symmetrical with respect to short and long exposure, which is in sharp contrast to many other categories of investors.

[51] Note that the shareholder receives a payment equal to the net amount immediately and a rebate at the end of the fiscal year. However, fiscally speaking, the rebate accrues to the holder of the shares on the ex-day. Therefore, the arbitrage only requires the lender to deliver shares for a few days around the ex-day.

[52] Note that the borrower has committed to the lender for a certain amount. If eventually the rebate allowance is insufficient, the borrower realizes a loss when he or she pays the original lender. Conversely, if an institution with a stock loan portfolio ends its fiscal year with a rebate allowance too low compared to what it could have claimed based on its taxable profits, it faces an opportunity loss because it could have been more aggressive in borrowing stocks.

pricing of 40 percent.[53] If the shares are being again lent away shortly after for a rebate of 60 percent, the net difference of 20 percent is a pure risk-free profit for the intermediary traders.[54] Why would somebody pay 60 percent? Because another institution may be in a position to claim 100 percent with little risk and be ready to pay 60 percent. The other natural question arising from this situation is why sell at 60 percent when the securities can be held through the ex-date and deliver 100 percent? For one, the overall rebate allowance at the end of the year may be uncertain or limited. And secondly, the 20 percent profit materializes in *cash* on the ex-date of the security, whereas the rebate is only a *deduction* months away.

Equity Financing

Equity financing transactions are essentially stock loans arranged exclusively for the purpose of borrowing cash.[55] These are therefore lender-initiated loans as opposed to securities-driven loans. The key difference in that context is the paramount importance of credit risk. As in any other deal, the borrower has a direct risk on the lender's credit, offset here by the delivery of securities. In equity financing, the ultimate commodity exchanged is cash, not equity; therefore the setup of these transactions usually implies a process more stringent with respect to credit lines. Not surprisingly, the counterparts involved in these deals are not necessarily identical to those engaged in securities-driven operations. For example, institutional investors like pension funds rarely need cash and would have a limited interest in lending their portfolio for this sole purpose.

This situation has two practical consequences: Transactions call for the introduction of a haircut rate designed to protect the cash lender, and the rating of the cash borrower is particularly important in setting the repo rate. The haircut works in the following way: The stock lender agrees to deliver a nominal higher than the cash he or she receives—for example, 110 percent—to protect the other party in case of

[53] As a reminder, this 40 percent indicates that 40 percent of the tax savings of €5 is being "reimbursed" to the lender.

[54] It should be apparent here that stock loan traders have a critical role to play in many respects, and they do engage in *trading* activities at least in areas where fiscal regulations make it appropriate. Note that in contrast to our description of an arbitrageur attending to his or her business quietly and discreetly, stock loan traders have an impact on the overall tax risk of their employer.

[55] Note that the stock borrower is the cash lender and vice versa.

liquidation.[56] The credit ratings of both parties become also extremely relevant. Consider, for example, a market participant lending stocks to a counterpart rated much higher, and assume that the traded repo is 0.50 percent. In essence, the cash borrower has obtained a loan at a rate 0.50 percent higher than the financing rate of its counterpart. If this counterpart as we assumed has a much better rating, a spread of 0.50 percent may indeed be a very good deal. Therefore, the repo in these cases is not so much related to the availability of shares in the market but rather to the creditworthiness of the cash borrower.

Margin Trades

As a general rule, every market transaction is supposed to be settled shortly after its execution, through delivery of shares and payment. However, most markets allow nonstandard transactions to occur, in which the seller does not deliver the shares—at least directly—and the buyer does not necessarily deliver the full amount. The general principle is that investors do not have to settle their purchases in full if they choose to, and can borrow the missing part from their broker.[57] Conversely in case of a sale, investors can choose to sell shares they don't hold, in which case the broker will deliver them instead, borrowing, for example, from another client. These trades are called *margin trades*, because the risk embedded in the open position creates a need for periodic margin calls. In addition, because they usually induce creation of credit, they are tightly regulated by central banks.

In the United States, for example, margin trades have to be booked on segregated accounts, and individuals can borrow up to 50 percent of their transactions.[58] The exchange does not know a margin trade from a regular one because the trade itself is settled as a standard transaction. The broker manages its clients' margins and positions, and naturally charges a fee for these services.

Margin trades are of little interest, in general, to professionals because they have cheaper alternatives. However, the overall balance of margin transactions, usually published by exchanges regularly for a large number of stocks, can be highly indicative of a widespread mar-

---

[56] This protection is meant to cover the possible market impact if the securities need to be liquidated in a very short period of time.

[57] Naturally this borrowing is not free; indeed, it is rather expensive. This type of trade is therefore almost exclusively used by individuals who cannot, or do not want to, commit significant capital to their portfolio.

[58] Because margin trades induce creation of credit, their regulation—that is, required coverage—falls under the jurisdiction of the Federal Reserve.

ket sentiment. It is therefore important to understand the fundamental underlying mechanisms.

TRADING

In this section we consider the practical side of stock transactions, specifically the structure of the market. Because of the wide diversity of systems and environments, this examination is meant to be a simple and broad introduction. There is no doubt that a clearer and more thorough understanding of many practical and technical details is tremendously important in day-to-day trading.

Market Microstructure: Dealer versus Auction, Floor versus Screen

Market microstructure is the "*study of the process and outcomes of exchanging assets under explicit trading rules.*"[59] Although the issues related to the design of an efficient market structure are not trivial, for our purpose we can schematically say that there are two main organizational structures: auction markets and dealer markets. Auction markets are order driven—that is, orders are executed through a set of liquidity providers that show their interest in a *limit-order book*. Most of the time these auction markets are continuous and electronic. Dealer markets, on the other hand, are quote driven: Liquidity is provided primarily by market makers who have no limit-order commitment but communicate instantaneous quotes for other participants to trade. Transactions are the result of a negotiation with the market maker and are still effected over the phone for large sizes. Nasdaq in the United States and SEAQ in the United Kingdom are two examples of dealer markets, with the particularity of providing electronic routing systems. The stock exchanges of Paris and Frankfurt are auction markets, while New York and London are a combination of both.[60] Tokyo became entirely electronic when it closed its trading floor in April 1999 after 120 years of service.

---

[59] Maureen O'Hara, *Market Microstructure Theory*, Blackwell Publishers, 1995, p. 1. This book contains a complete discussion of the market microstructure theory.

[60] London implemented the Stock Exchange Electronic Trading Service (SETS), a fully electronic trading system, in 1997 on the largest capitalizations included in the FTSE 100 index. This migration proved a success with more and more orders going through the electronic system, accounting for half the trading volume at the end of 1998.

Another dimension of market structure is the distinction between floor and screen markets, somewhat independent of the nature of the order matching process.[61] In a traditional floor market, all orders are brought to an open-outcry pit where brokers and market makers show their immediate interest with a complex set of hand gestures. In a screen-based model, orders are inputted into an electronic interface, regardless of the matching process.

With the volume of transactions growing dramatically over the years, the traditional floor has evolved into a modern version in which the floor still exists, but the open-outcry has been replaced by an electronic entry system. For example, on the NYSE, specialists have their dedicated booth, but there is no pit serving as a marketplace anymore. Indeed, most modern markets have now adopted a screen-based trading, in the sense that prices are available in real time on a screen and small orders can be routed electronically.[62] However, the degree of reliability of these prices depends highly on the nature of the underlying market. For example, Nasdaq is screen based, but arguably it is still difficult to rely on quoted prices. Therefore, for all practical purposes we can consider all the largest markets as screen based, at least for the stock side. The only exception of interest to us is Chicago for the S&P 500 futures, still traded in an open-outcry pit.[63]

In the interest of time and briefness, we will not go into much detail beyond this introductory description, which allows us to have a panoramic view, sufficient to serve our purpose. It is necessary to emphasize, however, that many issues related to market structure end up having a significant impact on arbitrageurs' ability to conduct their business profitably.

Circuit Breakers and Trading Halts

Circuit breakers and *trading halts* are mechanisms designed to moderate excessive volatility by interrupting the normal stock trading process for

---

[61] See, for example, Alexander Kempf, "Trading System and Market Integration," *Journal of Financial Intermediation*, 7, 1998, pp. 220–239, for an empirical discussion of floor- and screen-based trading systems.

[62] In the case of dealer markets, this is not true for sizable orders, and the phone call remains the only viable choice.

[63] The FTSE 100 Future in London was until May 1999 traded in an open-outcry pit as well. It is now traded on LIFFE-Connect, the electronic trading platform developed by the London International Financial Futures Exchange (LIFFE).

a period of time.[64] Circuit breakers are used throughout the market and were originally proposed by the U.S. Securities and Exchange Commission in 1987 on the grounds that had such measures been in place earlier, they would have significantly reduced the magnitude of the October crash. Trading halts are market suspensions on individual securities, to allow, for example, fair dissemination of new information. Both types of suspensions can be information based or rule based. Information-based interruptions are activated under the exchange discretionary power to reflect the fact that important new information has the potential to change prices significantly and should therefore be disseminated fairly to all market participants. Rule-based interruptions are systematic interruptions based on a set of rules fixed in advance and communicated to all participants. Table 2-3 gives an overview of all categories.

Intentional market interruptions implemented by exchanges are highly controversial and the subject of much debate because of the underlying practical and philosophical justifications advanced in both camps. On one side, regulators and exchanges overwhelmingly cite protection of investors' interests as the ultimate goal of circuit breakers and trading halts, and many people truly believe they appropriately serve this very goal. On the other side, academic research has attempted, and failed in most instances, to prove that these mechanisms have been beneficial to the stated purpose. Indeed, some studies

TABLE 2-3

	Information Based	Rule Based
Trading halt	For individual securities: dissemination of information, clarification of rumor, violation of exchange rules	For individual securities: trading outside of a predetermined percentage or point variation based on the previous day's close, current day's open, or a moving average of trading band
Circuit breaker	For the entire market: national emergency	For the entire market: trading outside of a predetermined percentage or point variation based on previous day's close for an index, current day's open, or moving average of trading band

(*Source*: Joshua Galper, *Managing Market Volatility: A Report to the FIBV Working Committee for the Focus Group Study*, FIBV Working Paper, 1999.)

---

[64] For a review of stock exchange practices throughout the world, see Joshua Galper, *Managing Market Volatility: A Report to the FIBV Working Committee for the Focus Group Study*, FIBV Working Paper, 1999.

seem to support the opposite view, that trading halts, even systematically implemented without any surprise effect, are actually detrimental and create an additional layer of volatility.[65] Beyond these arguments the fundamental philosophical question is whether stock exchanges have any responsibility to protect investors against themselves and whether the existence of such an explicit protection might create moral hazard and encourage irresponsible trading behavior.

Naturally, the question of the very existence of circuit breakers, and even more their appropriate design, is of critical importance to arbitrageurs, as to any other investor. Like market structure, the problem is far-reaching and the solutions adopted throughout the world vary depending on a number of factors, including cultural preferences and legal environments. This diversity prevents us here again from drawing any general conclusion, except that these devices should be very clearly identified and understood by traders on their market.

Beyond the interruption of trading, other devices and mechanisms have been proposed and implemented to address the same issue of investor protection against excessive volatility. Two examples will illustrate this point: the United States and Japan.

U.S. Controls on Excessive Volatility

Two particular trading rules have been in existence for some time in the United States to control two possible sources of excessive volatility: short selling and index arbitrage. The first is Rule 10a-1, the so-called up-tick rule, and the second is Rule 80a, the so-called trading collars rule.

The *up-tick rule* was enacted in 1938 by the Securities and Exchange Commission, and it forbids short selling of exchange-listed securities on a down-tick or zero-minus tick.[66] This is extremely painful in terms of trading because it effectively prevents execution to occur, regardless of the price. The United States is the only market to have implemented such a drastic measure; European exchanges having nothing similar.

---

[65] See, for example, Kryzanowski Lawrence, "The Efficacy of Trading Suspensions: A Regulatory Action Designed to Prevent the Exploitation of Monopoly Information," *Journal of Finance*, 35, 5, 1979; Charles Lee, Mark Ready, and Paul Seguin, "Volume, Volatility and the New York Stock Exchange Trading Halts," *Journal of Political Economy*, 85, 3, 1997; Matthew Harrison, "Stopping the Market," *The Stock Exchange of Hong Kong Regional Monitor*, 7, 1997; or Mason Gerety and Harold Mulherin, "An Analysis of Volume at the Open and the Close," *Journal of Finance*, 47, 1992, for a discussion of these issues and more.

[66] A *down-tick* is a transaction that occurs at a price strictly lower than the last traded price. A *zero-minus tick* is a transaction that occurs at the last traded price, when the first previous transaction effected at a different price was at a higher price.

This is also a decision that has been openly criticized over the years because several studies suggest that it does not achieve its stated goal of preventing market manipulation while preserving execution quality. For example, it appears that it actually damages the execution quality of short sell orders even in advancing markets.[67]

The *trading collars* rule was originally implemented on the New York Stock Exchange in 1988 as a result of the October 1987 events.[68] In 1990, it was revised and strengthened, in a move prompted again by unusual market circumstances, this time the 1989 minicrash.[69] The rationale behind the original proposition and subsequent amendment was to reduce market volatility associated with program trading and specifically index arbitrage. The rule states that index arbitrage trades are subject to a "tick test" if the Dow Jones index has moved by 50 points or more compared to its previous close during a session.[70] A buy program has to be executed on a down-tick if the move is upward, and a sell program on an up-tick if the market move is downward. The tick test is lifted if the Dow Jones comes back to a 25-point range from its previous close. The 50-point limit was originally intended to isolate days with excessive volatility, but with the uninterrupted bull market of late, it has become a common move and the collars have been triggered very regularly over the past few years—sometimes several times a day, and occasionally both ways on the same day.[71] This state of affairs prompted a revision of the rule, which went into effect at the beginning of 1999. The threshold is now variable, set at 2 percent, and revised every quarter. As an example, it was 210 points for the last quarter of 1999, with the collars lifted if the market came back to 100 points above or below

---

[67] See, for example, Gordon J. Alexander, "Short Selling on the New York Stock Exchange and the Effects of the Uptick Rule," *Journal of Financial Intermediation*, 8, 1999, pp. 90–116.

[68] The up-tick rule is a marketwide rule, and it is effective on stocks listed on any exchange. The trading collars rule, however, has been implemented by the New York Stock Exchange only.

[69] For a detailed chronological table of these developments, see G. J. Santoni and Tung Lui, "Circuit Breakers and Stock Market Volatility," *The Journal of Futures Markets*, 13, 1993, pp. 261–277.

[70] *Index arbitrage* here is loosely defined as the sale or purchase of 15 or more securities, for a total nominal of $1 million or more, if this basket is executed in conjunction with the sale or purchase of an index derivative—futures or option.

[71] They were triggered 29 times on 28 days in 1995, 119 times on 101 days in 1996, and 303 times on 219 days in 1997. Out of 250 open days, 219 days represents around 87 percent, fairly close to "almost every day" (*Source*: NYSE).

its previous close.[72] As was the case with the short sell rule, there is evidence that the collars do not necessarily perform as expected in reducing volatility.[73]

Not surprisingly, short sell and index arbitrage restrictions have a significant impact on investors and particularly arbitrageurs because by nature they always end up with a short, either stock or future. In either case one of the rules potentially makes transactions difficult to execute in volatile markets, at a time when arbitrageurs may be needed most to help the market keep its consistency and coherence. Furthermore, it is interesting to note that the trading collars, unlike any other restrictions—even those in Tokyo, detailed below—have the questionable privilege of segregating market participants in distinct categories. This raises again an interesting point about whether an exchange has a mandate to interfere and effectively discriminate among its market participants.

Japanese Controls on Excessive Volatility

Tokyo has a slightly different mechanism than New York. Functionally the purpose is identical, to slow trading down to prevent manipulation and allow investors to react appropriately while the price is under control. The adopted solution consists of "real-time price limits": If an order—market or limit—cannot be fulfilled at three ticks above or below the last traded price, the stock acquires a particular status—W for waiting, or SP for special if the imbalance is sizable—and no trade is effected for three minutes.[74] After that interval, the stock is authorized to trade at a price above or below these three ticks, under the condition that outstanding orders be fulfilled within six ticks. If that is not possible, three more minutes have to lapse before a trade is authorized within nine ticks. The process is reiterated until the imbalance disappears, or the absolute price limit for the day is reached.

There would be much to say about the actual effects of these limits as opposed to their expected benefits. Obviously if the intent is to slow the market, they are a success. However it is uncertain that they do attract more liquidity, and above all, they induce a high level of uncertainty because it is extremely difficult in many cases to gauge the new

---

[72] See the NYSE Web site for more details. The Rule 80b, also called the *side-car provision*, which stated that index arbitrage orders would be automatically delayed by five minutes in certain circumstances, has been abolished.

[73] See, for example, "Circuit Breakers and Market Volatility," footnote 69.

[74] This time interval has changed over the years. It has been reduced from six to three minutes in the mid-1990s.

price equilibrium when a stock is W or SP. In effect, it becomes impossible to price some stocks for periods of three minutes at a time,[75] which can be a real problem given that investors in general do not like price uncertainty, even less than volatility. The W or SP status is particularly painful at the close. If the imbalance persists then, or if one appears because market-on-close orders are not balanced within three ticks of the last traded price, the stock does not close and orders are left unexecuted.[76] This simply means that it is virtually impossible to execute large sizes on the close, because an imbalance is almost certain to develop for many stocks.

Overall it is fair to say that the United States and Japan share the particularity of a high level of exchange intervention in the day-to-day workings of their markets because Europe has really no similar mechanism in place.[77] It can be argued that these are the two largest markets, and in case of major crisis, the price discovery—that is, crash—would spread from one of them or both. Therefore, it makes sense to "protect" them more than secondary markets, which then are also implicitly protected. Beyond the obvious flaws of this argument, the recurrent question of the ideal involvement of exchanges in their market is still looming on the horizon. It would be preposterous to advance any definitive argument here, but the problem should be recognized for what it is, much more political and philosophical than anything else.

CAPITAL STRUCTURE: OUTSTANDING NUMBER OF SHARES

Introduction

The outstanding number of shares has a particular importance in the context of arbitrage. We mentioned earlier that such positions did not

[75] The tick size on the TSE is set in relation to the price of the stock. Most stocks priced below ¥1,000 have a tick size of ¥1. The average price of a Nikkei 225 constituent is ¥800, for reasons we will develop later. Therefore, the uncertainty is ¥3 over ¥800—that is, 0.375 percent. This can be quite uncomfortable at times, especially if a lot of stocks acquire a W or SP status at the same time.

[76] In fact, the situation is more complex than that. There is a set of rules to close a stock SP; outstanding orders are executed following a proration of the unbalanced side. For example, if a stock is SP-up, there are more buys than sells. An investor with 10 percent of all buy orders would receive an execution on 10 percent of the total size offered in the market. The same rules apply to Nikkei 225 futures.

[77] In addition, both Japanese and U.S. regulators require a high level of disclosure from arbitrageurs in terms of trading volumes and positions. Again no similar reporting is imposed in Europe.

necessitate any trading activity from initiation to maturity, except for minor adjustments. It would appear from this statement that an arbitrage position ought to be left aside without any particular monitoring effort.

In fact, as one would expect, the situation is not that simple. Schematically speaking, a stock position is characterized by a price and a number of shares. The nature of arbitrage is such that movements in price do not have any significant effect if the position is properly hedged. As far as the number of shares is concerned, it is susceptible to change to reflect adjustments in the capital structure of the company, even without any trading activity.

The nature of corporate events susceptible to affect the capital structure, and by extension the outstanding number of shares, is extremely diverse. From simple situations like splits or mergers to more complex recapitalizations or buyouts, each particular event has an impact on the corporation's debt and equity, in turn affecting holders of these securities in different ways.

It is by no means our intention here to enter a detailed examination of these different categories. For one thing we are concerned only with equity and then only with those events that are quite common on the markets we consider. Therefore, we will offer two specific examples and extract from these a general framework applicable to most.

- Splits and reverse splits
- Mergers and acquisitions

Other events, such as spin-off, conversion of convertible securities, capital increase or share buybacks, will be left out in the interest of time although they could be described by the same formalism.

Outstanding Number of Shares

When a company constitutes its capital, it usually issues shares through an *initial public offering* (IPO).[78] The total number of shares issued is referred to as the *total outstanding number of shares*, by opposition to the *authorized number of shares* stated in the corporate charter.

---

[78] This is the usual procedure but not the only one by far. An alternative is, for example, a private placement, in which only a handful of investors buys shares. In the United States, these shares are not registered with the Securities and Exchange Commission, making the whole issuance significantly cheaper. There is a hidden cost to this, however, and that is liquidity because unregistered shares cannot be sold outside another private placement.

Not all the shares are necessarily tradable, however. Large state-owned companies may have their shares listed, but part of those shares may not be tradable because large chunks are still held by the government.[79] Another example is the case of *employee stock ownership programs* (ESOPs) in which shares are allocated to employees but are not tradable for some time—typically five years. Even corporations for which these two situations do not apply may decide to offer only a part of their capitalization to the public market. The number of shares actually tradable, and therefore available to investors, is called the *float*.[80] Index sponsors as a general rule use the outstanding number of shares to compute the capitalization of a company and accordingly manage its ranking in the indices in which it is included.[81]

The outstanding number of shares and the float are the most important pieces of information arbitrageurs need to follow. Both evolve through the life of the corporation in distinct ways and constitute clear signals of the corporate strategy vis-à-vis its capital and ownership structure and, by extension, economic perspectives.

Following these two figures is essentially an exercise in arithmetic. All corporate events separate the time line into two periods—before and after—and the most critical aspect from a trader's perspective is to follow the overall capitalization, as measured by the outstanding number of shares, through these two periods. A change in capitalization, whether an increase or a decrease, usually creates a risk and should be understood and monitored carefully.[82] This is precisely what we will

---

[79] This is typically the result of a partial privatization, very common nowadays with the progressive disengagement of many governments from their domestic economic activity.

[80] The ratio of float to outstanding shares is important because it indicates the relative liquidity of the stock. Many high-technology corporations have floats of around 10 to 20 percent of their total outstanding shares number, which is relatively low. As a result, any news on the company is likely to move the stock significantly just because the tradable market is very thin.

[81] There may be different types of shares, for example common or preferred, and each type may also have several classes with its particular outstanding portion and float. Only one class, however, is included in a given index.

In agreement with market practice, we define the *capitalization of a corporation* as its outstanding number of shares times the last traded price of its stock. It is wrong from the standpoint of corporate finance—which includes market value of debt as well—but this is really what matters to an arbitrageur.

[82] Note that even capitalization-constant events may induce a risk—for example, a split in an index arbitrage position on a price-weighted index such as the Dow Jones or Nikkei 225. Cf. the chapter dedicated to index arbitrage.

do in our examples: follow the number of shares and extract the changes in capitalization associated with them.

Split and Reverse Splits

A *split* is an issuance of new—and free—shares in exact proration of the existing outstanding position. In effect, for each share held, shareholders receive a fixed number of additional shares. Because no payment is made for these shares, shareholders' wealth ought to remain unchanged through the split, and the price of the stock is necessarily adjusted. In a 2-for-1 split for example, it is divided by 2 on the day the split is effective, before the opening of the market.[83]

From a corporation's standpoint, a split has several convenient features:

- It does not modify the relative partition of equity. The total capitalization of the company remains unchanged, and so does a shareholder's stake in the company.
- The price of the stock appears "miraculously" affordable again. For individual or small investors, this is extremely important.[84]
- At the same time the new level of price attracts more—and smaller—investors in the shareholder pool, which may have a positive effect on the stock price.[85]

Splits are considered a sign of healthy growth, and as such are naturally much more common from high-tech companies than from blue chips, but both categories understand its formidable psychologi-

---

[83] All outstanding orders are also automatically adjusted with regard to size and price by the exchange trading system.

[84] Microsoft exemplifies this property: Having split numerous times on its way to the largest capitalization on the United States market and therefore worldwide, its price rarely exceeded $100. When it did so, it was only because its fantastic ascension went faster than its split pattern—that is, recently. The beauty of it is that investors often feel they are buying "cheap," even if per-share data remain absolutely unaffected by successive splits.

[85] This is especially true when the exchange trading rules are not friendly to small investors—for example, through high minimum trading units as in Japan. Indeed, one recent study covering Japan concluded that *"a reduction in the minimum trading unit greatly increases a firm's base of individual investors and its stock liquidity, and is associated with a significant increase in the stock price."* See Yakov Amihud, Haim Mendelson, and Jun Uno, "Number of Shareholders and Stock Prices: Evidence from Japan," *Journal of Finance*, 1999, 54, pp. 1169–1184. For other examinations of this issue, see Paul Schultz, "Stock Splits, Tick Size and Sponsorship," *Journal of Finance*, 55, pp. 429–440, or Marc Lipson, "Stock Splits, Liquidity and Limit Orders," NYSE Working Paper 99-04, 1999.

cal and signaling effect. Investors—particularly in the United States where splits are very frequent—have become so accustomed to that process that the very announcement of a split usually lifts prices significantly.

Splits are essentially mechanical processes, and resemble dividend distributions in many ways:

- The split calendar also includes an announcement date, last trading date, and ex-date.
- There is no cash flow, so the payment date is replaced by an effective date—that is, the date on which an investor will see an adjusted stock position. In the United States, the delay between the ex and effective dates is generally two to three weeks.
- Investors' positions are automatically adjusted according to their balance—short or long.
- There is usually no direct risk associated with a split, except in some atypical situations.[86] Therefore, prediction of a stock split is by and large irrelevant.
- *An n-for-m—also noted n:m—split will multiply the outstanding number of shares by a factor of n/m, and divide its price by the same factor.*

By convention, if the number of free shares is larger than 1, the split is described by a ratio above 1—2:1, 3:2, and so on. If it is smaller than 1, it is described in percentage terms—10 percent, 15 percent, and so on.[87]

It is convenient to introduce here a formalism, shown in Table 2-4, that will be extensively used later: W stands for the stock outstanding number of shares,[88] C for its capitalization, P for its price, and r for the relevant split ratio.[89] The prime sign indicates the same variables *after* the split. Note that implicitly W and P represent the number of outstanding shares and their price on the close of the last trading day, or equivalently on the morning of the ex-day before open. The capitalization is constant through the event ($C = C'$), and the char-

---

[86] Note that because new shares are not received for some time, they cannot be sold and delivered. The liquidation of a long position between the ex and effective dates thus creates a short sell on part of the position—half, for example, in the case of a 2-for-1 split. This is a punctual problem, but it generates extra costs because the missing shares must be borrowed.

[87] A stock dividend is exactly identical to a stock split; therefore, this notation is used indifferently for both.

[88] We will occasionally refer to the outstanding number of shares as the *weight* of the stock in an index. Hence the W.

[89] In an $n : m$ split, $r = n/m$.

acteristics of the capitalization after—W' and P'—are directly available as functions of the characteristics before—W and P.

These relationships hold for the total capitalization of the corporation, but it is important to realize that they do as well for any stockholder's position. In particular, if we denote Q as the number of shares an investor holds, the split will transform this number in a similar way: $Q' = Q \cdot r$. From there it is possible to analyze precisely what the impact of the split is on the position and act accordingly. In particular, a short position does not generate any specific difficulty through the split compared to a long.

Reverse splits, much less frequent, are the exact opposite of splits: The number of shares is decreased by a given ratio, and the price adjusted upward.

Mergers and Acquisitions

We will dedicate a full chapter to the examination of mergers and acquisitions from an arbitrageur's perspective. Therefore, these lines constitute only an introductory presentation in the broad context of corporate events. The general process can be described as the absorption of one corporation by another, and the merger of the two stocks into one.

There are many ways through which these transactions are effected in the marketplace. The most common forms are equity exchange and cash tender offer. In the first case the acquirer offers to exchange its own equity for the outstanding equity of the target company; in the second case it offers to pay cash at a preset price. Nowadays, with equity valuations at all-time highs, most transactions are taking place through exchange offers.[90]

As we did above, we want to consider the total capitalization to analyze the situation, and we need to include both companies. Let A be the index of acquirer and T that of the target. r is the exchange ratio: at

TABLE 2-4

Before	After
$C = W \cdot P$	$C' = W' \cdot P' = (W \cdot r) \cdot (P/r) = C$

[90] Taxes have also a direct impact on the financing structure. A tender offer for cash creates a taxable capital gain whereas an equity exchange usually does not create any tax liability.

maturity, holders of 1 share of T receive r shares of A. Finally, let C_T be the amount of the cash tender offer, if any.[91] Under these terms, $C_T = P_O \cdot W_T$, where P_O is the tender offer price.

Before the conclusion of the transaction, both organizations are independent and the total capitalization is the sum of the two. On the effective date, the W_T shares of T are transformed into $r \cdot W_T$ shares of A, at a price equal to that of A. Table 2-5 summarizes these changes. For C' to be equal to C, we need: $W_T \cdot (r \cdot P_A - P_T) + C_T = 0$. In the very common situation where $C_T = 0$, this simplifies into $P_T = r \cdot P_A$, which is a well-known relation for mergers. In other words, if $P_T \neq r \cdot P_A$ on the close of the last trading day before the merger goes ex, the capitalization of the transaction is not constant. The change in total capitalization, ΔC, can be expressed as:

$$\Delta C = C' - C = (r \cdot P_A - P_T + P_O) \cdot W_T$$

This important result is critical in many respects because it lays the foundations for a profitable arbitrage. Consider, for example, the cases of a cash tender offer $\Delta C = (P_O - P_T) \cdot W_T$, or a straightforward equity exchange $\Delta C = (r \cdot P_A - P_T) \cdot W_T$. In both these instances, ΔC is a difference, meaning that the total capitalization is not necessarily continuous through the merger. Specifically, if the tender price is higher than the market price at the time the offer expires, the difference ΔC materializes into a risk-free profit for whoever buys the shares in the market and tenders them. Similarly, if $P_T < r \cdot P_A$, an arbitrageur can buy 1 share of T, sell r shares of A and lock a risk-free profit. In a general case in which the transaction is not a straight tender or exchange, an opportunity might exist as well if ΔC is distinct from zero.

In practice, ΔC is almost always positive and one of the above conditions is true because the market is usually not fully pricing mer-

TABLE 2-5

Before	After
$C = W_A \cdot P_A + W_T \cdot P_T$	$C' = (W_A + r \cdot W_T) \cdot P_A + C_T$

[91] Note that this formalism captures most situations. If the offer is an exchange only, then $C_T = 0$. On the contrary, if it is a cash tender only, then $r = 0$. Cases in which it is partially both are also included and occur from time to time in reality. More complex situations, for example, a merger combined with a spinoff, occur as well.

gers or acquisitions.[92] The reason for this is embedded in what we termed *explicit convergence*. In contrast to dividends or splits, mergers come in general as a surprise, and the final approval from both public authorities and shareholders is not certain until the deal is actually put to a vote. Even in situations in which both companies have expressed satisfaction with the project, it may still be questioned again by one of the parties before completion. Therefore, market participants are reluctant to price the deal at its "fair" value and prefer to keep a safety cushion, which is taken advantage of by arbitrageurs ready to carry the full risk of the transaction.

The question of what happens to short sellers in that context is interesting. In a situation in which an investor is short the acquirer before the merger is effective, there is nothing special for him or her to do. The shares of A are not affected in any way, so the short position survives the merger with no particular intervention. However, a short-seller of T would be in trouble.

If we assume that the merger goes through, the lender of T should automatically receive shares of A if he or she held his or her original position. Therefore, the borrower of T must deliver shares of A if the borrowing position is closed after the merger ex-date.[93] The same reasoning that led us to the conclusion that a risk arbitrageur would realize a profit of ΔC being long T shows that a short seller of T actually loses ΔC. *A short seller of T automatically realizes a loss if the short is carried through the merger when $\Delta C > 0$.* In the case of a cash tender offer the loss is even more obvious. If the stock tendered trades below its tender price, which is usually the case, it seems obvious that a short seller would lose the difference if he or she carried the short through.

Conclusion on Corporate Events

We have examined and formalized a small fraction of corporate events on large mature organizations. To summarize, the following is a general description of what needs to be considered in the unlikely case of an event totally unheard of:

- *Schedule*: This is a critical aspect because it dictates the urgency of the situation. All corporate events have detailed schedules attached to them. If any action is required or advisable, a trader should have

---

[92] Even if ΔC were negative, an arbitrage would still be possible.

[93] In practice, the stock lender must be consulted to confirm that he or she would tender his or her shares, if there is a doubt about the completion of the acquisition.

a fair idea about deadlines to make a decision. The worst thing that can happen is to miss an event altogether. Consequences range from possibly profitable—mergers—to neutral—split or conversions of bonds—to disastrous—short positions in several instances.[94]

- *Creation of new shares, delisting of existing ones*: It is extremely important to determine when and how different entities are coming to life or, conversely, when and how existing ones disappear. Typically, it is necessary to make a distinction between the listing date and effective delivery. Listing of when-issued securities,[95] for example, allows market forces to shape the supply-demand curve with the consequence of imposing market prices when the transaction becomes effective. Delivery can be important, for example, to short sellers who need to assess the duration of their liabilities.
- *Risk of short selling*: This is particularly important because most events tend to be advantageous to shareholders and therefore risky to short sellers. As we indicated on many occasions, parameters to include in evaluating these situations are extremely diverse. Intrinsically, most risks associated with short positions cannot be hedged away—like the risk of recall from the lender.
- *Conservation of capitalization, price adjustment, and distribution of cash*: These are by far the most important points. The purpose of the formalism we adopted through the use of simple capitalization diagrams was to force us to develop a systematic analysis routine. In the same way that most problems in modern mechanics can be handled through the appropriate use of energy conservation laws, most problems in understanding corporate events can be solved with an analogous conservation law, this time applied to capitalization. Events for which capitalization are not constant often implicitly create arbitrage opportunities and therefore induce risks.
- *Execution*: Beyond the development of a complete understanding, if it is determined that an opportunity or a risk exists, execution is always a concern. Naturally important in the case of a risk arbitrage position, it is also critical in other settings. For example, what is the most appropriate execution strategy to sell an unwanted

[94] A logical consequence of all this analysis is that short sellers should definitely be much more cautious with respect to getting the right information at the right time.

[95] When-issued securities are securities traded before they have been issued. In some spin-off situations, for example, shares of the company spin-off trade before the effective date of the spin-off.

position in a spun-off company? To the extent that this position is small, this may not be a great concern. However, it should never be overlooked.

- *Risk-reward analysis*: As is the case with any other form of trading, an arbitrage should be entered only if its risk profile is adequate considering the trader's constraints and targets. Conversely, if a risk is predictable in the near future that cannot be dealt with in a satisfactory way, carrying it should be carefully weighted.

Depending on the market and the underlying set of stocks within an arbitrageur's universe, corporate events may be a secondary concern or, on the other hand, a primary focus. In any case, it is always preferable to be adequately prepared than to react at the last minute with the risk of missing the point.

3

FUTURES AND RELATED INSTRUMENTS

INTRODUCTION

In the same way that we opened the previous chapter with an overview of the world equity capitalization, we will open this chapter by examining the biggest markets with respect to futures liquidity. The adequate measure here is not capitalization anymore because we focus on derivatives, but rather outstanding position or open interest. The open interest indicates the number of contracts outstanding at a given time, and it suits our purpose perfectly.

Figure 3-1 presents the total open interest converted in U.S. dollars over the last five years of the Nikkei 225, DAX 30, FTSE 100, CAC 40, and S&P 500 futures. The U.S. market is undoubtedly dominant again with respect to futures trading, and indeed the ratios between the different open interests are of the same order of magnitude as for the exchanges' relative capitalization. For example, the open interest for the S&P 500 futures at the end of 1999 was around 10 times that of the CAC 40.

If we take a broader perspective, however, the situation changes slightly. First, these contracts are not the most liquid by far because equity futures are traded much less actively than interest rate products in general. For example, the eurodollar futures in Chicago have an average daily volume of $368.7 billion, and they had an average open interest of $2,976.4 billion in 1999, more than 20 times that of the S&P 500. Indeed, this situation is true on a larger scale and on options as well, as shown in Table 3-1.

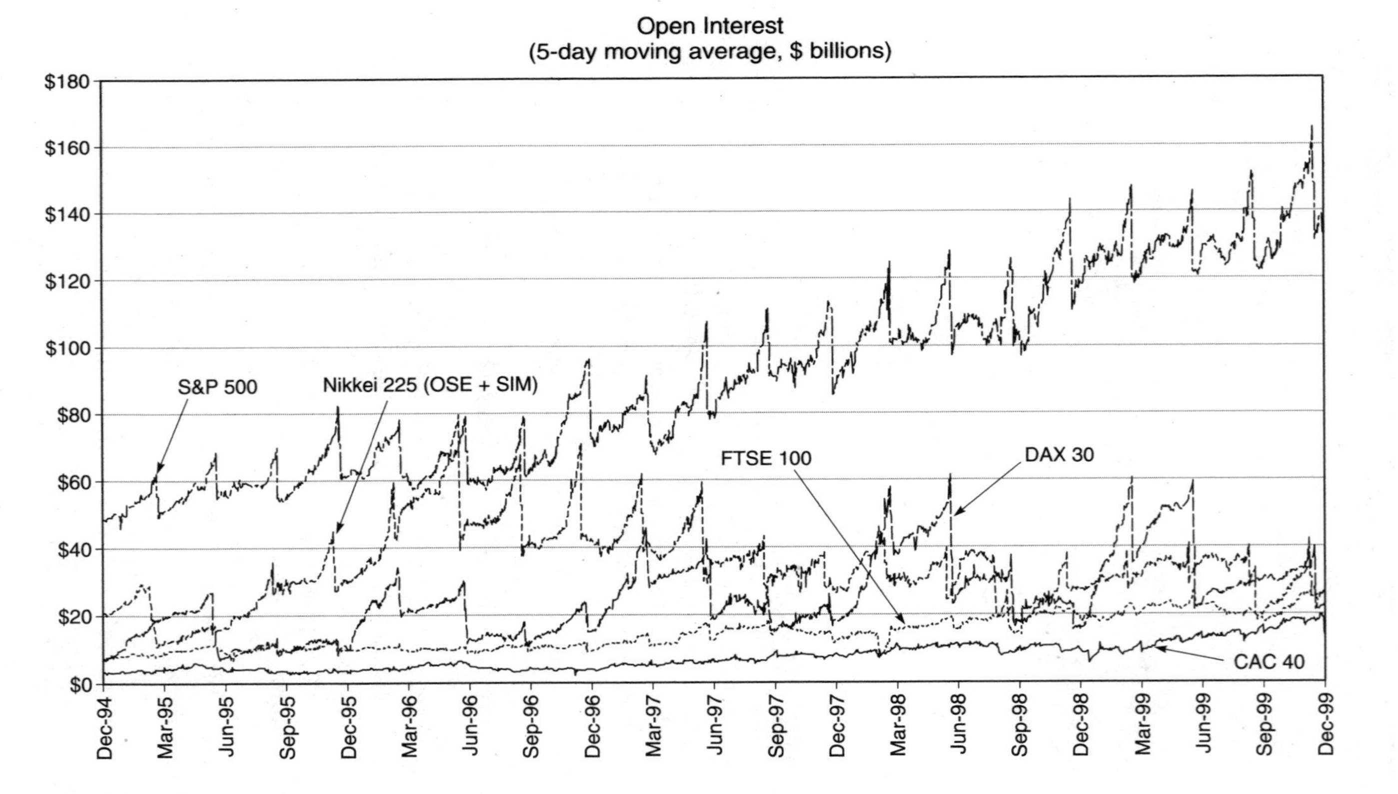

Figure 3-1 Open Interest
(*Source*: Compiled by author from Datastream data.)
The nominal data have been calculated using a monthly exchange rate. At year-end 1998, 1USD = 5.8262FRF, 1USD = 112.8JPY, 1USD = 1.6656DEM, 1USD = 0.6011GBP.

To be representative of total interest on the index, the Nikkei 225 futures open interest includes both the Japanese contract listed in Osaka (OSE) and the Singapore contract (SIM).

TABLE 3-1 Derivative Financial Instruments Traded on Organized Exchanges by Instrument and Location (Notational principal in billions of U.S. dollars)

	Amounts Outstanding				Turnover					
Instruments/Location	**1997 Dec.**	**1998 Dec.**	**1999 Sept.**	**1999 Dec.**	**1998 Year**	**1999 Year**	**1999 Q1**	**1999 Q2**	**1999 Q3**	**1999 Q4**
Futures										
All markets	**7,752.7**	**8,061.2**	**8,958.2**	**8,266.8**	**318,611.0**	**287,958.2**	**72,872.2**	**76,421.6**	**78,840.7**	**61,821.8**
Interest rate	7,489.2	7,702.2	8,605.1	7,897.3	294,792.6	283,718.1	87,068.1	70,492.4	70,848.0	55,309.8
Currency	51.9	38.1	44.6	36.5	3.068.4	2.573.2	609.2	648.4	715.8	599.7
Equity index	211.5	321.0	308.5	333.1	20,750.1	21,666.9	5,194.9	5,280.8	5,278.7	5,912.5
North America	**3,233.9**	**3,536.8**	**3,651.7**	**3,550.6**	**151,928.1**	**134,258.0**	**33,612.9**	**36,737.1**	**34,622.7**	**29,285.3**
Interest rate	3,082.6	3,365.3	3,468.1	3,357.3	139,326.0	120,681.6	30,355.7	33,319.6	31,227.2	25,779.1
Currency	48.5	38.9	40.4	32.0	2,868.7	2,239.1	542.8	566.5	615.0	514.8
Equity index	102.9	134.7	143.2	161.3	9.733.3	11,337.4	2,714.4	2,851.0	2,780.5	2,991.4
Europe	**2,550.3**	**2,914.1**	**2,842.7**	**2,371.4**	**117,396.1**	**104,547.6**	**27,948.1**	**27,178.4**	**28,309.5**	**21,111.6**
Interest rate	2,496.2	2,788.4	2,759.0	2,274.2	109,134.5	98,088.1	28,259.1	25,737.2	26,743.5	19,346.4
Currency	1.1	0.3	0.7	0.6	10.2	9.1	0.4	1.2	4.1	3.4
Equity index	53.1	127.5	83.0	96.7	8,251.5	8,452.3	1,688.6	1,440.0	1,561.9	1,761.8
Asia and Pacific	**1,928.9**	**1,581.2**	**2,283.6**	**2,146.6**	**47,285.6**	**47,114.2**	**10,886.7**	**11,994.5**	**13,370.6**	**10,862.5**
Interest rate	1,876.1	1,523.9	2,203.4	2,073.0	44,797.1	43,341.1	10,120.0	11,035.2	12,455.2	9,730.7
Currency	0.1	0.1	0.8	1.1	3.8	14.8	0.6	1.6	5.8	6.9
Equity index	52.8	57.2	79.4	72.4	2,484.7	3,758.3	766.2	957.7	909.8	1,124.9
Other Markets	**39.6**	**29.0**	**180.2**	**198.3**	**2,001.2**	**2,038.4**	**424.5**	**511.6**	**537.9**	**562.4**
Interest rate	34.4	26.7	174.6	192.9	1,534.9	1,607.4	333.4	400.4	420.1	453.4
Currency	2.3	0.8	2.7	2.8	185.7	310.2	65.4	79.0	91.1	74.6
Equity index	2.9	1.5	2.8	2.8	280.5	118.9	25.7	32.1	26.7	34.4
Options										
All markets	**4,449.6**	**5,487.9**	**5,755.0**	**5,234.2**	**69,088.1**	**62,042.8**	**18,268.8**	**16,805.2**	**14,860.1**	**14,110.7**
Intrerest rate	3,839.8	4,602.8	4,352.8	3,754.7	55,480.4	45,625.7	12,850.3	12,709.6	10,772.2	9,293.8
Currency	33.2	18.7	31.8	22.4	397.8	289.0	70.4	70.0	81.8	68.8
Equity index	776.5	866.5	1,370.4	1,457.2	13,209.9	18,128.1	3,346.2	4,025.5	4,008.1	4,750.2
North America	**3,092.6**	**3,780.9**	**3,572.0**	**3,380.8**	**47,605.5**	**41,166.5**	**10,899.9**	**11,523.1**	**9,546.7**	**9,196.7**
Interest rate	2,438.5	3,123.7	2,458.3	2,259.3	38,599.1	29,745.0	8,435.3	8,534.8	8,731.7	6,043.2
Currency	32.1	18.3	18.8	13.1	379.5	219.9	56.6	54.1	61.7	47.5
Equity index	621.9	639.0	1,094.9	1,108.5	8,626.9	11,201.6	2,408.1	2,934.2	2,753.3	3,106.0
Europe	**1,037.1**	**1,497.8**	**1,915.1**	**1,581.2**	**17,225.5**	**16,955.2**	**4,438.6**	**4,254.1**	**4,355.4**	**3,907.1**
Interest rate	917.6	1,309.9	1,695.4	1,299.9	14,152.4	14,034.1	3,873.5	3,641.0	3,601.2	2,918.4
Currency	0.2	—	0.5	0.5	0.9	2.0	0.3	0.3	0.6	0.7
Equity index	119.3	187.8	219.3	280.9	3,072.2	2,919.1	584.7	612.8	753.7	987.9
Asia and Pacific	**301.0**	**196.5**	**238.6**	**234.8**	**3,998.5**	**3,623.2**	**687.3**	**959.2**	**881.2**	**895.5**
Interest rate	279.5	187.5	196.3	191.1	2,590.9	1,796.8	533.7	518.3	428.7	316.1
Currency	—	—	—	0.1	—	0.6	—	0.1	0.3	0.2
Equity index	21.5	28.0	42.3	43.7	1,407.7	1,825.8	353.6	440.8	452.2	579.2
Other Markets	**18.9**	**13.7**	**29.2**	**37.3**	**258.5**	**297.9**	**41.0**	**68.8**	**76.7**	**111.4**
Interest rate	4.2	1.7	2.8	4.5	138.0	49.9	7.8	15.6	10.6	15.9
Currency	0.9	0.4	12.5	8.7	17.4	66.4	13.4	15.5	19.1	18.4
Equity index	13.8	11.8	13.9	24.1	103.1	181.8	19.8	37.8	46.9	77.1

(*Source*: Bank of International Settlements, *Statistical Annex to the Quarterly Review on International Banking and Financial Market Developments*, February 2000.)

The second interesting point is that in terms of contract turnover, the United States is in fact far behind Europe, as shown in Table 3-2. Among possible explanations for this situation is the fact that futures contracts in Europe tend to have a smaller size than they have in the United States. In any case, the German derivative exchange, Eurex, has since 1999 become the most active exchange in the world, in front of the CBOT with 379 million versus 255 million contracts traded, as shown in Figure 3-2.

Finally, for the sake of completeness, let's take an even broader perspective and replace these figures in the overall market for futures trading, as shown in Table 3-3. Financial futures are clearly dominant in the marketplace compared to agricultural or commodity futures, expanding from 59.5 to 65.5 percent of the aggregate open interest in the United States.

DEFINITIONS

A *futures contract* is a binding agreement between two parties to exchange certain goods, at a certain price, known on the day the transaction is effected and called the *futures price*, at a certain date in the future, known as the *expiration* or *expiry date*.[1] When the goods exchanged are monetary flows, the futures contract is said to have a *cash settlement* and is qualified as a financial futures.

Consider, for example, a transaction on a corn futures contract.[2] By convention, the buyer of the contract is the party receiving the goods upon delivery, against payment. The terms of the contract include its main characteristics—namely, the quantity and price of corn deliverable and the date of the delivery. Before that date, no exchange whatsoever is necessary between the parties. On expiry, the buyer pays for the corn and the seller delivers it.

For contracts listed on an exchange, the terms are standardized and include several more parameters, for example, the grade and

[1] The expiry date is the day on which the claim on the underlying goods becomes effective. Actual delivery usually follows by a few days, and the exact date on which it occurs is called the *settlement date* or *delivery date* depending on the context.

[2] Commodity futures are indeed a classic example because they were the first futures developed in history. This explains why Chicago, which has long been an important trading center in the midwest, imposed itself as a financial center as well very early on. It now houses the most important derivative exchanges in the United States and in the world.

TABLE 3-2 Derivative Financial Instruments Traded on Organized Exchanges by Instrument and Location (number of contracts in millions)

	Contracts Outstanding				Turnover					
Instruments/Location	1997 Dec.	1998 Dec.	1999 Sept.	1999 Dec.	1998 Year	1999 Year	1999 Q1	1999 Q2	1999 Q3	1999 Q4
Futures										
All markets	**23.4**	**20.7**	**22.3**	**21.3**	**992.5**	**914.7**	**231.6**	**237.8**	**238.6**	**206.6**
Interest rate	19.4	17.3	18.2	17.5	760.0	672.7	168.4	178.4	178.0	147.9
Currency	2.0	0.8	0.6	0.7	54.5	37.1	8.7	9.5	10.2	8.8
Equity index	2.0	2.6	3.5	3.1	178.0	204.9	54.5	49.9	50.5	49.9
North America	**5.2**	**5.5**	**5.7**	**5.4**	**357.7**	**319.9**	**83.9**	**85.9**	**80.7**	**69.5**
Interest rate	4.3	4.6	4.7	4.5	287.9	248.6	66.8	68.0	61.9	52.0
Currency	0.4	0.3	0.4	0.3	27.0	23.9	8.0	6.3	6.3	5.3
Equity index	0.5	0.5	0.5	0.6	42.8	47.5	11.1	11.8	12.5	12.2
Europe	**6.9**	**6.2**	**6.1**	**6.5**	**423.1**	**417.9**	**106.6**	**105.9**	**111.1**	**94.3**
Interest rate	5.0	4.7	4.3	3.6	345.1	322.9	78.6	84.8	88.3	71.4
Currency	1.4	0.4	0.1	0.2	8.9	1.8	0.4	0.4	0.2	0.5
Equity index	0.5	1.1	1.7	1.6	68.2	93.4	27.5	21.0	22.5	22.4
Asia and Pacific	**3.6**	**3.1**	**4.0**	**3.3**	**128.4**	**115.8**	**28.6**	**30.9**	**30.3**	**28.0**
Interest rate	2.8	2.2	3.0	2.5	76.7	65.9	16.1	17.5	18.2	14.1
Currency	—	—	—	—	0.1	0.3	—	—	0.1	0.1
Equity index	0.8	0.9	1.0	0.7	49.6	49.5	12.5	13.3	12.0	11.7
Other Markets	**7.8**	**6.0**	**6.5**	**7.1**	**85.3**	**61.1**	**12.5**	**15.2**	**16.8**	**16.8**
Interest rate	7.3	5.7	6.1	6.8	49.4	35.2	6.9	8.3	9.5	10.3
Currency	0.3	0.1	0.1	0.1	18.8	11.4	2.3	2.8	3.5	2.9
Equity index	0.2	0.2	0.3	0.2	17.4	14.5	3.4	4.0	3.5	3.8
Memorandum Items:										
Commodity Contracts	**6.1**	**6.3**	**7.1**	**6.5**	**306.9**	**327.5**	**82.0**	**81.5**	**86.8**	**77.2**
U.S. markets	2.7	2.8	3.3	2.9	153.4	165.6	40.2	41.7	44.9	38.7
Other markets	3.4	3.5	3.8	3.6	153.4	162.0	41.8	39.8	41.9	38.6
Options										
All Markets	**17.4**	**17.4**	**27.4**	**27.1**	**336.8**	**447.3**	**102.2**	**110.8**	**111.4**	**122.9**
Interest rate	6.0	6.9	6.7	5.6	129.7	118.0	31.5	32.5	28.2	25.7
Currency	2.4	0.9	0.7	0.5	12.1	6.8	1.6	1.6	1.9	1.7
Equity index	9.0	9.8	20.1	21.0	195.0	322.5	69.1	76.8	81.3	95.5
North America	**7.8**	**8.6**	**8.8**	**7.5**	**172.3**	**142.9**	**39.3**	**38.3**	**34.4**	**31.0**
Interest rate	3.4	4.5	3.7	3.2	86.1	72.2	21.1	20.9	16.4	13.8
Currency	0.4	0.2	0.2	0.1	5.4	2.8	0.8	0.7	0.8	0.5
Equity index	3.9	3.8	4.8	4.2	80.7	67.9	17.4	16.6	17.2	18.7
Europe	**5.6**	**6.0**	**15.8**	**16.3**	**102.8**	**186.8**	**37.7**	**43.1**	**48.1**	**57.7**
Interest rate	2.0	2.1	2.7	2.1	37.4	41.7	9.3	10.5	10.9	11.1
Currency	0.1	—	—	—	0.4	0.1	—	—	—	—
Equity index	3.5	3.9	13.1	14.1	65.0	144.9	28.4	32.7	37.2	48.8
Asia and Pacific	**1.0**	**0.8**	**1.1**	**1.0**	**44.8**	**91.9**	**20.0**	**22.6**	**22.9**	**28.5**
Interest rate	0.5	0.2	0.2	0.2	4.5	3.0	0.9	0.9	0.7	0.5
Currency	—	—	—	—	—	0.1	—	—	—	—
Equity index	0.5	0.6	0.9	0.8	40.1	88.8	19.0	21.7	22.2	25.9
Other Markets	**3.0**	**2.1**	**1.8**	**2.2**	**17.1**	**26.7**	**5.2**	**6.8**	**6.0**	**7.7**
Interest rate	0.1	—	0.1	0.1	1.7	1.0	0.2	0.3	0.2	0.3
Currency	1.9	0.7	0.5	0.3	6.3	3.8	0.8	0.8	1.1	1.1
Equity index	1.1	1.4	1.3	1.8	9.2	20.9	4.3	5.6	4.7	6.3
Memorandum Items:										
Commodity Contracts	**2.7**	**2.7**	**4.1**	**3.6**	**38.6**	**41.4**	**9.0**	**9.7**	**12.1**	**10.6**
U.S. markets	2.4	2.4	3.6	3.1	32.5	35.5	7.8	8.3	10.6	8.8
Other markets	0.3	0.3	0.5	0.6	4.1	5.9	1.3	1.4	1.5	1.9
Single Equity Contracts	**43.8**	**68.2**	**128.9**	**169.4**	**501.4**	**700.3**	**158.0**	**165.4**	**167.2**	**209.7**
U.S. markets	31.5	44.7	91.9	121.9	325.8	443.8	95.7	100.0	105.5	142.6
Other markets	12.3	23.5	35.0	37.5	175.7	256.6	62.4	65.4	61.8	87.1

(*Source*: Bank of International Settlements, *Statistical Annex to the Quarterly Review on International Banking and Financial Market Developments*, February 2000.)

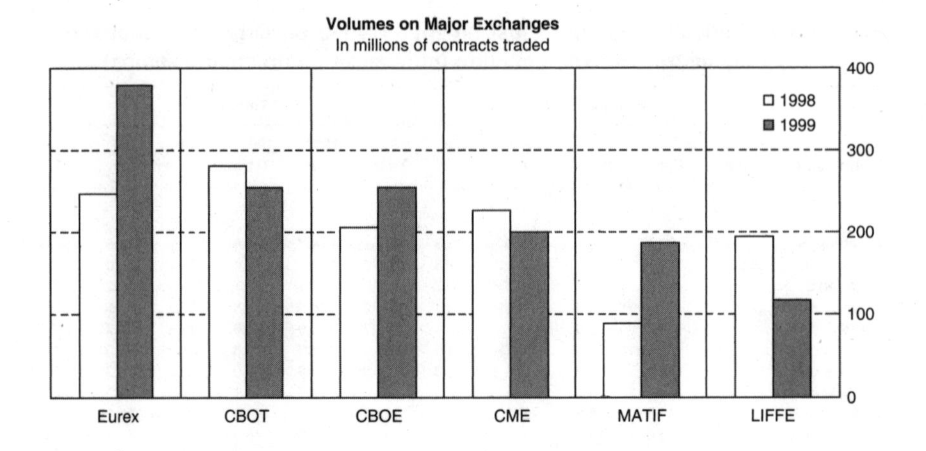

Figure 3-2 Future Exchanges
(*Source*: Bank of International Settlements, *Quarterly Review on International Banking and Financial Market Developments*, February 2000.)
CBOE: Chicago Board Options Exchange; CBOT: Chicago Board of Trade; CME: Chicago Mercantile Exchange; LIFFE: London International Financial Futures and Options Exchange; MATIF: Marché à Terme International de France.

quality of the corn and the delivery location. As a general rule, futures contracts on commodities are worded in such a way as to reduce ambiguities to a minimum and allow all transactions to be effected on a single fully fungible underlying. In fact, this necessity goes beyond commodity futures to all futures with a physical delivery, which is, for example, the case for futures on U.S. treasury bonds. The bonds acceptable for delivery are clearly specified in the terms of the contract.

Therefore a futures contract is really nothing more than a simple deferred transaction, but:

- On expiration day, if we assume that corn can always be bought for immediate delivery at any time, the futures contract does not provide any benefit compared to *cash* corn—that is corn bought for a delivery the same day.[3] At that time, nobody would be ready to

[3] We assume here that corn bought today can be delivered today. This is naturally a simplification because of the difference between operation date and settlement date.

This is the very first important characteristic of a futures contract: To price it, we must constantly refer to the price of the underlying commodity. Futures are derivative products, and their existence is subordinated to the existence of a cash market for the underlying.

TABLE 3-3 Futures—Average Month-End Open Interest, Number of Contracts Traded, and Number of Contracts Settled by Delivery or Cash Settlement by Major Groups, All Markets Combined, FY 1993–FY 1999

Fiscal Year	Total	Grain	Oilseed Products	Livestock Products	Other Agricul-turals	Energy/ Wood Products	Metals	Financial Instru-ments	Currencies
Average Month-End Open Interest (In Contracts)									
1993	5,164,957	365,751	301,492	116,640	292,869	697,275	314,421	2,758,539	317,970
1994	6,508,063	422,468	323,368	125,664	328,149	807,177	383,406	3,799,004	338,829
1995	6,434,175	502,955	332,115	118,664	357,332	695,734	378,352	3,749,845	299,178
1996	6,671,956	594,283	383,027	149,110	357,039	707,515	368,788	3,778,614	335,580
1997	7,035,190	484,878	378,005	158,554	399,845	793,050	355,152	4,052,556	413,150
1998	*8,734,778	561,318	419,055	156,097	*425,208	969,274	351,300	*5,337,352	*515,176
1999	8,927,497	581,590	420,159	178,617	395,387	1,140,329	381,265	5,372,623	477,527
Number of Contracts Traded									
1993	325,515,261	16,006,104	20,738,245	5,770,835	10,754,864	42,841,813	15,197,631	185,397,113	28,808,456
1994	411,056,929	19,970,008	20,988,318	6,137,105	12,318,572	50,460,607	18,231,411	252,579,136	30,371,774
1995	409,420,428	21,093,086	20,687,820	6,238,509	12,744,901	47,944,153	17,393,317	259,024,379	24,293,461
1996	394,182,422	30,217,442	25,591,703	7,048,534	12,018,522	46,891,524	16,938,969	234,261,790	21,213,938
1997	417,341,601	25,507,498	27,132,483	7,550,556	13,190,755	51,512,419	17,093,481	250,143,412	25,210,997
1998	*500,676,345	28,139,049	26,854,245	7,385,569	14,039,615	81,705,146	17,044,818	*319,916,853	*27,590,350
1999	491,137,790	26,860,264	25,625,245	7,438,875	13,753,993	72,941,784	17,294,322	303,684,764	23,558,563
Number of Contracts Settled by Delivery/Cash Settlement									
1993	2,082,970	48,573	179,284	11,695	56,840	62,744	184,621	1,035,375	503,838
1994	2,873,454	76,737	88,741	8,368	44,373	78,108	189,502	1,809,418	578,209
1995	2,995,958	70,548	158,003	12,900	60,593	75,209	157,323	1,939,908	521,473
1996	2,890,187	38,228	172,442	13,384	39,406	87,777	132,507	1,903,974	502,451
1997	3,559,079	36,589	148,703	29,883	38,015	119,505	129,977	2,385,886	670,721
1998	4,186,908	131,357	116,412	42,230	31,828	129,586	163,804	2,705,700	865,921
1999	3,631,918	120,775	106,364	44,129	32,282	131,905	128,557	2,230,017	837,687

*Revised since FY 1998 annual report.

Note: The number of contracts settled by delivery or cash settlement indicates the number of contracts actually expiring as opposed to the positions traded and liquidated or rolled over before expiry.

(*Source*: Commodity Futures Trading Commission, *Annual Report 1999*, www.cftc.org. Data for U.S. markets only.)

pay more for a futures contract than for the underlying cash product, and conversely. It follows that *a futures contract has a price equal to its underlying cash price on expiration day*. This price is usually referred to as the *special quotation (SQ) price*.

- Because cash corn is available for purchase at any time, the potential buyer of a futures contract has always an explicit choice between futures and cash. If he or she buys cash corn, he or she receives delivery the same day, loses the benefit of the cash he or she disbursed, and has to store the corn if he or she does not have an immediate use for it. On the other hand, if he or she buys the futures contract, he or she earns interests on the cash saved until expiry and does not have any storage cost. Furthermore, he or she is still certain to receive corn but at a future date that may be more suitable to his or her needs. Therefore, his or her decision to buy a futures contract will necessarily include these three components: interest rates, storage, and convenience.[4] But the problem has one more dimension because cash corn will also be available at the expiry of the future. The potential buyer could do nothing, wait, and buy cash corn later, at a price unknown as of today with the risk that it will be more expensive than the cash price or the futures price today. Therefore, the buyer should enter a transaction today, either cash or futures, only if he or she expects the price of corn to go up in the future. Now consider that he or she buys a future at $20 per unit, and at expiry of the futures the cash corn sells for $15 per unit. Because the futures is an obligation, the $5 potential savings is lost no matter what. The general conclusion is that *a futures contract induces an exposure on the underlying cash price,* despite the fact that no exchange of any sort has taken place before expiration date. Note that the $5 opportunity lost to the buyer accrues to the seller. This is a zero-sum game, like all futures transactions.

- There is no payment of nominal between the transaction date and settlement, as we mentioned.[5] Suppose that a futures contract seller loses its whole corn reserve in a fire. He will be unable to deliver corn on the expiration date and will have to buy cash corn at market price because he has an obligation to deliver. Therefore, he carries an additional risk if he is not able to deliver for any reason.[6] This situation is described as a *naked position*—that is, a derivative position without the protection of the underlying asset, as opposed to a *covered position* in which he would be able to deliver corn he owned. Our simple analysis shows that there is a critical difference between the two. A position in a future entered to offset an opposite exposure on the underlying is a covered transaction, in

---

[4] Financial futures have a different nomenclature. The convenience aspect is captured by the monetary flows expected during the life of the contract for a holder of the underlying asset. In the case of equities these flows are primarily dividends, including the tax rebate if there is one. Storage costs are the costs or benefits of holding a portfolio. For a short position, this cost is a borrowing fee; otherwise, it is the potential revenue generated by lending the stocks out. Note that storage costs are always an outflow for a commodity but can be of any sign with a financial asset.

[5] Futures listed on organized market have intermediate flows as we will see, the margin calls. In our case the nominal payment of the corn underlying the contract is not made until expiry.

[6] It looks as though this risk is particular to the seller and that the buyer is immune to it. In fact, it is not exactly true because the buyer may need the corn before expiry, which would force him or her to buy it in the cash market. He or she would then, at the expiration of the futures, have to sell the corn delivered back in the market.

which the portfolio is hedged and global risk decreased.[7] A naked futures position gives rise only to a speculative risk.

- Each party is exposed to the risk that its counterpart will fail to honor its contract upon settlement, notably because of a possible bankruptcy. The longer the maturity of the futures contract, the more serious the risk. To address this specific problem, exchanges throughout the world have set up clearinghouses and margin mechanisms designed to force market participants to cover their losses as frequently as possible, in practice every day. The consequence of that intermediation has been the standardization of the contracts to simplify procedures. It is naturally always possible to enter any type of contract off the floor of an exchange—that is, over the counter (OTC)—in which case, each party faces a full-fledged credit risk.

The case of commodity futures is particularly instructive because it is easy to understand why a corn grower would want to sell his or her soon-to-come harvest now for delivery later. He or she gets the benefit of a good price without the constraint of delivering corn that he or she does not own today but will harvest in the near future.

However, in comparison to financial futures, commodity futures in general represent nowadays only a relatively minor fraction of the total amount of futures traded throughout the world. We need to consider these futures in more detail, and we will focus on stock index futures that have probably the largest applications in equity arbitrage:

- A stock index future is a financial futures; therefore, it is cash settled. Its underlying is not one security in particular but a stock index.
- The contract is standardized in every respect. The underlying is clearly identified and unique. Expiration dates are fixed according to a rolling cycle—for example, the third Friday of March, June, September, and December for the S&P 500 index futures.[8]

---

[7] Note that a futures contract can also hedge a position that is not necessarily its underlying. In that case the correlation between that position and the futures underlying also plays a role in the overall profitability on the hedge.

[8] If this Friday is not a business day, expiry is usually the day before. Index futures in Germany, Japan, and the United Kingdom also have a quarterly schedule. France has a monthly schedule.

There are usually five expirations opened for trading at the same time. For example, if the first expiry is March 2000, the last future available for trading is March 2001. The first expiry, called the *front month,* is by far the most liquid. The second expiry, the *back month,* starts trading actively around two weeks prior to the expiration of the current front month.

- An index futures contract is also characterized by its point value, which is a coefficient that indicates the variation in hard currency associated with a variation in the quoted price. For example, the point value is $250 for the S&P 500, therefore every variation of $1 in the price of the futures contract induces a variation of $250 in the dollar value of the position.
- The SQ price of an index futures contract is usually defined with reference to a particular time. For example, on the S&P 500, the SQ is the value of the index computed with all the opening prices of its constituents on expiration date.[9] The Nikkei 225 index expires on a similar reference. Some European indices, however, have different conventions. For example, in France and the United Kingdom, the SQ is computed as an average on the underlying index prices over a short period of time.
- To ensure the financial integrity of all participants, clearinghouses have been instituted as necessary intermediaries, as we mentioned earlier. Every trade is actually carried out with a clearinghouse as a counterpart, which in turn has the legal responsibility and power to collect dues. In order to do so, clearinghouses have instituted an automatic margining system in which losses have to be systematically covered; if they are not covered, the positions are liquidated.[10] Futures being a zero-sum game, payments to cover losses on one account are necessarily credited to another account with an opposite position.
- The exposure created by a futures position is highly leveraged because of the specifics of the margining system. Whereas buying

[9] Note that this price has nothing to do with the value published by major data providers as the opening price for the index. The SQ price is known only when all stocks have opened, which may take several minutes. The opening price contributed by vendors is usually computed with opening prices for those stocks that have opened and previous closing prices for those that have not traded yet.

[10] Naturally there are other measures to limit the amount of losses a participant is susceptible to accumulate. For example, open positions are monitored carefully and restricted within certain limits.

The failure of a member is a rare event but not unheard of. In 1995, for example, the British merchant bank Barings collapsed due to fraudulent trading by one of its employees on the Singapore Monetary Exchange (SIMEX). What happens in such a case depends on the exchange. Japanese exchanges, for example, collect a small fee on every transaction—typically 0.001 percent—segregated in a dedicated safety fund to be used to cover extraordinary losses. The Chicago Mercantile Exchange, on the other hand, does not have a similar measure. Its rules state that members are responsible for every dollar of extraordinary losses in proration to their open positions.

$100 of stocks requires $100 of cash,[11] buying the equivalent of $100 of futures requires only a safety deposit that is much smaller than the traded nominal. If this deposit is, for example 20 percent, the same gain of $1 will appear as a poor 1 percent return in the case of a fully financed stock position, and an honest 5 percent in the case of leveraged futures. Therefore, futures are clearly attractive vehicles for fast, aggressive, and speculative gains.[12]

- Like stocks, futures are also subject to specific rules and are settled within a specific settlement cycle. The actual flows are due a certain number of days after the position has been traded in the market: $D+1$ in the United Kingdom and Germany, $D+2$ in the United States, $D+3$ in Japan, and so on.

We will revisit many of these issues in detail; meanwhile Table 3-4 gives a summarized view of the largest markets.

CLEARINGHOUSES, MARGIN CALLS, AND DEPOSITS

The clearinghouse acts as an intermediary in each and every transaction and is legally entitled to take action to ensure the financial integrity of the marketplace. Market participants are required to maintain a certain amount of financial resources with their broker, and the broker in turn is required to redirect a sizable fraction of these resources to the clearinghouse.

There are two important notions in defining the definitions of these requirements:

- An initial requirement, always due at the opening of the position, which represents the minimum balance to be maintained on the account

---

[11] Or $50 in a margin purchase in the United States where the requirement is 50 percent. Essentially stock margin transactions are similar to futures in that they also raise the need of a safety net in the form of regular margin calls. They differ, however, in the level of initial margin needed: Futures have a much lower requirement, allowing higher leverage.

[12] Note that we said "the equivalent of $100 of futures." When buying $100 in stocks, the nominal settled is $100 for the delivery of the shares. When buying a futures contract, the nominal of the transaction is the market price of the futures contract times its point value. This nominal, however, is not exchanged; only the deposit requirement is actually paid. Therefore, the $100 nominal in that case does not correspond to a physical flow. It is sometimes referred to as a *notional amount*.

TABLE 3-4

Index	Exchange[a]	Point Value	Cycle[b]	Expiry	Settlement Rule	Tick[c]	Special Quotation	Margin Requirement[d]	Margin Calculation
FTSE 100	LIFFE	£10	Quarterly	Third Friday	D + 1	£0.5	EDSP average[e]	£3,000	SPAN[f]
DAX 30	Eurex	€25	Quarterly	Third Friday	D + 1	€0.5	Intraday auction	€8,500	Other[g]
Nikkei 225	OSE	¥1,000	Quarterly	Second Friday	D + 3	¥10	Opening auction	¥1,000,000	Other
Nikkei 225	SIMEX	¥500	Quarterly	Second Friday	D + 2	¥5	Equal to OSE's	¥562,500	SPAN
S&P 500	CME	$250	Quarterly	Third Friday	D + 2	$0.5	Opening auction	$23,438	SPAN
CAC 40	MATIF	€10	Monthly	Last trading day	D + 1	€0.5	Average	€2,000	SPAN

[a] LIFFE, London International Financial Futures Exchange; Eurex, European Exchange; OSE, Osaka Securities Exchange; Simex, Singapore International Monetary Exchange; MATIF, Marché à Terme International de France.

[b] Quarterly: March, June, September, December.

[c] The tick value is the minimum variation in the quoted price of the future.

[d] Initial margin—that is, the minimum amount of money required on the account to authorize trading for one contract.

[e] EDSP, Exchange delivery settlement price.

[f] SPAN, Standard Portfolio Analysis of Risk, a margining system designed by the CME and very broadly used by clearing corporations worldwide.

[g] The Eurex runs its proprietary risk procedure, called "Risk-Based Margining." Margin requirements are recomputed every day for several classes of assets, in a way similar to SPAN evaluations.

(*Source*: Exchanges respective Web sites, www.liffe.com, www.eurexchange.com, www.ose.or.jp, www.simex.com, www.cme.com, www.matif.fr, and Bloomberg.)

- An incremental requirement, payable or receivable depending on market movements

These two quantities carry several names, like *initial* and *maintenance margin*, or *initial deposit* and *minimum margin call*. Beyond the labels, the difference resides in the fact that the initial margin covers the position as it is opened and must always be met after subsequent market moves. The maintenance margin, by contrast, is the minimum incremental amount that can move in and out of the account in order to keep the account in good standing. For example, the requirements for the CME S&P 500 are as follows: $23,438 per contract upon initiation, $18,750 for maintenance for *outright* positions.[13] The distinction of *outright position* is necessary because specific rules allow investors to decrease their margin calls if a position results in lower market risk than a straightforward futures exposure. For example, a calendar spread—that is, long one expiry and short another—is considered

[13] An outright position has one leg only, in contrast to a spread that has two opposite legs.

much less risky and the deposit requirement is smaller: $219 upon initiation and $175 for maintenance.

The existence of margin calls is an important parameter to consider when trading futures. The cash flows necessary to maintain a futures account generate treasury movements that need to be accounted for carefully, if only because of the financing entries they create.[14] It is therefore necessary here to achieve a clear understanding of the margining system. By and large all margining systems function in a similar way, so we will consider from now on the example of the S&P 500 futures to illustrate our discussion.

Consider an investor trading futures with the following transactions:

- On January 14, she has no preexisting position and she buys 100 S&P 500 futures at $1,250, with the market closing at $1,255.
- The next day with the market up, she decides to liquidate 25 futures at $1,265, but at the and of the day, buys 50 more on the close at $1,240.
- Finally, on January 16 she liquidates everything—that is, 125 contracts, at a market price of $1,230.

Table 3-5 summarizes his or her trading activity. Every day this investor faces potential profits or losses due to the difference between the market closing price and the historical trades in her portfolio. In addition, because she is still trading during the period, some of these profits or losses actually materialize.

The process of comparing an existing position to its value in the market is known as a *mark-to-market valuation*. This is the most basic function performed by a clearinghouse, after which it is in a position to call some accounts on margin while crediting others by an equal amount.

TABLE 3-5

Date	Position (at Open)	Buys	Sells	Close
Jan. 14	—	100 @ $1,250	—	$1,255
Jan. 15	100	50 @ $1,240	25 @ $1,265	$1,240
Jan. 16	125	—	125 @ $1,230	—

[14] Remember that from our trading perspective, every dollar needed is borrowed; therefore, margin calls are borrowed or invested at market rates.

TABLE 3-6

Date	Beginning-of Day Position	End-of-Day Position	Initial Requirement	Profit/Loss	Margin Call[a]	Account Balance after Margin Calls
Jan. 14	—	100	$2,343,800	$125,000[(1)]	−$2,218,800[(2)]	$2,343,800
Jan. 15	100	125	$2,929,750	−$218,750[(3)]	−$804,700[(4)]	$2,929,750
Jan. 16	125	—	—	−$312,500[(5)]	$2,617,250[(6)]	—

[a] The convention adopted here is the investor's view: a negative margin call is cash going out the door.

Table 3-6 shows the margin calls and the account balance. The figures result from the following calculations:

- **(1)** At the end of the day, the investor has a potential profit of $125,000 because she bought at $1,250 a position valued at $1,255 ($\$5 * 100 * \$250 = \$125{,}000$, $250 is the S&P 500 point value). Her *mark-to-market valuation* is positive. She has not locked this profit, however, because she still holds the position: This is an *unrealized* profit.
- **(2)** $\$2{,}218{,}800 = 100 * \$23{,}438 - \$125{,}000 =$ initial requirement for opening the position, minus the unrealized gain. This amount is larger than the maintenance requirement, $18,750, so it is claimed in full by the broker.
- **(3)** The in and out on 25 futures during the day at $1,240 and $1,265 generated $25 * \$25 * \$250 = \$156{,}250$. The unrealized profit on the 25 lots bought at the end of the day is 0 because they were traded at $1,240. Finally, the 100 futures carried overnight have a mark-to-market of $-\$375{,}000$ $(= -\$15 * 100 * \$250)$. In total, the loss for the day is $\$156{,}250 - \$375{,}000 = -\$218{,}750$.
- **(4)** The total initial requirement for 125 futures at the end of the day is $2,929,750. Considering the investor has a total mark-to-market of −$218,750, she has to pay $\$2{,}929{,}750 - (-\$218{,}750) - \$2{,}343{,}800 = \$804{,}700$.
- **(5)** The investor is closing 125 futures at $1,230. These futures were marked to market at $1,240 the previous night. The *realized* loss is therefore: $-\$10 * 125 * \$250 = -\$312{,}500$
- **(6)** The investor receives what is remaining on the account as a final flow, that is the previous balance $2,929,750 minus the current loss $312,500.
- The total loss for the whole period is given by the sum of all margin calls, or by the sum of all daily losses, in both cases −$406,250 here.

Note that all the margin calls paid out during the period come back except for the realized loss.[15]

- The total interest charge for the period is $728, which is relatively minor.[16] However, suppose that January 16 is a Friday and the final trading day is therefore postponed until January 19. The financing charge then becomes $1,382; it is still low but it is growing fast.

We have assumed here that payments are all settled in cash, but this is not the general case. In fact, because of the interest charges on margin calls, cash is very rarely used, and most clearinghouses accept alternative assets such as bonds issued by their domestic government. Most of them also accept U.S. treasury bonds. Some also accept domestic shares or other forms of collateral—letters of credit, for example.

In any case, there is a direct cost associated with a deposit requirement, even when cash is not used. If an arbitrageur wants to deposit bonds or stocks, he or she has to borrow them.[17] Against this borrowing, he or she will have to deliver a cash collateral, but the total cost of the operation is much lower than depositing cash directly at the clearinghouse. If he or she wants to use a letter of credit, the issuer of the letter will also claim a fee for this service. If the arbitrageur held some stocks, which is often the case by nature of the position, he or she could deposit them and apparently save the fee. At the same time he or she would not be able to lend these stocks, which would result in an *opportunity* cost.

Because of the amounts involved, it is extremely important for an arbitrageur to secure the cheapest deposit possible and to make sure

---

[15] Note also that on a given day, the total profit and loss for the position is the sum of a realized part, arising from deals effected on that day, and an unrealized part, the outstanding position carried over from the previous day.

[16] The calculation is as follows: Assuming a 5 percent interest rate, $2,218,800 is borrowed from January 14 to January 16 when the position is closed. The interest charge is ($2,218,800 × 5 percent × 2 days) / 360 = $616. An additional $804,700 is borrowed from January 15 to 16, at a cost of $112. The total is $728. Each additional day the position is kept costs $420 if the market is unchanged.

The reason this is a charge is that clearinghouses, and more generally brokers, are usually not allowed to pay interest on the money they receive as collateral for derivative positions. This interdiction arises from the fact they are not financial institutions in the business of managing money. Therefore, depositing money as a result of a margin call generates a pure financing loss.

[17] If he or she buys them, he or she carries the market risk over a period that can be significant. Borrowing does not transfer market risk, which remains with the lender.

that the flows generated by the market movements get accurately described and accounted for.

GENERAL MARGIN CALL FORMULA

We have explained how a margin call is computed on the basis of a mark-to-market valuation, but we implicitly effected a LIFO matching between open positions.[18] In computing a profit and loss for the day on January 15, we matched the 25 lots sold to the 50 lots bought on the same day. That is, we matched the latest purchase deals to offset the sale of 25 lots. Alternatively, we could have chosen the long position outstanding from the previous day, and matched the sale against these. This method would have been a FIFO matching because the position opened on the January 14 preexisted the purchase made on January 15.

The situation is therefore more complex than it appears. Indeed, there are essentially two generic ways to manage a futures account:

- *Position carried at market, no historical matching*: In that scenario, the outstanding position is reevaluated every day at close. Deals for a particular day are matched entirely, and they create a profit or a loss that is fully reflected in the margin call.[19] This is essentially what we did above. In that situation, the historical information about past transactions is irrelevant. All deals prior to today are evaluated as if they had been executed at yesterday's closing price. The margin call encompasses both realized and unrealized P&L with no further distinction.
- *Position carried at cost, specific matching rule:* In that scenario, all deals are carried at cost and ranked according to a specific key. This ranking is necessary to pair deals and offset sales and purchases in order to leave the account with one outstanding aggregate position, long or short.[20] In a FIFO matching, the oldest deal is retrieved and matched first. In a LIFO matching, the most recent deal is retrieved and matched first.[21] Historical information for

---

[18] LIFO = Last in first out, as opposed to FIFO, first in first out.

[19] *Profit and loss* will be abbreviated P&L from now on.

[20] This procedure is called *netting*, and is not always compulsory or automatic. In Japan, for example, it is possible to carry both long and short positions on the same account, without their being matched.

[21] For example, assume that we carry a long position, and today we sell one contract. A FIFO matching pairs today's sale with the oldest purchase available. A LIFO matching would pair the same sale with the most recent purchase.

each deal is critical in order to effect the matching properly. The margin call is the sum of realized and unrealized P&L, and it is naturally identical to the previous method. However, the key difference is the amount of realized P&L, which may have a significant impact on the taxation of the position.[22]

Differences between the two methods are not fundamental if we neglect the problem of accounting and taxes because overall the monetary flows are identical. They are only distinct formats presenting essentially the same information.

The following equations present a formalization of these results:

$$\mathrm{PL}_{t-1\to t} = \mathrm{PV}\left[P_t \cdot C_t - P_{t-1} \cdot C_{t-1} - \sum_{\text{today's deals}} Q \cdot P\right]$$

$$\mathrm{MC}_{t-1\to t} = \begin{cases} 0 & \text{if} |(P_{t-1} - P_t) \cdot \mathrm{IM} + \mathrm{PL}_{t-1\to t}| < \mathrm{MM} \\ (P_{t-1} - P_t) \cdot \mathrm{IM} + \mathrm{PL}_{t-1\to t} & \text{otherwise} \end{cases}$$

$$\mathrm{PL}^{\text{realized}}_{t-1\to t} + \mathrm{PL}^{\text{unrealized}}_{t-1\to t} = \mathrm{MC}_{t-1\to t}$$

where $\mathrm{PL}_{t-1\to t}$ = total P&L from yesterday to today[23]
$\mathrm{MC}_{t-1\to t}$ = margin call from yesterday to today
IM = initial margin requirement[24]
MM = maintenance margin requirement
PV = future point value
P_t, C_t = outstanding position and closing price today, respectively[25]
Q, P = quantities and prices for today's deals, respectively
realized, unrealized = realized and unrealized parts of $\mathrm{PL}_{t-1\to t}$[26]

---

[22] Another form of matching is called *best*: The deals are matched in order to realize the maximum amount of profit, or the minimum amount of loss. Again this mode has an impact on tax calculations.

[23] $\mathrm{PL}_{t-1\to t} > 0$ indicates that the position shows a profit. By the same token, $\mathrm{MC}_{t-1\to t} > 0$ indicates a positive flow—that is, a payment to the account holder.

[24] In some rare cases, IM is a percentage of the current market price and is not a fixed amount.

[25] By convention P is an algebraic number: $P > 0$ indicates a long. Along the same lines, Q is also algebraic and follows a similar convention: $Q > 0$ indicates a purchase. These conventions imply that $P_t - P_{t-1} = \sum_{\text{today's deals}} Q$.

[26] Note that getting an exact expression of $\mathrm{PL}^{\text{realized}}_{t-1\to t}$ and $\mathrm{PL}^{\text{unrealized}}_{t-1\to t}$ is not possible without a historical breakdown of deals.

The margin call is therefore composed of two terms:

- $(P_t - P_{t-1}) \cdot \text{IM}$: minimum required balance for the current size of the position
- $\text{PL}_{t-1 \to t}$: dependent upon the day-to-day trading activity and market level

As an application, consider our previous example and the margin call from January 14 to January 15. Here t = January 15:

- Outstanding position: $P_{t-1} = 100$, $P_t = 125$, $\text{IM} = \$23{,}438$
- Today's deals: $Q_B = 50$, $P_B = \$1{,}240$, $Q_S = -25$, $P_S = \$1{,}265$
- Closing prices: $C_{t-1} = \$1{,}255$, $C_t = \$1{,}240$

Therefore:

$$\text{PL}_{t-1 \to t} = 250 \cdot (125 * \$1{,}240 - 100 * \$1{,}255 - 50 * \$1{,}240 + 25 * \$1{,}265)$$

which becomes:

$$\text{PL}_{t-1 \to t} = 250 \cdot (\$155{,}000 - \$125{,}500 - \$62{,}000 + \$31{,}625) = -\$218{,}750$$

And the margin call is given by:

$$\text{MC}_{t-1 \to t} = (100 - 125) \cdot \$23{,}438 - \$218{,}750 = -\$804{,}700$$

Both figures are equal to those we obtained before.

Our presentation can be simplified further because we adopt the perspective of an arbitrageur, and we do not expect to have any trading activity once the position is set up. Under this steady-state assumption, $P_t = P_{t-1}$ and $\sum_{\text{today's sell}} Q \cdot P = \sum_{\text{today's buy}} Q \cdot P = 0$ because there is no trading activity. The above equation becomes:[27]

$$\text{MC}_{t-1 \to t} = \text{PL}_{t-1 \to t} = \text{PV}(C_t - C_{t-1})P_t$$

The margin call from yesterday to today is directly proportional to the variation of the market.[28] This result is fundamental because it gives a precise expression of the necessary flows to maintain the future position, and shows that these flows depend on market movements.

---

[27] For all practical purposes, the term MM is negligible in front of $(P_{t-1} - P_t) \cdot \text{IM} + PL_{t-1 \to t}$ in the calculation; therefore, we assume the condition $(P_{t-1} - P_t) \cdot \text{IM} + \text{PL}_{t-1 \to t} > \text{MM}$ is always true.

[28] It is certainly a natural and intuitive result, but interestingly it holds despite the rather complex margining structure.

We will develop further this argument in the examination of index arbitrage.

CUSTOMER MARGIN CALLS VERSUS EXCHANGE MARGIN CALLS

So far we have not made any distinction among market participants with respect to clearing procedures. In practice only exchange members are allowed to maintain an account directly with the clearinghouse. Other institutions have to have intermediaries to clear their trades.

Therefore, the margin calls managed by the clearinghouse are in fact aggregated over a large number of individual accounts, as shown in Figure 3-3. In that situation, the failure of a member has a potentially much more devastating effect than the failure of a single participant, which explains the high level of regulation imposed on financial institutions engaged in trading activities for customers.[29]

At the same time, to provide members with a safety cushion, the requirements on customer margin calls are often more stringent than those set by the exchange for its members.[30] Typically customers' deposits are higher and must be more liquid. The extreme example is an individual investor, for whom the types of deposits allowed to trade futures are often cash or money market funds only.

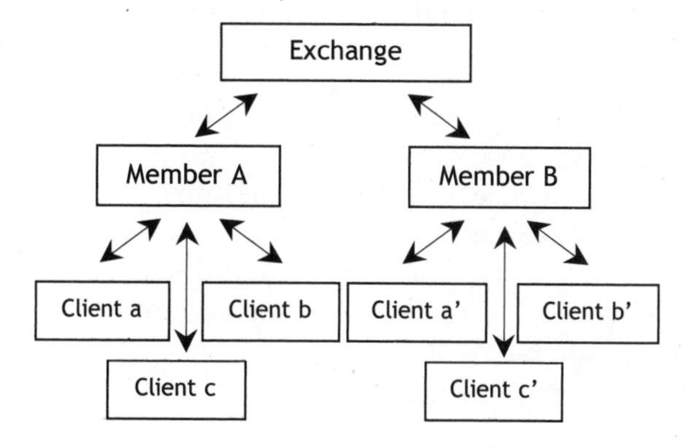

Figure 3-3 Client versus Broker MC

[29] Notably the diverse regulations call for a complete segregation of customers' assets to avoid a situation in which a rogue institution settles and disguises its own losses at the expense of its account holders.

[30] In some examples, Japan notably, an additional protection feature is that customer margins are due one day before exchange margins, and paid one day after.

STANDARD PORTFOLIO ANALYSIS OF RISK

The Standard Portfolio Analysis of Risk (SPAN) is a risk evaluation system originally developed by the Chicago Mercantile Exchange in 1988. It was designed to solve simple problems related to margining rules for derivative portfolios.

Consider, for example, a portfolio with a long position in a call option, and a short in a futures contract on the same underlying. Long positions in options do not create any margin requirement because once the option is paid for, the holder has no subsequent risk. On the other hand, the short leg of the position presents, in itself, a significant exposure and should consequently be margined appropriately. However, when put together, it can be argued that the call "protects" the short to some extent, and therefore the whole portfolio is less risky than an outright futures position. In fact, if the call is in-the-money, the portfolio is indeed completely protected and presents a very low level of risk. Regular margining rules would charge this portfolio with a requirement derived from the futures position although it may be almost perfectly hedged in practice.

Therefore, applying margining calculations instrument by instrument lead to requirements much too high and inappropriate with respect to the actual level of risk. An alternative approach is to consider each portfolio as a whole and run risk scenarios to identify potential losses arising from different market situations. This is exactly what SPAN does, running the following 16 scenarios[31]:

- Futures unchanged, volatility up and down
- Futures up 1/3 range, volatility up and down
- Futures down 1/3 range, volatility up and down
- Futures up 2/3 range, volatility up and down
- Futures down 2/3 range, volatility up and down
- Futures up 3/3 range, volatility up and down
- Futures down 3/3 range, volatility up and down
- Futures up extreme move
- Futures down extreme move

The margin requirement is then set to the maximum loss under any of the 16 scenarios.

---

[31] The futures "range" is the amplitude of the price movement creating a change in the value of the position equal to the maintenance margin, and the "extreme move" is twice that range. Volatility analysis is meant to capture the risk on option positions.

From a local initiative, SPAN has expanded to become an industry standard, and nowadays numerous derivative exchanges use it to evaluate margin requirements. SPAN has been adopted both by clearinghouses for their members, and by brokers-dealers for their customers.

Under a SPAN margining system, our simplified margin formalism does not necessarily apply because of cross hedging between different instruments. It is valid as a first approximation if futures constitute the main source of derivative risk in the portfolio.

SPECIAL QUOTATION CALCULATION AND CONVERGENCE REVISITED

In the case of index futures, there are two primary types of SQ[32]: straight reference and average. A straight reference is obtained by computing the index with a particular type of price for each stock. In that category, we find the S&P 500, Nikkei 225, and DAX 30. The first two have an SQ equal to the *price of the index computed using the opening price of each component on expiration day*, and the DAX futures settles on an intraday auction. An average SQ is obtained by taking the average of index prices measured periodically over a short period of time. Consider, for example, the official definition as given by the London futures exchange for FTSE 100:

> *Exchange Delivery Settlement Price (EDSP): The EDSP is based on the average values of the FTSE 100 Index every 15 seconds inclusively between 10.10 and 10.30 (London time) on the Last Trading Day. Of the 81 measured values, the highest 12 and lowest 12 will be discarded and the remaining 57 will be used to calculate the EDSP. Where necessary, the calculation will be rounded to the nearest half index point.*[33]

France falls into that category as well with an average on 20 minutes at the end of the expiration day.

To understand why these definitions are what they are, we need to realize that an SQ *must* be a "realizable" price because futures holders *must* be able to transfer their positions to cash on expiration.[34]

---

[32] As a reminder, the *special quotation* is the final settlement value of a futures contract.

[33] LIFFE Web site.

[34] *Realizable* means that the price can be reproduced through a reasonably low-risk trading strategy. This is the practical consequence of the absolute convergence that exists between a futures contract and its underlying.

Therefore, the final reference must be chosen so that all outstanding positions can be transferred to the underlying stocks with an adequate level of liquidity, without any dramatic impact on the market.

The closing price, which looks like a natural choice, is not a valid option because if an important unbalance materializes between buyers and sellers, the trading system may be unable to match them properly. In that case, the "fair" price of the stock—that is, the price that matches all present interests—is impossible to establish, and the SQ is not representative of the latest market conditions. In addition, investors are potentially left with sizable unexecuted orders that need to be carried over to the next day. Along the same lines, expiry on a single point in time during the day is difficult to implement with continuous trading systems, except if the system is appropriately equipped to handle exceptional punctual levels of liquidity, as, for example, in Germany.

Overall the solution that has been adopted is to spread liquidity over a short period of time. In the case of an SQ at open, the aggregation of orders is such that liquidity can flow to and from a particular stock before it actually opens. Because it is an auction, all orders are necessarily executed removing any execution risk.[35] The other implementation calls for an average over time so that the market can absorb the exceptional liquidity despite the fact that the process takes place during a regular continuous session without any auction. In other words, an SQ at open spreads liquidity over price, whereas an average spreads it over time.

Each of the two methods provides continuity and liquidity for SQ calculation and realization, and there is not much of a choice beyond them. It is interesting to note the repartition of the two groups: the United States, Japan, and Germany have opted for an auction reference while the United Kingdom and France have chosen an average. It is certain that transparency and simplicity are two powerful requirements for investors, and in these respects, opening SQs may appear less representative than averages but are far simpler and safer to manage.

What are the consequences of these definitions for investors and arbitrageurs? In the case of an opening, SQ realization is straightfor-

[35] It is extremely rare but not impossible for a stock not to open at all because of a market imbalance. We will see an example of that later in the chapter dedicated to index arbitrage. Therefore, the nonexecution risk still exists, but it is very small.

ward, whereas for an average things get much more complex. In order to realize the SQ price, a trader needs to replicate every price in the calculation sequence. For example, in the case of the FTSE 100, there needs to be partial executions every 15 seconds. The whole position must be partitioned into 81 parts, each executed separately, with the hope that the truncature of the 12 highest and lowest will not result in a large deviation.[36] Obviously the overall risk is significant, and managing an expiry on an average requires a lot of skill and a fairly decent nominal.[37]

It would already be difficult to calibrate an execution on 81 prints in a friendly market, but it gets even more risky because futures trading is a zero-sum game: For each buyer, there is a seller of equal size. Therefore, each player buying cash on expiration to cover for a long futures expiring is potentially confronted by a seller covering a short position. This remark leads to the following conclusion: If a trader is trying to manage an expiry by replicating the calculation sequence one way, somebody else is trying the other way.[38] It is exactly like two people pushing the same sliding wall from each side at the same time periodically. The strongest eventually wins; however, the weakest may push earlier—or later—from time to time and significantly "disturb" the mechanism the other is trying to develop. Thus, if trading itself is strictly zero-sum, it is not true for expirations: On average both lose because they are not the only ones anyway at a given time.[39] For all these reasons, it is always wise to consider all available options before deciding to "shoot" for cash on expiration on an averaged SQ.

---

[36] The truncature problem is subtle. Skipping one print on the expectation that it will be eliminated is a risky proposition at the beginning of the interval, much less so at the end. Experience is a powerful help in these cases.

[37] A large nominal to execute allows much more flexibility during the 20-minute interval because slices can be of different sizes and timed precisely. With the execution of a small nominal, it may not even be possible to slice executions into 81 parts, and only a passive strategy is possible.

[38] The good thing is that if one arbitrageur—typically an index arbitrageur—decides to intervene massively in the cash market at expiry, others involved in similar strategies most probably have the same interest for the same reasons. It is fair then to expect a significant aggregation of trading power in the same direction. However, arbitrageurs are not the largest participants by far, so it is presumptuous to make hasty conclusions even in that case.

[39] This statement is naturally an exaggeration, but it is extremely difficult to manage an average expiration "properly." If there are indeed several players in opposite camps and fairly large equal trading power, then most probably everybody loses.

FINAL SETTLEMENTS

The margin call is known at the end of each trading day, once the closing price of the day is officially available from the exchange. On expiration day, the position is liquidated with the final reference price being the SQ price. If we go back to our previous example, we are long 125 futures on January 16. We assume that the closing price on January 16 is $1,235 and that we hold the 125 futures instead of selling them. On January 17, the futures contract expires at $1,241.54, and we let the position expire, as shown in Table 3-7.

The margin call (1) is derived from the formula we introduced previously: The closing price changes from $1,240 to $1,235, and 125 futures lose $\$5 * \$250 * 125 = \$156{,}250$. The account balance (2) is identical to what it was on January 15: the additional amount injected by the margin call into the account has been consumed by mark-to-market losses.

The final margin call is the sum of the mark-to-market P&L of the position and of its total unused deposit. From $1,235 to $1,241.54, the position made $204,375, which represents the P&L part. The sum $2,929,750 represents the excess deposit because the position has been liquidated. Therefore, the total margin call is $3,134,125, which is flow (3). The general mechanism of final settlement is exactly equivalent to a final closing sale—or purchase—of the position.

EXPOSURE VERSUS INVESTMENT

Futures, and more generally derivative positions, have an interesting characteristic: Because they are traded on margin, the amount of money needed to enter a position is much smaller than the nominal risk created by this position. For a stock transaction, every variation in the price of the stock results in a 1-to-1 variation in the value of the position. If the stock is paid in full, exposure and investment are

TABLE 3-7

Date	Position Beginning of Day	Position End of Day	Initial Requirement	Closing Price	Margin Call	Account Balance
Jan. 16	125	125	$2,929,750	$1,235	−$156,250(1)	$2,929,750(2)
Jan. 17	125	—	—	$1,241.54	$3,134,125(3)	—

equal and move together. In the case of a margin trade, we have to settle only 50 percent of the full amount to enter the same position; the remaining 50 percent are borrowed from the institution managing the account. In that case, our profit is still exactly equal to any variation in the price, but our investment is half what it was.

For futures this difference is even higher because margin requirements are much smaller than 50 percent. In the case of the S&P 500, a requirement of $23,438 is less than 7 percent of the nominal of a futures contract at $1,400: an investment of $23,438 allows an exposure of $350,000. This well-known property is called *financial leverage,* which we define here as the ratio between exposure, that is, the nominal at risk, and investment, that is, the capital required. Table 3-8 is the current leverage of different futures.

Leverage is particularly important for many investors and particularly speculators. However, from an arbitrageur's point of view it is a given of no particular importance beyond the underlying margining system:

- Costs associated to the carry of the position are generated by margin requirements only; therefore, what is really important is the absolute amount of collateral requested, not the leverage resulting from it.
- The ultimate object of our attention is exposure. In an index arbitrage position, for example, we need to compare what is comparable—that is, exposure on each leg, not invested capital.
- Arbitrage is not speculation but a trading strategy, usually practiced in a specific context where capital is readily available. As a device to reduce capital requirements, leverage is therefore relatively unimportant.

TABLE 3-8

Index	Current Market Price	Point Value	Margin Requirement	Contract Nominal	Leverage Ratio[a]
FTSE 100	£6,100	£10	£3,000	£60,000	20:1
DAX 30	€7,500	€25	€8,500	€187,500	22:1
Nikkei 225 (OSE)	¥20,000	¥1,000	¥1,000,000	¥20,000,000	20:1
Nikkei 225 (SIM)	¥20,000	¥500	¥562,500	¥10,000,000	18:1
S&P 500	$1,350	$250	$23,438	$337,500	14:1
CAC 40	€6,000	€10	€2,000	€60,000	30:1

[a] Note that the leverage ratio depends on the current market price because margin requirements are usually constant through a long period of time.

CROSS LISTINGS

What is true for stocks is also true of futures: More and more exchanges worldwide cross list identical or similar contracts. There are two critical differences, however, with respect to cross-listed derivatives compared to stocks.

First, cross-listing initiatives for derivatives usually do not need any sponsorship because of the nature of the instruments: No corporation is in a position to claim "ownership" of a futures contract and sponsor a cross listing. Furthermore, many of these listings effectively result in additional competition for liquidity, which may or may not be well perceived by the institution that listed the original futures.

Second, the clearing part is critically important with respect to derivatives because of margin requirements. Suppose that the same contract is listed in the United States and United Kingdom, or in the United Kingdom and continental Europe. If the contracts are recognized as fully fungible, an investor can intervene indifferently on both markets with similar requirements, and all trades can be netted on a single account regardless of where they were actually effected. On the other hand, if the contracts have similar characteristics but are not fungible, each has to be margined and managed independently.

In characterizing two fungible contracts, there are four important conditions:

- *Identical underlying,* which seems a very natural prerequisite.
- *Identical SQ definition,* for its expiry dates as well as calculation method.
- *Similar characteristics,* not directly related to underlying, expiry, and SQ prices: point value, deposit requirements, settlement cycle, currency used for margin calls, and so on.
- *Reciprocal clearing agreements* between exchanges. This is actually the most important condition to ensure that the contracts can be traded indifferently. There may be cost differentials associated with trading one as opposed to the other, notably in terms of brokerage fees, but they are automatically netted on clearing statements.

The last condition is the most difficult to satisfy because it requires more than a paper agreement: There must be an electronic link between the different clearinghouses. This is exactly why fungibility is far from being the rule, and remains still an exception.[40] Most cross-listed contracts are listed on different exchanges without being fungible. In these cases they actually compete for liquidity because investors have an objective choice between two distinct instruments, usually designed to be very close.

There can be two main reasons for cross listing, quite different from those underlying corporate decisions to list a stock in different countries:

- *Market accessibility*: For structural reasons, a market is difficult or expensive to access. Another exchange with some type of competitive advantage, usually in the same geographical area, will seize the opportunity and list a contract under conditions that tend to improve accessibility. It is easy to find examples of this with Japan that long remained an inefficient fortress. The Singapore Monetary Exchange realized there was an opportunity and listed a contract on the Nikkei 225 index, which in effect became a direct competitor to the "official" contract listed in Osaka.[41]
- *Round-the-clock trading*: The need for continuous trading has been clearer and clearer over the years, notably because of unavoidable time differences between geographical zones. Even though it is unrealistic to expect liquidity to be equal in all parts of the world, at least the opportunity to trade, even small-size orders, is better than no market at all. The Chicago Mercantile Exchange, for example, listed a Nikkei 225 contract to address this concern and made it a dollar-denominated contract to solve at the same time the problem of currency conversion. Other answers to the same question have prompted the development of electronic

[40] In fact, no index futures contract in the list of those we consider has a fungible cross-listed contract. This situation is more frequent, however, on interest rate futures. The euroyen contracts listed on the Tokyo International Financial Futures Exchange (TIFFE) and the London International Financial Futures Exchange (LIFFE) are fully fungible, as are the eurodollar on the Chicago Mercantile Exchange (CME) and Singapore International Monetary Exchange (SIMEX).

[41] For several years the Singapore futures expired on a reference different from that of its Osaka counterpart, probably to avoid being so obvious a competitor. Eventually the SIMEX revised its rule and adopted the same reference. Still the two contracts are not fungible, notably because of their respective point values.

trading systems like Globex offering a wide range of contracts during and after regular hours.[42]

Let's explore now two particular examples of cross-listed index futures.

Nikkei 225 on the Osaka Stock Exchange versus Nikkei 225 on the Singapore International Monetary Exchange

Japan has traditionally been very rigid about and very protective of its securities industry. Policymakers today face a considerable task in reforming and deregulating, starting with the gigantic and almighty Ministry of Finance. Transactions on stocks and futures, for example, were taxed significantly, and brokerage commissions for trading stocks or futures were set for the whole industry and largely nonnegotiable.[43] Along the same lines many other parameters—typically margin requirements—have long been relatively high compared to other financial centers.[44]

The combination of high commissions and high holding costs made Japan an expensive market. This was seen as an opportunity by Singapore, which listed an identical Nikkei 225 contract in a ''friendlier'' environment:

- The contract has the same maturity cycle and SQ calculation. Its actual definition states equality between its SQ and OSEs. It is consequently also settled in Japanese yen.
- Deposit requirements do not call for cash. SIMEX allows other securities—U.S. treasury bonds, for example—and other types of

[42] The S&P 500 future, for example, is available on Globex but only after normal trading hours in order to avoid direct competition with the floor. It opens at 4:45 p.m. EST, 30 minutes after the floor closing, and closes in the morning at 9:15 a.m. EST. Globex also accepts orders for the E-Mini, an S&P 500 contract with a point value of $50. E-Mini is traded only on Globex and order size is electronically limited to 30 lots to deter trading by professionals and institutional investors.

[43] The same legal situation prevailed in the United States at the beginning of the 1970s. There have been considerable changes in Japan over the last decade, so many—but not all—of these direct or indirect costs have disappeared today.

[44] In particular, until a few years ago the OSE requested its members to deposit cash for a sizable portion of the deposit requirements. In turn, brokers also had to request cash from their customers for an even higher fraction.

collateral—letters of credit. Holding a SIMEX position is therefore significantly cheaper than holding an OSE position.[45]

- The size of the contract is smaller (point value of ¥500 instead of ¥1,000), and its tick value is smaller as well (¥5 instead of ¥10). Literally: 1 OSE = 2 SIMEX.
- Trading limits—highest and lowest prices allowed daily—are beyond those set by the OSE rules.[46]
- A few years ago SIMEX decided to open its Nikkei 225 five minutes before the OSE—8:55 a.m. instead of 9:00 a.m. In addition, for a long time SIMEX has been closing 15 minutes after the OSE—3:15 p.m. instead of 3:00 p.m.[47]
- Commissions in Singapore are not regulated at all as opposed to those in Japan.
- In order to attract more than futures traders, SIMEX also listed a whole series of options on the Nikkei 225, identical to the OSE's with minor differences, notably lot sizes.

The natural question at this point is whether the SIMEX initiative drained significant volume away from Japan, and as of today the answer is most definitively yes. As an example, Figure 3-4 shows the repartition of trading volume between the two marketplaces through 1999.[48] Even on a longer time frame, and considering open interest instead of traded volume, SIMEX seems to have unequivocally conquered its place under the sun, as shown in Figure 3-5.

Overall market shares look reasonably stable, with SIMEX holding a fair 25 percent of the total volume and open interest. It can be argued that 25 percent is indeed a sizable presence in what could have been virtually a captive market, and one can wonder to what extent the OSE simply failed to adapt and contain this slow drain. Nonetheless, both markets are now clearly established in the marketplace and trade with

[45] This induced a difference between the trading prices of the two contracts. They were continuously trading at a ¥5 difference. This discrepancy somewhat disappeared when the OSE lowered its deposit requirements.

[46] This particular point was made very clear in 1995 after the Kobe earthquake and when the Barings collapsed. The SIMEX contract traded at its limit down price several times during that period when the OSE futures were also limit down at a much higher price. The limit on SIMEX was ¥1,000 below the previous day's close, whereas the OSE's was ¥600.

[47] More recently the OSE extended trading hours to 3:10 p.m., prompting SIMEX to extend further from 3:15 p.m. to 3:25 p.m. in a move to offer the extra mile of trading.

[48] The trading volume of SIMEX has been divided by 2 in the chart to reflect its nominal size compared to the OSE.

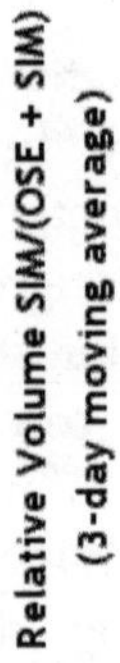

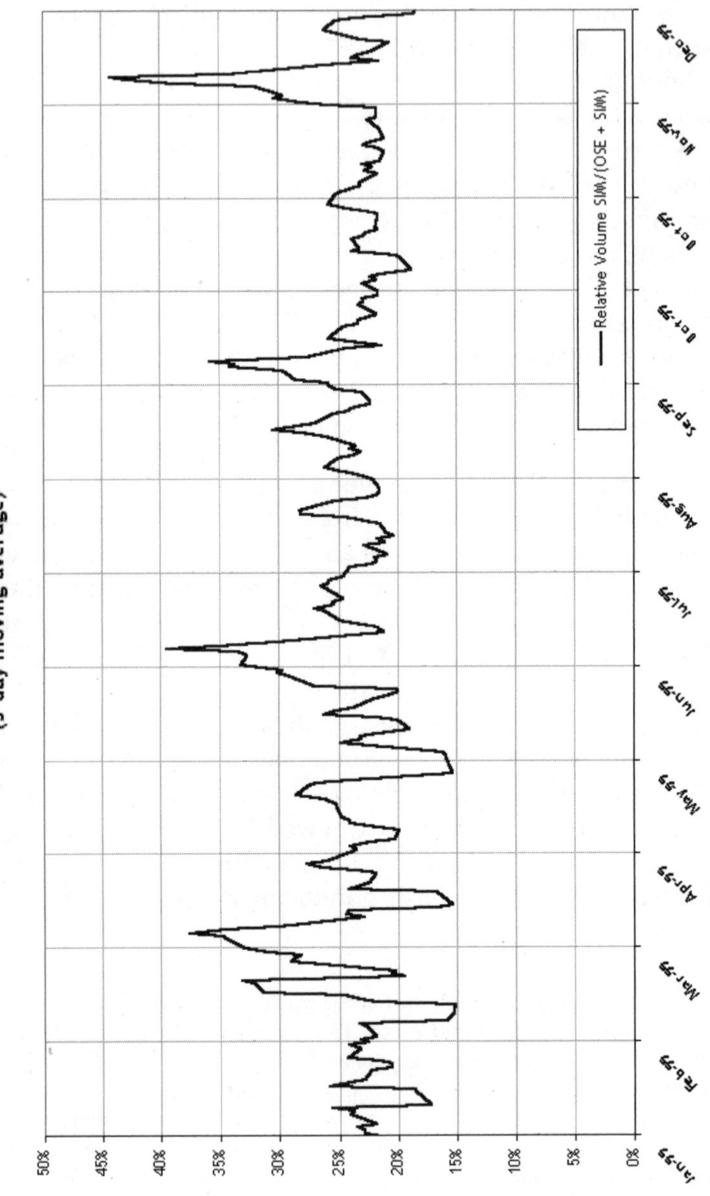

Figure 3-4 Volume on the SIM and OSE
(*Source:* Compiled by author from Datastream data.)

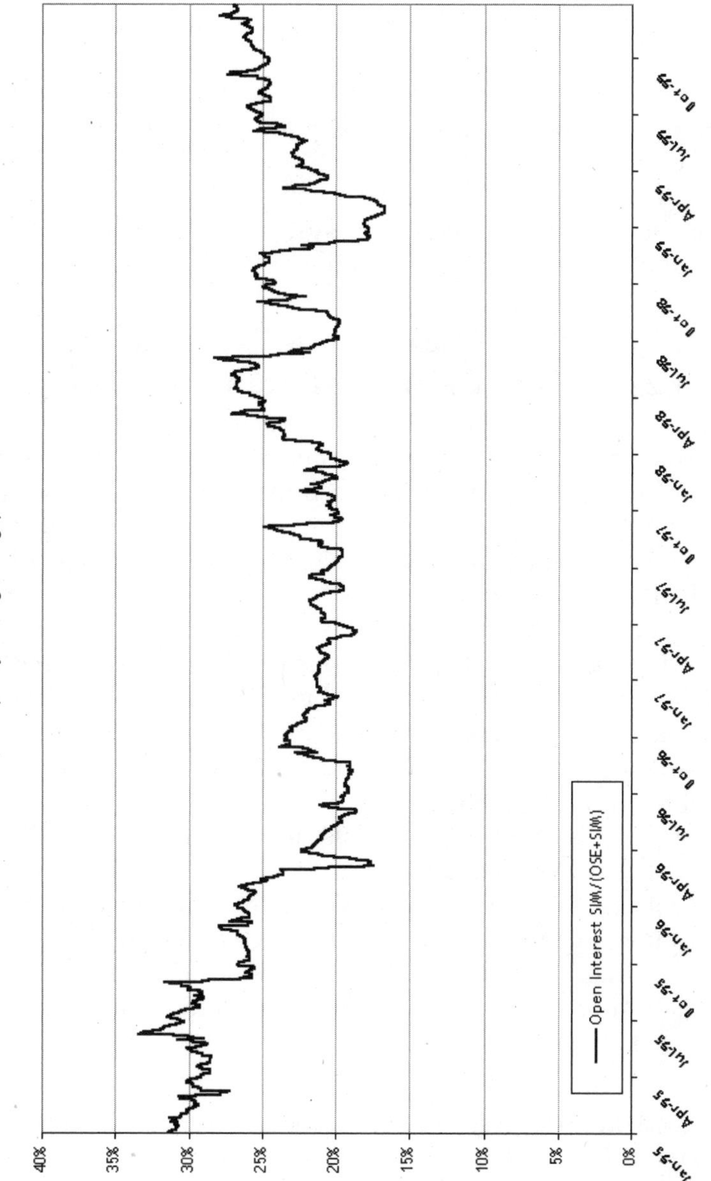

Figure 3-5 Open Interest on the SIM and the OSE
(*Source:* Compiled by author from Datastream data.)

a fairly adequate liquidity. Figure 3-6 shows the average price difference between the two futures over 1999. Despite the 10 minutes difference in closing times—OSE closes at 3:10 p.m. and SIMEX at 3:25 p.m.—prices are fairly close. The average over 1999 was −¥3.4, showing that OSE is trading at a small discount compared to the SIMEX.[49]

From an arbitrageur's perspective this situation is extremely convenient and comfortable. Both markets are essentially open over the same periods, and one is a floor (SIMEX) while the other is electronic (OSE). A trader gets all the possible benefits: a dual source of liquidity, the user-friendliness of an electronic system on the main market, and the volatility and opportunities of a floor.

Nikkei 225 on the Osaka Stock Exchange and Nikkei 225 on the Chicago Mercantile Exchange

The CME contract on the Nikkei 225 is an interesting example of unconventional contract. It was primarily listed for convenience because of the time difference between the United States and Japan. Naturally, because it attracts investors mostly outside Japan, its liquidity is very poor, but again it offers an option for late trading, which is better than no market at all.[50]

It is unconventional because it is an ADR-like futures contract: Listed in U.S. dollars with a point value of $5, all flows are settled in U.S. dollars, but the contract is quoted in Japanese yen. This last point is particularly important because standard ADRs are listed and quoted in the same currency. The CME contract therefore is similar but not identical to an ADR structure.

One OSE futures contract is ¥17,000,000 in nominal for a Nikkei at ¥17,000.[51] If the market moves from ¥17,000 to ¥17,100, an investor holding one contract makes ¥100,000. If the same investor holds a CME position instead, the nominal is $85,000 (= $5 * ¥17,000), and for the same market move the total profit is $500. This calculation may appear flawed because we apparently extract a dollar nominal from a price quoted in yen.

---

[49] The discount should definitely be measured more accurately with simultaneous data. But, as we mentioned earlier, it may very well be the result of structural differences between the two markets.

[50] Trading volume on the CME contract averages less than 2,000 contracts per session. Accounting for the difference in nominal, this is equivalent to 1,000 OSE contracts, which is tiny: the OSE customarily trades more than 25,000 contracts a day.

[51] ¥17,000,000 = ¥17,000 * ¥1,000. ¥1,000 is the point value.

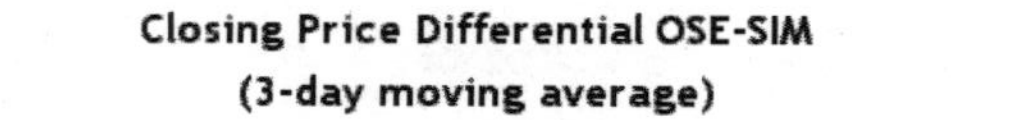

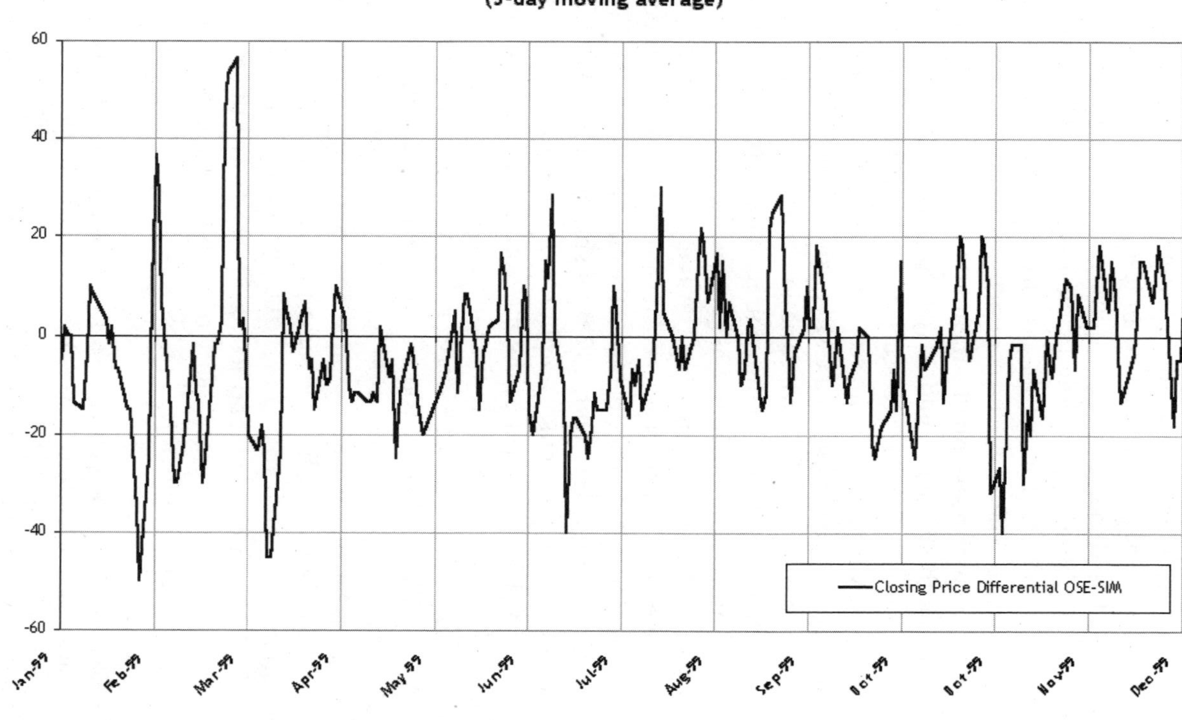

Figure 3-6 Price Differential on the SIM and the OSE
(*Source*: Compiled by author from Datastream data.)

The source of the possible confusion is the convention to express market prices with a currency sign. Under that convention, a price quoted in yen appears as ¥17,000. This is a strict representation of reality for a stock because the shares can be truly acquired at that price, but it is inadequate for a futures contract because there is no acquisition underlying a transaction. Indeed, the quoted price of a futures contract is dimensionless, acquiring a dimension exclusively when multiplied by a point value. In the case of the CME contract, the price is 17,000 *units*, each of these units in turn being "exchangeable" for $5 in cash. Therefore, the contract itself is "exchangeable" for $85,000 in cash, which essentially means that if its price went to 0 instantaneously, the holder would have to pay $85,000.

This long conversation is necessary to understand the mechanics underlying the CME behavior with respect to the $/¥ exchange rate. In fact, we proved that the holder of a CME position is *not* exposed to any variation in exchange rate, only to a variation in price. By extension, this explains why the quoted price of the contract is equal to that of the OSE futures.[52] As an illustration, Figure 3-7 shows the closing price difference between the two futures in 1999. The average difference is −¥29.5, but we cannot make any significant conclusion from this figure because of the important time difference between the closing prices: The CME is trading on U.S. time—that is, with a 12-hour shift from Japan.[53] It is fair to say, however, that the average amplitude of this differential and the apparent symmetry above and below the horizontal axis indicate that the CME and OSE are reasonably tracking each other.

This is not the end of the story, however, because trading the Nikkei 225 in Chicago does indeed create an exposure to the exchange rate, but in the particular situation in which an investor is also trading the OSE contract. Consider, for example, the following position: long 1 OSE at ¥17,000, short 2 CME at the same price. Assuming the Japanese market and the CME both go up to ¥17,100 the next day, this position is making ¥100,000 on one leg, and losing $1,000 on the other leg. We cannot conclude as to the profitability of the whole operation until we know the current exchange rate.[54]

---

[52] By contrast, consider a Japanese stock quoted ¥1,000 in Japan. Its ADR listed in the United States would trade at $9.09 if the exchange rate were ¥110 for $1. In contrast, if the OSE Nikkei 225 futures trade at ¥17,000, the CME trades at the *same* price.

[53] An interesting question, however, would be to explore to what extent the CME follows moves initiated in Osaka or anticipates variations to come to Osaka the next day. Regardless of the answer, if it is stable enough through time, there may be an arbitrage opportunity.

[54] Note that we need the rate after the move, not when the position is actually taken.

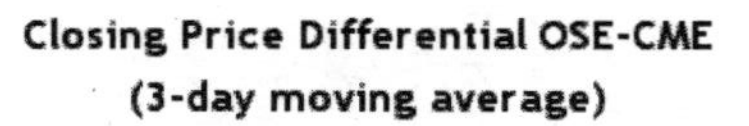

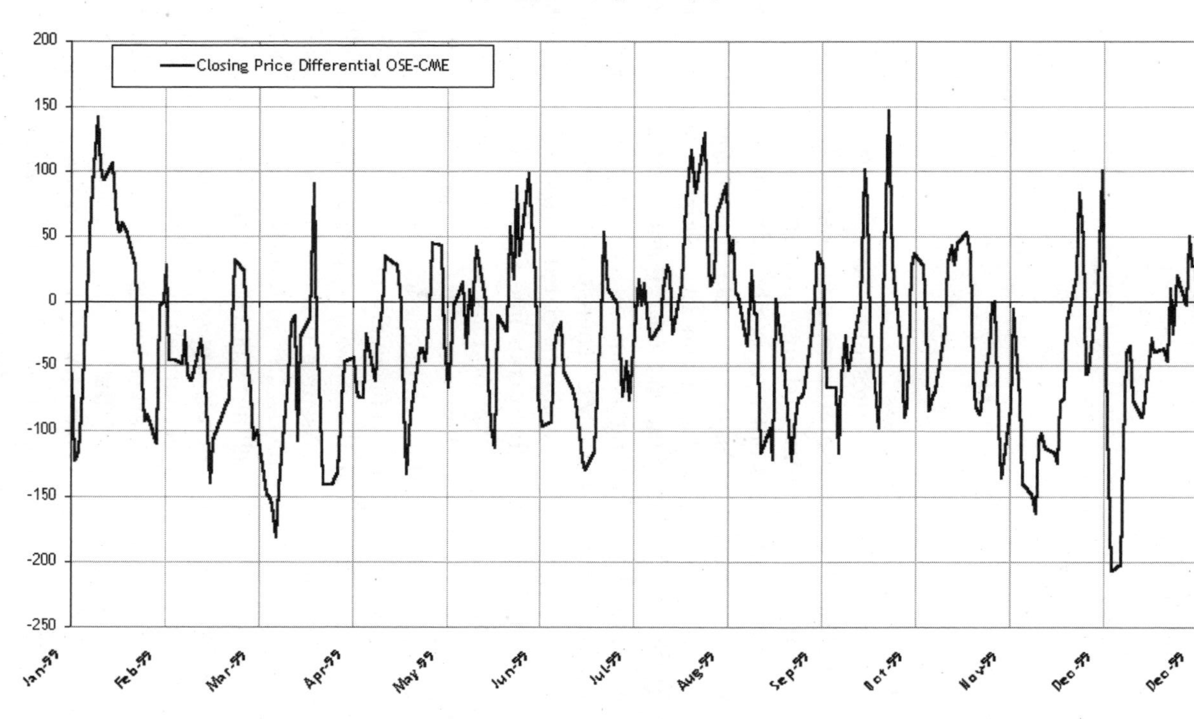

Figure 3-7 Price Differential CME/OSE
(*Source:* Compiled by author from Datastream data.)

Assume this rate is ¥110 for $1. The position is then losing ¥10,000 or $90.9 depending on which currency we want to focus on. The next day, if both contracts come back to ¥17,000, the position loses ¥100,000 and makes $1,000 back and is even. The general formula to describe the P&L is therefore:

$$P_{\$} = ¥1{,}000 * (P_{OSE} - ¥17{,}000)/f_{¥/\$} - \$5 * 2 * (P_{CME} - ¥17{,}000)$$

or

$$P_{¥} = P_{\$} \cdot f_{¥/\$} = ¥1{,}000 * (P_{OSE} - ¥17{,}000) - \$5 * 2 * (P_{CME} - ¥17{,}000) * f_{¥/\$}$$

with self-explanatory notations.

Essentially each bracket represents a domestic P&L. The exchange rate intervenes only because at some point one of them needs to be repatriated through a foreign exchange conversion.

However, reality does not necessarily match this simple description because of margin calls. For example, consider an investor trading both on the CME and OSE on two separate accounts in the United States and Japan. If the market is going up, the excess deposit available from the OSE long is not directly available to cover the deficit for the short on the CME. Therefore, the investor faces additional margin requirements with associated financing costs. In fact, if the position is large enough to consume significant amounts of collateral on each side, the investor may want to effectively transfer liquidity back and forth between the accounts regularly. These flows have a very important consequence: They transform the P&L from unrealized to realized, effectively creating a foreign exchange exposure. Consider again the previous spread position, with both futures closing at ¥17,100. Assume that the investor is based in the United States, and he or she decides to transfer the profit of ¥100,000 to the United States by selling ¥100,000 against $909.1 at ¥110/$1. Effectively, the account in yen is empty—except for the initial margin requirement—and the U.S. account shows a loss of $909.1 – $1,000 = –$90.9. The next day the market comes back to ¥17,000, and both futures close there; however, the exchange rate moves to ¥105/$1. The OSE position shows a loss of ¥100,000, and the other leg a profit of $1,000. This time the investor has to cover the shortfall on the OSE account, and he or she buys ¥100,000 for $952.4 at ¥105/$1. Overall, even if both markets have come back to their original level, the U.S. account is left with a loss of –$90.9 + ($1,000 – $952.4) = –$43.3. Therefore, the existence of intermediary flows has resulted in a foreign exchange loss of $43.3 despite the fact that the two contracts have the same index underlying and no exposure in and of themselves to foreign exchange.

Generally speaking, even if the P&L generated by differences in the exchange rate remains unrealized, it exists at all times because of the two distinct treasury needs, in yen and in dollars. This becomes apparent if we consider, for example, the variation in P&L only resulting from a change in $f_{¥/\$}$:

$$f_{¥/\$} = 110 \Rightarrow P_{\$} = -\$90.9, \qquad \mathrm{P}_{¥} = -\$10{,}000$$

$$f_{¥/\$} = 130 \Rightarrow P_{\$} = -\$230.8, \qquad \mathrm{P}_{¥} = -\$30{,}000$$

A depreciation of the yen compared to the dollar results in a potential loss—and therefore margin calls—even in the absence of a market movement. If we wanted to hedge this exposure, we would have to enter a foreign exchange position such that a variation from ¥110/$1 to ¥130/$1 would generate ¥20,000.

In fact, the exact formulation of a foreign exchange hedge for this arbitrage is a nontrivial exercise because the problem depends now on multiple stochastic variables, the exchange rate, and the futures prices. We will not enter into unnecessary details here, but it is important to realize that despite the similarities in definitions and trading prices, the two Nikkei 225 contracts are truly distinct.

TRADING

The variety of order types available to futures traders is similar to that available to stock traders. On electronic markets, the situation is therefore very straightforward: Futures are only one more regular instrument to trade. For the S&P 500, however, certain types of theoretically efficient orders do not translate in practice into precise executions because of the nature of the floor market. For example, opening or closing orders are extremely difficult to execute, and brokers on the floor will accept such orders on a best-effort basis only. They cannot guarantee any price, so the average executed price for an entire order may well be extremely different from the official opening or closing prices. The same phenomenon occurs with market orders. The execution of a sizable order at market may be virtually "all over the place."

At the same time, because orders flow through brokers, it is possible for a customer to require specific strategies or combinations. This added flexibility is unavailable in an electronic system in which orders usually have to be kept simple and elementary.

The net effect is nevertheless a lack of predictability in execution, magnified when orders grow in size or when the market gets particularly volatile. Accordingly, many traders will prefer to work their orders one by one, using small sizes and price limits rather than giving brokers autonomy in execution.

Real-Time Information

Even if real-time information for futures is theoretically equivalent to that available for stocks, there are important drawbacks when the future is not traded electronically. For example, bid-ask prices are provided in real time on the S&P 500 futures index, but they can hardly be trusted. The best and only way to get a reliable market quote is to get somebody on the floor on a phone line. And this is not necessarily a satisfactory solution because regardless of who gives a quote, the nature of the marketplace makes it impossible to know precisely where the market is during volatile sessions.

This is even more true for market depth available from brokers on the floor, which it is absolutely useless. There is indeed an incredible liquidity in that market, but the bulk of it is not visible: Orders get filled and absorbed by the crowd as they appear, but it is virtually impossible at any given time to predict what will be the impact of a fairly large transaction.

Beyond common data available on stocks, there is one piece of information particular to derivatives and extremely useful: the open interest. It indicates the total number of contracts outstanding for the *whole market*.[55] It is not a real-time number, but computed by the exchange every day. Consider, for example, the S&P 500 open interest for the first and second expirations over 1999 as shown in Figure 3-8.

This pattern of interrupted waves was clearly visible earlier in the introduction, on all futures alike. Just before a futures contract is about to expire, its successor gains momentum and the combined open interest shows a sharp spike. The reasons behind this spike can be multiple, but clearly there is a systematic excess exposure concentrated around expiration dates. We will come back to that phenomenon for a more detailed analysis when studying index arbitrage.

---

[55] Sometimes more details are available. In Japan, for example, this figure is also published weekly broken down by member firms.

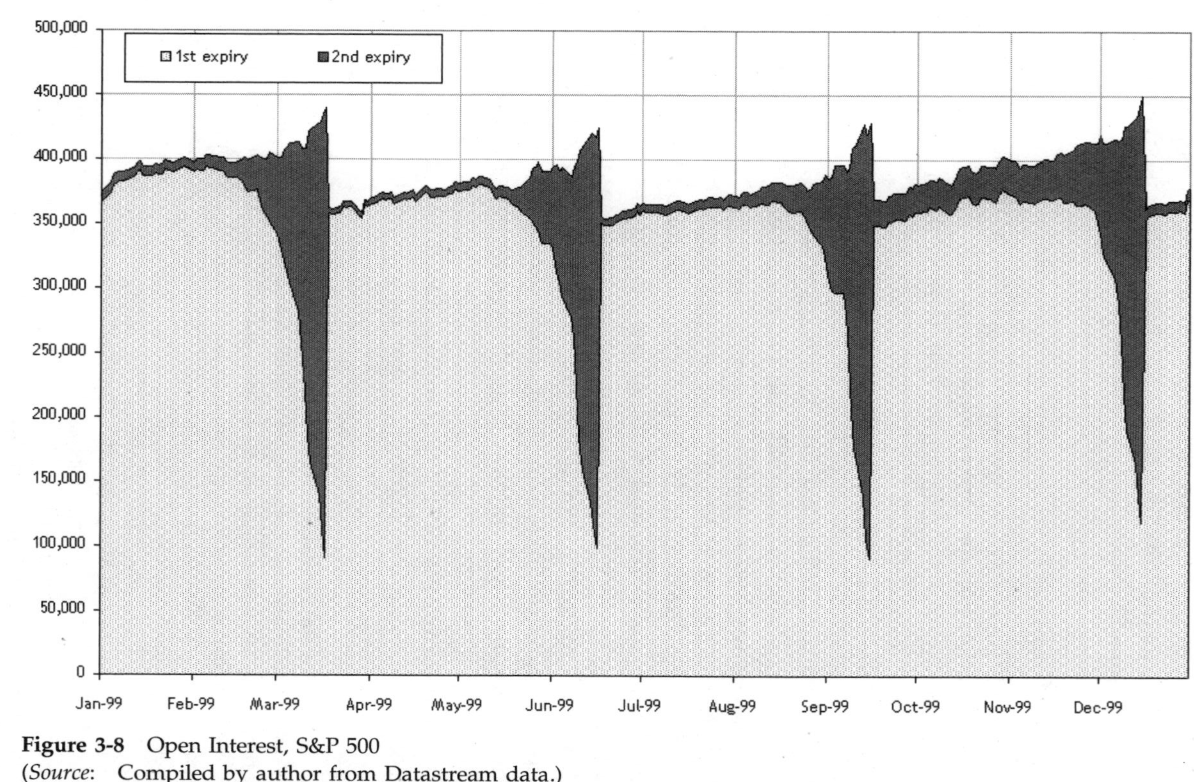

Figure 3-8 Open Interest, S&P 500
(*Source*: Compiled by author from Datastream data.)
This chart indicates the open interest for the nearest two expirations. For example, before the March contract expires, first and second futures represent, respectively, March and June. On the day the March contract expires, first and second come to represent June and September, respectively.

OTHER FORMS OF FIRST-ORDER EXPOSURE

Futures can be used to create a market exposure as if we were holding stocks. Similarly, there exist other instruments that create first-order exposure, and this part presents some of them. We focus primarily on instruments functionally identical to futures—that is, without any option component.

Forward Contracts

A *forward contract* is exactly equivalent to a futures; the only difference is that it is traded between two counterparts over the counter without the convenience of a clearinghouse. This is typically a private agreement in every respect.[56]

This has several important consequences:

- The forward is not listed and is not reported to any regulatory body.[57] In other words, only the parties involved are aware of the transaction and its details.[58]
- The characteristics of the contract are negotiated entirely between the parties. In particular, the underlying, initiation price, expiration and settlement dates, and nominal are tailored to the needs of the transacting traders. In practice, many forwards are traded because they cover maturities not available in the futures market. It is common, for example, to see one-year and two-year forwards on major indices because it is difficult to find the adequate liquidity in the future—if it is even listed.
- The whole purpose of listing futures is to remove the counterpart risk by imposing the clearinghouse as an intermediary in all trans-

[56] As such, it is the responsibility of each party to make sure that the contract includes satisfactory provisions, for example, with respect to credit risk. By and large legal enforcement is the most critical aspect of these transactions, and the current regulatory environment is considered by some to be inadequate and outdated for that purpose. For an examination of these issues, see, for example, Robert M. McLaughlin, *Over-the-Counter Derivative Products, A Guide to Business and Legal Risk Management and Documentation* (New York: McGraw-Hill, 1998) or "Over-the-Counter Derivatives Markets and the Commodity Exchange Act," *Report of the President's Working Group on Financial Markets* (Washington, D.C.: Government Printing Office, November 1999).

[57] Like many other derivative instruments, it does not even appear on the balance sheet on the transacting parties.

[58] Many of these transactions are traded through the mediation of a broker, and as such, they may be visible to the crowd. Even in that case, however, they are usually not subject to any official regulation.

actions. Forward contracts, therefore, are fully exposed to credit risk and as such are totally dependent on the general credit agreements and ratings between the parties. These agreements may or may not institute margin calls, and even if they do, their frequency may be lower than that of a regular clearinghouse—weekly versus daily, for example. Nowadays the trend is towards generalized margin calls, in which both parties aggregate all their OTC contracts regardless of the underlying, and agree to be called on margin frequently on a net amount.

In terms of market risk, futures and forwards are exactly identical except naturally for margin calls. Because these flows disappear, there is no financing cost associated with a forward position.[59] Consequently, a forward should be theoretically cheaper than a futures contract: For the exact same characteristics, it is more advantageous to hold. However, this difference is occulted by the fact that the absence of margin calls reactivates the impact of credit risk, even between the strongest counterparts.[60]

Equity-Linked Swaps

An *equity-linked swap* (ELS) is one of a family of financial instruments called *swaps*. In a swap, two counterparts have an agreement to exchange a certain number of flows on a set of dates in the future.

This definition is broad enough to include numerous applications on equities, fixed incomes, interest rates, foreign exchanges, and credit derivatives. We want to focus here exclusively on equity-linked swaps.

These swaps involve the exchange of one leg pegged to the performance of a security or basket of securities, the other leg being the financing of this performance. Consider an investor trying to be exposed on General Electric (GE) for a year. Buying GE outright, say, at $100, requires $100 in capital.[61] Depending on where this capital is coming from—borrowing versus in-house—the outflow is associated

---

[59] Also the leverage of a forward position is essentially infinite because there is no upfront payment.

[60] The problem of a possible price difference between futures and forwards has been studied extensively. The key consideration is the stochastic nature of interest rates, which has a critical impact on the financing of margin calls. See, for example, Simon Benninga and Aris Protopapadakis, "Forward and Futures Prices with Markovian Interest-Rate Processes," *Journal of Business*, 67, 1994, pp. 401–421.

[61] Or less on margin. However, the idea is the same: there is a significant capital outflow for a straight purchase.

with actual interest payments or a capital cost. At the end of this period, the investor realizes the full extent of price appreciation, plus the accumulated dividends, if any were paid. The total gain is therefore the price appreciation plus dividends minus financing.

Now assume that the same investor does not want to hold the stock himself. There are numerous reasons for doing so: Finding someone with a better access to the market or better financing rate, or the need to have this transaction outside his own book.[62] He has to enter an agreement with a third party who will take the position and do exactly what he would have done. This agreement is typically an ELS, and therefore receiving the performance and dividends on GE requires him to pay the financing in return. At the same time, he avoids the initial payment of $100.[63]

By convention, the buyer of an ELS receives the performance of the underlying security. The payments are usually scheduled every three months, at which time the price of the underlying instrument is used to compute the performance, while the current prevailing three-month interest rate is used on the financing side. Dividends are paid on the same dates regardless of when they were actually received.

Pricing an ELS is not an easy exercise. It is interesting to note that there are mainly three parts in the process: interest rates, dividends, and market performance. Because the behavior of an ELS creates a market exposure by definition, and because it has an expiry, it is equivalent to a futures contract. There is no futures contract on GE, and this is indeed one more advantage to trading an ELS: It creates an instrument very similar to futures on securities that do not have any such contracts listed.[64]

But not quite identical though. Pricing a future involves the same three components: interest rates, dividends, and market exposure. However, the risks in holding a futures contract versus an ELS are

---

[62] ELSs are considered derivative products, and as such they are not recorded on the balance sheet, unlike stocks.

[63] Futures are called on margin every day, forwards never. ELSs are somewhere in between because intermediary flows occur regularly but not daily. These flows are not referred to as "margin calls"; however, they are functionally equivalent because the performance of the underlying is exchanged in full, effectively resetting the risk of the structure.

[64] Note that ELSs are also very useful in the context of stock loans. If the seller of a swap purchases the securities from the buyer instead of going to the market, the whole transaction becomes a stock loan. The seller essentially borrows the securities and delivers cash in lieu of collateral.

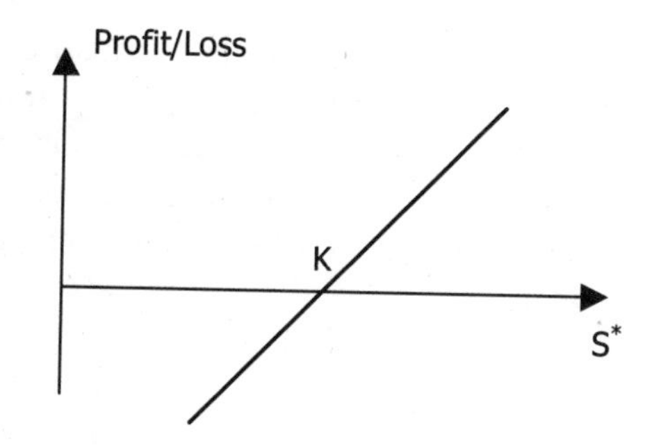

Figure 3-9 Synthetic Futures Contract

not the same. The ELS has interest rate payments embedded in its structure, at a variable rate reset periodically. The futures contract does not have any of these payments, and neither does it include dividends. Therefore, an ELS and a futures contract are functionally equivalent, but they are different in terms of flows and peripheral risks.

Synthetic Futures (Options)

If we combine a long call position with a short put, both having same strike and expiry, we get the profile at expiry shown in Figure 3-9. This is exactly the profile generated by a long position in the underlying security. Conversely, if we buy a put and sell a call of the same maturity and strike, we have built the equivalent of a short position.[65]

The structure formed by the difference between a call and a put of same strike and maturity is called a *synthetic futures contract*, because the market exposure resulting from that position is equivalent to that of a regular futures contract. There is one fundamental difference, however. The holder of a long position of a synthetic futures contract is short a put. If the put is American, it can be exercised at any time prior to maturity. If it does get exercised, the put disappears, and so does the synthetic future. Only the call remains, and the resulting payoff does not match that of a futures contract anymore. In this situation the writer of the put has two choices: Either sell back the call, or replace the put by another equivalent contract. Intuitively any of these opera-

[65] Indeed, the put-call parity for European options states that $C + Ke^{-rt} = P + S$, where Ke^{-rt} represents the present value of the exercise price. Therefore, $C - P = S - Ke^{-rt}$: The structure "call minus put" is essentially functionally equivalent to a futures contract.

tions has to be done at a particular price to ensure that the overall position does not suffer a loss, which may or may not be possible. In fact, chances are that it is not; otherwise, the exercise would not have been profitable in the first place. Therefore, synthetic futures contracts based on American options, as the ones trading on S&P 100, induce an additional risk of early exercise.

4

MONEY MARKETS

INTRODUCTION

The term *money market* describes transactions related to the flows and uses of money for a defined period of time. Typically, these are borrowing or lending operations of a given amount on terms negotiated between two parties. These operations are critical because arbitrageurs have to borrow every dollar they put at risk by nature of their business.[1]

It may appear strange, however, to consider money markets extensively in the context of equity arbitrage. There are two reasons for that. First, many arbitrage strategies call upon derivatives, notably futures, because derivatives are often the source of absolute convergence opportunities. As opposed to stock, futures typically carry a number of additional risks, for example, those related to interest rates and overnight financing, and we need to be equipped to understand and manage these risks appropriately. The second reason deals with the day-to-day funding of an arbitrage activity. Regardless of the instruments traded, treasury management is a critical part of the overall profitability.

This chapter will examine the fundamental characteristics of this market and a variety of instruments related to it. It is the first chapter in this book to call upon advanced formalism recurrently, specifically flow diagrams. From the mechanics of the cash market, we introduce the notion of zero-coupon rates and explain why these rates have a

[1] This distinction between proprietary traders and fund managers was explored in depth in Chapter 1.

particular role to play. We turn then to a certain number of derivative instruments essential to managing interest rates—namely, swaps and short-term interest rate futures.

MONEY MARKETS AND GOVERNMENT INSTITUTIONS

The creation of money and the monetary policy, as one would expect, are tightly regulated in a modern economy and are usually performed by a unique central entity, the central bank. Regardless of its name, structure, or legal status, it performs the same basic functions everywhere.[2]

These regulatory functions apply to the amount of money and its cost in the economy, with the ultimate goal of ensuring price stability. The tools and levers a central bank has the latitude to use are diverse, but they are primarily of two sorts: policy-setting devices and open-market operations. A policy-setting device is, for example, the general level of interest rates the bank applies when dealing with third parties. In the United States, this rate and other important benchmarks are fixed by the bank at the Federal Open Market Committee (FOMC), which also defines the stance of the Federal Reserve with respect to macroeconomic conditions.[3] Open-market operations, on the other hand, typically encompass day-to-day activities in terms of amounts and characteristics of transactions in the marketplace.

It is not necessary here to enter into lengthier details because all we need is to identify the central bank as the lender of last resort. Major financial institutions are required to maintain an account and a certain level of reserves with the bank, and they may obtain or dispose of liquidity when needed, for example, through short-term loans. For

[2] In the United States the actual printing of money is performed by Bureau of Engraving and Printing, under the responsibility of the Treasury Department, while the monetary policy—that is, the creation and management of credit—is strictly under the supervision of the Federal Reserve System. For a comprehensive description of the Federal Reserve System in the United States, see *The Federal Reserve System, Purposes & Functions*, (Washington D.C.: Board of Governors of the Federal Reserve System, 1994), available online at www.federalreserve.gov. For information on foreign central banks, see www.boj.or.jp, www.bundesbank.de, www.banque-france.fr, www.bankofengland.-co.uk, and www.ecb.int for the European Central Bank.

[3] The stance indicates the direction of the fed efforts. Until the end of 2000, this indicator had evolved from "Neutral" to "Inflation," clearly pointing toward a more restrictive credit policy and higher interest rates to fight inflationary pressures in the U.S. economy.

all practical purposes, the national monetary policy is exogenous to our conception of the equity market, which essentially means that there is no conditional relationship between the two.[4]

INTERBANK MARKETS AND INTEREST RATES

The above description is naturally very simplified, but it is sufficient because financial institutions deal relatively infrequently with the central authority directly except for the maintenance of the mandatory reserve requirements. Much more often they deal among themselves to cover their need for liquidity, and these flows constitute what we call the *interbank money market*. In practice, each of these institutions maintains a treasury department that determines its financing needs on a daily basis and manages cash excesses or shortfalls by entering transactions with another market participant.

The interest rates in general vary primarily because of two major mechanisms. The central bank on one side manages the cost of money through a set of reference rates, which we termed earlier *policy-setting devices*—for example, in the United States the Discount Rate for transactions with member banks and the prime rate as a base reference for general-purpose, private bank loans. A change in these rates is the result of a macroeconomic adjustment, for example, to counter inflationary pressures developing in the economy.

At the same time interest rates react naturally to market conditions—that is, to the prevalent supply-demand equilibrium for money across the term structure.[5] Except when dictated by the monetary policy it is trying to enforce, the central bank does not interfere with these mechanisms on a day-to-day basis and acts only as a sidelines player. Therefore, the money market is an interesting marketplace where by and large market forces drive prices and interest rates but where at the same time one particular player has the ultimate authority and power to enforce its strategy—and infrequently uses this power.

---

[4] In other words, a given move in the equity market does have the same probability to occur regardless of the prevailing monetary policy, and vice versa. It does not mean, however, that the overall correlation is nil, which we know would be obviously wrong. For a discussion of that last point, see, for example, Frank Smets, "*Financial Asset Prices and Monetary Policy: Theory and Evidence*," Working Paper No.47, September 1997, Bank of International Settlements.

[5] The *term structure* denotes the whole set of interest rates from overnight to far maturities, typically 30 years. The set is also referred to as the *yield curve*.

The term structure itself can be regarded as three distinct sets of rates of somewhat different natures: overnight, under one year, and over one year. These rates differ primarily by the type of risk associated with each maturity, but also by the dynamics of each segment. Overnight financing has very little credit risk and is essentially the result of liquidity management. For transactions under one year, credit risk is more important, but it is still fairly easy to monitor, and the need for cash results essentially from predictable activity and forward liquidity management. For time horizons over a year, credit exposure becomes a major concern, and transactions are often the result of strategic financing decisions. Taking the example of a nonfinancial institution, the long-term capital structure typically involves long-term transactions and instruments, for example, bonds, as opposed to short- and medium-term financing needs arising from continuing operations—working capital, for example, often managing with revolving credit lines.

Because each segment serves different needs, the instruments involved are fundamentally different. *Overnight* is exclusively a cash transaction because transacting institutions actually *need* to receive or dispose of a certain amount of cash. *Short-term* is most often also cash driven, although other options are also available, such as swaps and interest rate futures. As for *long-term management* in the context of a trading floor, virtually all transactions are swaps because they do not involve cash and decrease the magnitude of the credit risk.[6]

CREDIT RISK

The issue of credit risk, although already important with respect to derivative products, becomes absolutely critical on money market transactions. In contrast to a futures position, for example, a lender is typically fully exposed on the credit of his or her counterpart without the safety net of a clearinghouse.

This risk has two practical consequences for borrowers: Liquidity may be difficult to obtain, and even if it is not, it may be expensive due to relatively poor credit ratings. One convenient feature about the environment we focus on is that both concerns virtually disappear.

[6] In contrast, nonfinancial institutions usually finance their long-term development through issuance of equity or debt rather than pure money market transactions or swaps. Again it is necessary to realize here that we focus on swaps because of the particular context in which we are working.

All major financial institutions maintain, as we said, a treasury department, effectively engaged in the central management of funding needs. Traders in need of liquidity can always turn to this internal source to obtain funding.[7] Naturally transactions have to be executed at market rates, but there is no credit spread, which means that traders essentially get liquidity, when needed, at interbank rates. Obviously if the credit rating of the institution as a whole is poor, prices quoted by the treasury manager already reflect the spread resulting from this rating. However, we have restricted our universe to large and adequately capitalized financial institutions, which means that credit rating is probably not an issue.[8]

What applies to cash transactions also applies to money market derivatives such as swaps. Again major banks and money market participants maintain a swap-trading desk, and traders throughout the institution are usually required to get their quotes from this desk. As a result, the rates quoted are also usually free of any credit risk premium.

It is necessary to emphasize again that such an environment is extremely favorable in terms of funding cost because of the backing of a strong balance sheet. All the formal developments we will carry out in this chapter are still valid in any other environment, but actual prices can be significantly higher.

OVERNIGHT

Out of the typical money market transactions, overnight loans have a particular importance because all financial institutions are required to cover their treasury needs on a daily basis. Cash deficits have to be covered with a borrowing, whereas excesses have to be lent away. The reason the overnight market is particularly active is related to the unpredictability of flows: Banks, for example, cannot generally determine accurately their customers' flows long in advance. In order to avoid borrowing or lending too much, at the risk of an opposite transaction the next day, the treasurer covers their exact needs, as long as they can actually estimate them. The calculation of interest is very

[7] In fact, they have no other choice. The purpose of the central treasury management is to aggregate flows and liquidity needs; therefore, every money market transaction for an internal client has to go through it.

[8] In the case of hedge funds engaged in various arbitrage activities, this statement is obviously inaccurate and credit risk reappears.

straightforward: The money is made available today and returned tomorrow with the interest.

In the United States the overnight market is traded in conjunction with the *fed funds market*. All depository institutions are required by federal law to maintain a certain amount of reserves at a federal bank,[9] dependent upon the type of deposits held, notably in terms of liquidity and duration. The reserves must be cash held in a vault or non-interest-bearing deposits at a federal bank, which essentially represents a net cost to the institution. Broadly speaking, reserves requirements range from 0 to 14 percent depending on the specifics of the liabilities held, with an average value around 10 percent.

Fed fund rates are the rates charged on money lent by banks with excess reserves at a federal reserve bank to banks with a reserve deficit.[10] Typically these transactions serve as a reference for the broader overnight market, which includes not only reserve requirements but also all sorts of transactions, for example, stock loans. The fed funds rate is quoted in real time by major data providers, and the Federal Reserve also publishes a daily weighted average of all reserve-related transactions effected on that day, called the *effective rate* (see Figure 4-1).

The fundamental mechanism of the overnight market is similar in many countries. Banks need to maintain reserves with the central monetary institution and at the same time trade frequently with each other to cover their needs. In Europe, for example, the European Banking Federation computes a rate called *eonia* (euro overnight index average), as the weighted average of all overnight unsecured lending transactions entered by its members.[11] Figures 4-2 through

---

[9] Depository institutions include commercial banks, savings banks, savings and loans, credit unions, U.S. agencies and branches of foreign banks, and Edge Act and agreement corporations, regardless of their membership in the Federal Reserve System. At the end of 1993, 4,148 member banks, 6,042 nonmember banks, 495 branches and agencies of foreign banks, 61 Edge Act and agreement corporations, and 3,238 thrift institutions were subject to reserve requirements. [Source: *The Federal Reserve System, Purposes & Functions*, (Washington D.C., 1994). Board of Governors of the Federal Reserve System.]

[10] The operating procedure for reserves is worth mentioning. To provide banks with flexibility, the requirement sets a target on average over a maintenance period of two weeks, instead of on a daily balance. A bank may have an excess or deficit for several days in a row as long as it maintains the minimum reserve balance on average over the maintenance period. This calculation method has been proposed as an explanation for the high volatility of fed fund rates every other week. Cf. footnote 13.

[11] Note that this figure is inclusive of all transactions, whereas the figure reported by the Federal Reserve aggregates reserve requirements only. Unsecured transactions are loans with no collateral; thus stock loans are excluded.

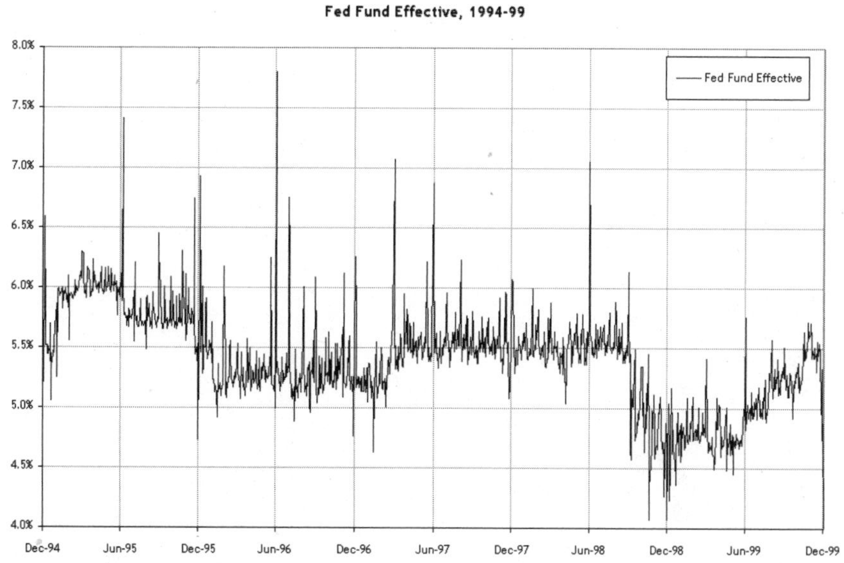

Figure 4-1 Fed Fund Effective Rates
(*Source*: Compiled by author from Datastream data.)

4-5 show for example domestic overnight rates over recent years in Tokyo, London, Frankfurt, and Paris. Clearly the overnight markets throughout the world have very different behaviors, and we need to keep this particular point in mind when examining financing-intensive activities such as index arbitrage.

The overnight rate is not the only very short term rate in the market: To cover a shortage of funds predictable one day in advance, treasury managers can trade the *tom-next rate*, from tomorrow to the next day. The overnight (O/N) and tom-next (T/N) are usually equal except in particular situations—for example, if tomorrow is the end of a corporate fiscal year. Most corporations and financial institutions end their fiscal year on December 31, and at that time they settle many flows and cover their treasury needs very precisely.[12] The accumulation of these events

[12] Research suggests that end-of-year adjustments also include window dressing on the part of banks in advance of required financial disclosure. See, for example, Linda Allen and Anthony Saunders, "Bank Window Dressing: Theory and Evidence," *Journal of Banking and Finance*, 16, 1992, pp. 585–623. For a more general examination of the end-of-year effect, see Craig H. Furfine, *The Price of Risk at Year-End: Evidence from Interbank Lending*, Working Paper No. 76, October 1999, Bank of International Settlements.

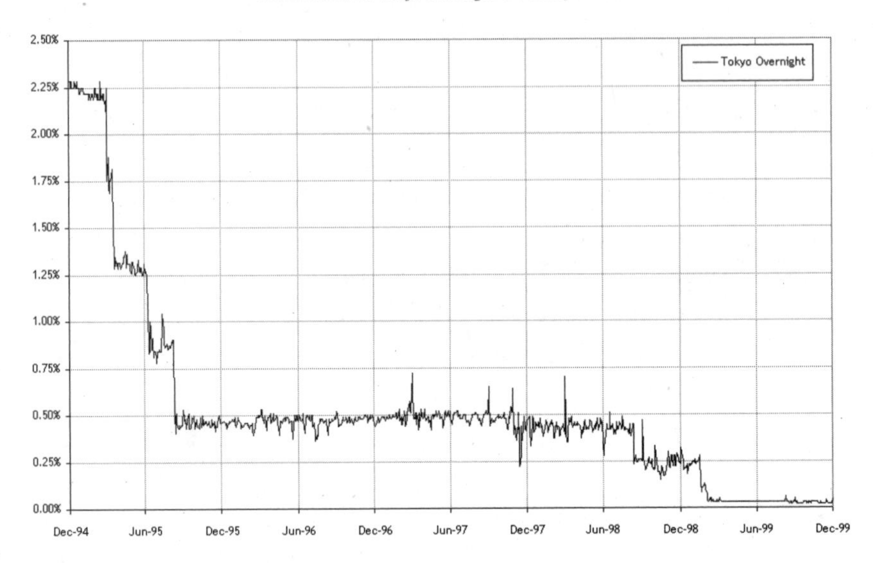

Figure 4-2 Overnight JPY
(*Source*: Compiled by author from Datastream data. From January 1, 1999, the data for the DEM and FRF rates are eonia rates computed by the Central European Bank.)

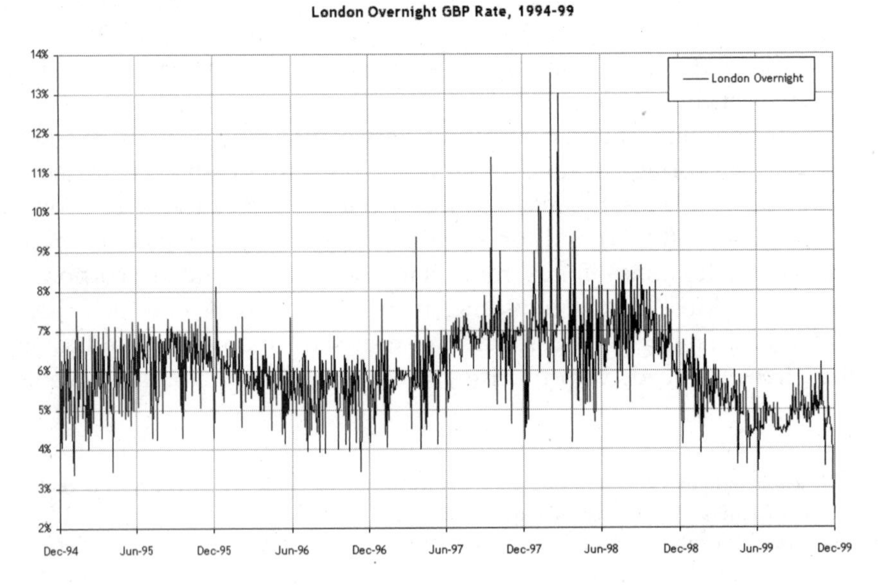

Figure 4-3 Overnight GBP
(*Source*: Compiled by author from Datastream data. From January 1, 1999, the data for the DEM and FRF rates are eonia rates computed by the Central European Bank.)

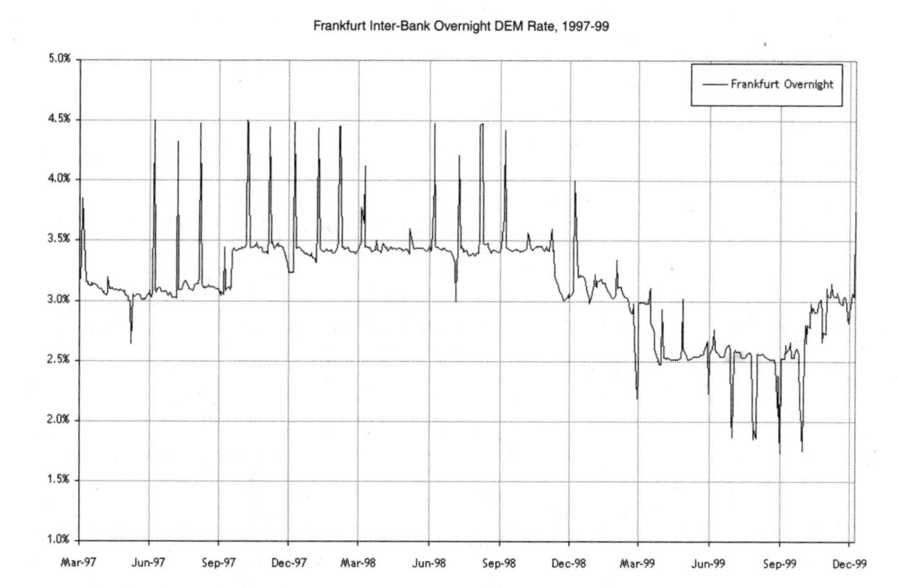

Figure 4-4 Overnight DEM
(*Source*: Compiled by author from Datastream data. From January 1, 1999, the data for the DEM and FRF rates are eonia rates computed by the Central European Bank.)

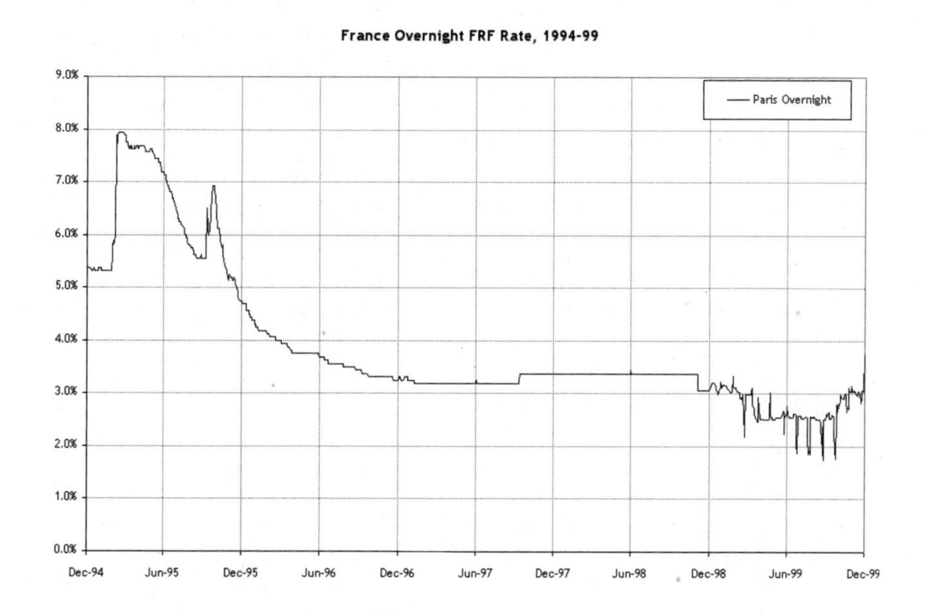

Figure 4-5 Overnight FRF
(*Source*: Compiled by author from Datastream data. From January 1, 1999, the data for the DEM and FRF rates are eonia rates computed by the Central European Bank.)

creates a high demand for funds over a single day. The overnight rate usually shoots up, and the tom-next does the same one day before. For similar reasons, a spike in the overnight is common at the end of the interim period on the last open day of June, and to a lesser extent at the end of each calendar month.[13] This effect is not equal in magnitude everywhere; it is, for example, particularly visible in the DEM overnight chart in Figure 4-4, and nonexistent in the case of FRF rates.

TREASURY MANAGEMENT VERSUS INTEREST RATE EXPOSURE

If overnight is a fundamental requirement to square the books every day, leaving little liberty for planning, short-term money market transactions—say, between a few days and several months—generally offer much more latitude in their execution and usually result from cash management decisions. In other words, beyond the immediate need for cash, treasurers are responsible for optimizing all short-term flows, trying to take advantage of opportunities or reduce risk.

Even if the vast majority of cash flows are necessarily uncertain, a skilled treasury manager has a fairly good idea about the aggregate commitments resulting from day-to-day operations. In addition, under a time horizon of one year the macroeconomic environment is relatively well known, and interest rates tend to be predictable. Naturally, there may be a Federal Open Market Committee—or its equivalent in a foreign market—here and there, and the threat of an adverse move. But overall it is possible to build a reliable intuition about the market, and optimizing flows based on that intuition helps manage the need for cash in a cost-efficient manner.

Longer term, the situation changes significantly.[14] Cash is not the main concern anymore because it does not make sense to start plan-

[13] Indeed the dynamics of the overnight market in the United States have been studied extensively. The rates exhibit strong temporal variation, even day-of-the-week effects. Proposed explanations include regulatory and accounting conventions—see, for example, "The Micromechanics of the Federal Funds Market: Implications for Day-of-the-Week Effects in Funds Rates Variability," *Journal of Financial and Quantitative Analysis*, 23, 1988—and bank payment activity—see, for example, Craig H. Furfine, "Interbank Payments and the Daily Federal Funds Rate," Federal Reserve Board of Governors Finance and Economics Discussion Series No. 1998-31.

[14] The widespread market convention is to introduce swap rates in the yield curve for maturities over one year. Therefore, our interpretation of "long-term" will typically be "over one year."

ning flows two years ahead. The general level of interest rates is much more important because under that time horizon it cannot be considered stable anymore. Furthermore, the fundamental question of solvency takes a whole new dimension, again because of the uncertainties related to the financial strengths of participants over a long period.

Whereas cash transactions rule the short-term money market world, swaps dominate unchallenged the longer-term money market world because they offer a remedy to this situation by considerably lowering the amount of credit risk. The need here is to manage an exposure to interest rates rather than a stream of cash flows. Swaps are particularly well suited for this task because they are relatively simple instruments offering a lot of flexibility in decoupling the two.

The distinction between cash management and interest rate risk management is indeed capital. It is already apparent from the above discussion that the yield curve can be segmented on the basis of this metric and that the instruments involved have fundamentally different properties. One is no substitute for the other, meaning it is possible to lose money every day from inadequate overnight management while protected from an overall move in interest rates. In addition, it is extremely important to dissociate the two in the risk management analysis. Index arbitrage will provide a good example of such dichotomy.

LONDON INTER-BANK OFFERED RATE

The theory of market efficiency, and by extension modern financial theory, relies heavily on information availability. In that respect, London played a major role over the centuries, until it lost its position as the world banking center to New York in the aftermath of World War II. It is still today a major financial center in the sense that transactions may not originate there, but prices of international commodities are for the most part available and quoted there. Gold markets, for example, are located in London, which made the British capital a focus point for 40 years after the Bretton Woods agreement on the Gold Standard.

For all these reasons, London still plays a privileged role in conveying market information, and that is particularly true on the money market. The British Bankers Association (BBA) publishes everyday a set of interest rates known as the London Inter-Bank Offered Rate (LIBOR). As their names indicate, these rates represent a market indication of the rates at which it is possible for financial institutions to procure a particular currency over a given period. They are collected every day from a list of 16 financial institutions, chosen according to certain criteria—for example, their main place of business or the main place of business of their parent company. For instance, on the dollar, U.S. organizations are naturally considered, as well as non-U.S. institutions at least in equal number, to offer a rate as indicative as possible of a broad market. Thirteen rates are collected in total—1 week, 1 and 1 to 12 months. The higher and lower four indications are removed for each maturity, and the remaining eight numbers are averaged to obtain the final figure. This whole process is repeated every day for a number of currencies, at 11:00 a.m., London time. Results are available usually around 12:00 p.m. from data providers. Table 4-1 shows, for example, the LIBOR rates as of September 13, 1999.

Why are these rates so important? The main reason is that they are widely accepted as being a fair indication of the interbank market, and they have become highly visible over the years, even if many individual countries have come up with daily rates as well on their own currency. Paris, for example, publishes a PIBOR, Frankfurt a FIBOR, Tokyo a TIBOR, Hong-Kong a HIBOR, and so on. In the vast majority of cases, indications from London are in perfect coherence with local figures. If differences appear, they are an indication of possible inefficiencies in the flows of money. Not surprisingly, during the Japan premium crisis, TIBOR rates reflected domestic market conditions

TABLE 4-1

Maturity[a]	USD	GBP	JPY	EUR
1WK	5.35625	5.00000	0.06125	2.54813
1MO	5.38000	5.24000	0.07250	2.58125
2MO	5.44000	5.36922	0.08000	2.64250
3MO	5.51000	5.47938	0.08750	2.68938
4MO	5.96375	5.81969	0.02200	3.08000
5MO	5.95000	5.87500	0.21750	3.09688
6MO	5.94125	5.94156	0.21750	3.11250
7MO	5.94625	6.00000	0.22375	3.13750
8MO	5.95125	6.06094	0.22500	3.16813
9MO	5.95750	6.11625	0.22625	3.20000
10MO	5.98500	6.17906	0.22875	3.23588
11MO	6.01500	6.25000	0.23375	3.27525
12MO	6.04750	6.30688	0.23625	3.31563

[a] The end of the year falls somewhere between 3 and 4 months. Note the "jump" between the rates for these two dates: 0.45375 percent for USD, for example, when at the same time the ampitude of the change from 4 to 12 months is only 0.10 percent.

(*Source*: Compiled by author from Bloomberg data.)

and were significantly higher than LIBOR.[15] At that point, anybody would have picked up an inconsistency just by looking at a financial paper.

Recently, the emergence of the Euro zone in Europe has reduced the need for independent calculations, and the European Banking Association (EBA) has undertaken a campaign to promote the euro as a reference currency in international money markets. In particular, the EBA publishes now a set of rates termed EURIBOR computed in a manner similar to the LIBOR.[16] The rates are published every day at 11:00 a.m. Brussels time, and the sample of banks include 47 banks of the European Union from countries participating in the euro from the outset, four banks from EU countries not participating in the euro, and six non-EU banks with important Euro zone operations. The results are trimmed to remove highest and lowest rates, and the average is published. From the beginning of 1999, the EURIBOR has replaced the historical rates published as PIBOR and FIBOR. Table 4-2 shows euro rates from EURIBOR and LIBOR on September 13, 1999.

The table shows clearly that while being very close, both sets are not identical. The choice of contributing institutions is the main source of differences, and it can be argued that because the EURIBOR has a larger base, it is somewhat closer to being a broad market indication. On the other hand, LIBOR has been in existence for much longer and has an established "mind share." Above all the BBA has the indisputable advantage of consisting of a large panel of currencies, which provides worldwide money managers with a one-stop reference.

DOMESTIC VERSUS INTERNATIONAL RATES

The market for a particular currency is by nature a worldwide market, but it is not necessarily homogeneous. There sometimes exists significant differences between the availability of funds within the domestic economy and the international markets. A simple example will illustrate this situation: Japan levies a withholding tax on foreign borrow-

---

[15] The *Japan premium* refers to the premium charged to Japanese borrowers due to worries about the developing bad-loan problem in Japan. Cf. next section "Domestic versus International Rates."

[16] Naturally, because the United Kingdom is not in the European Monetary Union, the BBA has maintained its LIBOR calculations. Considering, however, the financial weight of the Euro zone and of its banking association, it remains to be seen if LIBOR rates will keep their predominant role as reference figures.

TABLE 4-2

Maturity	Euro LIBOR	EURIBOR
1WK	2.54813	2.547
1MO	2.58125	2.584
2MO	2.64250	2.644
3MO	2.68938	2.693
4MO	3.08000	3.081
5MO	3.09688	3.096
6MO	3.11250	3.114
7MO	3.13750	3.139
8MO	3.16813	3.167
9MO	3.20000	3.202
10MO	3.23588	3.237
11MO	3.27525	3.277
12MO	3.31563	3.314

(*Source*: Compiled by author from Bloomberg data.)

ings, and an international corporation or institution lending yens to a domestic counterpart is taxed on the interest. For this reason, international participants will try to structure their transactions to avoid that tax, for example, in trading with an offshore subsidiary of the borrower. In any case, this situation tends to constrain the money flows in and out of Japan from offshore entities.

Beyond fiscal disadvantages, international and domestic markets may differ for other reasons, and Japan will give again a good illustration with the apparition of the "Japan premium" in 1995 and again in 1998. After the collapse of the stock and real estate market at the end of the 1980s, the Japanese banking system was left with an extraordinary amount of under-performing debt. As a result, the rate of default in the economy increased sharply, causing seven mortgage companies—known as *jusen corporations*—to fail at the same time. A wave of panic spread around the world, and Japan's solvency became the concern of the day. All major creditors worldwide put Japan on the red list of unwelcome borrowers. The resulting credit crunch forced the Bank of Japan to massively inject liquidity into the financial system, creating virtually a dual money market. Domestically, institutions and corporations had access to funds at normal interest rates—that is, rates that were more or less in line with what they were before the crisis. Internationally, however, all credit lines were dramatically reduced to Japanese borrowers, which had to pay huge premiums to finance their operations and eventually were unable to borrow as existing credit lines were rapidly exhausted. The lack of free flows between the domestic and international yen markets also meant that international yen lenders, with no access to domestic borrowers, and unwilling to extend more credit to Japanese institutions offshore, were ready to accept low rates from offshore counterparts. Therefore, whereas the domestic three-month rate was still around 0.50 percent, the same maturity was trading at 0.15 percent to about 0.20 percent internationally between counterparts with the adequate ratings—that is, not Japanese. The same difference prevailed across the whole term structure and remained in existence for several months, as shown in Figure 4-6.[17]

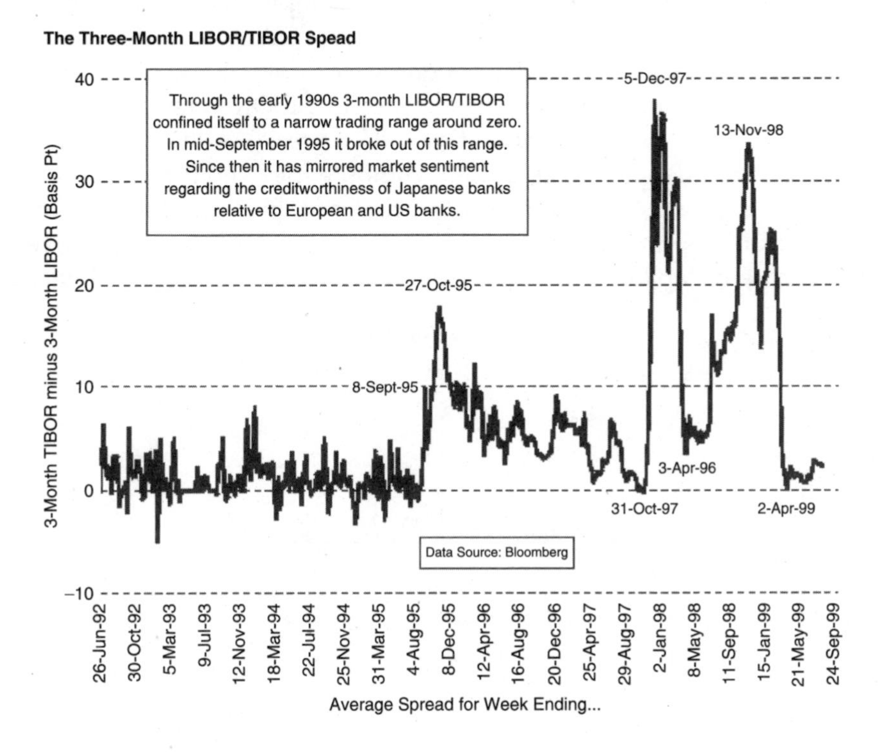

Figure 4-6 LIBOR/TIBOR
(*Source*: Fred Sturm, "Opportunities in the Euroyen LIBOR/TIBOR Spread," *Carr Futures*, www.carrfut.com. Reprinted with permission.)

[17] The premium was naturally visible in other markets as well, notably in the dollar-yen swap rates and corporate bond yields. See, for example, Tetsuro Hanajiri, *Three Japan Premiums in Autumn 1997 and Autumn 1998: Why Did Premiums Differ Between Markets?* Financial Markets Department Working Paper Series 99-E-1, Bank of Japan, August 1999, and Akira Leda and Toshikazu, *Recent Trends in the Spread over LIBOR on the Domestic Straight Bond Trading Market in Japan, Monetary and Economic Studies*, Bank of Japan, December 1998. Both papers are available online from www.boj.co.jp.

Even if this situation resulted from a crisis and is indeed an extreme example, in general interest rates are not the same between domestic and international players. As an additional illustration, consider the differences between the three-month domestic rates from Germany and France—respectively, the Frankfurt Interbank Offered Rate (FIBOR) and the Paris Interbank Offered Rate (PIBOR)—and the same rates quoted in London (LIBOR), as shown in Figures 4-7 and 4-8.

Broadly speaking, the differences—generally small but frequent—reflect numerous factors, notably comparative advantages of participants in their respective marketplaces. For example, French or German institutions may have more visibility when dealing with European counterparts, even for dollar-denominated operations, than they would with Japanese entities. In the case of LIBOR versus domestic rates, other reasons may include time differences,[18] or the non-homogeneity of the sample banks used to compute the averages.

An interesting question naturally arises as to whether these differences can be captured for a profit, and clearly the answer was positive in the case of Japan. An international organization with a subsidiary

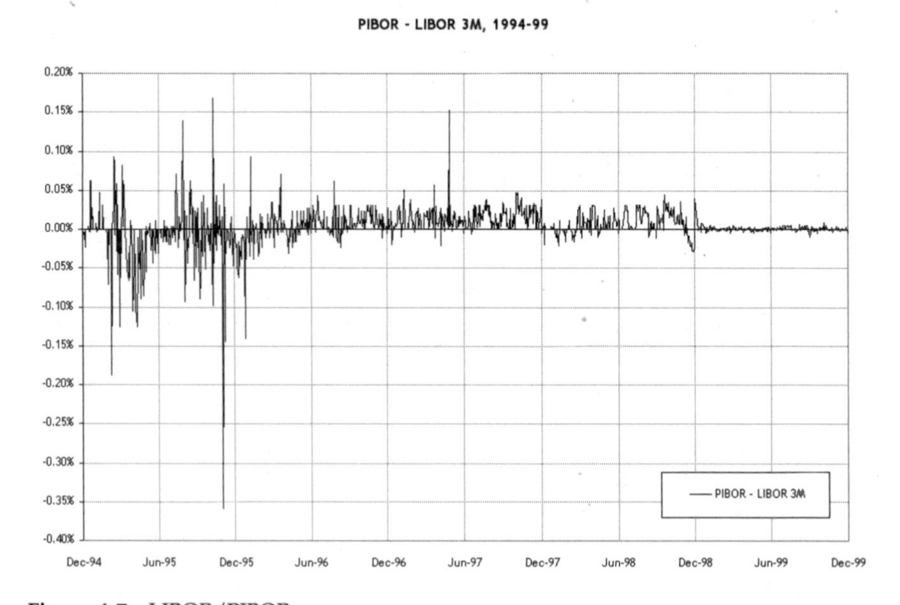

Figure 4-7 LIBOR/PIBOR
(*Source*: Compiled by author from Datastream data. From January 1, 1999, all rates are euribor rates for the euro.)

[18] The FIBOR and PIBOR are computed at 11:00 a.m. in France and Germany, whereas the LIBOR is computed at 11:00 a.m. London time—that is, one hour earlier.

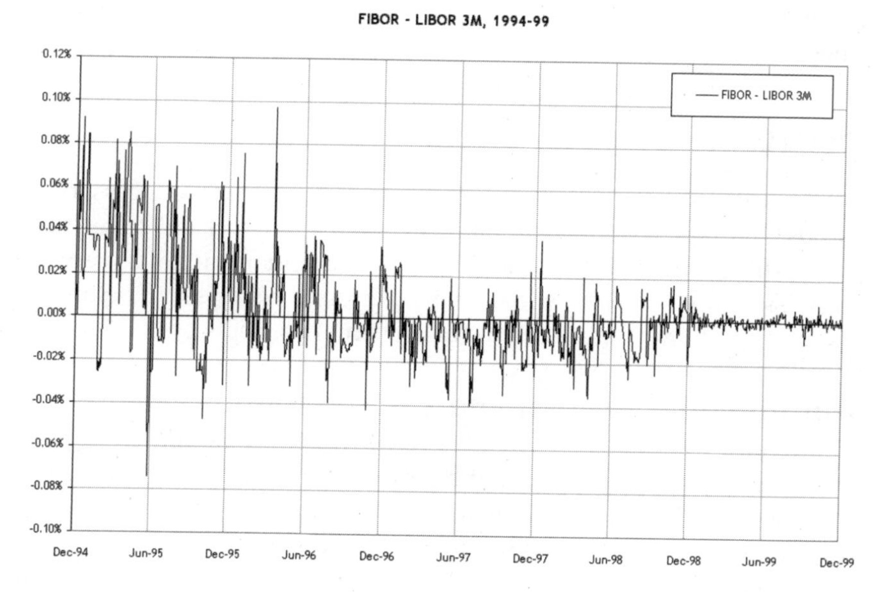

Figure 4-8 LIBOR/FIBOR
(*Source*: Compiled by author from Datastream data. From January 1, 1999, all rates are EURIBOR rates for the euro.)

and treasury management in Japan could borrow at 0.15 to 20 percent on one hand and lend away at 0.50 percent on the other. Even assuming taxes, the operation turned out to be quite profitable, under the—reasonable—assumption that the Japan premium was grossly mispriced and that Japan was in no danger of default as a country. Individual institutions, however, were, and some of them did default over the years, so this arbitrage was not exactly risk free. Still over a three-month period it can be argued that credit visibility is high, and in any case the Ministry of Finance would never have let a major institution go bust at that particular moment. Ironically the credit of large Japanese banks may not have been better than during this crisis because they probably enjoyed a—discrete but real—de facto guarantee from the government. As far as Europe is concerned, however, it is much less clear that what we see between PIBOR, FIBOR, and LIBOR can be translated into profitable arbitrage.

In the near future, closer integration of world capital markets will probably reduce the discrepancies between the diverse sets of rates applicable to a particular currency. Note, for example, in Figures 4-7 and 4-8 that the divergence between the LIBOR and EURIBOR rates is considerably smaller after January 1, 1999, showing indeed that the implementation of a single currency helped integrate markets in continental Europe.

CONVENTIONS

Before any further discussion about interest rates, it is necessary to discuss market conventions because interest rate calculations vary wildly from one country to another. The important notions we need to consider are *time basis*, *accrual convention*, and *holidays*, but before we do so we will introduce several fundamental concepts.

Introduction: Accrual and Compounding

Intuitively it is very clear that the borrower of a certain amount of money should pay interest on the period over which he or she enjoys that money. This fundamental concept is very simple, yet accounting for it may be tricky. Consider, for example, a loan of $100 at 6 percent for six months. Should the borrower pay $6 or $3 of interest at the end of six months? The answer naturally depends on the terms of the loan, but each amount is theoretically acceptable. If 6 percent is the appropriate six-month rate, $6 is the correct amount of interest due. On the other hand, if 6 percent is an annual rate, the borrower is liable for $3 because the period is half a year.

More generally, an interest rate is useless in and of itself if its underlying definition is not specified or implicit. Specifically, the operative information is the period on which it is *accruing*, as opposed to the period over which it is *applied*. For example, a six-month rate of 6 percent yields close to 12 percent in return over one year because it is accruing over six months—that is, twice in a year. A 6 percent annual rate, on the other hand, yields a return of 6 percent over a year because it is accruing only once.

To complicate things further, consider now the notion of compounding. Compounding describes an investment that is automatically reinvested periodically. For example, a six-month loan at a six-month rate of 6 percent compounded every three months yields: $(1 + 6 \text{ percent}/2)^2 - 1 = 6.09$ percent. At the end of three months, the principal—$100—and interest—$100 * 6 percent/2—are reinvested at the same rate. At the end of six months, the final flow is $\$100 * (1 + 6 \text{ percent}/2)^2$ from which we deduct the above yield.[19] The square is therefore a

---

[19] Specifically, we receive $\$100 * (1 + 6 \text{ percent}/2)^2$ for an initial investment of $100. Therefore, the yield is $[\$100 * (1 + 6 \text{ percent}/2)^2 - \$100]/\$100 = 6.09$ percent.

result of the compounding period of three months, whereas the 1/2 factor is a result of the fact that the rate is a six-month rate, and we need to divide by 2 to get a three-month equivalent. If we had taken an annual rate of 6 percent and had kept the same period and compounding, the yield would have been: $(1 + 6 \text{ percent}/4)^2 - 1 = 3.02$ percent. The square is still necessary to account for the compounding, but the relevant three-month rate is now 6 percent/4.

Thus there is a need for a rigorous nomenclature: We define the *accrual period* as the fundamental period over which the rate is accrued. An *annual* rate, for example, has an accrual period of *one year*. The *maturity* is the period over which the investment or transaction is traded. The *compounding factor* is the number of times reinvestment is made during this period.

Unless specified otherwise, all rates from now on will be annual rates.

Time Basis

With a better understanding of the accrual concept, consider now the *time basis*, which refers to the way days are accumulated in the interest calculations. There are four major basis used:

- **Actual/360**: The time fraction between two dates is the actual number of days divided by 360. For example, between February 10, 1999, and February 15, 1999, the number of days is 5, which would give a fraction of 5/360 in the interest calculation. Under this system one year is more than 1 in the interest formula.
- **Actual/365**: The fraction is computed the same way, but the total number of days in a year is 365. One year gives an exact fraction of 1.
- **Actual/actual**: This is an extension of the previous basis. The denominator is 366 when the period bridges over February 29 in a leap year; it is 365 otherwise.
- **30/360**: The number of days is computed assuming that *all months have exactly 30 days*. For example, in that format the number of days between January 18, 1999, and February 18, 1999, is 30, whereas in reality it is 31. In practice, this system is almost equivalent to the actual/365.

These different "accounting" systems have historically been used in different countries, and each of them still remains prevalent in certain parts of the world. In addition, different maturities or instruments do not use the same basis. For example, short-term regular deposits in Japan[20] and France[21] use actual/365, whereas longer-term—that is, above one year—use 30/360. In the United States all deposits carry an actual/360 basis, whereas most bonds use a 30/360 basis. Certain interest rate swaps in France use an actual/actual basis, while swaps in the United States use 30/360. The enumeration is convincing: Traders need to make sure that they are familiar with the conventions before trading any money market products.[22]

Conversion from one basis to another is relatively straightforward. If t represents the time fraction on a given number of days, then:

$$t_{30/360} \approx t_{\text{act}/365} \qquad t_{\text{act}/360} = t_{\text{act}/365} * \frac{365}{360} \qquad t_{\text{act}/\text{act}} \approx t_{\text{act}/365}$$

Accrual Convention

The *accrual convention* refers to the mathematical formulation of interest accumulation over time. The financial literature in general uses an exponential accrual: \$1,000 invested at 5 percent over a year yields \$1,000 * (1 + 5 percent) = \$1,050. If the same amount is invested over six months and renewed at the same rate, the final flow is \$1,000 * (1 + 5 percent/2)^2 = \$1,050.63. In general, for an investment over d days, compounded every n days at an annual rate r, the accrual factor is[23]:

$$f = \left(1 + \frac{n \cdot r}{360}\right)^{d/n}$$

If we consider a yearly compounding over two years—$n = 360$, $d = 720$—f becomes: $f = (1 + r)^2$. Conversely, for a semiannual compounding over a year, $n = 180$, $d = 360$, and $f = (1 + r/2)^2$. At the limit where n is one single day, that is, for an overnight compounding, $f = (1 + r/360)^d$.

A second convention, *continuous compounding*, is used in continuous finance theory, and it is an extension of the above formalism. It

---

[20] Interestingly in Japan short-term deposits are actual/365 when quoted domestically, actual/360 when quoted internationally.

[21] France, pre-euro introduction. After January 1, 1999, all euro market participants adopted similar conventions.

[22] Act/360 and act/365 are the two systems used most widely. Act/act was used in France exclusively and will probably disappear with the introduction of the euro.

[23] Note that we implicitly use an act/360 basis.

rests on the assumption that compounding is effected more and more frequently over shorter and shorter periods of time—that is, n gets smaller and smaller. Taken to the limit, interest compounds continuously, and the algebraic expression of f becomes[24]:

$$f = e^{d \cdot r/360}$$

Under this convention, a one-year investment of \$1,000 at 5 percent yields $\$1,000 * e^{5\%} = \$1,051.27$, more than an annual and semiannual compounding.[25]

There is, however, a much more practical accrual method, commonly referred to as *zero coupon*.[26] The idea is to substitute a linear relationship in place of an exponential expression and eliminate interim compounding. Thus, with the same notations, we want:

$$f = \left(1 + \frac{d \cdot r'}{360}\right)$$

By construction, r' is different from r, and we have to establish the relationships between the two, which we will do shortly. It is important, however, to note that none of these notations is right or wrong. Different needs require different tools, and many traders find it easier to manipulate zero coupon rates, whereas academics usually rely on continuous compounding because it is convenient from an algebraic and theoretical point of view.[27]

Out of the practicalities we derive from zero coupons, four are particularly interesting: homogeneity within the term structure, inclu-

---

[24] This accrual factor is based on the following result:

$$(1 + n \cdot h)^{1/n} \underset{n \to 0}{\longrightarrow} e^h$$

which applied to:

$$f = \left(1 + \frac{n \cdot r}{360}\right)^{d/n}$$

gives:

$$\left(1 + \frac{n \cdot r}{360}\right)^{d/n} \underset{n \to 0}{\longrightarrow} e^{d \cdot r/360}$$

[25] This is a general result: Everything else being equal, more frequent compounding yields a higher payoff at maturity. Therefore, continuous compounding yields the highest possible payoff at maturity.

[26] The term *zero coupon* was originally used to characterize bonds that do not pay any interim interest, but rather a lump sum upon redemption. By extension, it now describes all money market transactions in which no interim flows occur, regardless of the nature of the transaction. There are, for example, zero-coupon swaps.

[27] Note that the time basis is entirely independent from the linear or exponential nature of the accrual formulation.

sion of the reinvestment risk, simplified treatment of nonstandard maturities, and homogeneity across currencies.[28]

Transactions maturing before one year usually do not have any interim reinvestment, in which case $n = d =$ maturity of the transaction and the accrual factor is simply: $f = 1 + d \cdot r/360$. In these situations, zero coupon rates are exactly equal to "standard" rates—$r' = r$—and therefore all rates below one year can be considered zero coupon and in practice are quoted as such. In particular, the LIBORs are quoted as zero coupons.

If we take a maturity beyond one year, say, two years, an annual compounding has a known exponential form $f = (1 + r)^2$ because in most cases reinvestment occurs yearly. A zero coupon, on the other hand, has the form: $f = (1 + 2 \cdot r')$ by definition. Interestingly, this second expression is homogeneous to the shorter-term linear notation. Therefore, if we can convert long-term rates to zero-coupon equivalents, the resulting term structure is homogeneous below and above one year and easier to manipulate.

In addition, because there is no physical flow before maturity, the zero-coupon rate, if calculated properly, accounts for the reinvestment rate as opposed to the implicit assumption in the expression $(1 + r)^2$ that we can reinvest for the second period at the same rate we did for the first.

As far as nonstandard maturities are concerned, note that the LIBOR term structure shows 13 discrete maturities from 1 week to 12 months. However, if now is exactly three months before a futures expiry, two weeks later we will find ourselves 2½ months before, and we still need to compute an interest rate accurately. We would therefore appreciate a continuous-term structure, which would provide access to rates not-included in the standard set of LIBORs.

The natural inclination is to state that the 2½-month rate is somewhere between the 2- and 3-month rates. Market practice has institutionalized this reasoning, and traders customarily compute linear estimations for broken maturities. The problem gets more complex, however, if we consider a 2½-year rate for which we have to account for annual reinvestments when rates are derived from an exponential accrual method. Therefore, this averaging is truly simple only when applied to zero-coupon rates.

Zero coupons are also helpful in comparing across markets because without consistent conventions it is not possible to effectively assess

---

[28] Practically speaking, the absence of interim payments before maturity also translates into a much simpler treasury management.

relative funding costs. In particular, when pricing multicurrency products such as foreign exchange swaps, the adoption of zero-coupon rates on each side significantly simplifies the calculation.

Unfortunately, however, zero coupons are rarely quoted directly in the marketplace, and they must be deducted from other rates. There are typically two main extraction processes: from swap rates or from short-term interest rate futures contracts.[29]

Holidays

Finally, it is necessary to say a word about holidays. All countries have traditional customs associated with national holidays. It is not always easy to know in advance all the days that markets will be closed in the years ahead, and the further we look, the more difficult it gets. For that reason, money market traders have adopted a general convention that simplifies date calculations related to unexpected holidays. This rule is known as the *next business-day convention*: If a transaction generates a flow on a nonbusiness day, this flow is automatically delayed until the *next* business day. A variant includes the possibility of bridging the end of a month when postponing the flow. For fiscal, legal, or accounting reasons, this may not be beneficial to one of the parties. Thus the *modified next-business-day rule* states the flow has to be postponed if it falls on a national holiday unless it crosses the end of a month, in which case it has to be settled on the first business day *prior to* its original date.

Conventions: Why Bother?

This whole discussion about conventions may seem somehow unnecessary, but it is needed because money market transactions presuppose a deep knowledge of the marketplace. Who, as a junior trader, has not confused actual/360 with 30/360 or actual/365 and taken a humiliating loss as a result? The intrinsic value of these conventions will become even more apparent in the following example: Suppose that as a treasurer, you need to finance $1,000,000 for three years. If this deal is taking place in the United States, chances are that the basis is by default

---

[29] In the United States many government bonds can be "stripped" from their coupon payments, which in practice means that the notional payment on expiry is traded distinctly from the stream of coupon payments. The zero coupon is then implicit in the stripped structure although it is quoted as a discount, not as an outright rate. We concentrate on swaps and short-term interest rate futures because they have wider market usage—that is, higher liquidity.

30/360. You do not have to worry about any holiday within the next three years because you and your counterpart will default to the same calculations. Finally, if you want to avoid a reinvestment risk, you may want to trade a zero coupon, and the trader in front of you knows exactly what you mean and will quote one at your request. In the process, both parties have saved considerable time. There is not much theory behind these conventions, only a practical standardization.

NOTATIONS

Paradoxically, despite the seemingly complex nature of the above conventions, we will generally not indicate which basis or accrual method is used in a particular instance from now on. Most often we will use zero coupons, but there may be situations in which exponential compounding is warranted. The context dictates which method is more appropriate, and the notations reflect the specifics of that method. With respect to the calculation basis, it mostly depends on the country we operate in and possibly on the structure of the transaction we examine. Therefore, to remain relatively unspecialized, we have to leave this particularity aside, except in numerical applications in which we will take the U.S. conventions.

Furthermore, for the sake of simplification, we adopt the following shortcut: r alternatively describes the actual interest rate or the same rate already adjusted by the necessary time fraction. For example, assume we consider a three-month arbitrage opportunity and want to compute the associated financing cost. If the three-month current rate is 5 percent, and the number of days to maturity is 90 (actual/360), the interest calculation incorporates a time fraction of 90/360. In our convention, the symbol r indifferently refers to 5 percent or $90/360 * 5$ percent depending on the context. For example, if we note $(1+r)$ the accrual factor, r clearly has to be interpreted as $90/360 * 5$ percent.

Once we know how to obtain zero-coupon rates, this shortcut means that our accrual factor will almost always be $(1+r)$. If we consider a two-year 5 percent zero-coupon rate, this notation would translate into $(1 + 2 * 5 \text{ percent}) = 1.10$. If we considered a one-week deposit at 4 percent, it would be $(1 + 7 * 4 \text{ percent}/360) = 1.00077$. All these manipulations may appear painful and useless, but they will be quite useful in keeping the notations simple when we get to more complex formulas.

SETTLEMENT

It should not be surprising to discover that different currencies tend to have different settlement conventions. The most common is $T + 2$: The cash flow resulting from a transaction is exchanged two days after the transaction has been agreed upon. This effective date marks the beginning of interest accrual calculation. The British pound is the only major exception with transactions settled at $T + 1$.[30]

Obviously, overnight transactions do not follow these rules and are settled on the exact day they are traded. To allow the necessary wire transfers to take place properly, most players try to complete them as early as possible, typically before noon.

It is important to notice here that a rate quoted today does not *accrue* from today. If we take the general case of a $T + 2$ settlement, a one-week 5 percent rate indicates the cost of money for a period of one week from today's settlement date. For example, if today is Wednesday, this 5 percent indicates an operation from Friday to Friday next week. If we were to trade on a Thursday, the operation would start next Monday to the following Monday. Note also that an overnight contracted on a Friday is effective on three days, until the next Monday. All this goes without saying for those familiar with the conventions and calculations. For everybody else, it is important to realize the amount of details necessary to manage such transactions. Despite the high level of standardization, it is extremely easy to misprice or mismanage one.

SPREAD AND MIDMARKET

The LIBOR is by definition an offered rate, a rate at which bankers offer liquidity to the market—that is, lend. The price at which they are willing to borrow is sometimes referred to a "LIBID," which is not an acronym but a convenient shortcut.

As a general rule, the same way stocks trade with a bid-offer spread, interest rates exhibit spreads between the prices at which a trader is ready to borrow or lend. The typical spread on the NYSE,

---

[30] All this is very flexible, however. It is usually possible in practice to negotiate non-standard terms with a counterpart, for example, a U.S. dollar–denominated operation lasting 2½ months and effective three days from now. In that case the rate quoted is not a standard rate, and it may be different from a LIBOR, for example.

for example is 1/8, or $0.125.[31] The typical LIBOR spread is also 1/8—that is, 0.125 percent. This is recognized as "market practice": There is no obligation for a treasury manager to quote a 1/8 spread, and he or she may not do so if the market conditions do not allow him or her to do so. On the other hand, most participants are used to that figure. The spread obviously depends in a large part on the liquidity in the underlying currency, and the difference between the domestic and the international markets plays a role as well.[32]

For all practical purposes, the spread is a transaction cost, and there are basically two ways to handle it. Consider an index arbitrage situation: As we will see, such positions are usually long and have to be refinanced regularly, typically every three months at the expiration of the futures contract. Because of this structural characteristic, an index arbitrageur would tend to use an offered rate. Exceptionally, if he or she is in a position to lend, he or she has to be aware that the rate he or she uses most often is not appropriate and should be corrected by 0.125 percent. This is a conservative approach, in which the activity's treasury management is based on the side of the spread that is most frequently used. Any transaction on the opposite side creates a loss equal to the spread.

The second way to consider the situation is to base all interest rate calculations on the midmarket rate—that is, the average between the bid and offer. In that case, every treasury operation incurs a transaction cost equal to 0.0625 percent because the rate at which it is effected differs from the rate used for evaluation by this amount. Naturally the choice of one convention or the other is based on a relative appreciation of the activity and of the magnitude of the risk associated with interest rates in general.[33]

---

[31] What we call "typical spread" is different from tick value: The tick value on the NYSE is 1/16 ($0.0625), the minimum difference in price accepted by the system. Large caps trade with a 1⁄16 spread, but the vast majority in general still has a spread of 1⁄8.

[32] To put 0.125 percent in perspective, consider what happens with a bank account. Most banks in the United States pay currently between 2 and 4 percent interest on savings, while general-purpose loans are priced somewhere between 8 and 10 percent. The resulting spread is somewhere between 4 and 6 percent.

[33] A natural question here is why didn't we mention the spread on stock prices as being a transaction cost. In reality it is, but the situation is fundamentally different from that of interest rates. Because equity markets close every day with a unique reference price—typically the price of the last transaction—there is no spread attached to this final price. In contrast, money market operations *always* involve a spread because the market virtually never closes on a unique rate. If we ever get to a point where stocks trade 24 hours a day with no interruption and no discontinuity in liquidity, the inclusion of market spread in formal valuations will probably be advisable. A second

NONSTANDARD MATURITY

We already mentioned that a simple linear estimation was a convenient way to compute a nonstandard rate, assuming we are dealing with zero-coupon rates.[34] Specifically, consider that we are looking for the rate r of a transaction on n days. We know the rates r_1 and r_2 for the two closest standard maturities n_1 and n_2, respectively, with $n_1 < n < n_2$. A linear interpolation gives:

$$r = \frac{(n_2 - n) \cdot r_1 + (n - n_1) \cdot r_2}{n_2 - n_1}$$

This result happens to be independent from the time basis used as long as it is homogeneous among all components and can be used between any two rates in the term structure.[35]

Note, however, that this calculation is by definition an approximation: If r_1 and r_2 are quoted directly in the marketplace, nothing indicates that anybody will be willing to trade at the rate r derived from the interpolation.[36] Therefore, this method should be applied to obtain a "best" estimate of a *missing* rate, not to reconfirm an existing quoted maturity.

INTEREST RATE SWAPS

Definitions and Markets

A *swap* is a financial instrument whereby two parties enter an agreement to exchange a certain number of flows at specified dates in the

(Footnote continued)
reason deals with the magnitude of the cost. A 12.5 cents spread on a $20 stock is 0.63 percent, whereas 0.125 percent is 2.5 percent of a 5 percent rate. If transaction costs on stocks were to reach the 2.5 percent level, it would be absolutely necessary to include them in any formal valuation.

[34] It is a common estimation but not necessarily the best one. In practice, cubic splines are also frequently used because they are more accurate. The general problem of interpolating rates is not clearcut as we have intentionally presented it. There are several other interpolation methods possible, polynomial, for example. A weighted average has the important advantage of being simple.

[35] For example, if r_1 is quoted as actual/365, and r_2 as actual/360, one of them has to be transformed for the formula to be coherent.

[36] If this equation held consistently, the two-year rate would always be the arithmetic average of one- and three-year rates. It is not always the case in practice, and the difference indicates the extent to which this interpolation is reliable.

future. The amounts of these flows are not necessarily known at the time of the transaction, but both parties have agreed on their calculations and on the relevant parameters entering into these calculations. Swaps are derivative products, similar to futures in that there is no exchange of money at initiation, and transactions are governed by over-the-counter contracts between the parties.[37]

As an illustration of the widespread uses of swaps, Table 4-3 gives the details of OTC outstanding positions and gross market values for 1998 and 1999.[38] Swaps are clearly traded on a diverse set of underlying securities, from foreign exchange to gold. In each category they represent a sizable fraction of the outstanding notional, for example, 80 and 70 percent, respectively, in foreign exchange and interest rate activity.

Interest rate swaps fall under the generic definition: Each party pays the other a leg of the swap computed from a notional amount and a reference interest rate. For example, one side might pay annual flows while the other will pay monthly payments. The rates used may be fixed at the time of the transaction or reset regularly. If reset during the life of the swap, they match the frequency associated with the schedule: In the above example, we would use a variable one-month rate to compute the monthly flows. The notional amount is traditionally fixed throughout the life of the transaction, although "amortizing" swaps—in which the notional is amortized progressively—are also traded.

As was clearly visible in Table 4-3, interest rate derivatives are by far the most liquid instruments in the OTC market. Tables 4-4 and 4-5 give more details about the volume and characteristics of the market.

All together, the four most traded currencies account for 89 percent of the total outstanding notional in June 1999, and their aggregate transactions represent a little less than $54 billion a day in 1997. Interestingly, swaps are still mostly used by financial institutions (89

---

[37] However, this is probably less true nowadays. For example, realizing the fact that many swaps transactions could be standardized, the London International Financial Future Exchange listed a futures contract on swap in 1998—see www.liffe.com for details. In general, the swap market is certainly mature enough to undergo a wave of standardization, which would possibly transfer some of the traditional OTC products to exchange floors.

[38] The *gross market value* is the profit or loss generated by a variation in the market parameters. Swaps, like futures, are zero-sum instruments; therefore the gross market values indicate the amount of profit transferred from one of the parties to the other from the transaction's inception date.

TABLE 4-3 The Global Over-the-Counter (OTC) Derivatives Markets[a] (Amounts outstanding in billions of U.S. dollars)

	Notational Amounts			Gross Market Values		
	End June 1998	**End Dec. 1998**	**End June 1999**	**End June 1998**	**End Dec. 1998**	**End June 1999**
A. Foreign exchange contracts	**18,719**	**18,011**	**14,899**	**799**	**786**	**582**
Outright forwards and forex swaps	12,149	12,063	9,541	476	491	329
Currency swaps	1,947	2,253	2,350	208	200	192
Options	4,623	3,695	3,009	115	96	61
B. Interest rate contracts[b]	**42,368**	**50,015**	**54,072**	**1,160**	**1,675**	**1,357**
FRAs	5,147	5,756	7,137	33	15	12
Swaps	29,363	36,262	38,372	1,018	1,509	1,222
Options	7,858	7,997	8,562	108	152	123
C. Equity-linked contracts	**1,274**	**1,488**	**1,511**	**190**	**236**	**244**
Forwards and swaps	154	146	198	20	44	52
Options	1,120	1,342	1,313	170	192	193
D. Commodity contracts[c]	**451**	**415**	**441**	**38**	**43**	**44**
Gold	193	182	189	10	13	23
Other	258	233	252	28	30	22
Forwards and swaps	153	137	127	—	—	—
Options	106	97	125	—	—	—
E. Other[d]	**9,331**	**10,388**	**10,536**	**393**	**492**	**400**
Grand total	**72,143**	**80,317**	**81,458**	**2,580**	**3,231**	**2,628**
Gross credit exposure[e]				1,203	1,329	1,119
Memorandum Item:						
Exchange-traded contracts[f]	*14,256*	*13,549*	*17,262*	—	—	—

[a] All figures are adjusted for double-counting. Notational amounts outstanding have been adjusted by halving positions vis-à-vis other reporting dealers. Gross market values have been calculated as the sum of the total gross positive market value of contracts and the absolute value of the gross negative market value of contracts with non-reporting counterparties.

[b] Single-currency contracts only.

[c] Adjustments for double-counting estimated.

[d] For end-June 1998: positions reported by non-regular reporting institutions in the context of the triennial Central Bank Survey of Foreign Exchange and Derivatives Market Activity at end-June 1998; for subsequent periods; estimated positions of non-regular reporting institutions.

[e] Gross market values after taking into account legally enforceable bilateral netting agreements.

[f] Sources: FOW TRADEdata; Futures Industry Association; various futures and options exchanges.

(*Source*: Bank of International Settlements, "The Global OTC Derivatives Market at end of June 1999," www.bis.org.)

Note: For an exhaustive introduction to OTC derivatives, see, for example, Robert McLaughlin, *Over-the-Counter Derivative Products: A Guide to Business and Legal Risk Management and Documentation* (New York: McGraw-Hill, 1998).

TABLE 4-4

Currency	Notional Volume, 1997, $US billions	Share of Total	Outstanding Notional, Year-End 1997, $US billions	Share of Total
USD	$4,386	25.7%	$6,078	27.3%
JPY	$2,899	17.0%	$4,313	19.3%
DEM	$2,593	15.1%	$3,278	14.7%
FRF	$2,518	14.8%	$2,377	10.7%
GBP	$1,034	6.1%	$1,456	6.5%
Other	$3,637	21.3%	$4,789	21.5%
Total	$17,067	100%	$22,291	100%

(*Source*: International Swaps and Derivatives Association, www.isda.org.)

TABLE 4-5 The Global OTC Interest Rate Derivatives Markets[a] (Amounts outstanding in billions of U.S. dollars)

	Notational Amounts			Gross Market Values		
	End June 1998	End Dec. 1998	End June 1999	End June 1998	End Dec. 1998	End June 1999
Total contracts	**42,368**	**50,015**	**54,072**	**1,160**	**1,675**	**1,357**
With other reporting dealers	18,244	24,442	27,059	463	748	634
With other financial institutions	18,694	19,790	21,149	515	683	559
With nonfinancial customers	5,430	5,783	5,863	182	244	164
Up to one year[b]	17,422	18,185	20,287	—	—	—
Between one and five years[b]	16,805	21,405	21,985	—	—	—
Over five years[b]	8,141	10,420	11,800	—	—	—
U.S. dollar	13,214	13,763	16,073	311	370	337
Euro[c]	13,576	16,461	17,483	476	786	584
Japanese yen	7,164	9,763	10,207	194	212	192
Pound sterling	3,288	3,911	4,398	59	130	103
Swiss franc	1,055	1,320	1,404	19	31	27
Canadian dollar	770	747	814	14	18	16
Swedish krona	826	939	1,122	19	25	21
Other	2,475	3,113	2,570	68	102	77
Memorandum item:						
Exchange-traded contracts[d]	*13,107*	*12,305*	*13,810*	—	—	—

[a] See footnote a to Table 4-3.
[b] Residual maturity.
[c] Before end-June 1999; legacy currencies of the euro.
[d] See footnote f to Table 4-3.

(*Source*: Bank of International Settlements, "The Global OTC Derivatives Market at End of June 1999.")

percent), for maturities over one year (62 percent). Note as well the total outstanding notional for listed products, one quarter the size of the OTC market.

Structures

Interest rate swaps can be seen as two money market operations back to back: Party *A* lends the notional amount to party *B* according to a set of negotiated terms, while party *B* lends the same exact amount back to *A* with a somewhat different structure. Accordingly, there is no need for an exchange of notional at any time; only interest payments are settled regularly.

The most common type of swaps involves fixed versus variable payments.[39] The reasons that two parties may be willing to enter such an agreement are diverse and depend on the type of institutions involved. A manufacturing corporation and an insurance company certainly have different needs to fulfill in their day-to-day business; nevertheless, both may use swaps at some point for a common purpose: to manage an interest rate exposure.

Consider, for example, a corporation that has funded its growth through debt issuance at a time of low interest rates. This corporation may have been in a situation in which a variable coupon was its best option, and thus it carries an exposure to interest rates that may prove painful: In a context of tightening monetary policy or rising interest rates, its interest burden will increase significantly. In that situation, the company could potentially get rid of this undesired exposure through an appropriate swap. If it pays fixed interests and receives variable payments matching its variable coupon, the variable risk goes away and the company has secured its financing cost once and for all. Here, the swap provides a protection against a rise in interest rates.

The opposite situation is also frequent. Consider the case of an insurance company receiving premiums from its customers on a monthly basis. This money has to be invested at the prevalent interest rate, with the risk that these rates may go down. Lending at a fixed rate and borrowing the variable side of a swap would offer the money managers a convenient protection, providing a secured rate over the life of the swap.

---

[39] Other types of swaps: For example, in the United States, LIBOR 1M versus 3M or 3M versus 6M, LIBOR 6M versus fed funds, prime versus 3M.

A broad discussion about the intrinsic power of swap transactions is beyond our scope, but we have to dedicate a significant amount of time to their pricing methodology. On one side they represent a huge amount of trading activity in the OTC market, and at the same time they have direct applications in the world of arbitrage from a risk management perspective.

In particular, they have three powerful features: They give easy and cheap access to long-term financing, provide a short path to a zero-coupon term structure, and constitute the simplest and cheapest way to manage an exposure to interest rates.

Conventions

The same way established conventions prevail in cash transactions, the swap market is heavily permeated by standards, norms, and conventions. For example, U.S. dollar–denominated swaps are usually semiannual on the fixed side, indexed on three-month LIBORs,[40] and use the 30/360 basis. In other words, payments on the fixed side occur twice a year and four times a year on the variable leg. Following this path, many other markets have adopted similar conventions, as seen in Table 4-6.

Settlement is dependent upon the currency, usually $T+2, T+1$ for the British pound. It is customary to refer to the fixed side to design the way the swap has been traded: A fixed-rate payer has "bought" or "borrowed" the swap. Bid-ask spreads are generally much smaller

TABLE 4-6

Country	Short-Term Deposit Basis	Swap Basis	Fixed Frequency	Variable Reference
U.S.	Act/360	30/360	Semiannual	3M LIBOR
U.K.	Act/365	Act/365	Semiannual	6M LIBOR
Japan	Act/360	Act/365	Semiannual	6M LIBOR
Euro zone	Act/360	30/360	Annual	6M EURIBOR

(*Source*: Compiled by author from Bloomberg data.)

[40] Annual and semiannual with respect to the legs of a swap indicate the frequency of payments. Rates are still fundamentally annual with respect to their accrual period, as we defined it earlier. For example, if a semiannual payment is due with a rate of 6 percent, the payment is 6 percent/2 = 3 percent of the notional.

than for cash deposits: typically 0.03 to 0.06 percent and we will see specifically why this is so.

Regarding the inclusion of holidays in the date calculations, swaps behave in the exact same way as cash transactions: They follow the next business day rule or its modified version.[41]

Long-Term Financing

Consider the following "standard" two-year swap: fixed annual versus six-month variable. We buy this swap—that is, borrow the fixed rate, paying 5 percent every year for two years. Against these flows, we receive a six-month rate two times a year.

In parallel, we borrow an amount equal to the notional of the swap every six months for six months, at a rate as close as possible to the swap reference—that is, at a six-month LIBOR. The LIBOR being an offered rate, this operation presents no difficulty. The resulting structure is a portfolio in which all variable flows match and disappear: It is a plain two-year borrowing at a rate equal to the fixed leg of the swap.

This construction is extremely interesting for two reasons:

- To secure a term loan over a period of two years, any serious lender will request piles of financial information and would price the loan according to the perceived credit risk. In addition to being expensive, this path may be long and painful because every dollar lent is at risk for a period of two years. Comparatively, consider the swap transaction: The notional is not at risk, and the credit exposure for both parties is limited to interest payments—that is, a fraction of the notional. Credit is still an issue, but to a much smaller extent. The cash loan still occurs, but every six months for a period of six months: Credit requirements are less stringent, and the borrower will find lenders much more easily.[42]

[41] Swaps have been massively standardized over the years by the International Swaps and Derivatives Association (ISDA, www.isda.org). The ISDA has issued generic guidelines on all aspects of these transactions over the years, and most legal confirmations nowadays reference these guidelines as being the governing defaults.

[42] We see again the distinction between interest rate exposure and cash management. Despite the existence of the swap, a short-term loan is necessary to gain access to cash.

- The borrower keeps its financial flexibility. For example, if for some reason the loan is not needed anymore, the transaction can be closed every six months by simply unwinding the swap; and because the swap market is extremely liquid, the total cost to exit is very low. If interest rates have moved from the original time of the transaction, exiting may generate a profit or a loss, but this effect would have been identical with a two-year term loan. Therefore, nothing fundamental is changed with a swap structure except that the overall funding operation leaves more flexibility and is certainly cheaper.

Naturally, the actual borrowing must occur four times, every six months. This is certainly a constraint, and the inclusion of a swap component is not suited for all financing needs. However, it is a convenient way to achieve equivalent results, provided the overall situation allows it.

Swaps and Zero Coupons

Because swap rates are essentially long-term borrowing rates when linked to short-term loans, we will consider them as a *direct and most accurate indication of the prevalent interest rates for money market transactions of the corresponding maturity*. For example, a two-year fixed annual swap price of 5 percent indicates that the cost of borrowing over two years is 5 percent annually, regardless of the variable schedule. In fact, because we accept the constraint to adapt to the variable schedule, it totally disappears from our considerations.[43]

Now consider the same swap without the fixed flow at the end of the first year. The rate we would pay to enter this structure is exactly the two-year zero-coupon rate because we would pay interest only once at maturity. The same reasoning can be applied to longer maturity: Remove the two intermediate payments from a three-year fixed annual swap and you get a three-year zero coupon. This tweaking is

[43] It is very important here again to refer to the context in which we make this statement. An arbitrageur has access to an internal swap desk to price and trade these instruments. In addition, the credit rating of this institution is usually good enough for him or her to access LIBORs without any credit spread. For all these reasons entering a two-year swap is exactly equivalent to borrowing on a term of two years. For any other participants not in the same environment, the cost of borrowing for the same term may be significantly higher.

exactly the trick we need to translate a swap term structure into a zero-coupon yield curve. Furthermore, because swaps are so liquid and quoted for a diversity of maturities and currencies, their prices tend to be extremely accurate as to the overall market expectations, making them a very reliable source of information.

Swaps and Risk Management

The example of the corporation entering a swap to hedge its interest charge is a perfect example of the uses of swaps to hedge miscellaneous risks attached to interest rates. Considering how liquid the swap market has become, and the fact that prices are widely available from information providers such as Reuters and Bloomberg, swaps have become by far the cheapest way to hedge—or create—a medium- to long-term exposure. In particular, in the context of index arbitrage, we will see that they are widely used in conjunction with and complement to short-term futures contracts.

ZERO-COUPON TERM STRUCTURE

Swap Asymmetries and Bid-Ask Spreads

Swaps are interest rate derivative products, but compared to other derivatives we have seen, they have an exotic feature: They are not symmetrical with respect to the price of their underlying. Specifically, because swap variable rates are usually indexed against the LIBOR, which is an offered rate, swaps implicitly take the perspective of a borrower of liquidity.

In all our discussions so far, we have neglected this point, as we have systematically described swaps as practical vehicles for *borrowers*, and only occasionally for lenders. For lenders, there are extra costs associated with trading swaps—namely, the bid-ask spread on cash deposits. If we want to borrow liquidity for two years, for example, we know we can enter a swap—which does not provide cash in and of itself—and renew a short-term borrowing operation at every reset on the variable leg. The borrowing is always possible, and it is cost free if we can do it at the price of the variable leg—usually the LIBOR. Now if we were to trade the other way and sell the swap to lend liquidity for two years, we would have to renew a loan regularly at every reset on the variable leg, and this would cost us an extra 0.125 percent of the bid-ask spread. This cost of 0.125 percent appears in addition to the spread on the swap, which is usually relatively low, typically below 1/16—that is, 0.0625 percent.[44] For example, selling a swap with quarterly variable resets and lending cash at the LIBID every three months will generate costs of 0.125 percent divided by 4, four times a year.

The convention behind this asymmetry is essentially historical. Swaps originally were promoted to nonfinancial corporations as tools for risk management purposes. Because nonfinancial institutions tend to be overwhelmingly borrowers to fund future industrial development, it was indeed a natural thing to consider an offered rate as the appropriate benchmark.

With respect to zero coupons, the existence of this asymmetry is not practical because it potentially complicates significantly the algebra. There are three simple ways to solve this difficulty. One is to ignore it altogether and decide that we do not need to include LIBOR-LIBID spreads on the variable leg in zero-coupon calculation. The second is algebraic and involves a simple approximation. In this approach, we neglect the compounding of the 0.125 percent cost. In effect, regardless of the frequency of variable resets, we assume that the overall cost to lend regularly is 0.125 percent annually.[45]

The third approach, more qualitative, is different in nature. Consider, for example, an index arbitrage activity, which is often structurally a borrower of cash. The "working capital" of the arbitrage is highly negative, and in the vast majority of cases the refinancing cycle is very short term—typically from futures expiry to futures expiry. In that environment, if we need periodically to lend money because of a swap, the cash is not actually lent away but rather deducted from the outstanding balance that has to be borrowed periodically. In other words, the loan matching the variable leg of a swap is in fact a deduc-

---

[44] As a general rule, the same asymmetry exists with all other interest rate derivative products indexed on a reference rate, either a bid or an offer such as the LIBOR. This problem does not surface with stocks because of the existence of a unique reference price at the close, which is neither a bid nor an offer.

The fact that the swap is no substitute for cash also explains why spreads are much lower than that of money market transactions, 1/16 instead of 1/8. There is no exchange of liquidity—usually the scarce resource—only a contractual commitment, which does not require the same margin.

[45] This approximation is relatively benign. With a semiannual compounding, assuming market rates at 5 percent, the annual cost is 0.1265 percent versus our assumption of 0.125 percent. With quarterly compounding, the cost becomes 0.1273 percent. These errors represent respectively $15,000 and $23,000 annually on a $1 billion notional.

tion from a borrowing operation that would be traded presumably at the LIBOR: It can be considered as a virtual loan at the LIBOR. The zero-coupon calculation is therefore very straightforward, we consider that we can effectively lend at the LIBOR.[46]

The important part in this reasoning is to understand that zero-coupons are context dependent. If we use swaps to manage an interest rate exposure, with no particular emphasis on treasury management, we do not even need to care about the money market spread in any way. If, on the other hand, liquidity is an issue, then we need to incorporate the overall funding need of the trading activity. If it happens to be on the borrowing side, again the spread can be neglected. If it is on the other side or unclear, we still need to make sure we account for the situation properly.

In the following we will essentially ignore the spread to keep calculations to their simplest expression. The zero-coupon rates we will obtain, therefore, will be a general approximation, sufficient for our purpose.

Pricing

In our definition, zero coupons are money market transactions during which no interim payment is made and for which interest accrues linearly. Regardless of the maturity, all the interests and principal are repaid in one lump sum at expiry.

Let's denote $r_{\text{ZC-6M}}, r_{\text{ZC-1Y}}$ the zero-coupon rates for six months and one year. We know these rates from market quotes because the LIBOR are for zero coupons and include maturities up to one year. If we denote $r_{\text{SW-1Y}}$ as the one-year annual swap rate, we know that $r_{\text{SW-1Y}} = r_{\text{ZC-1Y}}$ because there is no interim fixed payment on the swap. Now consider a two-year term loan built from an annual swap priced at $r_{\text{SW-2Y}}$, and the flow diagram shown in Figure 4-9. (Note that the variable leg being ignored here, we indicate only the frequency of the fixed leg in the denomination of swaps.)

Assume we borrow \$1 from this two-year structure: We receive \$1 today, and we pay the intermediate interest payment of $\$1 * r_{\text{SW-2Y}}$ by definition of the swap and the final payment $\$1 * (1+r_{\text{SW-2Y}})$. These flows are represented in bold lines. At the same time, we lend an amount equal to $\$1 * r_{\text{SW-2Y}}/(1 + r_{\text{ZC-1Y}})$ for one year, so that the

[46] The opposite situation in which a trading activity would have a positive working capital is naturally different. In that case we would still need to account for the cost of the spread.

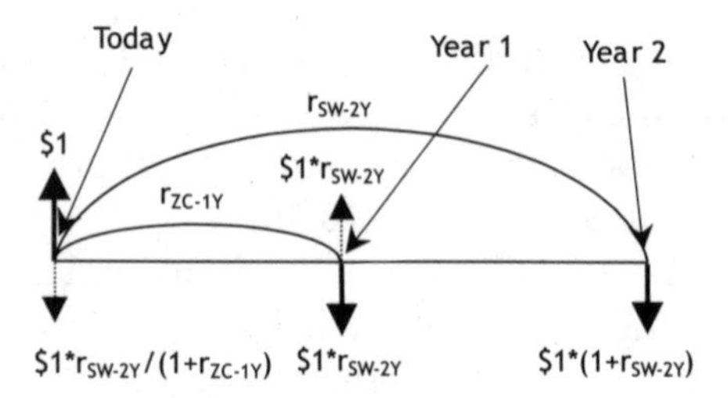

Figure 4-9 Zero Coupon, Two Years

final payment of this flow falls on the same date as the swap interim interest payment. These flows are represented in dashed lines.

The net effect of this structure is given in Figure 4-10.

We have eliminated the intermediate flow, and the resulting rate is therefore a two-year zero coupon: The nominal transacted is $\$1 - \$1 * r_{\text{SW-2Y}}/(1 + r_{\text{ZC-1Y}})$, and the net interest at expiry is $r_{\text{SW-2Y}}$. Therefore[47]:

$$\left(1 - \frac{r_{SW-2Y}}{1 + r_{ZC-1Y}}\right)(1 + r_{\text{ZC-2Y}}) = 1 + r_{\text{SW-2Y}}$$

As we mentioned, we removed the explicit basis for the date calculations. It is worth coming back to this issue for a second. Consider, for example, that today's settlement date is January 15, 1998—therefore, we are two days before, January 13. The swap is two years and therefore ends on January 15, 2000. The interim payment is due on January 15, 1999. The one-year zero coupon is 4.5 percent, the swap fixed rate is 5 percent, and all dates are considered to be actual/360.

In the diagram, the $r_{\text{SW-2Y}}$ on the left side of the above equation applies to the period 1998 to 1999, while on the right side it applies to the period 1999 to 2000. There are 365 days between January 15, 1998,

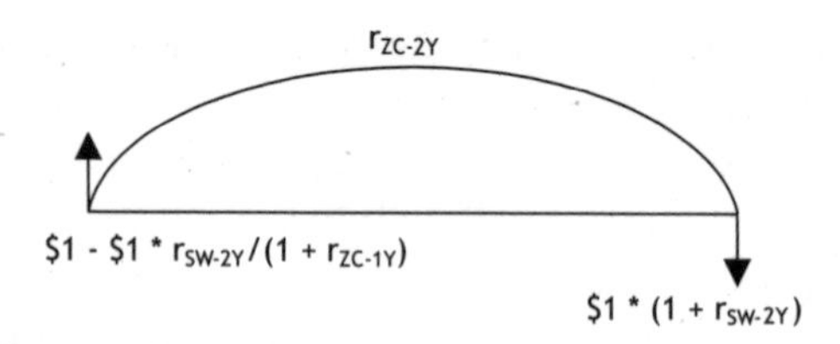

Figure 4-10 Net Zero Coupon, Two Years

[47] In agreement with what was announced earlier, the term $1 + r_{\text{ZC-2Y}}$ actually incorporates the time fraction. Alternatively, it could have been written $1 + 2 \cdot r_{\text{ZC-2Y}}$ because it is a two-year zero coupon.

and January 15, 1999. January 15, 2000, being a Saturday, the flow is postponed to January 17, 2000—that is, 367 days from January 15, 1999.

In other words, the above equation should be written as:

$$\left(1-\frac{\frac{365\times 5\%}{360}}{1+\frac{365\times 4.5\%}{360}}\right)\left(1+\frac{732\cdot r_{ZC\text{-}2Y}}{360}\right)=1+\frac{367\times 5\%}{360}$$

which gives $r_{ZC\text{-}2Y} \approx 5.14$ percent. The numeric value has little importance, but two points are worth noticing in this example:

- This relation $r_{ZC\text{-}2Y} > r_{SW\text{-}2Y}$ is expected considering that with no interim payment, a zero coupon should pay more at the end.
- Rigorous analysis matters tremendously when manipulating interest rate calculations, specifically in an environment in which non-explicit conventions are frequent.

It follows that:

$$r_{ZC-2Y}=\frac{1+r_{SW-2Y}}{1-\left(\frac{r_{SW-2Y}}{1+r_{ZC-1Y}}\right)}-1$$

To anchor the approach, consider now a three-year swap and similar interim zero coupon lending to remove the swap fixed payments, as shown in Figure 4-11. The same conclusion holds as to the structure resulting from our superposition. It is a three-year zero coupon, and its price is given by:

$$\left(1-\frac{r_{SW-3Y}}{1+r_{ZC-1Y}}-\frac{r_{SW-3Y}}{1+r_{ZC-2Y}}\right)(1+r_{ZC-3Y})=1+r_{SW-3Y}$$

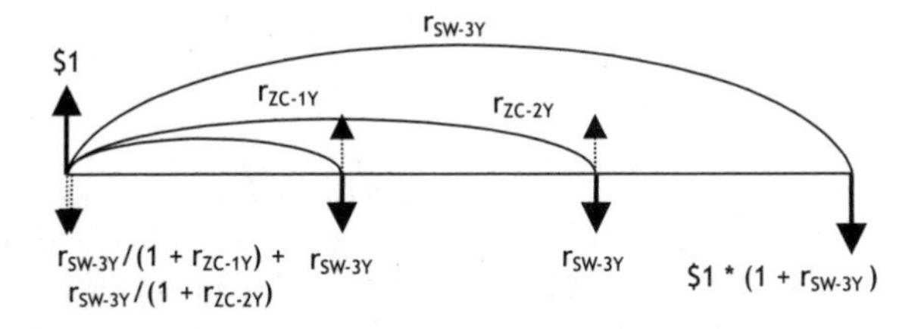

Figure 4-11 Zero Coupon, Three Years

And:

$$r_{ZC-3Y} = \frac{1 + r_{SW-3Y}}{1 - \left(\frac{r_{SW-3Y}}{1 + r_{ZC-1Y}}\right) - \left(\frac{r_{SW-3Y}}{1 + r_{ZC-2Y}}\right)} - 1$$

$$r_{ZC-nY} = \frac{1 + r_{SW-nY}}{1 - \left(\sum_{i=1}^{n-1} \frac{r_{SW-nY}}{1 + r_{ZC-iY}}\right)} - 1$$

If we denote:

$$\Sigma_n = \sum_{i=1}^{n-1} \frac{r_{SW-nY}}{1 + r_{ZC-iY}}$$

the generic formula becomes[48]:

$$r_{ZC-nY} = \frac{1 + r_{SW-nY}}{1 - \Sigma_n} - 1$$

Are we done with the computation of a zero coupon term structure? Recall that swaps in the United States are conventionally quoted as semiannual fixed payments, and our formula has been derived from annual fixed swaps.

Instead of manipulating algebra, let's introduce a small approximation frequently used. Knowing the price r_S of a semiannual swap, the equivalent annual rate r_A can be derived from[49]:

---

[48] It is easy from there to compute $r_{ZC\text{-}nY} - r_{SW\text{-}nY}$:

$$r_{ZC-nY} - r_{SW\text{-}nY} = \sum_{n} \frac{1 + r_{SW-nY}}{1 - \Sigma_n}$$

which shows unequivocally what we suspected: $r_{ZC\text{-}nY} > r_{SW\text{-}nY}$. Furthermore in general $\Sigma_n > \Sigma_m$ if $n > m$, which indicates that for $n > m, r_{ZC\text{-}nY} - r_{SW\text{-}nY} > r_{ZC-mY} - r_{SW-mY}$: the zero-coupon rates diverge from their swap equivalent. The further ahead we look, the higher the zero-coupon yield compared to the swap rate of same maturity.

[49] Note that the factor ½ in ½r_S should have been omitted because it represents the time basis for the date calculation, and we stated earlier that we would not exteriorize these fractions. We include it only to emphasize the semiannual to annual transformation. To be extremely rigorous, note also that ½ is not accurate because through the life of a swap there may be six-month periods longer or shorter ½ a year. Therefore, the formula is a simplifying approximation in many respects.

$$\left(1+\frac{r_S}{2}\right)^2=1+r_A$$

This formula is not rigorously correct because it supposes that the interim payment is reinvested at the exact same rate r_S for all interim six-month periods. For our purposes, however, it is sufficiently accurate, and we can use it as a small trick to convert semiannual swaps to an annual schedule and then perform the zero-coupon analysis presented above.

The final issue pending is the question of the spread.[50] If we denote "ask" as the rate at which we are likely to borrow, and "bid" as the one at which we are likely to lend, the zero-coupon formula becomes:

$$r_{\mathrm{ZC}-n\mathrm{Y}}^{\mathrm{ask}}=\frac{1+r_{\mathrm{SW}-n\mathrm{Y}}^{\mathrm{ask}}}{1-\Sigma_n^{\mathrm{ask}}}-1 \qquad \Sigma_n^{\mathrm{ask}}=\sum_1^{n-1}\frac{r_{\mathrm{SW}-n\mathrm{Y}}^{\mathrm{ask}}}{1+r_{\mathrm{ZC}-i\mathrm{Y}}^{\mathrm{bid}}}$$

The bid side is obtained by inverting the ask and bid rates in these formulas.

Table 4-7 is an illustration of those results and shows the zero-coupon yield curve for the U.S. dollar. For the purpose of these calculations, today is September 13, 1999. The settlement is September 15, 1999. To make things clearer, here are the major steps in the process:

- Gray-shaded areas indicate market rates as obtained in real time from major information providers (Bloomberg, Reuters, Telerate, BRIDGE, and so on). LIBORs are contributed by the British Bankers Association, whereas swap rates are available from specialized brokers.
- Maturity dates are calculated by adding the relevant number of months and years to the settlement date and adjusting for holidays. For example, September 15, 1999, + 4 months = January 15, 2000, which is a Saturday. The flow is postponed to the following Monday, January 17, 2000.[51] All date calculations below one year are on actual/360 basis. Over one year, swaps are 30/360 and zero

[50] The spread here refers to the bid-ask spread on the fixed leg of the swap. The spread we mentioned earlier in reference to swap asymmetry was due to the variable leg of the swap. It is being ignored here as we indicated.

[51] For simplification, we ignored banking holidays. If by any chance one of our maturities is a banking holiday, the flow has to be postponed one more day.

TABLE 4-7

Maturity	Date	Nb Days	USD LIBID	USD LIBOR	Swap Semiannual		Swap Annual		Sigma n		Zero Coupon	
					Bid	Ask	Bid	Ask	Bid	Ask	Bid	Ask
1WK	Sep. 22, 1999	7	5.2313%	5.3563%							5.2313%	5.3563%
1MO	Oct. 15, 1999	30	5.2550%	5.3800%							5.2550%	5.3800%
2MO	Nov. 15, 1999	61	5.3150%	5.4400%							5.3150%	5.4400%
3MO	Dec. 15, 1999	91	5.3850%	5.5100%							5.3850%	5.5100%
4MO	Jan. 17, 2000	124	5.8388%	5.9638%							5.8388%	5.9638%
5MO	Feb. 15, 2000	153	5.8250%	5.9500%							5.8250%	5.9500%
6MO	Mar. 15, 2000	182	5.8163%	5.9413%							5.8163%	5.9513%
7MO	Apr. 17, 2000	215	5.8213%	5.9463%							5.8213%	5.9463%
8MO	May 15, 2000	243	5.8263%	5.9513%							5.8263%	5.9513%
9MO	Jun. 15, 2000	274	5.8325%	5.9575%							5.8325%	5.9575%
10MO	Jul. 17, 2000	306	5.8600%	5.9850%							5.8600%	5.9850%
11MO	Aug. 15, 2000	335	5.8900%	6.0150%							5.8900%	6.0150%
12MO	Sep. 15, 2000	366	5.9225%	6.0475%							5.9225%	6.0475%
2Y	Sep. 17, 2001	733			6.2500%	6.2900%	6.3477%	6.3889%	6.00%	6.04%	6.4674%	6.5165%
3Y	Sep. 16, 2002	1,097			6.4000%	6.4400%	6.5024%	6.5437%	11.91%	12.00%	6.8548%	6.9099%
4Y	Sep. 15, 2003	1,461			6.5100%	6.5500%	6.6160%	6.6573%	17.57%	17.70%	7.2256%	7.2883%
5Y	Sep. 15, 2004	1,827			6.6000%	6.6400%	6.7089%	6.7502%	23.01%	23.18%	7.6114%	7.6834%
6Y	Sep. 15, 2005	2,192			6.6800%	6,7200%	6.7916%	6.8329%	28.18%	28.40%	7.9975%	8.0806%
7Y	Sep. 15, 2006	2,557			6,7400%	6,7800%	6.8536%	6.8949%	33.03%	33.29%	8.3854%	8.4816%
8Y	Sep. 17, 2007	2,924			6,7900%	6.8300%	6.9053%	6.9466%	37.61%	37.92%	8.7934%	8.9053%
9Y	Sep. 15, 2008	3,288			6,8400%	6,8800%	6.9570%	6.9983%	41.92%	42.27%	9.2110%	9.3414%
10Y	Sep. 15, 2009	3,653			6.8800%	6.9100%	6.9983%	7.0294%	45.95%	46.28%	9.6531%	9.7787%

(*Source*: Compiled by author from Bloomberg data.)

coupons are on actual/360 basis. For simplification purposes we consider that 30/360 is equivalent to actual/365 and use the latter.

- The semiannual swap rate is converted into an annual rate using the approximation introduced above. For example, the six-month offered rate of 6.72 percent is considered equivalent to 6.8329 percent annually.
- Σ_n is computed step by step for each maturity. For example:

$$\Sigma_2^{\text{ask}} = \frac{r_{\text{SW-2Y}}^{\text{ask}}}{1 + r_{\text{ZC-1Y}}^{\text{bid}}} = \frac{\dfrac{366 * 6.3889\%}{365}}{1 + \dfrac{366 * 5.9225\%}{360}} = 6.04\%$$

$$\Sigma_3^{\text{bid}} = \frac{r_{\text{SW-3Y}}^{\text{bid}}}{1 + r_{\text{ZC-1Y}}^{ask}} + \frac{r_{\text{SW-3Y}}^{bid}}{1 + r_{\text{ZC-2Y}}^{\text{ask}}} = \frac{\dfrac{366 * 6.5024\%}{365}}{1 + \dfrac{366 * 6.0475\%}{360}}$$

$$+ \frac{\dfrac{(733 - 366) * 6.5024\%}{365}}{1 + \dfrac{733 * 6.5165\%}{360}} = 11.91\%$$

Note that in each of these equations, $r_{\text{SW-}n\text{Y}}$ denotes a different interim flow. In Σ_2 this flow occurs on September 15, 2000, and interest accrues from September 15, 1999—that is, 366 days on actual/365 basis. In Σ_3, the first $r_{\text{SW-}n\text{Y}}$ occurs on September 15, 2000, for 366 days as well, but the second appears on September 17, 2001, and interest accrues from September 15, 2000—that is, 733 – 366 = 367 days. As for $r_{\text{ZC-}i\text{Y}}$, it accrues from the very beginning of the swap—that is, today's settlement date—to each interim flow date.

- The rates $r_{\text{ZC-}n\text{Y}}$ are computed using Σ_n according to the formula given earlier. For example:

$$\frac{733 \cdot r_{\text{ZC-2Y}}^{\text{ask}}}{360} = \frac{1 + r_{\text{SW-2Y}}^{\text{ask}}}{1 - \Sigma_2^{\text{ask}}} - 1 = \frac{1 + \dfrac{(733 - 366) * 6.3889\%}{365}}{1 - 6.04\%} - 1$$

$$= 13.26\% \Rightarrow r_{\text{ZC-2Y}}^{\text{ask}} = 6.5165\%$$

$$\frac{1{,}097 \cdot r_{\text{ZC-3Y}}^{\text{bid}}}{360} = \frac{1 + r_{\text{SW-3Y}}^{\text{bid}}}{1 - \Sigma_3^{\text{bid}}} - 1 = \frac{1 + \frac{(1{,}097 - 733) * 6.5024\%}{365}}{1 - 11.91\%} - 1$$

$$= 20.89\% \Rightarrow r_{\text{ZC-3Y}}^{\text{bid}} = 6.8548\%$$

Here $r_{SW\text{-}nY}$ describes the last flow of the swap, from September 15, 2000, to September 17, 2001 (733 – 366 = 367 days) in $r_{ZC\text{-}2Y}$ and from September 17, 2001, to September 16, 2002 (1,097 – 733 = 364 days) in $r_{ZC\text{-}3Y}$.

If we plot the market rates on one side and zero coupons on the other, we get a better picture of the relative yield curves and actual cost of money, as shown in Figures 4-12 and 4-13. Note in these charts that the zero-coupon yield curve is remarkably linear, which is not the case of the market curve.

FORWARD RATE AGREEMENTS

Consider a situation of relatively low interest rates in which, as a corporation, you know that you will need a significant amount of money in six months. You would like to secure a rate now, but borrowing now is inappropriate because you have no need for the cash. The solution is to enter an agreement in which you borrow money at a rate fixed today, but settlement is postponed for six months. This type of

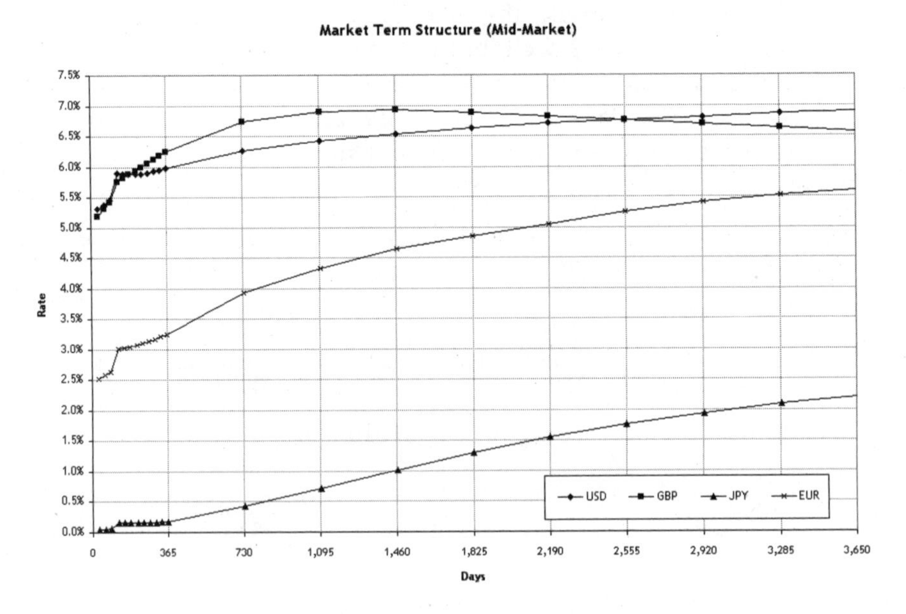

Figure 4-12 Zero-Coupon Curve, USD Chart

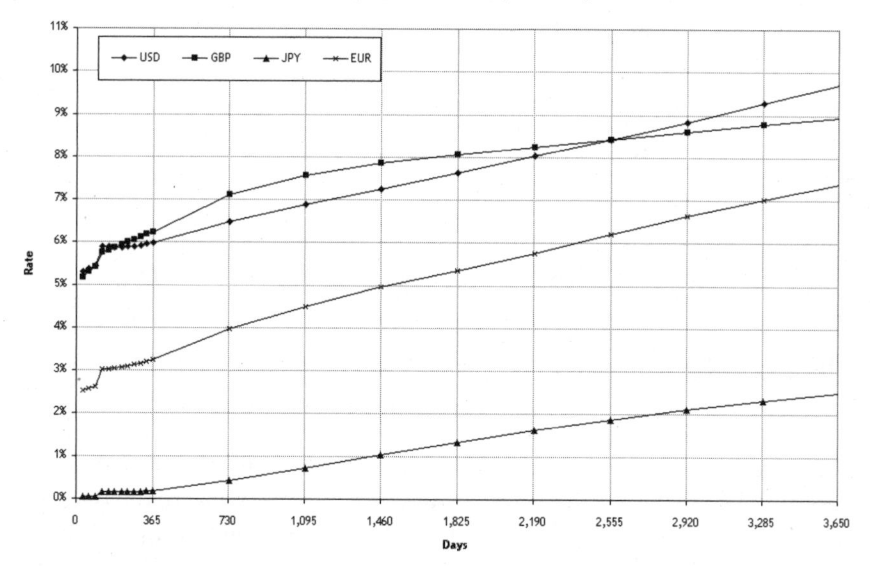

Figure 4-13 Zero-Coupon Curve, USD Chart

agreement is called a *forward rate agreement* (FRA). It is exactly a forward contract on interest rates.

Because the deal is actually done today, the negotiated rate has to be a function of the current term structure. Indeed, consider the diagram in Figure 4-14. Assume we borrow a \$1 zero coupon up to the maturity needed, at a rate r_M (these flows are represented in bold lines). We lend the same amount \$1 up to the settlement desired for the FRA, in our case six months from now at a rate r_S (these flows are represented in dashed lines). The net effect of these two operations is a wash: There is no flow today. On the date of the settlement of the FRA, we receive a payment equal to $\$1 * (1 + r_S)$, including the interest on the dollar lent. At maturity we still have to pay back $\$1 * (1 + r_M)$.

The net operation is exactly the FRA we are looking for. We receive $\$1 * (1 + r_S)$ on settlement and pay back $\$1 * (1 + r_M)$ on maturity. By definition, the rate for this composite operation is the FRA r_F:

$$(1 + r_S) \cdot (1 + r_F) = (1 + r_M) \quad \Rightarrow \quad r_F = \frac{1 + r_M}{1 + r_S} - 1 = \frac{r_M - r_S}{1 + r_S}$$

If we introduce the bid-ask spread, things get slightly more complex:

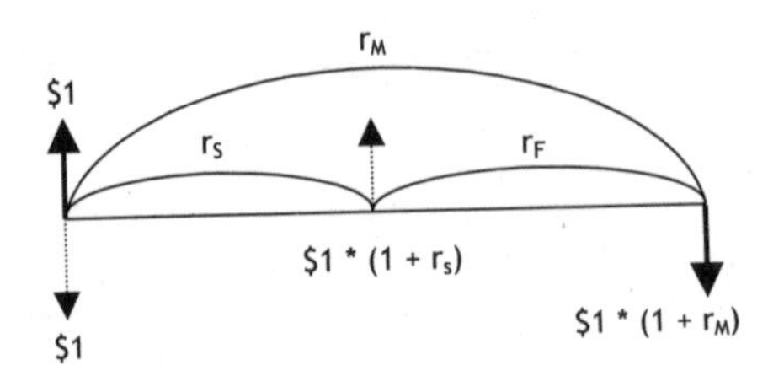

Figure 4-14 FRA

$$(1 + r_S^{\text{bid}}) \cdot (1 + r_F^{\text{ask}}) = (1 + r_M^{\text{ask}}) \quad \Rightarrow \quad r_F^{\text{ask}} = \frac{r_M^{\text{ask}} - r_S^{\text{bid}}}{1 + r_S^{\text{bid}}}$$

These equations are extremely useful as we will see shortly.

Beyond the algebra, it is interesting to investigate the relationship between the rate for a settlement now or postponed. Consider, for example, an identical operation settled today, in three and in six months. The different rates are shown in Table 4-8. Clearly the deferred settlement has an impact on the cost of financing, even more visible in Figure 4-15.

The effect visible here is a manifestation of a more general rule because forward rates depend essentially on the slope of the yield curve. In an upward-sloping environment, which is the case above, FRAs are more expensive than spot rates, and vice versa. If we took an hypothetical downward-sloping curve such as shown in Table 4-9, the FRA prices would be cheaper than the spot rates, as shown in Figure 4-16.

A final word about terminology. FRAs are quoted using a convention "$n \times m$": n indicates the settlement in months, m the expiry. A 2×6 FRA is a rate for a transaction of four months in two months. Table 4-10 is an example page of quotes from Bloomberg on September 13, 1999, U.S. dollars. Note that the quotes are ranked by maturity: From 1×4 to 9×12, all deposits are 3M; from 1×7 to 18×24, they are 6M; and so on, and that the bid-ask spread is 0.04 percent systematically.

TABLE 4-8

Maturity	End Date	Nb. Days	Regular Settlement, Mid	Settlement in 3M, Mid	Settlement in 6M, Mid
1MO	Oct. 15, 1999	30	5.32%	7.06%	5.74%
2MO	Nov. 15, 1999	61	5.38%	6.44%	5.75%
3MO	Dec. 15, 1999	91	5.45%	6.22%	5.76%
4MO	Jan. 17, 2000	124	5.90%	6.12%	5.81%
5MO	Feb. 15, 2000	153	5.89%	6.07%	5.87%
6MO	Mar. 15, 2000	182	5.88%	6.03%	5.91%

Note: For simplicity, the rates indicated are midmarket.

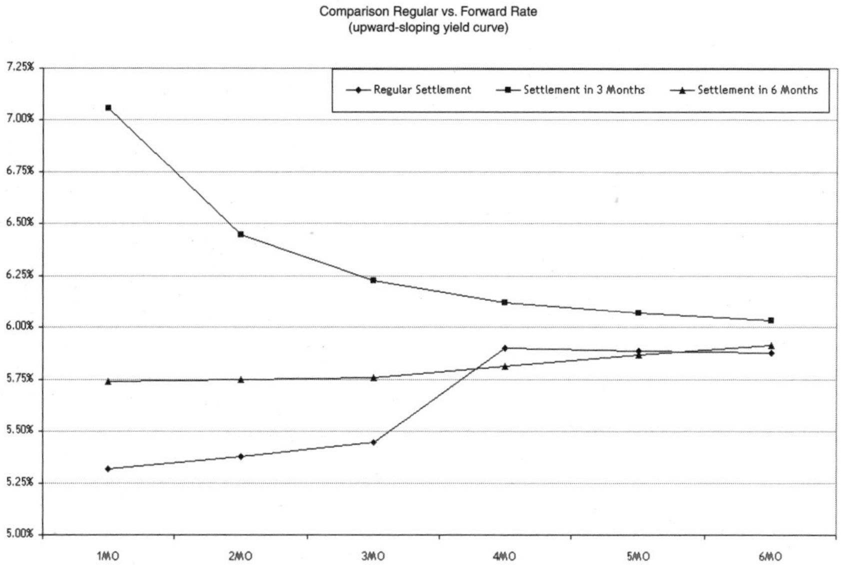

Comparison Regular vs. Forward Rate
(upward-sloping yield curve)

Figure 4-15 FRA versus Spot

SWAP PRICING

Variable Flows

The formula for forward rates will lead us to another interesting result, extremely useful to derive a general swap formula.[52] Consider a variable payment at some point in the future life of a swap. By definition, this flow is unknown because the rate has not been fixed as of today. It

TABLE 4-9

Maturity	End Date	Nb. Days	Regular Settlement, Mid	Settlement in 3M, Mid	Settlement in 6M, Mid
1MO	Oct. 15, 1999	30	5.99%	4.09%	5.25%
2MO	Nov. 15, 1999	61	5.93%	4.70%	5.24%
3MO	Dec. 15, 1999	91	5.86%	4.92%	5.23%
4MO	Jan. 17, 2000	124	5.40%	5.02%	5.17%
5MO	Feb. 15, 2000	153	5.42%	5.07%	5.12%
6MO	Mar. 15, 2000	182	5.42%	5.11%	5.07%

[52] We ignored the variable leg in the calculation of zero coupons, because we assumed swaps gave us access to money market rates. From now on we are more focused on swaps as stand-alone instruments, and we need to reinstate the variable leg in our analysis to price it accurately.

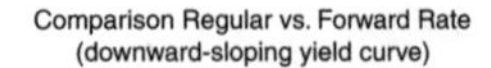

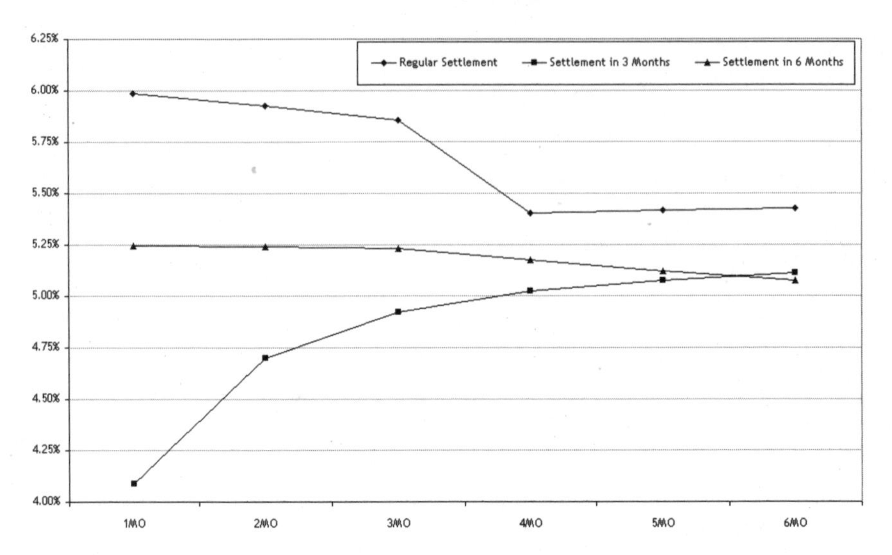

Figure 4-16 FRA versus Spot

is possible, however, to compute a forward rate based on today's term structure and to use it as an estimate of the unknown rate.

Figure 4-17 shows a variable payment on a notional of $1 at r_F, today's forward rate, used as a proxy for the unknown variable rate. The term r_M stands for the zero coupon from today to the payment date of the flow. The present value PV_1 of this variable flow is: $PV_1 = r_F/(1 + r_M)$. Now consider the situation in Figure 4-18, in

TABLE 4-10

Maturity	Bid-Ask	Maturity	Bid-Ask
1 × 4	5.88/92	3 × 9	5.93/97
2 × 5	5.86/90	4 × 10	5.86/90
3 × 6	5.88/92	5 × 11	5.91/95
4 × 7	5.70/74	6 × 12	5.99/03
5 × 8	5.80/84	12 × 18	6.40/44
6 × 9	5.85/89	18 × 24	6.55/59
7 × 10	5.92/96	1 × 10	5.89/93
8 × 11	5.99/03	2 × 11	5.95/99
9 × 12	6.08/12	3 × 12	6.02/06
1 × 7	5.89/93	6 × 18	6.30/34
2 × 8	5.91/95	12 × 24	6.58/62

(*Source*: Compiled by author from Bloomberg data.)

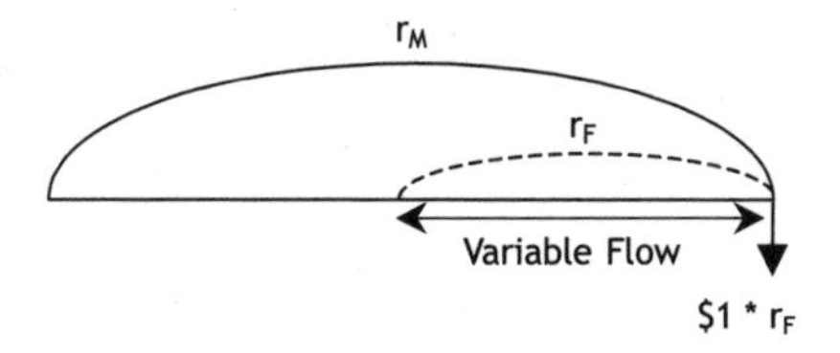

Figure 4-17 Swap Variable

which two equal flows of \$1 are set at the beginning and end of the period on which the same variable flow accrues.

The present value PV_2 of these flows is $PV_2 = \$1/(1 + r_S) - \$1/(1 + r_M)$, where r_S stands for the zero coupon up to the beginning of the period. Considering the definition of r_F, it follows that:

$$\begin{aligned} PV_1 &= \frac{r_F}{1 + r_M} = \frac{r_M - r_S}{(1 + r_S) \cdot (1 + r_M)} = \frac{(1 + r_M) - (1 + r_S)}{(1 + r_S) \cdot (1 + r_M)} \\ &= \frac{1}{1 + r_S} - \frac{1}{1 + r_M} = PV_2 \end{aligned}$$

This result can be stated in the following manner: *An unknown variable-rate payment can be estimated as of today by a set of two flows of notional of opposite direction respectively at the beginning and end of the variable accrual period.*

Consider now two successive variable payments, as shown in Figure 4-19.

And operate the above transformation, as shown in Figure 4-20. The \$1 interim flows cancel out, and we are left with only the *first and last of these flows to consider*. In other words, whatever the variable schedule is, we can accurately price it if we include two flows of notional of opposite directions at the beginning and at the end of the sequence.

Pricing

From this point a generic pricing formula will be straightforward. A swap is a succession of flows, some of them fixed, some of them variable. *Its value today is therefore the net present value of all these flows.*

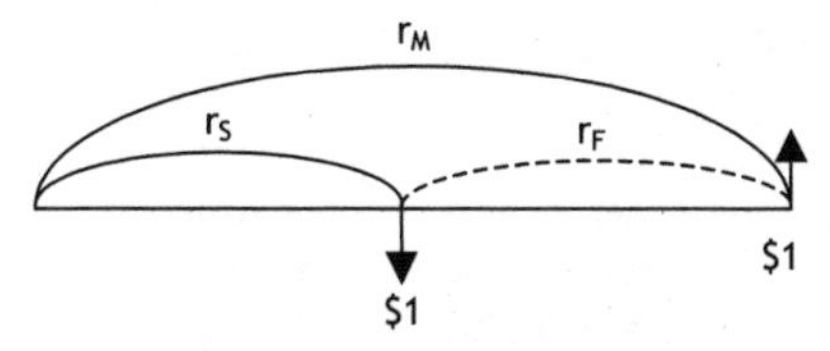

Figure 4-18 Swap Variable Nominal

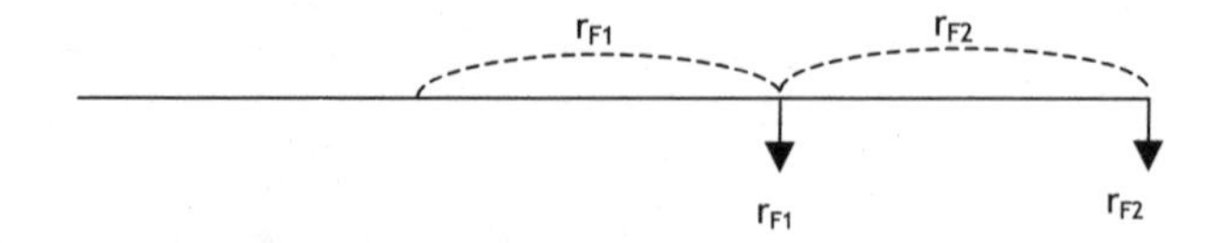

Figure 4-19 Swap Variable Nominal

Consider as an illustration the two-year annual swap with a six-month variable schedule on a $1 notional, as shown in Figure 4-21.

Let r_{vi} stand for the—unknown—variable rates, r_1 and r_2 for the zero coupon up to the payment dates of fixed flows, and r_{SW} for the fixed rate of the swap.[53] Next we operate the transformation of the variable leg, and we get rid of interim variable flows, as shown in Figure 4-22. We are left with four flows in total, two annual resulting from the fixed leg, two at each end resulting from the collapse of the variable leg. The value V of this swap is therefore:

$$V = \left(\frac{r_{\mathrm{SW}}}{1+r_1} + \frac{r_{\mathrm{SW}}}{1+r_2}\right) + \left(\frac{1}{1+r_2} - 1\right) = \left(\frac{r_{\mathrm{SW}}}{1+r_1}\right) + \left(\frac{r_{\mathrm{SW}}}{1+r_2}\right) - \left(\frac{r_2}{1+r_2}\right)$$

The first two terms in parentheses is the valuation of fixed payments, and the third represents the two notional flows resulting from the aggregation of the variable schedule.

From there the generic formula for a swap of notional N, fixed annual rate r_{SW}, and duration n years is one step away:

$$V = N \cdot \left[r_{\mathrm{SW}} \cdot \sum_{i=1}^{n} \frac{1}{1+r_i} - \frac{r_n}{1+r_n} \right]$$

where r_i stands for the zero-coupon rates at each fixed payment date.

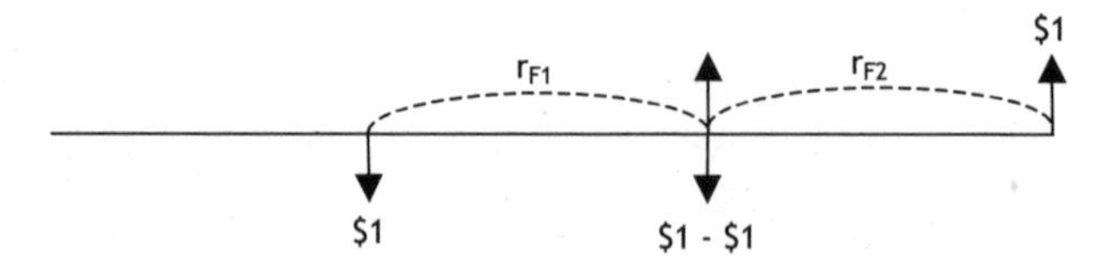

Figure 4-20 Swap Variable Nominal

[53] We implicitly assume here that r_1 and r_2 are midmarket rates; therefore, we get a midmarket swap rate. It is relatively straightforward to price independently the bid and ask sides of the swap, so we don't detail all calculations and focus on midmarket for simplicity.

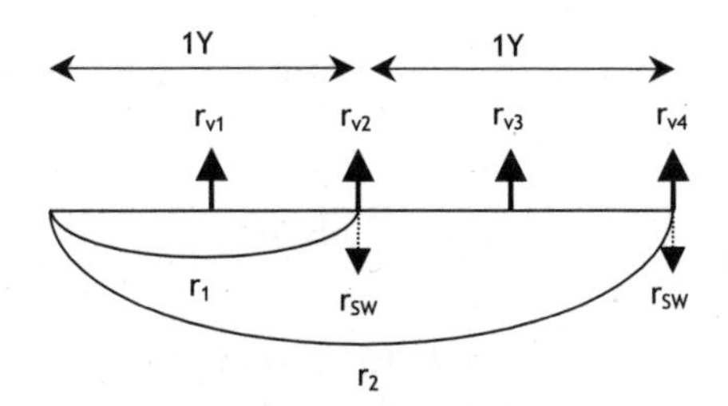

Figure 4-21 Swap Pricing

Several remarks can be made regarding this formula:

- Semiannual swaps are slightly more complex, but the principle remains the same. Indeed, the formula remains the same if we stipulate that r_i stands for the zero coupon up to the ith fixed payment, whenever that payment occurs. There is no need to consider even regular payments on either the fixed or variable side. The formula above applies to any type of schedule, regardless of its frequency or regularity, as long as zero coupons and date calculations are handled properly.[54]
- The term $1/(1 + r_i)$ is trickier than it looks: Because of our choice to suppress time fractions, we did not care about date calculations. The numerator 1 is not equal to the numeral 1; it is in fact a succession of $n_i/360$ where n_i stands for the number of days between two successive fixed payments. By the same token, the denominator $1 + r_i$ is in fact $1 + (d_i/360) \cdot r_i$, where d_i there stands for the number of days between today and the successive fixed payment dates.
- This result can be used in a different way: Given a schedule of fixed and variable payments, we can price the structure and extract a value V. Conversely, if we force V to be zero, we get the *fair value* of

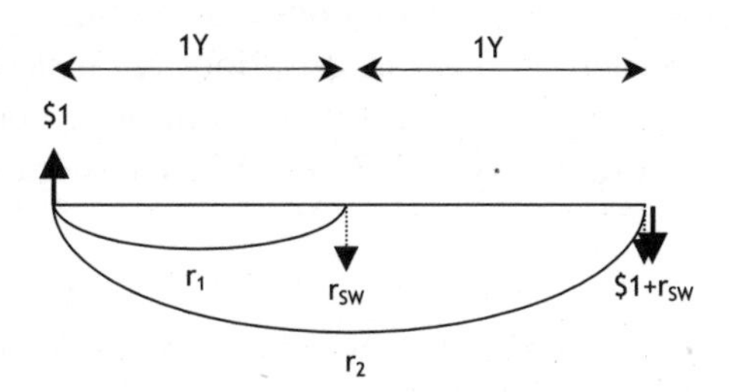

Figure 4-22 Swap Pricing

[54] The same exact formula can be used for a forward swap—that is, a swap negotiated today but whose accrual period starts at some point in the future.

this structure—that is, the swap rate that best reflects current market conditions:

$$r_{SW} = \frac{1}{\Sigma_n} \cdot \left(\frac{r_n}{1+r_n}\right) \qquad \text{where} \quad \Sigma_n = \sum_{i=1}^{n} \frac{1}{1+r_n}$$

At this point we know how to extract zero coupons from swaps and conversely price standard and nonstandard swaps from zero coupons. As a consistency check, it is always possible to reprice a swap quoted in the market with the prevalent zero coupons, which we might do just to verify that the price we compute is in line with the market. If it is not, it may very well be there is an arbitrage opportunity, although a calculation error is much more likely because in general, swap and cash markets are very closely integrated.

SHORT-TERM INTEREST RATE FUTURES CONTRACTS

Definitions

A short-term interest rate futures contract—commonly labeled a *eurofuture*—is a listed forward rate agreement.[55] By trading a contract, each party enters a forward money market transaction at a rate set by the price of the futures contract. We know from the previous chapter the defining characteristics of a listed futures contract:

- As financial futures, eurofutures are cash settled. No security is delivered on expiry.
- As listed products, they are standardized with respect to the terms of the underlying money market operation. Most eurofutures are three-month FRAs, but some are one-month or one-year.[56] A three-month FRA is *always* 90 days in duration, regardless of the actual number of calendar days in a full three-month period. The time fraction is therefore always 90/360 = ¼. The notional amount of

[55] The market terminology with regard to individual contracts depends on the underlying currency. Eurodollar contracts are futures on the U.S. dollar, whereas eurosterling and euroyen are respectively contracts on the British pound and Japanese yen. The exception is the euro, for which the contract has been named *euribor*.

[56] Eurodollar contracts are mostly three-month FRAs, but a one-month contract is also listed on the Chicago Mercantile Exchange. Similarly for the euroyen in Tokyo, the most liquid futures contract is a three-month FRA, but a one-year FRA is also listed.

the FRA is fixed for each contract—for example, \$1,000,000 for eurodollars, ¥100,000,000 for euroyen, and £500,000 for eurosterling.

- Eurofutures are quoted as 100 minus the rate of the FRA. For example, if the FRA is 5 percent, the price of the futures contract is $100 - 5 = 95$.
- The tick value is usually 0.005, but 0.01 and 0.0025 also exist.
- The expiry cycle is usually quarterly—March, June, September, and December. Most exchanges list in addition interim maturities—for example, monthly contracts—until the second quarterly expiry.[57]
- As listed products, they are subject to margin requirements and margin calls.
- The final settlement, often referred to as the SQ by analogy with index futures, is often the current LIBOR.[58]
- Eurofutures in general are wildly and aggressively cross listed, which was not the case for index futures, for example. In particular, the most liquid contracts, such as eurodollar, euroyen, and euribor, are listed on multiple exchanges in the United States, Europe, and Asia.

The only characteristic we have not included is the point value, which is here a consequence of the definition of the contracts, not an arbitrary figure. In order to illustrate this point, consider the diagram in Figure 4-23, which represents the FRA underlying a eurofuture. By definition, the forward cash transaction starts upon expiry of the futures contract and accrues typically for three months. Its price is r_F, which is 100 minus the price at which the future has been traded. If the FRA transaction were actually taking place, two flows equal to the notional of the

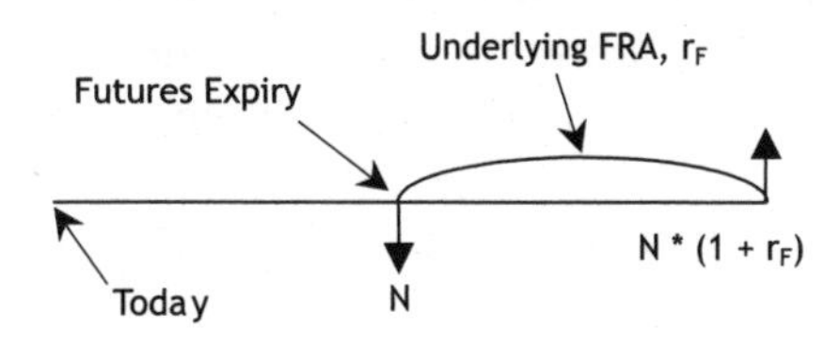

Figure 4-23 Eurofuture

[57] If we are today in January 2000, the first two quarterly futures are March and June, but January, February, April, and May are also listed. When March expires, two more monthly contracts are listed—July and August—to complete the monthly cycle until the second quarterly expiry again. Note that the interim contracts are also three-month FRAs.

[58] Therefore, eurofutures, like swaps, are not symmetrical as well with respect to LIBID-LIBOR spreads.

contract, N, would be exchanged at the beginning and at the end of the FRA. However, because the futures is cash settled at expiry, the notional is never exchanged, and instead r_F is compared to the LIBOR on expiry, and the difference is settled in cash.

Back to the point value: Consider a euroyen contract quoted at 99.70. If the tick size is 0.01, each move in price equal to the tick size modifies the FRA rate by 0.01 percent. The FRA is a three-month transaction on ¥100,000,000 at 100 – 99.70 = 0.30 percent by definition, thus a move of 0.01 percent results in a change in value equal to ¥100,000,000 * 0.01 percent * (90/360) = ¥2,500. Each move of 0.01 in the quoted price of the futures contract results in a variation of ¥2,500 in the value of the underlying position. If upon expiry the three-month LIBOR is 0.35 percent, the difference 0.35 percent – 0.30 percent = 5 ticks results in a total variation of 5 * ¥2,500 = ¥12,500 in the value of the position. ¥12,500 are therefore exchanged between the two transacting parties, and there is no additional flow afterwards. As a result of this definition, a *buyer* of the future is exposed on interest rates going *up* because a rise in the rates implies a drop in the future price. Conversely, sellers benefit from an increase in the short-term rates.

Fed Fund Futures

Fed fund futures are an interesting variant of eurofutures. Their periodicity is monthly, and they are settled on the last day of each month on the simple arithmetic average of the effective fed fund rate for that month. For example, on the fifteenth of a given month, because all fed fund rates are already known from the beginning of the month, 50 percent of the final settlement rate of the futures contract is also known. Obviously the futures contract loses its liquidity toward the end of each month because the averaging makes it very unlikely that a move just before expiry will significantly change the settlement value.

Markets

Despite the seemingly complex mechanics, eurofutures are extremely simple and powerful instruments. They have been designed with the same inverse relationship with respect to interest rates that bonds have, but they are much simpler to trade, and indeed they have become over the years the most liquid futures contracts across all categories. Figure 4-24, for example, shows the open interest of the five biggest currency markets from 1994 to 1999.

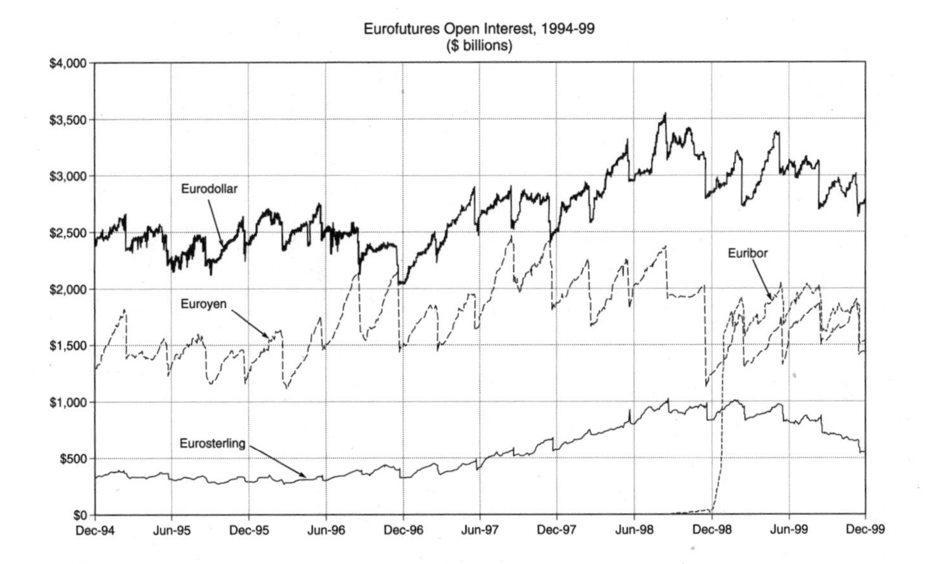

Figure 4-24 Eurofuture Open Interest
(*Source*: Compiled by author from Datastream data.)
Note: Data unavailable for EURIBOR prior to January 1999. Data include all major exchanges for a given contract. For euroyen, the LIBOR and TIBOR contracts have been aggregated to reflect the overall amount of activity on Japanese interest rates.

As one would expect, eurodollars are clearly ahead in terms of market activity, with euroyen and euribor contracts hovering much lower. Note the spikes visible for each quarterly expiry, a phenomenon that was present already with index futures and to which we will come back later.

Cross Listings

As we mentioned earlier, cross listing is widespread with eurofutures. Considering the typical turnover in all these contracts, competition is fierce to attract volume. Table 4-11 presents an overview of the cross-listing network.

Interestingly, despite identical characteristics, different exchanges have adopted significantly different margin requirements. Often these discrepancies have resulted in liquidity flowing to the cheapest market.[59]

---

[59] With respect to euroyen contracts, the LIFFE and TIFFE have implemented a clearing agreement in which all trades on the LIFFE are automatically cleared on the TIFFE. Therefore, historical data for the LIFFE euroyen show a trading volume and open interest at zero because both are automatically aggregated in the statistics reported by the TIFFE.

TABLE 4-11

Contract	Listed	Notional	Tick	Cycle	Point Value[a]	Special Quotation	Final Settlement	Initial Margin
Fed fund	CME	$3,000,000	0.005	Monthly	$25	Simple average	Last day of month	$135
Fed fund	CBOT	$5,000,000	0.005	Monthly	$41.66[b]	Simple average	Last day of month	$270
Eurodollar	CME SIMEX	$1,000,000	0.0025 (CME) 0.005 (SIMEX)	Quarterly	$25	3M LIBOR	Third Wednesday	$675
TIBOR Euroyen	TIFFE SIMEX LIFFE CME	¥100,000,000	0.005	Quarterly	¥2,500	3M TIBOR	Third Wednesday	¥16,200 (CME) ¥23,625 (TIFFE) ¥18,900 (SIMEX)
LIBOR Euroyen	TIFFE SIMEX LIFFE CME	¥100,000,000	0.005 (LIFFE, CME, SIMEX) 0.01 (TIFFE)	Quarterly	¥2,500	3M LIBOR	Third Wednesday	¥37,800 (CME) ¥80,000 (TIFFE) ¥10,800 (SIMEX)
Eurosterling	TIFFE	£500,000	0.005	Quarterly	£12.5	3M LIBOR	Third Wednesday	£350
EURIBOR	EUREX MATIF LIFFE	€1,000,000	0.002 (MATIF) 0.005 (EUREX, LIFFE)	Quarterly	€25	3M EURIBOR	Third Wednesday	€500 (MATIF, LIFFE) €750 (EUREX)
Euro LIBOR	LIFFE	€1,000,000	0.005	Quarterly	€25	3M LIBOR	Third Wednesday	€500

Note: Chicago Mercantile Exchange; CBOT, Chicago Board of Trade; SIMEX, Singapore International Monetary Exchange; LIFFE London International Financial Futures Exchange; TIFFE, Tokyo International Financial Futures Exchange; MATIF, Marché à Terme International de France; and EUREX, European Exchange.

[a] For a move of 0.01 point in the quoted price.

[b] The notional FRA is always 30 days long; therefore, the point value is $5,000,000 * 30/360 * 0.01 percent = $41.66.

(*Source*: Compiled by author from Bloomberg data.)

As we did earlier with the Nikkei 225 futures contract, it is quite instructive to look at the market share of SIMEX versus TIFFE with respect to euroyen open interest, and at the difference in price between the two markets,[60] as shown in Figures 4-25 and 4-26. The SIMEX seems to have captured over the years a reasonable market share, around 25 percent similar to that of the Nikkei contract. At the same time, both euroyen contracts appear to be trading relatively closely, although differences are clearly apparent from time to time. Naturally it remains to be seen if these differences will create profitable arbitrage opportunities.

Yield Curves and Eurofutures

Besides swaps, eurofutures are the second-best source of information to extract a zero-coupon yield curve. Their liquidity makes them

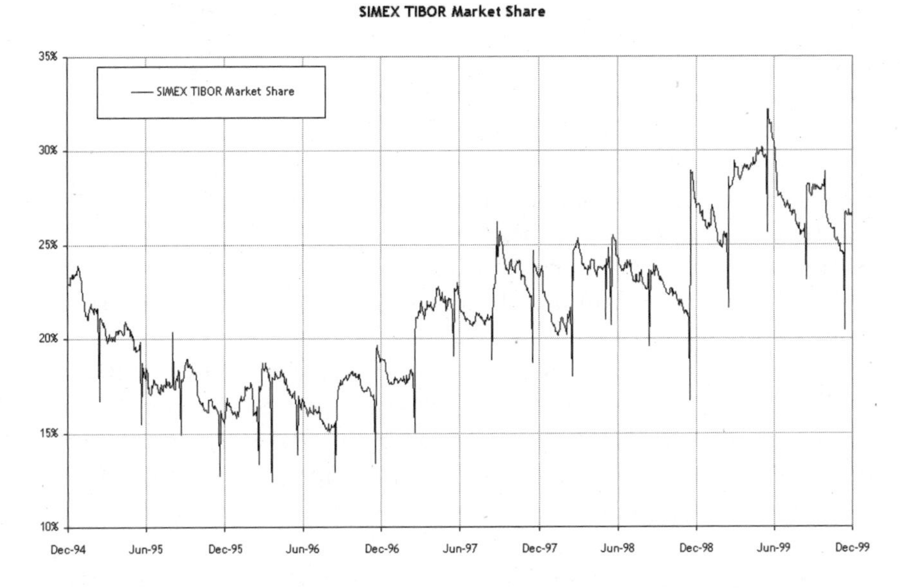

Figure 4-25 TIBOR Market Share
(*Source*: Compiled by author from Datastream data.)

---

[60] Eurodollars are overwhelmingly traded in the United States (≈ 97 percent in volume over 1994 through 1999), whereas the biggest share of EURIBOR is traded in London (≈ 88 percent over 1999). SIMEX/TIFFE is therefore the only example of a sizable repartition of liquidity.

The charts show respectively the open interest on SIMEX as a percentage of the total open interest (SIMEX + TIFFE), and the difference closing price of SIMEX minus the closing price of TIFFE.

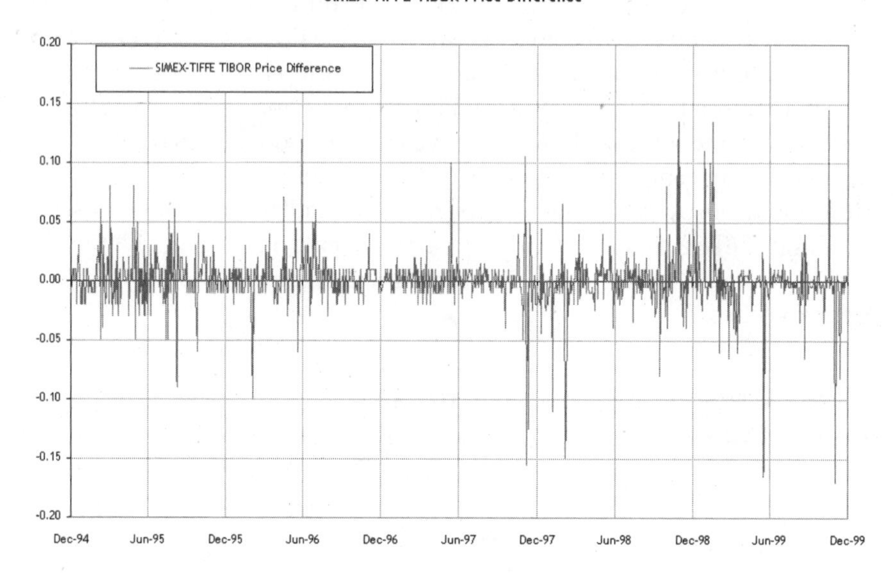

Figure 4-26 TIBOR Price Difference
(*Source*: Compiled by author from Datastream data.)

ideal in terms of informational content, and the overall calculation is much simpler than for swaps. There is a small caveat, however: Far maturities tend to be much less liquid; therefore, medium- to long-term swaps do remain the best option to access long-term zero coupons.

Transforming euro rates into zero-coupon rates is based on a bootstrap method. We consider all euro contracts to be chained together, and because we know each individual rate, we can compound these rates and extract zero coupons for each future maturity. From there, a simple linear interpolation leads to the standard yield curve.

As an illustration, consider the spreadsheet in Table 4-12 with market prices of eurodollar contracts. Each contract has a final settlement on the second Wednesday of March, June, September, and December. Settlement convention is $T + 2$; therefore, the March 2000 contract expiring on March 15, 2000, trades until March 13, 2000. From there we apply the following calculations:

- The bid and ask shaded prices are market prices. Three-month rates are deducted from the definition: 100− price. Because of the subtraction, a "bid" price on the future is an "ask" price on the rate. We

TABLE 4-12

(Today: February 15, 2000. Settlement: February 17, 2000.)

Expiry	Settlement	Price Bid	Price Ask	Rate Bid	Rate Ask	Days	From Today	Factor Bid	Factor Ask	ZC Bid	ZC Ask
Mar. 13, 2000	Mar. 15, 2000	93.8400	93.8450	6.155%	6.160%		27	1.00418	1.00428	5.575%	5.700%
Jun. 19, 2000	Jun. 21, 2000	93.4350	93.4400	6.560%	6.565%	98	125	1.02101	1.02112	6.050%	6.081%
Sep. 18, 2000	Sep. 20, 2000	93.1700	93.1750	6.825%	6.830%	91	216	1.03794	1.03806	6.323%	6.343%
Dec. 18, 2000	Dec. 20, 2000	92.9550	92.9600	7.040%	7.045%	91	307	1.05584	1.05598	6.548%	6.565%
Mar. 19, 2001	Mar. 21, 2001	92.8650	92.8700	7.130%	7.135%	91	398	1.07463	1.07479	6.751%	6.765%
Jun. 18, 2001	Jun. 20, 2001	92.7650	92.7750	7.225%	7.235%	91	489	1.09400	1.09417	6.920%	6.933%
Sep. 17, 2001	Sep. 19, 2001	92.7100	92.7200	7.280%	7.290%	91	580	1.11398	1.11418	7.075%	7.087%
Dec. 17, 2001	Dec. 19, 2001	92.6350	92.6450	7.355%	7.365%	91	671	1.13448	1.13471	7.215%	7.228%
Mar. 18, 2002	Mar. 20, 2002					91	762	1.15557	1.15584	7.350%	7.363%

consider these rates to be actual/360 and make the approximation that they are valid for the full period between each settlement date.[61]

- The first line of ZC rates are deducted from the prevalent short-term money-market rates, typically the LIBOR. We need them because we have to have a rate up to the first contract's settlement.
- "Days" represents the number of days from contract settlement date to contract settlement date. "From today" refers to the number of days from today's settlement date, February 17, 2000, to each contract's settlement date.
- "Factor bid" ("factor ask") represents the compounding factor. For example, for the June expiry, we have to compound 5.575 percent (5.7 percent) on 27 days, 6.155 percent (6.16 percent) on 98 days, according to the diagram in Figure 4-27.

$$F_1^{\text{bid}} = \left(1 + \frac{27 * 5.575\%}{360}\right) \cdot \left(1 + \frac{98 * 6.155\%}{360}\right) = 1.02101$$

$$F_1^{\text{ask}} = \left(1 + \frac{27 * 5.7\%}{360}\right) \cdot \left(1 + \frac{98 * 6.16\%}{360}\right) = 1.02112$$

Similarly:

$$F_2^{\text{bid}} = \left(1 + \frac{27 * 5.575\%}{360}\right) \cdot \left(1 + \frac{98 * 6.155\%}{360}\right) \cdot \left(1 + \frac{91 * 6.56\%}{360}\right) = 1.03794$$

$$F_2^{\text{ask}} = \left(1 + \frac{27 * 5.7\%}{360}\right) \cdot \left(1 + \frac{98 * 6.16\%}{360}\right) \cdot \left(1 + \frac{91 * 6.565\%}{360}\right) = 1.03806$$

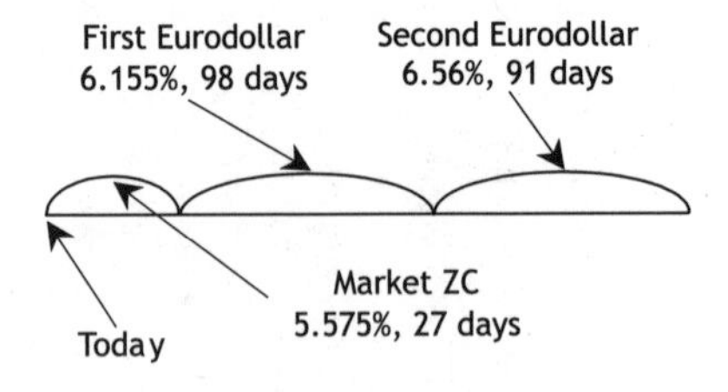

Figure 4-27 ZC from Euro

[61] This is an approximation because rigorously speaking, three-month eurodollars are exactly 90 days, no more, no less. Here we consider that the rate embedded, for example, in the March contract is valid from March 15, 2000, to June 21, 2000—that is, 98 days.

- The ZC is then extracted from the compound factor, taking into account the total number of days:

$$r^{\text{bid}}_{\text{ZC-1st euro}} = (1.02101 - 1) * \left(\frac{360}{27 + 98}\right) = 6.05\%$$

$$r^{\text{ask}}_{\text{ZC-1st euro}} = (1.02112 - 1) * \left(\frac{360}{27 + 98}\right) = 6.081\%$$

$$r^{\text{bid}}_{\text{ZC-2nd euro}} = (1.03794 - 1) * \left(\frac{360}{27 + 98 + 91}\right) = 6.323\%$$

$$r^{\text{ask}}_{\text{Z -2nd euro}} = (1.03806 - 1) * \left(\frac{360}{27 + 98 + 91}\right) = 6.343\%$$

From there we obtain a first zero-coupon yield curve based on euro-futures expiries. The next step is to translate this curve into a standard set of expiries—1M, 2M, 6M, and so on—through a linear interpolation, as shown in Figure 4-28. For example, we know the rate for 27 days (5.574 percent/5.70 percent) and 125 days (6.05 percent/6.081 percent); therefore, it is easy to average them to obtain the rate for 29 days, which is exactly one month from today (February 17, 2000, to March 17, 2000):

$$r^{\text{bid}}_{\text{ZC-1M}} = \frac{(125 - 29) * 5.575\% + (29 - 27) * 6.05\%}{125 - 27} = 5.585\%$$

$$r^{\text{ask}}_{\text{ZC-1M}} = \frac{(125 - 29) * 5.70\% + (29 - 27) * 6.081\%}{125 - 27} = 5.708\%$$

and for two months:

$$r^{\text{bid}}_{\text{ZC-2M}} = \frac{(125 - 60) * 5.575\% + (60 - 27) * 6.05\%}{125 - 27} = 5.735\%$$

$$r^{\text{ask}}_{\text{ZC-2M}} = \frac{(125 - 60) * 5.70\% + (60 - 27) * 6.081\%}{125 - 27} = 5.828\%$$

Applying the interpolation to all maturities leads to the result shown in Table 4-13. The only difficulty in that approach is that we need four

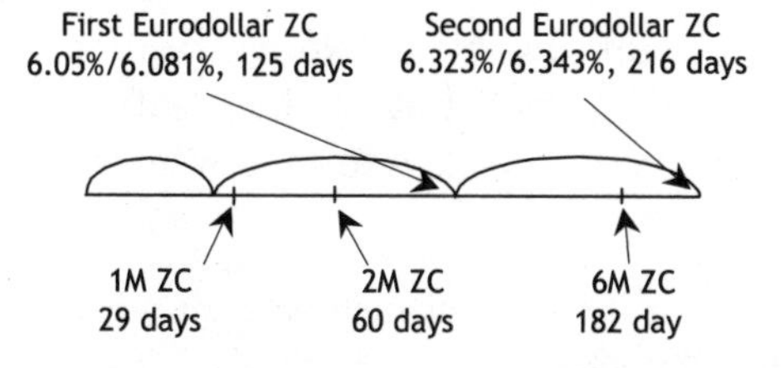

Figure 4-28 ZC from Euro

TABLE 4-13

Expiry	Settlement	Days	ZC Bid	ZC Ask
1M	Mar. 17, 2000	29	5.585%	5.708%
2M	Apr. 17, 2000	60	5.735%	5.828%
3M	May 17, 2000	90	5.880%	5.945%
6M	Aug. 17, 2000	182	6.221%	6.246%
9M	Nov. 17, 2000	274	6.467%	6.485%
1Y	Feb. 19, 2001	368	6.684%	6.699%
2Y	Feb. 18, 2002	732	7.305%	7.318%

eurofutures for each year we look ahead because eurofutures "price" rates three months at a time. For eurodollars this is a minor issue because more than 40 expiries trade at any given time; therefore, we can accurately extract zero coupons for the next 10 years. For other currencies, however, euro contracts are not listed so far in the future or they are too illiquid to really be indicative, and in that case, swaps remain the only reliable source of information. Generally speaking the yield curve deducted from eurofutures should be very close to that extracted from swap rates.

Eurofutures Basis

As regular futures, euro contracts trade at a price different from the price of their underlying. It is particularly interesting to examine closely the magnitude and sign of this difference, an exercise we will practice with index futures also when considering index arbitrage. In Figures 4-29 through 4-32 are, for example, the differences between three-month contracts and the corresponding short-term rates for eurodollar, euroyen, eurosterling, and euribor futures[62]:

Despite many particularities relative to each individual market, in general a negative basis tends to be associated with decreasing interest rates and vice versa. This situation indicates that the futures contract is widely used by market participants as a proxy for how the current rates will evolve in the future, definitely something to keep in mind when trading interest rate products. Note also that the existence of a liquid cash and futures market potentially creates arbitrage opportunities for whoever has cheap access to money markets.

[62] The term *basis* in the charts refers to the difference between the rate implied by the future price minus the prevalent three-month rate. It is positive if the FRA implied by the future is higher than the current money market rate, and negative otherwise.

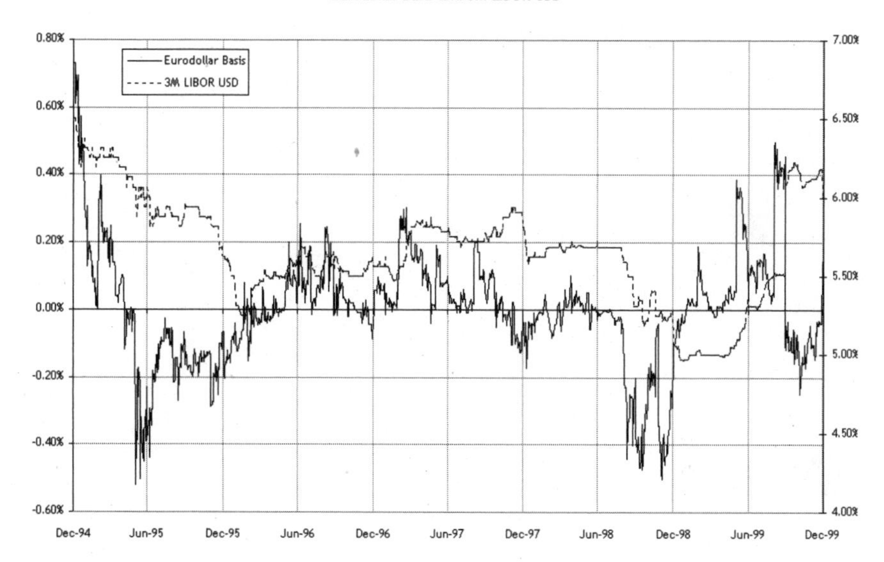

Figure 4-29 Euro Basis, USD
(*Source*: Compiled by author from Datastream data.)

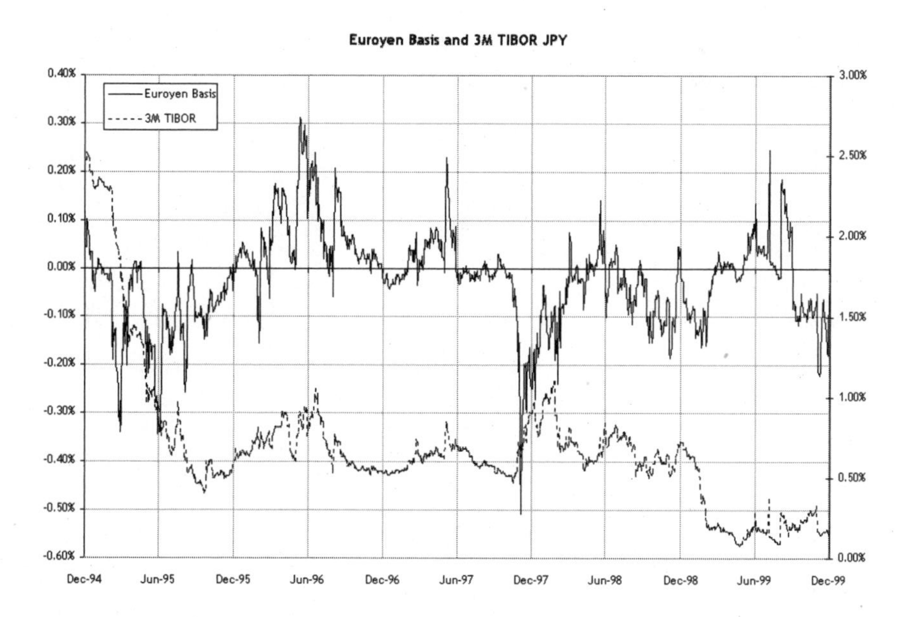

Figure 4-30 Euro Basis, YEN
(*Source*: Compiled by author from Datastream data.)

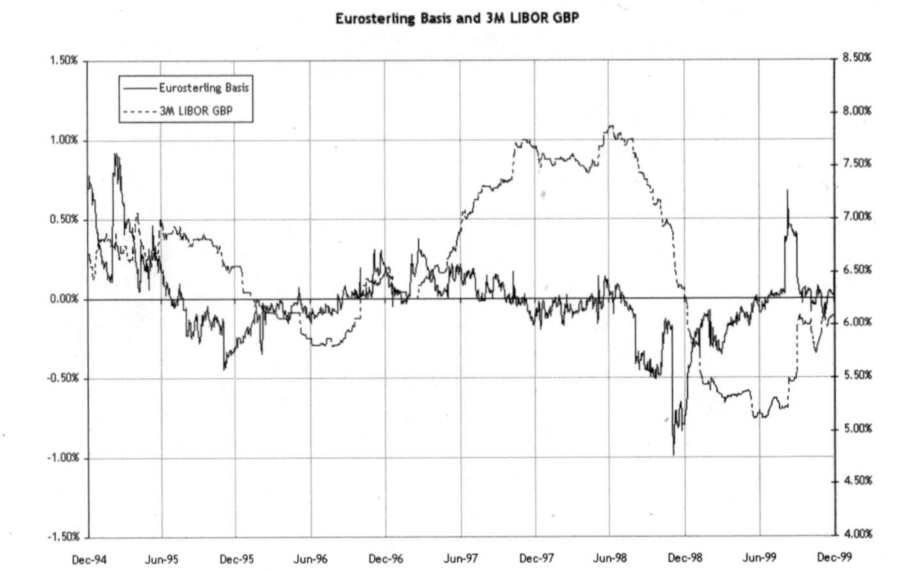

Figure 4-31 Euro Basis, GBP
(*Source*: Compiled by author from Datastream data.)

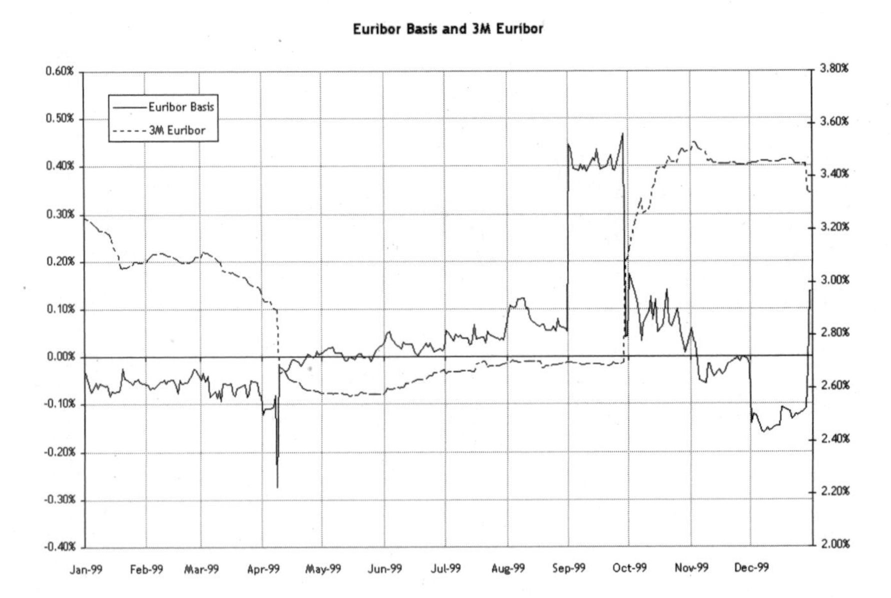

Figure 4-32 Euro Basis, EUR
(*Source*: Compiled by author from Datastream data.)

Eurofutures and Interest Rate Exposure

We mentioned earlier that eurofutures were often used as complements to swaps to manage interest rate exposure. In practice, this is done by trading a euro "strip"—that is, a series of chained contracts.[63]

Consider, for example, an investor who needs to borrow cash regularly over a given period and wants to be protected against an increase in short-term rates. The investor needs to enter into a transaction that will turn profitable if rates increase, offsetting the additional interest expense incurred on the loans. We saw earlier that a short position in eurodollars would behave exactly this way; therefore, the investor has the option to sell eurodollar futures—if the original exposure is in dollars. For example, if the rolling nominal at risk is $20,000,000 every three months for a total period of one year, 20 contracts need to be sold of the four nearest maturities to create an offsetting futures position[64] as shown in Figure 4-33.

Generally speaking, buying or selling a series of consecutive eurofutures protects against a decline or rise in interest rates for a period equal to the total period covered from the first to the last contract. To see this more clearly, consider, for example, the first contract. If it were traded at 95.00, the implied FRA would be 5 percent. Now suppose that the actual LIBOR is 5.5 percent upon expiration of the future. The final settlement price is 100 – 5.5 = 94.50. Assuming we were short at 95.00, the 0.5 percent difference in rate would generate a gain of 0.50 points per contract. If we borrow at the spot rate of 5.5 percent, this gain means that the effective borrowing cost is actually 5.5 percent–0.5

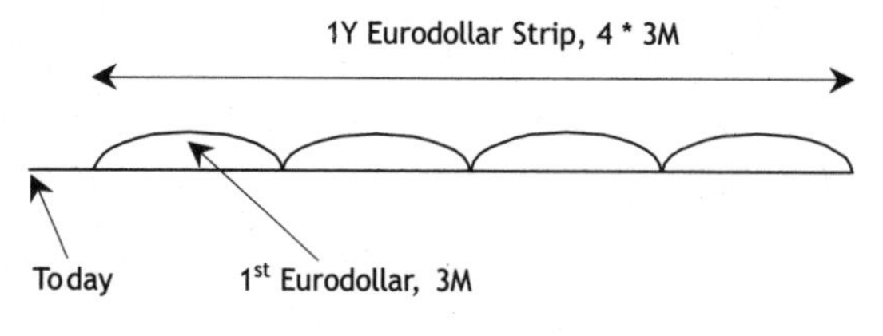

Figure 4-33 Euro Strip

[63] The terminology may be different in some cases. For example, the CME lists eurodollar "bundles" and "packs," which are essentially strips. Bundles are strips of an integer number of year—1, 2, 3, 5, 7, 10—whereas packs are strips of only four consecutive contracts. See the CME Web site for more details.

[64] In reality, the calculation would be more complex because there must be several adjustments to account for the mismatch in dates between the rolling loans and the two nearest future expiries.

percent = 5 percent, which was the original implied rate when the futures contract was sold. Applying the same reasoning to each individual contract shows that the rate for the entire period was indeed set upon selling the strip.

This strip protection covers a period of one year and therefore hedges a one-year rate. Furthermore, because it starts with the first maturity, which is typically less than three months away, the protection is effective against the current one-year rate because any move today in that rate would be reflected in the prices of the futures contracts. In contrast, if we started the strip with a contract in one year, we would still protect a one-year rate but one year away. In essence, the rate hedged is not the spot rate anymore but the FRA, as shown in Figure 4-34. Naturally there are many other variations possible using eurofutures, which is why these contracts are so popular and so widely used.

Eurofutures and Swaps

Consider again a regular one-year euro strip, as shown in Figure 4-35. Assume we sell the strip and that at each and every expiry, we enter a borrowing transaction equal to the notional of the strip. The result is a one-year money market operation at a rate fixed by the compounded implied rates of each contract.

This operating mode—regular borrowing at market rates—is exactly equivalent to borrowing liquidity through a swap with a variable leg matching the eurofutures schedule. In terms of risk and exposure, swaps and eurofutures strips are therefore *exactly equivalent*, but they differ in the implementation of this exposure. Because swaps have two legs, they are priced such that the net present value of all flows is zero at the time of the transaction.[65] A eurofutures strip, on the other

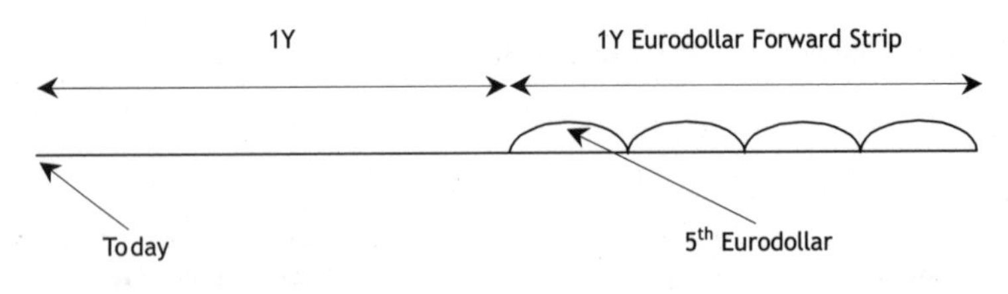

Figure 4-34 Euro Strip

[65] Note that this is generally true of all derivative contracts because their pricing is by definition based on an absolute convergence—that is, an arbitrage-free situation.

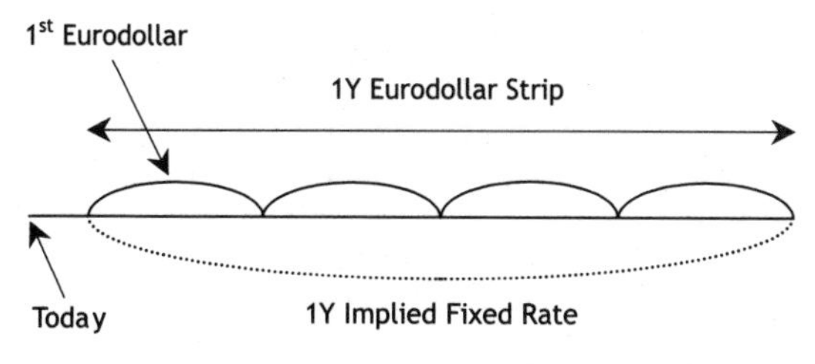

Figure 4-35 Euro Strip

hand, is not a two-legged product, so its net present value at initiation is equal to the borrowing cost over the period—that is, the implied fixed rate from the compounding of each individual contract.

Because of the differences between the swap and eurofutures markets, notably the fact that one is an OTC market while the other is listed, one may be more appropriate to trade than the other depending on the particular circumstances and on the nature of the transacting institution. However, from a functional perspective, they are entirely equivalent even though the actual flows resulting from each are different.

FOREIGN-EXCHANGE SWAPS AND FORWARDS

Definitions

Foreign exchange swaps are exactly identical in principle to interest rate swaps, but each leg is pegged to a different currency. For example, a dollar/yen swap is a transaction in which one party agrees to pay a given interest rate on a dollar notional, while the other agrees to pay a yen interest rate on an equivalent notional in yen. A forward is simply a deferred foreign exchange transaction at an exchange rate set today.

Foreign exchange derivatives are slightly more complex than straight interest rate products because of the introduction of an additional currency, which implies that the spot exchange rate and a second set of interest rates must be included in the pricing of the product. As an illustration, consider, for example, a simple one-year dollar/yen swap, a three-month LIBOR on each side, for a notional of $N_\$$, as shown in Figure 4-36.[66] Nothing is exchanged today, and only the interest is paid every three months. If we denote $f_{¥/\$}$ as the current yen/dollar exchange rate, we have the additional relationship

[66] A variant of this swap would include the actual exchange of $N_{¥}$ for $N_\$$ at initiation and conversely at expiry. The inclusion of these flows depends on the particular need of the transacting parties.

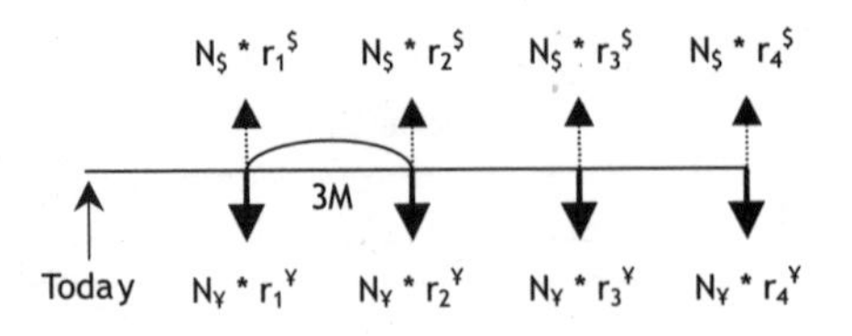

Figure 4-36 Forex

$N_{¥} = N_{\$} * f_{¥/\$}$. There are multiple variations of this simple structure, notably in terms of frequency and rate reference. For example, one of the legs may be a fixed rate or a six-month LIBOR.

Markets

Even more than interest rate derivatives, foreign exchange transactions are mostly traded over the counter (OTC). However, outstanding positions are significantly lower with $14,899 billion as of June 1999 versus $54,072 billion for interest rate products as a whole. The U.S. dollar is not surprisingly, even more dominant with a market share of 44 versus 30 percent for interest rates. Table 4-14 presents an overview of the market.

Interestingly the vast majority of foreign exchange contracts are short-term products: 83.5 percent of outstanding positions are below one year versus 37.5 percent for interest rates. It also appears that market participation is broader, with reporting financial institutions holding only 36.7 percent of outstanding positions. This is in contrast to the ratio of 50 percent for interest rate transactions. Nonfinancial institutions are also more actively involved: 20.2 percent versus 10.8 percent.

These statistics show clearly that the market for foreign exchange derivatives is significantly different from that of interest rate products. The nature of the needs and of the population they serve are different, if only because numerous nonfinancial corporations are exposed to foreign currencies as part of their day-to-day business. In contrast the interest rate market is a more delineated arena in which traders and speculators have a larger share.

Pricing

Swaps

Foreign exchange swaps are fairly straightforward to price by discounting all flows at the prevailing zero-coupon rates, as shown in Figure 4-37. If $F_i^{\$}$ and $F_i^{¥}$ stand for the flows on each leg, N for their

TABLE 4-14 The Global OTC Foreign Exchange Derivatives Markets[a,b] (Amounts outstanding in billions of U.S. dollars)

	Notional Amounts			Gross Market Values		
	End June 1998	End Dec. 1998	End June 1999	End June 1998	End Dec. 1998	End June 1999
Total contracts	**18,719**	**18,011**	**14,899**	**799**	**786**	**582**
With other reporting dealers	7,406	7,284	5,464	314	336	200
With other financial institutions	7,048	7,440	6,429	299	297	246
With nonfinancial customers	4,264	3,288	3,007	186	153	136
Up to one year[c]	16,292	15,791	12,444	—	—	—
Between one and five years[c]	1,832	1,624	1,772	—	—	—
Over five years[c]	595	592	683	—	—	—
U.S. dollar	16,167	15,810	13,181	747	698	519
Euro[d]	8,168	7,658	4,998	193	223	206
Japanese yen	5,579	5,319	4,641	351	370	171
Pound sterling	2,391	2,612	2,281	55	62	63
Swiss franc	1,104	937	823	35	30	33
Canadian dollar	660	594	636	29	34	27
Swedish krona	351	419	435	11	9	14
Other	3,019	2,674	2,805	179	146	130
Memorandum item:						
Exchange-traded contracts[e]	*103*	*57*	*80*	—	—	—

[a] See footnote a to Table 4-3.
[b] Counting both currency sides of every foreign exchange transaction means that the currency breakdown scans to 200% of the aggregate.
[c] Residual maturity.
[d] Before end-June 1999; legacy currencies of the euro.
[e] See footnote f to Table 4-3.

(*Source*: Bank of International Settlements, "The Global OTC Derivatives Market at the End of June 1999.")

number, $r_i^{\$}$ and $r_i^{¥}$ for the corresponding zero-coupon rates, and $f_{¥/\$}$ for the current exchange rate, the value V of the swap is simply[67]:

$$V_{\$} = f_{\$/¥} \cdot V = \sum_{i=1}^{N} \left(\frac{F_i^{\$}}{1 + r_i^{\$}} \right) - f_{\$/¥} \cdot \sum_{i=1}^{N} \left(\frac{F_i^{¥}}{1 + r_i^{¥}} \right)$$

[67] \$ and ¥ have been chosen for simplicity as a generic notation for any two currencies. We employ indifferently $f_{¥/\$}$ and $f_{\$/¥}$ with $f_{¥/\$} = 1/f_{\$/¥}$.

As we did for a generic interest rate swap pricing formula, we implicitly consider that all rates are midmarket; therefore, $V_{\$}$ is also a midmarket valuation.

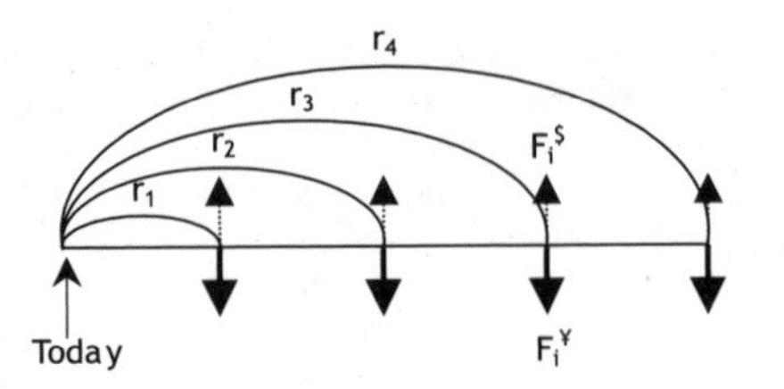

Figure 4-37 Forex Swap

Incidentally, this formula can be generalized to handle any type of swap, regardless of its characteristics. If N denotes the number of flows on one leg, M the number on the other leg, V becomes:

$$V_{\$} = f_{\$/¥} \cdot V_{¥} = \sum_{i=1}^{N} \left(\frac{F_i^{\$}}{1 + r_i^{\$}} \right) - f_{\$/¥} \cdot \sum_{i=1}^{M} \left(\frac{F_i^{¥}}{1 + r_i^{¥}} \right)$$

where $F_i^{\$}$ and $F_i^{¥}$ may have totally different schedules or even calculation methods—fixed versus variable—provided that $r_i^{\$}$ and $r_i^{¥}$ are chosen appropriately for each flow.

In the particular case of each leg being pegged to a variable rate, for example, the LIBOR, we can operate the same simplification we used for the variable leg of an interest rate swap and substitute two flows of notional to each unknown variable flow.[68] The whole structure becomes as shown in Figure 4-38.

In the figure, r_{ZC} stands now for the zero-coupon rate until maturity. V can be expressed here as:

$$V_{\$} = f_{\$/¥} \cdot V_{¥} = \left(N_{\$} - \frac{N_{\$}}{1 + r_{ZC}^{\$}} \right) - f_{\$/¥} \cdot \left(N_{¥} - \frac{N_{¥}}{1 + r_{ZC}^{¥}} \right)$$

Considering that $N_{\$} = f_{\$/¥} * N_{¥}$, this expression can be further simplified:

$$V_{\$} = N_{\$} \cdot \left(\frac{r_{ZC}^{\$}}{1 + r_{ZC}^{\$}} - \frac{r_{ZC}^{¥}}{1 + r_{ZC}^{¥}} \right) = N_{\$} \cdot \frac{r_{ZC}^{¥} - r_{ZC}^{\$}}{(1 + r_{ZC}^{¥}) \cdot (1 + r_{ZC}^{\$})}$$

The valuation of the swap depends on the interest rate differential between the two currencies.[69]

---

[68] Note that the transformation requires only that each leg be reset on a market variable rate. Therefore, both sides need not have the same frequency.

[69] Note that in a variant of the swap where $N_{¥}$ and $N_{\$}$ would be exchanged at initiation and back at expiry, the value of the swap would be exactly 0 because all flows disappear from the structure.

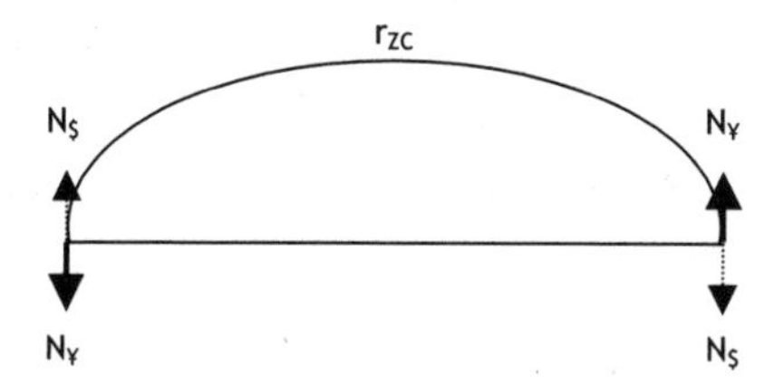

Figure 4-38 Forex Swap

As a numerical application, consider a one-year dollar/yen swap for $1,000,000, for which $r_{ZC}^{¥} = 0.29$ percent and $r_{ZC}^{\$} = 6.87$ percent. If we apply the formula for $V_{\$}$, we get:

$$V_{\$} = \$1{,}000{,}000 * \frac{\left(\frac{0.29\% * 365}{360}\right) - \left(\frac{6.87\% * 365}{360}\right)}{\left(1 + \frac{0.29\% * 365}{360}\right) * \left(1 + \frac{6.87\% * 365}{360}\right)} = -\$62{,}175.66$$

$V_{\$} < 0$ indicates that the buyer of this swap—that is, the receiver of dollar rates/the payer of yen rates—would have to pay close to $62,176 to enter the transaction. This is a very intuitive result: Considering the difference between 0.29 percent and 6.87 percent, it only seems natural that the differential appears very clearly in the value of the deal.

FUTURES REVISITED

The payoff to the holder of a future position can be expressed as:

$$P = Q \cdot (F_{SQ} - F_H)$$

Q is the number of units in contracts, F_{SQ} the final settlement value of the future, and F_H the price at which it was traded originally.[70] This payoff is usually denominated in the currency of the underlying, but there exist other options. We examine below three types of futures: standard, ADR, and quanto.

Standard Futures

To price a standard futures contract on a security S, consider the diagram in Figure 4-39 in which:

[70] We neglect again here the margin calls and deposits on the futures contract. As was mentioned on several occasions these flows only generate financing costs which we leave aside.

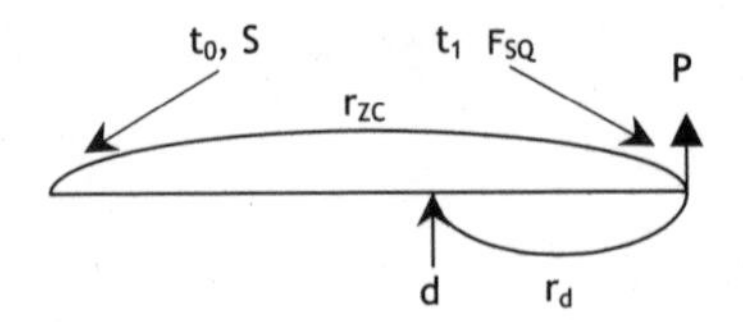

Figure 4-39 Futures Contract

- t_0 = time of pricing and transaction, typically today
- t_1 = expiry
- P = payoff to the holder of the future position
- d = dividend paid on the underlying security
- $r_{ZC=}$ zero-coupon rate from t_0 to t_1[71]
- r_d = forward zero-coupon rate from the dividend payment date to t_1[72]
- S = price of the underlying security on t_0
- F_{SQ} = price of the underlying security on expiry—that is, future SQ price
- Q = number of units of futures traded on t_0 at F_H

Consider now the following elementary transactions from the perspective of the seller of the future who needs to hedge the short:

On t_0:

- Borrow an amount $N = Q * S$ from t_0 to t_1 @ r_{ZC}.
- Buy Q units of S @ S_0, for a total nominal N.
- Sell one future @ F_H.

The resulting cash flow is:

$$C_0 = +N - Q * S = 0$$

On t_1:

- Pay back loan $N * (1 + r_{ZC})$.
- Sell Q units of S @ F_{SQ}.

---

[71] Rigorously speaking, r_{ZC} is the relevant rate from today's stock settlement date to the stock settlement date on the futures expiry.

[72] Note that r_d is from the payment date, not the ex-date, to expiry. In Japan, for example, dividends are typically paid three to four months after ex; therefore, the payment date may very well be after expiry.

- Pay equity performance $P = Q * (F_{SQ} - F_H)$
- Receive accumulated capitalized dividends $Q * d.^{*}$[73]

The resulting cash flow is:

$$\begin{aligned} C_1 &= -N * (1 + r_{ZC}) + Q * F_{SQ} - Q * (F_{SQ} - F_H) + Q * d^* \\ &= -N * (1 + r_{ZC}) + Q * F_H + Q * d^* \end{aligned}$$

For the seller and the buyer to be willing to enter the contract, we need to have $C_1 = 0$[74]:

$$F_H = S \cdot (1 + r_{ZC}) - d^*$$

This simple formula is consistent with our expectations: F_H is proportional to S, ascending with r_{ZC} and descending with $d.^{*}$[75]

Each term of this expression needs to be examined carefully. The spot price S is the price at which the underlying is trading today. If S is a single stock and if we price during market hours, it is necessary to account for the market spread in calculating S. Selling the future requires buying the underlying security, which has to be done at the market offered price. r_{ZC} is a zero-coupon rate, but the direction of the trade dictates if we need to include a bid or ask price. The seller of the future is borrowing cash to cover the purchase of the underlying; therefore, an offered price here is necessary again. d^* represents an amount

---

[73] The symbol * is often used to denote the capitalization of a series of flows until a certain date. In the case of dividends, we do not know exactly when they are paid, but presumably they are spread out all across the life of the future. d^* represents all the dividends that have been paid between t_0 and t_1 for one unit of underlying and for which we have received interest by lending the cash until t_1. For example, if there is a single dividend d, then $d^* = d * (1 + r_d)$. Rigorously speaking, we should enter today into an FRA between the dividend payment date and the expiry of the future to lock r_d. If we do not, the actual rate of financing of dividends between payment date and expiry may be different from r_d, resulting in a profit or a loss.

[74] What we did is essentially construct a replicating portfolio for the futures contract and apply absolute convergence reasoning. The price at which both parties are indifferent between the futures contract and its replicating portfolio is the fair price of the transaction.

[75] The formula we obtain for F_H is derived from a cost-of-carry model. In the framework we consider this approach to be absolutely satisfactory because in a real arbitrage situation we would actually replicate the underlying portfolio and carry it. There are, however, alternative models derived from specific hypotheses, notably on interest rates. See, for example, Eduardo Schwartz, "The Stochastic Behavior of Commodity Prices: Implications for Valuation and Hedging," *Journal of Finance*, 52, 1997, pp. 923-973 or Michael Hemler and Francis Longstaff, "General Equilibrium Stock Index Futures Prices: Theoretical and Empirical Evidence," *Journal of Financial and Quantitative Analysis*, 26, 1991, pp. 287–308.

of accumulated dividends. In contrast to S and r_{ZC}, which are known fairly precisely at the time of pricing, d^* is not known for sure, only estimated. If after the trade the amount of dividends paid is not equal to what was expected, the difference is a profit or a loss to each party. Specifically, if dividends increase, the seller of the futures contract, being also the holder of the underlying, receives more cash than expected and realizes a profit. In contrast, the buyer does not realize a loss directly but paid too high a price for the futures contract in the first place.

As a numerical illustration, consider the S&P 500 index at $1,400. Assume a three-month expiry, $r_{ZC} = 6$ percent, and $d^* = \$4.5$. F_H has the following value:

$$F_H = \$1{,}400 * \left(1 + \frac{6\% * 90}{360}\right) - \$4.5 = \$1{,}416.5$$

The difference $1,416.5 – $1,400 = $16.5 is referred to as the *theoretical basis* of the futures contract, or as its *fair value*. It indicates the amount by which the future price differs from the price of its underlying. Because of the financing bracket $(1 + r_{ZC})$ in F_H, the fair value is generally positive unless the amount of dividends is such that $d^* > S * r_{ZC}$. Note also that because d^* is usually fairly constant, the term $(1 + r_{ZC})$ decreases with time as we get closer to expiry.

We will revisit many of these issues when dealing with index arbitrage, but it is useful to keep in mind that a future position creates a side exposure to interest rates and dividends.

ADR Futures

An ADR futures contract is a bicurrency futures contract in which the performance is paid in a currency different from that of the underlying.[76] Specifically, the payoff formula is modified and becomes:

$$P = Q \cdot (f_1^{¥/\$} \cdot F_{SQ} - f_0^{¥/\$} \cdot F_H)$$

where $f_0^{¥/\$}$ and $f_1^{¥/\$}$ represent the exchange rate between two generic currencies yen and dollars, respectively, on t_0 and t_1. The operating mode to hedge this type of futures is quite similar to that of the previous case:

[76] In reality, there is no listed ADR or quanto futures contract. These particular structures are almost always traded OTC, which means that they are forwards rather than futures.

On t_0:

- Borrow an amount $N^{¥}$ from t_0 to t_1 @ $r_{ZC}{}^{¥}$.
- Change $N^{¥}$ into $N^{\$}$ @ $f_0^{¥/\$}$.
- Buy Q unit of S @ S_0, for a total nominal $N^{\$}$.
- Sell one future @ F_H.

The resulting cash flows are:

$$C_0^{¥} = +N^{¥} - N^{¥} = 0$$
$$C_0^{\$} = +N^{\$} - Q * S = 0$$

On t_1:

- Pay back loan $N^{¥} * (1 + r_{ZC}^{¥})$.
- Sell Q units of S @ F_{SQ}.
- Change $Q * F_{SQ}$ in yen to $Q * f_1^{¥/\$} * F_{SQ}$.
- Pay equity performance $P = Q * (f_1^{¥/\$} * F_{SQ} - f_0^{¥/\$} * F_H)$.
- Receive accumulated capitalized dividends in dollars and change them to $Q * f_1^{¥/\$} * d^*$.

The resulting cash flows are:

$$\begin{aligned} C_1^{¥} &= -N^{¥} * (1 + r_{ZC}^{¥}) + Q * f_1^{¥/\$} * F_{SQ} - Q * (f_1^{¥/\$} * F_{SQ} - f_0^{¥/\$} * F_{H}) \\ &\quad + Q * f_1^{¥/\$} * d^* = -N^{¥} * (1 + r_{ZC}^{¥}) + Q * f_0^{¥/\$} * F_H + Q * f_1^{¥/\$} * d^* \\ C_1^{\$} &= +Q * F_{SQ} - Q * F_{SQ} + Q * d^* - Q * d^* = 0 \end{aligned}$$

because every flow cancels out on the dollar side.

Again both parties are indifferent if $C_1^{¥} = 0$. Therefore:

$$F_H = S \cdot \left(1 + r_{ZC}^{¥}\right) - \left(\frac{f_1^{¥/\$}}{f_0^{¥/\$}}\right) \cdot d^*$$

The financing cost has been transferred to the second currency, and the dividend payment is modified to account for the change in exchange rates between initiation and expiry. This last point, however, poses a problem because $f_1^{¥/\$}$ is not known on t_0. We can easily solve this difficulty by exchanging d today at the *forward exchange rate* $f_d^{¥/\$}$, as shown in Figure 4-40.

The foreign exchange risk on $d^{¥}$ disappears and $C_1^{¥}$ then becomes:

$$C_1^{¥} = -N^{¥} * (1 + r_{ZC}^{¥}) + Q * f_0^{¥/\$} * F_H + Q * d^{¥*}$$

It follows that:

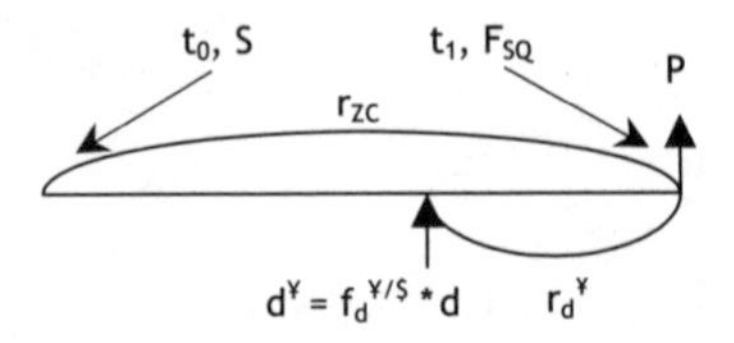

Figure 4-40 ADR Futures Contract

$$F_H = S \cdot \left(1 + r_{ZC}^{¥}\right) - \left(\frac{d^{¥*}}{f_0^{¥/\$}}\right)$$

in which all parameters are known on t_0.

The ADR futures contract keeps the same risks as its standard counterpart in terms of interest rate and dividends. There are two differences, however. First, the relevant interest rate is that of the currency in which the payoff is paid, not that of the underlying. Second, there is an additional risk on the exchange rate on the dividend side. If the amount of actual dividends is different from expectations, the difference—already a profit or loss—is in addition exposed to the difference in exchange rate, from the initial forward rate $f_d^{¥/\$}$ to the spot rate on payment date.

Quanto Futures

A quanto futures contract is bicurrency for which the payoff is locked with respect to the exchange rate[77]:

$$P = f_0^{¥/\$} \cdot Q \cdot (F_{SQ} - F_H)$$

It is relatively easy to build again a flow diagram based on this payoff, and the fair value of the futures contract has to be equal to the following:

$$F_H = S \cdot \left(1 + r_{ZC}^{¥}\right) - \left(\frac{f_1^{¥/\$} - f_0^{¥/\$}}{f_0^{¥/\$}}\right) \cdot F_{SQ} - \left(\frac{d^{¥*}}{f_0^{¥/\$}}\right)$$

This formula, however, is not as simple as those we obtained before. In particular, the middle term is problematic because it depends on the exchange rate as well as F_{SQ}. Although $f_0^{¥/\$}$ is known at t_0, neither $f_1^{¥/\$}$ nor F_{SQ} are. We could potentially use the forward rate

[77] The alternative formula $P = f_1^{¥/\$} * Q * (F_{SQ} - F_H)$ is of no particular interest because it is equivalent to a standard futures contract for which the equity payoff is exchanged on expiry at the spot exchange rate.

again to get rid of the uncertainty about $f_1^{¥/\$}$, except that this time we need to hedge F_{SQ}, which is not known today. In short, a quanto futures contract cannot be priced easily with a flow diagram, and we need more sophisticated tools.

We will not develop the pricing further, because we want to focus on relatively simple products, and quanto futures are indeed not such simple products.[78] This exercise is essentially useful as a demonstration of the limitations of the pricing procedure we have employed so far.

CONCLUSION

As it happens, the money market is a massive component of modern financial markets, and therefore a significant part of our attention needed to be devoted to the different instruments and practices. This may seem to be a contradiction to the original stated focus on equity markets, but in fact it is not.

Except for extremely specialized strategies like mutual funds—by and large limited to one single class of assets—every trader needs to have a clear and comprehensive knowledge of a multitude of products beyond his or her natural domain of expertise because rigorous risk management demands it. This is all the more true for a professional arbitrageur who may have a very broad mandate to focus loosely on equities and needs to be able to hedge other risks away.

For example, even a simple product like an index futures contract includes a significant risk to interest rates and dividends. Understanding these risks allows a trader to manage them actively—for example, in hedging them at a fair price. Out of all the risks likely to affect the trading environment, many are directly related to the money market, be it interest rate or foreign exchange, short term or long term. Therefore, the knowledge we built in this long and arguably painful examination is a prerequisite for all derivative traders alike.

[78] In fact, quanto futures can be priced very easily with a Black-Scholes model including a second currency.

5

AGGREGATE INDICATORS: STOCK INDICES

INTRODUCTION

Equity indices have been around for as long as equities have been around. They are designed to serve the purpose of aggregating information in a legible and meaningful way. There is a multitude of different indices nowadays, broad based as well as industry specific, and some have become milestones in the modern financial landscape—the Dow Jones Industrial Average or the Nasdaq Composite, for example.

Indices were originally developed to capture a relative appreciation, and in practice an index is really nothing more than a weighted arithmetic average of the prices of its components. As we will see, there are mainly two ways to consider the question of the weightings, but for all practical purposes computing an index is a very simple exercise. Difficulties arise only from corporate events affecting component companies. On one side, index sponsors have to monitor carefully the general market trends to identify what the best candidates for inclusion are. An illustration of this point was made very clear when Dow Jones decided to include Nasdaq stocks in its industrial average for the first time in mid-1999. The move was long overdue for some, but in any case it reflected the reality of today's markets—technology stocks are here to stay. On the other hand, individual corporate events must be tracked in a meaningful and timely manner if the index is to remain representative of the activity taking place in its portfolio base.

From our perspective, indices represent important instruments because a significant fraction of the world's most liquid equity financial products is index related, be it futures or options. This concentration is largely explained by fundamental corporate finance theory, notably the *capital asset pricing model* (CAPM), but also by more down-to-earth considerations. The CAPM states that investors are not rewarded for unsystematic risk—that is, risk that can be diversified away with a larger portfolio. The ultimate diversified portfolio is the market, and broad-based indices in general capture a sizable fraction of the overall capitalization, making them ideal vehicles for investors trying to diversify their assets. On the other hand, because index futures are extremely simple and cheap to trade, many investors look no further to take speculative positions. Even emerging markets have fairly liquid index futures; therefore, investors unable to find liquidity on individual issues always have the option to use these.

DEFINITIONS

Rigorously speaking, an index is a measure of relative value. It captures the appreciation of a reference set of securities from a base period:

$$I = \frac{\sum_i w_i \cdot P_i}{\sum_i w_i \cdot P_i^O}$$

where w_i stands for the individual weight of each component today, P_i for its price, and P_i^O for its original base price. This definition implies that I is a dimensionless figure, being the ratio of two capitalizations.

There may be variations of this simple formulation—for example, the Laspeyres or Paäsche formulas, each one named after the economist that first proposed it in the mid-nineteenth century. Differences reside notably in the weights used in the denominator. The above convention, $\sum_i w_i \cdot P_i^O$, means that I captures a change in overall capitalization due exclusively to a change in price because the same current weights are used in both numerator and denominator. An alternative would be $\sum_i w_i^O \cdot P_i^O$, which means that I now reflects a change in overall capitalization, due either to w_i or P_i.

In any case the above formula is not extremely practical and needs to be refined slightly because nobody wants to keep track of base prices of 50 years ago, for example. We transform the numerator into a more generic quantity, which we call the *divisor* of the index, and which we denote as D:

$$I = \frac{\sum_i w_i \cdot P_i}{D}$$

The divisor plays a fundamental role in the life and continuity of the index, as we will see shortly. Depending on the exact definition and properties of w_i, the index can be capitalization weighted, price weighted, or total return.

Capitalization-Weighted Indices

In a *capitalization-weighted index,* w_i is the outstanding number of shares. We denote this weight W_i, and the index becomes:

$$I = \frac{\sum_i W_i \cdot P_i}{D}$$

The reason that the index is called "capitalization-weighted" is related to the variation in I with respect to a variation in one of the prices, P_i. Specifically the definition of I implies that:

$$\frac{\Delta I}{\Delta P_i} = \frac{W_i}{D} = \frac{W_i \cdot I}{\sum_i W_i \cdot P_i}$$

if ΔP_i denotes a variation in the market price of the ith component. This result can be written as:

$$\frac{\Delta I}{I} = \left(\frac{W_i \cdot P_i}{\sum_i W_i \cdot P_i}\right) \cdot \frac{\Delta P_i}{P_i}$$

In other words, the relative variation of I following a move of one of its components is equal to the relative variation of that component times its relative capitalization in the index.

Price-Weighted Indices

In a *price-weighted index,* w_i is a fixed weight, usually identical for all components. The characterization "price weighted" comes from the dependence of I on each component's price. The above formula expressing a relative variation in I is still arithmetically valid:

$$\frac{\Delta I}{I} = \left(\frac{w_i \cdot P_i}{\sum_i w_i \cdot P_i}\right) \cdot \frac{\Delta P_i}{P_i}$$

but all w_i are equal; therefore, this expression simplifies to:

$$\frac{\Delta I}{I} = \left(\frac{P_i}{\sum_i P_i}\right) \cdot \frac{\Delta P_i}{P_i}$$

which shows that $\Delta I/I$ is proportional to $\Delta P_i/P_i$ again, but the ratio is now the relative *price* of the ith component in the index.

In practice, there are only a few price-weighted indices in the world, and only two we want to consider—the Dow Jones Industrial Average and the Nikkei 225. The weight of Dow's constituents are 1, and its divisor is 0.20145 as of April 2000. For the Nikkei 225 the situation is slightly different: 222 components have a weight equal to 1,000, 2 have a weight of 100, 1 has a weight of 1, and the divisor is 10,179.8. The reason behind the difference in weight is the disproportionate price of some stocks. Nippon Telephone & Telegraph (NTT), for example, has a price around ¥1,600,000, whereas most other stocks are below ¥10,000, which essentially means that without any adjustment, NTT would drive the index entirely.

Even if the Dow Jones is considered a worldwide reference, the fact that until recently no derivative was listed on it is clearly indicative of the relative lack of interest price-weighted indices have received in general. The calculation method accounts for a large part of this relative indifference because small stocks have a disproportionate impact. The Nikkei 225 is the only exception, and even if the Tokyo Stock Exchange also lists two capitalization-weighted indices—the Tokyo Price Index (TOPIX) and Nikkei 300—the Nikkei 225 remains the flagship market aggregate.[1]

Total Return Indices: Dividend Reinvestments

A *total return index* lists stocks for which dividends are systematically reinvested. Because the weight of a stock going ex is affected by the reinvestment, total return indices are necessarily capitalization weighted.

Consider a stock with a weight W and a price P that is going ex-dividend today by an amount d. If Y and T respectively stand for yesterday and today, the ex-dividend effect implies:

$$P_T = P_Y - d$$

The "fair" price of the stock today is its price yesterday adjusted for the dividend.[2] For the capitalization of the stock to reflect the decrease in price, we need to increase the weight W by an equivalent amount, which we denote $\delta * W$. If we consider this increase to occur as of yesterday's close, the following relationship holds:

---

[1] The reason for this is probably the size of the TOPIX, more than 1,600 stocks. When the Nikkei 300 was listed, it should have corrected this situation; however, its listing occurred in the middle of the Japanese financial and economic crisis, which may explain the lack of interest it received.

[2] Naturally, this relationship is valid only before the opening, the difference between the actual opening price and $P_Y - d$ being unpredictable. Note that d here is a gross amount and that the tax status of investors transacting the stock at open will effectively set the value of the opening discount. Cf. the discussion on dividend arbitrage in the first part.

$$P_Y * \delta * W = W * (1 + \delta) * d$$

This equation states that the incremental capitalization captured by $\delta * W$ as of yesterday is equal to the total amount of dividend received today on $W * (1 + \delta)$ shares. δ is then simple to extract:

$$\delta = \frac{d}{P_Y - d}$$

Therefore, for a stock going ex, the weight in a total return index is increased to W', where:

$$W' = W * \left(\frac{P_Y}{P_Y - d}\right)$$

In that case, although the index is still capitalization weighted, each weight is not equal to the outstanding number of shares anymore but adjusted every ex date. The DAX 30 is the only major total return index in our list.[3]

Dividend Yields

Let's extend the above definitions and denote:

$$d_I = \frac{\sum_i w_i \cdot d_i}{D}$$

where d_i stands for all the individual dividends paid by the index constituents over an identical period of time, typically a year. Regardless of whether the index is price or capitalization weighted, d_I represents the total amount of dividends paid by the underlying universe of stocks expressed in index points. The dividend yield y_I is then simply defined as:

$$y_I = \frac{d_I}{I}$$

d_I and y_I are particularly important with respect to the fair value of index derivative products, especially futures. When applied to an index, the futures pricing formula becomes:

$$F_H = I * (1 + r_{ZC}) - d_I^*$$

[3] The fact that all dividends are reinvested has a significant effect on the DAX futures calculation. Recall the pricing formulas for a standard futures contract, which explicitly included capitalized dividend payments on expiry. In the case of a total return index, these payments do not occur anymore because they are reinvested before; therefore, the fair value of the future is only the financing cost until expiry.

where r_{ZC} is the relevant zero-coupon rate to expiry. d_I^* is here an extension of d to account for the capitalization of all dividends to expiry:

$$d_I^* = \frac{\sum_i w_i \cdot d_i^*}{D}$$

Alternatively, F_H can be expressed as:

$$F_H = I * (1 + r_{ZC} - y_I^*)$$

where y_I^* is also an extension of y_I to account for the financing on dividend payments.

The choice of one particular formula for F_H depends on the repartition of dividends through time. If dividends are relatively homogeneously distributed until expiry, then the use of y_I^* is acceptable and indeed simplifies practical calculations. On the other hand, if dividends tend to cluster around particular periods, using y_I^* leads to a possible mispricing in F_H.[4]

MAJOR INDICES

Introduction

Table 5-1 gives an overview of the major stock indices in the United States, Europe, and Japan. Interestingly, many indices appeared during the eighties and therefore are quite young by many standards.

Concentration

Indices are usually constructed in order of descending capitalization and "chained" to cover different segments of the stock universe. For example, in Germany, the DAX 100 is constituted from the stocks of the DAX 30—the 30 biggest capitalizations—and those of the MDAX—the next 70. (See Figures 5-1 through 5-5, for diagrams of the German, French, U.K., Japanese, and U.S. indices.)

[4] As a general rule, y_I^* is used relatively rarely on equities, except for back-of-the-envelope approximations. In Japan, for example, dividends are highly concentrated around the end of the fiscal year—March 31—or interim period—September 30 for a large number of corporations. In the United States, although dividends are relatively homogeneous, most traders still use d_I^*. In the United Kingdom dividends usually go ex on Mondays, but their amount is not steadily distributed; therefore y_I^* is not really applicable either. In France, dividends are also concentrated, around the second quarter of each calendar year.

TABLE 5-1

Name	Exchange[a]	Sponsor	Number of Components[b]	Value on Dec, 31, 1999	10-Year CAGR[c]	Method[d]	Instituted[e]	Base Value
FTSE 100	LSE	Financial Times	100	£6,930.20	11.08%	CW	Jan. 3, 1984	£1,000
FTSE 250	LSE	Financial Times	250	£6,444.90	9.31%	CW	Dec. 31, 1985	£1,412.60
FTSE 350	LSE	Financial Times	350	£3,327.00	10.68%	CW	Dec. 21, 1985	£682.94
FTSE All Share	LSE	Financial Times	797	£3,242.06	13.56%[f]	CW	Apr. 10, 1962	£100
FTSE Small Cap	LSE	Financial Times	444	£3,097.80	12.43%	CW	Dec. 31, 1992	£1,363.79
DAX	FSE	FSE	30	€6,958.14	14.54%	TR[g]	Dec. 31, 1987	€1,000
DAX Mid-Cap	FSE	FSE	70	€4,103.82	6.77%	TR[g]	Dec. 31, 1987	€1,000
DAX 100	FSE	FSE	100	€3,293.54	13.40%	TR[g]	Dec. 31, 1987	€500
Dow Industrial	NYSE	Dow Jones	30	$11,497.10	15.36%	PW	Oct. 1, 1928	—
S&P 100	NYSE	S&P	100	$792.83	17.02%	CW	Jan. 2, 1976	$50
S&P 500	NYSE	S&P	500	$1,469.50	15.31%	CW	1941–1943	$10
S&P 400	NYSE	S&P	400	$444.67	18.03%	CW	Dec. 31, 1990	$100
S&P 600	NYSE	S&P	600	$197.79	12.04%	CW	Dec. 31, 1993	$100
S&P Composite	NYSE	S&P	1,500	$308.89	25.30%	CW	Dec. 31, 1994	$100
Russell 3,000®	NYSE	F. Russell Company	3,000	$1,457.72	14.93%	CW	Dec. 31, 1986	$140
Nasdaq 100	Nasdaq	Nasdaq	100	$3,707.83	32.41%	CW	Feb. 1, 1985	$250
Nasdaq Composite	Nasdaq	Nasdaq	4,739	$4,069.31	24.50%	CW	Feb. 5, 1971	$100
Nikkei 50	TSE	Nikkei	50	¥2,008.78	−0.69%	PW	Jul. 4, 1988	¥1,000
Nikkei 225	TSE	TSE	225	¥18,934.34	−6.95%	PW	May 16, 1949	¥176.21
Nikkei 300	TSE	TSE	300	¥324.26	−4.64%	CW	Oct. 1, 1982	¥100
TOPIX	TSE	TSE	1,358	¥1,722.20	−5.01%	CW	Jan. 4, 1968	¥100
TSE2	TSE	TSE	506	¥2,609.73	0.85%[h]	CW	Jan. 4, 1968	¥100
CAC	SBF	SBF	40	€5,958.32	11.53%	CW	Dec. 31, 1987	€1,000

(continued)

TABLE 5-1 (*continued*)

Name	Exchange[a]	Sponsor	Number of Components[b]	Value on Dec, 31, 1999	10-Year CAGR[c]	Method[d]	Instituted[e]	Base Value
SBF 80	SBF	SBF	80	€4,217.58	17.34%	CW	Dec. 31, 1990	€1,000
SBF 120	SBF	SBF	120	€4,052.58	16.82%	CW	Dec. 28, 1990	€1,000
SBF 250	SBF	SBF	250	€3,810.86	16.03%	CW	Dec. 28, 1990	€1,000

[a] LSE, London Stock Exchange; FSE, Frankfurt Stock Exchange; NYSE, New York Stock Exchange; Nasdaq, National Association of Securities Dealers Automated Quotation; TSE, Tokyo Stock Exchange; and SBF, Société des Bourses Françaises.

[b] As of third quarter 1999.

[c] Ten-year compounded annual growth rate as of December 31, 1999. For indices instituted after December 31, 1989, the rate is from inception.

[d] CW, capitalization weighted; TR, total return; and PW, price weighted.

[e] "Instituted" may be different from "listed." For example, the Nikkei 300 was instituted as of 1982 but listed in 1995. The date of institution indicates the date upon which the index is based. On that particular date, its value is equal to the base value.

[f] From December 31, 1990.

[g] Note that the total return feature of the DAX makes a direct comparison of returns impossible with other indices.

[h] From December 31, 1991.

Source: Compiled by author from exchanges' respective Web sites and Bloomberg.

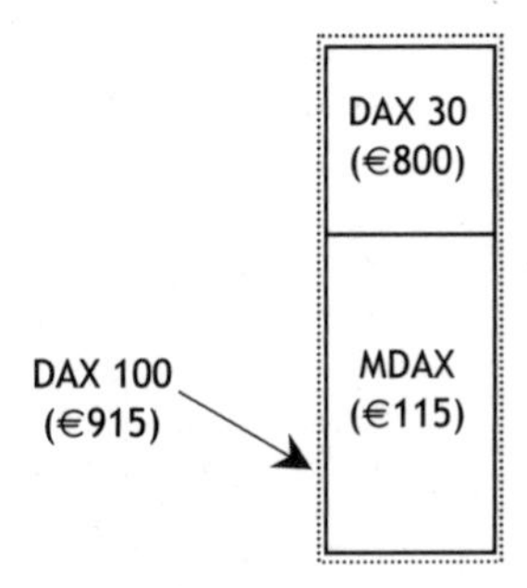

Figure 5-1 DAX
(*Note*: All figures are the total capitalization of the index as of August 31, 1999, in billions.)
(*Source*: Author's estimates and Bloomberg except Russell data, Frank Russell Company, reprinted with permission.)

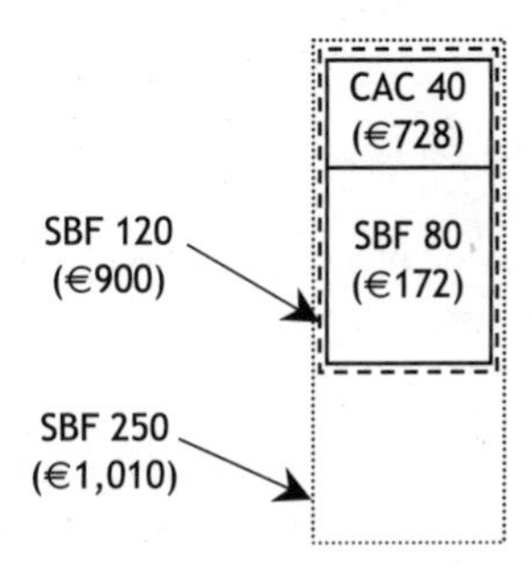

Figure 5-2 CAC
(*Note*: All figures are the total capitalization of the index as of August 31, 1999, in billions.)
(*Source*: Author's estimates and Bloomberg except Russell data, Frank Russell Company, reprinted with permission.)

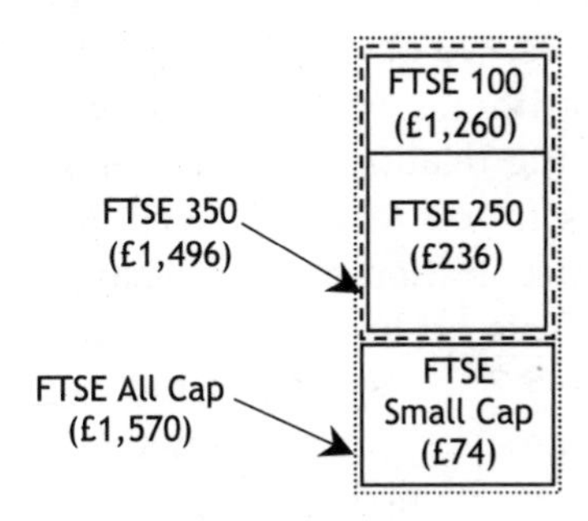

Figure 5-3 FTSE
(*Note*: All figures are the total capitalization of the index as of August 31, 1999, in billions.)
(*Source*: Author's estimates and Bloomberg except Russell data, Frank Russell Company, reprinted with permission.)

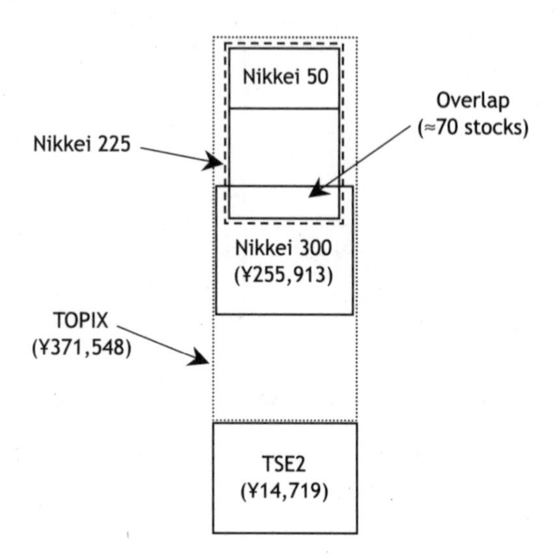

Figure 5-4 NIK
(*Note*: All figures are the total capitalization of the index as of August 31, 1999, in billions.)
(*Source*: Author's estimates and Bloomberg except Russell data, Frank Russell Company, reprinted with permission.)

Based on these diagrams, it is particularly interesting to push a little further and examine the relative concentration of each index. With 500 constituents, for example, the S&P 500 encompasses $10,414 billion in capitalization whereas the S&P 1500 Composite has three times as many constituents with only $1,190 billion in additional capitalization. Presented otherwise, with 33.3 percent of the stock base of the S&P 1500, the S&P 500 captures 89.7 percent of the overall capitalization. Table 5-2 reproduces the same calculation for most of the above indices. If we plot these figures, we obtain the chart in Figure 5-6. The dashed line represents a logarithmic regression and gives an idea of a possible shape of the underlying relationship between the two variables.

The regression is fitting relatively well and can be interpreted as showing that the concentration of capitalization tends to be similar in every major index. This is, however, true only for large indices, as illustrated in Figure 5-7. It represents the percentage of the overall capitalization of each market captured by the 5 percent largest companies. When only so few companies are included, there are wide disparities in the total capitalization they capture, which indicates that similar concentrations between the different markets appear indeed only for large indices. Note that the trend is unambiguously toward more concentration across the board.

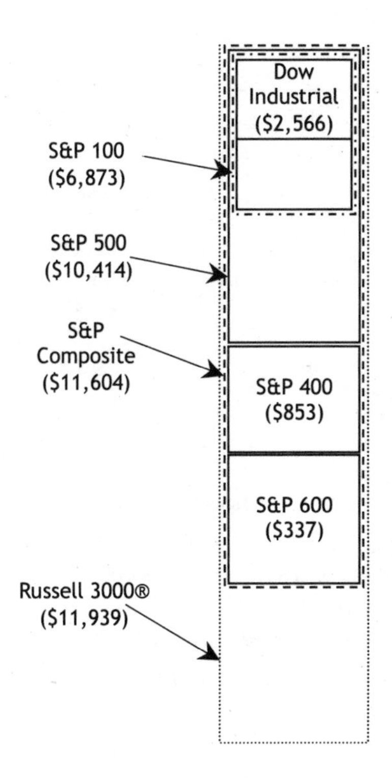

Figure 5-5 S&P
(*Note*: All figures are the total capitalization of the index as of August 31, 1999, in billions.)
(*Source*: Author's estimates and Bloomberg except Russell data, Frank Russell Company, reprinted with permission.)

The overall issue of concentration is particularly important when designing or managing an index because too much capitalization in a small number of stocks makes the index relatively skewed and less representative. For example, France Telecom and TotalFina in France or Deutsche Telekom and Allianz in Germany account for more than 25 percent of the CAC 40 and DAX 30 indices, a proportion that is arguably too high to consider both indices as true broad based indicators.

SPONSORSHIP

A *sponsor* is an institution responsible for the constitution and the calculation of an index. In some cases these roles are assumed by the exchange or an institution affiliated with it—France, Germany, or the TOPIX in Tokyo—but most often a third (private) party is undertaking

TABLE 5-2

Index	Stock	Capitalization	Reference
Dow Jones	2.0%	22.1%	S&P 1500
S&P 100	6.7%	59.2%	S&P 1500
S&P 500	33.3%	89.7%	S&P 1500
FTSE 100	12.6%	80.2%	FTSE All Share
FTSE 350	43.9%	95.3%	FTSE All Share
DAX	30.0%	87.4%	DAX 100
CAC	16.0%	72.1%	SBF 250
SBF 120	48.0%	89.1%	SBF 250

these tasks—*Financial Times,* Nikkei, or Standard & Poor's. The calculation is a fairly straightforward responsibility, but managing the constitution, in contrast, is a much more sensitive issue.

There are numerous aspects to this—notably concentration as we indicated, or industry representation—but the most important is transparency, which essentially means that clear standards and rigorous disclosure procedures should be set with respect to inclusions and deletions. The standard is necessary so that investors at large know what to expect throughout the life of the index in terms of composition

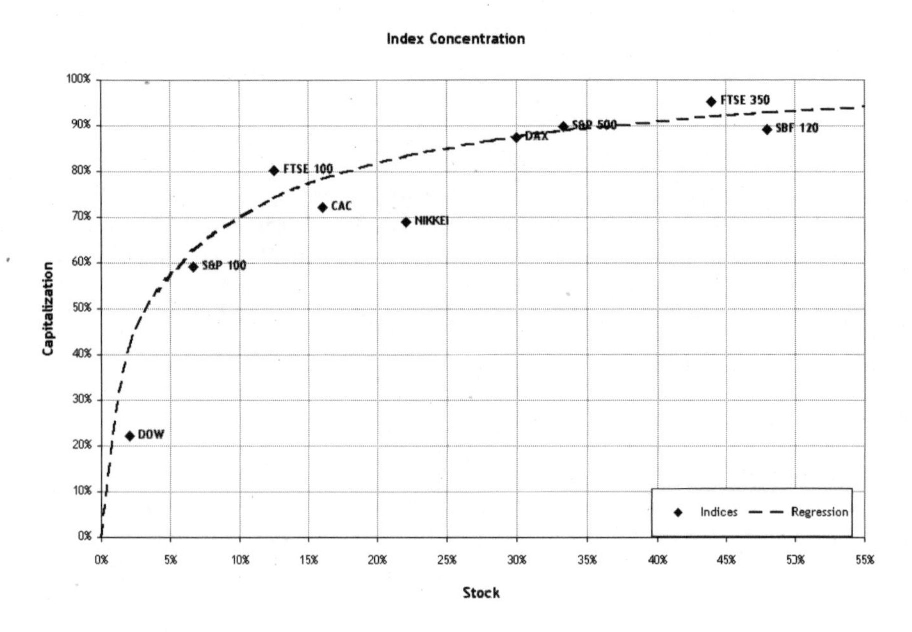

Figure 5-6 Concentration

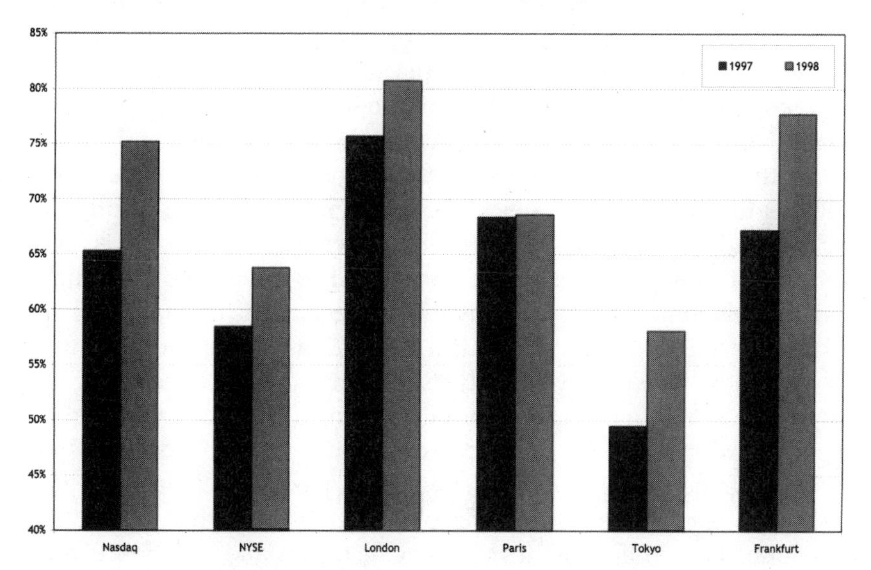

Figure 5-7 Capitalization
(*Source*: Compiled by author from FIBV data.)

and may react accordingly.[5] Failure to maintain such a standard results in a lot of volatility when announcements are actually made, when in fact most of this volatility could be avoided.[6]

Disclosure is also critical because of the importance of maintaining an index on which it is possible to trade continuously. In many cases sponsors have established explicit rules; for example, disclosure happens a certain number of days before the inclusion or dele-

---

[5] For descriptions of addition and deletion standards, see, for example, www.nikkei.co.jp for Nikkei 225 and 300, www.dj.com for Dow Jones, www.spglobal.com for the family of S&P indices, www.exchange.de for the family of DAX indices, and www.ftse.com for the family of FTSE indices.

[6] In general, many broad-based indices effectively serve as benchmarks to a whole set of strategies, and inclusion of a new stock usually creates a lot of demand—that is, buying pressure—whereas exclusion has the opposite effect. Obviously index arbitrageurs are first in line to act on these events because the nature of their position requires them to track the index rigorously. "Index funds"—that is, mutual funds tracking a given index—are probably next in line, and they have more and more impact considering their size has grown explosively over the past decade. Beyond these, many investors are also more or less directly benchmarking against specific indices. For an examination of inclusions and deletions with respect to institutional ownership, see, for example, Stephen W. Pruitt and K. C. John Wei, "Institutional Ownership and

(continued)

tion is effective.[7] It is necessary to realize here that early announcement, although necessary, is very costly in terms of index return. Consider, for example, an index replacing one of its components *A*, by a stock *B*. When the switch is announced, assume that *A* loses 5 percent and *B* rises by 10 percent. If the announcement is made before the effective date, the rise of *B* is not included in the index, whereas the decline of *A* is. Therefore, the index officially captures a decline and misses the corresponding increase. In fact, it is even worse because in practice many stocks tend to "overshoot" on inclusion or deletion. Traders will overbuy the entrant and oversell the stock replaced, often resulting in a correction on the morning after the switch is effective. Not only is the index return recording the original loss and missing the original gain, it is also recording the correction, during which *A* is included and potentially declines and *B* is not included anymore and potentially recovers. Naturally, it is difficult to generalize from these observations, but there cannot be any doubt that indices with recurrent inclusion and deletion events, like the S&P 500, suffer significantly from the price movements between an announcement and its effective date.

The alternative is to disclose the inclusion or deletion event after the fact—for example, just after the close on effective date. As it happens, Standard and Poor's used this procedure commonly before 1989, when it decided to revise it toward a fixed delay of five days. The case also presented itself in Japan with the Nikkatsu bankruptcy, and we will detail the exact situation in the chapter dedicated to

---

(Footnote continued)
Changes in the S&P 500, " *Journal of Finance*, 44, 1989, pp. 509–513. See also Andrei Shleifer, "Do Demand Curves for Stocks Slope Down?" *Journal of Finance*, 41, 1986, pp. 579–590. Stocks recently included in the index are found to present an abnormal return of 2.79 percent.

The very existence of an "inclusion premium" is directly dependent upon the level of index arbitrage activity. For example, the Dow Jones until recently did not have any futures contracts, and newly included stocks were not under price pressure. See, for example, Messod Beneish and John Gardner, "Information Costs and Liquidity Effects from Changes in the Dow Jones Industrial Average List," *Journal of Financial and Quantitative Analysis*, 30, 1995, pp. 135–157.

[7] See, for example, Messod Beneish and Robert Whaley, "An Anatomy of the 'S&P Game': The Effects of Changing the Rules," *Journal of Finance*, 51, 1996, pp. 1909–1930, for a complete discussion of the S&P 500 and its disclosure policy.

In addition to disclosing inclusion and deletion, transparency also refers the availability of weights and divisor on a regular basis. Many exchanges have set up automatic systems through which market participants can query constituents' characteristics when needed.

index arbitrage because it constitutes undoubtedly a risk to arbitrageurs. To set the stage, let's say that Nikkatsu was a Japanese movie production corporation that went bankrupt very suddenly in 1993. It had been in a very poor financial condition for some time, but its bankruptcy came as a surprise. Even more surprising, however, was the fact that Nikkei decided to remove the stock from the Nikkei 225 immediately but announced it *after* the close.[8] The stock went from ¥229 to ¥25 (−89 percent) the next day, while the entrant company, Shionogi & Co., rose from ¥985 to ¥1,050 (+6.6 percent). Both moves constituted a pure loss to index arbitrageurs and more generally to holders of benchmarked positions. To make matters worse, there were rumors at the time of inside trading, notably on Nikkatsu, because the chart reflected a selling pressure shortly before the announcement.

Interestingly, what was common practice in the United States until 1989 was extremely ill perceived in 1993 in Japan. Nikkei's decision proved disastrous in terms of public confidence and started a wave of protests against its irresponsibility and total disregard of investors' interests. Clearly, the development of index arbitrage, practiced profitably by the largest—and most influential—securities houses, and the aggressive growth of index funds have made a late announcement an unambiguous liability to the sponsor, even though it had been commonly accepted.[9] Therefore, it is unlikely that a Nikkatsu situation will occur ever again, at least on a major marketplace.[10]

---

[8] The major criterion for inclusion in the Nikkei 225 is liquidity, measured broadly speaking by the traded volume. This selection mechanism, coupled to very rare alterations of the index constitution, leads to the awkward situation in which many companies with a fairly decent capitalization are excluded from the Nikkei 225 while some stocks with declining, and eventually very poor liquidity, are not deleted for quite some time.

[9] Index arbitrage was for a long time the biggest loser in a situation of late announcement. Today the total amounts invested in index funds dwarf those allocated to arbitrage, and the biggest loss is undoubtedly transferred to index funds holders, at least in the United States. A Nikkatsu-like decision today would prove primarily unpopular to individual investors, not arbitrageurs, and would consequently not be very smart from a commercial standpoint.

[10] Interestingly, faced with a similar situation in September 1990 with a failure of one of its constituents—Prime Motors Corp.—Standard and Poor's removed it on a short notice from the S&P 500 but left one full trading day between announcement and effective date.

INDEX TRADING AND FUTURES HEDGING

Index Trading

Consider a portfolio set with the explicit strategy of tracking an index I, defined by its weights W_i and divisor D. It is very clear that we need to include all the index components in the portfolio, so let's denote Q_i the quantity for each of them. The value V of the portfolio is therefore:

$$V = \sum_i Q_i \cdot P_i$$

and I is still defined by:

$$I = \frac{\sum_i W_i \cdot P_i}{D}$$

The analogy between the two formulas suggests that we consider setting $Q_i = W_i/D$. The quantity $W_{i,}/D$ can then be interpreted as the implicit number of shares of the ith component of the index. The convention generally accepted is to refer to a portfolio constituted with W_i/D shares of each stock as a portfolio equal to 1 index. A portfolio equal to 10 indices would then be defined by $10 * (W_i/D)$ shares of each stock.

A simple numerical application will illustrate the point. Consider a simple index constituted by two stocks A and B, such that $W_A = 1{,}000$, $W_B = 2{,}000$, $\mathrm{P}_A = \$15$, $P_B = \$25$, and $D = 100$. I is then equal to:

$$I = \frac{1{,}000 * 15 + 2{,}000 * 25}{100} = 650$$

Consider now a portfolio P of 10 shares of A and 20 shares of B. The value V of this portfolio is:

$$V = 10 * \$15 + 20 * \$25 = \$150 + \$500 = \$650$$

It is very easy to verify also that the capitalization of A in I $(= 1{,}000 * \$15/\$65{,}000)$ is equal to that of A in the portfolio $(= 10 * \$15/\$650)$. We conclude that P is rigorously tracking I, and by convention we refer to P as *1 index*.

Now say that we have \$100,000 to invest in P, and we would like to find what is the appropriate number of shares for A and B. Knowing that 1 index is worth \$650, \$100,000 represents 153.8 indices $(= \$100{,}000/\$650)$, which in turn translates into 1,538 shares of A $(= 10 * 153.8)$ and 3,076 shares of $B(= 20 * 153.8)$. Therefore, given a nominal N, we know that we need N/I units of the elementary portfolio P, or $(N/I) *(W_I/D)$ shares of each component i. By extension, this convention gives a meaning to the expression "trading the index" because we can reconstruct fairly easily an equivalent portfolio.

If we take the real example of General Electric (GE) within the S&P 500, for example, $W = 3{,}295{,}312{,}000$ and $D = 8{,}565{,}281{,}030$; therefore one index contains 0.385 shares of GE. The second biggest capitalization in the S&P 500 is Cisco (CSCO), which has $W = 6{,}937{,}630{,}000$. Therefore, one index contains 0.81 shares of CSCO. Within the Dow Jones, $W = 1$ and $D = 0.20145$; therefore, one Dow Jones index contains 4.964 shares of GE.

Futures Hedging

Let's take again the typical arbitrage situation in which we buy an index today and sell its futures contract at the same time. Specifically, we buy a portfolio P and Q_i shares for each stock and sell it back on expiry. On the futures side, we want to know what is the appropriate quantity of futures to sell, and we denote it δ. With the same notations we used earlier for a standard futures, we arrive at the following.

On t_0:

- Borrow an amount $N = \sum Q_i * P_i$ from t_0 to t_1 @ r_{ZC}.
- Buy 1 index @ I_0, for a total nominal $N(= I_0)$.
- Sell δ future @ F_H.

The resulting cash flow is:

$$C_0 = +N - \sum Q_i * P_i = 0$$

On t_1:

- Pay back loan $N + (1 + r_{ZC})$.
- Sell 1 index @ I_{SQ}.
- Sell futures at expiry $\delta * \mathrm{PV}_F * (F_{SQ} - F_H)$, where PV_F is the future's point value.
- Receive accumulated capitalized dividends d^*.

The resulting cash flow is:

$$C_1 = -N * (1 + r_{ZC}) + \sum Q_i * P_i^{SQ} - \delta * \mathrm{PV}_F * F_{SQ} + \delta * PV_F * F_H + d^*$$

We know by definition that:

$$F_{SQ} = I_{SQ} = \frac{\sum_i W_i \cdot P_i^{SQ}}{D} = \sum\nolimits_i \left(\frac{W_i}{D}\right) \cdot P_i^{SQ} = \sum\nolimits_i Q_i \cdot P_i^{SQ}$$

which leads to:

$$C_1 = -N * (1 + r_{ZC}) + \sum Q_i * P_i^{SQ} * (1 - \delta * \mathrm{PV}_F) + \delta * \mathrm{PV}_F * F_H + d^*$$

Setting $\delta = 1/\mathrm{PV}_F$ is a convenient way to set C_1 exactly equal to what it was for a single security, with the same expression for F_H. Therefore, the appropriate number of futures to hedge a portfolio equal to 1 index is exactly $1/\mathrm{PV}_F$ where PV_F is the point value of the future. Formulated differently, 1 future hedges PV_F indices.[11]

Taking the numerical example of the S&P 500, $\mathrm{PV}_F = \$250$; therefore, 1 future hedges 250 indices. In other words, because 1 index contains 0.385 shares of GE and 0.81 shares of CSCO, 1 future hedges exactly 96.25 shares of GE and 202.5 shares of CSCO. For the Dow Jones, $\mathrm{PV}_F = \$10$; therefore, 1 future hedges 10 indices, or 49.64 shares of GE.

INDEX CONTINUITY

Introduction

Continuity refers to the chaining of the index value from today to tomorrow. In practice, it means that today's closing price as of today should be equal to yesterday's closing price as of tomorrow. The reason for such continuity is the importance of maintaining a tradable index, which goes back to the functions it is meant to serve.

As we said, indices serve the purpose of aggregating market information in a convenient and meaningful way, and this has numerous implications. On one side, the informational role of such an aggregation is clear because it serves as a lighthouse and revelator of market activity. Continuity is then a logical requirement because over a period during which the market is closed, an index simply cannot change in value. At the same time this informational content is insufficient in practice if it is not supported by the possibility to invest in it.[12]

[11] This result is obviously dependent upon the set of conventions used to define the notion of "1 index." In many cases 1 index is alternatively defined as a portfolio equal to $Q_i = \mathrm{PV}_F * W_i/D$ with the stated purpose of instituting a "1 index $\Leftrightarrow$ 1 futures correspondence."

[12] Index sponsors in general generate revenues by licensing their intellectual property—namely, their indices. A nontradable index has less licensing value; therefore, continuity is also an economical requirement.

Continuity is synonymous here with *traceable changes*, changes that can be reproduced at no cost in a portfolio tracking the index.[13]

It is therefore necessary for us to consider the question of continuity in detail from the dual perspective of numerical value and tradability, with respect to the different types of events likely to affect the index composition.

Inclusions and/or Deletions

Arithmetic

Consider a very simple index with two components, A and B. W_A, W_B, P_A, and P_B denote respectively A and B's weight and price today. I is then given by:

$$I = \frac{W_A \cdot P_A + W_B \cdot P_B}{D}$$

Suppose now that B is replaced by C, effective on today's close. As of tomorrow morning, I becomes:

$$I = \frac{W_A \cdot P_A + W_C \cdot P_C}{D'}$$

Clearly $D' \neq D$ because otherwise I would not keep the same numerical value. This very simple example shows the exact role of D: *The divisor is the critical adjustment parameter to ensure numerical continuity of the index*. In addition, D changes in value only if $W_c \cdot P_c \neq W_B \cdot P_B$—that is, if the total capitalization included in the index is not constant throughout the substitution.

Tradability

The above reasoning can be extended to a more general case:

$$I = \frac{\sum_{i \neq j} W_i \cdot P_i + W_j \cdot P_j}{D} = \frac{\sum_{i \neq j} W_i \cdot P_i + W'_j \cdot P'_j}{D'}$$

where W_j, P_j, W'_j, and P'_j represent the characteristics of the stock deleted and included respectively. This formula is generally used to compute D' from D.

Now let's consider a replicating portfolio P, constituted of n indices. If we denote Q_i the quantity held for each individual stock, the value V of the portfolio on the close before substitution is:

---

[13] In the example of Nikkatsu, the nondisclosure did not jeopardize the numerical continuity on the Nikkei 225, but its tradability. The change could not be reproduced at no cost.

$$V = \sum_{i \neq j} Q_i \cdot P_i + Q_j \cdot P_j \qquad \text{where} \quad Q_i = n \cdot \left(\frac{W_i}{D}\right)$$

After the substitution, the number of shares to be held in a perfectly replicating portfolio is changed to:

$$Q_i' = n \cdot \left(\frac{W_i}{D'}\right)$$

for every single constituent. Because $D' \neq D \quad \Rightarrow \quad Q_i' \neq Q_i$, we need to actually adjust every single position in the portfolio. There is, however, a way around that, by considering that the number of units n is not constant. Let's suppose that n is changed to n' after the substitution, and let's make n' such that:

$$Q_i' = n' \cdot \left(\frac{W_i}{D'}\right) = n \cdot \left(\frac{W_i}{D}\right) = Q_i$$

which implies:

$$n' = n \cdot \left(\frac{D'}{D}\right)$$

This relationship is convenient because we do not need to adjust all the Q_i anymore; therefore, the major part of the portfolio is unchanged through the substitution. In that case the only thing we need to do is get rid of Q_j and acquire Q_j', given by:

$$Q_j = n \cdot \left(\frac{W_j}{D}\right) \qquad Q_j' = n' \cdot \left(\frac{W_j'}{D'}\right)$$

In other words, *we can "trade" the substitution by simply selling the entire position—Q_j shares—of the deleted stock, and buying Q_j' shares of the newly included one. As a consequence of the substitution, the number of index units in the portfolio is changed to n'.*

This result shows that the substitution is tradable provided that it is announced prior to being effective. It does not say anything, however, about the cost of this trading. Consider, for example, that we sell Q_j at $p_j \neq P_j$, and buy Q_j' at $p_j' \neq P_j'$.

If the substitution is effective tonight and we trade it, the value of the portfolio after the close becomes:

$$V = \sum_{i \neq j} Q_i \cdot P_i + Q_j' \cdot P_j'$$

The term $Q_j \cdot P_j$ has disappeared, having been replaced by $Q_j' \cdot P_j'$. Meanwhile by selling Q_j, we received $Q_j \cdot p_j$, and buying Q_j' cost $Q_j' \cdot p_j'$. It is very clear that if $p_j \neq P_j$, and $p_j' \neq P_j'$, the change in value

V is not compensated by the amount of cash required to settle the trades. Therefore, we need to trade the substitution at the exact price used in the index calculation—that is, the closing price.

This is exactly what proved impossible in the case of Nikkatsu because the announcement was made too late, after the close. The next day the substitution was effective, and investors realized a loss because prices had moved significantly from P_j and P'_j.[14] Note that the defining parameter here is the divisor. Because D' is computed with P_j and P'_j, these prices are literally set in stone for the substitution.

As a numerical application, consider the case of the substitution of four constituents of the Dow Jones operated in November 1999. Chevron, Goodyear Tire, Sears, and Union Carbide were removed, to be replaced by Home Depot, Intel, Microsoft, and SBC Communications, effective on November 1, 1999. Table 5-3 presents all relevant prices as of October 29, 1999.

The first 26 stocks remain unchanged, and the weighted average of this "core" is simply the sum of all prices, \$1,896.75. The group of four stocks being deleted accounts for \$221.81, and those about to be added, \$296.63. The divisor before the change was 0.19740; therefore, computing the new divisor is relatively simple:

$$I = \frac{\$1{,}896.75 + \$221.81}{0.19740} = \frac{\$1{,}896.75 + \$296.63}{D'} \qquad \Rightarrow \qquad D' = 0.20437$$

In reality, the new divisor given by Dow Jones was 0.20436, the difference being a rounding error. If we had a replicating portfolio of 100 indices before, we have now $n' = n \cdot (D'/D) = 103.53$ units, but the number of shares for each stock remains identical at 506.58.[15]

Corporate Events

As we did earlier with the examination of the impact of corporate events on the outstanding number of shares, we need to consider here the impact of these same events with respect to index tradability. The formalism we used before will be entirely relevant, and in general

---

[14] In a "normal" addition and deletion process, newly included stocks usually appreciate until the effective date and then correct slightly. Therefore, deciding not to buy Q'_j until after effective date can also be a very conscious trading decision. It constitutes a possible source of profit or loss, but it can be actively managed.

[15] The role of the number of units may appear unclear in this example. It is in fact easy to show that it is proportional to the number of futures necessary to hedge the position. Therefore, an increased number of units simply indicates that the position would have to be hedged by more futures because its total nominal increased.

TABLE 5-3

Name	Ticker		Closing Price
Alcoa	AA		60.7500
AT&T Corp.	T		46.7500
AlliedSignal Inc.	ALD		56.9375
American Express Co.	AXP		154.0000
Boeing Co.	BA		46.0625
Caterpillar Inc.	CAT		55.3125
Citigroup	C		54.2500
Coca-Cola Co.	KO		59.0000
E.I. Du Pont de Nemours & Co.	DD		64.4375
Eastman Kodak Co.	EK		68.9375
Exxon Corp.	XON		74.0625
General Electric Co.	GE		135.5000
General Motors Corp.	GM		70.4375
Hewlett-Packard Co.	HWP		74.1875
International Business Machines Corp.	IBM		98.2500
International Paper Co.	IP		52.6250
J. P. Morgan & Co.	JPM		130.8750
Johnson & Johnson	JNJ		104.7500
McDonald's Corp.	MCD		41.2500
Merck & Co.	MRK		79.5625
Minnesota Mining & Manufacturing Co.	MMM		95.0625
Philip Morris Cos.	MO		25.1875
Procter & Gamble Co.	PG		104.8750
United Technologies Corp.	UTX		60.5000
Wal-Mart Stores Inc.	WMT		56.6875
Walt Disney Co.	DIS		26.5000
		Core:	**1,896.75**
Goodyear Tire & Rubber Co.	GT		41.3125
Chevron Corp.	CHV		91.3125
Sears, Roebuck & Co.	S		28.1875
Union Carbide Corp.	UK		61.0000
		Out:	**221.81**
Home Depot Inc.	HD		75.7500
Intel Corp.	INTC		77.4375
Microsoft Corp.	MSFT		92.5625
SBC Communications	SBC		50.8750
		In:	**296.63**

(*Source*: Compiled by author from Datastream data.)

it is not surprising to find that virtually all events are tradable quite simply, provided that the information is available in a timely manner.

The general idea is that corporate events are never price driven. In other words, if the capitalization of a particular stock is affected by a specific capital operation, the index should not be because it is meant to record only price appreciation. Therefore, the divisor of an index is adjusted following a corporate event in such a way as to ensure continuity and make the event invisible in the index performance.

Dividends

Dividend payments are recorded only in total return indices, and the weight is modified in the following way:

$$W' = W * \left(\frac{P_Y}{P_Y - d}\right)$$

Therefore, for a total return index, a dividend ex-amount is recorded with the following adjustment:

$$I = \frac{\sum_{i \neq j} W_i \cdot P_i + W_j \cdot P_j}{D} = \frac{\sum_{i \neq j} W_i \cdot P_i + W_j \cdot \left(\frac{P_j}{P_j - d}\right) \cdot P_j}{D'}$$

As we observed for an inclusion or deletion, $D' \neq D$ means that we potentially need to adjust the entire portfolio stock by stock.[16] We solve this difficulty in the same manner by saying that the number of index units n has been changed to n' due to the dividend ex-date. Therefore, the quantity Q_j we should hold is modified accordingly to Q'_j:

$$Q_j = n \cdot \left(\frac{W_j}{D}\right) \qquad Q'_j = n' \cdot \left(\frac{W'_j}{D'}\right) = n' \cdot \left(\frac{W_j}{D'}\right) \cdot \left(\frac{P_j}{P_j - d}\right)$$

Because of the relationship between n and n', Q'_j becomes:

$$Q'_j = n \cdot \left(\frac{W_j}{D}\right) \cdot \left(\frac{P_j}{P_j - d}\right) = Q_j \cdot \left(\frac{P_j}{P_j - d}\right)$$

This very simple result means that the adjustment taking place in the index is directly replicable within the position. We need to buy only a small additional quantity ΔQ_j of the stock going ex, equal to:

[16] Note that in the case of an inclusion or deletion, we cannot be sure that $D' > D$. In the case of an ex-dividend event for a total return index, this is always true.

$$\Delta Q_j = Q_j' - Q_j = Q_j \cdot \left(\frac{P_j}{P_j - d}\right) - Q_j = Q_j \cdot \left(\frac{d}{P_j - d}\right)$$

It would be very simple as well to show that ΔQ_i must be bought at the close P_j or at the "fair" opening price $P_j - d$. In practice, because the actual opening price may be significantly different from $P_j - d$, it is always safer to buy ΔQ_j at the close of the last trading day.

Splits

Splits are extremely straightforward events with regard to index behavior. If r denotes the split ratio, we know that $Q_j' = r \cdot Q_j$ and $P_j' = P_j/r$. Therefore, the index is simply not affected in any way:

$$I = \frac{\sum_{i \neq j} W_i \cdot P_i + W_j \cdot P_j}{D} = \frac{\sum_{i \neq j} W_i \cdot P_i + (W_j \cdot r)\left(\frac{P_j}{r}\right)}{D'}$$

$D' = D$, and the replicating portfolio is unaffected. There is really nothing particular to do except passively record the changes in W_j and P_j.

This development is true for capitalization-weighted indices but not for price-weighted indices. In the case of a price-weighted index, the weight W_j remains unchanged through the split:

$$I = \frac{\sum_{i \neq j} W_i \cdot P_i + W_j \cdot P_j}{D} = \frac{\sum_{i \neq j} W_i \cdot P_i + W_j \cdot \left(\frac{P_j}{r}\right)}{D'}$$

Here $D' \neq D$, and for this reason the number of units again changes to $n' = n \cdot (D'/D)$. The new theoretical quantity Q_j' is equal to Q_j:

$$Q_j' = n' \cdot \left(\frac{W_j'}{D'}\right) = n' \cdot \left(\frac{W_j}{D'}\right) = n \cdot \left(\frac{W_j}{D}\right) = Q_j$$

but we still have a problem because we receive a distribution of $(r - 1) \cdot Q_j$ free shares due to the split, and we need to sell these shares on the effective day of the split. They need to be sold at the price P_j/r, which is the fair price of the stock after the split but before the open. Again we do not know for sure the exact opening price; therefore, it is more prudent to sell them the day before on the close, automatically realizing the price P_j used in the divisor adjustment.

If we denote δ the proportion of shares we actually need to sell, the new position held is $Q_j \cdot (1 - \delta)$ on the close. The number of free shares we receive is then $Q_j \cdot (1 - \delta) \cdot (r - 1)$, and the total position is $Q_j \cdot (1 - \delta) \cdot r$. This total position should be equal to Q_j' for the portfolio to be a perfectly replicating portfolio again:

$$\begin{cases} Q_j \cdot (1-\delta) \cdot r = Q'_j \\ Q'_j = Q_j \end{cases} \quad \Rightarrow \quad \delta = \frac{r-1}{r}$$

This result means that to remain perfectly hedged after a split in a price-weighted index, we need to sell $(r-1)/r \cdot Q_j$ shares of the stock to be split at the close of the last trading day of the split.

Consider as an illustration a portfolio of 100 Dow Jones indices, and the split 3:2 of Home Depot (HD) on December 31, 1999. As of December 30, the Dow divisor was 0.20436, and each constituent had an equivalent quantity of 4.893 shares. A portfolio of 100 indices would have held 489.33 shares of HD. HD closed at \$100.1875, and the next morning after the split its fair price was \$66.7917 (= \$100.1875 * 2/3). At the same time, the Dow closed at \$11,452.86, indicating a total weighted average of all constituents of \$2,340.50 (= \$11,452.86* 0.20436). The new divisor D' is then given by:

$$I = \frac{\$2{,}340.50}{0.20436} = \frac{\$2{,}340.50 - \$100.1875 + \$66.7917}{D'} \quad \Rightarrow D' = 0.20144$$

Therefore, the next day we hold $n' = n \cdot (D'/D) = 98.57$ indices, and we need to have 489.33 (= 98.57/0.20144) shares of each constituent, which is the case already except for HD. For HD we have now 734 shares (= 3/2 * 489.33) due to the distribution of free shares after the split. To remain hedged, we should hold 489.33 shares only, which means 244.67 shares in excess. We can sell those shares at the open on the ex-date at the risk that the opening price is lower than \$66.8125, or we can decide to sell them preemptively on the close of the last trading day.[17] In that case, we sell $\delta \cdot Q_j = 163.1 (= 0.33 * 489.33)$ shares, after which we have 326.22 left. These 326.22 generate 163.11 free shares with the split, reconstituting the needed 389.33 position. Figure 5-8 is a quick diagram to help in visualizing the situation.

Mergers and Acquisitions

Mergers and acquisitions are complex events with respect to index composition and behavior. On one side, the stocks involved may or may not trade at par with respect to the terms of the transaction, which potentially creates an opportunity—and a risk. The second dimension of the event is which stock will remain in the index after the transaction. Not surprisingly, different configurations lead to different results, but more interestingly some of these may be profitable.

---

[17] As it happens, the actual opening price on December 31 was \$67.4375, 62.5 cents higher than its fair value. The value \$66.8125 is different from the theoretical fair price \$66.7917 because of the rounding to the nearest 16th.

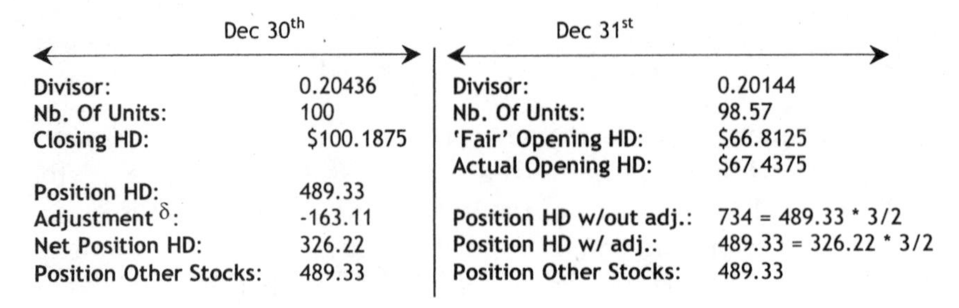

Figure 5-8 Substitution

As an illustration, consider a capitalization-weighted index constituted of three stocks, out of a universe set to A, B, C, or D. We consider that A absorbs B with a ratio r, meaning that at maturity holders of B receive r shares of A for each share they hold. In terms of index composition, four scenarios are possible:

- A, B, and C in the index; no stock is added after the merger.
- A, B, and C in the index; D is added.
- A, C, and D in the index.
- B, C, and D in the index.

Let's examine each situation in detail and draw some generalizations from there.

A *and* B *Included, No Addition*[18]

If the index is A, B, and C, continuity is expressed by:

$$I = \frac{W_A \cdot P_A + W_B \cdot P_B + W_C \cdot P_C}{D} = \frac{W'_A \cdot P_A + W_C \cdot P_C}{D'}$$
$$= \frac{(W_A + r \cdot W_B) \cdot P_A + W_C \cdot P_C}{D'}$$

The number of units in our portfolio is changed to $n' = n \cdot (D'/D)$ only if $P_B \neq r \cdot P_A$—that is, if both stocks are not trading at par. Its value is also modified just by virtue of the merger from:

$$V = Q_A \cdot P_A + Q_B \cdot P_B + Q_C \cdot P_C$$

to:

$$V' = (Q_A + r \cdot Q_B) \cdot P_A + Q_C \cdot P_C$$

[18] This situation occurs, for example, when the index is all-inclusive, like the TOPIX in Japan. When two stocks merge, there is not necessarily a replacement immediately.

Because of the relationship between n' and n, it is very simple to check that the portfolio remains a perfect replication of the index without any further adjustment. In addition, there is a creation of value if A is trading above par with respect to B:

$$V' - V = (r \cdot P_A - P_B) \cdot Q_B$$

In other words, the holders of a portfolio replicating an index passively benefit from the risk arbitrage opportunity created by the merger. Note, however, that the benefit occurs only on the last trading day of the merger, when the difference with par is probably small.

A *and* B *Included,* B *Replaced*

This situation is very similar to the one before. Continuity is given by:

$$I = \frac{W_A \cdot P_A + W_B \cdot P_B + W_C \cdot P_C}{D}$$
$$= \frac{(W_A + r \cdot W_B) \cdot P_A + W_C \cdot P_C + W_D \cdot P_D}{D'}$$

assuming B is replaced by D. Again we have $n' = n \cdot (D'/D)$, and the same mechanical effect of the merger creates a passive profit or loss upon expiry. The only difference from the previous case is that D needs to be bought on the close of the last trading day of the merger, with:

$$Q'_D = n' \cdot \left(\frac{W_D}{D'}\right) = n \cdot \left(\frac{W_D}{D}\right)$$

A *Only Included*

Continuity here is given by:

$$I = \frac{W_A \cdot P_A + W_C \cdot P_C + W_D \cdot P_D}{D}$$
$$= \frac{(W_A + r \cdot W_B) \cdot P_A + W_C \cdot P_C + W_D \cdot P_D}{D'}$$

This situation requires us to buy additional shares of A because its weight increases in the index. Although before we held B as part of our replicating portfolio, we do not here, which means that the difference with par does not automatically materialize in the position on expiry. If we buy an additional quantity ΔQ_A number of shares at the close, the position is perfectly hedged with respect to the index, at no cost or profit:

$$\Delta Q_A = Q'_A - Q_A = n' \cdot \left(\frac{W_A + r \cdot W_B}{D'}\right) - Q_A$$
$$= n' \cdot \left(\frac{W_A}{D'}\right) + n' \cdot r \cdot \left(\frac{W_B}{D'}\right) - Q_A = n \cdot r \cdot \left(\frac{W_B}{D}\right)$$

based again on the fact that $n' = n \cdot (D'/D)$.

B *Only Included*

This case is particularly interesting because although relatively infrequent. Continuity here is given by:

$$I = \frac{W_B \cdot P_B + W_C \cdot P_C + W_D \cdot P_D}{D}$$
$$= \frac{(W_A + r \cdot W_B) \cdot P_A + W_C \cdot P_C + W_D \cdot P_D}{D'}$$

Because we hold B before the merger, we benefit again automatically from a difference with par between P_A and P_B. We still need to buy shares of A to adjust the portfolio because the transformation of B shares into A shares provides only a fraction of the capitalization we need:

$$Q'_A = n' \cdot \left(\frac{W_A + r \cdot W_B}{D'}\right) = n' \cdot \left(\frac{W_A}{D'}\right) + n' \cdot r \cdot \left(\frac{W_B}{D'}\right)$$
$$= n \cdot \left(\frac{W_A}{D}\right) + r \cdot Q_B$$

$r \cdot Q_B$ is what we receive in A shares due to B's position, but $n \cdot (W_A/D)$ is missing and must be bought at the close of the last trading day.

Summary

Table 5-4 presents a rapid summary of the different alternatives. The Π column represents the "Automatic win" profit or loss. In cases **1**, **2**, and **4**, because of a native position in B, an index-replicating portfolio automatically and passively benefits from a merger if the price relationship between A and B is such that $r \cdot P_A - P_B > 0$ on expiry. In practice, this relationship is almost always true because it simply indicates that B is trading at a discount to its fair acquisition price. However, if for some exceptional reason P_B were trading at a premium, Π would be negative and a replicating portfolio would then automatically record a loss. The only way to hedge against this loss is to trade the risk arbitrage before at a favorable price. Case **3** is very similar to cases **1** and **2** and benefits from the merger, but the arbitrage has to be implemented manually because it is not automatically reflected in the divisor's adjustment.

TABLE 5-4

Situation	Π	Adjustment	Risk Arbitrage "Free" Option	"Automatic Win"	"Double Chance"
1 *A* and *B* in, no addition	$\Pi = (r \cdot P_A - P_B) \cdot Q_B$	Ø	Yes	Yes	—
2 *A* and *B* in, *D* added	$\Pi = (r \cdot P_A - P_B) \cdot Q_B$	Buy $Q'_D = n \cdot \left(\frac{W_D}{D}\right)$	Yes	Yes	—
3 *A* in, remains in	$\Pi = 0$	Buy $\Delta Q_A = n \cdot r \cdot \left(\frac{W_B}{D}\right)$	Yes	—	Yes
4 *B* in, replaced by *A*	$\Pi = (r \cdot P_A - P_B) \cdot Q_B$	Buy $\Delta Q_A = n \cdot \left(\frac{W_A}{D}\right)$	—	Yes	Yes

The "Risk arbitrage option" describes the option embedded in the position to benefit from the merger *before* expiry. In three out of four situations, we hold A as part of the replicating portfolio; therefore, if the arbitrage of the merger is profitable, we can trade it very easily, without having to borrow A, which can be difficult and expensive.[19]

In short, the first generalization we can make is that *it is always possible for the holder of a replicating portfolio to benefit from a merger situation within an index*. In cases **1** and **2**, the arbitrage can be implemented any time before expiry, and in any case, accrues automatically anyway on the last trading day. In **3** the arbitrage is also possible at any time, but it does not materialize automatically. In **4**, the arbitrage is automatic on expiry, but it is not necessarily possible before because we do not hold A.

Now consider cases **3** and **4**, and the "Double chance" feature. In both situations we have to buy A upon expiry of the merger, as part of the normal life cycle of the index. However, buying A is not necessarily optimal because we can trade B instead and tender the shares to the merger on the effective date. Therefore, we have an *additional option to benefit from the merger*, in addition to the full extent of the position we already hold. In **3**, instead of buying $n \cdot r \cdot (W_B/D)$ shares of A, we can buy $n \cdot r \cdot (W_B/D)/r = n \cdot (W_B/D)$ shares of B at a better price if B trades at a discount. Similarly, in **4** we can buy $n \cdot (W_A/D)/r$ shares of B instead of $n \cdot (W_A/D)$ shares of A.

The difference between cases **3** and **4** is only a question of magnitude in the "Double chance" opportunity. For example, in **3**, if we decide to buy $n \cdot (W_B/D)$ shares of B, the nominal of this trade is:

$$N_3 = n \cdot \left(\frac{W_B}{D}\right) \cdot P_B = \left(\frac{n}{D}\right) \cdot (W_B \cdot P_B)$$

whereas in **4**, if we buy $n \cdot (W_A/D)/r$ shares of B, it is:

$$N_4 = \left(\frac{n}{r}\right) \cdot \left(\frac{W_A}{D}\right) \cdot P_B = \left(\frac{n}{D}\right) \cdot \left(W_A \cdot \frac{P_B}{r}\right) \approx \left(\frac{n}{D}\right) \cdot (W_A \cdot P_A)$$

if we assume for simplicity that $r \cdot P_A = P_B$. It is apparent that N_3 is proportional to the total capitalization of B—$W_B \cdot P_B$—whereas N_4 is proportional to that of A—$W_A \cdot P_A$. If the merger is a merger of equal entities, there is no significant difference between N_3 and N_4. In gen-

[19] Note that the automatic win or risk arbitrage options are nonexclusive. In **1** and **2** it is possible to enter arbitrage before expiry and still benefit from the automatic win at expiry.

eral, however, B tends to be smaller than A, which means that the "Double chance" in **3** is usually smaller than in **4**.

This discussion leads to the second generalization: *If one of the merging companies is not included in the index at the time of the merger, there is an additional opportunity to arbitrage the event, the most advantageous situation being that of a substitution operated in parallel to the merger—that is, event* **4**.

Price-Weighted Indices

Let's examine the different cases again, this time from the perspective of a price-weighted index:

A *and* B *In, No Addition*[20]*:*

$$I = \frac{W_A \cdot P_A + W_B \cdot P_B + W_C \cdot P_C}{D} = \frac{W_A \cdot P_A + W_c \cdot P_C}{D'}$$

but we know that $W_A = W_B = W_C = W$, so:

$$I = \left(\frac{W}{D}\right) \cdot (P_A + P_B + P_C) = \left(\frac{W}{D'}\right) \cdot (P_A + P_C)$$

A *and* B *In,* D *Added:*

$$I = \frac{W_A \cdot P_A + W_B \cdot P_B + W_C \cdot P_C}{D} = \frac{W_A \cdot P_A + W_C \cdot P_C + W_D \cdot P_D}{D'}$$

which simplifies to:

$$I = \left(\frac{W}{D}\right) \cdot (P_A + P_B + P_C) = \left(\frac{W}{D'}\right) \cdot (P_A + P_C + P_D)$$

A *In, Remains In:*

$$I = \frac{W_A \cdot P_A + W_C \cdot P_C + W_D \cdot P_D}{D} = \frac{W_A \cdot P_A + W_C \cdot P_C + W_D \cdot P_D}{D'}$$

and clearly $D' = D$.

B *In, Replaced by* A*:*

$$I = \frac{W_B \cdot P_B + W_C \cdot P_C + W_D \cdot P_D}{D} = \frac{W_A \cdot P_A + W_C \cdot P_C + W_D \cdot P_D}{D'}$$

again simplifies to:

[20] In the case of the Dow Jones or Nikkei 225, the merger would result in one less constituent; therefore, this case is practically impossible.

$$I = \left(\frac{W}{D}\right) \cdot (P_B + P_C + P_D) = \left(\frac{W}{D'}\right) \cdot (P_A + P_C + P_D)$$

If we draw a table similar to the one above, it would result in the summary shown in Table 5-5.

In cases **1** and **2**, the weight of A is unchanged by the merger, and we need to sell B because it is not part of the index anymore. We still have the option to arbitrage the merger because of a native position Q_A, but there is no automatic win anymore. On the surface it looks as though there is potential for a "Double chance" because we need to sell Q_B, and we could decide to sell A instead and enter the arbitrage. In practice, however, if we take advantage of the arbitrage before expiry to the full extent of what the position allows, we do not hold A anymore on expiry. Therefore, if we want to sell more shares of A instead of Q_B, we need to borrow them, which may be impossible or expensive. Therefore, the double chance is in fact uncertain.

Case **3** is really a nonevent because the index is absolutely unchanged with $D' = D$, and so is the replicating portfolio.

Case **4** is more interesting because there is a need for adjustment in the position. If we do nothing, the position Q_B is automatically transferred to an equivalent $r \cdot Q_B$ shares of A, which creates an "Automatic win." However, this quantity is not necessarily equal to what we should have: $Q'_A = n' \cdot (W/D') = n \cdot (W/D) = Q_B$. Therefore, we must sell $\delta \cdot Q_B$ shares of B so that after the merger, $r \cdot (1 - \delta) \cdot Q_B$ is equal to Q'_A[21]:

$$r \cdot (1 - \delta) \cdot Q_B = Q'_A = Q_B \qquad \Rightarrow \qquad \delta = \frac{r - 1}{r}$$

At the time the merger is effective, the position in B is reduced to $(1 - \delta) \cdot Q_B = Q_B/r$, and the profit generated by the automatic win is then:

$$\Pi = (r \cdot P_A - P_B) \cdot \left(\frac{Q_B}{r}\right)$$

Because we can sell $r \cdot \delta \cdot Q_B$ shares of A instead of $\delta \cdot Q_B$ shares of B to adjust the position, the situation presents a possible double chance feature. In fact, if $r \geq 1$, we need to sell A, which we do not hold and have to borrow. Therefore, the double chance is uncertain because we are not assured that we can find the shares. If $r < 1$,

[21] In general, $r \geq 1$, which means $\delta > 0$. However, $r < 1$ also occurs, in which case we need to *buy* $(-\delta \cdot Q_B)$ shares.

TABLE 5-5

Situation	Π	Adjustment	Risk Arbitrage "Free" Option	"Automatic Win"	"Double Chance"
1 *A* and *B* in, no addition	$\Pi = 0$	Sell Q_B	Yes	—	Uncertain
2 *A* and *B* in, *D* added	$\Pi = 0$	Sell Q_B Buy Q_D	Yes	—	Uncertain
3 *A* in, remains in	$\Pi = 0$	Ø	Yes	—	—
4 *B* in, replaced by *A*	$\Pi = (r \cdot P_A - P_B) \cdot \left(\frac{Q_B}{r}\right)$	Sell $\Delta Q_B = \left(\frac{n}{D}\right) \cdot \left(\frac{r-1}{r}\right) \cdot W$	—	Yes	Uncertain

we need to buy B, which is always possible, and the double chance is then certain.

Conclusion

This detailed examination of corporate events explains in a large part why we focused heavily on understanding them in the first place. It can be argued that only index arbitrageurs and index fund managers really care about index-replicating portfolios, but the reality is much broader.

Indeed, any arbitrage position for which one of the legs is an index futures contract is potentially affected by a corporate event. Because it is possible to associate each futures contract to an elementary quantity of each constituent in the index, a futures contract is also a form of replicating a portfolio and needs to be managed accordingly. The rigorous exercise of precisely tracking opportunities based on a simple arithmetic definition is also extremely useful in many other settings where the same type of analysis must be performed.

CORRELATIONS

As was indicated before, many indices are chained to include and segment as many constituents as possible within the underlying universe of listed stocks. Therefore, it is interesting to consider the relative behavior of embedded indices more generally.

Consider, for example, two indices I_1 and I_2 constituted of m_1 and m_2 securities, such that I_1 is included in I_2. By definition:

$$I_1 = \frac{\sum_{i=1}^{m_1} w_1 \cdot P_i}{D_1} \quad \text{and} \quad I_2 = \frac{\sum_{i=1}^{m_2} w_i \cdot P_i}{D_2}$$

if I_1 and I_2 are computed according to the same averaging rule. If we rank the stocks according to their inclusion in I_1, we can write:

$$I_2 = \frac{\sum_{i=1}^{m_2} w_i \cdot P_i}{D_2} = \frac{\sum_{i=1}^{m_1} w_i \cdot P_i + \sum_{i=m_1+1}^{m_2} w_i \cdot P_i}{D_2}$$

$$= \frac{D_1 \cdot I_1 + \sum_{i=m_1+1}^{m_2} w_i \cdot P_i}{D_2} = \left(\frac{D_1}{D_2}\right) \cdot I_1 + \frac{\sum_{i=m_1+1}^{m_2} w_i \cdot P_i}{D_2}$$

If we denote:

$$C_{1/2} = \frac{\sum_{i=m_1+1}^{m_2} w_i \cdot P_i}{D_2}$$

the above expression becomes:

$$I_2 = \left(\frac{D_1}{D_2}\right) \cdot I_1 + C_{1/2}$$

This simple relationship indicates how we can transfer a position on I_1 to I_2 and vice versa. To illustrate this point, consider we hold n_1 indices I_1. For each stock in I_1, the number of shares in the portfolio is:

$$Q_i^1 = n \cdot \left(\frac{W_i}{D_1}\right)$$

This number of shares is equal to what we would hold if we had n_2 indices I_2 in portfolio, with n_2 such that $n_2 = n_1 \cdot (D_2/D_1)$. However, to have a complete I_2 position, we should also hold stocks that are not included in I_1 for an amount equal to:

$$Q_i^2 = n_2 \cdot \left(\frac{w_i}{D_2}\right) \qquad \text{for} \quad m_1 + 1 \leq i \leq m_2$$

This is exactly the quantity associated with $C_{1/2}$, if $C_{1/2}$ is considered an independent index. Therefore, to transform n_1 indices I_1 into n_2 indices I_2, we need to trade n_2 indices $C_{1/2}$ as if it were itself a third distinct index. Naturally the reverse transformation is exactly the opposite.

This result is not extraordinarily surprising, but it is interesting in at least three aspects. First, it opens the door to cross-index arbitrage. We know how to transform I_1 into I_2, which means that if both indices have listed futures, we can indifferently trade any of them and operate a transformation when needed. Second, we have implicitly created a new index, strictly equal to $I_2 - I_1$. If needed, we can use it to take a position on the difference $I_2 - I_1$, for example, to benefit from an expected appreciation of small capitalization stocks compared to traditional larger companies. Finally, we even have a futures contract on this new index because the difference $F_1 - (D_1/D_2) \cdot F_2$ behaves exactly like a futures contract on $C_{1/2}$. In the United States, for example, the existence of a long series of embedded indices offers a certain number of opportunities for investors trying to build nonconventional index positions.

CONCLUSION

This chapter covers many of the technicalities necessary to manage a portfolio replicating a given index. In fact, beyond that specific case applicable to index arbitrageurs, the day-to-day maintenance of a stock portfolio requires a precise understanding of the mechanics, and more importantly the opportunities, attached to corporate events. The formalism we went through should enable a rigorous analysis of any situation, from the most common to the least frequent, giving solid tools to understand the details and benefit from them.

Part II

FINANCIAL VALUATION AND RISK ANALYSIS

6

VALUATIONS

INTRODUCTION

After the exhaustive examination of all the instruments independently of each other, we must now turn to the issue of evaluating an entire position. The underlying assumption in all prior analytical results was a *static forward-looking perspective*: All products were about to be traded, and we systematically examined how they should be priced in order to determine their fair value at the time of the trade.

The perspective we want to take now is that of a live position, established at various points in the past. It is a collection of various instruments of different nature, notably in terms of payment schedule. This situation corresponds to the reality of a trading desk where transactions are accumulated day after day and where we must be able to value incoming trades as well as established positions. Furthermore, we must design a unified process so that all instruments can be systematically valued, in such a way that the figure we obtain is reliable and meaningful. *Reliability* is here an internal metric and points toward rigorous pricing procedure, with the lowest possible level of uncertainty. *Meaningfulness*, on the other hand, refers to the overall environment and implies that valuation parameters be chosen wisely to be as representative as possible. For example, there cannot be much debate about the value of a futures contract based on a cost-of-carry model, but there may be more discussion about the relevant amount of dividends or the right interest rate to use. Clearly the futures contract can be priced rigorously with any choice of parameters, but its value is not meaningful if it is not specifically tailored to the characteristics of the underlying position and market environment.[1]

Another dimension of a valuation statement is that it is distributed to a relatively broad audience. Traders have full responsibility for the day-to-day management of their position, but the valuation is always an absolute reporting requirement to senior management and other departments such as internal control and audit. A practical consequence of this requirement is that the valuation document should be readily understandable by nontraders and furthermore should also accommodate different formats. Typically the back-office department in charge of clearing and settling trades performs its own valuation every day, necessarily different from the front-office figure because of distinct conventions. The best illustration of this situation is the difference between a mark-to-market and theoretical figure: The mark-to-market calculation reflects market conditions and arguably is more valid than any sort of convergence assumption. At the same time an absolute convergence is a unique characteristic that should be incorporated in the valuation, making the theoretical value more representative. In fact, reliability and meaningfulness sometimes conflict, and when this is the case, it is usually better to produce two documents rather than try to impose one of them as the absolute truth.

Finally, it is necessary to mention that the framework we develop here goes far beyond the sphere of pure arbitrage. Indeed, we would argue that any type of financial valuation should be based on the same principles because traders are generally looking for similar information regardless of the products they trade. For the same reasons we do not make any distinction for geographic particularities because there should be few, if any.

To build a valuation procedure on solid ground, we adopt a staged approach. First, we develop a certain number of general and fundamental principles with a clear emphasis on the underlying need they serve. As a second step, we take a standard portfolio and apply these principles systematically to every instrument. Before we do that, however, let's define clearly what we call *valuation*.

---

[1] A principle very well known in a variety of other settings as *GIGO*: garbage in, garbage out.

DEFINITIONS

The valuation of a financial position is equal to the cash flow generated by a full liquidation of this position at its fair market value. The concept is very simple and very straightforward: We liquidate every single instrument in the portfolio at a price as close as possible to its fair market value and derive the total amount of money brought in by this liquidation.

This definition has two practical consequences. On one side, a valuation is a static figure. Although the position itself is constantly evolving, performing a valuation means freezing its constitution and parameters at the same moment. Therefore, any possible variation of any of these parameters is not reflected in the valuation figure itself. There is indeed a need for a dynamic analysis, which we call a *risk analysis* and describe in the next chapter. The other side of the definition is that we do not know how to account for noncash items if they cannot be turned into cash. A typical example would be the possibility of a system failure on a futures expiry. At this time the inability to transmit orders to the stock exchange could prove disastrous. We do not really know how to value this risk, and accordingly we cannot incorporate it in the total valuation although it is extremely real.

PRINCIPLES

Liquidation, Cash, and Present Value

In performing a valuation, cash is the only object of interest. The purpose of the operation is to compute the net present value of all liquidating flows, regardless of their effective date. The term *liquidation* has therefore a dual meaning. On one side it means that we have to neutralize unknown flows still dependent on the market, and on the other side we must ensure that they are adequately offset by a money market operation. At the end of the liquidation, *there is no more uncertain flow in the future, as every single one of them has been "canceled out" and discounted today*.

To better understand the implication of this procedure, consider a long forward position. If we sell the forward today, the settlement flow of this transaction will take place at expiry, as opposed to a futures contract for which the settlement would have taken place in the next days with the margin call. The sale does neutralize the forward because the final flow is thereafter known with certainty. The second step requires us to borrow or lend today the amount associated with the forward flow, so that its value is canceled out. If we were supposed to receive $1,000,000 as a final settlement in two months, we would have to borrow today an amount such that we have to reimburse exactly $1,000,000 in two months. The amount we borrow, which is exactly the amount of cash generated by the liquidation of the forward, is the valuation we are looking for. After we secure both the sale and the borrowing, we still have to settle two flows on expiry—$1,000,000 on the forward side and the opposite amount on the money market. However, at this time the settlement is only a technical formality.

For reasons that will become apparent later, it is often practical to choose the date on which all flows are discounted to be the regular settlement date on futures; $D+1$, for example, in the United States. It is relatively unimportant as long as it is consistent within a given portfolio.

Continuity and Time Partition

Continuity refers to the consistency of the valuation through time. Typically professional traders have to run a valuation on their position every day, and the difference between two of these figures represents the profit or loss generated over the period.[2] This P&L is critical in many respects because it determines the performance of the trading activity and needs to be examined thoroughly.

There are many pieces of information we want to extract from the P&L statement—notably a decomposition by instrument—but we are concerned here with the chronological analysis. This layer tries to determine what is the fraction of the P&L generated by new transactions as opposed to the carry of preexisting ones.

Consider as an illustration that we hold a position of 1 share of S, priced at $100, $110, and $95 over a three-day period. The P&L, with obvious notations, is $\Delta V_{1\to 2} = +\$10$, $\Delta V_{2\to 3} = -\$15$. Now assume that we buy 1 additional share of S on Day 2 at $105. At the end of Day 2, we have now 2 shares, and the P&L becomes: $\Delta V_{1\to 2} = +\$15$, $\Delta V_{2\to 3} = -\$30$. $\Delta V_{1\to 2}$ has increased by $5 due to the purchase of 1 additional share, but this figure itself does not allow for any distinction between preexisting and newly acquired positions. Therefore, in computing our P&L, we want to introduce the notion of a preexisting position, and we write:

$$\Delta V_{1\to 2} = \Delta V_{1\to 2}^{\text{preexisting}} + \Delta V_2^{\text{new}}$$

[2] More generally we define a *profit and loss* as a difference of two valuations.

which would translate here into: $\Delta V_{1\to2}{}^{\text{preexisting}} = +\$10$, $\Delta V_2^{\text{new}} = +\$5$.

In practice, this equation can be generalized and written as:

$$\Delta V_{Y\to T} = \Delta V_{Y\to T}^{YP} + \Delta V^{TD}$$

The total valuation from yesterday to today is equal to the valuation generated by the position carried over plus the increment due to today's transactions. The denominations "yesterday" and "today" are commonly used to describe any day such that yesterday < today.

Parametric Valuations

As we indicated, we want to consider only cash when evaluating a position. Another way of specifying the same constraint is to impose our valuation to be *parametric*, which essentially means that its mathematical formulation is exclusively built upon numerical parameters known with certainty at the time of valuation. These parameters can be market parameters such as interest rates, closing prices, internal costs such as that of capital, or external constants such as the tax rate on distributed income. In any case, our valuation will take the form $V = f(P_1, P_2, P_3, \ldots, P_n)$ where $P_1, \ldots, P_n$ represents the parameters we deem relevant.

This formalism is a direct consequence of the fundamental characteristic we postulated. If we care about cash and cash only, we should be able to associate each component in the valuation to a numerical descriptor. It is also extremely convenient because we want the valuation process to reflect accurately current market conditions and more generally the specifics of the position as of today. Therefore, we impose an algebraic formulation such that all these characteristics are captured into a set of parameters. If at a future date we want to re-create the market as we know it today, we know we can reuse today's parameters. Along the same lines, if we are trying to compare two different dates, we know this comparison is reduced to a set of parameters and can be automated relatively simply.

Overnight Financing

A valuation breaks the time line in two, before and after. In terms of cash flows, this separation has a very tangible consequence because most of the flows "after" are unknown and in any case not received yet, whereas all the flows "before" are known and have actually been received.

If we look precisely at the amount of money on balance in the account associated with the trading activity, there are two different sets of flows. Certain flows result from the life cycle of a traded instrument, whatever it is, and we call them *settlement flows*. Others are interest payments resulting from the carry of the entire balance from one day to the next, and we refer to these as *overnight financing expenses*. Suppose, for example, that today is a forward expiry and that we are due to receive $1,000,000 from the counterpart as settlement of the forward tomorrow. This payment is clearly a direct result of a traded position and thus is a settlement flow. Once the payment is received, it will earn interest at the overnight rate, for example, 5 percent from tomorrow to the day after tomorrow. At that time the balance amounts to $1,000,138.89, adding $138.89 of interest (= 5 percent/360 * $1,000,000).[3] This amount of interest is a financing flow because it is associated to an overnight money market operation. Because of the difference in nature between settlement and financing, we need to make a distinction and track them separately. Settlement flows are critically important because they must be exchanged with third parties and thus they must be easily accessible. Financing flows, which are exclusively the results of overnight transactions, must also be accounted for because their incidence on the overall result of the activity is not negligible, and yet they are not necessarily the result of any active trading decision.

If we denote C and I the overall balances due respectively to settlement flows and overnight interests, the following relationships formalize our discussion:

$$I_T = I_Y + (I_Y + C_Y) * r_O \qquad C_T = C_Y + \Sigma\, CF_T$$

I_Y and I_T represent respectively the accumulated amount of financing flows for yesterday and today; C_Y and C_T, on the other hand, are the accumulated amount of settlement flows.[4] $\Sigma\, CF_T$ is a generic term describing the algebraic sum of all settlement flows receivable and

[3] If in contrast we had lent the same $1,000,000 for a week through a money market operation, the final interest payment would have been a settlement, not a financing flow, because it would have been the result of a particular transaction, as opposed to money left on the account after every claim had been settled.

[4] The notion of an accumulated amount implies a time origin on which the accumulation started. In practice, this time is often the beginning of each fiscal year for the institution performing the valuation.

payable today. r_O is the relevant overnight rate from yesterday to today.

In short, *the balance of financing interests today is equal to yesterday's plus yesterday's total balance carried at the overnight rate*. Along the same line the *total balance of settlement flows today is yesterday's balance combined to all flows expected on today's settlement date*.[5] In practice, C and I are computed instrument by instrument and aggregated over the entire position.

Despite the somehow artificial nature of this formalism, it is essential because it corresponds to an internal reality. In many institutions, different departments are responsible for managing C and I independently. As we mentioned earlier, treasury departments are usually in charge of overnight financing, which in practice means managing I for all sorts of activities within the institution.[6] C, on the other hand, is usually monitored by the back office because it includes flows that have to be paid and received in a timely manner.

Front Office versus Back Office

Distinction

As we mentioned already, the existence of distinct internal control procedures requires the presentation and reconciliation of different perspectives from different parties. A very clear illustration of the risk created by a failure to design and implement such independent procedures, was, for example, the collapse of Baring's in 1995. Nick Leeson at that time was head of both the back and front offices,[7] and he was in a position to dissimulate losing trades on a large scale, a privilege that he used and abused over and over again.

---

[5] It is important to note that C and I are defined as of today's settlement date. In the example of the $1,000,000 forward settlement tomorrow, I_T is the *overnight financing charge payable or receivable on the day after tomorrow, on tomorrow's balance, due to the expiry today*. Because it appears due to today's activity, we defined it as today's overnight charge although the overnight charge actually paid today is different and is the result of the trading activity a few days ago.

[6] Treasury management has in fact two layers. A trader is naturally involved in optimizing his or her own treasury, whereas the treasury department has a broader mandate with respect to optimizing cash requirements for the institution at large.

[7] *Front office* refers to the trading and personnel infrastructure dealing directly with the market. *Back office*, on the other hand, denotes the organizational structure dealing with clearing, settlement, and accounting procedures. In some instances there exists an intermediate step not surprisingly called *middle office*, for preprocessing information between the front and back offices.

In the context of a closely monitored professional trading floor, traders and back-office risk managers produce their own independent P&L statements. Requirements for each of these may vary from one institution to the next, but in general back-office figures tend to be much more conservative, notably in their appreciation of cash flows.

Consider as an illustration the case of a one-month money market transaction entered today at a rate of 5 percent. If the traded nominal is \$1,000,000, we receive that amount today and pay back \$1,004,167 one month from now. One week later, let's look at the valuation of the same operation assuming that the three-week rate is still at 5 percent. According to our principles, we enter an offsetting money market operation to match the \$1,004,167 flow in three weeks, so there is no more flow on expiry. Therefore, the total P&L generated by the two opposite transactions is[8]:

$$P = \$1{,}000{,}000 - \frac{\$1{,}004{,}167}{1 + \left(\frac{3 * 5\%}{48}\right)} = -\$1{,}038.42$$

This amount corresponds to the implicit interest charge incurred over the week elapsed from the initial operation and is exactly the front-office valuation.

A back-office valuation would look at the same situation from an accounting perspective and associate the valuation to the current cost of the operation.[9] In other words, if we have to pay \$4,167 over a month to use \$1,000,000, for a week, we should pay one fourth. Therefore, the P&L is here:

$$P = \frac{-\$4{,}167}{4} = -\$1{,}041.75$$

Both figures are very close, but they are not equal. The difference is even accentuated if interest rates move. In a front-office valuation, assuming the three-week interest rate changes to 6 percent, the P&L becomes:

---

[8] For simplicity, we assumed a year is 12 months, and 4 * 12 = 48 weeks. We also neglected overnight financing for the \$1,000,000 sitting on the account.

[9] Readers familiar with accounting know that one of the most fundamental principles in accounting is the *going concern*: An economic entity should be considered from the perspective of an ongoing business. Front-office financial valuation, on the other hand, is very clearly focused on immediate liquidation. Hence a lot of basic differences between the two points of view.

$$P = \$1{,}000{,}000 - \frac{\$1{,}004{,}167}{1 + \left(\frac{3 * 6\%}{48}\right)} = -\$415.11$$

The loss has decreased because the present value of the final flow is lower. The back-office figure, however, is unchanged because the current cost remains identical.

There can be little argument about the necessity to include changes in interest rates to accurately value a money market transaction from a front-office perspective. The fundamental principle of meaningfulness simply requires it. On the other hand, the back-office and accounting figures fulfill different needs, and these needs are better served with different conventions. Naturally there is no doubt that these differences should be reconciliated very precisely, and this situation opens the door to long and intricate explanations if both parties do not recognize from the start their distinct nature. In general, financial controllers and risk managers are highly influential in this respect because it is their primary responsibility to ensure that reliable figures get reported every day.[10]

Mark to Market versus Theoretical

It is always possible to argue in any trading situation about the *fair* price of a particular instrument, as opposed to the price at which it is trading in the marketplace, based on some sort of proprietary knowledge or expertise. After all, nobody would ever buy a stock without the conviction that it is priced too low.

A valuation based on some esoteric justification can be characterized as *theoretical*, in contrast to a valuation *marked-to-market*. In general, sound risk management requires regarding the whole theoretical argument with a lot of suspicion and basically denying it systematically except in a certain number of well-defined situations. In other words, the market is always right, and whatever its price is, there is no way around it.

As it happens, many of the well-defined situations in which a theoretical valuation is warranted, if not necessary, are arbitrage related. As we explained before, an absolute convergence has some unique features that make its theoretical valuation a requirement. Therefore, in the particular context in which we evolve, we need to provide an alternative theoretical valuation when necessary.

---

[10] A sound risk management practice is to extract P&L figures from statements produced by financial controllers, which forces traders to justify their own results, especially if they are higher.

However, even if a theoretical valuation has to be called upon, for example, for futures and forwards, in principle it is, and will always remain, a financial monster because it relies on the assumption that the market is "wrong." For that reason, a back-office P&L will not surprisingly always use exclusively mark-to-market prices, which is commonly one of the major differences with front-office results. Problems here are much more acute than pure methodology differences for two reasons. On one side, a theoretical valuation substitutes nonobservable "arbitrary" prices to observable immediate prices. And it also introduces a disconnection with reality that may have far-reaching consequences.

To illustrate both points, consider a futures contract on the S&P 500. Assume that the index closes at $1,400 today, with a basis of $15. Fair value for the futures is therefore $1,415, but assume it closes at $1,418 in the market. The theoretical futures in that situation are valued at $1,415 whereas the mark-to-market price is $1,418. If we are long one future, the theoretical valuation will be lower than the mark-to-market one by $3—that is, $750 (= $3 * $250). For a large position this difference might represent a sizable amount of money, with the consequence of disconnecting risk managers' and traders' figures. In addition, the margin call of the futures contract is computed on $1,418 as opposed to $1,415. Therefore, valuing the position at $1,415 means that valuation is not in line anymore with actual monetary flows, which is disturbing because we specifically requested the valuation process to care only about actual cash flows. This apparent contradiction disappears on expiry because the futures contract comes in line with cash and the final margin call matches the theoretical valuation of the position perfectly. Still, at any time before we can have no certainty about actual margin calls versus theoretical valuation, and we have to be aware of that.

Therefore, introducing theoretical valuations is a dangerous exercise, and it should be practiced recurrently as we said only in well-known situations, such as absolute convergence situations. When necessary, we will present both formulations for each instrument.

Valuations and Random Variables

By and large, all market prices can be considered random variables, and rigorous option pricing, for example, is highly dependent on the assumed distributions of these variables. The different models used nowadays differ on the characteristics of each particular parameter behavior, as well as on a number of simplifying assumptions. For example, the Black and Scholes option model treats stock prices as random walks but does not account for a stochastic interest rate, and it has been adapted since.[11]

Therefore, it is a natural question to ask about the existence of a stochastic valuation. By definition, such a calculation would account for the variability in all market parameters in a mathematically satisfactory way, producing a valuation figure potentially more accurate. Clearly, the choice we have made to freeze a position before valuing its components is not an accurate reflection of the reality of the marketplace.

Generally speaking, there can be two ways to deal with this problem. On one side, we can freeze the market, value our position, and account for variability in a second step, which we called a *risk analysis*. Varying each parameter within a given range and measuring the effect on the position then gives a simple picture of the underlying parametric risks. If we detect, for example, an increase in valuation as a result of an increase in the price of a given security, we conclude that we are long this security and may decide to hedge the position by selling an appropriate amount of it. This is essentially what we set out to do here. The second method would be to embed variability in the valuation, trying to come up with an expected valuation and a distribution for this figure. This is what a *value-at-risk* does, and we will consider this methodology in more detail shortly.

Each method has its strengths and weaknesses, but arguably the first one is the most useful from a front-office perspective. A critical aspect of managing a trading position is differentiating sources of risk in an intelligible way, so that each risk can be independently monitored and managed. This may not be always possible because many risks are entangled and correlated, but the ultimate goal should be to carry only those risks that we really want to carry, leaving to the market those we do not care about. In that perspective a two-staged approach explicitly breaks the valuation into a series of elementary processes, each one focusing exclusively on one category of risk. Incidentally, this operating procedure has a very well known mathematical counterpart, called a partial *derivative*. If we denote f a function of two variables x and y, an elementary variation in f, denoted df, is a function of an elementary variation dx or dy:

[11] The case of interest rates is indeed particularly meaningful because numerous models have been proposed over the years, probably more than for equities.

$$df(x_0, y_0) \approx \left(\frac{\partial f}{\partial x}\right)_{(x_0,y_0)} dx + \left(\frac{\partial f}{\partial y}\right)_{(x_0,y_0)} dy$$

The notation

$$\left(\frac{\partial f}{\partial x}\right)_{(x_0,y_0)}$$

describes an elementary variation in f due to a move in x, around the point (x_0, y_0), assuming y is constant. Respectively,

$$\left(\frac{\partial f}{\partial y}\right)_{(x_0,y_0)}$$

assumes x is constant and measures an elementary variation in f due to a move in y. Overall the total variation df is a linear combination of both terms. This formalism is extremely useful in our context because it essentially means that a risk analysis is nothing more than the numerical estimation of partial derivative, a point that we will develop in the next section.

In contrast a value-at-risk—V@R—usually provides one single figure assorted of an expected probability. For example under a 95 percent certainty, the maximum loss or maximum profit of a given position is such and such. This massive aggregation of information is difficult to interpret at the trader's level because it incorporates many different types of uncertain parameters. For this exact reason, a V@R is in fact much more useful at the highest level of risk management, typically executive committees and eventually COO and CEO level. At the same time its methodology incorporates a certain number of technicalities clearly missing in a partial derivative analysis—notably the observed correlation between parameters.[12]

Therefore, it is fair to say that our choice of a frozen valuation is necessary in many respects because we place ourselves on the trading desk, but we should definitely be aware of its limitations. In the context

[12] Consider, for example, that we hold a position exposed on the 5-year and 10-year interest rates. Should these be considered independent parameters? No straight answer to this question is satisfactory because these rates are clearly closely correlated, but it is also very possible for one to change significantly without the other's being affected. A partial derivative approach would consider that they move independently, whereas a V@R would typically measure their correlation based on available historical data. The reality of the market is somewhere in between.

of arbitrage, optionality is very low or nonexistent and instruments relatively simple so these limitations are benign.

Partial Derivatives and Explanatory Valuations

Beside their fundamental application to risk management, partial derivatives have a lot to offer to traders with regard to the behavior of their position. Typically even if markets are relatively quiet, a lot of parameters change from one day to the next. A valuation process considers each class of assets distinctly, which can in turn be broken down into smaller categories to facilitate some fine-grain checking if necessary.

Consider, for example, a standard futures contract. Its theoretical price is a function of the price of its underlying, of the interest rate to maturity, and of the capitalized expected dividend amount until maturity. If all three change from today to tomorrow, the aggregate valuation as such does not provide a lot of details in and of itself. Still it is extremely useful, if not necessary, to isolate the impact of each one individually, as a safety check about what is really happening in the position.

An easy way to solve this difficulty is to perform a valuation independently on each parameter, which is equivalent to a partial derivative formulation.[13] If $P_1^Y, P_2^Y, \ldots, P_n^Y$ denotes the n valuation parameters as of yesterday, and $P_1^T, P_2^T, \ldots, P_n^T$ for their value today, we can write:

$$\Delta V_{Y \to T} = \left(\frac{\Delta V}{\Delta P_1}\right) \cdot \Delta P_1^{Y \to T} + \left(\frac{\Delta V}{\Delta P_2}\right) . \Delta P_2^{Y \to T} + \cdots + \left(\frac{\Delta V}{\Delta P_n}\right) \cdot \Delta P_n^{Y \to T}$$

Each term

$$\left(\frac{\Delta V}{\Delta P_i}\right) \cdot \Delta P_i^{Y \to T}$$

represents the partial valuation due to a change in P_i, and should be close to 0 for a position perfectly hedged with respect to P_i. It is computed very simply by running two valuations with slightly different parameters:

$$\left(\frac{\Delta V}{\Delta P_i}\right) = \frac{V(P_1^Y, \ldots, P_i^T, \ldots, P_n^Y) - V(P_1^Y, \ldots, P_i^Y, \ldots, P_n^Y)}{P_i^T - P_i^Y}$$

[13] Note that the implementation of this technique is possible because we imposed the valuation to have a closed parametric form.

The only parameter changed is P_i, which is taken as of today. All other P_i are kept equal to what they were yesterday. In practice, the partial valuation is performed only for the most important market variables, typically spot prices, interest rates, and time. By analogy to options pricing, the quantities computed are respectively called *delta*, *theta*, and *rho*.

Instruments versus Portfolio Valuations

As we indicated, it is relatively natural to perform an independent valuation for each specific class of instruments, but in many cases this approach does not look optimal. Recall, for example, how the SPAN margining system, by looking at the complete portfolio, led to a cheaper margin cost than that computed by looking at each individual component, notably because of cross-hedging opportunities. For an arbitrage valuation we can apply the same type of reasoning and come up with a similar conclusion because looking at only one leg of the arbitrage negates the original intent, which was to set up a fully hedged risk-free position.

Therefore, it would be tempting to tailor a generic valuation procedure to particular situations. For example, when considering an index arbitrage, we could measure the difference between cash and theoretical futures and base the overall valuation on this difference, instead of valuing each instrument independently. An extreme example of such a process would be to simply postulate this valuation to be zero, on the grounds that it is a risk-free situation by definition. Obviously, this proposition would not be very popular with risk managers.

Still it is absolutely legitimate to examine the issue of valuation between the whole and the parts. V@R techniques are indeed a partial answer to that concern, because by definition they explore a given portfolio as a whole, and they link distinct instruments through their historical correlation. However, we argue that *there should never be any portfolio aggregation for the purpose of evaluating a position*, because this is exactly what a theoretical valuation is meant to address.

Consider, for example, a situation of risk arbitrage in which the two merging stocks should be held in proportion to their merging ratio. If we were to take a portfolio approach, we would consider the two legs as one single position, and evaluate the spread compared to its expected value—that is, 0. Alternatively, we can value one of the stocks, for example, the acquirer, at its market price, while in contrast the acquisition target carries a theoretical price deducted from the merge ratio. Let's call A the acquirer, B the acquisition, and r the ratio, and assume that $P_A = \$100$, $P_B = \$49$, and $r = 1/2$. Looking at the portfolio as one single entity essentially means defining a new security S such that $S = P_B - r \cdot P_A = -\$1$. In that situation we are long 2 shares of B, and short 1 share of A, and the spread has a theoretical valuation of 0 and a mark to market of $-\$1$.[14] Alternatively, if we value A and B independently, we can attribute a theoretical value to B, P_B^{TH}, which would be in that case $\$50(= r \cdot P_A)$. The mark-to-market value for the entire position would still be $P_B - r \cdot P_A$ and its theoretical value, $P_B^{\text{TH}} - r \cdot P_A$. It is apparent that both methods lead to the same numerical values, but the second option is much more satisfactory for several reasons.

First, if only B carries the label "theoretical," we avoid the danger of a nongeneric valuation. Introducing particularities in financial valuations is always a dangerous exercise because it creates the risk of losing track of the market. The second reason is that it is simpler to implement and monitor. A price correction on one single security is very straightforward to perform, whereas a specific risk arbitrage software module designed to handle only certain situations would require custom development, possibly useless in nonstandard situations. Finally, and this is probably the most powerful argument, a price correction forces consistency as opposed to a valuation in which each portfolio would be considered an independent entity. Consider, for example, the case of two strategies trading the same stock, with the result that the net position in this stock is nil. If each strategy uses a specific valuation technique, the same stock will receive two different implicit prices, possibly different. This is obviously an absurd situation, even more so considering that the stock is not even part of the inventory. In contrast, if the question were to assign a single theoretical price for the stock, the structure of the valuation would at least ensure that a consistent answer is provided.[15]

[14] Note that S has been defined such that $S \leq 0$ indicates an opportunity to buy B, which is in practice the most common case.

[15] This example raises a whole set of interesting issues. We said earlier that a financial valuation should be meaningful with respect to the external environment, but it should naturally also be consistent with the internal environment. This problem is critical in large organizations in which traders on different desks may be trading the same instruments with different parameters.

The implicit recommendation here is that one stock should have a unique market price, and in some circumstances a unique theoretical price.

(continued)

Therefore, we will ignore the specifics of the trading strategy going forward, and we stick to a valuation performed instrument by instrument. When an adjustment is necessary to reflect a known singularity, it will be performed through a price revision and the introduction of a theoretical valuation.

Provisions on Anticipated Expenses

The question of transaction costs is particularly important when dealing with a valuation procedure. In general, these costs are relatively low and typically masked in most cases behind the expected profit of each transaction. If we have to liquidate the whole position, however, they take a new dimension.

Consider, for example, a $1 billion index arbitrage position on the S&P 500. With an index at $1,400, this position holds 2,857 futures, which represents a liquidation cost of $14,285 if we pay $5 per contract in execution commissions. Naturally, $14,285 may represent a ridiculous amount compared to the overall valuation, but in and of itself it is certainly not negligible. On the cash side, if we take the average price of a stock equal to that of the NYSE in 1999—that is, $43.88—we have 22,789,425 shares in position, and if execution costs amount to 1 cent per share—a reasonable assumption—the overall liquidation cost is close to $227,894.

This very simple example shows clearly that transaction costs cannot be neglected when dealing with the overall liquidation process. As we will see, there are different ways to account for them, notably in terms of realized versus expected value. As a general principle, they should be included as precisely as possible.

(Footnote continued)

In some circumstances, it is possible to have different front-office and back-office prices. This is the case, for example, in Japan, where stocks under a heavy unbalance of unexecuted orders move slowly up or down. If the unbalance persists at the time of closing, the last traded price may be far away from the current reference price that reflects the most current market conditions but for which no transaction has taken place yet because of the unbalance. The index calculation uses the reference price for those stocks that are included in an index. There is no doubt that the reference price is a better representation of the market, but the back office is under specific requirements to use the last price at which a transaction occurred.

INSTRUMENTS

Stocks

Introduction

Stocks are the easiest instruments to evaluate. If the valuation is performed after the close of the main market, the fair price of the stock is its closing price. The cash flow generated by liquidating a position is then exactly the position held times its price minus the establishment price:

$$V_T = Q_T \cdot \left(\frac{P_T - P_T^H}{1 + r_T} \right)$$

where Q_T denotes the number of shares held today, P_T^H the historical price paid to acquire today's position, and r_T the relevant zero-coupon rate between stock and future settlement dates.[16] If we consider the same position carried over between two days indexed as Y and T:

$$\Delta V_{Y \to T}^{YP} = Q_Y \cdot \left(\frac{P_T - P_Y^H}{1 + r_T} - \frac{P_Y - P_Y^H}{1 + r_Y} \right)$$

and again this flow occurs on today's future settlement.[17]

The term ΔV^{TD} represents the liquidating cash flow resulting from the incremental position we traded today, which can be expressed as:

$$\Delta V^{TD} = \frac{(Q_T - Q_Y) \cdot P_T + \sum CF_T}{1 + r_T}$$

where $\Sigma\ CF_T$ denotes the algebraic sum of all settlement flows due to today's deals. Therefore, it follows that:

$$\Delta V_{Y \to T} = \Delta V_{Y \to T}^{YP} + \Delta V^{TD} = Q_Y \cdot \left(\frac{P_T - P_Y^H}{1 + r_T} - \frac{P_Y - P_Y^H}{1 + r_Y} \right) + \frac{(Q_T - Q_Y).P_T + \sum CF_T}{1 + r_T}$$

[16] In general, futures are settled before stocks, which explains the form of the discount factor. The extreme example in that respect was France, where many stocks settled once a month but value date for the future is $D + 1$.

Note that the expression of V_T, correct here, is not consistent with other formulas used in prior chapters. These were simplified to make a particular point.

[17] Under the simplifying assumption $r_T \approx r_Y, P_H$ disappears from the formula. In other words, the valuation does not have any memory beyond the day of acquisition. This assumption is often used in practice because it is a second-order approximation.

If P_T^H denotes the average price as of today—that is, including today's transactions—we have the additional relation:

$$Q_T.P_T^H = Q_Y.P_Y^H - \sum CF_T$$

which leads to:

$$\Delta V_{Y \to T} = Q_T \cdot \left(\frac{P_T - P_T^H}{1 + r_t} \right) - Q_Y \cdot \left(\frac{P_Y - P_Y^H}{1 + r_Y} \right)$$

consistent with the initial definition of V. If we were to adopt the assumption $r_T \approx r_Y, \Delta V_{Y \to T}$ would simplify into:

$$\Delta V_{Y \to T} = \frac{Q_T \cdot P_T - Q_Y \cdot P_Y + \Sigma\ CF_T}{1 + r_T}$$

which is much simpler because it does not require any historical data about the position.[18]

Regarding the overnight financing charge, we have the following:

- C_T represents the balance of settlement flows: $C_T = C_Y + \Sigma\ CF_T$.
- I_T is given by $I_T = I_Y + (C_Y + I_Y) \cdot r_Y^O$, if r_Y^O stands for the appropriate overnight rate from yesterday to today.

Therefore, the final valuation looks like this:

$$\Delta V_{Y \to T} = Q_T \cdot \left(\frac{P_T - P_T^H}{1 + r_T} \right) - Q_Y \cdot \left(\frac{P_Y - P_Y^H}{1 + r_Y} \right) + (C_Y + I_Y) \cdot r_Y^O$$

This definition satisfies all the principles we highlighted: It is cash driven, continuous,[19] parametric, inclusive of overnight financing, and equal to a liquidation value. Above all, it is universal, which is of paramount importance. It applies to any type of situation, and it is the only tool we need to value a stock position.

Dividends

The inclusion of a dividend is fairly simple when valuing stocks. Because the closing price is what it is regardless of the dividend, a

---

[18] Note that the accuracy of $r_T \approx r_Y$ depends also on the number of days implied in the rate calculation. For example, consider that today is Wednesday. Yesterday's future settlement is today, and yesterday's stock settlement is Friday. Today's future settlement is tomorrow, and today's stock settlement has been pushed to Monday because of the weekend. Therefore, a factor $(1 + r_Y)$ would include a time fraction of 2/360 whereas the fraction in $(1 + r_T)$ is 4/360 due to the weekend.

[19] Note, for example, that $\Delta V_{T_1 \to T_3} = \Delta V_{T_1 \to T_2} + \Delta V_{T_2 \to T_3}$, which indicates that we can break a given time period into as many intervals as we want.

dividend going ex appears only as an additional expected cash flow. Assuming the ex-date is today, the term $\Delta V_{Y \to T}$ is modified and becomes[20]:

$$\Delta V_{Y \to T}^{YP} = Q_Y \cdot \left(\frac{P_T - P_Y^H}{1 + r_T} - \frac{P_Y - P_Y^H}{1 + r_Y} + d^* \right)$$

if d denotes the dividend per share. The asterisk indicates that the dividend needs to be adjusted to account for its payment date, which is after the ex-date. Therefore, $d^* = d/(1 + r)$, where r is the zero-coupon rate between the ex-date and the payment date. This formulation is potentially incomplete, however, because it does not reflect the existence of taxes on dividends. If we call t the effective tax rate, $(1 - t) \cdot d$ is the cash on payment date. The term $Q_Y \cdot d^*$ must then be replaced by $Q_Y \cdot (1 - t) \cdot d^*$.

Applications

Consider that we are trading a stock S over three days, and we execute the following transactions, settling at $D + 3$[21]:

- *Day 1*: Purchase of 100 shares at \$9¾, closing price \$10.
- *Day 2*: Purchase of 60 shares at \$9¾ and 35 more at \$10½, sale of 25 shares at \$9 and 20 more at \$11¼. Closing price \$11.
- *Day 3*: No trading, closing price \$10½.

Table 6-1 summarizes the different variables in the day-to-day valuation of this position.

The results in Table 6-1 are obtained from the following calculations:

- CF_T: On Day 1 we buy 100 shares at \$9¾, for a total amount of–\$975: $\Sigma\ CF_1 = -\$975$. The next day we buy 60 shares at the same price, and 35 more at \$10½. The purchase amount is therefore $60 * \$9¾ + 35 * \$10½ = \$952.5$. If we perform the same calculation on sales, we get in total $\Sigma\ CF_2 = -\$502.5$. These flows are accounted for on the day we trade but will actually settle on the settlement date—that is, Days 4 and 5, respectively.

[20] The dividend is included in $\Delta V_{Y \to T}^{YP}$ as opposed to ΔV^{TD} because it is a consequence of the existence of a position Q_Y as of yesterday.

[21] For simplicity, we neglect the discounting at $(1 + r_T)$ in this example.

TABLE 6-1

Variable	Day 1	Day 2	Day 3
Q_Y	—	100	150
Q_T	100	150	150
P_Y	—	$10	$11
P_T	$10	$11	$10½
CF_T—purchase	–$975	–$952.5	—
CF_T—sale	—	$450	—
CF_T	–$975	–$502.5	—
$\Delta V_{Y\to T}^{YP}$	—	$100	–$75
ΔV^{TD}	$25	$47.5	—
$\Delta V_{Y\to T}$ without overnight	**$25**	**$147.5**	**$75**
$\Delta C_{Y\to T}$	–$975	–$502.5	—
$\Delta I_{Y\to T}$	—	–$0.13	–$0.20
$\Delta V_{Y\to T}$ with overnight	**$25**	**$147.37**	**–$75.20**

- $\Delta V_{Y\to T}^{YP}$: On Day 2, applying the formula $\Delta V_{Y\to T}^{YP} = Q_Y \cdot (P_T - P_Y)$ leads to $\Delta V_{1\to 2}^{YP} = 100 * (\$11 - \$10) = \$100$. Similarly, $\Delta V_{2\to 3}^{YP} = 150 * (\$10½–\$11) = -\$75$.
- ΔV^{TD}: On Day 1, applying $\Delta V^{TD} = (Q_T - Q_Y) \cdot P_T + \sum CF_T$ gives $\Delta V^1 = 100 * \$10 - \$975 = \$25$. Similarly, $\Delta V^2 = (150 - 100) * \$11 - \$502.5 = \$47.5$, and $\Delta V^3 = 0$ because $Q_3 = Q_2$.
- $\Delta C_{Y\to T}$: On Day 1 we settle a flow equal to $-\$975$ for the purchase of 100 shares: $\Delta C_{0\to 1} = -\$975$. Similarly, on Day 2 we settle $-\$502.5$, $\Delta C_{1\to 2} = -\$502.5$, and $\Delta C_{2\to 3} = 0$. $\Delta C_{0\to 1}$ is physically settled on Day 4, $\Delta C_{1\to 2}$ on Day 5.
- $\Delta I_{Y\to T}$: The overnight cost is computed on the actual treasury balance $C + I$. Therefore, on Day 2, we owe $\$975 * 5\%/360 = 13.5$ cents for a 5 percent charge (actual/360). Similarly, on Day 3 we owe $(\$975.13 + \$502.5) * 5$ percent$/360 = 20.5$ cents. Note again that these flows are accounted for today but occur physically on Days 5 and 6 respectively.

This simple example provides a perfect illustration of the different principles we developed earlier. We have now a rigorous and systematic way to value any type of stock activity over a given period of time. Pertinent parameters driving the valuation are unambiguously identified. The total P&L can be precisely allocated between the recurrent trading activity and the carry of preexisting positions, and we have a clear vision of the treasury balance to monitor settlement details.

Theoretical Prices

Let's consider again a dividend distribution on a stock. If P denotes the price of the stock on the last trading day, it becomes $(P - d)$ the next day before the open. This modification is not arbitrary because it is simply the translation of price continuity between yesterday and today. Therefore, it is legitimate to define $(P - d)$ as the theoretical price of the stock on the ex-date, before the open. This price has a very short life span, however, because it disappears immediately when the market opens.

Similarly, there are other situations in which the introduction of a theoretical price may be legitimate. We mentioned before a merger situation, for which the price of the acquired company stock can be modified to account for the expected convergence on maturity. More generally any type of corporate event is likely to include a theoretical valuation, and Table 6-2 presents a summary of those we developed in a previous chapter. In most cases the theoretical substitution is relatively minor because it applies only to a short time span. The theoretical price is then an instantaneous representation for the purpose of performing a valuation.

In some cases—for example, cross listings or mergers or acquisitions—the theoretical price has a longer period of existence, typically from announcement to the effective date or even unlimited. This substitution, however, applies only to forward-looking prices, not to executed transactions. It has no effect on C or I.

Back-Office Valuations

Being much more conservative than its front-office counterpart, the back-office valuation ignores entirely the possibility of a theoretical

TABLE 6-2

Event[a]	Mark to Market	Theoretical	Validity
Dividend	P	$P' = P - d$	Before the open on the ex-date
Cross listing, ADR[b]	$P^{¥}$	$P^{\$}$	Any time
Split	P	$P' = \frac{P}{r}$	Before the open on the ex-date
Merger or acquisition[c]	P_B	$P'_B = \frac{P_A}{r}$	Until the effective date of the merger

[a] r represents the relevant ratio for each particular event.

[b] ¥ and \$ denote a generic pair of currencies, with \$ being the principal exchange.

[c] A is the acquirer, B the target company.

price. Along the same lines, the discount factor $(1 + r_T)$ is removed because there is no need to account for the difference in settlement between stocks and futures. Therefore, a back-office valuation can be formulated simply as:

$$\Delta V^{BO}_{Y \to T} = Q_T \cdot P_T - Q_Y \cdot P_Y + \sum CF_T$$

In the case of dividends, the difference is subtler, however. The back-office usually does not recognize a flow until it is actually paid; therefore the dividend does not appear on the ex-date but on the payment date. In between it necessarily does not match the front-office figure.

Futures and Forwards

Futures

The mark-to-market valuation of a futures contract is arithmetically strictly similar to that of a stock:

$$V_T = Q_T \cdot P_V \cdot \left(\frac{F_T - F^H_T}{1 + r_T} \right)$$

where F_T and F^H_T stand respectively for the market futures price and the historical cost of the position, and P_V is the point value of the futures contract.

However, the margining system is such that in reality we are marked to market every day, and we would like this fact to be reflected in the valuation. This is very simple to do, by setting the future settlement date as the effective date on which we perform the valuation. Under this assumption the discounting disappears, and V becomes:

$$V_T = Q_T \cdot P_V \cdot (F_T - F^H_T)$$

From there the differential valuation of a constant position is easy to express:

$$\Delta V^{YP}_{Y \to T} = Q_Y \cdot P_V \cdot \left[(F_T - F^H_Y) - (F_Y - F^H_Y) \right] = Q_Y \cdot P_V \cdot (F_T - F_Y)$$

As for today's activity, the expression of ΔV^{TD} is exactly identical to that of a stock position[22]:

$$\Delta V^{TD} = (Q_T - Q_Y) \cdot P_V \cdot F_T + \sum CF_T$$

[22] Note that CF_T does not represent actual flows because there is no flow associated to trading a futures contract. This is in fact a convenient notation used to describe the algebraic nominal sum of today's transactions.

which leads to:

$$\Delta V_{T \to T} = (Q_T \cdot F_T - Q_Y \cdot F_Y) \cdot P_V + \sum CF_T$$

This result is very simple and intuitive: *The mark-to-market valuation of a futures position from one day to the next is exactly equal to its margin call.*

This expression, however, seems to neglect the initial margin requirement. The initial margin is important only from a treasury perspective because we get it back in full when we close the position, which is the underlying process behind the valuation. It does not have to be included in V and can be handled by modifying C:

- $C_T = C_Y + MC_T + IC_T$ where $MC_T = (Q_T \cdot F_T - Q_Y \cdot F_Y) \cdot P_V + \Sigma\ CF_T$ is the maintenance margin, and $IC_T = IC_Y + (Q_T - Q_Y) \cdot IM$ is the initial margin.[23]
- I_T still given by $I_T = I_Y + (C_Y + I_Y) \cdot r_Y^O$.

It follows:

$$\Delta V_{Y \to T} = (Q_T \cdot F_T - Q_Y \cdot F_Y) \cdot P_V + \Sigma\ CF_T + (C_Y + I_Y) \cdot r_Y^O$$

Applications

Consider that we are trading an S&P 500 futures contract over three days, and we execute the following transactions, settled at $D + 1$:

- *Day 1*: Purchase of 10 futures at $1,400, closing price $1,408.
- *Day 2*: Purchase of 60 futures at $1,415 and 35 more at $1,397, sale of 25 futures at $1,420 and 20 more at $1,382. Closing price $1,402.
- *Day 3*: No trading, closing price $1,416.

Table 6-3 summarizes the different variables in the day-to-day valuation of this position. These results are obtained from the following calculations:

- CF_T: On Day 1 we buy 10 futures at $1,400, for a total notional amount of 10 * $250 * $1,400 = $3,500,000: $\Sigma\ CF_1 = -\$3{,}500{,}000$. The next day we buy 60 futures at $1,415, and 35 more at $1,397. The notional purchase amount is therefore 60 * $250 * $1,415 + 35 * $250 * $1,397 = $33,448,750. If we perform the same calculation on sales and add up the two, we get $\Sigma\ CF_2 = -\$17{,}663{,}750$. Note that despite the label "cash flow," these figures do not represent any payment of any sort. They are only a set of conventions used to facilitate the calculation process.

[23] IM is the initial margin requirement per contract—for example, $23,438 for the S&P 500 futures.

TABLE 6-3

Variable	Day 1	Day 2	Day 3
Q_Y	—	10	60
Q_T	10	60	60
P_Y	—	\$1,408	\$1,402
P_T	\$1,408	\$1,402	\$1,416
CF_T—purchase	–\$3,500,000	–\$33,448,750	—
CF_T—sale	—	\$15,785,000	—
CF_T	–\$3,500,000	–\$17,663,750	—
$\Delta V^{YP}_{Y\to T}$	—	–\$15,000	\$210,000
ΔV^{TD}	\$20,000	–\$138,750	—
$\Delta V_{Y\to T}$ without overnight	**\$20,000**	**–\$153,750**	**\$210,000**
$\Delta C_{Y\to T}$	–\$214,380	–\$1,325,650	\$210,000
$C_Y + I_Y$	—	–214,380	–\$1,325,679.78
$\Delta I_{Y\to T}$	—	–\$29.78	–\$213.90
$\Delta V_{Y\to T}$ with overnight	**\$20,000**	**-\$153,779.78**	**\$209,786.10**

- $\Delta V^{YP}_{Y\to T}$: On Day 2, applying the formula $\Delta V^{YP}_{Y\to T} = Q_Y \cdot P_V \cdot (F_T - F_Y)$ leads to $\Delta V^{YP}_{1\to 2} = 10 * \$250 * (\$1{,}402 – \$1{,}408) = -\$15{,}000$. Similarly, $\Delta V^{YP}_{2\to 3} = 60 * \$250 * (\$1{,}416 – \$1{,}402) = \$210{,}000$.
- ΔV^{TD}: On Day 1, applying $\Delta V^{TD} = (Q_T - Q_Y) \cdot P_V \cdot P_T + \Sigma\, CF_T$ gives: $\Delta V^1 = 10 * \$250 * \$1{,}408 – \$3{,}500{,}000 = \$20{,}000$. Similarly, on Day 2, $\Delta V^2 = (60 - 10) * \$250 * \$1{,}402 – \$17{,}663{,}750 = -\$138{,}750$, and $\Delta V^3 = 0$ because $Q_3 = Q_2$.
- $\Delta C_{Y\to T}$: On Day 1 the margin call is equal to \$20,000–\$234,380 = –\$214,380 because we have to include the initial margin on 10 futures. Similarly, on Days 2 and 3 the margin calls are, respectively, \$1,325,650 and \$210,000. These three flows are physically settled on $D+1$—respectively, Days 2, 3, and 4.
- $C_Y + I_Y$: The overnight cost is computed on the actual treasury balance $(C+1)$. On Day 2, we owe \$214,380 $*$ 5 percent/360 = –\$29.78 for a 5 percent charge (actual/360). Similarly, on Day 3 we owe: $(-\$214{,}380 - \$153{,}750 - \$1{,}171{,}900 - \$29.78) * 5$ percent/360 = –\$213.90. These financing charges physically appear on Days 3 and 4, respectively.

As it appears, the valuation of a futures contract is even simpler than that of a stock, and the principles are rigorously identical. We have now to consider to what extent a theoretical valuation changes the results.

Theoretical Values

The introduction of a theoretical valuation for a futures position is based on the cost-of-carry model $F_{\mathrm{TH}} = S \cdot (1 + r) - d^*$. Given the underlying S, if we carry a position until maturity, we pay exactly $r \cdot S$ (financing) and receive d^* (dividends). It would appear that, rigorously speaking, this formulation is valid only in the context of an index arbitrage situation because in any other setting the underlying stock position, if any, is not a rigorous index-replicating portfolio. In fact, all we need to use for the cost-of-carry model is the existence of arbitrageurs with sufficient capital to make the theoretical price a reality. Naturally we cannot be sure about the capital reserve available to arbitrageurs at any given time, but out of all arbitrage strategies, index arbitrage is probably one of the safest, which essentially validates the theoretical valuation.

Algebraically speaking, the theoretical valuation consists only in a substitution of prices, but this substitution must be done consistently. Because the cost-of-carry price implies the existence of a carry, the final settlement of a theoretical futures contract occurs necessarily on expiry. Therefore, if F_Y^{TH} and F_T^{TH} denote the theoretical prices yesterday and today:

$$\Delta V_{Y \to T}^{YP} = Q_Y . P_V \cdot \left(\frac{F_T^{\mathrm{TH}} - F_Y^H}{1 + r_T} - \frac{F_Y^{\mathrm{TH}} - F_Y^H}{1 + r_Y} \right)$$

$$\Delta V^{TD} = \frac{(Q_T - Q_Y) \cdot P_V \cdot F_T^{\mathrm{TH}} + \sum CF_T}{1 + r_T}$$

and thus:

$$\Delta V_{Y \to T} = Q_Y \cdot P_V \cdot \left(\frac{F_T^{\mathrm{TH}} - F_Y^H}{1 + r_T} - \frac{F_Y^{\mathrm{TH}} - F_Y^H}{1 + r_Y} \right) + \frac{(Q_T - Q_Y) \cdot P_V \cdot F_T + \sum CF_T}{1 + r_T}$$

$\Sigma\, CF_T$ remains naturally unchanged because it corresponds to the transactions of the day. As a result, I_T is also unchanged.

Consider, for example, a forward position on the S&P 500, expiring 60 days from today. Assume $F_T^{\mathrm{TH}} = \$1{,}405$, $F_Y^{\mathrm{TH}} = \$1{,}400$, $F_Y^H = \$1{,}370$, $Q_Y = Q_T = 1$, $P_V = \$250$, and $r_Y = r_T = 5$ percent. $\Delta V_{Y \to T}$ is then given by:

$$\Delta V_{Y\to T} = \$250 * \left(\frac{\$1{,}405 - \$1{,}370}{1 + \left(\frac{60 * 5\%}{360}\right)} - \frac{\$1{,}400 - \$1{,}370}{1 + \left(\frac{61 * 5\%}{360}\right)} \right)$$
$$= \$250 * (\$34.71 - \$29.75) = \$1{,}240.51$$

Without the discount factor, the difference in price is exactly \$5 between F_T^{TH} and F_Y^{TH}. This difference is reduced to \$4.96 because of the 1-day shift between yesterday and today (61 versus 60 days to maturity). Naturally if today is such that we bridge over a weekend, this difference is even larger because the time fraction loses 3 days at once.

This overall analysis is important because it confirms two particularly important points. First, a theoretical valuation is always linked to a particular situation and to prevailing assumptions about that situation. On stocks the situation may be a corporate event, and on futures it is the existence of an active index arbitrage "industry." In both cases we do not necessarily need to be actively involved in any particular strategy, but we need to be certain that somebody else is.

Second, the valuation itself is very dependent on the rigorous analysis of the instrument, and it requires a close examination of issues related to treasury management.

Explanatory Valuations

Considering that we can express F_T^{TH} as a function of other parameters, let's develop the expression for $\Delta V_{Y\to T}^{YP}$ one step further:

$$\Delta V_{Y\to T}^{YP} = Q_Y \cdot P_V \cdot \left(\frac{F_T^{\mathrm{TH}} - F_Y^H}{1 + r_T} - \frac{F_Y^{\mathrm{TH}} - F_Y^H}{1 + r_Y} \right)$$
$$= Q_Y \cdot P_V \cdot \left(\frac{S_T \cdot (1 + r'_T) - d_T^* - F_Y^H}{1 + r_T} - \frac{S_Y \cdot (1 + r'_Y) - d_Y^* - F_Y^H}{1 + r_Y} \right)$$

r'_T and d_T^* denote respectively the relevant zero-coupon rate to expiry and capitalized dividend payment until then.[24] The expression of

[24] $r'_T \neq r_T$ because r'_T accrues from today's stock settlement to the stock settlement on SQ, whereas r_T accrues from today's future settlement to the future final settlement on SQ. If the settlement cycle is different on stocks and futures, these rates are not necessarily equal, although they are probably very close. It would be tempting to use an approximation and simplify the whole expression, but rigorously speaking, r'_T and r_T do not necessarily have the same number of days, notably around weekends.

$\Delta V^{YP}_{Y\to T}$ is then very clearly dependent on S, r, and d. To separate these components, we write:

$$\Delta V^{YP}_{Y\to T} = Q_Y \cdot P_V \cdot \left(\frac{S_T \cdot (1+r'_T)}{1+r_T} - \frac{d^*_T + F^H_Y}{1+r_T} - \frac{S_Y \cdot (1+r'_Y)}{1+r_Y} + \frac{d^*_Y + F^H_Y}{1+r_Y} \right)$$
$$= Q_Y \cdot P_V \cdot (\Delta S'_{Y\to T} - \Delta d^*_{Y\to T} - \Delta F^H_{Y\to T})$$

where:

- $\Delta S'_{Y\to T} = S_T.\left(\frac{1+r'_T}{1+r_T}\right) - S_Y.\left(\frac{1+r'_Y}{1+r_Y}\right)$

  is the movement in the underlying price, adjusted for the difference in effective financing periods.

- $\Delta d^*_{Y\to T} = \left(\frac{d^*_T}{1+r_T}\right) - \left(\frac{d^*_Y}{1+r_Y}\right)$

  is the difference in net present value of future dividend payments until expiry.

- $\Delta F^H_{Y\to T} = F^H_Y \cdot \frac{r_Y - r_T}{(1+r_T)\cdot(1+r_Y)}$

  is the difference in the position cost base.

This decomposition allows us to extract one more layer of information from the valuation process by breaking the total figure into buckets corresponding to different parameters. For example, assuming every parameter except S remains constant from yesterday to today, the fraction of the valuation exclusively due to a movement in the spot price is:

$$\Delta V^{YP}_{Y\to T} = Q_Y \cdot P_V \cdot \Delta S'_{Y\to T} \approx Q_Y \cdot P_V \cdot (S_T - S_Y)$$

Along the same line, the fraction of the valuation attributable to dividends only is:

$$\Delta V^{YP}_{Y\to T} = -Q_Y \cdot P_V \cdot \Delta d^*_{Y\to T}$$

Finally, we probably would like to know the impact of interest rates, but this is a little tricky. First of all, r appears everywhere in $\Delta V^{YP}_{Y\to T}$; therefore, there is no single term carrying the information we want. The more important difficulty, however, is the fact that r carries the time component. In effect, even if the interest rate is constant, in our formulas $r_T \neq r_Y$ because r_Y has one more day in the time fraction. To solve this problem, in practice the valuation is run keeping the rate constant with 1 day difference or with the same number of days and different rates. This procedure is simple to implement, but we will not develop the algebraic formulation here because it takes up space.

Instead, let's consider the question from another angle. The cost-of-carry model relates interest rates and the price of the futures contract; therefore, it is possible to extract the dependence with time from it. Specifically, if we express $F^{\mathrm{TH}} = C \cdot (1 + r \cdot n/360) - d^*$, then[25]:

$$\frac{\Delta F^{\mathrm{TH}}_{Y \to T}}{\Delta n} = \Theta_{Y \to T} = \frac{C \cdot r}{360}$$

In other words, the price of the theoretical futures contract decreases with time, by an increment exactly equal to the financing charge. This is naturally an approximation because theta here applies only to the futures price, not to the exact valuation as we defined it. However, it gives a very good sense of what is going on with respect to the carry.

Along the same lines:

$$\frac{\Delta F^{\mathrm{TH}}_{Y \to T}}{\Delta r} = \rho_{Y \to T} = \frac{C \cdot n}{360}$$

which indicates that the futures contract is exposed to interest rates on the full amount of the underlying cash, until expiry. Overall this explanatory valuation proves extremely useful in practice because it allows traders to track the behavior of their position with respect to each individual risk.

Forwards

The key difference between futures and forwards is the absence of margin calls, which means that a forward cannot be valued at a market price; its valuation is exclusively theoretical. Its expression is exactly equal to that of a regular theoretical future.[26] The final settlement flow is therefore always taking place at expiry, and it must be discounted to the appropriate valuation date.

$$\Delta V^{YP}_{Y \to T} = Q_Y \cdot P_V \cdot \left(\frac{F^{\mathrm{TH}}_T - F^H_Y}{1 + r_T} - \frac{F^{\mathrm{TH}}_Y - F^H_Y}{1 + r_Y} \right)$$

---

[25] Note that n is a number of days; therefore, $\Delta n = (n-1) - n = -1$ from today to tomorrow.

[26] Q denotes the number of contracts held. The product $Q \cdot P_V$ is often referred to as the *number of units* of the transaction.

$$\Delta V^{TD} = \frac{(Q_T - Q_Y) \cdot P_V \cdot F_T^{\mathrm{TH}} + \sum CF_T}{1 + r_T}$$

From a treasury perspective, there is no flow whatsoever at the initiation of the forward transaction, or during its life. Therefore, there is no overnight cost associated with the payment of daily margin calls.

Money Markets

Front Office

Consider a straight borrowing entered at some point in the past, at a rate r. Figure 6-1 shows a representation of all the flows. r_T is today's zero coupon to the maturity of the loan. Liquidating the position here means entering into another money market transaction, in which we receive $N \cdot (1 + r)$ on maturity, as shown in Figure 6-2. The valuation of the original transaction is therefore equal to:

$$V_T = N - N \cdot \left(\frac{1 + r}{1 + r_T}\right) = N \cdot \left(\frac{r_T - r}{1 + r_T}\right)$$

The term $(r_T - r)$ indicates that we are exposed to a variation in interest rates, which is highly intuitive. If we borrow today at 5 percent and the same rate goes down to 4 percent tomorrow, we lost 1 percent over the period because we are committed to paying 5 percent in a context where the market demands only 4 percent. For example, consider that we entered into a $1,000,000 borrowing operation 1 month ago—that is, 30 days—at 5 percent, for a maturity of six months—that is, 180 days. Assume that today the 5-month rate—that is, 150 days—is 4.5 percent. The valuation of this borrowing, which we expect to be negative, is:

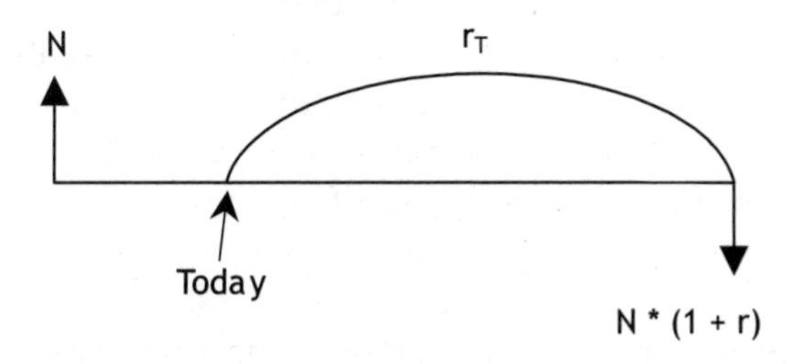

Figure 6-1 Money Market

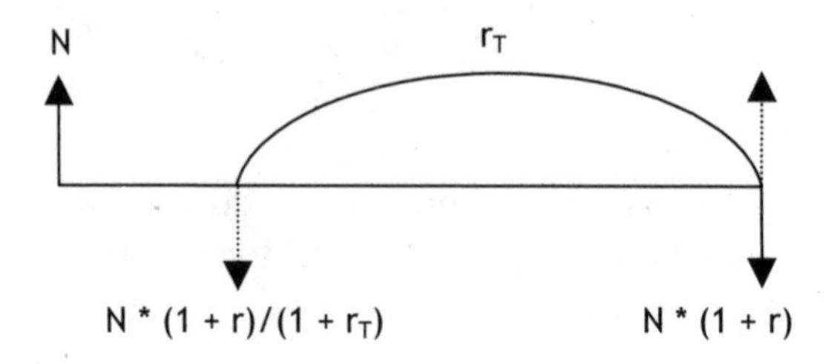

Figure 6-2 Money Market

$$V_T = \$1{,}000{,}000 * \frac{\left(\frac{150 * 4.5\%}{360}\right) - \left(\frac{180 * 5\%}{360}\right)}{\left(1 + \frac{150 * 4.5\%}{360}\right)} = -\$6{,}134.97$$

We can now express $\Delta V^{YP}_{Y \to T}$, which is simply:

$$\Delta V^{YP}_{Y \to T} = N \cdot \left[\frac{r_T - r}{1 + r_T} - \frac{r_Y - r}{1 + r_Y}\right] = N \cdot \frac{(r_T - r_Y) \cdot (1 + r)}{(1 + r_T) \cdot (1 + r_Y)}$$

As for ΔV^{TD}, it can be computed according to the same principle. If we call r_T^D the rate at which a transaction was executed today:

$$\Delta V^{TD} = N \cdot \left(\frac{r_T - r_T^D}{1 + r_T}\right)$$

Note that this formula applies to an *individual* transaction. In contrast to stocks and futures that we might trade very actively during a given day, in general, money markets are traded occasionally. Therefore, each operation is likely to have unique characteristics and should be treated independently.

The above formula provides a very clear illustration of the impact of the bid-ask spread on the valuation. If we use midmarket prices for the zero-coupon yield curve, the difference $r_T - r_T^D$ is probably close to -0.06 percent—assuming r_T^D is an offer price—which indicates $\Delta V^{TD} < 0$. *By evaluating all our position at a midmarket price, we book a loss equal to half the spread whenever we trade, regardless of the direction.* Conversely, if we chose r_T to be an offer price, we would not record any loss, but for every lending transaction, we would then have to recognize a loss of 0.125 percent.

From a treasury perspective, a money market operation has a well-defined impact because when a transaction has been made, no more flows occur until maturity. In other words, $C_T = C_Y + N$ on the day the money market is entered into, $C_T = C_Y - N \cdot (1 + r)$ when it expires, and $C_T = C_Y$ in between.

To illustrate the implications of this situation, consider an activity with a treasury balance equal to 0: $C_Y = 0$. Assume the trader enters today into a lending operation for a nominal N at a rate $r : C_T = -N$. For simplicity we consider that $r_T = r$, so that $\Delta V^{TD} = 0$.

The next day, $\Delta V^{YP}_{Y \to T}$ is given by[27]:

$$\Delta V^{YP}_{Y \to T} = -N \cdot \frac{(r_T - r_Y) \cdot (1 + r)}{(1 + r_T) \cdot (1 + r_Y)} \approx -N \cdot (r_T - r_Y) \approx \frac{N \cdot r_T}{360}$$

under the simplifying assumptions $(1 + r_Y) \approx (1 + r_T) \approx (1 + r) \approx 1$, and $r_T \approx r_Y$. The difference $(r_T - r_Y)$ can then be simplified into $r_T/360$ because there is exactly 1 day difference between yesterday and today.[28] The total valuation includes the overnight and is thus equal to:

$$\Delta V_{Y \to T} = \frac{N \cdot r_T}{360} + (C_Y + I_Y) \cdot r^O_Y = \frac{N \cdot r_T}{360} - \frac{N \cdot r^O_Y}{360} = N \cdot \left(\frac{r_T - r^O_Y}{360} \right)$$

This interesting result shows that the exposure created by the transaction is a differential risk, between the rate remaining to maturity and the overnight. In other words, this risk is of the second order. In contrast, if we buy a stock outright, the risk created is of the first order, directly on the price of the stock.

Applications

As a numerical application, consider the same money market operation we used above. Its valuation today is $V_T = -\$6,134.97$. Let's imagine now that the next day the market rate has changed to 4.6 percent. $\Delta V^{YP}_{Y \to T}$ is equal to:

$$\Delta V^{YP}_{Y \to T} = \$1{,}000{,}000 * \frac{\left(\frac{149 * 4.6\%}{360} - \frac{150 * 4.5\%}{360} \right) * \left(1 + \frac{180 * 5\%}{360} \right)}{\left(1 + \frac{149 * 4.6\%}{360} \right) * \left(1 + \frac{150 * 4.5\%}{360} \right)}$$

$$= \$285.23$$

[27] Note that we value a lending transaction; therefore, the formula has been adapted from N to $-N$.

[28] Naturally if there were a banking holiday or a weekend between yesterday and today, the difference would be more than 1 day.

A direct calculation gives $V_T = -\$5{,}849.74$—that is, an equal difference of \$285.23.

Explanatory Valuations

The above difference of \$285.23 between yesterday and today is the result of two effects, change in time and in interest rates. As we did for a theoretical future, it is useful here to introduce again an explanatory valuation and try to break the overall figure into several boxes. If n denotes the number of days between today and the money market expiry, we have[29]:

$$V_T = N \cdot \left(\frac{r_T - r}{1 + r_T}\right) = N \cdot \frac{\left(\dfrac{n \cdot r_T - m \cdot r}{360}\right)}{1 + \left(\dfrac{n \cdot r_T}{360}\right)}$$

where m stands for the total number of days accruing over the entire life of the loan. Therefore:

$$\Delta V_{Y \to T}^{YP} = N \cdot \frac{\left(\dfrac{n \cdot r_T - m \cdot r}{360}\right)}{1 + \left(\dfrac{n \cdot r_T}{360}\right)} - N \cdot \frac{\left(\dfrac{(n+1) \cdot r_Y - m \cdot r}{360}\right)}{1 + \left(\dfrac{(n+1) \cdot r_Y}{360}\right)}$$

assuming for simplification that the actual number of days until expiry was $(n + 1)$ yesterday. If we want to isolate the effect of time, we keep the interest rate constant equal to r_Y:

$$\Delta V_{Y \to T}^{YP} = N \cdot \frac{\left(\dfrac{n \cdot r_Y - m \cdot r}{360}\right)}{1 + \left(\dfrac{n \cdot r_Y}{360}\right)} - N \cdot \frac{\left(\dfrac{(n+1) \cdot r_Y - m \cdot r}{360}\right)}{1 + \left(\dfrac{(n+1) \cdot r_Y}{360}\right)}$$

$$= -N \cdot \left(\frac{r_Y}{360}\right) . \frac{\left(1 + \dfrac{m \cdot r}{360}\right)}{\left(1 + \dfrac{n \cdot r_Y}{360}\right) . \left(1 + \dfrac{(n+1) \cdot r_Y}{360}\right)}$$

This quantity is called the *theta* (Θ) of the position by analogy to the theta of an option. It represents the variation in valuation due exclusively to the passage of time. In the example above, $r = 5$ percent on $m = 180$ days and $r_Y = 4.5$ percent on $n = 150$ days. Therefore:

---

[29] Note that we used a shortcut: n is in fact the number of days from today's money market settlement date to the money market settlement date of the loan.

$$\Theta_{Y\to T} = -\$1{,}000{,}000 * \left(\frac{4.5\%}{360}\right) * \frac{\left(1+\frac{180*5\%}{360}\right)}{\left(1+\frac{149*4.5\%}{360}\right)*\left(1+\frac{150*4.5\%}{360}\right)}$$
$$= -\$123.47$$

If we want now to evaluate the effect of r, we have to keep the time constant:

$$\Delta V^{YP}_{Y\to T} = N\cdot\frac{\left(\frac{(n+1)\cdot r_T - m\cdot r}{360}\right)}{1+\left(\frac{(n+1)\cdot r_T}{360}\right)} - N\cdot\frac{\left(\frac{(n+1)\cdot r_Y - m\cdot r}{360}\right)}{1+\left(\frac{(n+1)\cdot r_Y}{360}\right)}$$
$$= N\cdot(n+1)\cdot\left(\frac{r_T - r_Y}{360}\right)\cdot\frac{\left(1+\frac{m\cdot r}{360}\right)}{\left(1+\frac{(n+1)\cdot r_T}{360}\right)\cdot\left(1+\frac{(n+1)\cdot r_Y}{360}\right)}$$

This quantity represents the variation in valuation due to a change in interest rate, and it is used to compute the rho of the position:

$$\rho_{Y\to T} = \frac{\Delta V^{YP}_{Y\to T}}{r_T - r_Y}$$

Numerically:

$$\Delta V^{YP}_{Y\to T} = \$1{,}000{,}000 * 150 * \left(\frac{4.6\% - 4.5\%}{360}\right)$$
$$* \frac{\left(1+\frac{180*5\%}{360}\right)}{\left(1+\frac{150*4.6\%}{360}\right)*\left(1+\frac{150*4.5\%}{360}\right)} = \$411.34$$

which leads to[30]:

$$\rho_{Y\to T} = \frac{\$411.34}{0.10\%} = \$411{,}340$$

From there we can reconstruct $\Delta V^{YP}_{Y\to T} = \Theta_{Y\to T} + (r_T - r_Y)\cdot \rho_{Y\to T} = -\$123.47 + \$411.34 = \$287.87$. This value is slightly different

[30] For back-of-the-envelope estimates, theta and rho can be approximated to the first order:

$$\Theta_{Y\to T} = -N\cdot\left(\frac{r_Y}{360}\right) \qquad \rho_{Y\to T} = N\cdot\left(\frac{n+1}{360}\right)$$

from the one we computed before, $285.23, because the methodology we followed is an approximation of more complex differential calculus. Considering that theta and rho need to be informative and not absolutely exact here, these results are in fact acceptable.

Finally, it is important to note the respective sign of theta and rho. In our example, theta is negative, which is consistent with the fact that we carry a loan, and each day we owe one more day of interest. Rho, on the other hand, is positive because the rate to maturity increases from 4.5 percent to 4.6 percent, which means that the loan we carry is more valuable.

Back Office

Because of its simplicity and unambiguous formalization, there is no theoretical valuation on a money market transaction, but there is a distinct back-office presentation as we mentioned earlier. The principle is derived from an accounting perspective, based on cost. To illustrate the point, consider Figure 6-3. The total loan lasts m days, of which p have lapsed already and there remains n until expiry ($m = p + n$). Considering that we have to pay $m \cdot r \cdot N/360$ in interest at maturity, the accrued cost as of today is $p \cdot r \cdot N/360$. The valuation is therefore:

$$V_T^{BO} = -\frac{p \cdot r \cdot N}{360}$$

Naturally on expiration both valuations come together because there is no discounting anymore in V_T:

$$V_T = N - N \cdot (1 + r) = -r \cdot N$$

The back-office valuation is flawed from a front-office perspective because it does not incorporate the market. It simply considers that the operation is carried to maturity.

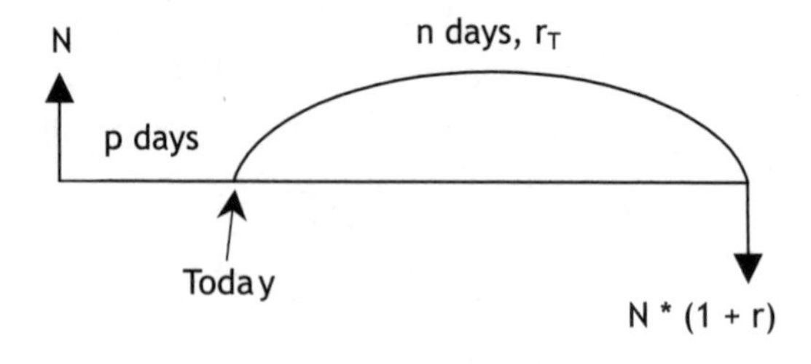

Figure 6-3 Money Market

Interest Rate Swaps

Front Office

Consider a 6M two-year annual swap against LIBOR, a notional N, traded at r_{SW}, as shown in Figure 6-4. Both flows r_{SW} are known today because they are fixed. r_{V1}, r_{V2} are also known, but only r_{V1} has been paid. As we did earlier when pricing a swap, we operate a transformation of the two unknown variable flows r_{V3} and r_{V4}, as shown in Figure 6-5. In this last structure there is no more unknown flow, so the liquidation is simply a discounting of all future payments at the current market rate. The valuation is then equal to:

$$V_T = N \cdot \left(\frac{r_{SW} - r_{V2} - 1}{1 + r_1^T} \right) + N \cdot \left(\frac{r_{SW} + 1}{1 + r_2^T} \right) - N \cdot r_{V1}$$

The first bracket is the present value of the flows on the next reset, whereas the second bracket is the present value of the last reset. This expression can be generalized and written as:

$$V_T = N \cdot r_{SW} \cdot \sum_{i=1}^{n} \frac{1}{1 + r_i^T} - N \cdot \left(\frac{r_V^{\text{next}}}{1 + r_1^T} \right) - N \cdot \left(\frac{1}{1 + r_1^T} - \frac{1}{1 + r_n^T} \right) + \sum CF_{\text{past}}$$

where:

- $i = 1 \ldots n$ is used to index all future fixed flows and the corresponding zero-coupon market rates.
- $N \cdot r_{SW} \cdot \sum_{i=1}^{n} \frac{1}{1 + r_i^T}$

  is the valuation of the remaining fixed flows.
- $-N \cdot \left(\frac{r_V^{\text{next}}}{1 + r_1^T} \right)$

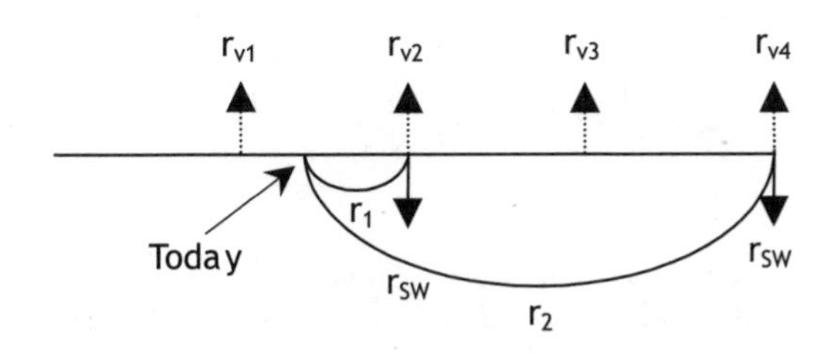

Figure 6-4 Swap

Note: The diagram's convention is that we receive r_{SW}—that is, we sold—the swap.

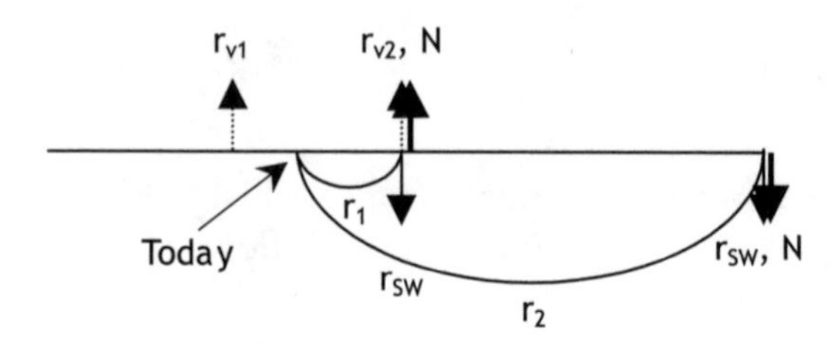

Figure 6-5 Swap

is the valuation of the next variable flow, which is the only known flow on the variable side.

- $-N \cdot \left(\frac{1}{1+r_1^T} - \frac{1}{1+r_n^T}\right)$

  is the valuation of the variable side, excluding the next flow.

- $\sum CF_{\text{past}}$ is the algebraic sum of all flows paid to date, fixed or variable.[31]

From there it is easy to express $\Delta V_{Y \to T}^{YP}$:

$$\Delta V_{Y \to T}^{YP} = N \cdot r_{SW} \cdot \sum_{i=1}^{n} \left(\frac{1}{1+r_i^T} - \frac{1}{1+r_i^Y}\right) - N \cdot r_V^{\text{next}} \left(\frac{1}{1+r_1^T} - \frac{1}{1+r_1^Y}\right)$$
$$- N \cdot \left(\frac{1}{1+r_1^T} - \frac{1}{1+r_1^Y}\right) + N \cdot \left(\frac{1}{1+r_n^T} - \frac{1}{1+r_n^Y}\right)$$

which can be simplified to:

$$\Delta V_{Y \to T}^{YP} = N \cdot r_{SW} \cdot \sum_{i=1}^{n} \frac{r_i^Y - r_i^T}{(1+r_i^T) \cdot (1+r_i^Y)} - N \cdot \frac{(r_V^{\text{next}} + 1) \cdot (r_1^Y - r_1^T)}{(1+r_1^T) \cdot (1+r_1^Y)}$$
$$+ N \cdot \frac{r_n^Y - r_n^T}{(1+r_n^T) \cdot (1+r_n^Y)}$$

[31] The inclusion of past flows may seem relatively surprising for a valuation today based on the liquidation of the position. The reason that they must be included is *continuity*. If we perform a valuation over a period during which payments are exchanged, we have to include them after they have been paid because they were estimated before.

As for today's deals, ΔV^{TD} is given by the pricing formula we introduced in the part dedicated to swaps in the money market chapter[32]:

$$\Delta V^{TD} = N \cdot \left[r_{SW} \cdot \sum_{i=1}^{n} \frac{1}{1 + r_i^T} - \frac{r_n^T}{1 + r_n^T} \right]$$

where r_{SW} is the fixed priced at which the swap has been traded, and r_i^T denotes the mid-market zero coupon until the ith fixed payment date. If we call r_{SW}^T the fair market price of the swap today, we know that:

$$r_{SW}^T = \frac{1}{\Sigma_n} \cdot \left(\frac{r_n^T}{1 + r_n^T} \right) \qquad \text{with} \quad \Sigma_n = \sum_{i=1}^{n} \frac{1}{1 + r_i^T}$$

which leads to:

$$\Delta V^{TD} = N \cdot \left(r_{SW} \cdot \Sigma_n - r_{SW}^T \cdot \Sigma_n \right) = N \cdot \Sigma_n \cdot \left(r_{SW} - r_{SW}^T \right)$$

In other words, the valuation is directly proportional to the difference $(r_{SW} - r_{SW}^T)$. This difference is usually equal to half the market spread because r_{SW}^T is a midmarket price, between 0.01 and 0.02 percent.

From a treasury perspective, nothing happens when a swap is traded because there is no exchange of notional. Therefore, the swap does not have any overnight financing associated until flows are actually received or paid on each side. On each payment date, $C_T = C_Y + \Sigma\, CF$, and the overnight charge can be assessed on the total balance C_T.

Applications

As a numerical application, consider that we want to value the swap shown in Figure 6-6. We assume $r_{V1} = 4.7$ percent, $r_{V2} = 5.1$ percent, $r_{SW} = 5$ percent, $r_1 = 4.8$ percent, $r_2 = 5.5$ percent, and $N = \$1{,}000{,}000$. Based on these parameters, the flows r_{V1}, r_{V2}, and r_{SW} are known: $r_V1 = -\$1{,}000{,}000 * 180/360 * 4.7$ percent $= -\$23{,}500$, $r_{V2} = -\$1{,}000{,}000 * 180/360 * 5.1$ percent $= -\$25{,}500$, and $r_{SW} = \$1{,}000{,}000 * 360/360 * 5$ percent $= \$50{,}000$.[33]

---

[32] Note that the valuation process has to be carried out swap by swap as for money market operations, and a given swap is either preexisting or traded today.

[33] We sell the swap—that is, receive the fixed and pay the variable side—and for simplicity all variable flows are separated by 180 days.

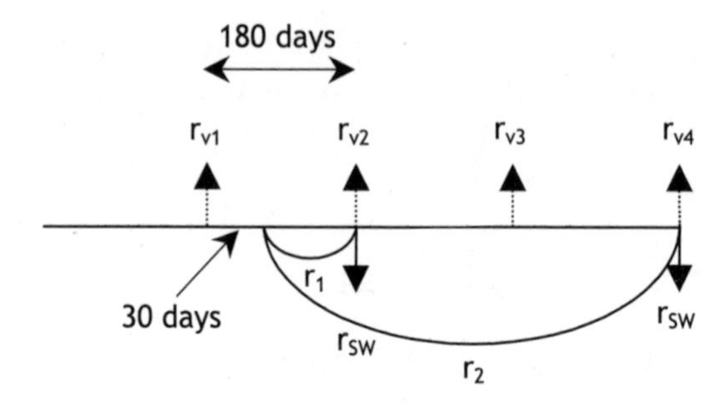

Figure 6-6 Swap Valuation

The different terms in V_T are respectively equal to:

- $N \cdot r_{SW} \cdot \sum_i \frac{1}{1+r_i^T} = \frac{\$50{,}000}{1+\left(\frac{150 * 4.8\%}{360}\right)} + \frac{\$50{,}000}{1+\left(\frac{510 * 5.5\%}{360}\right)} = \$95{,}405.38$
- $-N \cdot \left(\frac{r_V^{\text{next}}}{1+r_1^T}\right) = -\frac{\$25{,}500}{1+\left(\frac{150 * 4.8\%}{360}\right)} = -\$25{,}000$
- $-N \cdot \left(\frac{1}{1+r_1^T} - \frac{1}{1+r_2^T}\right) = -\$1{,}000{,}000$

$$* \left[\frac{1}{1+\left(\frac{150 * 4.8\%}{360}\right)} - \frac{1}{1+\left(\frac{510 * 5.5\%}{360}\right)}\right] = -\$52{,}676.66$$

- $\sum CF = -N \cdot r_{V1} = -\$23{,}500$

Finally:

$$V_T = \$95{,}405.38 - \$25{,}000 - \$52{,}676.66 - \$23{,}500 = -\$5{,}771.28$$

This figure is negative because we traded at 5 percent when the current long-term market rate is 5.5 percent. We receive the fixed side, which is *less* than the market.

Now consider that we value the same swap tomorrow, with slightly different parameters: $r_1 = 4.85$ percent and $r_2 = 5.45$ percent. $\Delta V_{Y \to T}^{YP}$ is then the sum of three terms:

- $$N \cdot r_{SW} \cdot \sum_i \frac{r_i^Y - r_i^T}{(1+r_i^T) \cdot (1+r_i^Y)} = v_1 + v_2$$

where:

- $v_1 = \$50{,}000 * \dfrac{\left(\dfrac{150 * 4.8\%}{360}\right) - \left(\dfrac{149 * 4.85\%}{360}\right)}{\left(1 + \dfrac{150 * 4.8\%}{360}\right) * \left(1 + \dfrac{149 * 4.85\%}{360}\right)} = -\$3.54$

- $v_2 = \$50{,}000 * \dfrac{\left(\dfrac{510 * 5.5\%}{360}\right) - \left(\dfrac{509 * 5.45\%}{360}\right)}{\left(1 + \dfrac{510 * 5.5\%}{360}\right) * \left(1 + \dfrac{509 * 5.45\%}{360}\right)} = \$37.03$

- $-N \cdot \dfrac{(1 + r_V^{\text{next}}) \cdot (r_1^Y - r_1^T)}{(1 + r_1^T) \cdot (1 + r_1^Y)} = -\$1{,}000{,}000$

$$* \frac{\left(1 + \dfrac{180 * 5.1\%}{360}\right) * \left(\dfrac{150 * 4.8\%}{360} - \dfrac{149 * 4.85\ \%}{360}\right)}{\left(1 + \dfrac{150 * 4.8\%}{360}\right) * \left(1 + \dfrac{149 * 4.85\%}{360}\right)} = \$72.55$$

- $N \cdot \dfrac{r_2^Y - r_2^T}{(1 + r_2^T) \cdot (1 + r_2^Y)} = \$1{,}000{,}000 * \dfrac{\left(\dfrac{510 * 5.5\%}{360}\right) - \left(\dfrac{509 * 5.45\%}{360}\right)}{\left(1 + \dfrac{509 * 5.45\%}{360}\right) * \left(1 + \dfrac{510 * 5.5\%}{360}\right)}$

$$= \$740.52$$

which finally leads to:

$$\Delta V_{Y \to T}^{YP} = -\$3.54 + \$37.03 + \$72.55 + \$740.52 = \$846.56$$

A direct calculation gives $V_T = -\$4{,}924.72$—that is, an identical difference of \$846.56. The P&L is positive here because the market rate went down from 5.5 to 5.45 percent.

Explanatory Valuations

The breakdown of a swap valuation into distinct components is tedious, so we will keep the algebra to a minimum. Recall the expression of $\Delta V_{Y \to T}^{YP}$:

$$\Delta V_{Y \to T}^{YP} = N \cdot r_{\text{SW}} \cdot \sum_i \frac{r_i^Y - r_i^T}{(1 + r_i^T) \cdot (1 + r_i^Y)} - N \cdot \frac{(r_V^{\text{next}} + 1) \cdot (r_1^Y - r_1^T)}{(1 + r_1^T) \cdot (1 + r_1^Y)}$$
$$+ N \cdot \frac{r_n^Y - r_n^T}{(1 + r_n^T) \cdot (1 + r_n^Y)}$$

for which we want to keep alternatively the time and interest rates constant. Assuming first that rates are constant—that is, $r_i^Y = r_i^T$—the terms $(r_i^Y - r_i^T)$ and $(1 + r_i^Y) \cdot (1 + r_i^T)$ can be written as[34]:

$$r_i^Y - r_i^T = \frac{(n_i + 1) \cdot r_i^Y - n_i \cdot r_i^Y}{360} = \frac{r_i^Y}{360}$$

$$\left(1 + r_i^Y\right) \cdot \left(1 + r_i^T\right) = \left(1 + \frac{(n_i + 1) \cdot r_i^Y}{360}\right) \cdot \left(1 + \frac{n_i \cdot r_i^Y}{360}\right)$$

assuming n_i denotes the number of days between today and the ith fixed flow.

If we take the example we used before, $r_1^Y = 4.8$ percent, $r_2^Y = 5.5$ percent, $n_1 = 149$, and $n_2 = 509$, we have:

$$\left(1 + r_1^Y\right) \cdot \left(1 + r_1^T\right) = \left(1 + \frac{150 * 4.8\%}{360}\right) * \left(1 + \frac{149 * 4.8\%}{360}\right) = 1.04026$$

$$\left(1 + r_2^Y\right) \cdot \left(1 + r_2^T\right) = \left(1 + \frac{510 * 5.5\%}{360}\right) * \left(1 + \frac{509 * 5.5\%}{360}\right) = 1.16174$$

and:

$$N \cdot r_{SW} \cdot \sum_i \frac{r_i^Y - r_i^T}{(1 + r_i^T) \cdot (1 + r_i^Y)} = \frac{\$50{,}000 * \left(\frac{4.8\%}{360}\right)}{1.04026} + \frac{\$50{,}000 * \left(\frac{5.5\%}{360}\right)}{1.16174}$$
$$= \$12.98$$

$$-N \cdot \frac{(r_V^{\text{next}} + 1) \cdot (r_1^Y - r_1^T)}{(1 + r_1^T) \cdot (1 + r_1^Y)} = -\frac{(\$25{,}500 + \$1{,}000{,}000) * \left(\frac{4.8\%}{360}\right)}{1.04026}$$
$$= -\$131.44$$

$$N \cdot \frac{r_n^Y - r_n^T}{(1 + r_n^T) \cdot (1 + r_n^Y)} = \$1{,}000{,}000 * \frac{\left(\frac{5.5\%}{360}\right)}{1.16174} = \$131.51$$

Finally, we can extract a value for theta:

$$\Theta_{Y \to T} = \$12.98 - \$131.44 + \$131.51 = \$13.05$$

If we keep now the time constant and change interest rates, we have:

[34] We assume again for simplicity a 1-day difference between yesterday and today.

$$r_i^Y - r_i^T = \frac{(n_i+1)\cdot r_i^Y - (n_i+1)\cdot r_i^T}{360} = \frac{(n_i+1).\left(r_i^Y - r_i^T\right)}{360}$$

and:

$$\left(1+r_i^Y\right)\cdot\left(1+r_i^T\right) = \left(1+\frac{(n_i+1)\cdot r_i^Y}{360}\right)\cdot\left(1+\frac{(n_i+1)\cdot r_i^T}{360}\right)$$

With $r_1^Y = 4.85$ percent, $r_2^Y = 5.55$ percent, we have:

$$\left(1+r_1^Y\right)\cdot\left(1+r_1^T\right) = \left(1+\frac{150 * 4.8\%}{360}\right) * \left(1+\frac{150 * 4.85\%}{360}\right) = 1.04061$$

$$\left(1+r_2^Y\right)\cdot\left(1+r_2^T\right) = \left(1+\frac{510 * 5.5\%}{360}\right) * \left(1+\frac{510 * 5.45\%}{360}\right) = 1.16114$$

and:

$$N\cdot r_{\text{SW}}\cdot\sum_i \frac{r_i^Y - r_i^T}{(1+r_i^T)\cdot(1+r_i^Y)} = \$50{,}000*$$

$$\left[\frac{150 * \left(\frac{4.8\% - 4.85\%}{360}\right)}{1.04061} + \frac{510 * \left(\frac{5.5\% - 5.45\ \%}{360}\right)}{1.16114}\right] = \$20.49$$

$$-N\cdot\frac{(r_V^{\text{next}}+1)\cdot(r_1^Y - r_1^T)}{(1+r_1^T)\cdot(1+r_1^Y)}$$

$$= -\frac{(\$25{,}500 + \$1{,}000{,}000) * 150 * \left(\frac{4.8\% - 4.85\%}{360}\right)}{1.04061} = \$205.31$$

$$N\cdot\frac{r_n^Y - r_n^T}{(1+r_n^T)\cdot(1+r_n^Y)} = \$1{,}000{,}000 * 510 * \frac{\left(\frac{5.5\% - 5.45\%}{360}\right)}{1.16114} = \$610.03$$

and finally:

$$\rho_{Y\to T} = \$20.49 + \$205.31 + \$610.03 = \$835.83$$

From there we can rebuild $\Delta V_{Y\to T}^{YP} = \Theta_{Y\to T} + \rho_{Y\to T} = \$13.05$ + \$835.83 = \$848.88 compared to a value of \$846.56 before, and again the difference is due to the methodology which is only an approximation of derivative calculus. Note that the definition of rho has changed slightly here. Because we have two rates—r_1 and r_2—changing at the same time, it is not possible anymore to define rho homogeneously by

$\Delta V_{Y \to T}^{YP} / (r_T - r_Y)$. Therefore, we consider that rho simply denotes the incremental valuation due to the changes in rates. In contrast to a money market, it is important to notice that the theta of a swap is in general relatively low because both sides cancel out for the largest part. This property is equivalent to saying that the largest part of a swap valuation comes from an interest rate variation, which makes swaps ideal instruments to hedge interest rate-related risks.

Back Office

A back-office valuation for a swap is a strange proposition. On one side the back-office requirements are to include only flows known with certainty, which is why we had to use future market prices or interest expense on a money market. On swaps, however, variable flows are not known before they are set, which potentially poses a problem.

In practice, the easiest way to address the situation is to adopt a hybrid formulation, in which known flows are accounted for on a cost basis, while unknown flows are evaluated on a front-office methodology. The result is somewhat unpractical, but it has the advantage of meeting accounting requirements while keeping all the legs of the transaction included.

FRAs and Eurofutures

FRAs

FRAs are extremely simple to evaluate because they are very simple instruments to begin with. Their valuation is exclusively mark to market, and there is no distinction between back office and front office because there is no flow until the FRA begins, at which point it becomes a regular money market operation.

Assume, for example, that we enter an FRA borrowing for a nominal N, at a rate r_F, and value the position some time later. The expected flows are shown in Figure 6-7 where r_1 and r_2 denote respectively the zero-coupon mid-market rates to the effective and expiry dates of the FRA. The valuation V_T of this structure is very straightforward:

$$V_T = \frac{N}{1 + r_1} - \frac{N \cdot (1 + r_F)}{1 + r_2}$$

Considering that the current market FRA r_F^T is given by:

$$1 + r_F^T = \frac{1 + r_2}{1 + r_1}$$

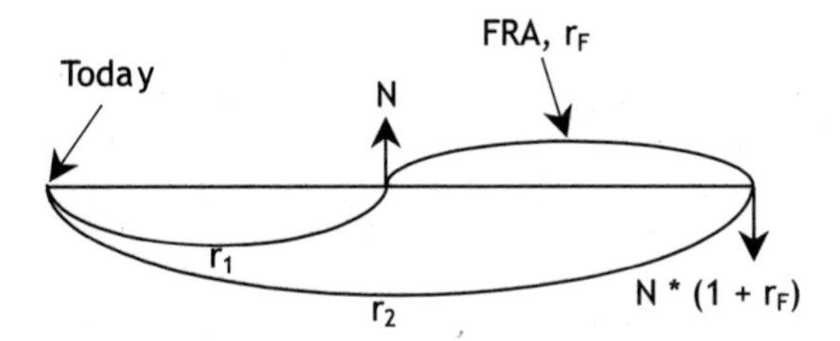

Figure 6-7 FRA

V_T can be simplified to:

$$V_T = N \cdot \left(\frac{r_F^T - r_F}{1 + r_2} \right)$$

From there we can easily express the time components of $\Delta V_{Y \to T}$:

$$\Delta V_{Y \to T}^{YP} = N \cdot \left(\frac{r_F^T - r_F}{1 + r_2^T} \right) - N \cdot \left(\frac{r_F^Y - r_F}{1 + r_2^Y} \right)$$

$$\Delta V^{TD} = N \cdot \left(\frac{r_F^T - r_F}{1 + r_2^T} \right)$$

Naturally these expressions are valid only if the FRA has not started yet, but if it has, it can be valued as a regular money market anyway. It is then very straightforward to extract from these equations the values of theta and rho:

$$\Theta_{Y \to T} = N \cdot \frac{\left(\frac{r_1^Y}{360} \right)}{\left[1 + \frac{(n_1 + 1) \cdot r_1^Y}{360} \right] \cdot \left(1 + \frac{n_1 \cdot r_1^Y}{360} \right)}$$

$$- N \cdot \frac{(1 + r_F) \cdot \left(\frac{r_2^Y}{360} \right)}{\left[1 + \frac{(n_2 + 1) \cdot r_2^Y}{360} \right] \cdot \left(1 + \frac{n_2 \cdot r_2^Y}{360} \right)}$$

$$\rho_{Y \to T} = N \cdot \frac{\dfrac{(n_1+1) \cdot \left(r_1^Y - r_1^T\right)}{360}}{\left[1 + \dfrac{(n_1+1) \cdot r_1^Y}{360}\right] \cdot \left[1 + \dfrac{(n_1+1) \cdot r_1^T}{360}\right]}$$

$$- N \cdot \frac{(1+r_F) \cdot \dfrac{(n_2+1) \cdot \left(r_2^Y - r_2^T\right)}{360}}{\left[1 + \dfrac{(n_2+1) \cdot r_2^Y}{360}\right] \cdot \left[1 + \dfrac{(n_2+1) \cdot r_2^T}{360}\right]}$$

Consider, for example, a 4×7 FRA at 5 percent. If we buy the FRA, we borrow at 5 percent 4 months from now, for a period of 3 months. Assuming we entered this transaction 1 month ago (30 days), the rates have changed and we have now $r_1 = 5$ percent (90 days) and $r_2 = 5.5$ percent (180 days). The flow diagram for this situation is shown in Figure 6-8. The new market FRA is therefore:

$$1 + \frac{(180-90)}{360} * r_F^T = \frac{\left(1 + \dfrac{180 * 5.5\%}{360}\right)}{\left(1 + \dfrac{90 * 5\%}{360}\right)} \quad \Rightarrow \quad r_F^T = 5.93\%$$

and the valuation of the transaction can be calculated from there:

$$V_T = N \cdot \left(\frac{r_F^T - r_F}{1 + r_2}\right) = \$1{,}000{,}000 * \frac{\dfrac{90 * (5.93\% - 5\%)}{360}}{1 + \dfrac{90 * 5\%}{360}} = \$2{,}286.24$$

This figure is positive, consistent with the fact that we originally borrowed and the rate increased. Suppose now that the next day $r_1 = 5.1$ percent and $r_2 = 5.4$ percent. The new market FRA valuation from yesterday to today is:

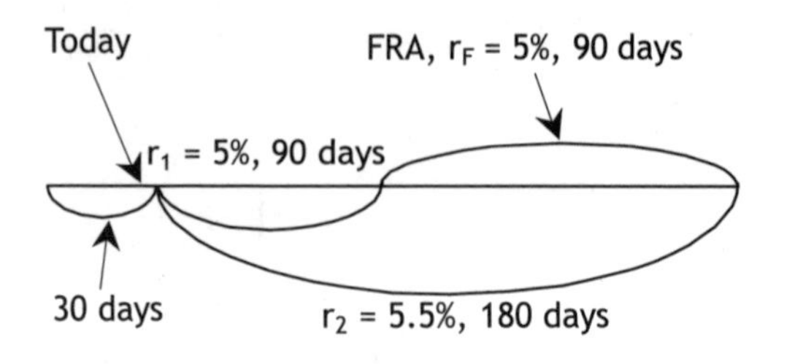

Figure 6-8 FRA

$$1+\frac{(180-90)}{360}*r_F^T=\frac{\left(1+\frac{179*5.4\%}{360}\right)}{\left(1+\frac{89*5.1\%}{360}\right)} \quad\Rightarrow\quad r_F^T=5.63\%$$

$$\Delta V_{Y\to T}^{YP}=\$1{,}000{,}000*\left[\frac{\frac{90*(5.63\%-5\%)}{360}}{1+\frac{89*5.1\%}{360}}-\frac{\frac{90*(5.93\%-5\%)}{360}}{1+\frac{90*5\%}{360}}\right]$$

$$=-\$741.38$$

r_F^M went down so the valuation is negative as expected. If we decompose it into theta and rho:

$$\Theta_{Y\to T}=\$1,000,000*\left[\frac{\left(\frac{5\%}{360}\right)}{\left(1+\frac{90*5\%}{360}\right)\cdot\left(1+\frac{89*5\%}{360}\right)}\right.$$

$$\left.-\frac{\left(1+\frac{90*5\%}{360}\right)*\left(\frac{5.5\%}{360}\right)}{\left(1+\frac{180*5.5\%}{360}\right)\cdot\left(1+\frac{179*5.5\%}{360}\right)}\right]=-\$11.04$$

$$\rho_{Y\to T}=\$1{,}000{,}000*\left[\frac{\frac{90*(5\%-5.1\%)}{360}}{\left(1+\frac{90*5\%}{360}\right)\cdot\left(1+\frac{90*5.1\%}{360}\right)}\right.$$

$$\left.-\frac{\frac{180}{360}*\left(1+\frac{90*5\%}{360}\right)*(5.5\%-5.4\%)}{\left(1+\frac{180*5.5\%}{360}\right)\cdot\left(1+\frac{180*5.4\%}{360}\right)}\right]=-\$723.55$$

The total is then –\$11.04 – \$723.55 = –\$734.59, an approximation of the accurate figure of –\$741.38. We find again that the theta is much smaller than rho, indicating again that FRAs are essentially dependent on interest rates.

Eurofutures

In contrast with FRAs, eurofutures are listed, and there can be a mark-to-market valuation based on closing prices. There are therefore two ways to value them: theoretical, which essentially comes back to a FRA, and mark to market, like a regular futures contract. Not surprisingly the mark to market is predominantly used as a back-office figure.

Theoretical Valuations

In a theoretical valuation, the theoretical price of the futures is the current market FRA, but the flow resulting from the liquidation appears on expiry, not at the end of the FRA. Consider, for example, that we bought a euro contract at a historical price P^H. If r_F^T is the current market FRA, $P_F^T = 100 - r_F^T$ is the current theoretical price for the futures contract, and the liquidation flow is exactly $P_V \cdot (P_F^T - P^H)$, occurring at the expiry of the contract—that is, at the beginning of the FRA.[35] Figure 6-9 represents this situation. The valuation of the futures is then:

$$V_T = Q_T \cdot P_V \cdot \left(\frac{P_F^T - P^H}{1 + r_1^T} \right) = Q_T \cdot P_V \cdot \left(\frac{r^H - r_F^T}{1 + r_1^T} \right)$$

And the components are easy to express:

$$\Delta V_{Y \to T}^{YP} = Q_Y \cdot P_V \cdot \left(\frac{P_F^T - P^H}{1 + r_1^T} - \frac{P_F^Y - P^H}{1 + r_1^Y} \right)$$

$$\Delta V^{TD} = \frac{(Q_T - Q_Y) \cdot P_V \cdot P_F^T + \sum CF_T}{1 + r_1^T}$$

The term $\Sigma\ CF_T$ reflects the fact that we can aggregate all trades during a single trading day because listed contracts of the same maturity are fungible. From there all other components of the valuation, notably theta and rho, are easily accessible and similar to those of a regular FRA.

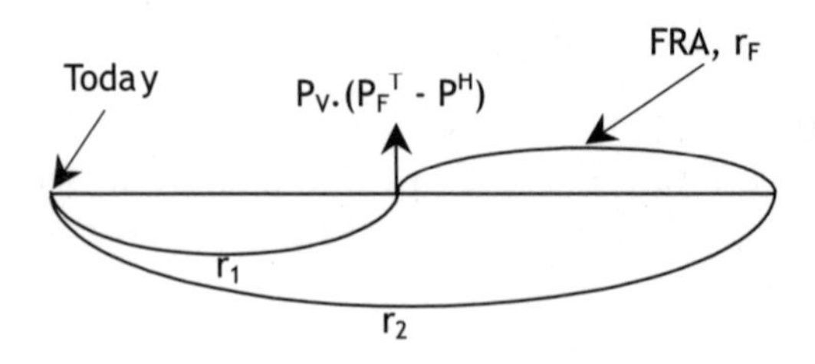

Figure 6-9 Eurofutures

[35] Note that P_F^T is a *theoretical "market" price*: It is derived from actual market rates, but it is theoretical in nature because the futures does have a market price that may be different.

Mark-to-Market Valuations

As we indicated, eurofutures are listed products, so they have a market price possibly different from their theoretical one. It is possible to perform a mark-to-market valuation, which is actually similar to that of an index future:

$$V_T = Q_T \cdot P_V \cdot \left(\frac{P_F^T - P^H}{1 + r^T} \right) = Q_T \cdot P_V \cdot \left(\frac{r^H - r_F^T}{1 + r^T} \right)$$

where P_F^T is now the futures market price, Q_T the position held, P_V the futures point value, and r is the market rate from the eurofutures settlement date to the relevant discount date for the valuation.[36] r^H and r_F^T represent respectively the FRAs associated with the current market price of the futures and the price at which it was traded in the past—that is, $P_F^T = 100 - r_F^T$ and $P^H = 100 - r^H$.

$\Delta V_{Y \to T}^{YP}$ and ΔV^{TD} are then equal to:

$$\Delta V_{Y \to T}^{YP} = Q_Y \cdot P_V \cdot \left(\frac{P_F^T - P^H}{1 + r^T} - \frac{P_F^Y - P^H}{1 + r^Y} \right)$$

$$\Delta V^{TD} = \frac{(Q_T - Q_Y) \cdot P_V \cdot P_F^T + \sum CF_T}{1 + r^T}$$

If we were to adopt the simplifying assumption $r_T \approx r_Y$, we would find again that the valuation of the position to be very close to the margin call:

$$\Delta V_{Y \to T} = \frac{\left(Q_T \cdot P_F^T - Q_Y \cdot P_F^Y \right) \cdot P_V + \sum CF_T}{1 + r^T}$$

This expression is, not surprisingly, similar to that of an index future.

On the treasury side, because of the existence of margin calls, we also have a situation similar to that of a regular futures contract:

- $C_T = C_Y + MC_T + IC_T$ where $MC_T = (Q_T \cdot P_F^T - Q_Y \cdot P_F^Y) \cdot P_V + \Sigma\, CF_T$ is the maintenance margin, and $IC_T = IC_Y + (Q_T - Q_Y) \cdot IM$ is the initial margin.
- I_T still given by $I_T = I_Y + (C_Y + I_Y) \cdot r_Y^O$.

[36] In the United States, for example, index and eurofutures are settled at $D + 1$; therefore, $r = 0$ and $V_T = Q_T \cdot P_V \cdot (P_F^T - P^H)$ if the relevant discount date is the futures settlement date.

And the complete valuation is therefore:

$$\Delta V_{Y \to T} = \frac{\left(Q_T \cdot P_F^T - Q_Y \cdot P_F^Y\right) \cdot P_V + \sum CF_T}{1 + r^T} + (C_Y + I_Y) \cdot r_Y^O$$

where r_Y^O is the relevant overnight rate from yesterday to today.

Foreign Exchange Forwards and Swaps

Swaps

Consider the swap ¥/$ shown in Figure 6-10. Assuming we receive the yen payments, the valuation of this swap is in principle exactly equivalent to that of a transaction with only one currency—that is, we discount all expected flows at the prevalent zero-coupon mid-market rate:

$$V_T^{\$} = \frac{1}{f_{¥/\$}^{\mathrm{T}}} \cdot \left(\sum_{i=2}^{4} \frac{CF_i^{¥}}{1 + r_i^{¥}} + CF_1^{¥}\right) - \left(\sum_{i=2}^{4} \frac{CF_i^{\$}}{1 + r_i^{\$}} + CF_1^{\$}\right)$$

If we take the specific case of a variable-variable structure, we can operate as we did before a transformation of the variable sides, as shown in Figure 6-11. The valuation becomes:

$$V_T^{\$} = \frac{1}{f_{¥/\$}^{\mathrm{T}}} \cdot \left(\frac{CF_2^{¥} + N_{¥}}{1 + r_2^{¥}} - \frac{N_{¥}}{1 + r_4^{¥}} + CF_1^{¥}\right) - \left(\frac{CF_2^{\$} + N_{\$}}{1 + r_2^{\$}} - \frac{N_{\$}}{1 + r_4^{\$}} + CF_1^{\$}\right)$$

which can be generalized to any number of flows:

$$V_T^{\$} = \frac{1}{f_{¥/\$}^{T}} \cdot \left[N \cdot \frac{r_{V,\mathrm{next}}^{¥}}{1 + r_1^{¥,T}} + N_{¥} \cdot \left(\frac{1}{1 + r_1^{¥,T}} - \frac{1}{1 + r_n^{¥,T}}\right) + \sum CF_{\mathrm{past}}^{¥}\right]$$
$$- \left[N_{\$} \cdot \frac{r_{V,\mathrm{next}}^{\$}}{1 + r_1^{\$,T}} + N_{\$} \cdot \left(\frac{1}{1 + r_1^{\$,T}} - \frac{1}{1 + r_n^{\$,T}}\right) + \sum CF_{\mathrm{past}}^{\$}\right]$$

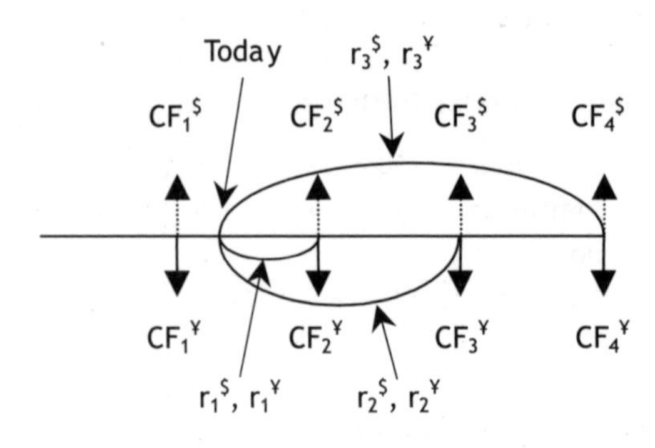

Figure 6-10 Forex Swap

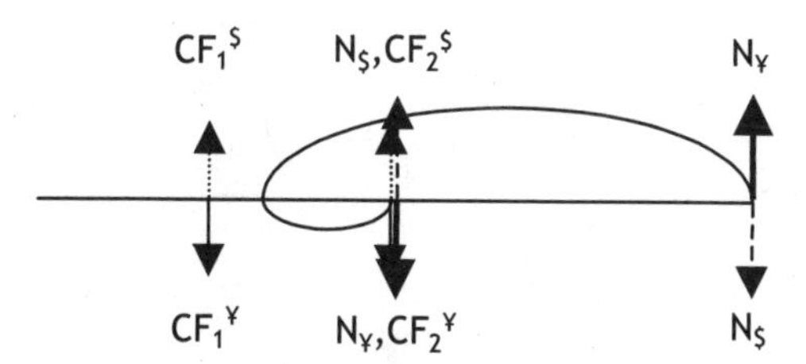

Figure 6-11 Forex Swap

where:

- $N_{¥} \cdot \dfrac{r_{V,\text{next}}^{¥}}{1+r_1^{¥,T}}$ and $N_{\$} \cdot \dfrac{r_{V,\text{next}}^{\$}}{1+r_1^{\$,T}}$

represent the present value of the next variable flows.

- $N_{¥} \cdot \left(\dfrac{1}{1+r_1^{¥,T}} - \dfrac{1}{1+r_n^{¥,T}}\right)$ and $N_{\$} \cdot \left(\dfrac{1}{1+r_1^{\$,T}} - \dfrac{1}{1+r_n^{\$,T}}\right)$

represent the present value of the remaining unknown variable flows.

- $\sum CF_{\text{past}}^{¥}$ and $\sum CF_{\text{past}}^{\$}$ represent the algebraic sum of all flows paid to date on each leg.
- $N_{¥}$ and $N_{\$}$ denote the notional of the swap, with $N_{¥} = f_{¥/\$}^{H}, N_{\$}, f_{¥/\$}^{H}$ as the spot exchange rate at the time the swap was traded.

In terms of treasury, a foreign exchange swap is identical to a regular swap in that the flows accumulate in C_T when they are paid—that is, on each payment date. From there the overnight financing is straightforward to compute, with the small subtlety that it requires keeping track of dollars and yen separately.

As it appears, the expression of $V_T^{\$}$ hardly fits in a full page and is far from being user friendly in any way. Considering that we have already developed all the pieces of the formalism earlier, in the interest of time and space, we will not develop the valuation further but rather concentrate on a numerical application.

Consider a structure similar to the one above, in which $N_{\$} = \$1{,}000{,}000$, $N_{¥} = ¥107{,}000{,}000$, $CF_1^{\$} = -\$13{,}750$ (5.5 percent on 90 days), $CF_2^{\$} = -\$15{,}000$ (6 percent on 90 days), $CF_1^{¥} = ¥40{,}125$ (0.15 percent on 90 days), $CF_2^{¥} = ¥42{,}800$ (0.16 percent on 90 days), $r_1^{\$} = 5.8$ percent, $r_3^{\$} = 6.5$ percent, $r_1^{¥} = 0.15$ percent, $r_3^{¥} = 0.20$ percent, and $f_{¥/\$}^{T} = ¥108$, as shown in Figure 6.12. The dollar leg is valued at:

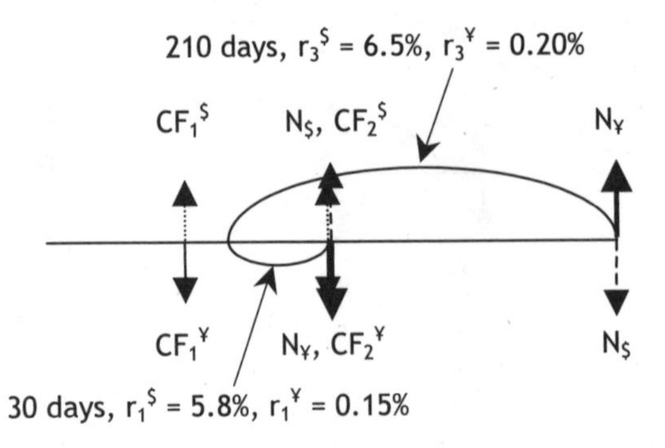

Figure 6-12 Forex Swap

$$V_{T,1}^{\$} = -\frac{\$15{,}000}{\left(1+\frac{30*5.8\%}{360}\right)} + \$1{,}000{,}000 * \left(\frac{1}{1+\frac{210*6.5\%}{360}} - \frac{1}{1+\frac{30*5.8\%}{360}}\right) - \$13{,}750 = -\$60{,}399.28$$

The yen leg is valued at:

$$V_{T,2}^{\$} = \frac{1}{108} * \left[\frac{¥42{,}800}{1+\frac{30*0.15\%}{360}} + ¥107{,}000{,}000 * \left(\frac{1}{1+\frac{30*0.15\%}{360}} - \frac{1}{1+\frac{210*0.20\%}{360}}\right) + ¥40{,}125\right] = \$1{,}798.46$$

Which leads to the valuation of the entire swap:

$$V_T^{\$} = V_{T,1}^{\$} + V_{T,2}^{\$} = -\$60{,}399.28 + \$1{,}798.46 = -\$58{,}600.82$$

This valuation is negative because we are paying interest rates on the dollar notional and receiving yen interest in exchange, at a much lower rate. If parameters were to change tomorrow to $r_1^{\$} = 5.9$ percent, $r_3^{\$} =$ 6.6 percent, $r_1^{¥} = 0.15$ percent, $r_3^{¥} = 0.25$ percent, and $f_{¥/\$}^{T} = ¥107.5$, the valuation would become:

$$V_{T,1}^{\$} = -\frac{\$15{,}000}{\left(1+\frac{29*5.9\%}{360}\right)} + \$1{,}000{,}000 * \left(\frac{1}{1+\frac{209*6.6\%}{360}} - \frac{1}{1+\frac{29*5.9\%}{360}}\right) - \$13{,}750 = -\$60{,}851.43$$

and:

$$V_{T,2}^{\$} = \frac{1}{107.5} * \left[\frac{¥42,800}{1 + \frac{29 * 0.15\%}{360}} + ¥107,000,000 * \left(\frac{1}{1 + \frac{29 * 0.15\%}{360}} - \frac{1}{1 + \frac{209 * 0.25\%}{360}} \right) + ¥40,125 \right] = \$2,093.6$$

Finally:

$$V_T^{\$} = V_{T,1}^{\$} + V_{T,2}^{\$} = -\$60,851.43 + \$2,093.64 = -\$58,757.79$$

The difference between the two dates is −\$156.97, and if we want to understand the source of this difference, we need to dig one more layer in the valuation. Indeed, if we compute theta, delta, and rho, we have[37]:

$$\begin{bmatrix} \Theta_{Y \to T} = \$4.28 \\ \rho_{Y \to T} = -\$169.21 \\ \Delta_{Y \to T} = \$8.36 \end{bmatrix}$$

which gives a value of −\$156.57 for $\Delta V_{Y \to T}$, close to the actual figure of −\$157.97. The largest piece is rho, negative because rates are going up by a higher increment on the dollar side.[38]

COSTS AND FEES

Introduction

The examination of costs and fees related to establishing and maintaining a trading position may appear somehow misplaced here. It is fair to say that in general trading costs associated to financial instruments are relatively low, especially in a high-volume professional environment.

From the perspective of a rigorous valuation, however, it is necessary to revisit these issues, for three reasons. First, because we consider the liquidation of the entire position as a starting point, expenses negligible for an individual transaction may become significant and should

[37] Delta denotes the variation with the spot exchange rate, $f_{¥/\$}^{T}$.

[38] The impact of $r_1^{\$}$ and $r_1^{¥}$ is relatively minor; only $r_2^{\$}$ and $r_2^{¥}$ make a difference: $r_2^{\$}$ goes up by 0.10 percent from 6.5 percent to 6.6 percent, $r_2^{¥}$ by 0.05 percent only.

be accounted for. Second, we need to explore the proper accounting of transaction costs in general, and from there the notion of provisioned costs. Finally, and this is clearly the most important aspect, expenses may be fixed or variable, in which case they can and probably should be hedged appropriately because they represent in effect an additional risk.

Realized versus Provisioned

Consider that we build today an index arbitrage position on the S&P 500 for a nominal of $100,000,000. At an assumed average price of $43.88, we buy an approximate market of 2,300,000 shares, and sell 286 futures if the index is around $1,400. If we consider that the total trading cost is 3 cents per share and $5 per contract, the total establishment cost is $70,430. This amount is due as a result of today's activity; therefore, it is a realized cost and should be accounted for as a pure outflow in the valuation.

There are basically two ways to incorporate this information. On one hand, we can add 3 cents to the price of each share bought, and subtract 2 cents from the price of each futures sold. In so doing, transaction costs are embedded in the transactions' market prices and do not need to be kept separate. On the other hand, it is possible to establish a separate account, dedicated to trading costs that would show a loss of $70,430, partitioned into $69,000 and $1,430 to reflect cash and derivative activity.

If, technically speaking, both approaches are valid, the second has much more appeal because it allows an evaluation of the trading expenses for what they are—peripheral costs not necessarily related to the fundamental business. In particular, a distinct accounting keeps the P&L statement clean and gives access to the intrinsic profitability of the activity. If this profitability is mediocre, trading should be adjusted accordingly. This type of fine-tuned analysis is not possible without an explicit and distinct tracking mechanism.

Now consider the evolution of the position. At some point it will have to be reversed, even if we do not have any idea about when this will happen. The bottom line is, trading costs will accrue again, as far as we can tell to an equal amount. Therefore, there should be $70,430 provisioned somewhere. When the position is actually unwound, this provision is reincorporated into the P&L, and actual costs are deducted as regular expenses. Figure 6-13 illustrates the process. In essence, we take a double loss today and "save" transaction costs when the position is decreased or closed.

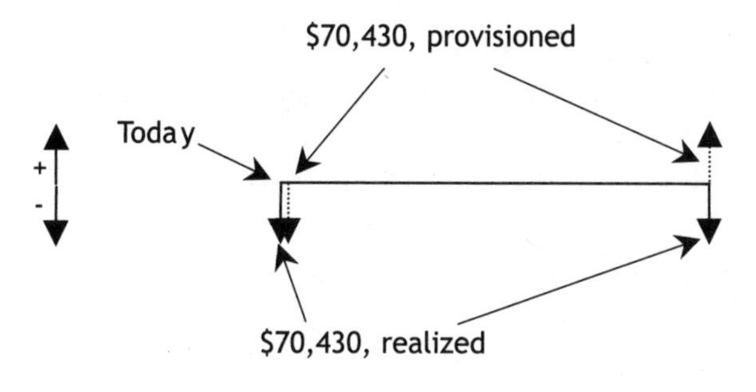

Figure 6-13 Fees

This operating mode is not a requirement but has the advantage of being conservative and accurate. However, it should be noted that it does not apply to all instruments. Money market loans, for example, cannot be described this way because the transaction cost is included in the bid-ask spread, not captured in a commission as for stocks and futures.

Fixed versus Variable

In the above example, the trading costs associated with stocks and futures are variable because their magnitude depends on the size of the position, but in the absence of trading, they remain fixed. Consider now the case of a brokerage cost proportional to the nominal traded, say, 0.10 percent. The total amount of transaction costs varies with the size of the position and the level of the market. If we do keep the same accounting mode of provisioning future expenses known today, we pay $100,000 for a $100 million position, and we should charge $100,000 more in anticipation of the unwinding. This simple calculation, however, does not solve the problem entirely, because if the market is 50 percent higher at the time we eventually sell, the total charge will be $150,000, not $100,000.

This trivial example shows that the 0.10 percent cost is more than a trading cost; it is truly a risk that we should track daily and hedge by taking a long position of 0.29 future (= 0.10 percent * $100,000,000/($1,400 * $250)). If the original amount of $100 million is increased to $150 million, the gain on the future is ($2,100 – $1,400) * 0.29 * $250 = $50,000—that is, exactly equal to the incremental trading expenses.

In reality, the situation may be even subtler because some costs are asymmetric. The "selling tax" in Japan, for example, applied before it disappeared only to the sale, not purchase, of stocks. If we buy ¥100 million worth of Japanese stocks today, we do not pay any tax, but we should still provision an amount equal to the selling tax and hedge it again with the appropriate long position. If we were now to take a short position, there would be no need to account for any transaction tax anymore because buying back the short will not create any tax liability. However, the borrowing fee, usually charged as a percentage of the position periodically, would then need to be provisioned and hedged.

Conclusion

This simple discussion of costs and fees is not meant to be an exhaustive description of the costs associated with maintaining a trading position, arbitrage related or not. In practice, each market has its own particularities in the types and magnitude of trading fees. It is useful, however, in presenting the issues associated with these costs from a valuation and risk perspective. It shows clearly that a careful analysis of the nature and behavior of all trading expenses is necessary to manage the overall position rigorously.

COST OF CAPITAL

Introduction: The 1988 Basle Accord

In 1988 after more than a year of negotiations, the Basle Committee on Banking Supervision of the Bank of International Settlements (BIS) reached an agreement among its members on an international regulatory framework for bank capital requirements. This agreement marked an important phase in the development of international regulatory guidelines because it included the 12 leading industrial countries and bridged over numerous legal and accounting differences.

The goal of the committee was twofold: on one side, protect the international financial system by imposing an international norm for capital requirement, and level the playing field with respect to bank lending.[39] The first point is relatively straightforward to understand because imposing a minimal capital requirement results in a better protection of creditors—that is, depositors. The second argument is based on the competitive advantage created by a lack of harmoniza-

[39] In particular, because Japanese banks had been aggressively taking advantage of the lack of harmonization in banking regulation to underprice their competitors and acquire market share. See, for example, John Wagster, "Impact of the 1988 Basle Accord on International Banks," *Journal of Finance*, 51, 4, 1996.

Bank A

Assets	Liabilities + Equity
$100	$90
	$10

Bank B

Assets	Liabilities + Equity
$50	$40
	$10

Figure 6-14 Balance Sheet

tion. Consider, for example, two banks with the same amount of equity capital, $10. Bank *A* has no minimum capital whereas bank *B* must hold 20 percent of its total assets in the form of equity. Without any set limit bank *A* can lend and grow its balance sheet significantly, while bank *B* is limited to $50 in assets because of its 20 percent requirement. Figure 6-14 shows an example of the two balance sheets. If both banks want to present a return on equity of 15 percent to their shareholders, they must realize a profit of $1.5. On an asset base of $100, bank *A* needs a return of 1.5 percent, while bank *B* needs for the same performance a return of 3 percent (= $1.5/$50). Therefore bank *A* has more pricing power than bank *B*, and can gain market share without damaging its reported profitability.

The trick here is that *A*'s equity is much more risky than *B*'s because the level of debt is much higher. In other words, any downturn in the market may force *A* out of business while *B* would have less exposure and remain solvent. To compensate for this higher risk, *A*'s shareholders would not be satisfied with a return on equity close to that of *B* but would demand much higher. This simple example shows that a minimum capital requirement has a significant impact on the economic and competitive situation of a bank.

The Basle agreement was designed to address these issues and impose a minimum capital requirement for banking institutions. The principle adopted was to divide the equity part of a balance sheet into two tiers and define a maximum asset coverage for this capital. Tier 1 capital represents "pure" equity—that is, paid-up share capital for common stocks and disclosed reserves. Tier 2 includes capital assimilated to equity under specific conditions: undisclosed reserves, asset reevaluation reserves, general provisions and general loan-loss reserves, hybrid (debt-equity) capital instruments, and subordinated debt.[40] In front of the total capital available in each of these groups,

---

[40] For specific details of these categories, see Basle Committee on Banking Supervision, *International Convergence of Capital Measurement and Capital Standards*, 1988.

the Basle committee defined risk weightings to apply to each asset class, with the recommendation that the weighted asset nominal be matched with at least 8 percent equity, out of which 4 percent should be Tier 1. For example, in the case of bank *A*, assuming \$50 of the \$100 assets are risk weighted at 100 percent and the \$50 remaining are risk weighted at 50 percent, the minimum capital is 8 percent $*$ (\$50 $*$ 100 percent + \$50 $*$ 50 percent) = \$6, out of which \$3 should be Tier 1—that is, pure equity.

This framework has a significant impact on the management of a banking institution because it transforms equity into a scarce resource. Every dollar of asset on the balance sheet must have an equity base, which in turn means that this asset has to have a minimum return commensurate with the institution's cost of capital. For example, if equity holders expect 15 percent from their investment, a low-risk asset weighted at 20 percent has to have a minimum return of 0.24 percent (= 20 percent $*$ 8 percent $*$ 15 percent), while a risky asset weighted at 100 percent would have to have a minimum return of 1.2 percent (= 100 percent $*$ 8 percent $*$ 15 percent). In effect, the rule serves as an incentive for banks to preferably hold low-risk assets unless they are compensated with an appropriate return.

Despite its general nature, this discussion has far-reaching consequences in the day-to-day business of most professional proprietary traders. As we indicated before, many securities houses are subsidiaries of large banks, and they are therefore fully consolidated in the bank's balance sheet. All the assets held by the trading subsidiary are incorporated in the minimum capital rule, which essentially means that traders are also subject to a strict capital allocation monitoring. The total capital consumption associated with a particular activity leads to a cost that has to be subtracted from the activity's profits. If these profits are insufficient to sustain profitability after the cost of equity, then the entire activity should be redesigned or interrupted.

In practice, the minimum-capital rule is extremely complex to implement, for many reasons. First, a bank always evolves in its own domestic regulatory environment, which may impose further restrictions and disclosure than those set in the BIS recommendations.[41] In addition, the allocation process is a firm-wide undertaking, which means that every individual activity should theoretically review its required return and consumption of capital regularly and base its

---

[41] The Basle Accord imposes minimum standards but leaves entire latitude to domestic regulatory authorities to go further in strengthening capital requirements.

investment decisions on the result of this examination.[42] Finally, by nature, trading positions fluctuate wildly in size or composition, and it can be therefore extremely difficult to compute or estimate a reliable risk-weighted asset nominal.[43]

Arbitrage and Capital

Being part of a larger trading floor, arbitrageurs are naturally affected by the BIS guidelines. However, arbitrage positions are by definition always perfectly hedged or hedgeable, and it is therefore tempting to argue that their intrinsic risk is lower, justifying a lower cost of capital than a regular equity position. Consider, for example, a fully hedged \$100 stock position. Under a generic capital calculation, each leg is accounted for separately, and if their risk weight is 50 percent, the total requirement is \$8 [= (\$100 + \$100) $*$ 50 percent $*$ 8 percent]. Alternatively, if the position is a real arbitrage, it might be already very conservative to charge capital on one leg only, or even less than that.

Consider, for example, an index arbitrage position we denote N. Assume the risk weight for stocks is 15 percent and 7 percent on futures.[44] The total capital need C is given by $C = 8$ percent $*$ (15 percent $* N + 7$ percent $* N$) if we consider the position as a juxtaposition of stocks and futures. C is therefore equal to 1.76 percent of the total nominal. If we require a return of 15 percent on this capital, the total charge on the arbitrage activity is 0.264 percent (= 1.76 percent $*$ 15 percent). In other words, to carry a \$1 billion position, the trader

---

[42] In many institutions the cost-of-capital allocation process is run periodically, from once a year to once a month. At this time a snapshot is taken of all the assets of the banks, and each activity is internally "charged" its capital consumption.

[43] There is a fourth component to that complexity in countries like Japan and the United States where securities houses are subject to specific regulation. Usually subsidiaries of large banks, these institutions must satisfy their own sets of solvency criteria and fit within those imposed to their parent companies because they are consolidated in their balance sheet. We leave that layer of complexity aside. For more information about the regulation of financial institutions in the United States, see, for example, Clifford Ball and Hans Stoll, "Regulatory Capital of Financial Institutions: A Comparative Analysis," *Financial Markets, Institutions and Instruments*, New York University Salomon Center, 1998. For a comparative analysis of capital requirements in the United Kingdom, Europe, and the United States, see Elroy Dimson and Paul Marsh, "Capital Requirement for Securities Firms," *Journal of Finance*, 50, 3, 1995.

[44] Fifteen percent is the actual weighting required by the Securities and Exchange Commission for liquid stocks, and 7 percent corresponds to the margin deposit on the S&P 500 assuming an index close to \$1,400.

should generate at least $2.64 million in profit, and his or her personal performance will be evaluated only above that threshold. On the other hand, if the position was recognized for an arbitrage and risk weighted accordingly, the net-capital requirement would be significantly smaller and the trader's variable compensation would kick in much faster.

Indeed, this example reflects one of the criticisms of the Basle framework; it is very capital intensive because it does not recognize any correlation between the assets in their risk weighting.[45] An alternative could be to allow arbitrage positions to be recognized as logical "components" of an entire portfolio and compute a capital consumption accordingly. Japan is an interesting example in that respect because it does allow securities houses to reduce their capital requirement by presenting index arbitrage positions as "integrated." C is then computed with:

$$C = r_C * (r_M * M + r_U * U)$$

where U and M represent the nominal respectively unmatched and matched within the position, while r_M, r_U are their respective risk weightings. r_C is the overall capital ratio, 8 percent. The principle of matching used to make a distinction between M and U based on the number of futures in the position, n_F. For each futures contract, we should hold a rigorous number of shares of each constituent of the index if the portfolio is to be perfectly replicating. Let's denote Q_i^{TH} this quantity, and Q_i the actual quantity held. M and U are defined respectively as:

$$M = \sum_i \min\left(Q_i, n_F \cdot Q_i^{\mathrm{TH}}\right) \cdot P_i \qquad U = \sum_i \left|Q_i - n_F \cdot Q_i^{\mathrm{TH}}\right| \cdot P_i$$

where i covers the number of securities in the portfolio, and P_i is the relevant market price or the ith security. M captures the nominal entirely matched between the futures contract and stock position. U, on the other hand, captures the mismatch between the two, either because the portfolio is not perfectly replicating the index or because we do not have the appropriate number of futures to cover the stock position. If $Q_i = n_F \cdot Q_i^{\mathrm{TH}}$, which is supposed to be the case, then $U = 0$ and $M = N$.

Naturally U is included in C to introduce a penalty for a position that is not perfectly maintained with respect to its underlying index. This is done by setting $r_U > r_M$. Indeed, typically $r_U = 100$ percent,

[45] This criticism is examined from the perspective of an arbitrageur, but it extends naturally way beyond this type of trading strategy.

which is a reflection of the fact that the unmatched nominal is unhedged and entirely at risk. In contrast, r_M can be quite low—for example, 10 percent—to incorporate the stability and low level of risk expected from a true arbitrage position. Under these assumptions the penalty due to U can be quite important. Consider, for example, a situation in which $M = 95$ percent $* N$ and $U = 5$ percent $* N$. If the position were entirely matched, the cost C would be $C = 8$ percent $*$ (10 percent $*$ M) $= 0.8$ percent $* N$. If $r_E = 15$ percent is the expected return on equity, the cost of capital K_E is $K_E = r_E \cdot C$—that is, $K_E/N = 0.12$ percent. If we incorporate now the unmatched part $U, C = 8$ percent $*$ (10 percent $* M + 100$ percent $* U$) $= 8$ percent $*$ (10 percent $*$ 95 percent $* N + 100$ percent $*$ 5 percent $* N$) $= 1.16$ percent $* N$. In that situation, $K_E/N = 0.174$ percent. The difference of 0.054 percent is an increase of 45 percent in the total cost of capital, amounting to $540,000 for a $1 billion total position. A slight deviation of 5 percent in the management of the position has therefore a huge impact on the cost charged on the activity under capital consumption, providing the trader with a significant incentive to monitor the position correctly.

The cost of capital is an important notion for a proprietary trading activity because of its implication in terms of expected and minimum profitability. Rigorously speaking, it should be monitored every day, but in reality, it is measured only infrequently. It does impact day-to-day trading decisions, however, because traders have to make sure that they pursue the most profitable opportunity for a given amount of capital put at risk. Arbitrageurs should even be more focused when their strategy is highly capital intensive, such as index arbitrage.

7

RISK ANALYSIS

INTRODUCTION

In common nomenclature, *risk* is defined as the possible occurrence of an unfavorable event. For example, a poker gambler may take the risk that someone else at the table has a better hand. Alternatively a pedestrian crossing a street with heavy traffic takes the risk of being hit by a car. In essence, the notion of risk is often associated with a negative outcome. In the world of financial markets, risk is a symmetrical concept referring to the randomness embedded in markets and assets prices. A risk can lead to positive as well as negative outcomes and still be considered inappropriate.[1] Indeed, even if there exist many risks leading primarily to negative events, the vast majority of them can evolve both ways. The added value of a trader is then to choose and manage those that he or she is in a position to understand.

The notion of risk is the ultimate concern on a trading floor, and it is arguably far more important than being able to evaluate precisely an opportunity, for example. This point is particularly clear in the official mandate most traders receive from their employers: They are given P&L *objectives* but risk *limits*. In other words, it is acceptable to lose money or fail to meet a profit target—to a certain point at least—but it is an absolute requirement to monitor the level of risk and maintain it under a fixed limit. In a period of troubled or volatile markets, traders may not know precisely how much they lose because the market

[1] For example, a trader taking a huge risk as a result of mismanagement will probably be sanctioned even if the firm turns a profit.

moves too fast, but they will never get away with not knowing how much they *can possibly* lose if everything goes wrong. Incidentally, emphasizing maximum loss instead of expected profit is a sound risk management practice, valid far beyond the world of finance.

Risks come in many shapes and forms, and cataloguing them is a difficult task because the perception of a particular event as a risk is very subjective and highly dependent on the internal and external context. It is trivial to say that the buyer and seller of a given security do not perceive the risks in the same way, but it should nevertheless be kept in mind. The same trivial idea leads to the recognition that arbitrageurs in general love volatility whereas investors at large tend to consider it a risk and a nuisance, and this difference has had a long-standing influence on regulating authorities.

From our perspective we focus primarily on market risks, although we shortly examine other risks as well. In contrast to a valuation procedure, we cannot base the discussion here on a distinction by instruments because many products carry several classes of risk. Therefore, we adopt a functional presentation, in which we classify and discuss risk type by type. Furthermore, a risk in itself is only accessible through risk measurement mechanics, the same way a distant star can be seen in detail only through a magnifying telescope. The quality of the telescope has a huge impact on the ability of scientists to draw conclusions about the star, and this is also true of the risk management system that conditions the ability of a trader to make the right decision. In addition, it is necessary to note that the proposed framework is not meant to embody the ultimate truth, but rather to be one robust and relatively simple alternative. If there can be little debate on the market price of a stock, a risk analysis may be performed under different mathematical formulations or models, with different results, in turn leading to adequate decisions along different paths. Before we start, however, a few words are necessary on the ability of human beings to take and handle risks in general.

RISK AND HUMAN PSYCHOLOGY

It is a very clear and known fact that risk is not handled the same way by different individuals. For example, assume that you play heads or tails with a friend and that you pay \$6 if you lose and receive \$10 if you win. The probability of each outcome is 50 percent; therefore, the fair value of the game from your perspective is \$2 (= \$10 $*$ 50 percent — \$6 $*$ 50 percent). In other words, you would be ready to pay your friend $2 to enter the game, and he should consider the deal a fair one. In reality, three types of reactions are possible with respect to such a game. *Risk-neutral individuals* will figure out the math and accept the fair price, $2, to carry the risk of paying $6 for a total upside of $10. *Risk-averse individuals* will not be willing to enter the bet at fair price, so they will either refuse or expect more than $2. *Risk-seeking individuals* will be willing to receive less than $2 for the opportunity to receive $6.

If this simple example underlines the principle behind the notion of risk aversity, there are naturally many nuances and refinements. Clearly the willingness to carry risk depends on a number of factors, including sociodemographic elements such as age or income, but also an innate inclination that pushes individuals one way or the other. Beyond acceptance, another dimension is the ability of individuals to *handle* risk and uncertainty. In the above example the result of the bet is available immediately, and the amount is small. In other instances, if the amount were significant and the outcome uncertain for some time, even somebody with an inclination to take the bet in its original form would probably think twice to account for the persistent uncertainties.

This discussion is naturally nothing more than an introduction to the complex problems behind human psychology, but it is essential to keep it in mind when examining the notion of risk.[2] In contrast to a portfolio evaluation, which is by and large a mechanical process, risk management calls upon intrinsic individual characteristics and behavior. A good trader is not necessarily someone with a Fields Medal or Nobel Prize, but he or she must have the ability to evaluate, assume, and handle risks consistently.[3] In practice, this often translates into the ability to withstand heavy losses without losing sight of the best decision at a given time. Therefore, even the best risk management system is no substitute for judgment and experience. We try to present the whole process as highly rigorous and analytical, which it is, but more than in any other part in this book, the mechanics we present are tools and should be taken as the necessary first step, not as an end in and of themselves.

---

[2] For a short discussion about anomalies in financial markets, see, for example, Jayendu Patel, Richard Zeckhauser, and Darryl Hendricks, "The Rationality Struggle," *The American Economic Review*, 81, 2, 1991.

[3] This last characteristic is particularly important because most people tend to be risk averse in bad times and risk seeking in good times, which more often than not leads to an inconsistent set of decisions and accumulating losses.

PRINCIPLES

Purpose

In our approach, a risk analysis is nothing more than a dynamic valuation—that is, a valuation carried out for an incremental variation in trading parameters. As such, a risk analysis shares the fundamental characteristics of a valuation: It is essentially cash driven and presents relevant information as of today. There is, however, a significant difference in principle. If the valuation assumes liquidation, a risk analysis assumes continuation in the position, even though it uses liquidation because it is based on a standard valuation. Its purpose is to identify and quantify risks, *risk* being defined as any random occurrence of events with an impact on the overall P&L. Its results must allow a trader to make the appropriate decisions to carry the position with the best chances of realizing a profit or avoiding a loss.

This definition means that a risk analysis is a parametric procedure like a regular valuation, and indeed the reason we imposed a valuation to be parametric in the first place was to simplify the risk analysis process. In contrast to a valuation, however, a thorough analysis of risk must also account in some form for nonparametric sources of risks. Earlier we gave the example of a system failure, but there are many other sources that could be included, and some will be explored later on.

The problem with nonparametric random events is that they are extremely difficult to quantify accurately. For example, in the case of a system failure, depending on the magnitude of the failure, the consequences may be devastating or relatively minor. In practice, there are no specific rules to deal with these risks but rather a few general principles, and being paranoid is one of them. In the case of a system failure, a thorough evaluation of contingency plans and alternative execution routing systems would be a good place to start, making sure that these plans are well known and regularly tested and updated.[4] "Expect the unexpected" and plan accordingly is indeed the best way to address these potential problems, keeping in mind that the cost of carrying some of these risks may be prohibitively expensive.

---

[4] The system failure is indeed a very serious problem for financial institutions. The 1995 Kobe earthquake in Japan, or the fire at the Credit Lyonnais headquarters in 1996 in France, for example, reminded market participants that natural disasters were a true possibility. Virtually all trading firms maintain secret fully functional alternative trading floors, to be used in case of emergency.

Isolation of Individual Risks and Hedging

Principles

In a risk analysis, we compute the change in the value of the position based on a unitary variation in each of its underlying parameters. A *unitary variation* in our context is a variation small enough that a Taylor expansion of the valuation V is acceptable to the first order.

The principle is identical to an explanatory valuation but implemented differently. An explanatory valuation is meant to break $\Delta V_{Y \to T}$ into distinct parts:

$$\Delta V_{Y \to T} = \left(\frac{\Delta V}{\Delta P_1}\right) \cdot \Delta P_1^{Y \to T} + \left(\frac{\Delta V}{\Delta P_2}\right) \cdot \Delta P_2^{Y \to T} + \cdots + \left(\frac{\Delta V}{\Delta P_n}\right) \cdot \Delta P_n^{Y \to T}$$

where:

$$\left(\frac{\Delta V}{\Delta P_i}\right) = \frac{V(P_1^Y, \ldots, P_i^T, \ldots, P_n^Y) - V(P_1^Y, \ldots, P_i^Y, \ldots, P_n^Y)}{P_i^T - P_i^Y}$$

A risk analysis is meant to access R_i, the ith risk factor, defined by:

$$R_i = \left(\frac{\Delta V}{\Delta P_i}\right) = \frac{V(P_1^T, \ldots, P_i^T + \delta_i, \ldots, P_n^T) - V(P_1^T, \ldots, P_i^T, \ldots, P_n^T)}{\delta_i}$$
$$= \frac{V(P_i^T + \delta_i) - V(P_i^T)}{\delta_i}$$

where δ_i is arbitrarily small. This process reduces V into a number of independent linear functions, each carrying the impact of the variation of one particular parameter:

$$V(P_i^T + \delta_i) - V(P_i^T) = R_i \cdot \delta_i$$

This relationship is used in turn to evaluate the extent of the P&L associated with any value δ_i. Graphically, the approach can be represented as shown in Figure 7-1. The actual dependency of V is approximated wherever necessary by a straight line, with a slope equal to R_i.

Hedging a risk in that representation is equivalent to trading an additional instrument in the position so that R_i is neutralized. If v is the incremental valuation due to this additional instrument, we would ideally want to have:

$$v(P_i^T) \geq 0 \qquad \text{and} \qquad v(P_i^T + \delta_i) - v(P_i^T) = -R_i \cdot \delta_i$$

so that the addition of v turns out to be both profitable and risk reducing. Naturally, in general, these relations are difficult to combine, and hedging an unwanted risk may turn out to be extremely costly. Furthermore, the inclusion of one instrument to hedge a given class

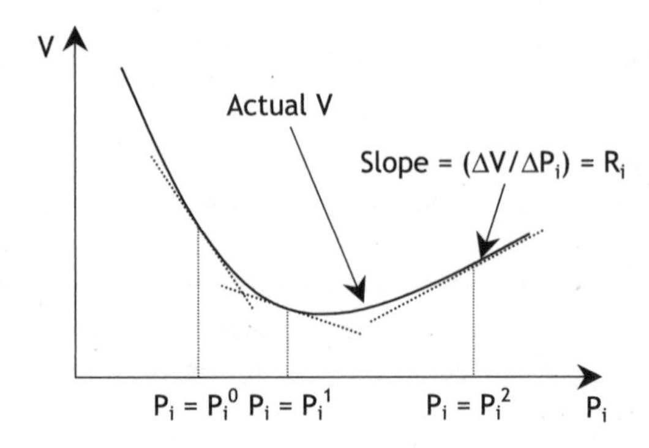

Figure 7-1 Risk Factor

of risk may have the effect of creating risk of another type. Therefore, if on paper the procedure is fairly simple, it is much less so to implement in reality. In any case, this approach illustrates the key benefits of handling risk through a partial derivative framework: Each type of risk is systematically quantifiable, allowing a rigorous and tailored risk management.

Difficulties

Naturally this method has clear limitations, visible, for example, in Figure 7-1. The linear approximation is only truly valid in the neighborhood of the point around which it is calculated, which means that if the market moves significantly from that point, the actual P&L may be different from the one calculated. This difficulty can be solved by sampling more points like P_i^0, P_i^1, and P_i^2 in Figure 7-1, at the expense of computing time.

A more serious problem, however, comes from the assumed independence between variables. Varying a single parameter at a time while keeping all the others constant is inaccurate because it does not reflect the reality of the marketplace. For example, interest rates exhibit a cross dependency throughout the yield curve; therefore, keeping each one of them independent can give inconsistent results. Even for instruments as simple as stocks, varying the price of one while keeping the others constant in a portfolio is a strange proposition.

There can be two broad solutions to this problem. On one side, it is possible to assume "rigid" relationships between parameters, implying that a cross correlation is always equal to 1. The second option is to incorporate correlations into the model and proceed with a more complex mathematical framework. The V@R was derived from the latter perspective, so we will develop it when examining V@R in details.

As an illustration of the first approach, consider that we hold two stocks S_1 and S_2. Assuming they are independent, we would define R_1 and R_2 as:

$$V(S_1 + \delta_1) - V(S_1) = R_1 \cdot \delta_1 \qquad V(S_2 + \delta_2) - V(S_2) = R_2 \cdot \delta_2$$

with δ_1 and δ_2 defined arbitrarily small, possibly equal. In that case a global variation in V is simply a linear combination of these two terms, and we can hedge the position if necessary independently on S_1 and S_2.

If we were to adopt a rigid correlation between S_1 and S_2, we would assume that S_1 and S_2 move in parallel—that is, a move of δ percent on S_1 gets exactly reflected on S_2 because the entire market is affected equally. We then define an aggregate risk factor R as:

$$R = \frac{V[S_1 \cdot (1+\delta), S_2 \cdot (1+\delta)] - V(S_1, S_2)}{\delta}$$

In that case, if we want to hedge the position, we cannot consider S_1 and S_2 individually because they are in fact part of a bigger market. We need to hedge against variability from the whole market, S_1 and S_2 being only two components of this market.

As an application, consider that we are long 5 shares of S_1 and short 6 shares of S_2. If we were to consider S_1 and S_2 independently, we would have:

$$R_1 = \frac{V(S_1 + \delta_1) - V(S_1)}{\delta_1} = \frac{5 * (S_1 + \delta_1) - 5 * S_1}{\delta_1} = 5$$

and similarly $R_2 = -6$. R_1 and R_2 are here homogeneous to a number of shares. If we wanted to hedge V against a move in S_1 we would have to sell 5 shares of S_1 or buy 6 shares of S_2 for a protection against a move of S_2.

On the other hand, if S_1 and S_2 are rigidly linked, R becomes:

$$R = \frac{5 * S_1 * (1+\delta) - 5 * S_1 - 6 * S_2 * (1+\delta) + 6 * S_2}{\delta} = 5 * S_1 - 6 * S_2$$

Here R is homogeneous to a nominal, not to a number of shares anymore. This nominal could be hedged with S_1, S_2, another asset, or a combination of other assets. R is used here to hedge an entire class of risks, those related to equity prices, not those created by a particular instrument in that class.[5]

---

[5] In some cases, for example, index arbitrage in which the portfolio is supposed to be a perfect replication of an index, the calculation of each individual R_i may be useful in addition to that of R to identify which, if any, stock position deviates from its perfect value.

This same framework can be used to handle interest rate risk because again it is difficult to separate one particular rate from another. However, we have here one additional difficulty because to hedge the position, we need to enter a money market operation of a given maturity; therefore, we have to know what maturity is most exposed in the position. The solution is to complement R by each individual R_i. R captures the exposure of the position to a general move in the level of interest rates, while the series R_i shows very clearly the maturities at risk in the yield curve. For example, consider a position holding different instruments of maturities below 5 years. V is dependent upon the entire yield curve below 5 years:

$$V = V(r_{1\,\mathrm{WK}}, r_{1\,\mathrm{MO}}, r_{2\,\mathrm{MO}}, r_{3\,\mathrm{MO}}, \ldots, r_{2\,\mathrm{Y}}, r_{3\,\mathrm{Y}}, r_{4\,\mathrm{Y}}, r_{5\,\mathrm{Y}})$$

R_i and R are respectively defined by:

$$R_{1\,WK} = \frac{V(r_{1\,\mathrm{WK}} + \delta, r_{1\,\mathrm{MO}}, r_{2\,\mathrm{MO}}, \ldots, r_{5\,\mathrm{Y}}) - V(r_{1\,\mathrm{WK}}, r_{1\,\mathrm{MO}}, r_{2\,\mathrm{MO}}, \ldots, r_{5\,\mathrm{Y}})}{\delta}$$

$$\vdots$$

$$R_{5\,\mathrm{Y}} = \frac{V(r_{1\,\mathrm{WK}}, r_{1\,\mathrm{MO}}, r_{2\,\mathrm{MO}}, \ldots, r_{5\,\mathrm{Y}} + \delta) - V(r_{1\,\mathrm{WK}}, r_{1\,\mathrm{MO}}, r_{2\,\mathrm{MO}}, \ldots, r_{5\,\mathrm{Y}})}{\delta}$$

$$R = \frac{\begin{array}{c} V(r_{1\,\mathrm{WK}} + \delta, r_{1\,\mathrm{MO}} + \delta, r_{2\,\mathrm{MO}} + \delta + \ldots + r_{5\,\mathrm{Y}} + \delta) \\ -V(r_{1\,\mathrm{WK}}, r_{1\,\mathrm{MO}}, r_{2\,\mathrm{MO}}, \ldots, r_{5\,\mathrm{Y}}) \end{array}}{\delta}$$

If each rate were independent, we would have $R = R_{1\,\mathrm{WK}} + R_{1\,\mathrm{MO}} + \cdots + R_{5\,\mathrm{Y}} = \Sigma\, R_i$, but in general this relation does not hold.[6] Looking at the R_i, it is now possible to determine what is the implicit exposure in the portfolio and hedge it. For example, if we determine that $R_{12\,\mathrm{MO}}$ is the predominant element in the series, we know that probably the whole portfolio should be hedged with a maturity close to 12 months. As for the nominal at risk, it depends on the expected behavior of the actual market curve.[7] If it is probable that a punctual move will affect $r_{12\mathrm{MO}}$ specifically while leaving the remaining part of

---

[6] To see why this is possibly so, consider a 3½-year loan. The relevant rate to value this loan is an interpolation of the 3- and 4-year rates. If this interpolation is linear—$r_{3\frac{1}{2}} = (r_3 + r_4)/2$—and the risk analysis is also linear, then $R = R_{3\mathrm{Y}} + R_{4\mathrm{Y}}$. If, however, the interpolation is not linear—polynomial, for example—then, $R \neq R_{3\mathrm{Y}} + R_{4\mathrm{Y}}$.

[7] Although R_i and R can be homogeneous to a number of shares or nominal when computed in stocks, for example, on interest rates they are always homogeneous to a nominal, representing the nominal at risk in the position for a move in interest rates equal to δ.

the curve relatively unchanged, we should use $R_{12\,\text{MO}}$ as an exact indication of the nominal to hedge. If, on the other hand, we expect a general move, we should probably use R, with the underlying assumption that the entire position will be adequately hedged by taking care only of its most sensitive maturity.

Conclusion

The above discussion shows that a risk analysis process is not as clear-cut as a valuation because of the subtleties of the mandate and the difficulties to describe appropriately the intrinsic randomness of the market. In particular, two of the fundamental principles we used to perform a valuation are not valid anymore. On one side, we cannot consider each instrument independently but rather we need to treat the portfolio as a whole and identify classes of risk across all assets. Similarly, depending on the type of position held, the methodology will be different. For example, for a large portfolio it probably makes more sense to compute a global R, assuming that risk is accurately described from the perspective of the entire market shifting in the same direction. For a small position, a stock-by-stock perspective may be warranted, in which case the portfolio risk is more appropriately described by the family of R_i.

In fact, an identical underlying may be analyzed differently in two distinct positions. If it is held as part of an arbitrage, the assumed convergence will dictate the type of analysis performed, in contrast to another type of strategy. Assume, for example, that we try to evaluate the risk embedded in a risk arbitrage between two stocks A and B. We can compute three risk factors R_A, R_B, and R on this portfolio, each capturing a different side of the risk exposure. However, none of these does a good job at looking at the most important risk, the fact that the spread between A and B might evolve unfavorably. The metrics necessary to account for that particular risk is the arithmetic quantity $S = r \cdot P_A - P_B$ where r is the merger ratio. If at the same time somebody else on the trading floor is looking at A and B from a general perspective—that is, without any emphasis on the planned merger—the corresponding risk analysis would not use S but simply P_A and P_B.

A risk analysis is therefore inherently highly context sensitive, in sharp contrast to a valuation that we presented as an "absolute" process. If the purpose—allowing a trader to make a relevant decision—is universal, and the tools—partial derivatives—commonly used, the implementation should be tailored to the situation. Back to the risk arbitrage example: R_A, R_B, and R do not serve the purpose adequately, but R_S does if R_S is defined by:

$$R_S = \frac{V(S+\delta) - V(S)}{\delta}$$

In essence, the risk analysis should extract the relevant information from the position, and it belongs to the trader to make sure that this is truly the case. Thus, our enumeration of risks cannot possibly be exhaustive but will present the most important categories and those directly relevant to arbitrage opportunities.

Risk Management and Reporting

Internal Risk Management

Like a valuation, a risk analysis is reported every day from each individual trading desk to the management of the firm, with a degree of aggregation depending upon the target audience. For example, the head of an equity trading department will be interested in how each individual activity contributes to the risk of the entire floor, which desk is most heavily exposed, and which risk factor is most critical. As a result of this information, he or she acquires a vision broader than that of individual traders and may be able to optimize the overall exposure.[8] Higher in the hierarchy, the information needs to be compacted even more—for example, to include fixed income and foreign exchange as well as equity. Finally, at the higher executive level, the CEO, CFO, or COO are most probably interested in a maximum loss, in addition to the recurrent level of risk carried by the firm as part of its day-to-day business.

This situation is very similar to what happens with a valuation statement, with two major differences: The first one is that a risk analysis is essentially a forward-looking prescriptive document because its entire purpose is to enable hedging. A valuation statement, on the other hand, is usually backward looking and descriptive, and it does not call for action. Furthermore the ability to execute on the risk analysis disappears rapidly when going up the hierarchy. For example, the

[8] Consider, for example, that two traders have an opposite exposure on a given risk factor. Independently each one would be tempted to hedge and possibly pay a fee to a third party for that. If they traded internally, on the other hand, they could price the transaction at fair value so that each is appropriately hedged at zero cost.

Needless to say, this broader vision is also absolutely necessary in evaluating individual performances.

head of a trading floor may be in a position to recommend specific trades, but the CEO will simply comment on the level of risk. Therefore, even though valuation and risk statements tend to travel together throughout a firm, they cannot be aggregated in a similar way.[9]

The second is related to the fact that a risk analysis is highly dependent on a strategy and its particular management, and therefore it carries much more potential for misunderstanding. In other words, it is possible to reconcile and explain a valuation, good or bad, based on facts, but much more difficult to justify a level of risk that might depend on the specific nature of the position as well as a market opportunity. Index arbitrage is an excellent example of this potential for conflict. In general, positions of that type reach several billion dollars, and such an amount tends to make risk managers nervous. At the same time, when properly hedged and managed, the intrinsic risk here is much smaller than that, for example, of an option position on a much smaller nominal.

To understand a valuation, a risk manager needs to be familiar only with instruments and products, whereas when dealing with reported risk analyses, he or she has to understand the underlying trading strategy and its implications on the management of the position. This specific knowledge is hard to acquire without practical trading experience, which makes the task of nontrader risk managers all the more demanding.

Time Horizons

Another important aspect of a risk analysis is its time horizon. A valuation is a snapshot as of today, and it does not have any time component because the position is liquidated immediately. A risk analysis, in contrast, should have a time component because risk is likely to evolve in the future. Typically the expiry of an instrument, derivative or not, at a given time significantly alters the risk profile of the entire portfolio.

This problem can be addressed in two ways. On one hand, although the purpose of a risk report is to enable trading immediately, it should at the very least present a detailed schedule of expected expirations and other relevant events. Indeed, it should ideally provide the trader with an exhaustive calendar of events likely to affect the position one way or another. Such a calendar would, for example, include corporate events—dividends, splits, and so on—index inclu-

[9] Typically a dollar earned is a dollar earned anywhere in a firm. In contrast, a dollar at risk is not the same depending on which activity carries it.

sions and/or deletions, and expirations of, say, money markets, stock loan agreements, and futures. Naturally monitoring such a diverse universe is a difficult task, and in practice, many traders manage this process themselves, in general manually.

On the other hand, and this is the most important aspect, some risk factors are likely to depend on time and should be organized in a term structure, similar to that of interest rates. The best example of this is volatility, used to value an options position, but the same reasoning applies also to the repo rate for stock loans and other parameters. Volatility is highly dependent on maturity, the same way interest rates are, and an accurate description of the associated risk requires several estimators based on different expiries. Therefore, it is not one volatility risk factor but several that must be included and analyzed together if the position is to be hedged correctly.

Magnitudes

A risk factor is characterized by two elements: its magnitude and its probability. In a risk analysis performed with partial derivatives, the notion of probability is relatively silent because we fix the elementary variation we want to use, and we do not really need to know the associated probability. On the other hand, the probability becomes extremely important in a V@R, as we will see.

Therefore, we will focus primarily on the order of magnitude of a given class of risk. To illustrate this notion, consider a $100 million position on stocks. If the market loses 10 percent tomorrow, the portfolio is likely to lose close to $10 million. If the portfolio is instead a loan for 1 year on $100 million with a market rate of 5 percent, a change of 10 percent in the rate leads to a loss of $500,000 (= $100,000,000 * 5 percent * 10 percent). Finally, if we hold again a stock position but this time the dividend yield—assumed equal to 2 percent—varies unfavorably by 10 percent, the total loss is $200,000 (= $100,000,000 * 2 percent * 10 percent).

This short example shows that the absolute magnitude of the risk depends on the nominal of the position but more importantly on the nature of the risk examined. It is customary to refer to the magnitude of a given exposure as its *order*. In the above example the market risk related to asset prices is clearly of the first order, interest rates of the second order, and dividends, the third order. This nomenclature is highly subjective, however. For a treasury manager, interest rates clearly represent a first-order concern, while perfectly hedged index arbitrageurs, on the other hand, would consider the change in asset prices as of the second order because their exposure is usually differential, not outright.

The purpose of this labeling is essentially practical. When dealing with a particular position, it is essential, especially for junior traders, to make very quickly a distinction between the different layers of risk, which is exactly what the notion of "order" tries to describe. In the following examination of market risks, and even more in the last part presenting specific arbitrage situations, we will try to qualify risks by their order of magnitude, to make their relative importance and impact clear.[10]

Interest Rates

In contrast to a valuation, the yield curve in a risk analysis does not need to be zero coupon. All valuations are usually performed with zero coupons, but the parameters used to represent interest rate risk—that is, P_i—do not have to be. To understand what this means, we denote r_i^{ZC} the zero-coupon yield curve and r_i the market curve, made of swaps, eurofutures, or any other relevant product. We saw in a previous section how to derive the series r_i^{ZC} from r_i, a process we summarize by a function g such that:

$$(r_1^{ZC}, \ldots, r_n^{ZC}) = g(r_1, \ldots, r_n)$$

We know that V uses r_i^{ZC}, so we can define the "natural" ith risk factor R_i as:

$$R_i = \frac{V(r_1^{ZC}, \ldots, r_i^{ZC} + \delta, \ldots, r_n^{ZC}) - V(r_1^{ZC}, \ldots, r_i^{ZC}, \ldots, r_n^{ZC})}{\delta}$$

However, if we want to use the market yield curve, we can use:

$$R_i' = \frac{V[g(r_1, \ldots, r_i + \delta, \ldots, r_n)] - V[g(r_1, \ldots, r_i, \ldots, r_n)]}{\delta}$$

R_i' is different from R_i because we apply the same change in rate, δ, but not on the same curve; a shift of, for example, 0.10 percent of the market curve is not equivalent to a shift of 0.10 percent on the zero coupons.

The reason behind this transformation is primarily practical. Even though zero coupons are essential in a valuation, the most liquid rates actually traded in the market are swaps and eurofutures. Therefore,

---

[10] Alternatively, a first-order risk is a risk to which the entire nominal of the position is exposed. A second-order risk is a risk to which only a fraction of the position is exposed, and so on for subsequent orders. This is consistent with the original discussion introduced in the first chapter about nominal versus differential exposure.

using a market rate as P_i gives a result that is directly relevant to market instruments. Consider, for example, that we determine a possible loss of $-\$500,000$ to an increase of 0.20 percent in the two-year zero-coupon rate. To hedge this risk, we would need to enter a two-year zero coupon such that an increase of 0.20 percent in the rate generates $500,000 in additional profit. However, it may be difficult, or expensive, to trade this type of zero coupon in the market, whereas two-year swaps are readily available. Assuming that a variation of 0.20 percent in the two-year zero coupon is equivalent to the same variation in the two-year swap is a mistake because the relationship between the two is not linear. Therefore, we have no easy way to perform a hedge, and we need to translate the incremental 0.20 percent in swap prices. If, in contrast, the risk analysis had been carried out originally on swap prices, we would have the information necessary to hedge directly available.

In the remainder of this chapter, we do not specify if interest rates P_i are zero coupon or market. Except for the intricacies of translating one into the other, the fundamental results and analysis are independent from the reference yield curve.

MARKET RISKS

Market risks incorporate all risks that are dependent upon one or a set of market parameters. For our purpose, a market parameter is a numerical quantity varying randomly continuously.[11] For example, the price of a stock is known today, but it is unknown tomorrow or at any later date for that matter. More generally, the price discovery process occurring in the market is such that asset prices are always instantaneously available, but they are systematically unknown for any future period. In contrast, other risks do not depend on the market and may not even be parametric. For example, the risk of a system failure is uncorrelated to the market level and difficult to describe with a single figure.

Market risks are the primary focus of risk managers' attention, if only because these risks need to be monitored at least daily. In contrast, nonmarket risks often tend to be overlooked, despite the fact that in

[11] Note that the variable may be discrete or continuous, and in fact, it does not need to vary very often, although the higher the variability, the more important the associated risk. Dividends, for example, vary only episodically and generally on the upside and still they generate a risk that must be accounted for.

some instances their magnitude is equivalent. Back to the example of a system failure, a power outage, for example, on a futures expiry can very well lead to significant losses if a large number of orders cannot be sent to the market at the right time or price.[12]

In the following discussion, we separate market and nonmarket risks, and we tend to discuss the former in more detail. The reason for this choice is the perspective we have chosen from the start. A trader is directly accountable for the management of the market risks in his or her position, but his or her sphere of influence and responsibility is rapidly constrained for nonmarket risks. Although they certainly should be kept in mind, they are usually better handled by more qualified parties. The legal and contractual aspect of OTC trades, for example, should be proofed by experienced lawyers.

Prices

Delta and Gamma

The most important market risk is a first-order risk related to the price of an asset. This asset may be a stock, bond, or foreign currency, and in all cases its price varies continuously and has a direct impact on the exposure of the position. By analogy to the Greek used in an options position, this risk is often referred to as the *delta of the position*:

$$\Delta = \left(\frac{\Delta V}{\Delta S}\right) = \frac{V(S+\delta) - V(S)}{\delta}$$

As we mentioned earlier, the delta may be computed asset by asset, or on the entire position at once. Similarly, it can be expressed as a number of units or nominal, depending on the environment. For example, if the position examined is a foreign exchange or a treasury portfolio, the relevant unit of measure is a nominal figure. This risk is very simple to track and understand. In an arbitrage situation it corresponds to a position for which the legs are not properly matched, in number of units or nominal.

If today $S = S_0$ and we do not hedge a move from S_0 to S_1, the valuation V of the position becomes:

$$V(S_1) = V(S_0) + (S_1 - S_0) \cdot \Delta_0$$

[12] An interesting example is the Y2K phenomenon. Financial institutions worldwide spent hundreds of millions to alleviate their fears of an unrecoverable failure in the system.

As long as delta is constant and small, the hedge can be executed at any time, and the incremental valuation will probably remain relatively small. A problem occurs, however, if delta is large or not constant.

The case of delta's being too large indicates a position that was not hedged in the first place, which may be the result of a mistake or an intentional choice to "play" the market in a given direction. More interesting is a situation in which delta is not constant and varies with the market. This phenomenon is typical of an options position, but it may be found in "standard" positions as well.[13] The variation of delta is described with another Greek letter borrowed from options theory, *gamma*:

$$\Gamma = \left(\frac{\Delta^2 V}{\Delta S^2}\right) = \frac{\Delta(S+\delta) - \Delta(S)}{\delta}$$

Gamma makes a position much more difficult to manage, and for all purposes much more risky, because the P&L generated by an error in gamma grows with the square of market movements:

$$V(S_1) = V(S_0) + (S_1 - S_0) \cdot \Delta_0 + ½ \cdot (S_1 - S_0)^2 \cdot \Gamma_0$$

In practice, the existence of a gamma exposure means that the position should be hedged very often in periods of volatile markets because the term $(S_1 - S_0)^2$ may become significant. Ideally the hedge should be continuous, but due to transaction costs, this is impossible, and the best compromise may be to hedge several times a day.

Correlation and Convergence

Correlations

The correlation risk is a second-order risk coming from the mismatch of two assets that should fluctuate very close to each other. If we use the framework we introduced earlier for a generic spread position in two assets A and B, with a nominal such that $N_A = N_B + \Delta N$, the valuation is given by:

$$\Delta V = p_A \cdot N_A - p_B \cdot N_B = (p_A - p_B) \cdot N_B + p_A \cdot \Delta_N$$

where $p_A = \Delta P_A / P_A$ and $p_B = \Delta P_B / P_B$ denote the percentage variations of A and B. Assuming the position is originally hedged in nominal, $N_A = N_B = N, \Delta V$ is then:

---

[13] For example, we showed how the arbitrage between the Nikkei 225 in Osaka and Chicago required the management of a foreign exchange position with a delta depending on the current spot rate and the level of the Nikkei 225.

$$\Delta V = (p_A - p_B) \cdot N$$

The dependence of ΔV on a differential performance creates a second-order exposure, which is exactly the overall correlation of A and B. Considering what an arbitrage position is built upon, this risk is particularly relevant to our enterprise and, as we will see, it takes a slightly different form depending on the situation.

Convergences

A convergence risk is nothing more than an extreme form of correlation exposure. When considering the dynamic relationship of two assets, we can make a distinction between a one-time equality—convergence—and the existence of an ongoing pattern of similar returns—correlation. We know already that if a convergence exists, the correlation should be very high as is the case in index or risk arbitrage. The reciprocal relation is not true, however, because two assets may exhibit a strong historical relationship without converging with any certainty. This is typically what pair or technical trading is about.

Convergence and correlation tend to evolve in the same direction but do not capture the same information. Except for situations of absolute convergence in which both are relatively benign in magnitude, a trader would care more about one dimension than about the other. In risk arbitrage, for example, convergence is dominant because if it breaks, correlation will automatically collapse. In contrast, pair or technical trading would focus more on correlation because convergence is highly uncertain. As with all other risks, the focus is dictated by the underlying strategy.

Corporate Events

Corporate events constitute a risk only rarely, and usually only for holders of short positions.[14] When terms are available in a timely manner, which is almost always the case, arbitrageurs have plenty of time to analyze the proposed event and make the necessary adjustments to their position. Short sellers, however, may be squeezed in specific situations, unable to close the risk at a reasonable price.

In many cases an additional layer of risk comes from the uncertainty attached to the general acceptance of the event. If, for example, distribution of new shares in a rights offering is prorated based on the

---

[14] Naturally risk arbitrage is based on a corporate event, but we consider here only "incidental" corporate events—that is, events affecting a position built for the purpose of pursuing a specific and distinct strategy.

overall subscription ratio, an arbitrageur may have to hedge a position unknown at the time of the hedge.[15]

Clearly the best way to protect a position against unforeseen difficulties, especially on the short side, is to monitor announcements and events very closely. First, a deep understanding of the details will lead to an appropriate decision and a clear assessment of the risks involved. Then it may be more economically efficient to close the relevant position early than to try to carry it through.

Interest Rates

In general, interest rate risk is relatively straightforward to handle, given adequate information. Depending on the maturity, swaps, eurofutures, or money market deposits can provide the necessary hedge, with or without actually changing the treasury balance. However, getting the adequate information is not easy considering the number of dimensions involved and the possible movements within the yield curve. For a money market trader, hedging interest rate exposure may be a complex process because of the multitude of instruments and maturities involved. For an equity trader, on the other hand, the management of this risk is simpler because it always appears as a byproduct of the main trading activity. Typically the interest rate risk created by trading a futures contract or forward, for example, is easy to identify and neutralize because these are instruments with a defined expiry.

In fact, in many instances the interest rate risk is simply ignored because it is not relevant considering the specifics of the position. For example, a trader using an index futures contract only infrequently to hedge a minor part of his or her portfolio would probably not feel the need to enter a short-term hedge on interest rates for the induced exposure. Even if futures or other instruments such as foreign exchange derivatives are used often and for a large volume, if the time horizon of a strategy is short enough, the real risk becomes very small.[16]

We do not mean to imply that risks associated with interest rates should be neglected but rather that they can probably be considered

---

[15] A proration indicates an allocation of shares on a certain criterion. A company may decide, for example, that a rights subscription is canceled if a certain threshold has not been met. In that case, the arbitrageur may have hedged the entire number of shares he or she exercised and will eventually receive nothing.

[16] For a position of typical life span equal to three months, for example, even a 0.50 percent move in interest rates, fairly large, would create a risk of only 0.125 percent (= 0.50 percent/4) on the total nominal.

from a distance in the particular context of an equity trading desk. Therefore, judgment and experience appear once more to be very valuable in making the most appropriate and "cheapest" decision by weighting the different factors.

Financing Risk

Financing risk is a subset of interest rate exposure, and it refers to the P&L generated in the very short term, typically because of the monetary balance carried overnight. This risk can be of two types: outright and spread. An outright exposure indicates an additional financing cost that needs to be accounted for and monitored. An example of this is typically the margin calls of futures. A spread exposure arises when the overnight financing is carried at a rate possibly different from what has been implicitly priced in a traded instrument. The overnight *squeeze* at the end of a fiscal year will serve as an example here.

Outright Risk

Suppose we buy 10 S&P 500 futures at $1,400, a position for which we have to pay initial and maintenance margin calls every day. The initial margin is 10 * $20,438 = $204,380, payable in cash or acceptable securities, typically treasury bills. If this position is kept for a week and exited at $1,400, the realized P&L is zero because the market did not move. However, we had to pay financing on $204,438 for a week. The cost associated may be a cash market rate if we deposited cash or a borrowing fee if we borrowed securities. Therefore, the magnitude varies, but the cost exists in both cases and applies to the entire initial margin.

If the market moves over the week, we pay or receive in addition maintenance margins, for which again the deposit needs to be borrowed or lent. Here the funding cost may actually be a profit if we receive margin payments. In any case, these daily payments vary with the market level and as such can and should be hedged. In contrast, initial margin payments depend on the size of the position, not the level of the market and therefore cannot be hedged.

To establish the algebraic expression of the hedge ratio, consider a long position of n futures. The market prices are respectively F_Y and F_T for yesterday and today. Let r be the zero-coupon rate from today until the expiry of the futures. If we held n futures yesterday and the market moved from F_Y to F_T, the maintenance margin call would be:

$$MC_T = PV \cdot (F_T - F_Y) \cdot n$$

where PV is the futures point value. If the market remains unchanged until the expiry, the financing generated by this margin call is $MC_T \cdot r$. In order for us to be hedged, we need to take an additional futures position δ such that a move from F_Y to F_T generates a loss equal to the financing of the margin call. δ is then given by:

$$\delta \cdot PV \cdot (F_T - F_Y) = -PV \cdot (F_T - F_Y) \cdot (n + \delta) \cdot r$$

The left term is the additional P&L generated by δ futures, and the right term is the financing on the margin call on $(n + \delta)$ futures. This leads to:

$$\delta = -\left(\frac{r}{1+r}\right) \cdot n$$

which in turn gives:

$$\delta + n = n \cdot \left(\frac{1}{1+r}\right)$$

This result indicates that *hedging the margin call financing of a futures position requires changing the number of futures from n to n/(1 + r).*[17] If we take $r = 5$ percent over two months, $1/(1+r) = 1/(1+5 \text{ percent} * 2/12) = 0.99173$. For a \$1 billion position—that is, 2,857 futures—the adjustment is 23.6 futures, big enough to warrant attention.

This example of "parasitic" financing and the necessary hedge is very common and widely used by futures traders.[18] Note that this adjustment is not necessary with forwards because of the absence of margin calls.

Spread Risk

Consider a portfolio in which we entered a swap to cover long-term financing needs. Having bought the swap, we pay the fixed rate, receive the variable rate, and borrow periodically at the LIBOR. The interests paid on the LIBOR loans match exactly the variable payments from the swap, which means that the effective borrowing cost of the

---

[17] The same result can be obtained using the risk framework we introduced before. If V is the valuation of a position of $(n+\delta)$ futures, its delta is $\Delta V/\Delta S = (n+\delta) \cdot \Delta F/\Delta S = (n+\delta) \cdot r$ because $F = S \cdot (1+r) - d^*$. Hedging $\Delta V/\Delta S$ means setting δ so that $\Delta V/\Delta S + \delta = 0$. This is true if $(n+\delta) \cdot r = -\delta \quad \Rightarrow \quad \delta = -n \cdot r/(1+r)$.

[18] In addition, note that the hedge ratio changes with maturity. For example, if we take a five-month futures contract it becomes $[= 1/(1 + 5 \text{ percent} * 5/12)] = 0.97959$.

The process by which the number of hedging futures is changed is usually referred to as *tailing the hedge*. The *tail* denotes the small fraction of the hedge covering the margin calls. See, for example, Ira G. Kawaller, "Tailing Futures Hedges/Tailing Spreads," *The Journal of Derivatives*, October 1997.

structure is the fixed rate of the swap. We described this approach earlier.

Now consider that we forget or intentionally forego entering one of the LIBOR loans. Assuming we need the cash, the shortfall will be covered day to day by an overnight carry. In contrast to the LIBOR, which would have been known for the entire three months, the overnight rate is known with certainty only from one day to the next, and it can vary significantly depending on the liquidity instantaneously available in the marketplace. As a result of this variability, the effective cost of carrying the overnight for three months might end up being different from the original three months' LIBOR at which we should have traded. Indeed, because of its particular nature, the overnight rate can be affected by a number of factors including day-of-the-week or end-of-month effects. Consider as an illustration the five charts in Figures 7-2 through 7-6 giving overnight and three months' LIBOR for USD, GBP, FRF, DEM, and JPY.

These charts show the immediate difference between a three-month LIBOR and the overnight. Clearly there are systematic differences between the two rates, and their relative behavior is highly dependent on the market. What is not directly available, however, is the actual differential cost of carrying a position overnight instead of hedging it at a three-month LIBOR. Figure 7-7 presents exactly that information. It is obtained by compounding the overnight over a three-month period, and comparing the compounded return to the three-month LIBOR at the beginning of the period. It therefore represents a direct P&L for somebody who would have made a choice to stay at the overnight.[19]

Interestingly, the chart is most often under the x axis, which indicates that for a borrower it is often better to carry the overnight risk than to hedge with the three-month LIBOR. Conversely, a lender would have a strong interest in entering a term loan. It appears that the shape of the chart changes with the country, but in general the same conclusion holds: It is cheaper for borrowers to carry the overnight risk. This risk is not entirely free, however, because if the overnight shoots up suddenly for one or several days, the total cost advantage might disappear very quickly.

Another example of spread risk can be found in the United States with the fed fund futures contracts. As we have seen, the fed fund futures are settled on the average effective fed fund rate every month. The effective fed fund is a weighted average of all the trades

[19] A negative figure indicates that the compounded overnight is below the three-month rate at the beginning of the compounding period.

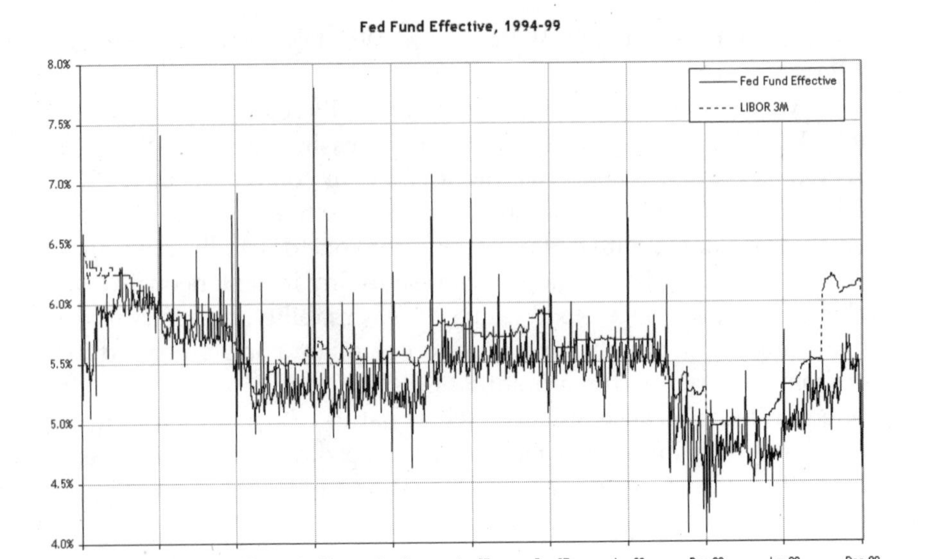

Figure 7-2 Fed Fund
(*Source*: Compiled by author from Datastream data.)

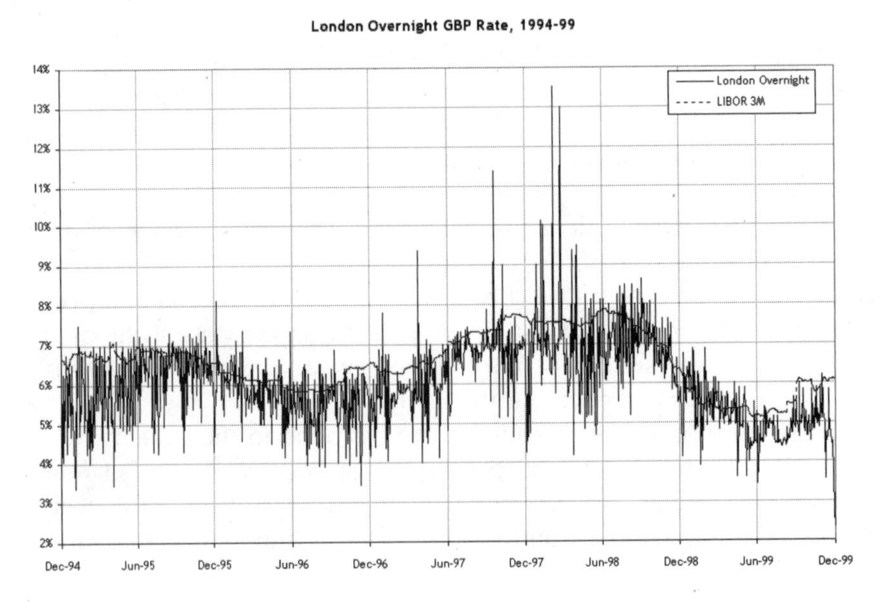

Figure 7-3 Overnight GBP
(*Source*: Compiled by author from Datastream data.)

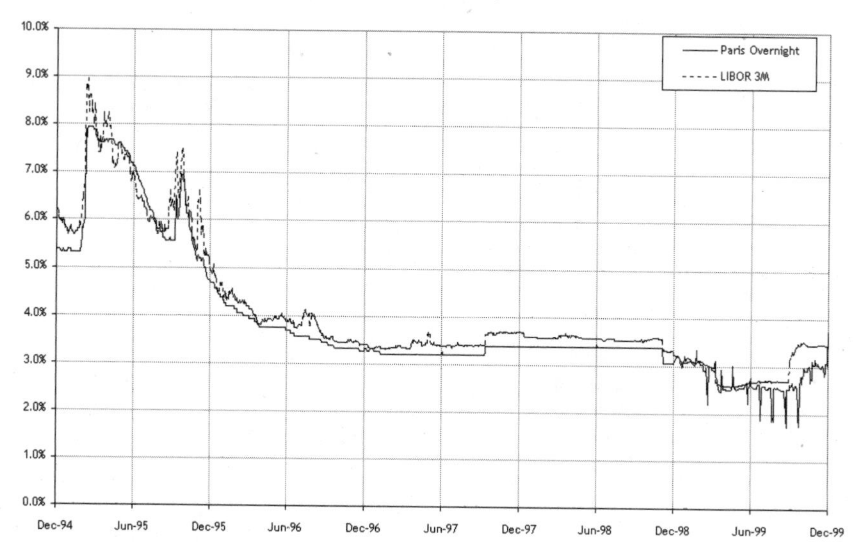

Figure 7-4 Overnight FRF
(*Source*: Compiled by author from Datastream data.)

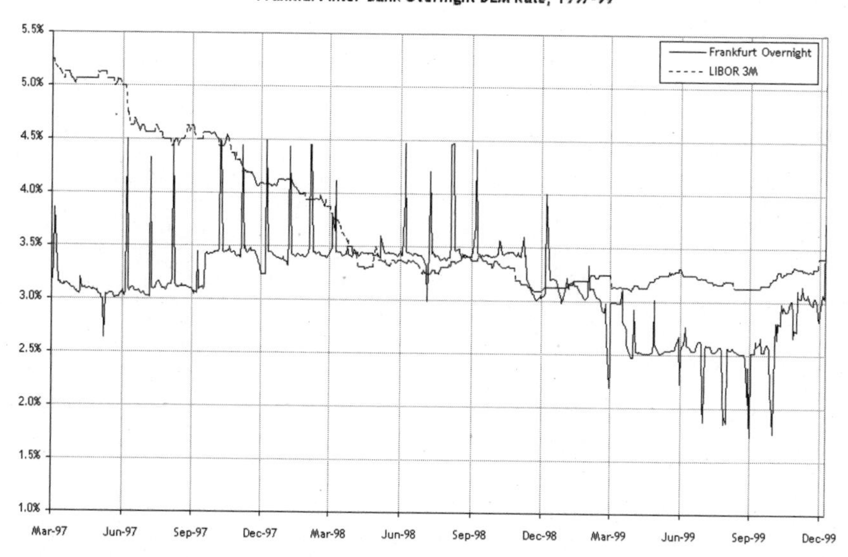

Figure 7-5 Overnight DEM
(*Source*: Compiled by author from Datastream data.)

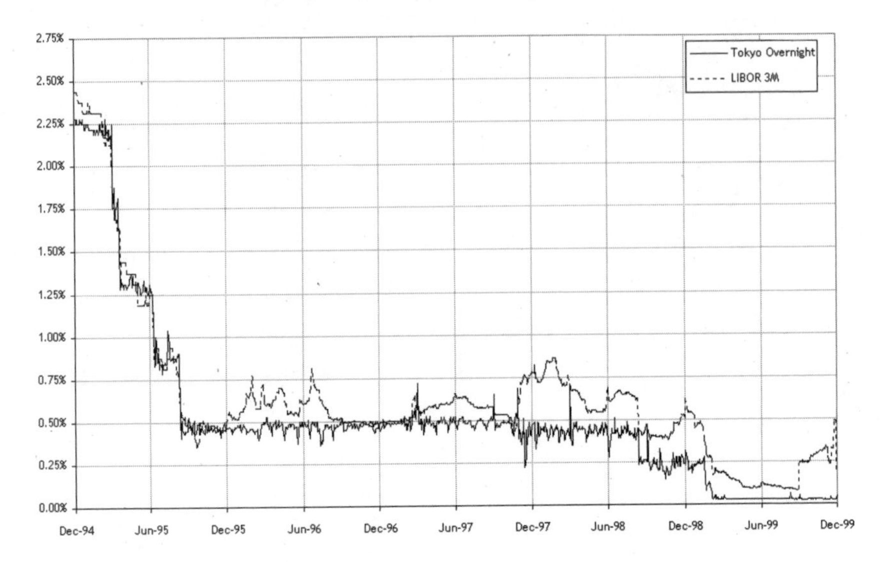

Figure 7-6 Overnight JPY
(*Source*: Compiled by author from Datastream data.)

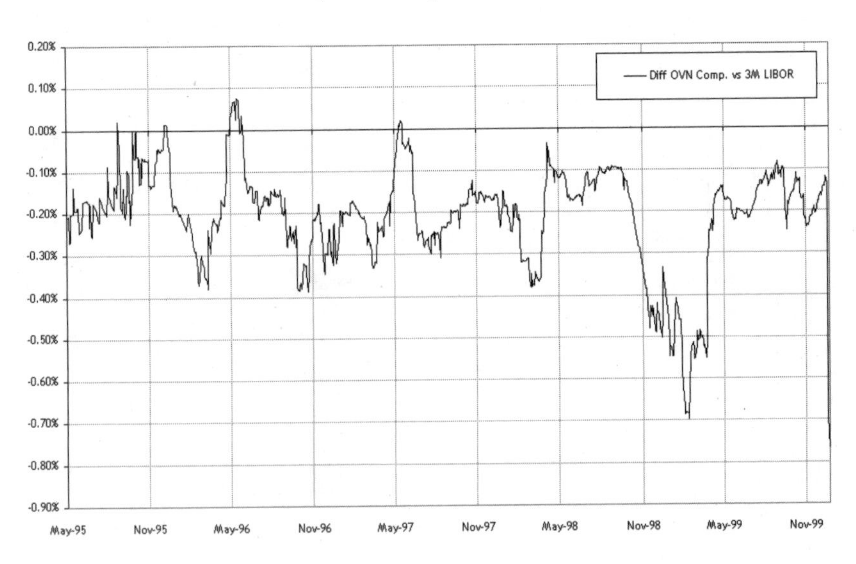

Figure 7-7 Compounded Overnight USD
(*Source*: Compiled by author from Datastream data.)

of the day; therefore, it is different from the close which represents a snapshot of the price traded at the end of each day. The difference between these two rates can be significant, both ways, as shown in Figure 7-8. Somebody hedging a treasury position with a fed fund futures contract but executing overnight transactions toward the end of each day would effectively carry the spread risk between the two. In fact, even trading earlier during the day would not remove the risk because there cannot be any guarantee that the effective rate for the day will be equal to the rate traded at some particular time.

Dividends

The dividend risk arises essentially because of a difference between expected and actual values for dividend payments. As we have described, the procedure by which dividends are set implies that the actual amount is unknown until a few days before it is actually paid. If this amount had to be estimated before, and there are numerous situations in which it is necessary to do so, any difference between expectations and actual values results in a profit or a loss.

Consider, for example, a risk arbitrage in which the target company B and acquirer A have similar historical nominal dividend payments, say, $0.10 per quarter. If we take a typical merger arbitrage situation, the target company B is trading at a discount compared to the terms of the

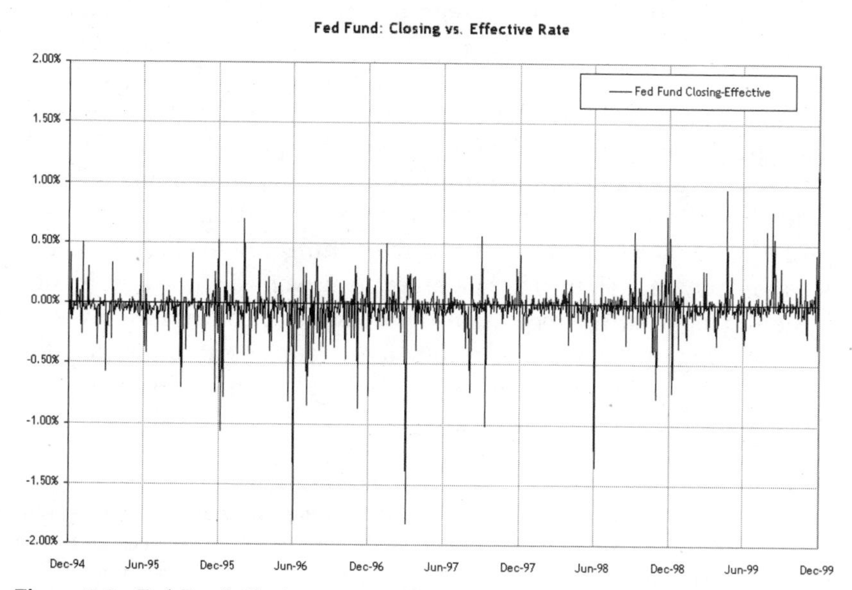

Figure 7-8 Fed Fund Closing versus Effective
(*Source*: Compiled by author from Datastream data.)

acquisition. Assuming for simplicity a merger ratio of 1, we are long *B* and short *A* for the same number of shares. In that scenario, when we entered the spread, dividend payments were expected to cancel out: +\$0.10 every quarter from *B*, −\$0.10 with the same frequency on *A*. The first possible problem is a sequencing issue. If dividend ex-dates do not occur at the same time, we may have to pay more on *A* than we receive on *B*, if, for example, more ex-dates of *A* are included in the period until maturity. This difference would naturally have to be included in the arbitrage profitability. More generally, assume that the ex-dates coincide, so that we are perfectly matched. The risk here is an increase in *A*'s dividends, or alternatively, a decrease in *B*'s. If, for example, *A* went up from \$0.10 to \$0.12 and *B* down from \$0.10 to \$0.05, we would realize a loss of \$0.07 (= \$0.02 + \$0.05) per share of *A* and B. In practice, downward revisions of dividends are not well perceived in the marketplace, so a company involved in a merger would certainly avoid that option. However, an increase is always possible, especially if *A* wants to show its financial strength and emphasize what it perceives to be a significant positive event, namely, the merger.

There is no easy way to hedge this risk because dividend payments are set by the board and the information related to the decision process is highly proprietary. Many companies have adopted consistent and transparent policies, making their decisions relatively predictable. When a large number of companies is involved, however, such as with an index arbitrage position, on average it is not possible to consider the dividends really predictable. This situation makes any hedge problematic because the underlying variable does not fit a traditional pattern.

Interestingly, a dividend exposure may exist even without explicit equity exposure. If we take the example of a portfolio hedged with index futures, the value of the futures is highly dependent on the index dividend expectations, whereas the underlying portfolio may not be a replicating portfolio. In that case, if the futures are evaluated with a cash-and-carry model, they create an exposure on the index dividends despite the fact that the index is not necessarily a concern in any way for the trading strategy. As a result, the overall portfolio carries the dividend risk of the actual stock position, plus an exposure on the index dividends through the futures position.[20]

---

[20] Note that even if futures are held as a hedge, the dividend exposure on each leg is in the same direction. Consider, for example, that the portfolio is long stock and short futures. If dividends go up on the stocks and on the index, the portfolio will show a profit on both legs because the theoretical value of the futures goes down, which results in a profit on a short position.

Short Squeezes

We already gave one example of a short squeeze on the financing side, although it carried another name: "end-of-month effect." Demand for liquidity is so high in some instances that the market price of this liquidity exhibits an abnormal spike to reflect the shortage of the scarce resource. Despite its abnormal nature and possible magnitude, this spike is in general relatively benign because central banks are available to attenuate its effect as part of their regular market interventions.

More interesting and more costly is a short squeeze on stocks for short sellers. We evoked this risk in several instances already, notably with regard to corporate events. The extreme form is a squeeze in which the price of the scarce resource—that is, the borrowing fee—becomes irrelevant because there are simply no more shares available in the marketplace. The effect can be devastating because short sellers have no choice but to close their positions at the current market price.

Consider, for example, the situation of an arbitrageur of closed-end funds. Trying to capture a premium, the arbitrageur would short sell the fund and hedge with a replicating portfolio of some sort. If the fund premium starts widening, the arbitrageur is losing on the spread, and at some point if the fund becomes really expensive relative to its underlying assets, holders will be tempted to sell, and to do so they will have to recall the shares they have lent out. Naturally, because the total number of shares is fixed, the arbitrageur should be able to find another counterpart ready to lend a replacement position. In practice, for a short time it is extremely possible that all holders will recall their shares at once to sell them, and during that period the arbitrageur will be unable to keep the short position. If sellers do rush to the market, the premium will collapse again, at which time the arbitrageur will find new shares to borrow, having been forced out of the market at the worst time.

A short squeeze occurs when a scarce resource becomes even more scarce, which essentially means that it becomes impossible to acquire when it is most needed. Due to its nature, it is also extremely difficult to hedge and, in the particular case of borrowed securities, virtually impossible because lenders usually keep the ultimate privilege to recall their shares when needed.

Execution

We exposed earlier the fundamental risk of execution related to the expiry of a futures contract on an average value. Similarly, when creating synthetic futures with American options, like those on the S&P 100, the risk of exercise on one of the legs creates an execution risk because the leg must be replaced, at a price likely to be different from its fair value when originally acquired.

More generally, we define *execution risk* as the need to execute in the market a parameter that is already implicitly or explicitly priced in an existing position. This parameter may be a stock price or any other market price. For example, if a swap structure is used to borrow cash over a long period of time, the implicit assumption is that it will always be possible to borrow short-term liquidity at the reset price of the variable leg—that is, the LIBOR. This assumption creates precisely an execution risk because any difference between the LIBOR and the actual loan rate at a reset date will result in a profit or a loss, unaccounted for previously.[21]

In many instances, and arbitrage is a powerful example, execution is a risk but at the same time the primary driver of profitability. Indeed, arbitrageurs act as cross-security market makers and as such profit from instantaneous price discrepancies. Because the two legs of a position can never be really executed at the same time, the necessary time lag between them creates an execution risk, which should constitute the only significant risk in the strategy if it is truly an arbitrage. Therefore, execution, more than any other, is a risk we do not necessarily want to hedge away, even if we were able to.

Other Risks

Despite the fact that they are less visible, nonmarket risks are extremely important in many respects. Clearly, their magnitude and monitoring are much more difficult to assess with an adequate level of comfort, which makes them sometimes even difficult to define. More importantly, however, their main characteristic is their discrete nature.

Although a market price is relatively continuous, nonmarket risks are of a different nature because they essentially boil down to "all or none." In the case of credit risk, for example, if a counterpart fails before final settlement, chances are that the claim on its assets will be difficult and painful to recover, to the point where it may be wiser to write it off. On the other hand, if its financial strength is adequate, payment will occur with no particular difficulty. Therefore, except

---

[21] If we knew from the very beginning that we would have to pay more than the LIBOR, this difference would not be a risk because it would be entirely predictable.

for somebody in the business of explicitly trading it, this risk is not welcome in general because it is extremely difficult to encapsulate in a risk analysis framework.[22]

The same is true of a larger set of risks, some of which are not even tradable in the market. Considering what our perspective has been from the very beginning, the following presentation will be essentially an introduction.

Credit Risks

Credit risk denotes the risk that a counterpart fails to settle its liabilities when they come due. For example, if a corporation fails to meet a covenant attached to one of its obligations, bond holders may have the option to force it into receivership or bankruptcy.[23] In virtually all cases, however, default is defined with respect to financial strength, not operating performance. This last point is critical because it means that power to trigger judicial action rests with a particular category of investors—debt holders.[24] In that situation, stockholders' rights are subordinated to those of debt holders and creditors, and this precedence is well known. In other words, the failure of a corporation creates a credit risk to creditors but a market risk to shareholders because the two groups have different rights and expectations from their investment.

Generally speaking, credit risk is probably the most pervasive type of risk beyond that created directly by a market exposure. Virtually every single flow expected at one particular moment is potentially at risk, regardless of its nature and paying party. Naturally numerous safeguards have been implemented over the years at every key juncture in the financial system, such as the

---

[22] Naturally it is possible to follow and closely watch for degradation of financial strength in many institutions because a situation of default naturally does not appear overnight. Such ongoing monitoring requires skills and resources not necessarily available to the population of traders we focus on, which is why it is necessary to make a distinction between professionals explicitly focused on credit issues and other nonexperts.

[23] Bankruptcy law differs widely in many countries. In some instances, it implies liquidation, while in others, like the United States, the corporation is temporarily protected from its debt holders and creditors and allowed to remain in business under appropriate judicial control.

[24] Naturally shareholders have full latitude to judge the performance of the management team and accordingly take legal steps to protect their interests. Bond holders have additional rights because of their status when the solvency of the corporation is under scrutiny.

execution, clearing, and settlement infrastructure for publicly traded securities. Even if the situation is not perfect, it is reasonable to consider that in many countries the appropriate controls and procedures are in place to guarantee that investors carry credit risk as a choice, not as a necessity.

In the trading world of an equity arbitrageur, credit risk is primarily arising from transactions entered over the counter. These can be money market or derivative, but in all cases a natural hedge against credit risk, more and more used, is a reciprocal margining agreement between counterparts that are used to trading with each other. The model is that of margin calls on futures and options, and it is a natural step to take even if it is administratively expensive because all parties have a strong interest in protecting themselves.[25]

Legal and Compliance Risks

Legal and compliance departments are extremely important in securities dealing institutions, especially in the United States, where the securities law is complex and intricate. It requires financial institutions to monitor themselves on numerous dimensions, from training and registration of their personnel to disclosure guidelines and ethical requirements when dealing with investors and clients.

Broadly speaking, legal risk arises on two dimensions: compliance with the prevalent securities law and enforcement of private contracts. Naturally both aspects are highly dependent on the country's legal structure and maturity of the capital market, which makes it impossible to offer a generic description here. As an example of the intricacies involved, we consider briefly the case of the United States.

In the United States, the regulatory framework for financial market participants establishes two major regulatory institutions. The Securities and Exchange Commission (SEC), on one side, regulates the market for securities, and options on securities. The Commodity Futures Trading Commission (CFTC), on the other hand, regulates the market for commodity futures and options on futures, where the term *commodity* includes a wide range of assets, physical as

[25] The market for credit risk derivatives has grown tremendously in size and maturity over the years, and there are now sophisticated products to address some of the needs of market participants. Still the principle of preemptive margins is widespread because of its simplicity and appeal. For example, some bond covenants force the issuing corporation to establish a "sinking fund" to progressively cover the principal redemption payment at maturity.

well as financial. The SEC was established in 1933 as a result of the debacle of 1929, whereas the CFTC was established in 1974 by the Commodity Futures Trading Commission Act, as a significant revision to the previously existing Commodity Exchange Act (CEA). Despite the apparently well defined jurisdictional frontier between the two institutions, the legal environment has been characterized by fierce battles between them, often considered as pure "turf battles." The current state of affairs is certainly not written in stone as more and more complex instruments present blended characteristics, making any definite classification extremely difficult. In addition to federal-level regulations, a number of other rules apply to market participants, notably state laws, also known as *blue sky laws*. Other self-regulated organizations (SROs), such as the National Association of Securities Dealers (NASD) or New York Stock Exchange (NYSE) impose in addition their own requirements on their members. The result of this patchwork is a complex set of issues, making compliance a nontrivial challenge and an expensive—but necessary—proposition.

Given the context, enforcement of private contracts is not surprisingly also a complex issue. Depending on the financial structure of a particular product, any one of the two agencies can legitimately claim jurisdictional power, in which case the original legal framing of the transaction may prove inadequate. It is therefore possible to refute a liability on the grounds that it was not properly qualified to start with and that the losing party did not receive appropriate information and/or advice. An example of such an attempt is the highly publicized Procter and Gamble (P&G) swap with Bankers Trust (BT) in 1993. P&G entered at that time into a speculative and highly leveraged swap on interest rates, which ended up losing almost $160 million. The loss prompted P&G to sue BT on several accounts, notably breach of fiduciary duty, negligent misrepresentation, and fraud. P&G also tried to have the transaction requalified as a security under SEC jurisdiction, which would have been much more sympathetic to end-user concerns. This requalification, however, was denied, and the rulings of the judge in 1996 also found that the swap was exempt from exchange-listing requirements under the Swaps Exemption of the CEA. Denying that the swap was actionable under the CEA or securities laws, the judge essentially upheld the legality of the original transaction in the context in which it had been traded—that is, a swap documented by a standard form ISDA master agreement. Eventually P&G and BT reached a negotiated agreement ending the legal battle, but the case served in many respects as a road map of the legal intricacies attached to complex OTC structures.[26]

This short digression is highly illustrative of the complexity of the issues in OTC contracts and more generally of the prevalent legal framework applicable to derivative products. In our context, the legal risk is mitigated by the fact that OTC transactions are usually entered between traders with similar and straightforward objectives, a situation with two practical consequences. First, the traded structures are usually fairly simple—standard forwards or swaps. More importantly, because both parties have arguably the same high level of understanding in the technicalities of the products, it is difficult for either of them to sue the other for misrepresentation, for example.

Other Risks

Beyond credit and compliance, there are numerous other possible sources of risk within a trading institution. Even if individual traders do not necessarily feel they are concerned, risk managers have to have a view broad enough to encompass as many uncertain or unexpected events as possible.

For example, reconsider the case of the tax rebate. We detailed earlier how fiscal arbitrage was widespread in countries where tax authorities implicitly or explicitly permit it. This arbitrage naturally is not risk free, and here the risk can be qualified as fiscal risk—that is, the possibility that actual tax liabilities may end up being higher than expected. Equivalently, the rebate effectively available may turn out to be lower than originally planned, resulting in a pure loss.

Other areas of uncertainty and risk are the operational performance of a given institution, or its IT infrastructure. The previous example of a failure in the order execution system just before an expiry is only a small illustration of this particular category. Miscommunication between internal departments may also result in wrong information being passed along, which could in turn result in a disastrous trading decision or conversely in no decision when one would have been necessary. Consider, for example, the impact of corporate events on stock portfolios, for which we mentioned several times that traders should at the very least follow the terms of the proposed transaction

[26] See, for example, Robert McLaughlin, "Over-the-Counter Derivative Products," (New York: McGraw-Hill, 1999) for a legal description of the case and of its implications.

very closely. In many cases an internal department, typically the back office, concentrates all the details and makes them broadly available to avoid a situation in which each individual trader would search for and track the same information independently. This aggregate internal source has to be particularly reliable and timely in the way it processes external information because a number of critical decisions depend on it.

It is fair to say then that establishing an exhaustive catalog of all possible sources of risk is extremely difficult. Clearly, risk is a pervasive notion, and even if we considered primarily its financial side, it is far from being the entire story.

VALUE-AT-RISK

Introduction

The notion of value-at-risk (V@R)[27] was first introduced by J. P. Morgan as an internal risk reporting metric. The idea was to provide an aggregate value of maximum loss under a given confidence interval. Instead of compiling pages and pages of charts and figures, the aggregation allowed the senior management of the bank to assess the bank-wide financial risk for the next day in just a simple figure. In 1994, J. P. Morgan started distributing its framework for free, accompanied by all the elements necessary to make it a turnkey solution—notably the variance-covariance matrices for different classes of assets. The framework was called *RiskMetrics*, and it has since been spun off from J. P. Morgan as an independent entity. Ultimately V@R has been adopted by the Bank of International Settlement (BIS) as a required firm-wide risk management system, indicating that it has now become a worldwide standard in risk management.

To understand what is behind a value-at-risk, consider a single asset—for example, a share of General Electric (GE). If we held 1 share of GE for a year until the beginning of May 2000, for example, the maximum daily profit or loss would simply be the highest change in the price of GE over the period. The histogram of daily returns looks like that shown in Figure 7-9. The line shows the distribution of normal returns, and it is apparent that there are significant differences between

---

[27] For an overview of the different risk management techniques and particularly V@R, see, for example, *VAR: Understanding and Applying Value-at-Risk* (New York: Risk Publications, 1997), or Philippe Jorion, *Value at Risk: The New Benchmark for Controlling Market Risk* (New York: McGraw-Hill, 1997.)

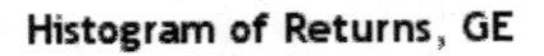

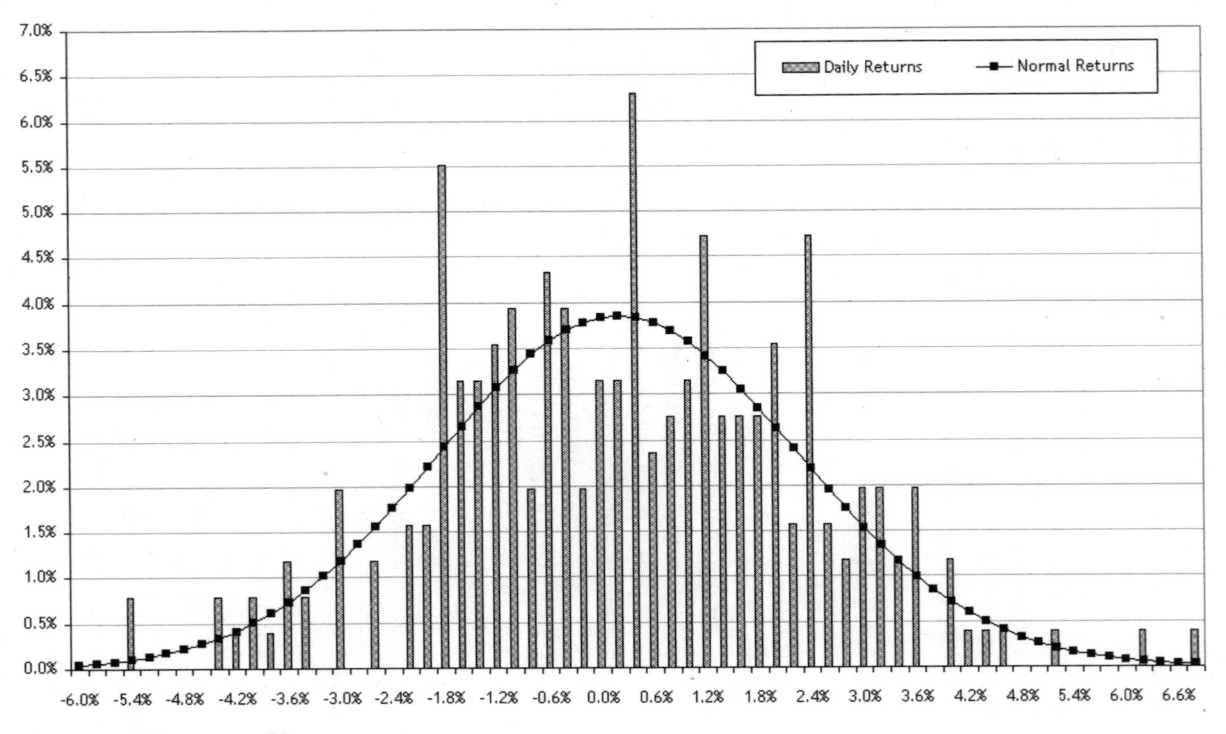

Figure 7-9 Histogram, GE
(*Source*: Compiled by author from Datastream data.)

the two curves although the shapes are similar, a point we will develop later. From this histogram, the value-at-risk is relatively easy to find because it represents the maximum loss for a given probability level. Visually, it is easier to extract from a cumulative distribution, as shown in Figure 7-10. Considering that 95 percent of the time the return is above −3.4 percent, at the 5 percent confidence level the value-at-risk is close to −3.4 percent.[28] If GE closes today at $150, for example, the nominal V@R is then $5.1 (= $150 * 3.4 percent).

Naturally even if the basic methodology holds in a wide range of applications, the actual calculation can be extremely complex if the portfolio is not held constant or if it contains several stocks or even more if it has sophisticated instruments such as bonds or options. Consider, for example, a situation in which we hold Microsoft (MSFT) in addition to GE. MSFT has its own return distribution and behaves in a way significantly different from GE. Therefore, the distribution of returns on the portfolio is a bivariate distribution where the correlation between MSFT and GE plays a particular role.

In fact, the approach we have taken, based on historical data, is not the only framework that has been proposed to answer the V@R question. Before we proceed to a more general discussion of V@R from a risk management perspective, let's examine the different alternatives.

Methodology

V@R calculations can be classified broadly in three categories: analytical method, historical method, and stochastic simulation method. The analytical method, essentially that developed originally by J. P. Morgan and embedded in RiskMetrics, makes the assumption that all assets have returns distributed normally. Under this umbrella, it is fairly easy to construct the distribution of returns of any portfolio because it is a linear combination of normal returns. Specifically, the variance of a portfolio is given by:

$$\sigma_P^2 = \sum_i (\alpha_i \cdot \sigma_i)^2 + 2 \cdot \sum_i \sum_j \alpha_i \cdot \alpha_j \cdot \rho_{ij} \cdot \sigma_i \cdot \sigma_j$$

where α_i is the weight of asset i, σ_i is the standard deviation of its return, and ρ_{ij} is the coefficient of correlation between assets i and j. The return of the portfolio is then normally distributed, and its cumulative distribution is available from a simple calculation when σ_P is known, which requires only the individual terms σ_i and ρ_{ij}.

[28] Rigorously speaking, the V@R is between −3.6 percent and −3.4 percent, and it can be obtained through a simple linear interpolation.

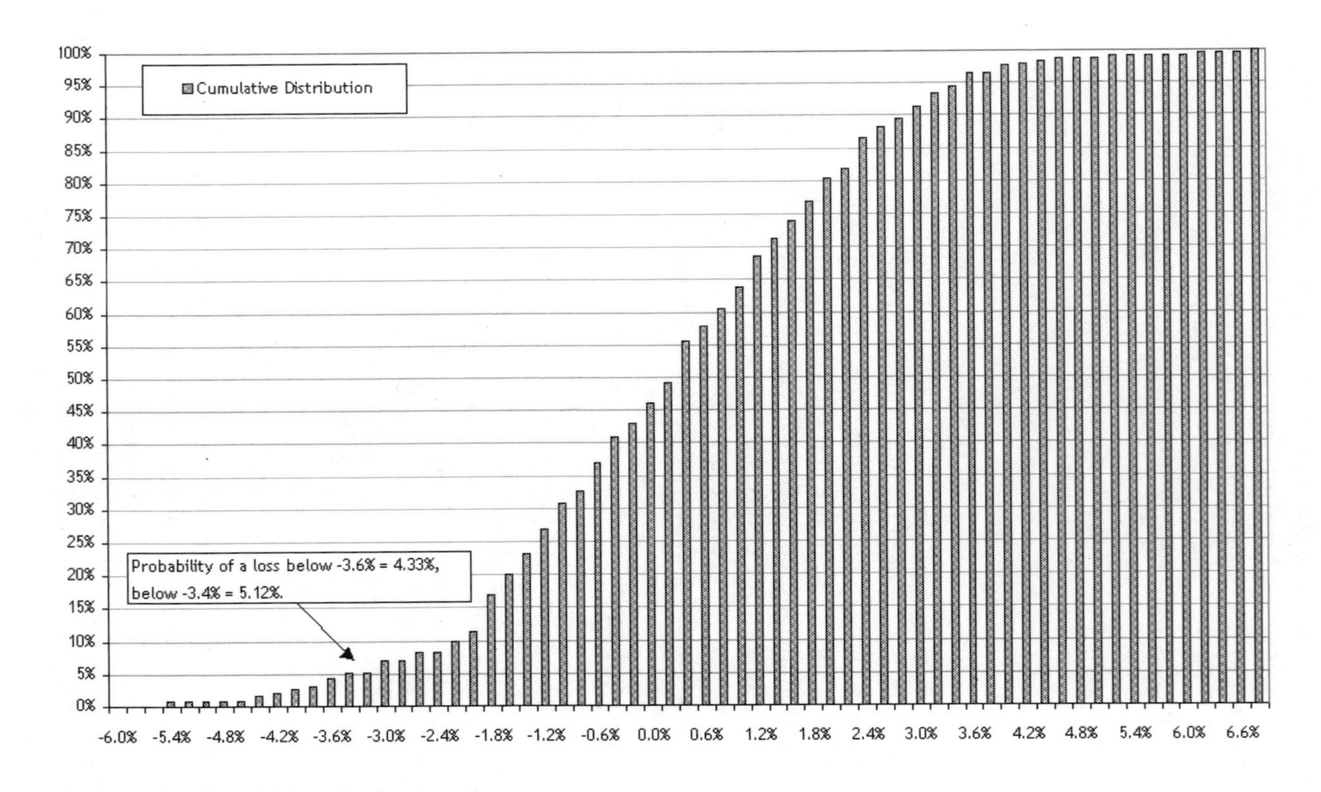

Figure 7-10 Cumulative Distribution, GE

Therefore, the RiskMetrics model conveniently requires only minimal input, and it applies quickly to a wide range of assets.

The historical method is the one we applied earlier to GE. It consists of assembling historical data over a relevant period for the portfolio under consideration and basing the cumulative histogram on these observed data points. It has the advantage of using actual data, removing the need to simplify the assumptions about normality. At the same time its principal drawback is that it does not properly incorporate sudden changes in the size of the portfolio or, in our example, in the number of shares we hold. As a remedy to this weakness, a model called *historic simulation* has been proposed. Instead of collecting only daily profit and losses for the portfolio, the historical simulation model is based on collecting historical market parameters. The parameters are then analyzed for their 95 percent confidence value, and the V@R is the valuation of the portfolio based on this new set of parameters.

The stochastic simulation method, based on a Monte Carlo simulation, is designed to incorporate "stress testing" in the risk management process. Traders know all too well that the past is usually not a reliable predictor of the future; therefore computing a V@R on any other sort of historical record is dangerous because it describes only "known risks"—that is, risks that have occurred already. A stochastic simulation is based on a set of randomly generated scenarios, for which a virtually unlimited number of hypotheses can be incorporated. This approach guarantees that the V@R truly reflects a large fraction of "unknown" behavior, possibly highly volatile.

Naturally these three methods have their strengths and weaknesses, and the above descriptions cover only their most fundamental principles. The most important of these is probably the tradeoff speed versus accuracy. The Monte Carlo simulation, for example, requires a tremendous number of runs to provide adequate precision, whereas a V@R assessment based on historical analysis and RiskMetrics can be computed in seconds. There is much more to say about each one; Table 7-1 presents a useful overview.

As it appears, there is no best answer here again for the "V@R problem." Risk is highly dependent on time and context, which has an impact on the choice of a particular method.

Value-at-Risk and Risk Management

We briefly mentioned earlier the key difference between a V@R approach and the one we chose based on partial derivatives. In essence, V@R has two main drawbacks, making it a powerful tool

TABLE 7-1 A Comparison of VAR Approaches

	Risk Metrics	Historical	Historical Simulation	Stochastic Simulation
Assumption about asset returns	Assumes normality	No assumption	No assumption	User-defined/flexible
Valuation model(s)	Not required	Not required	Required	Required
Cash flow mapping	Yes	No	No	No
Speed	Depends on the variety of assets present and the size of the corresponding variance/covariance matrix	Quick	Medium	Slow
Data requirement	Historical price/rate data of key market variables or J.P. Morgan's risk datasets to the extent that they cover all relevant assets in the portfolio	Historical P&L of portfolio	Historical price/rate data of key market variables	All historical market data that are necessary to estimate the parameters of the stochastic processes used in the risk modeling
Precision of risk measure	Depends on the validity of its main assumptions – stability of asset variances and correlations, normality of return distributions, lack of option components	Good if the portfolio composition is relatively constant over time and there is little ageing effect	Good if the historical path is representative of all future market behavior	Better precision to the extent that the stochastic simulation is more realistic and captures more market interactions and portfolio details
Best choice when ...	Portfolio assets/ liabilities have no optionality eg a portfolio of stocks, FX and/or spot commodities	Portfolio mix does not change over time and ageing effect is minimal	Portfolio has optionality and historical path is representative of all possibilities	Portfolio has substantial optionality and there are many possible sample paths, each representing a different risk
Worst choice when...	Portfolio has substantial optionality	Portfolio mix has changed substantially over time	Historical path is an outlier of all potential outcomes	The portfolio is enormous and the potential sample paths are many; hardware constraints
Representative user	J.P. Morgan, quantitative portfolio managers	Merrill Lynch uses a combination of the historical method (actual P&L distributions) and stress testing for risk measurement. See the company's 1995 annual report for details	Some commercial risk management systems vendors such as Algorithmics, LOR/ GB and Sailfish offer historical simulations as one of the options	Salomon, Bear Stearns, Enron

Note: "Cashflow mapping" indicates a simplifying treatment of cash flows within a portfolio, assumed to settle on a fixed number of days.

(*Source*: Kenneth Leong, "The Right Approach," *V@R: Understanding and Applying Value-at-Risk* [New York, KPHG Publications, June 1996.])

but relatively off target at the trader's level: The first one is aggregation and the second is its stochastic nature.

The purpose of a risk analysis is highly dependent on the target audience, and for a trader, a risk report must focus absolutely and primarily on the positions he or she is responsible for. In addition, a risk analysis should provide a clear view of each individual risk factor, such as stock prices, interest rates, and foreign exchange rates, because each category calls upon different techniques and instruments. In other words, the level of details he or she is looking for is inadequate for anybody else, even sometimes his or her direct manager. V@R has specifically been designed with aggregation as a stated purpose, which creates a conflict with individual traders' needs.

Beyond this problem, a more important "flaw" in V@R methodology has to do with the nature of the reported result. A V@R calculation incorporates the randomness of the market because this is what its users need. The sole function of a trader, on the other hand, is to "manage" this randomness because this is exactly how he or she makes money. Therefore, he or she needs it stripped away, and he or she will then make decisions based on this report and his or her own intuition. A V@R report is only descriptive whereas a trader needs a prescriptive document, packaging information in a way suitable to trade on it.

This is not to say that the two approaches are incompatible to the point where one represents the absolute truth and the other is plainly wrong. Incompatibilities do exist, but are dependent mainly on the audience's needs and not on the informational content. Typically, for example, an experienced trader is probably capable of estimating easily a V@R for the positions he or she knows and manages, which indicates how close the two information sets are.

It is important also to note that the use of different tools by different people leads to potential misunderstandings and conflicts, which constitutes another reason to investigate these tools. Consider, for example, a trader for whom risk limits are fixed in V@R terms. If this trader uses a partial derivative approach to monitoring risk, he or she faces a potential challenge in matching both methods and making the right decision at a given time.

CONCLUSION: THE LEPTOKURTIC CHALLENGE

Regardless of the method, risk is about predicting the unpredictable. And, as a general rule, the more unexpected the event, the larger the damages. The obvious example in the world of financial markets is a crash, and 1987 is a perfect illustration. In terms of statistical relevance, October 1987 was a 20+ standard deviation event, which, assuming a normal distribution, has a *very, very low* probability. By comparison, a probability of 1 occurrence in a 1,000 years is "only" 4.5 standard deviations.[29]

In fact, the recurrent occurrence of events that should statistically never happen is a well-known property of stock prices, and more generally of financial assets. It is indeed the major flaw in the assumption that asset returns are normally distributed and one reason why RiskMetrics has been consistently criticized over the years. Statistically speaking, distributions with that characteristic are known as *leptokurtic*, which essentially means that they have tails fatter than those of a normal distribution. As an illustration, consider the case of Microsoft (MSFT). Figure 7-11 shows the histogram of returns from December 31, 1993, to mid-May 2000.

The kurtosis of the distribution is 6.12, way higher than that of a normal distribution, 3.[30] The points on the left represent sharp overnight losses, with the minimum −15.60 percent on April 24, 2000. The second worst is −14.47 percent, on April 3, 2000. On the other side, the maximum is 9.88 percent on December 15, 1999, followed by 9.68 percent on April 18, 1997. At −3 standard deviations, the cumulative probability for MSFT is 0.437 percent, and the normal cumulative probability 0.106 percent. In other words, an unfavorable event on MSFT has 4.12 more chances (= 0.437 percent/0.106 percent) of happening on MSFT than on a normally distributed stock. Conversely, at +3 standard deviations, MSFT has a score of 0.25 percent, compared to 0.11 percent for a normal curve. Here the "likelihood" ratio is "only" 2.2.

Although MSFT is a striking example, the leptokurtic challenge is a much more general problem, arguably the most important in risk management. If market parameters follow stochastic processes relatively well known, virtually all of them are likely to exhibit leptokurtic distributions, with the consequence that out-of-sample observations are a reality, not a theoretical concept. Traders and risk managers should keep this particular fact in mind when assessing risk. Managing risk on a daily basis is certainly a challenging task, but it pales compared to managing out-of-sample observations. In fact, many such realizations,

---

[29] At 252 open days a year, 1,000 years have 252,000 open days. 1 in 252,000 is 0.000396825 percent, which in turn yields a Z score of −4.47 when plugged into a reverse normal cumulative distribution.

[30] The higher the kurtosis, the fatter the tails.

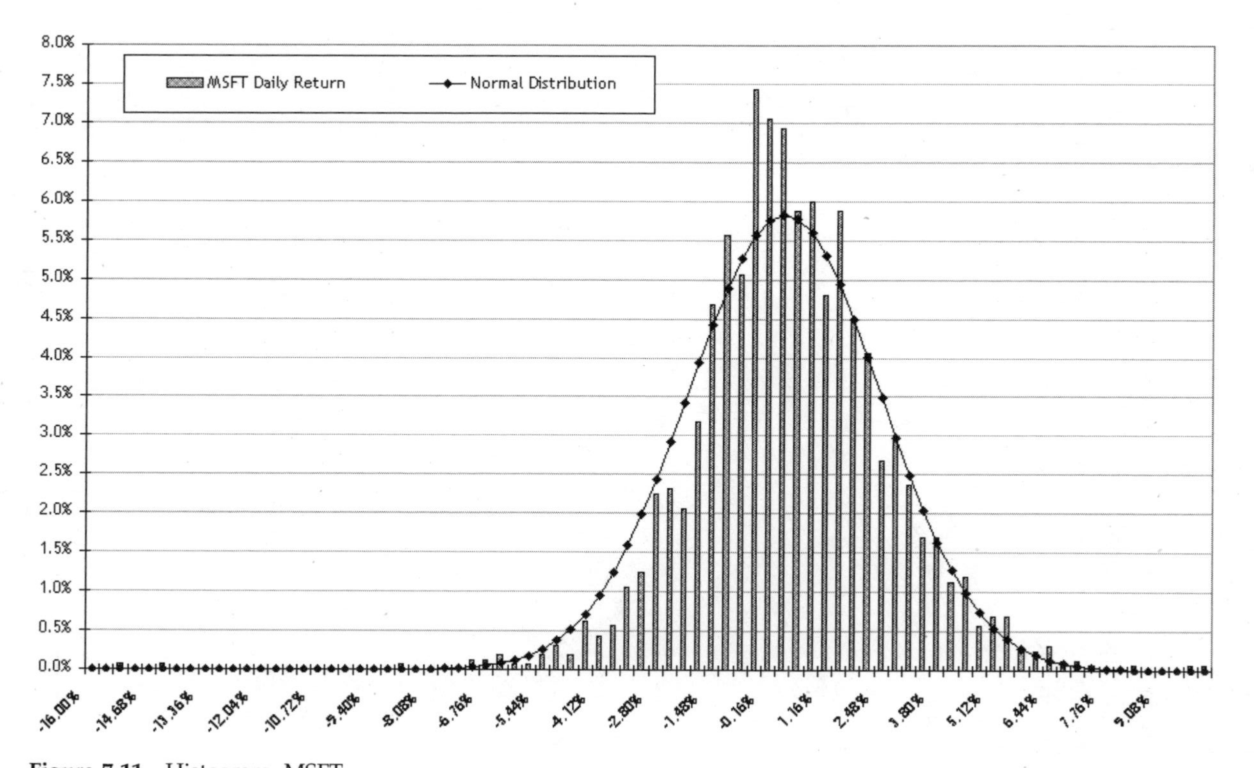

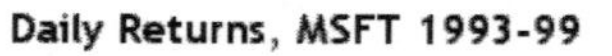

Figure 7-11 Histogram, MSFT
(*Source*: Compiled by author from Datastream data.)

albeit less dramatic than 1987, have been responsible for financial disasters, of which Barings is one example.[31]

The same remarks in fact apply to a number of risks, and probably most of them under one form or another. In general, unexpected events tend to alter and damage established processes, with the consequence of generating decisions that are suboptimal if not plainly wrong. Although rigorous analysis certainly helps, it is literally impossible to prepare for every contingency, and this is exactly where leptokurtic events tend to strike and make the most damage.

[31] The Barings collapsed in 1995 from heavy losses—$1.3 billion—in its Singapore subsidiary. A single trader, Nick Leeson, had taken excessive positions on the Nikkei 225 future in Osaka by forging and falsifying internal reporting documents. When the Kobe earthquake struck, the sudden drop in the market generated huge losses for which he was unable to meet the margin requirements.

PART III
COMMON ARBITRAGE SITUATIONS

8

Index Arbitrage

INTRODUCTION

Index arbitrage is the simultaneous sale and purchase of an index future and of a portfolio replicating the same index. At a given time, an opportunity exists if the futures is different from its theoretical value computed from a cost-of-carry model. Specifically, with the following set of notations:

- F_{TH}, F_M theoretical and market prices of the futures
- I current value of the index
- P_i current price of the ith component of the index
- W_i, D definition of the index (weights and divisor)
- r_F zero-coupon market rate from today's settlement date to the futures expiry date[1]
- d_i^* future value of the accumulated dividends paid by the ith index component, as of the future expiry date

An arbitrage situation in which we would buy the cash and sell the futures can be illustrated as shown in Figure 8-1 with:

$$F_{TH} = I \cdot (1 + r_F) - d^* \qquad I = \frac{\sum_i W_i \cdot P_i}{D} \qquad d^* = \frac{\sum_i W_i \cdot d_i^*}{D}$$

The difference $b_{TH} = F_{TH} - I = r_F \cdot I - d^*$ is called the *theoretical basis*, or the fair value of the futures. It indicates the amount by which the price

[1] That is, from today's settlement date to the last settlement date of the futures contract.

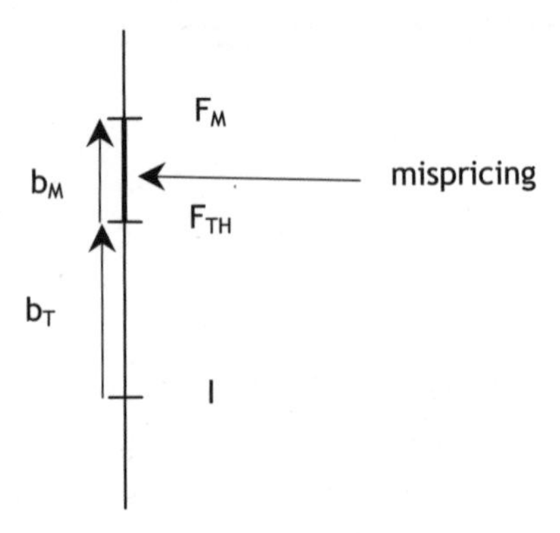

Figure 8-1 Arbitrage Situation

of the futures should exceed the price of its underlying.[2] The quantity $b_M = F_M - F_{TH}$ is often called the *market basis*, and it indicates the amount by which the futures market price exceeds its theoretical price at a given time. Therefore, an opportunity exists when $b_M \neq 0$. If $b_M > 0$, we buy a replicating portfolio and sell the futures, and vice versa if $b_M < 0$.

To understand why this is an opportunity, look at Figure 8-2 and recall the reasoning we used to establish F_{TH}. Assume we buy 1 index today (t_0) at I, and sell 1 futures at F_M. In order to cover the amount I, we borrow it at r_F until expiry. On expiry (t_1), the futures expires on its final settlement price (*Special quotation*, or SQ), and we sell the index portfolio while paying back the amount $I \cdot (1 + r_F)$ as repayment for the loan. There is no treasury balance on t_0 because we borrow exactly what we need, and the sale of the futures does not generate any cash flow—leaving aside margin calls for now. On t_1, the total cash flow on expiry is equal to:

$$CF = -I * (1 + r_F) + F_{SQ} - (F_{SQ} - F_M) + d^* = F_M - F_{TH}$$

The term $-I * (1 + r_F)$ is the payment of the loan including interest. The first F_{SQ} is the sale of the index replicating portfolio at the SQ price. The bracket $(F_{SQ} - F_M)$ is the flow generated by the expiry of the futures at F_{SQ} because we were short. Finally, d^* is the amount of dividend received through the life of the position, on which we have received interest day to day. In effect, the cash flow on expiry is exactly equal to

[2] The theoretical basis is in general a positive number, but it can very well be negative. This is the case, for example, in Japan just before some ex-dates because the interest rate r_F is smaller than the accumulated expected dividend d^*.

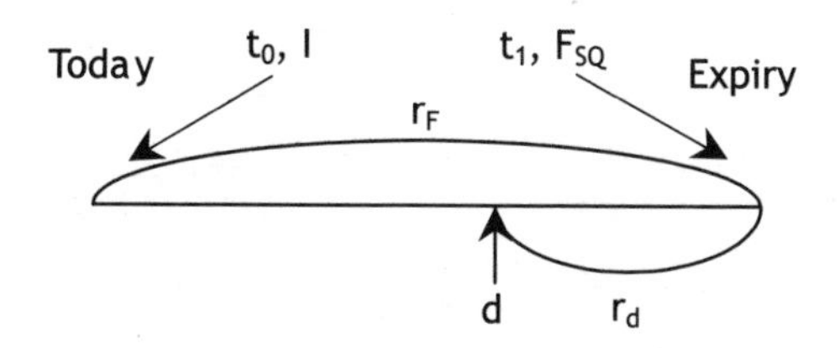

Figure 8-2 Cash and Carry

the market basis at initiation of the position. If positive, this amount is exactly the profit generated by the arbitrage. Note that it is not conditional in any way, which is why it is considered risk free. The only approximation is that we left margin calls aside temporarily, but we will revisit this issue.[3]

This presentation is all we need to understand the basics of index arbitrage, but in practice, it is necessary to examine a number of peripheral issues that make its implementation less straightforward. This detailed examination is exactly the purpose of the discussion below. After presenting all the tools and techniques independently in previous parts, we focus now on tying them together and try to complement the presentation with as many practical examples as possible.

ABSOLUTE CONVERGENCE

Index arbitrage is based on an absolute convergence, and this property has a number of consequences as we indicated very early. Recall the convergence continuum, as shown in Table 8-1. Because the convergence of a futures contract with its underlying cash is the "ultimate" convergence in terms of certainty, we do not need to spend a lot of time on items such as valuation, convergence type, or convergence risk. In doing so, we explicitly negate the possibility of a failure in the financial system, which would be the only reason why the futures contract does not converge to its underlying cash price on expiry—because this type of event is extremely unlikely on any of the markets we consider.

Once uncertainty about the convergence is cleared, we have to look for second-order risks. In this case, there are really three categories that should attract our attention: execution, hedge, and carry. Each of them needs a careful discussion and has implications in a number of direc-

[3] In addition, the stock position can be lent out partially or entirely, generating additional revenues. For simplicity, we leave this particular case out, but it would be simple to include in the overall valuation.

TABLE 8-1

Convergence	Absolute	Hypothetical
Valuation	Theoretical	Mark to market
Convergence type	Public	Highly proprietary
Convergence risk	Low to nonexistent	Critical
Execution risk	Critical	Low
Hedge	Fixed quantity	Fixed quantity or delta
Risk of carry	Important	Low
Time horizon	Known or bounded	Unknown
Window of opportunity	Very short	Longer
Profitability	10 × 1	1 × 10
Robustness	Strong	Weak
Implications	Pricing	None (Inefficient market?)

tions. Before diving into the subject, however, let's take a somewhat bird-eye's-view perspective and examine the notions of time horizon, window of opportunity, and profitability.

OPPORTUNITIES AND PROFITABILITY

Opportunities

As it appears, opportunities for an index arbitrageur seem relatively simple to identify: They are exactly equal to the difference between the futures market price and its fair value. Naturally a subsequent and important question is whether they can be captured, but if we simply chart the market basis, we should get a visualization of the market integration between cash and futures.

Figures 8-3 through 8-7 present exactly this information—the market basis—over a period of several years, at the close of each market. To improve visibility, the actual basis has been averaged over 40 days and represented as a percentage of the underlying index value, and the chart overlays the 40-day moving average value of the index as well.[4]

---

[4] The fair value charted in the figures is always computed on the nearest futures contract—the "front month"—and this may be inadequate just before an expiry when the following futures contract—that is, the "back month"—becomes more liquid. However, this is entirely sufficient for the purpose of the exercise, which is to get a sense of the respective behaviors of each market.

Figure 8-3 S&P 500 Market Basis
Note: Fair value is estimated with a standard cost-of-carry model.
(*Source*: Compiled by author from Datastream and Bloomberg data.)

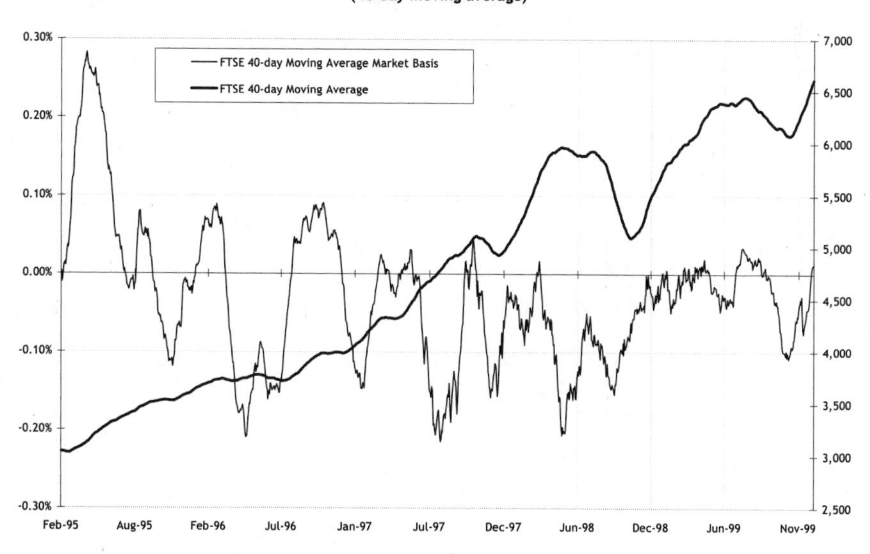

Figure 8-4 FTSE 100 Market Basis
Note: Fair value is estimated with a standard cost-of-carry model.
(*Source*: Compiled by author from Datastream and Bloomberg data.)

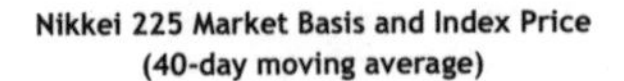

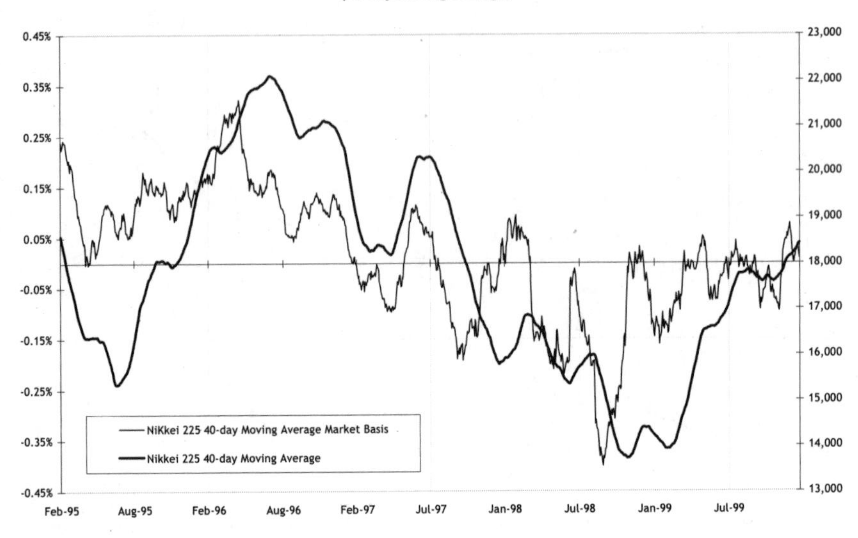

Figure 8-5 Nikkei 255 Market Basis
Note: Fair value is estimated with a standard cost-of-carry model.
(*Source*: Compiled by author from Datastream and Bloomberg data.)

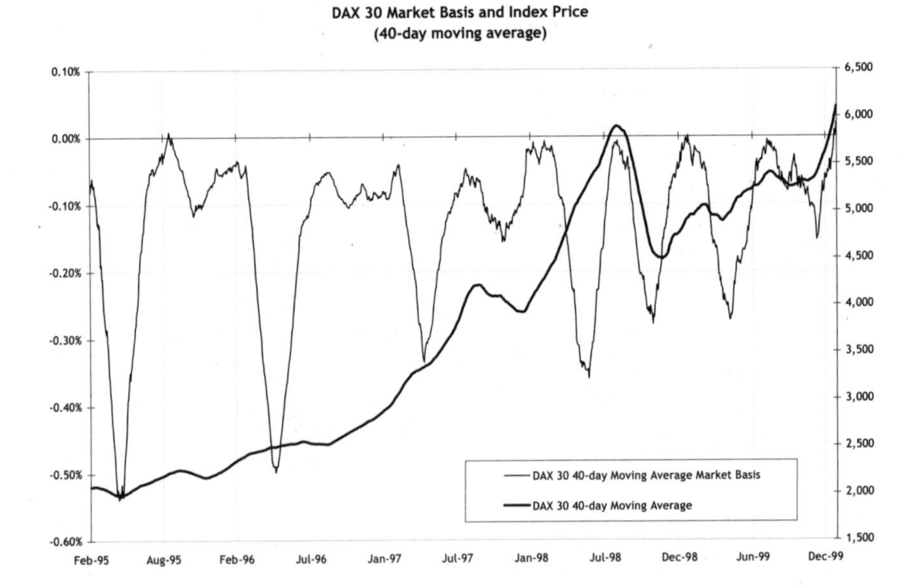

Figure 8-6 DAX 30 Market Basis
Note: Fair value is estimated with a standard cost-of-carry model.
(*Source*: Compiled by author from Datastream and Bloomberg data.)

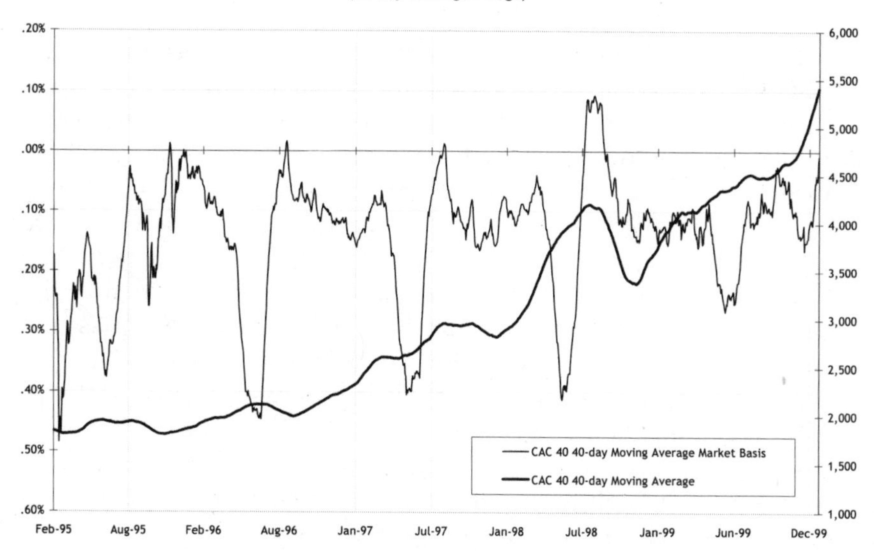

Figure 8-7 CAC 40 Market Basis
Note: Fair value is estimated with a standard cost-of-carry model.
(*Source*: Compiled by author from Datastream and Bloomberg data.)

Naturally these charts should be taken for what they are—that is, gross indications using rough estimates in terms of market parameters. Interest rates are LIBORs, and dividends are estimated from each index dividend yield, with no real correction for actual ex-dates. In addition, dividends are taken as approximate amounts regardless of any withholding tax or tax credit, and we know that in European markets notably these notions tend to have a significant impact on arbitrageurs and eventually on the market fair value.

As was already the case with interest rates, we definitively see different behaviors expressed in these charts, and accordingly, individual arbitrageurs on these markets will have different strategies to capture price discrepancies. Before we enter into details with respect to local particularities, the following two broad remarks should be made.

First, we are looking at the close, which is a very particular time of the trading day. It can be argued that because the market instantaneously closes at that time, arbitrage is extremely difficult if not impossible, and that is essentially the reason that the above charts show sizable price discrepancies recurrently. Indeed, in the case of the S&P 500, the problem is even worse because the futures close 15 minutes after the stocks; therefore, the chart in Figure 8-3 presents highly non-simultaneous data. Although there is substance and truth in these arguments, they do not explain why the market basis seems to follow a cyclical pattern in *every country*, nor do they tell us why this pattern of waves seems to be centered approximately on the x axis, which is precisely the no-arbitrage situation.[5] The reasonable conclusion to draw from these pictures, despite the apparent low significance of the data, is that the basis at close does capture information from the market, in the form of a "market sentiment." In a climate of pervasive selling pressure, for example, it is reasonable to assume that the futures, being more liquid, capture a larger share of that pressure, including at the close, which would essentially lead to a negative market basis at that time. This may seem like a purely speculative assumption; however, in practice, it is often the case that nervous markets tend to close with a negative basis and vice versa.[6] In turn, if this phenomenon is strong enough to find its way into the closing basis, it is not unreasonable to assume that it gets reflected somewhat in the intraday basis, creating opportunities also during the day. This short discussion brings to light a possible explanation for arbitrage opportunities in the presence of an absolute convergence: positive or negative expectations that get reflected more heavily in futures because of their intrinsic nature.

The second broad remark that needs to be made about these charts concerns their high level of legibility. Every single one of them contains a wealth of information about the underlying market, and each one should be carefully examined. The type of information extracted from the S&P 500 data has little in common with that obtained from looking at the DAX picture, but both tell us a lot. For example, the magnitude of the S&P 500 basis indicates that the U.S. market is by far the most efficient. Its deviation remains within −0.15 percent and 0.15 percent consistently, while others oscillate within wider bounds. The Nikkei 225 chart shows a remarkable relationship between the sign of the basis and the direction of the market, and this relationship could give an

[5] This last observation obviously does not appear to France and Germany because of strong dividend effects as we will see shortly. However, a wave pattern still develops in these markets.

[6] Indeed, there seems to be academic evidence of that property, well known from market practitioners. See, for example, Nai-fu Chen, Charles J. Cuny, and Robert A. Haugen, "Stock Volatility and the Levels of the Basis and Open Interest in Futures Contracts," *Journal of Finance*, 50, 1995, pp. 281–300. The article concludes that "empirical evidence confirms the model's prediction that increased volatility decreases the basis and increases the open interest."

indication as to whether the market basis can be used as an indication of things to come.

Figures 8-3 through 8-7 include five years of data, but longer time frames would give us an even better view of the underlying markets. As an illustration, consider the chart in Figure 8-8 showing the percent deviation from fair value from June 1982[7] to January 1999 for the S&P 500. Clearly, the basis reacted to periods of troubled markets like 1987 and 1989, but more generally it is fair to say that the trend is toward lower and lower discrepancies. If we compared the two periods 1982 through 1989 to 1995 through 1999, it is apparent that the magnitude of the market basis in the latter period is considerably

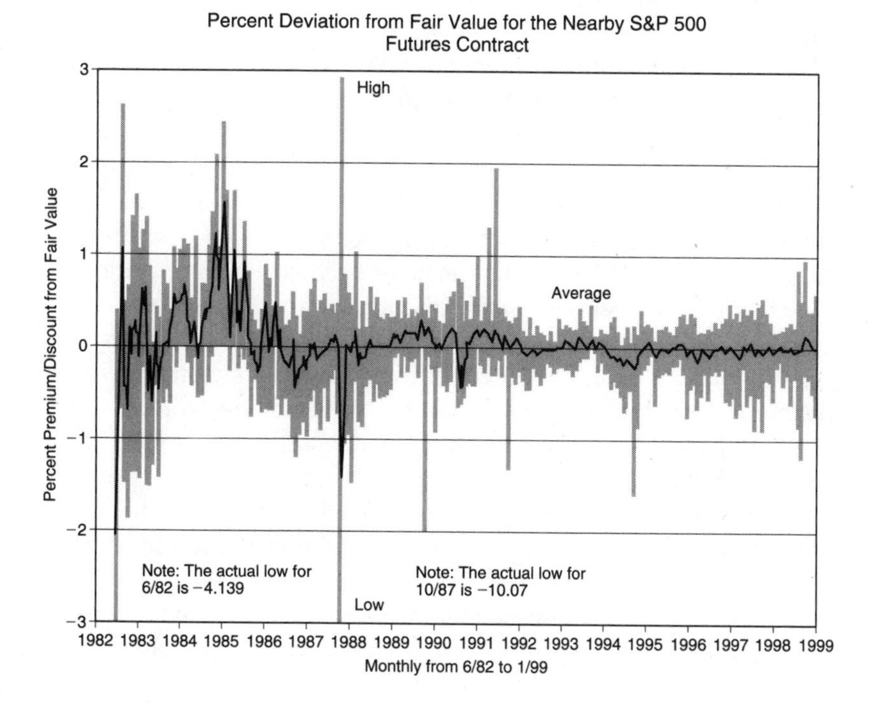

Figure 8-8 S&P 500 LT Market Basis
[*Source*: Jack C. Francis, William W. Toy, and J. Gregg Whittaker, *The Handbook of Equity Derivatives* (New York: John Wiley & Sons, 2000.)]

[7] June 1982 is the original date of listing of the S&P 500 contract on the Chicago Mercantile Exchange.

smaller than that of the previous one. There cannot be any doubt that this is the result of improved market efficiency and a better market-wide understanding of futures and their relationships to cash products.[8]

United States

The case of the United States is particularly interesting because it serves as a benchmark of sorts. The fact that the basis at close oscillates between −0.15 percent and +0.15 percent indicates that the market is probably more mature and efficient than anywhere else. Even if making such a conclusion is relatively far-fetched from close-to-close data, which we know are biased because of nonsimultaneous prices, experience shows that this is indeed a fair description of the marketplace.

Another interesting remark is the decorrelation between the sign of the basis and the direction of the market. We would expect the market to be headed downward in periods of low negative basis, and conversely in periods of high positive basis. The reasons for this are not as much related to the activity of arbitrageurs as to the notion that a relative buying or selling pressure tends to appear more rapidly on futures than on cash, creating punctual mispricings and driving the basis one way or the other. The absence of such correlation, combined with the fact that the basis is evenly distributed above and below the *x* axis, suggests that the market is efficient enough to be well arbitraged regardless of the overall market conditions. This last statement is confirmed by trading data available from the NYSE. During the period of June 1998 to June 2000 the total volume dedicated to program trading and index arbitrage was relatively steady beyond weekly variations, compared to the market performance or its basis.[9] Figure 8-9 shows the volume statistics, and it is relatively easy to compare it to the chart of the S&P 500 to come to this conclusion.

Taken all together, these elements point toward a market more efficient than its peers, in which participants adapt extremely rapidly to new market conditions without any visible effect on the basis, and for which the basis is relatively low and stable in absolute terms. It is

---

[8] There is theoretical evidence as well that index arbitrage reduces basis volatility. See, for example, Praveen Kumar and Duane J. Seppi, "Information and Index Arbitrage," *Journal of Business*, 67, 1994, pp. 481–509.

[9] The data are reported weekly by all members to the exchange. The index arbitrage volume is included in the total volume of program trading. For example, if program trading is 20 percent and index arbitrage 5 percent, then 25 percent (= 5 percent/20 percent) of all program trading transactions are index arbitrage.

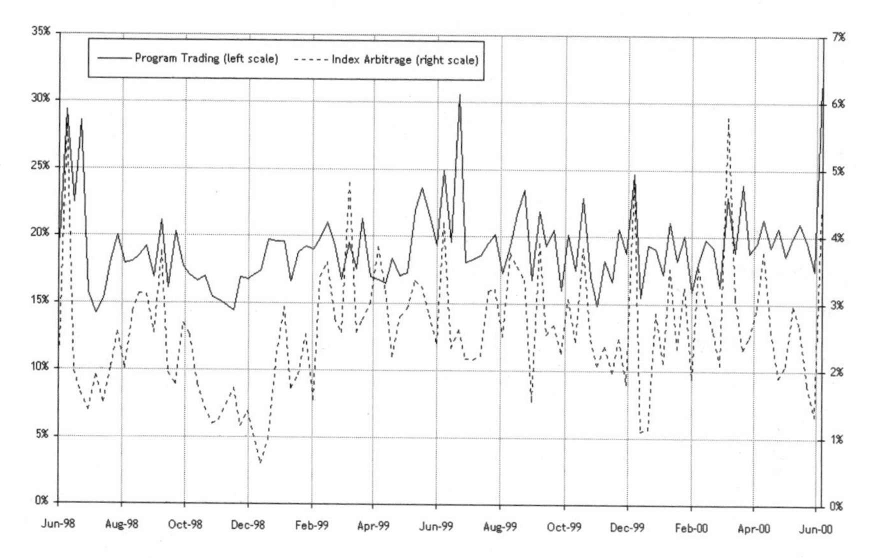

Figure 8-9 Program Trading
(*Source*: New York Stock Exchange, www.nyse.com.)

relatively natural from there to conclude that the United States represents the "ultimate" phase of index arbitrage maturity. The basis variability there is not due to a lack of efficiency but rather to the intrinsic level of noise embedded in the structure of the market, and due to the difference in liquidity and volatility between the futures and its underlying index. In other words, it is almost as if the market reached a steady state in which opportunities will persist indefinitely, but confined to an extremely narrow range.

Japan

Japan is also an extremely interesting case because none of the remarks we made for the United States truly applies. First, the magnitude of the basis variations tend to be larger, almost twice as large—between 0.20 percent and 0.30 percent. Experience shows indeed that index arbitrage is more profitable in percentage terms in Japan than in the United States. More interestingly, Japan is the only market in our list having experienced repeated sharp downturns over the past few years, which enables a more detailed examination of the correlation between basis and market performance. Indeed, Figure 8-5 shows a strong correlation, a rising market being accompanied almost always by a positive basis and vice versa. This particular relationship could suggest that arbitrageurs are driving the market; however, this is a grossly misstated conclusion because arbitrageurs are always hedged and have an equal nominal impact on both legs—for a net impact of zero. In fact, this property indicates that the "expectation model"—that is, the tendency of the basis to reflect market expectations—is stronger in Japan than anywhere else, a fact that is confirmed easily by experience.

United Kingdom

The case of the United Kingdom represents a curiosity because it adopted an electronic platform in October 1997. Prior to that date, equities were traded in a dealer market, where no central electronic system was available to receive and centralize orders. Without any electronic system, index arbitrage is extremely difficult and risky to implement because an arbitrageur needs to buy all the index constituents one by one. Furthermore, in a dealer market transactions typically take place over the phone, which makes the whole process unpractical to say the least. In that context, the introduction of an all-electronic marketplace has provided arbitrageurs with a much friendlier environment, in turn facilitating their job considerably. To a large extent, the U.K. basis mirrors this evolution of the market. Prior to October 1997 the basis shows wide swings, whereas after a short adaptation period toward the end of 1997, it evolves into a much narrower range.

As far as the direction of the market is concerned, the basis seems to have little correlation with the overall market, showing here a market closer to the United States than Japan in nature. Beyond these observations, the U.K. market is in fact interesting primarily as an illustration of the impact of modern trading technology on overall efficiency. Even if making definitive conclusions is probably far-fetched just by looking at one single chart, there cannot be any doubt that investors in general benefited largely from the introduction of an electronic and automated order-execution system, and arbitrageurs as well even if that meant more competition. This raises the interesting question of whether the United States, for example, would not benefit from a similar move, away from the Nasdaq dealer market.

Germany

Germany is, along with France, the most intriguing situation here. Figure 8-6 shows a number of regular crevasses resulting from the particularities in taxes and dividends. To understand why this is so, consider an index valued at $100, with a gross dividend yield of 2 percent and a corporate tax rate on dividends at 30 percent. For simplicity, assume that all the dividends are paid on the same ex-date.[10]

An off-shore investor will be subject to the 30 percent tax, so will receive a net amount of $1.4 (= $100 * 2 percent * 70 percent). If this investor—whom we denote I_O—is pricing a futures on this index before the ex-date with two months left until expiry and a rate of 4 percent, the fair value is:

$$b_{\text{off-shore}} = \$100 * (2 * 4 \text{ percent}/12) - \$1.4 = -\$0.73$$

Now consider a domestic investor—I_D—accredited to claim a tax rebate for the entire amount of tax, $0.6. This investor sees a fair value at:

$$b_{\text{domestic}} = \$100 * (2 * 4 \text{ percent}/12) - \$2 = -\$1.33$$

In other words, if the future is currently trading at $99, I_O sees a market basis of ($99 – $100) – (–$0.73) = –$0.27, while I_D sees ($99 – $100)– (–$1.33) = $0.33. Because the market basis is negative, I_O has an interest to sell his or her position, while I_D, on the other hand, has an interest to build one. This difference in market parameter has been described before, but what is interesting here is the practical consequence: The tax rebate creates an economic incentive for off-shore investors to sell their position to domestic ones. Intuitively this result makes a lot of sense because domestic investors are tax advantaged and have a strong interest in holding stocks.

Now let's consider one more dimension and allow I_O and I_D to enter a stock loan. If the tax rebate is priced at 50 percent in the transaction, I_O will lend his shares to I_D and receive 50 percent of the rebate on the ex-date. In practice, I_D acquires I_O's entire position just before the ex-date, claims the tax rebate due to his holding on the ex-date, and pays back 50 percent—that is, $0.3 to I_O at the expiry of the stock loan. Under these assumptions, let's revisit the fair value of each investor:

$$b_{\text{off-shore}} = \$100 * \left(\frac{2 * 4 \text{ percent}}{12}\right) - (\$1.4 + \$0.3) = -\$1.03$$

because I_O receives $0.3 more than before in dividends, and:

$$b_{\text{domestic}} = \$100 * \left(\frac{2 * 4 \text{ percent}}{12}\right) - (\$2 - \$0.3) = -\$1.03$$

[10] For simplicity as well we compute a standard cash-and-carry futures, although the DAX is a total return index. The actual calculation is slightly more complex but the conclusion is exactly the same.

because I_D has to pay \$0.3 back to I_O. Both investors see now an equal fair value, and accordingly with a future at \$99, will see a (\$99 – \$100) – (–\$1.03) = \$0.03 market basis. There is no more incentive to transfer stocks from one investor to the other in that environment.

This simple example illustrates perfectly the mechanic of the tax rebate and its impact on the fair value of distinct market participants. It is directly relevant to our original discussion because it helps understand the curious shape of the market basis in Germany. If we price the fair value with net dividends, a domestic investor will have an incentive to sell futures aggressively around the ex-date because he or she receives more than net dividends with the tax rebate. Therefore, to us the basis will appear sharply negative while for him or her, it will probably be fairly priced, which is exactly what is visible in Figure 8-6 considering that dividends are highly concentrated in the second quarter of the year in Germany.[11]

In fact, we can take a step further and even make quantitative conclusions. A domestic investor will sell futures as long as the expected tax rebate on borrowed stocks is higher than the expected rebate payment to the lender.[12] In Figure 8-6, the first valley in March through April 1995 is close to 0.50 percent deep, which is exactly the dividend advantage adjusted for the market-wide price of the rebate through stock loans. Assuming this pricing was close to 50 percent at that time, the total rebate benefit to stock borrowers was close to 1 percent (= 0.50 percent/50 percent). If we assume a tax rate of 30 percent, the total dividend yield at that time can be estimated at 3 percent (= 1 percent/30 percent).[13]

A second interesting observation from the chart is the decreasing amplitude of the "dividend valley." This is a result of a relative depreciation of the dividend yield because nominal dividends grew more slowly than the overall market. Indeed, in 1999, if we assumed dividends equal to those of 1995, a tax rebate of 50 percent, and a tax

[11] It would be tempting to conclude that the basis is negative because domestic investors are aggressively selling futures and have a natural control of their domestic market. This is not true: The negative basis is not the result of more aggressive allocation or easier availability of capital between domestic and off-shore investors. It is simply the equilibrium state of the market in the presence of fiscal arbitrage, which means that actions of all rational investors alike contribute to this equilibrium.

[12] Technically speaking, we should also account for the borrowing fee paid to the lender. In practice, many stock loans entered into for dividend purposes carry no borrowing fee as such; rather, it is embedded in the terms of the tax rebate.

[13] Note that this example is illustrative only, even though its results are reasonable.

bracket of 30 percent, we should have a basis negative by 0.29 percent (= 0.50 percent * 2,500/4,250)—that is, half that of 1995—to account for the fact that the market went up from 2,500 to 4,250. Naturally it is impossible to confirm this calculation just by looking at Figure 8-6, but interestingly enough the basis is 0.25 percent in 1999, which is not too far off.

With respect to the overall magnitude of the basis, the market is fairly priced outside the particular deviation due to dividends. Indeed, remove the valley from Figure 8-6, and all that is left is a flat line between −0.20 percent and 0. Experience confirms that it is indeed difficult to make money in Germany from trading only. There are two interesting points, however, in 1997 and 1998. At first glance the negative basis of fall 1997 and fall 1998 could be assimilated to a dividend basis, except that there were no dividends at those times. Those troubled periods correspond to the minicrash of October 1997 and to the Russian crisis and show clearly that the basis was reactive to the overall environment, even if this reactivity does not really materialize anywhere else in the entire five-year period.

Finally, it is worth mentioning that the basis in Germany is consistently negative outside dividend periods, which essentially means that index arbitrageurs are short, *on average*. The distinction "on average" is important because we see only close-to-close data, and it may very well be that the basis during the day offers opportunities to go long. In fact, it is true that arbitrageurs tend to be short in practice, with the associated complication of having to secure stock regularly from potential lenders. It may seem paradoxical to associate a market that provides an apparently strong economic incentive to go short with significant opportunities for stock holders during dividend periods, but in fact, both properties are one and the same. It is exactly because the entire market is eager to go long that futures tend to trade systematically at a discount because holding a position against a futures contract is the only way to eliminate the market risk while enjoying the benefits of holding the stocks. In other words, the futures contract is under consistent selling pressure from participants who are trying to maintain a stock inventory without carrying too much risk.

Clearly, the German market cannot be understood or traded without a prior understanding of dividends and the opportunities that exist because of them. These are in fact primarily available to domestic investors; therefore it has been necessary for foreign—and notably U.S.—securities firms to open subsidiaries there, and most of them have done so. This is an example of the structural competitive convergence we mentioned very early. Opening a domestic branch to benefit fully from market opportunities is a requirement, but all it accomplishes is to put all *domestic* competitors on equal footing without providing any further advantage.

France

With France we encounter a situation similar to that of Germany with respect to dividends. The same basis effect is visible around the second quarter of each year because dividends are also concentrated around that period. Indeed, the basis in France seems to be very similar to that in Germany, and the same cause having the same effects, clear opportunities exist to enter fiscal arbitrage. Outside dividends, pure trading is again difficult and largely on the short side, although the magnitude of the basis seems to be slightly higher than that on the DAX.

France has a particularity, however, because of its settlement system. Futures are rolling monthly, even if quarterly expiries are by far most liquid.[14] With a monthly settlement, index arbitrageurs do not have any financing to pay if they enter a position against the nearest futures. At the end of each month they can theoretically unwind their position without any financing expense. In practice, this operating mode is not as trivial because the future expires on an average, so it may very well be that a known financing charge to carry the position into the following month is better than an unknown execution risk on expiry.

Profitability

Profitability of index arbitrage is a particularly critical question. If it were highly profitable, we would indeed have identified a true money machine. In reality, it is not extraordinarily so, which explains why only few professionals really practice it as a stand-alone profit center.[15]

---

[14] This particular statement means that the chart for France should be interpreted more cautiously. It represents the market basis with respect to the nearest futures contract, which is not always the most liquid when it is not a quarterly expiry. Drawing conclusions about trading opportunities is then trickier because of frequent rollover between maturities.

[15] This point is extremely important. As we mentioned earlier with respect to Germany, index arbitrage is the best way to accumulate an inventory of stocks without carrying the market risk. Reasons for holding an inventory are diverse; dividends are certainly one but there are many others, like the ability to price requests from customers on particular stocks or sets of stocks. Generally speaking, inventory holders differ from pure arbitrageurs because their target is accumulation, so they may not be as aggressive, particularly on the selling side.

In fact, assessing real profitability is a challenge for an index arbitrage position because of the difficulty in tracking all parameters. Actual realized gains would be ideal, but these are highly proprietary figures in general. An alternative is to track gains from market data, trying, for example, to reconstitute opportunities as they appear in the marketplace. This method leads to interesting results, but it is extremely tedious because of the difficulty in tracking exact transaction data for a large number of stocks. When applied to the S&P 500, for example, this approach requires time-and-sales data for all constituents and for the futures, trying to compute the market basis as an arbitrageur would see it. From there, once an opportunity is identified, trades must be simulated as if effected in real time for each individual stock, and only then is it possible to extract a total profit estimate.

Despite the difficulty, this exercise has been carried out relatively frequently in the academic sphere, at a time when program trading, and particularly index arbitrage, were under a lot of scrutiny. At the end of the 1980s and beginning of the 1990s, academic research was focused on trying to identify the role of these strategies in the 1987 debacle and in the 1989 minicrash. Over recent years, however, these same questions have receded, and with them the overall assessment of program trading and index arbitrage as viable trading strategies. Therefore, whatever research is available is relatively outdated, although it may be worth a look.[16]

We will attack the question with a very empirical and broad-based approach. Because the United Kingdom is probably still undergoing transition following its adoption of an all electronic marketplace, it is probably not yet in a steady state with respect to index arbitrage, so we will leave it aside here. We will also leave France and Germany aside, but for different reasons. We have determined that both markets are "governed" by dividend and tax issues, which are nontrivial because they involve the ability of each individual institution to price, trade, and claim tax rebates. Although there may be relative uniformity among market participants in that respect, this question is really unrelated to index arbitrage per se. An arbitrage position may be built for the sole purpose of capturing a fiscal advantage, but we are primarily concerned here with trading profitability. Therefore, we will really focus on Japan and the United States, and adopt a similar framework for both.

---

[16] For a short bibliography, see the references at the end of the chapter.

The idea is to look at the best scenario from an arbitrageur's perspective. As we indicated in the section dedicated to index replicating portfolios, buying a portfolio means that all the constituents have to be purchased at the same time. The "best" scenario on the cash side is to buy each and every stock on the bid price, without having to pay as much as the offer price. Conversely, if we are selling cash, the best case is to be able to realize the ask price. With respect to the futures, the best-case scenario is also buying on the bid and selling on the offer.

Given this set of assumptions, consider now the practical case of the S&P 500. The real-time bid-ask price on the index is usually \$2, relatively steady and independent of the market direction. On the futures, the spread is much more volatile, but in general it is less than \$0.50. Therefore, the typical market situation can be described by the diagram in Figure 8-10 where I_{last}, I_{bid}, and I_{ask} denote respectively the index computed with last traded, bid, and ask prices. F_{last}, F_{bid}, and F_{ask} are the last traded, bid, and ask prices for the futures, and b_{TH} and b_M are respectively the theoretical and market basis.

If $F_{bid} - b_{TH}$ goes above I_{ask}, it becomes possible to lock a profit by buying all the stocks at their ask price, and selling the futures contract on its bid. Conversely, if $F_{ask} - b_{TH} \leq I_{bid}$, the opposite opportunity develops, and it is possible to sell all the stocks on their bid and buy the futures contract on its offer, locking the difference. Needless to say, these situations are extremely infrequent, and in most cases the following inequalities hold: $F_{bid} - b_{TH} \leq I_{ask}$, $F_{ask} - b_{TH} \geq I_{bid}$. Therefore, the best case for an arbitrageur is a situation in which $F_{bid} - b_{TH} \approx I_{ask}$ or $F_{ask} - b_{TH} \approx I_{bid}$, and the realized market basis is then between \$2 and \$2.5. Naturally in reality it is impossible to trade all stocks at the bid or offer because of execution lags. Therefore, \$2 to \$2.5 is a very optimistic

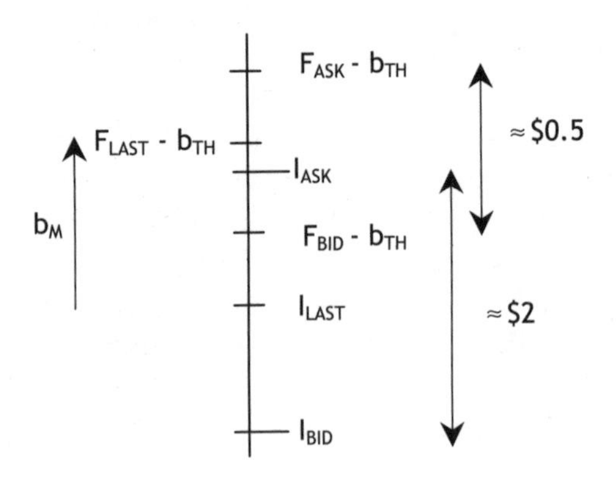

Figure 8-10 Bid-Ask Spread

figure, but it has a high relevance with what is happening in the marketplace. For simplicity, we neglect here transaction—and clearing—costs, which will give us an even more optimistic figure.

From there we conclude that a typical arbitrage trade yields a maximum of 0.14 to 0.17 percent (= $2/$1,400) with an index at $1,400.[17] However, this is not complete because of several additional elements. First and foremost, the position should be "turned" as often as possible to ensure that capital is used adequately. Then, arbitrageurs can make money on stock lending, provided that they are long, which is usually the case in the United States and Japan.[18] Finally, they benefit from rolling their position from one expiry to the next, a procedure we will detail shortly.

To account for the turnover, let's consider that there are no more than a dozen active arbitrageurs on the U.S. market, each with a position limit of $5 billion. This is possibly a high estimate, but it is not unreasonable considering the nature of the industry. Even if there are more than a dozen active players, what we really care about is the total amount of capital dedicated to index arbitrage, and $60 billion is a good place to start.[19] The NYSE statistics show that on average arbitrage-related trades account for 2.7 percent of the overall volume (June 1999 to June 2000). During the same period, the average daily volume was 912 million shares. If we assume in addition that the S&P 500 account for 90 percent of the total arbitrage volume, the daily average volume of index arbitrageurs is approximately 22.2 million shares (= 912 * 2.7 percent * 90 percent). To tie everything together, take the average NYSE stock price at $50. A total amount of $60 billion is then equivalent to 1.2 billion shares (= 60/50), which means that 2.4 billion shares must be traded for the position to "turn" entirely.[20] At 22.2 million shares per day, this turnover requires 108 days. In short, the entire capital dedicated to index arbitrage turns roughly 2.3 times a year (= 252 / 108), a figure we will round to 2.5 for convenience.

---

[17] 0.14 to 0.17 percent is a profit figure net of all direct costs except the cost of capital. It accounts for the fact that we pay the financing on the stock position because this financing is included in the fair value.

[18] Alternatively, they have to pay a borrowing fee if they are short. We primarily focus on the long side here, knowing that this would be again an overstatement if we were short.

[19] We consider here primarily arbitrage on the S&P 500 because it is a dominant strategy. Other possible indices include the Dow Jones, S&P 100 with "synthetic" futures created from options, and the Nasdaq 100 index.

[20] In other words, 2.4 billion shares must be traded for the position to be built and unwound entirely.

Therefore, a typical arbitrageur will turn the position 2.5 times a year, making between \$4 and \$5 for every roundtrip. On a \$5 billion position—that is, 14,285 futures (= \$5b / \$1,400 / 250)—this amounts to a total profit between \$35.7 and \$44.6 million. If we take \$40 million as an indicative midpoint, the return on invested nominal is 0.8 percent (= \$40 / \$5,000). We need to include now stock lending opportunities and the profit from the roll.

If the position turns entirely 2.5 times a year, we assume that on average it is around \$2.5 billion in nominal. Taking the typical fee to be close to 0.15 percent in the United States, lending the position out consistently yields an additional \$3.75 million. As far as the roll is concerned, let's consider that it adds \$0.25 every quarter, \$1 per year—that is, 0.07 percent on an average position of \$2.5 billion. We will detail and revisit this figure shortly.

Finally, we need to deduct the cost of capital associated with the solvency requirements. In the United States listed stocks are considered relatively low risk assets and weighted in the calculation at 15 percent. Taking the solvency ratio at 8 percent, and the return to shareholder capital at 15 percent, the total cost of capital is 0.18 percent (= 15 percent * 8 percent * 15 percent). All together the arbitrage position yields 0.73 percent (= 0.80 percent + 0.15 percent/2 + 0.07 percent/2 −0.18 percent) of the maximum authorized position, \$5 billion in our case.[21]

By and large, this is a relatively low figure, and we know from the many estimations we made it is probably an optimistic figure nevertheless. If we perform the same calculation for Japan, we find a slightly higher figure, close to 0.85 percent. Round-trip profit on the Nikkei is probably closer to 0.90 percent with turnover of twice a year, and the roll has been historically much higher, around 0.20 to 0.30 percent. Stock lending is relatively small, and we will consider it negligible. As far as the cost of capital is concerned, it can be considered equal, which gives a total of 0.85 percent (= 0.90 percent + 0.25 percent/2 − 0.18 percent).

Despite the obvious approximate nature of these figures, it is clear that index arbitrage is extremely capital intensive for the type of returns it provides. In addition, it is available only to institutions with low-cost funding, low-cost capital, and low transaction costs. In other words, it is really worth implementing only on a large scale,

[21] 0.15 percent/2 is the P&L from lending the stocks, \$5 billion in maximum amount, but \$5/2 billion on average. 0.07 percent/2 is the P&L from the rollover on a position which is \$5/2 billion on average.

which again explains why so few trading desks are actively practicing it and why in turn we have been so restrictive about the context.

RISKS

Execution

As we indicated earlier, execution is an important aspect of risk in an arbitrage strategy, and this is particularly true for index arbitrage because of the large number of instruments that must be transacted at the same time. In order to analyze that risk, we first present a general introduction in the context of a regular market, and we examine next an exceptional situation that could have resulted in significant losses to arbitrageurs.

Introduction

For an index arbitrage, the execution pattern is relatively simple. As soon as a trader identifies an opportunity, he or she tries to capture it by intervening in the market and sending orders simultaneously on the stocks and on the futures. As a result, the market basis tends to narrow because the executions on the stock move the last traded prices back within nonarbitrage boundaries. Visually, the basis looks like that shown in Figure 8-11. These charts represent the market basis averaged over a two-year period and 50,760 program trades, centered on the time at which the arbitrage event was supposed to have taken place.[22] The data are NYSE proprietary data on program trading and index arbitrage, which means that it is reliable to the extent that reporting institutions follow the reporting guidelines notably with respect to accurate time-stamping.[23] The wave and its amortization are particu-

[22] An *arbitrage event* is defined here as the reported time upon which an arbitrage transaction was initiated. The regressions mentioned in the legend are regressions of the minute-by-minute basis against the total nominal of arbitrage events. They look like $b_t = \alpha_i \cdot x_{t-i} + \beta_i$ where b_t is the market basis at time t, (α_i, β_i) are the regression coefficients, and x_t indicates the nominal of a program trade originated at time t. i is varied from -5 to $+30$, giving a total of 36 regressions. The chart plots $(\alpha_i + \beta_i)$ for $-5 \leq i \leq 30$. This methodology allows disentangling the effects of different programs initiated at different times.

[23] As a reminder, the difference in reporting between program trades and index arbitrage is related to the fact that index arbitrage involves an index derivative, futures, or options.

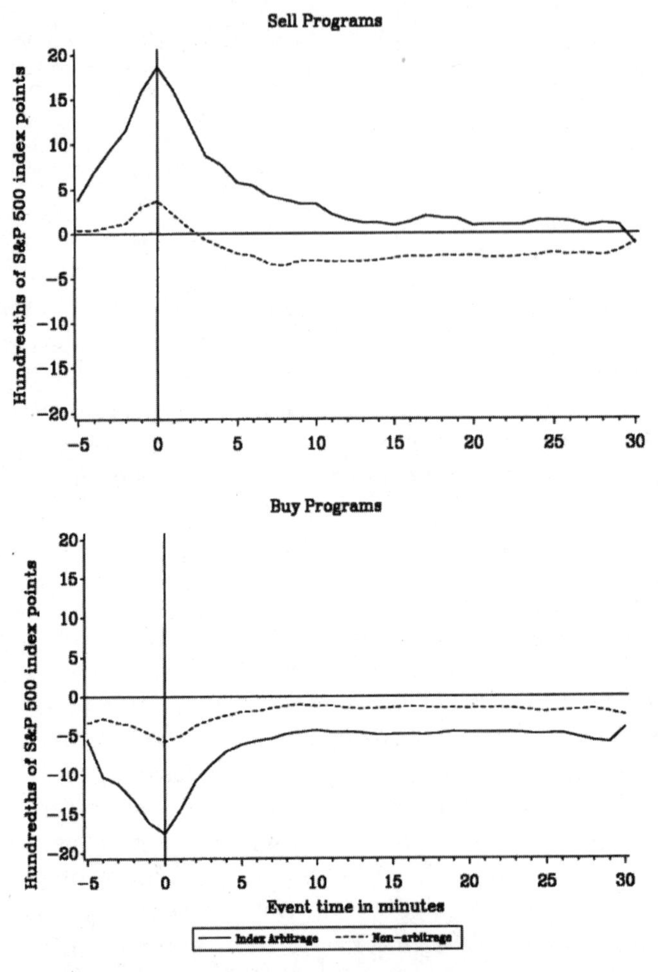

Event-time basis surrounding program trades for January 1989 through December 1990
Estimated basis surrounding $10 million program trades. The estimates plotted are regression coefficients (plus intercept) obtained from regressions of the minute-by-minute time series of the basis on 5 leads and 30 lags of index arbitrage buy-and-sell and nonarbitrage buy-and-sell program trades. The basis is the value of the S&P 500 index minus the price of the nearest S&P 500 futures contract plus a statistical estimate of the expected carrying cost.

Figure 8-11 Arbitrage Event
Note: The basis as it is charted here is the market basis as we defined it with opposite conventions. It is equal to the index price minus the futures market price plus a statistical estimate of the cost of carry—which we know is the theoretical basis. Therefore, a buy opportunity, which corresponds to a positive market basis for us, is charted as a negative value.
(*Source*: Lawrence Harris, George Sofianos, and James Shapiro, "Program Trading and Intraday Volatility," *Review of Financial Studies*, 7, 1994. Reprinted with permission.)

larly visible and show that a real opportunity does not seem to be available more than a few minutes.[24]

It is also interesting to look at the number of orders executed in the market at the time of an index arbitrage or program trade, which is available in Figure 8-12. Clearly, arbitrage events lead to larger numbers of orders at the same time, suggesting that arbitrageurs are indeed trying to execute as many orders as possible as quickly as possible. It could be inferred from Figure 8-12 that arbitrageurs have a disproportionate impact on the market in terms of outright direction or volume. In fact, it is not necessarily true because their net impact is zero if they maintain a nominal hedge in their position. As far as volume is concerned, index arbitrage averaged 2.5 percent of daily NYSE volume over the past two years—not exactly a large figure.

Another interesting remark can be made with respect to Figure 8-12: It is apparent and highly intuitive that index arbitrage trades are triggered by a basis mispricing. However, it is fair to say that nonarbitrage program trading is also somewhat correlated to the same

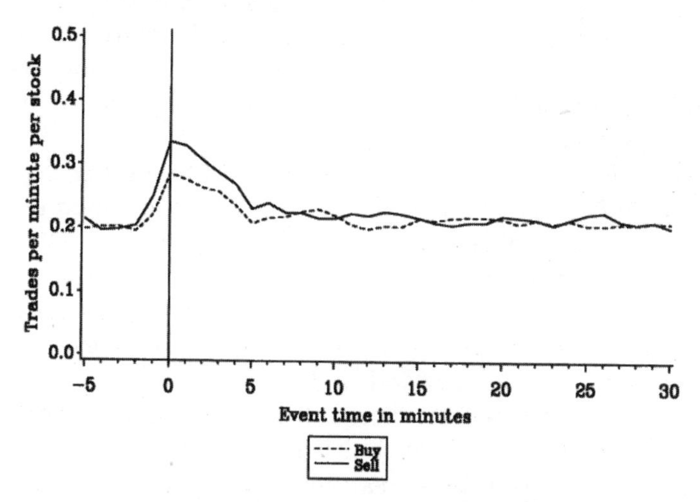

Event-time trades per minute per index stock surrounding index arbitrage program trades for June 1989

Estimated number of trades per minute per stock in the 457 NYSE S&P 500 stocks surrounding \$10 million buy-and-sell index arbitrage program trades. The estimates plotted are regression coefficients (plus the intercept) obtained from regressions of the minute-by-minute time series of number of trades on 5 leads and 30 lags of index arbitrage buy-and-sell and nonarbitrage buy-and-sell program trades.

Figure 8-12 Arbitrage Event Execution
(*Source*: Lawrence Harris, George Sofianos, and James Shapiro, "Program Trading and Intraday Volatility," *Review of Financial Studies*, 7, 1994. Reprinted with permission.)

[24] Because of the methodology in the study, the y axis does not represent the amplitude of the basis mispricing. It is therefore not directly comparable to the −0.15 percent we proposed earlier.

parameter. This particular phenomenon is an illustration of the distinction we made earlier between passive and active arbitrage. Index arbitrageurs are actively involved in capturing opportunities by trading both legs aggressively as often as possible. Program traders, however, are an example of passive arbitrageurs: They obviously adapt their execution strategy to the environment—that is, the level of market basis at the time of the trade—but they are not engaging in arbitrage per se because they do not hedge their position with futures or options. Considering that index arbitrage is around 13 percent of total program trading volume on average over the past two years, it is reasonable to conclude that passive arbitrage, in the form of program trading or otherwise, is much more powerful than active index arbitrage in keeping the market efficiently priced.

Percentage of Execution

The execution of an arbitrage trade requires trading at the same time the futures and index constituents in proportion to their weighting in the index. Therefore, execution risk can be considered from two different angles: on one hand, the nonsimultaneity of transactions between cash and futures, and on the other hand, the nonexecution of some stocks in the portfolio.

We will deal with the second possibility in the section dedicated to correlation because this is really what it is, a correlation exposure between the perfect replicating portfolio and the position we actually hold. With respect to the nonsimultaneity of transactions between cash and futures, it is useful to introduce the notion of percentage of execution as the fraction of the overall capitalization executed at a given time.[25] If we denote e_S and e_F these percentages on stocks and futures, respectively, the execution risk in an arbitrage event can be represented by a time diagram similar to the hypothetical example in Figure 8-13. At a given time, there may be a difference in executed nominal on both legs, and this difference can be interpreted as the effective execution risk at that particular moment. As a more dramatic illustration, consider the situation in Figure 8-14. In this particular case, execution on the cash side is lagging behind that on the futures.[26] The reasons behind an execution strategy of that type can be diverse, but it is usually meant to capture an anticipated move in

[25] All orders not already executed are said to be "working orders."

[26] This practice is generally referred to as *legging*—that is, the execution of the two legs at different paces.

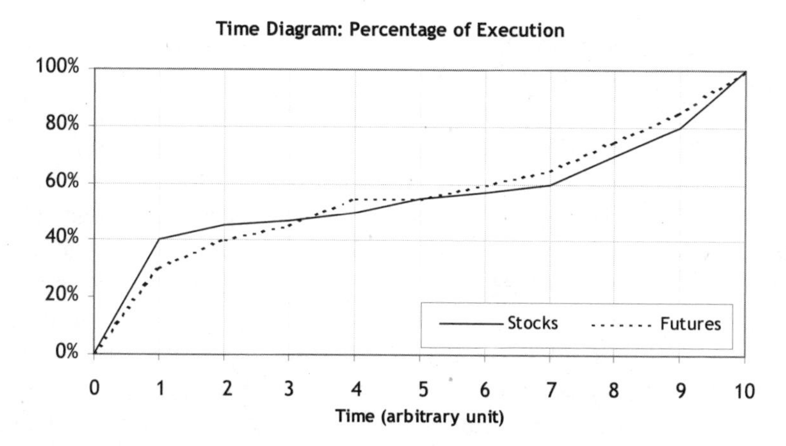

Figure 8-13 Percentage of Execution

the market. For example, if the above arbitrage is a buy trade, the arbitrageur is selling futures more aggressively than cash, hoping to buy cash a few minutes later at a lower price. Alternatively, if it is a sell trade, then the arbitrageur is buying futures in anticipation of a move up that would allow him or her to sell cash higher.

Regardless of the direction of the trade, during the first seven minutes of the arbitrage, the position is at risk from an unfavorable shift in the market. Assume, for example, that the total size is $15 million on the S&P 500—that is, 43 futures with an index at $1,400. For the first seven minutes the difference in executed percentages is relatively steady at around 30 percent—that is, 13 futures. If we take

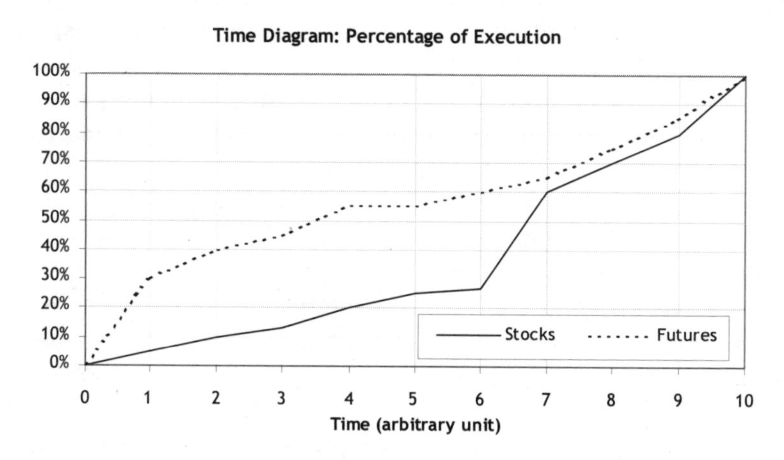

Figure 8-14 Percentage of Execution

the arbitrage to be a buy trade—that is, long cash and short futures—the arbitrageur is essentially short 13 futures for a period of seven minutes. If the market goes down during that interval, he or she can complete the cash side or buy back the extra futures at a profit. If the market goes up, however, he or she may end up losing a significant part of the anticipated profit, if not all. If the expected profit is $2.5 on 43 futures—that is, $26,875, which we know is a very optimistic figure on average—a move of $4 on the futures is enough to dissipate 50 percent of the original profit, and in fact $4 over a few minutes is extremely common. It is tempting to argue that if the futures went up, the arbitrageur would still have an opportunity to complete the cash side because it is presumably going up more slowly. This is true to a large extent, but it does not really change the outcome: The trade is much less profitable if not losing.

We argued earlier that nonsimultaneous execution was not entirely necessary and should even be avoided in a pure arbitrage situation. Indeed, if an arbitrageur built a short in his or her execution pattern because of an anticipated move, he or she might as well have taken a straight short position without bothering with the complications of a two-legged strategy. It is all too tempting to blend pure speculative positions—highly risky—to risk-free trades and try to make the best out of the combination. In practice, the result is rarely satisfactory because these strategies do not require the same skills, and blending them does not enable a trader to make an assessment of his or her ability to successfully trade one or the other.

Execution on Expiry: The Case of Sumitomo in June 1996

Beyond real-time execution another type of execution risk is related to the expiry of the futures. We mentioned before the case of an expiry on an average—for example, in France and the United Kingdom—as being more risky because of the nature of the averaging process. In fact, even futures expiring on outright prices such as opening can be tricky to execute under some circumstances.

An interesting case of this situation was illustrated by Sumitomo Corp. in Japan. Sumitomo is a large Japanese corporation involved in a number of commercial activities, and commodity trading is one of them. For years Sumitomo has been highly respected in the copper market because it employed one of the most renowned—and feared—copper traders, Yasuo Hamanaka. In June 1996, however, a major scandal broke out, bringing to light years of fraudulent activity on Hamanaka's part. Sumitomo originally declared losses of $1.8 billion, soon to grow to $3.5 billion by September.

On the day of the announcement, Friday, June 14, 1996, the Tokyo Stock Exchange suspended trading in Sumitomo (ticker: 8053) for the day.[27] As it happened, this particular day was a quarterly Nikkei 225 futures expiry, and Sumitomo was included in the index. Figure 8-15 shows Sumitomo's closing price over the period and its daily trading volume. The stock eventually opened on the following Monday to close at ¥1,010, losing 16.5 percent.[28] This particular gap is in itself an interesting example of a leptokurtic distribution, but more interesting to us, it had a significant impact on index arbitrageurs. Many arbitrageurs were planning to unwind their stock position at the open by realizing the SQ value of the futures. Because liquidity at open is usually plentiful, such an unwinding is easy to implement and risk free. The fact that Sumitomo was suspended, however, complicated the situation because the applicable rule stated that the price attributed to Sumitomo for the SQ calculation would be the last traded

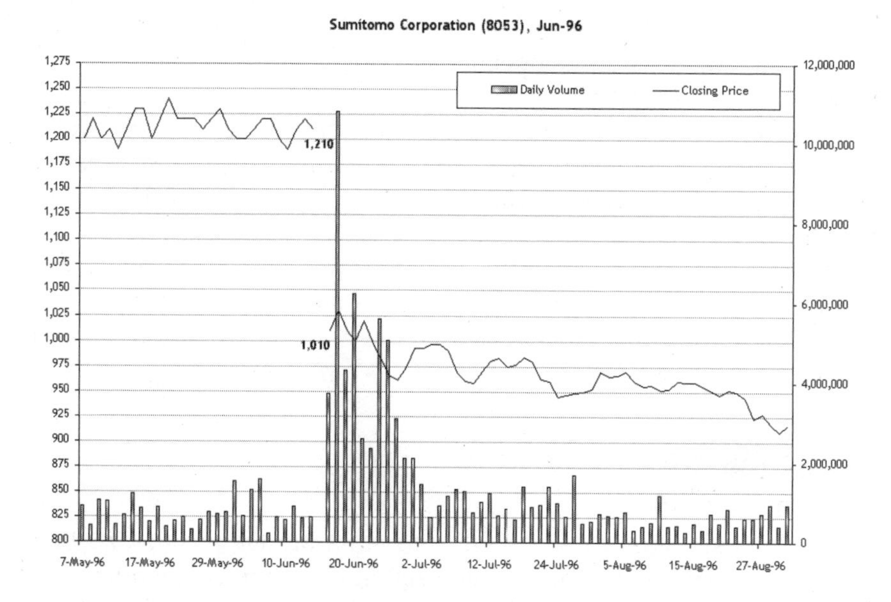

Figure 8-15 Sumitomo
(*Source*: Compiled by author from Bloomberg data.)

---

[27] See, for example, "Sumitomo Says Unauthorized Dealings in Copper Caused $1.8 Billion in Losses," *Wall Street Journal*, June 14, 1996, p. A3.

[28] Interestingly, it traded in London on June 14 at a price anywhere between −10 and −20 percent compared to the last traded price in Tokyo, ¥1,210.

price—that is, ¥1,210. In short, arbitrageurs were facing an SQ computed with Sumitomo at ¥1,210 but were unable to execute on that price. Furthermore, there was naturally a sense that Sumitomo would trade sharply lower, but in the absence of an active market, "sharply" could have meant anything. Buyers were in a relatively comfortable situation because any price lower than ¥1,210 was to their advantage. Sellers, on the other hand, were desperate, and many of them turned to London as soon as possible because Sumitomo was listed on the London foreign market.

To get a sense of the possible impact, assume a $1 billion position—that is, ¥100 billion if we take a convenient exchange rate of ¥100 for $1. With a Nikkei around ¥18,000, a ¥100 billion position is equivalent to 555,500 shares of Sumitomo.[29] Therefore, a drop of ¥200 in price if the position could not have been liquidated at ¥1,210 would have resulted in a net loss of ¥111 million—that is, $1.1 million. Assuming the overall profitability of the position was close to 0.85 percent as we proposed earlier, $1.1 million represents 13 percent of the overall total, $8.5 million. In other words, this particular event does not necessarily compromise the profitability of the activity, but it is serious enough to potentially wipe out a nonnegligible part of the expected profit for the entire year.

There is really no way to hedge against this particular risk because it depends on a number of factors typically impossible to predict. It is, however, particularly important to be aware of the exact rules for handling the SQ calculation under unusual circumstances. By and large, virtually all exchanges will use the latest traded price available when one particular index constituent is suspended, but they may differ significantly in the criteria applied to determine whether a stock should be suspended or not.

Time Diagrams and Rolls

Short-Term Rolls

Consider a situation in which we enter an arbitrage position by buying a stock replicating portfolio and selling the appropriate number of futures. Assuming we carry the entire position or part of it until the futures expiry, let's consider in detail what happens on that particular day.

---

[29] The weight of Sumitomo in the Nikkei 225 was 1,000, and the divisor ¥10,000. Therefore, ¥100 billion is equivalent to (1,000/¥10,000) $*$ (¥100,000,000,000/¥18,000) $\approx$ 555,500 shares of Sumitomo.

After the close of the previous day, the futures do not trade anymore, but technically speaking, they still exist because the expiry has not occurred yet. In essence, the expiry occurs when the SQ price is known with certainty because the futures contract is fully defined then and all flows can be settled. If we consider a market where the SQ is referenced at the open, the position is still technically hedged by a short position until that moment, although the futures leg cannot be traded anymore. Immediately after the open, when all stocks have opened, the SQ is known and the short leg simply disappears. The holder of an arbitrage position is then left with an outright stock position, suddenly not hedged anymore. This is clearly a problem because a $1 billion risk-free arbitrage position is an entirely different proposition from a $1 billion long stock portfolio. There are really only two solutions to that potential problem: Sell the portfolio at the SQ so that the expiry of the futures is matched by the realization of the same price by liquidating the portfolio, or trade the futures position away so that it disappears *before* expiry.

In the second case, to remain hedged, for every futures that we buy back, we need to sell an equivalent nominal of *something*, and if we determine that we want to keep the stock position intact through the SQ, we need to sell a futures of a later expiry. This type of calendar spread is commonly referred to as a *roll*, and the position has simply been rolled over to a further expiry. It is convenient and enlightening to represent the whole operation as a time diagram, as shown in Figure 8-16. When the position has been entirely rolled over, we do not hold the nearest futures anymore, but the entire stock position is now hedged with futures further away.

Because this type of spread is traded extremely frequently, it has become a listed instrument in and of itself. Typically two to three

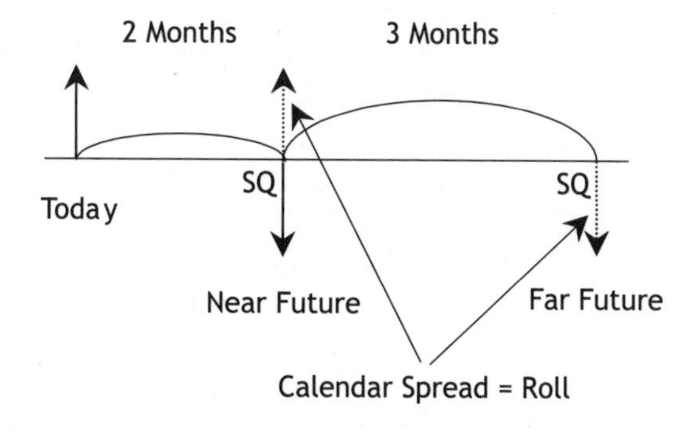

Figure 8-16 Roll

weeks before a futures expires, the next maturity becomes liquid and traders can get very deep market on the roll. The quote convention is "far minus near"—that is, a March to June roll quoted at $20 indicates that the June futures is quoted $20 above March. As a consequence, selling the roll means selling the far maturity—June, for example, in a March to June roll.

Although two futures on the same index clearly have common characteristics, they do not have the same price. The further away the futures, the larger the financing component in its price, which explains why in general far maturities are more expensive than near ones. Let's consider as an illustration a March to June spread with the following characteristics: $r_{Mar} = 6$ percent, $r_{Jun} = 6.5$ percent, $t_{Mar} = 5$ days, $t_{Jun} = 95$ days, $I = \$1{,}400$, $d^*_{Mar} = \$0.20$, $d^*_{Jun} = \$7$. The theoretical prices of each futures are as follows:

$$F^{TH}_{Mar} = \$1{,}400 * \left(1 + \frac{5 * 6\%}{360}\right) - \$0.20 = \$1{,}400.97$$

$$F^{TH}_{Jun} = \$1{,}400 * \left(1 + \frac{95 * 6.5\%}{360}\right) - \$7 = \$1{,}417.01$$

The theoretical roll is then $1,417.01 - $1,400.97 = $16.05. Naturally the roll can trade at a price different from its theoretical price, the same way a futures can trade above or below its theoretical price. The same causes having the same effects, there is an arbitrage opportunity if the roll is trading too far from its "fair" price.

Consider, for example, that the roll is too expensive compared to its theoretical value. Under these circumstances, it is very intuitive that arbitrageurs will be natural sellers. Imagine one of them, with no position, selling a March to June spread above its fair value.[30] Until the expiry of March, the spread position is exposed to the market through the quoted roll price. If the transaction was originally March to June at $16, and if the market quotes $17 on a given day, unwinding the position would create a loss of $1. If the spread is kept until March expires, we know that the occurrence of the SQ will require the arbitrageur to *buy something* to replace the expiry leg, or to sell the June futures in order to remain reasonably hedged.

---

[30] Naturally, the same applies to any investor in the market. An arbitrageur in that case may pursue the opportunity more aggressively, but the market at large is very likely to enter at least into a "passive arbitrage" mode.

The arbitrageur has two choices: Buy a replicating portfolio at the SQ price, or sell the June futures at a price as close as possible to the SQ. Buying a portfolio of stocks is a reasonably safe proposition in general; however, selling futures is highly uncertain because the market price of the contract depends on a number of factors and may be significantly different from the reference at which we need to trade.[31] In general, thus, arbitrageurs tend to buy cash, and this is all the more true if there is an additional advantage in holding stocks, like a tax rebate or incremental revenues from stock loans.

Obviously, traders are very aware of the possible difficulties associated with selling the roll in the first place, which means that in general the purpose of the sale is indeed to buy a replicating portfolio. This is in fact a very interesting and safe way of doing that because the position transforms itself into a fully hedged arbitrage portfolio on expiry of the long futures—March in our example. Conversely, buying the roll requires selling stocks on expiry, which in turns implies borrowing costs if the stocks are not held in the first place. Therefore, it is no surprise that the roll is in general used much more frequently to build a long stock position than the opposite.

Consider now the consequences of this discussion. If the roll is trading above fair value, arbitrageurs will probably sell it at first to roll their existing position. Once these are entirely rolled, they still have the option to roll more and to buy stocks on expiry. On each roll sold, they make a profit equal to the difference between the market price and the fair value of the roll. Alternatively, if the roll is trading below fair value, they will suffer a loss if they decide to roll existing positions anyway, which means that they will have to liquidate on SQ. They might even consider selling more than what they hold if the roll is sufficiently cheap. Therefore, an expensive roll usually creates a buying pressure on the SQ while a cheap roll has the opposite effect. Naturally these are not absolute rules, but they are fairly reasonable as far as arbitrageurs are concerned. With respect to the market at large, however, it is more difficult to draw conclusions, but we can safely assume

---

[31] Naturally, if the SQ is an average, as in France or the United Kingdom, we know that the situation is not as simple as it is on an opening. The problem then is to weigh the risk associated with the realization of the SQ on cash versus executing on the futures. Again experience is a helpful guide in these situations.

The price we need to realize on the cash is the SQ price of March contract. Therefore, the reference price on the June contract is *the theoretical price of the June futures based on an index price equal to the SQ.*

that "passive arbitrageurs" will have a similar analysis of the situation and similar conclusions.

Therefore, if there were a way to observe the level of roll in the market, we could then infer a number of conclusions for the next SQ, and possibly anticipate its direction. This type of focus on the SQ might appear surprising, but quarterly events of such nature are generally widely regarded as "signals" of things to come. In other words, a positive SQ—that is, an expiry for which stocks move up—is usually considered a bullish sign or at the very least a sign of confidence in the marketplace. Accordingly there is some value in trying to get a sense of SQ imbalances, and fortunately there is in fact a way to assess the level of roll in the market through the futures open interest.

Open Interest

The open interest indicates the number of open contracts in the market for a given expiry. If a buyer and a seller with no prior position trade a futures contract, the open interest of the contract is increased by 1 because this is a "new" commitment. If, in contrast, a contract is traded between two parties and closes a position that was opened before, the open interest is reduced by 1.

Consider now an investor with a long position in a particular contract, say, March. If the investor decides to roll the position into June, he or she buys the roll—that is, he or she sells his or her March contracts and buys an equal number of June contracts. In doing so, the aggregate open interest of March and June combined remains unchanged because one contract literally replaces the previous one. Consider now an arbitrageur selling the roll with no preexisting position in futures. The transaction leaves the aggregate open interest unchanged if the buyer closes a position or increases its absolute size because the arbitrageur is now long one March and short one June when he or she had no position before.

Therefore, we can draw conclusions from the aggregate level of open interest only if we have a sense of the preexisting positions. In practice, this is often the case because different classes of investors tend to have recurrent positions. Index arbitrageurs, for example, tend to be all on the same side. In the United States and Japan, they are long cash and short futures so they are natural sellers of the roll to keep their positions. In France and Germany, on the other hand, they are much more often short stocks and long futures; therefore, they would be natural buyers of the roll. Investors at large tend to be in general on the long side, except hedgers using the futures as a protective device. This schematic presentation is very useful in understanding the impact of the roll of the market in general and on the SQ in particular. If the roll is expensive and the aggregate open interest increases just before the SQ, chances are that arbitrageurs—and possibly other investors—are selling it aggressively, and on expiry they have to buy cash to replace the dying futures. The result is most probably a buying pressure building in the market on the SQ. The opposite conclusion could be made from observing a cheap roll and an increase in open interest. This situation is much less frequent, however.

As an illustration, Figures 8-17 through 8-21 present the aggregate open interests of several futures over the past year.[32] Beyond the numerical values that are relatively unimportant here, the shape of each chart reveals again a number of details about the underlying markets. Very regularly the aggregate open interest literally jumps before the SQ, to fall back again immediately after. This is an effect that is visible virtually everywhere, albeit with different magnitudes.

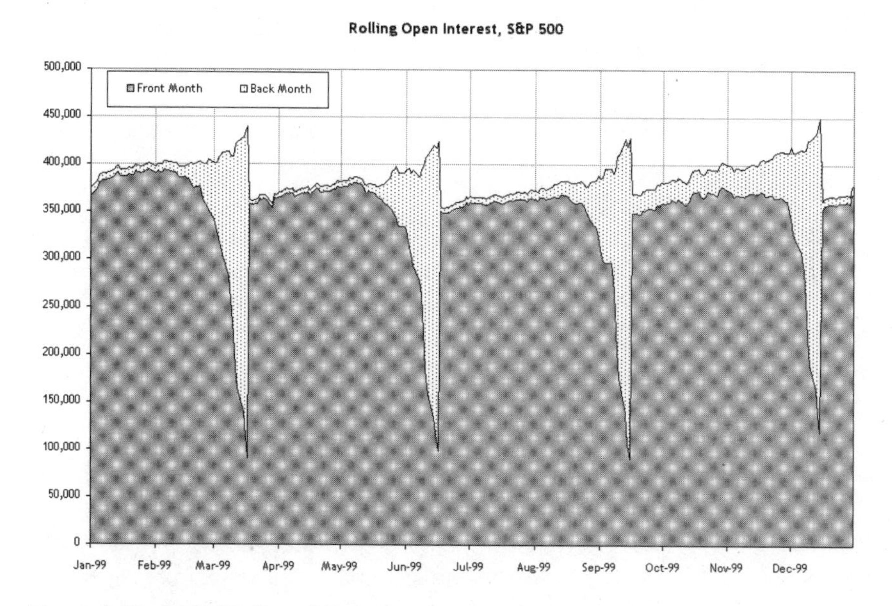

Figure 8-17 S&P 500 Open Interest
(*Source*: Compiled by author from Datastream data.)

[32] The *y* axis is the open interest in the number of contracts for each designated maturity. "First expiry" denotes the nearest futures contract, "second expiry," the next one. Note that the chart for the S&P 500 was presented in an earlier section. France has a monthly cycle; therefore, the second expiry includes also the third one corresponding to a quarterly cycle when necessary.

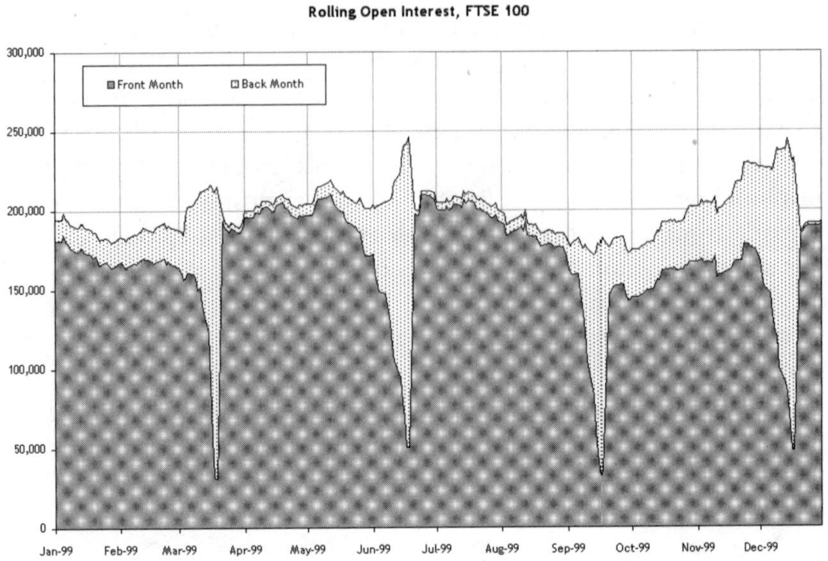

Rolling Open Interest, FTSE 100
Front Month
Back Month
300,000
250,000
200,000
150,000
100,000
50,000
0
Jan-99
Feb-99
Mar-99
Apr-99
May-99
Jun-99
Jul-99
Aug-99
Sep-99
Oct-99
Nov-99
Dec-99

Figure 8-18 FTSE 100 Open Interest
(*Source*: Compiled by author from Datastream data.)

Rolling Open Interest, Nikkei 225
Front Month
Back Month
400,000
350,000
300,000
250,000
200,000
150,000
100,000
50,000
0
Jan-99
Feb-99
Mar-99
Apr-99
May-99
Jun-99
Jul-99
Aug-99
Sep-99
Oct-99
Nov-99
Dec-99

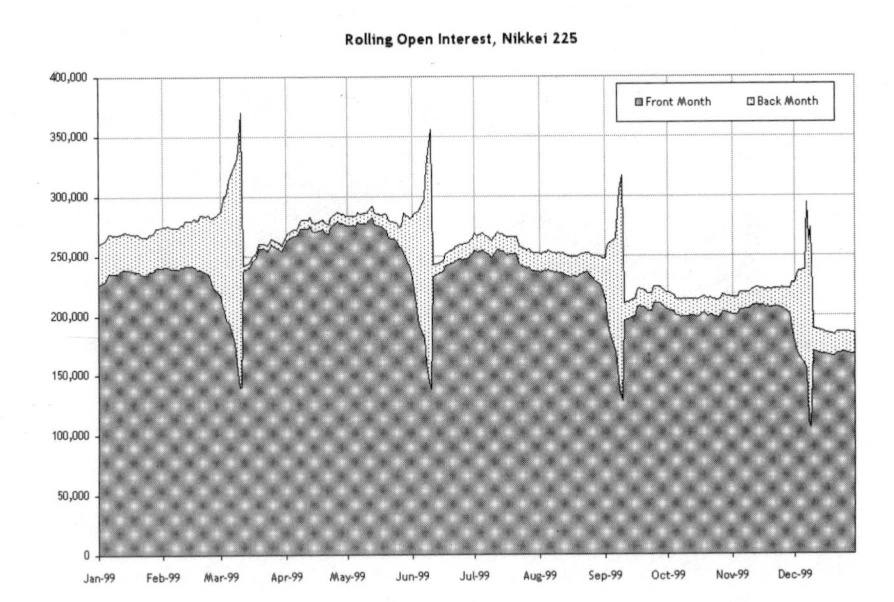

Figure 8-19 Nikkei 225 Open Interest
(*Source*: Compiled by author from Datastream data.)

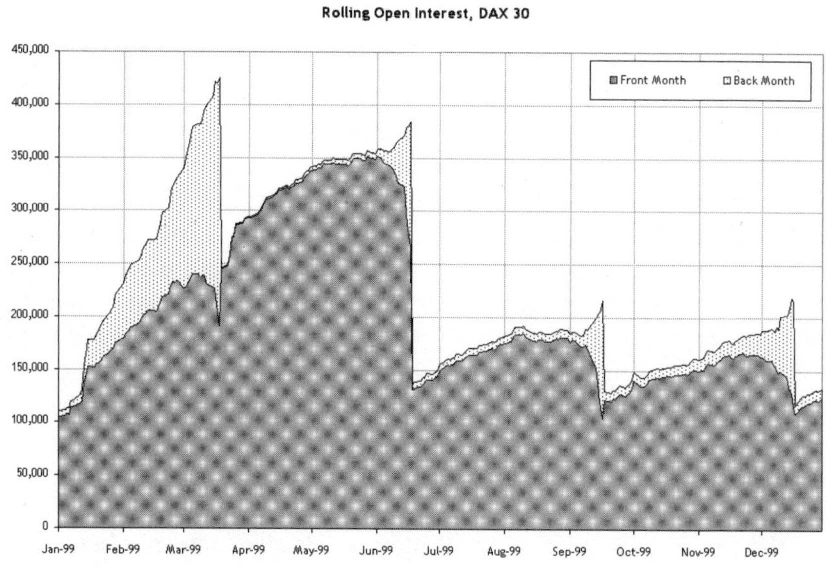

Rolling Open Interest, DAX 30
Front Month
Back Month
450,000
400,000
350,000
300,000
250,000
200,000
150,000
100,000
50,000
0
Jan-99
Feb-99
Mar-99
Apr-99
May-99
Jun-99
Jul-99
Aug-99
Sep-99
Oct-99
Nov-99
Dec-99

Figure 8-20 DAX 30 Open Interest
(*Source*: Compiled by author from Datastream data.)

Rolling Open Interest, CAC 40
Front Month
Back Month
300,000
250,000
200,000
150,000
100,000
50,000
0
Jan-99
Feb-99
Mar-99
Apr-99
May-99
Jun-99
Jul-99
Aug-99
Sep-99
Oct-99
Nov-99
Dec-99

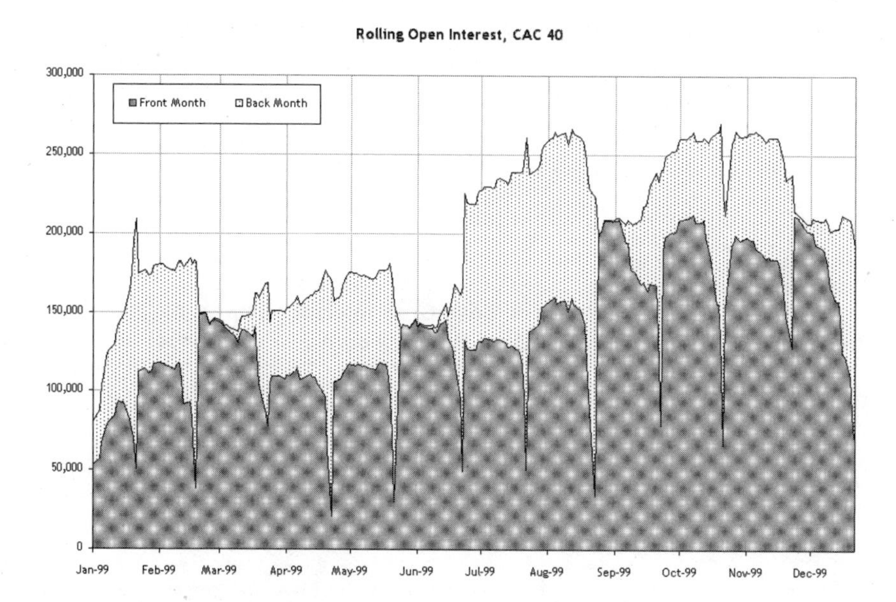

Figure 8-21 CAC 40 Open Interest
(*Source*: Compiled by author from Datastream data.)

This is clearly the sign that an unusually large number of contracts has been created just before the expiries.

To better understand the phenomenon, consider the case of the United States. On average, over the period the total open interest is between 350,000 and 400,000 contracts. Far from an expiry, only the front month is truly liquid; therefore, the open interest is heavily concentrated on this particular contract. As the expiry approaches, investors have four alternatives. They can unwind their front month position before the expiry, which does not increase the open interest.[33] They can roll their front month to the back month, which keeps the open interest exactly unchanged. They can decide to let their position expire on the SQ, with or without intervening in the cash market. This strategy would have no impact on the open interest before the SQ, but it would decrease it significantly on that particular day. And finally, they can *overroll*—that is, purchase or sell the roll beyond their original position. In both cases the open interest actually increases before the SQ and decreases again on the SQ when the front month expires. Table 8-2 shows a summary of the diverse strategies and their respective impact on the open interest.

The only decision that increases open interest is the last one, and it corresponds to a situation in which arbitrageurs and investors at large take a position on the roll beyond their natural need. This position may be speculative in the sense that arbitrageurs are trying to take advantage of the mispricing of the roll, or it may be more fundamental—if it is associated, for example, with the tax advantage due to dividends. In addition, we do not know just from the above charts if this position is built by selling or buying the roll because both lead to the same effect. By and large, selling is much more

TABLE 8-2

Decision	Impact on Total Open Interest (Front + Back Month) *before SQ*	Impact on Total Open Interest *on SQ*
Liquidate before SQ	– or Ø	Ø
No action, let it expire	Ø	–
Roll to back month	Ø	Ø
Overroll	+	–

[33] For example, if a long position is liquidated, if the buyer of the contracts is not liquidating a short position, the open interest is unchanged. If the buyer is liquidating a short, then the interest is decreased. In any case, it is never increased.

frequent, however, because it is a very simple and safe way to build a long stock position on the SQ.

As far as local particularities are concerned, experience shows that the roll has been historically much more often expensive than cheap in the United States and Japan, which unambiguously points toward arbitrageurs making profit every quarter on their existing position and probably buying more cash through the roll.[34] Incidentally, note that the overall level of total open interest remains relatively constant in the United States while it decreases slightly in Japan, which may be a sign of a general decrease in activity over the end of the year in that particular market.

In the United Kingdom the same conclusion does not hold, and in fact, the United Kingdom chart presents the only significant case of a flat aggregate open interest in September 1999. It is difficult to make any definitive conclusion, but the basis at that time was edging negative, and this may have caused arbitrageurs and investors in general to be less aggressive in their strategy on the SQ.

Germany presents a very interesting chart, consistent with the conclusions we made earlier. Considering that most dividends are concentrated during the second quarter of each year, the roll at that time was aggressively sold to allow arbitrageurs to buy stocks massively in anticipation of the dividend season. The total open interest dropped dramatically in June, which probably indicates that a sizable fraction of positions held after March were liquidated in June when the dividend game was over.

France also presents an interesting situation, primarily because the futures cycle is monthly, which means that we have 12 expiries instead of 4. In contrast to Germany, however, the dividend effect is relatively silent, and certainly insignificant compared to the sharp increase in open interest visible at the end of the year. This situation is difficult to interpret. Clearly, dividend advantages are pursued much less aggressively than in Germany, but beyond that preliminary conclusion, a more exhaustive examination of the market would be necessary to make better sense of the chart.

In conclusion, open interest constitutes another source of valuable information on the SQ but much more generally on market behavior in general. Naturally it should be examined in conjunction with the market basis because both present essentially complementary information.

---

[34] We included these profits when assessing the overall arbitrage profitability.

Hedge Ratios

We neglected in the above presentation an important factor about the roll, precisely the fact that different futures do not have the same hedge ratio. We mentioned in the chapter dedicated to risk analysis that hedging the financing of futures margin calls required a modification of the hedge ratio by a factor $1/(1 + r)$ where r denotes the relevant rate to the expiry.

Different maturities have different r; therefore, they should not be adjusted by the same factor. Numerically, consider the two futures mentioned earlier:

$$F_{\text{Mar}}^{TH} = \$1{,}400 * \left(1 + \frac{5 * 6\%}{360}\right) - \$0.20 = \$1{,}400.97$$

$$F_{\text{Jun}}^{\text{TH}} = \$1{,}400 * \left(1 + \frac{95 * 6.5\%}{360}\right) - \$7 = \$1{,}417.01$$

Every replicating portfolio equivalent to one future should in fact be hedged with:

$$\frac{1}{1+r} = \frac{1}{1 + \left(\frac{5 * 6\%}{360}\right)} = 0.999$$

March futures or:

$$\frac{1}{1+r} = \frac{1}{1 + \left(\frac{95 * 6.5\%}{360}\right)} = 0.983$$

June futures. Therefore, a March to June roll should be traded with a ratio of 0.984 June for 1 March (= 0.983/0.999). If we had to roll a $1 billion long position—that is, short 2,857 futures—from March to June, we would have to buy 2,857 March contracts and sell only 2,811.3 June contracts $(= 2,857 * 0.984)$. In practice, the roll is always traded in the market with the same number of contracts on each leg; therefore, we would have to sell 2,857 rolls and buy back 45.7 June contracts $(= 2.857 - 2,811.3)$ independently.

Long-Term Rolls

We've considered so far a short-term roll—that is, from one expiry to the next. Naturally longer maturities are also commonly traded, for example, March to September, or even June to September or June to December. However, it is sometimes interesting to roll the position longer term, typically beyond one year.

The reasons for doing that are multiple. First and foremost, rolling an existing position long term allows a trader to keep the benefits of holding this position for a longer period. For example, if dividends or opportunities to lend stocks are significant enough, an arbitrageur may decide that he or she would like to enjoy this rent for as long as possible. Alternatively, the price of a particular roll may be such that an arbitrageur will decide to buy it, rolling a short only because it makes economic sense. Overall, long-term rolls are interesting because they magnify the problems or opportunities associated with shorter ones, typically with respect to interest rates, stock loans, and dividends. For example, even if it does not necessarily create any profit immediately, a long-term roll may prove beneficial if it hedges or reduces an existing risk.

Because long-term rolls are usually not listed, they must be traded over the counter, as forwards, equity-linked swaps, or synthetic futures—that is, futures created by a call-put position. Depending on a number of factors, the market is more or less liquid, and credit risk reappears as a significant issue again. This is all the more true because long-term instruments of that nature tend to be bought by institutional investors rather than by traders.

All the markets we consider have fairly liquid OTC markets for long-term roll, typically up to two to three years. Beyond that term, trading depends on finding the right counterpart, which means that quoted prices may be less favorable.

Risks of Short Squeezes

Consider an arbitrage position with the time diagram shown in Figure 8-22. We are long 15 indices as of today, and against that short 25 futures and long 10 long-dated forwards.[35] Although it is not necessarily apparent immediately, this position carries the possibly significant risk of a short squeeze at some point in the future.

Consider, for example, that we liquidate the first 5 futures. At the close of the last trading day of the next futures, the diagram looks as it is shown in Figure 8-23. The expiry of the 20 futures tomorrow requires

[35] By "long 15 indices," we mean long a stock position replicating the index and such that the number of underlying indices is 15.

Note that the diagram is simplified and not rigorously accurate. The number of futures and forwards adds up to -15, which is the hedge against the stock position. However, the number of futures for each expiry should be adjusted by $1/(1+r)$ to reflect the hedge of the margin call financing. Forwards, however, are not subject to this adjustment because they are not marked to market every day.

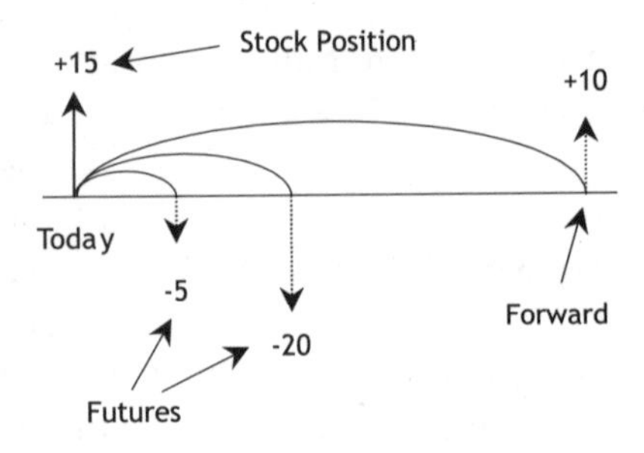

Figure 8-22 Roll

that we sell 20 more futures of a later expiry, or 20 indices at the SQ price. Alternatively, we could sell 10 indices and roll only 10 futures. There is apparently no difference compared to a standard futures expiry, but this is only superficially true. In general, an arbitrageur holding a long position against futures has entire latitude in deciding what should be rolled and what should be liquidated. In the particular case we are considering however, this is not true anymore because even if the stock position is liquidated, 10 more futures are expiring so the arbitrageur *has* to roll 10 futures, or sell 10 more indices short, to hedge the position adequately.

This obligation removes any opt-out possibility from the arbitrageur if the market is unfavorable. Typically when the roll is below par, arbitrageurs tend to liquidate their position if they are long and if they don't gain somewhere else—on dividends, for example. In the above situation, the arbitrageur would have no choice but to sell the roll, at any price; otherwise he or she would not be able to maintain a hedged position. If he or she wanted to sell stocks instead, he or she would face the risk that too many borrowers would appear at the same time, in effect making stock borrowings prohibitively expensive. This scenario is in fact extremely probable because, as we said many times earlier, index arbitrageurs tend to react at the same time in the same

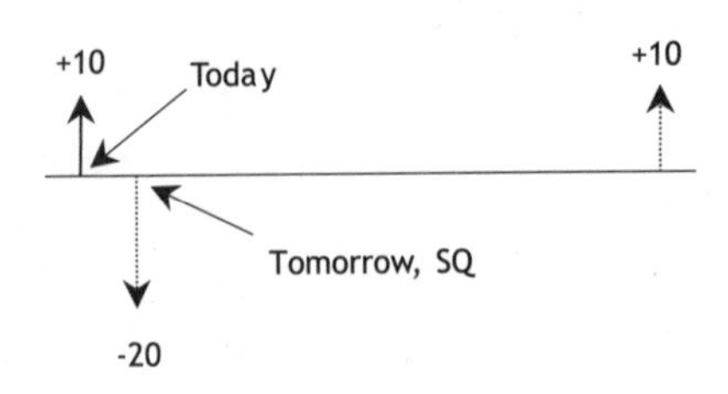

Figure 8-23 Short Squeeze

direction. Therefore, if one were facing a particularly unfavorable roll price, most certainly all of them would carry out the same analysis and make the same conclusion.

To make matters more complicated, it is important to realize that this type of situation can develop only under a specific set of circumstances. The arbitrageur must have been able to buy at some point in the past a long-term roll, probably at a profit or at least without any significant loss. If that is the case, the market was pricing at that time a long-term roll close or below par—that is, it was also implicitly pricing all the interim short-term rolls close to or below par. Therefore, buying a long-term roll cheap gives an early indication that interim rolls will most probably be cheap, in turn giving some substance to the risk of being squeezed at a later date.

To better understand the source of this risk, let's reconsider a standard roll position. Consider, for example, that we hold the exact opposite position, as shown in Figure 8-24. We can buy 20 rolls today, or 20 indices at the SQ, or choose any combination of the two. There is no problem whatsoever here because we can always buy stocks, at a maximum cost equal to the transaction costs.[36] Therefore, the difficulty appears only because going short on stocks is difficult and/or costly. This is particularly true in Japan, for example, where the securities loan market is not mature yet compared to that of the United States or Europe.

Interest Rates

As an illustration of the interest rate exposure inherent to an index arbitrage position, consider that we enter a trade today in which we buy a replicating portfolio at I and sell futures at their theoretical price

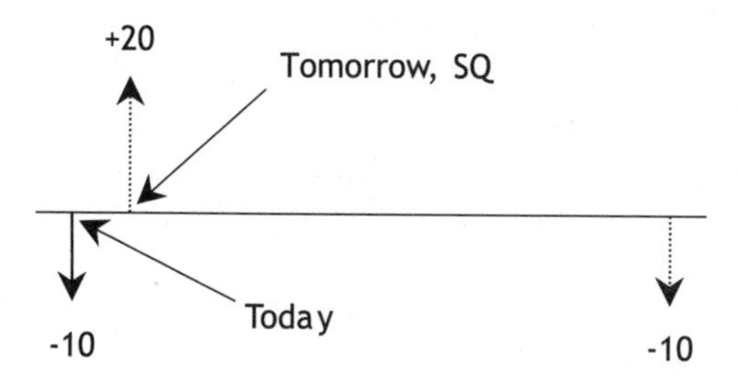

Figure 8-24 Short Squeeze

[36] This assumes naturally that we have the capital to buy additional shares—that is, that the current position has not reached a limit.

F_{TH}. If r denotes the interest rate from today's stock settlement date to the final settlement date of the futures, and d^* denotes the accumulated dividend amount expected until the expiry, then we know that $F_{TH} = I \cdot (1+r) - d^*$. This formula implies that we borrow an amount equal to the cash outlay necessary to establish the position—that is, I, at a rate r until the expiry. Consider now that we do not perform this money market transaction and that the interest rate changes to r' as of tomorrow.[37] If for the sake of simplicity we keep the stock market unchanged from today to tomorrow, we have no profit or loss on the stock side but possibly a P&L on the futures position. Along the same lines, we consider $d^* = d'^*$ for simplicity although this would probably not be true in practice. Today the short futures are valued at F_{TH}, and tomorrow at $F'_{TH} = I \cdot (1+r') - d^*$.

Specifically, if P_V denotes the point value of the futures and Q the position held, the P&L P is approximately equal to[38]:

$$P = Q \cdot P_V \cdot \left(\frac{F_{TH} - F'_{TH}}{1+r} \right) = Q \cdot P_V . I \cdot \left(\frac{r - r'}{1+r} \right)$$

To illustrate the magnitude of this risk, consider a \$1 billion S&P 500 position—that is, 2,857 futures with an index at \$1,400. We assume that the futures expiry is in two months and that $r = 6$ percent and $r' = 6.10$ percent. Under these assumptions, P is equal to:

$$P = 2{,}857 * \$250 * \$1{,}400 * \left[\frac{\frac{2 * (6\% - 6.1\%)}{12}}{1 + \frac{2 * 6\%}{12}} \right] = -\$165{,}008$$

If the position is optimistically expected to yield 0.73 percent over the course of a regular year—that is, \$7.3 million—a loss of \$165,000 represents approximately one week of trading (5.6 days = \$165,000/ \$7,300,000 * 250). Although it is probably nothing dramatic in absolute terms, this loss can be easily avoided by entering the appropriate

[37] If we do not perform the money market transaction, the position will still be financed but at the overnight rate. The result of the discussion does not change because we are still entirely exposed on a change in r.

[38] P is an approximation because we use $r \approx r'$ in order to simplify the expression. In theory, we should use:

$$P = Q \cdot P_V \cdot \left(\frac{F_{TH} - F_H}{1+r} - \frac{F'_{TH} - F_H}{1+r'} \right)$$

where F_H is the historical price at which the futures has originally been traded.

money market transaction because the −$165,000 is then offset by a profit from rising interest rates.[39]

This example is relatively straightforward and intuitive because it is apparent that we need to finance the carry of the stock position at a given rate. The same risk exists, however, in a situation in which we do not explicitly have to carry the position yet. Consider, for example, that we roll today part of our position through a one-year forward transaction. We buy a number of futures and sell an equivalent number of one-year forward contracts, resulting in Figure 8-25. The futures position is exposed on the two-month rate, r_{2M}. The forward, on the other hand, depends exclusively on the one-year rate, r_{1Y}. If the entire portfolio is properly hedged as of today before the forward is traded, it includes a replicating stock position, an equivalent short futures position, and a money market hedging the interest rate risk until expiry. When the forward is "substituted" to the futures,[40] the money market is not appropriate anymore to hedge the risk associated with r_{1Y}. This situation is another practical example of the distinction between treasury management and interest rate exposure. As of today the treasury balance is nil because the money market covers the entire amount of stock purchased, so there is no need for any adjustment on the treasury

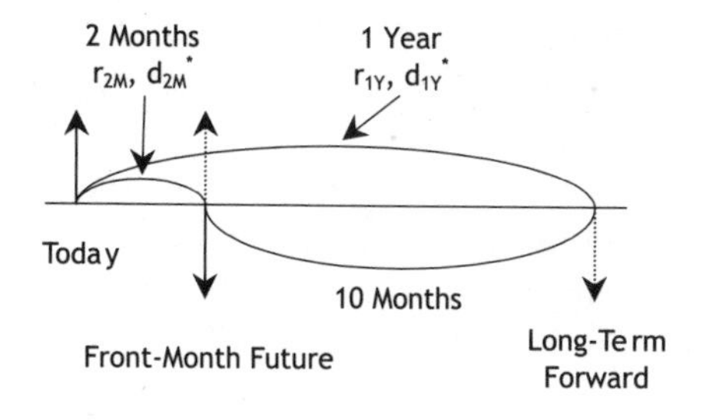

Figure 8-25 Interest Rate Risk

[39] Note that the magnitude of the loss depends as much on the absolute change in interest rates, 0.10 percent in our example, as it depends on the remaining time to expiry. If there were only one month left, the loss would be −$82,915, still significant but much less so.

[40] The forward is not *substituted* for the futures, but the net result of the roll—that is, a futures purchase and forward sale—can be seen as a substitution. Naturally, depending on the price at which each instrument is traded, the entire operation may result in a profit or a loss. We leave this particular element out here because we are concentrating on the interest rate component.

as a result of the forward trade. In contrast, the interest rate exposure of the entire portfolio has been significantly modified because r_{2M} is not the relevant variable anymore. To reestablish a satisfactory hedge, we need to enter into a transaction that has no effect on the treasury while simultaneously hedging a rate exposure.

In fact, the situation is slightly subtler than that because in 2 months the existing money market disappears. What we really need then is a transaction that allows us to access cash liquidity in 2 months at a rate set today, for a total maturity of 10 months. This is typically what a FRA is designed for, although a swap of eurofutures could be used as well.

The risk created by the forward transaction is not on the 2-month or 1-year rate but rather on the 2 × 12 FRA—that is, 10-month rate in 2 months. We can hedge it with a 2 × 12 FRA, or a swap starting on the futures expiry date, or a eurofutures strip starting on the futures expiry date as well. The best choice depends on a number of factors, the most important probably being the net cost to perform the hedge. FRAs being cash transactions, we know we can expect a wide bid-ask spread, and consequently they are unlikely to be the cheapest solution. Swaps are a very strong alternative, but for the particular case of a 10-month maturity, eurofutures are probably the most attractive considering their high liquidity and very low bid-ask spread. If the forward had been a longer-term transaction, for example, beyond 2 to 3 years, then a swap would have probably been the most likely—and in fact only—decision.

Naturally it is always possible to neglect that risk and keep the position unhedged. However, because the true maturity here is 10 months, the effect of an adverse move on interest rate can be sizable. If we recall the example we used before, a 0.10 percent move would in that case result in a loss of[41]:

$$P = \$1{,}000{,}000{,}000 * \left(\frac{-\dfrac{10 * 0.1\%}{12}}{1 + \dfrac{12 * 6\%}{12}} \right) = -\$786{,}163$$

These examples show clearly that interest rate risk can be significant, although relatively easy to manage in general.

---

[41] The term 10 ∗ 0.1 percent/12 corresponds to a loss of 0.10 percent in 10-months, while the discount factor (1 + 12 ∗ 6 percent/12) is necessary because the loss occurs in 12 months at the expiry of the futures. The formula is not exactly the forward valuation but an estimate of the loss associated with a change in the 2 × 12 market FRA.

Recomposition

By definition of index arbitrage, an arbitrageur is supposed to carry a replicating portfolio of the underlying index, which is the only way to guarantee that the futures hedge is effective. This operating mode implies a dynamic replication throughout the life of the position—that is, adjustments whenever the index itself is adjusted by its sponsor. Naturally the most important question here is whether these changes can be implemented at no cost—that is, if they are what we called "realizable." We argued in the chapter dedicated to indices that this property was a fundamental requirement for sponsors, in terms of consistency in the index behavior as much as from a purely economic perspective.

To assess the risk embedded in a recomposition event, let's consider again the case of Nikkatsu in 1993. Nikkatsu was a movie producer and went bankrupt suddenly in July, 1993. Although the company was known to be in financial difficulties, its collapse surprised the market. Nihon Keizei Shinbun, the Nikkei 225 sponsor, decided to remove Nikkatsu from the index on July 1, 1993, effective immediately, and replaced it with Shionogi Corporation. The change took place at the close of the day, and the new divisor was computed accordingly. At that point arbitrageurs faced a tough situation because they were naturally unable to realize the index substitution at a time the market was closed. Furthermore, it was quite certain that the price of Nikkatsu would fall sharply the next day, and indeed this is exactly what happened. Figure 8-26 shows closing prices for Nikkatsu and Shionogi over the period, scaled to 100 percent on the day of the announcement.

Arbitrageurs were still required to implement the adjustment in the index, so most of them tried to liquidate Nikkatsu and buy Shionogi the next day. In doing so, they incurred a significant loss, which we can estimate easily. Assuming a $1 billion position—that is, ¥100 billion—we know that we would have held close to 555,500 shares of Nikkatsu.[42] The price loss for Nikkatsu was ¥204, from ¥229 to ¥25, while Shionogi gained ¥65 from ¥985 to ¥1,050. In selling Nikkatsu, arbitrageurs thus lost ¥113.3 million, and ¥36.1 million more in buying Shionogi. The total loss, close to $1.5 million, represents 17.6 percent of the expected profit for the year if

[42] Cf. footnore 29. The Nikkei 225 is price weighted so that all components have the same weight.

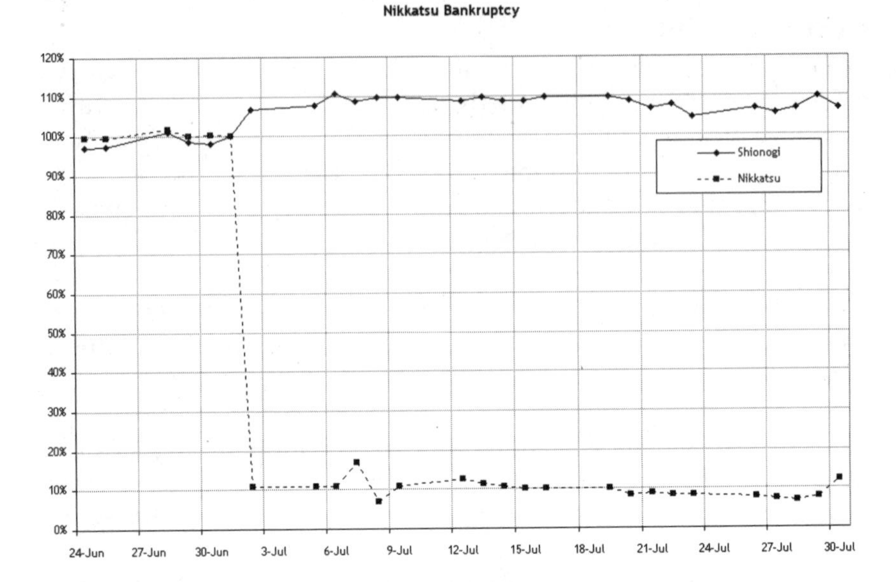

Figure 8-26 Nikkatsu
(*Source*: Compiled by author from Bloomberg data.)

we assume an overall profitability of 0.85 percent. As in the case of Sumitomo, this is not dramatic but it is certainly significant.

This is a very telling example of a situation that is virtually impossible to hedge, even though it may have a sizable negative impact. Nowadays examples of such adverse events are relatively rare, and the best way to prepare for them is to know the exact rules applied by a sponsor whenever an index member files for bankruptcy.

Correlation

Percentage of Execution Revisited

We have so far mentioned several times the notion of replicating portfolio, assuming that we would have at all times a perfect portfolio with the right number of shares for each constituent, based on the underlying index definition. It is now time to revisit this particular assumption and examine the correlation risk associated with an unperfect position.

Indeed, the constitution of a perfect portfolio is a relatively easy task theoretically, but it is more difficult in practice. As an illustration, let's revisit the execution risk and more particularly the measure of the percentage of execution. If we denote e_S this percentage on the cash side, e_S can be defined as[43]:

$$e_S = \frac{\sum_i Q_i^{\text{exec}} \cdot P_i^{\text{last}}}{\sum_i Q_i \cdot P_i^{\text{last}}}$$

where Q_i^{exec} and Q_i^{unexec} are the executed and unexecuted parts of the original quantity Q_i, P_i^{exec} is the average price of execution of executed orders,[44] and P_i^{last} is the last traded price of stocks for which there remains an unexecuted part. This definition does not make any difference for the relative executed position of each individual stock, however. If, for example, a small number of stocks are entirely executed, while a large fraction of the remaining portfolio is almost entirely unexecuted, e_S may be relatively high although the position is not what we would like it to be.

As a simple example, consider that we are buying an index with only two stocks, A and B, each with a weight of 50 percent. If A is entirely executed while B is entirely unexecuted, the total percentage of execution is 50 percent, which means that we would trade 50 percent of the total size on the futures leg. Naturally this is radically different from 50 percent executed on each stock, which would still require us to trade the same number of futures. To get a sense of the magnitude of the difference, let's call P_A and P_B the prices at which A and B trade when we execute A, and P'_A and P'_B the same prices when we execute B. If we assume for simplicity the index to be price weighted, the following relationships are true:

$$I = \frac{P_A + P_B}{2} \qquad I' = \frac{P'_A + P'_B}{2}$$

[43] Note that e_S is homogeneous to a capitalization. Therefore, e_S is really a price-weighted percentage of execution.

There is an alternative definition of e_S:

$$e_S = \frac{\sum_i Q_i^{\text{exec}} \cdot P_i^{\text{exec}}}{\sum_i Q_i^{\text{exec}} \cdot P_i^{\text{exec}} + \sum_i Q_i^{\text{unexec}} \cdot P_i^{\text{last}}}$$

If this last formula is used, the definitions of L and S later in the text should be modified accordingly.

e_F, the percentage of execution on futures, does not appear here because we consider a situation in which we are hedged at all times—that is, $e_F = e_S$.

[44] Therefore, at all times, $Q_i = Q_i^{\text{exec}} + Q_i^{\text{unexec}}$.

if I and I' respectively denote the instantaneous value of the index in the two instants when A and B are executed. If F and F' denote the price of the futures at these two moments, and b_{TH} is the fair value for the day, then we know that $F > I + b_{TH}$ because otherwise we would not have entered the arbitrage in the first place. Let's call b_M the market basis when we originally enter the arbitrage, $b_M = F - (I + b_{TH})$. In essence, this situation represents an opportunity—that is, b_M—we are trying to capture but for which only 50 percent of the portfolio is executed immediately—that is, A. To complete the picture, let's make the final assumption that the opportunity has disappeared when we finally execute B—that is, $F' = I' + b_{TH}$.

The purpose of the exercise is to show how the execution partition between A and B affects the overall profitability of the trade. If P&L stands for the expected profit for the trade, it is given by the difference between the realized value of the future and that of the index. If F_{exec} and I_{exec} respectively denote the executed prices on futures and index, then the P&L is given by:

$$\text{P\&L} = F_{exec} - (I_{exec} + b_{TH})$$

In addition, we know that:

$$I_{exec} = \frac{P_A + P'_B}{2}$$

$$F_{exec} = \frac{F + F'}{2} = \frac{(I + b_{TH} + b_M) + (I' + b_{TH})}{2} = \frac{I + b_M + I'}{2} + b_{TH}$$

I_{exec} is a result of the definition of P_A and P'_B, while F_{exec} results from the fact that we trade the total number of futures at two different prices F and F'. The total profit is then equal to:

$$\text{P\&L} = \frac{\left(\frac{P_A + P_B}{2}\right) + b_M + \left(\frac{P'_A + P'_B}{2}\right)}{2} + b_{TH} - \left(\frac{P_A + P'_B}{2} + b_{TH}\right)$$

which can be simplified into:

$$\text{P\&L} = \left(\frac{P_A + P_B}{4}\right) + \left(\frac{P'_A + P'_B}{4}\right) - \left(\frac{P_A + P'_B}{2}\right) + \frac{b_M}{2}$$

and finally:

$$\text{P\&L} = \left(\frac{P'_A - P_A}{4}\right) + \left(\frac{P_B - P'_B}{4}\right) + \frac{b_M}{2}$$

Interestingly, despite the fact that A is fully executed immediately, we still carry an exposure to its price through P'_A. Along the same lines, even if B is fully unexecuted when we initiate the trade, the total P&L is exposed on P_B as much as it is on P'_B.

Consider now a situation in which we execute half the total position on A and B instead of executing A only and the remaining halves instead of executing B. The only change is I_{exec}, which becomes:

$$I_{exec} = \frac{\left(\frac{P_A + P_B}{2}\right) + \left(\frac{P'_A + P'_B}{2}\right)}{2}$$

The total profit is naturally affected and is now equal to:

$$\text{P\&L} = \frac{\left(\frac{P_A + P_B}{2}\right) + b_M + \left(\frac{P'_A + P'_B}{2}\right)}{2} + b_{TH} - \left(\frac{\frac{P_A + P_B}{2} + \frac{P'_A + P'_B}{2}}{2} + b_{TH}\right)$$

Therefore:

$$\text{P\&L} = \frac{b_M}{2}$$

This formula is clearly much more attractive than the previous one because it depends only on the market basis, not on the prices of A or B anymore. In fact, the profit in that case is the average of the market basis when we executed the first 50 percent of the entire position—that is, b_M—and the market basis when we executed the remaining 50 percent—that is, 0: P&L = $(b_M + 0)/2$. This result is very intuitive and can be easily generalized: If execution within the position is homogeneous for each index constituent, the total profit on the entire trade is the average of the market basis throughout the execution period.[45] In contrast, if the execution is not homogeneous, then the overall profitability depends not only on the current price of each constituent but also on the price it was trading at if it is "overexecuted" or will be trading at if it is "underexecuted." This dependence is usually referred to as a *correlation risk between the portfolio and the index* because despite the fact that the portfolio is perfectly hedged against futures, it may not track the index accurately, and it may lose value compared to the futures due to its inexact composition.

The level of risk associated with correlation can be measured by two aggregate indicators, which we denote L and S. L is the total

[45] Rigorously speaking, the execution is homogeneous if, for example, at 10 percent of execution, every single component in the position has been executed at 10 percent of its entire size.

nominal created by overexecutions—that is, stocks for which we executed more than the overall percentage of execution. S is the similar nominal for stocks that have been underexecuted. Algebraically L and S can be written as[46]:

$$L = \sum_{Q_i^{exec} \geq e_S \cdot Q_i} (Q_i^{exec} - e_S \cdot Q_i) \cdot P_i^{last} \qquad S = \sum_{Q_i^{exec} < e_S \cdot Q_i} (e_S \cdot Q_i - Q_i^{exec}) \cdot P_i^{last}$$

Because we assume a position correctly hedged at all times, we know that we can expect $L \approx S$. However, what is important here is the magnitude of L and S compared to the original nominal, or the total nominal executed up to this point.[47] In fact, the situation is exactly equivalent to a perfect replicating portfolio of size $e_S \cdot Q_i$, hedged with the appropriate number of futures, and two additional opposite portfolios (l_i) and (s_i) with $l_i = Q_i^{exec} - e_S \cdot Q_i$ and $s_i = e_S \cdot Q_i - Q_i^{exec}$. L and S are the current nominal of each of these portfolios. This spread position between L and S is unwanted and the result of the random executions coming from the market. Ideally we want to have L and S as small as possible relative to the total executed position, but managing them in real time is not an easy task. In fact, the execution problem to minimize correlation risk can be formulated as trying to maximize e_S while b_M is advantageous while keeping L and S as low as possible. In the S&P 500, for example, it is difficult to follow 500 components at once, and this is all the more difficult if we require a homogeneous percentage of execution across the board. Therefore, in practice arbitrageurs try to achieve a homogeneous percentage within the largest capitalizations as fast as possible, knowing that the smallest components will have only a marginal effect on the overall profitability and risk. In other words, it is generally true that the overall profitability of a particular operation is determined within a few minutes of the oppor-

---

[46] Note that the alternative definition in which we would replace P_i^{last} by P_i^{exec} has no interest because we want to follow the evolution of L and S in real time.

[47]

$$L - S = \sum_{Q_i^{exec} \geq e_s \cdot Q_i} (Q_i^{exec} - e_s \cdot Q_i) \cdot P_i^{last} - \sum_{Q_i^{exec} < e_S \cdot Q_i} (e_S \cdot Q_i - Q_i^{exec}) \cdot P_i^{last}$$

which eventually leads to:

$$L - S = \sum_{Q_i^{exec} \geq e_S \cdot Q_i} Q_i^{exec} \cdot P_i^{last} + \sum_{Q_i^{exec} < e_S \cdot Q_i} Q_i^{exec} \cdot P_i^{last} - e_S \cdot \sum_i Q_i \cdot P_i^{last} =$$

$$\sum_i Q_i^{exec} \cdot P_i^{last} - e_S \cdot \sum_i Q_i \cdot P_i^{last} = 0$$

by definition of e_S.

tunity, even if the execution can spread through a much longer period of time.

Illustration

As a hypothetical numerical illustration of the discussion, consider a price weighted-index with three components, A, B, and C. Assume the three stocks have a weight of 100 in the index, and that the divisor is 1. If we want to buy one index we have to purchase 100 shares of each: $Q_A = 100$, $Q_B = 100$, and $Q_C = 100$. In addition we assume the following parameters: $Q_A^{exec} = 20$, $Q_B^{exec} = 80$, $Q_C^{exec} = 50$, $P_A = \$10$, $P_B = \$15$, and $P_C = \$30$. e_S, L, and S are easy to compute:

$$e_S = \frac{20 * \$10 + 80 * \$15 + 50 * \$30}{100 * \$10 + 100 * \$15 + 100 * \$30} = \frac{\$2{,}900}{\$5{,}500} = 52.7\%$$

$$L = (80 - 52.7) * \$15 = \$409.1$$
$$S = (52.7 - 20) * \$10 + (52.7 - 50) * \$30 = \$409.1$$

In essence, we have here a portfolio of 52.7 shares of A, B, and C perfectly hedged against the appropriate number of futures, and a spread position between 27.3 shares of A on one side and 32.7 shares of B and 2.7 shares of C on the other side. Because the perfect portfolio of 52.7 shares is a perfect replication of the index, its profitability is preserved as long as the market basis remains advantageous. However, if we wait too long to complete the trade, regardless of b_M, the spread between L and S may evolve unfavorably and dilapidate the original profit.

To evaluate if that scenario is potentially threatening, consider that we expect to realize a profit of 0.15 percent on this trade. With an index at \$5,500, 0.15 percent gives a nominal profit of \$8.25. In other words, the market basis is probably close to \$8 when we enter the arbitrage. The spread position between L and S has a nominal of \$409.1, which means that an adverse move of 1 percent on each leg would generate a loss equal to the expected profit on the entire portfolio. Despite the hypothetical nature of the argument, it is clear that a 1 percent move is very common, and the risk of losing the entire expected profit or even more is extremely real. The best way to diminish the risk here would be to buy A and C more aggressively to increase e_S and decrease L and S.[48]

[48] Alternatively we could sell B, but this does not really make sense because we would have to buy it back at some later point to complete the trade.

CONCLUSION

Here ends our discussion of index arbitrage. The reader should get a sense of the diverse dimensions involved in managing a position of that type, in terms of risk and opportunities. The difficulty naturally is to bring every aspect together in practice, incorporating all the valuation and risk analysis techniques to make the best decision at a given time. As always, judgment and experience are powerful allies, and a cross-border experience is particularly valuable to gain a broad view of issues such as execution, dividends, or correlation beyond one single market. This is exactly what we have attempted to achieve here, a global perspective hopefully rich in rewarding insights.

REFERENCES

The following are valuable resources on the subject of index arbitrage profitability:

George Sofianos, "Index Arbitrage Profitability," *The Journal of Derivatives*, fall 1993.

Wolfgang Buhler and Alexander Kempf, "DAX Index Futures: Mispricing and Arbitrage in German Markets," *Journal of Futures Markets*, 15, 1995.

Kee-Hong Bae, Kalok Chan, and Yan-Leung Cheung, "The Profitability of Index Futures Arbitrage: Evidence from Bid-Ask Quotes," *Journal of Futures Markets*, 18, 1998.

Michael Brennan and Eduardo Schwartz, "Arbitrage in Stock Index Futures," *Journal of Business*, 63, 1990.

Peter Chung, "A Transactions Data Test of Stock Index Futures Market Efficiency and Index Arbitrage Profitability," *Journal of Finance*, 46, 1991.

9

RISK ARBITRAGE

INTRODUCTION

In the most general sense, *risk arbitrage* describes trading strategies in which the entire profit is based on the assessment and trading of one particular class of risk. Over the years, however, the term has become more and more specific and now refers almost unequivocally to the systematic arbitrage of corporate events, most notably mergers and acquisitions. The underlying concept is even more straightforward than index arbitrage. The terms of the corporate event specify exactly what investors will receive in exchange for their holdings when the operation effectively closes: stocks, cash, or a combination of the two.

Let's denote, for example, A the acquirer, T the target, and r the exchange ratio—that is, 1 share of T is exchanged for r shares of A at expiry.[1] An arbitrage situation can be represented as shown in Figure 9-1, where P_A denotes the market price of A and P_T that of T. In this diagram P_T trades at a discount because $r \cdot P_A^{\text{Last}} > P_T^{\text{Last}}$, although if we account for the bid-ask spreads, the opportunity is not necessarily easy to capture.

It would appear that the total "available" profit is $r \cdot P_A^{\text{Last}} - P_T^{\text{Last}}$ or $r \cdot P_A{}^{\text{Bid}} - P_T^{\text{Ask}}$ if we incorporate the bid-ask spreads, but in fact, this is not rigorously true notably because of dividends and borrowing costs. To obtain a clear expression of the profitability, let's examine the situation more rigorously. Figure 9-2 shows the relevant parameters if we enter a position on t_0 and close it on expiry t_1. The initial trades are

[1] We implicitly assume that the operation is not a straight tender offer; otherwise, the discussion is trivial because investors just tender shares bought at a lower price. Along the same lines, the exchange might incorporate a cash part without any significant change in the reasoning.

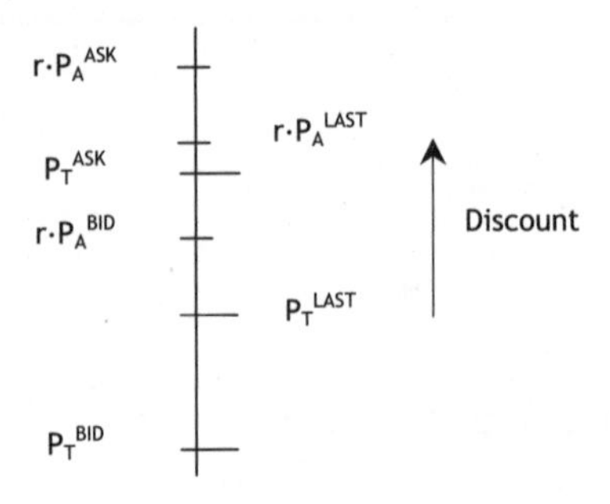

Figure 9-1 Arbitrage Situation

executed at P_A and P_T respectively. At expiry the closing prices[2] are respectively P'_A and P'_T. In addition, we call d_A, d_T, r_A, and r_T the dividends for A and T and the relevant zero coupons between the *payment* date and expiry. Finally, r_E, and b_A denote the zero coupon from t_0 to t_1 and the market borrowing cost for A.[3]

If we want to take advantage of the arbitrage, we need to enter the following transactions:

On t_0 :

- Buy 1 share of T at P_T.
- Secure a borrowing of r shares of A until expiry at b_A.[4]

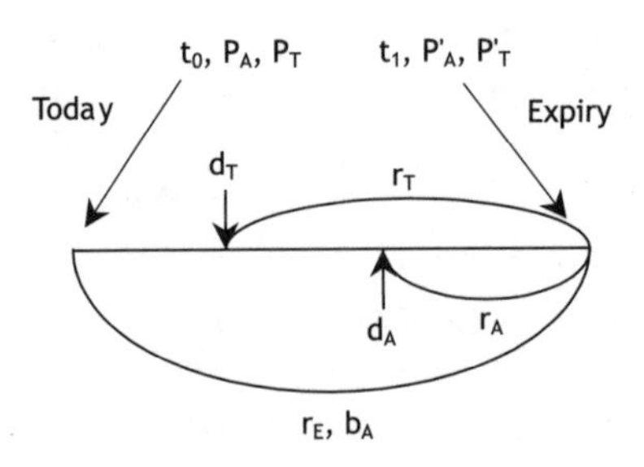

Figure 9-2 Arbitrage Cash Flow

[2] Note that we do not necessarily have $r \cdot P'_A = P'_T$. This is true only if the two stocks close at par on the last trading day before the merger is effective.

[3] This assumes that we sell A—that is, T trades at a discount—which is generally the case. However, if T were trading at a premium, we would have to consider b_T—that is, the cost of borrowing T, not A. The reasoning would be modified accordingly.

[4] Note that we could also include the revenue generated by lending T out. In practice, we know for a fact that we will have to pay a borrowing fee for A, but we cannot be sure that T can be lent out. Therefore, we leave this out for simplicity without any loss of generality. The total profit we obtain can be considered conservative.

- Sell r shares of A at P_A.[5]
- Lend an amount equal to $r \cdot P_A - P_T$ until exiry at r_E.

These operations generate a cash flow CF_0 equal to:

$$CF_0 = -P_T + r \cdot P_A - (r \cdot P_A - P_T) = 0$$

There is no cash flow at establishment of the position, so we do not have any overnight cost of carry. Alternatively, we would decide not to enter the money market transaction in which case the residual $r \cdot P_A - P_T$ would be carried at the overnight rate until expiry.

On t_1:

- Deliver r shares of A to the original lender.
- Receive r shares of A from the exchange of T.
- Receive $(r \cdot P_A - P_T) \cdot (1 + r_E)$.
- Pay borrowing fee $r \cdot b_A \cdot P_A$.
- Pay accumulated dividends on A to original lender: $r \cdot d_A^* = r \cdot (1 + r_A) \cdot d_A$.
- Receive accumulated dividends on $T : d_T^* = (1 + r_T) \cdot d_T$.

The cash flow CF_1 is:

$$CF_1 = (r \cdot P_A - P_T) \cdot (1 + r_E) - r \cdot b_A \cdot P_A - r \cdot d_A^* + d_T^*$$

This cash flow represents in fact the P&L associated with the entire arbitrage. The original indicator $r \cdot P_A - P_T$ has been modified to account for three distinct adjustments:

- The financing of the profit until maturity
- The costs associated to enter the arbitrage by borrowing A
- The opportunity cost—or profit—associated with the dividend differential between A and T

Out of these adjustments, it is important to make a distinction between what is a clear loss and what is a clear profit. The financing of $r \cdot P_A - P_T$ is undeniably a profit if we execute the arbitrage appropriately—that is, if $r \cdot P_A - P_T > 0$. The longer the carry of the position, the better for us because $(1 + r_E)$ increases with time.[6] In contrast, $-r \cdot b_A \cdot P_A$ is

[5] We implicitly assume that there is no payment flow required to enter the borrowing, only the delivery of a collateral equal to the nominal of the stocks borrowed, which is the case in practice. In other words, we get the full proceeds from the sale, and the fee is paid in full upon closing of the position.

[6] This financing term did not appear anywhere in an index arbitrage because the entire profit was realized on expiry, whereas here it effectively appears in treasury at the initiation of the arbitrage.

undeniably a cost and is also dependent on the time remaining until the expiry. Finally, the dividend differential ($d_T^* - r \cdot d_A^*$) can be positive or negative, and its dependence with time is limited to the frequency of dividend distributions. For example, in the United States dividends are paid quarterly, so the differential varies only quarter by quarter.

The purpose of this short discussion is to understand how the overall profit is dependent on time, precisely on "time to expiry," which is fundamentally different from an index arbitrage situation. We will come back to this particular issue, but it is already clear that the timing of the convergence should be considered as a new risk, in addition to its likelihood.

As a numerical illustration of a hypothetical arbitrage, consider the following set of parameters: $P_A = \$50$, $P_T = \$98$, $r = 2$, $r_E = 6$ percent, $t_1 - t_0 = 6$ months, $b_A = 0.30$ percent, $d_A^* = \$0.75$, and $d_T^* = \$0.99$. The total profit is then given by:

$$\text{P\&L} = CF_1 = (2 * \$50 - \$98) * \left(1 + \frac{6 * 6\ \%}{12}\right) - 2 * 0.30\ \% * \left(\frac{6}{12}\right) * \$50 - 2 * \$0.75 + \$0.99 = \$1.4$$

When compared to an initial nominal close to \$100, the arbitrage yields an annual return of 2.8 percent ($= \$1.4/\$100 * 12/6$). If, however, the entire position had to be kept for an entire year with the same nominal profit at initiation, the yield would be only 1.4 percent.

EXPLICIT CONVERGENCE

As an illustration of a class of arbitrage where convergence is not certain although it is highly likely, risk arbitrage should fall within the framework we introduced originally to consider arbitrage situations in general. Specifically, Table 9-1 shows the case of risk arbitrage, somewhere in between absolute and hypothetical. Considering that we are outside the safe harbor of an absolute convergence, we need to examine this particular risk and the implication it has in terms of valuation and risk analysis. We will naturally have to consider also execution, hedge, and risk of carry because these are important parameters albeit somewhat less critical than in the case of index arbitrage. Meanwhile, as we did in the previous section, let's start by a general

TABLE 9-1

Convergence	Absolute	Hypothetical	Risk Arbitrage
Valuation	Theoretical	Mark to market	Both should be performed.
Convergence type	Public	Highly proprietary	Public, but personal judgment is key.
Convergence risk	Low to nonexistent	Critical	Can be high, situation specific.
Execution risk	Critical	Low	Medium.
Hedge	Fixed quantity	Fixed quantity or delta	Fixed quantity (merger ratio).
Risk of carry	Important	Low	Can be high (stock borrowing cost).
Time horizon	Known or bounded	Unknown	Uncertain but estimated.
Window of opportunity	Very short	Longer	Relatively short.
Profitability	10 × 1	1 × 10	Situation specific.
Robustness	Strong	Weak	Medium.
Implications	Pricing	None (Inefficient market?)	Not really applicable.

discussion about typical opportunities and profitability for risk arbitrage strategies.

OPPORTUNITIES AND PROFITABILITY

Opportunity

It is an understatement to say that mergers and acquisitions have become a major component of the modern corporate landscape. In particular, in telecommunications, be it Internet or entertainment related, scale seems to be the credo of the day, and the amount and number of transactions is simply staggering. Figure 9-3, for example, shows the evolution of these two statistics over the past 30 years for transactions executed between U.S. companies.

Clearly, consolidation is happening at a faster rate today, and it is difficult to say exactly when and how it will stop. Furthermore, if this effect is clearly visible in the United States, it is more and more common on other continents like Europe or Asia. With the implementation of the single currency, Europe has finally progressed on its way to a deeper economic integration, even if political integration is still more a utopia than a reality. Takeovers, traditionally very infrequent, have

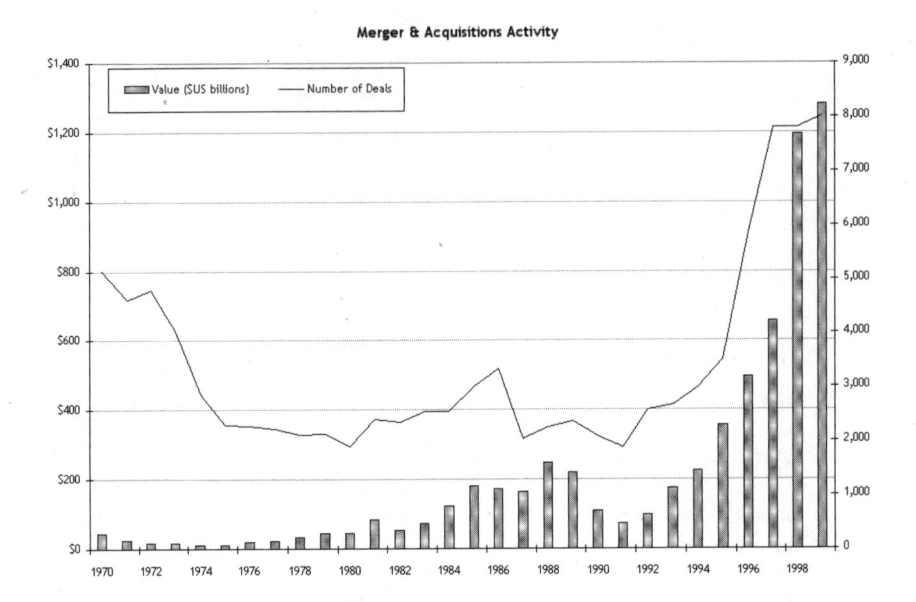

Figure 9-3 Mergers and Acquisitions
(*Source*: Mergerstat, www.mergerstat.com. Reprinted with permission. 1999 data up to October 1999.)

become relatively common, including across borders and in some cases on hostile terms. We will consider below one of these takeovers, the acquisition of Crédit Commercial de France (CCF) by Hong-Kong and Shanghai Bank (HSBC).

In Asia, industrial consolidation is also very active; however, it is not fueled by a modernization of the environment and a strengthening economic growth. Rather, the Asian crisis has led many developing countries to ask for help from international financial institutions such as the International Monetary Fund (IMF), and the money came under conditions of more transparency and more openness to foreign capital. As a result, Korea, for example, but also Thailand, Malaysia, and to a lesser extent Indonesia, have experienced a renewed interest from international investment bankers shopping around for valuable assets at postcrisis prices. Although Japan does not fall under this particular category of developing economy, the same scenario is unfolding there as well. The acquisition of Nissan by Renault is an example. France if anything had always been caricatured as a fortress of unionism and administrative inefficiency, and the automobile industry was certainly a very strong pocket of these. The Japanese economic crisis, however, was so strong and so pervasive following the market crash at the end of the 1980s that even legendary corporations such as Nissan were forced to look for financial support. Europe opened itself after decades of painful economic evolution, whereas Asia was forced into opening up because its economic model by and large proved unsustainable over the long run. Regardless, the market for corporate control is now more transparent and active than ever before, and investment banks in the United States and elsewhere probably have a few more fat years to come.

Indeed, Figure 9-4 provides a numerical illustration of capital concentration in different markets, and the trend is unambiguous. In Frankfurt, for example, the 5 percent largest listed companies accounted for 10 percent more of the total listed capitalization in 1998 than in 1997. Except for Nasdaq, where this particular statistic may be explained partly by an active listing of very small companies, everywhere else the primary explanation is a concentration of assets on the balance sheets of fewer and fewer entities.

For the risk arbitrageur, this discussion has several interesting implications. On one side, it is very clear that risk arbitrage opportunities have increased by several orders of magnitude, at least in number. Even if all transactions turn out to be unequally profitable, at least there are many more to choose from. From a relatively quiet and specialized activity, risk arbitrage has risen to the status of an industrial strategy with both more people and more capital committed.

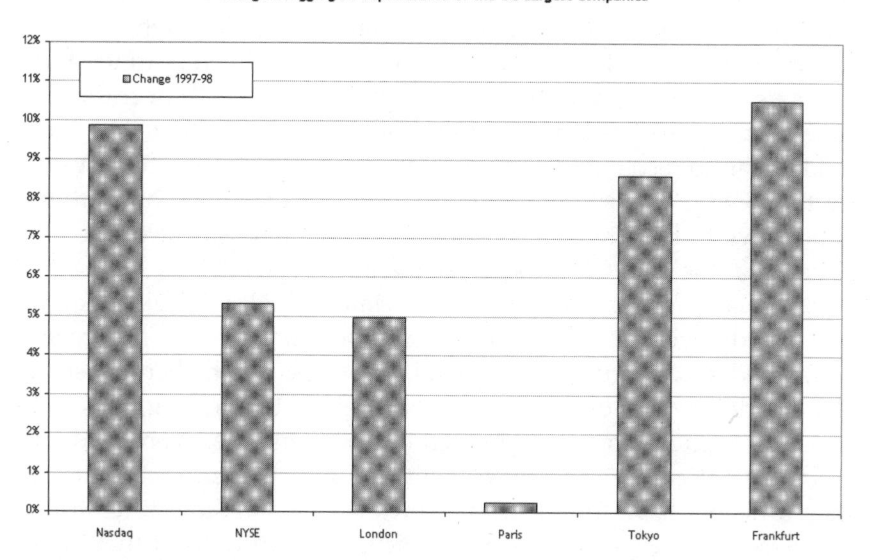

Figure 9-4 The 5 Percent Largest Listed Companies
(*Source*: Compiled by author from FIBV data.)

The second consequence is also relatively positive from an arbitrageur's perspective: The market is expanding and has become truly global over the past few years. A diversified risk arbitrageur should now be able to consider deals in Europe and Asia in addition to the United States, because the financial markets are probably less mature there and consequently opportunities should be more profitable, all else being equal.

Finally, the third consequence points toward more risk as a balance to more opportunities. This particular evolution can be perceived in two areas. On one hand, an accelerated increase in corporate concentration has to draw sooner or later the attention of regulators. Indeed, in the United States as well as Europe, even if bigger deals are occurring more frequently, both the Federal Trade Commission (FTC) and the European Commissioner in charge of monitoring competition within the Union have voiced concern over many proposed transactions, effectively preventing some of them from proceeding because they would have too significantly affected the competitive landscape within their industry. From a pure risk perspective, regulators are one more source of uncertainty, and in fact more and more so. On the other hand, the occurrence of more deals has changed the nature of the game because the average "quality" of each deal has probably decreased, making it more uncertain and risky. The term *acquisition strategy* is, for example, often used as a viable option to "buy growth." Beyond the fact that this view is debatable, integration is a legitimate concern because it is unclear that an acquisition can be digested soon enough and well enough to deliver its promises before the next one is consummated. Even if arbitrageurs are not exposed in any way to the risk that a merger fails over the long run, this delicate question has significantly increased the risk that shareholders fail to recognize the virtues of a particular transaction pushed by their CEO. This situation is more frequent than ever, and arbitrageurs have to be careful in making their own assessment of the likelihood that the deal will proceed as planned.

This last remark raises in fact an interesting ambiguity that we uncovered several times before. The expectations of an arbitrageur are related to the occurrence of a deal, regardless of whether it destroys shareholders' value or decreases social welfare by creating, for example, a de facto monopoly in a given industry. In other words, arbitrageurs do not care in any way about the industrial project, although they probably have to have some sort of understanding of its underlying economics. Here their interest differs radically from that of the investors of each firm, and from that of the investing community, assuming this community is more or less pursuing higher shareholders' value. By arbitraging the merger, they provide a service and make the market more efficient, even if their immediate target may be in direct conflict with the interests of much larger groups of investors.[7]

Profitability

Measuring profitability with risk arbitrage is an exercise more difficult than with index arbitrage. One important difference is the risky nature of the arbitrage. If we want to talk about profitability, we need to discount the results by the riskiness of each particular position, to obtain risk-adjusted returns, assuming we have all the data to make this transformation. In addition, there are less academic studies to offer a starting point for such a measurement. The world of corporate control is extremely well documented, and many researchers have tried to understand all the aspects of corporate events, from the original human or economic motivations to the postintegration life of the company. Still, risk arbitrage as a systematic trading strategy seems to be less documented especially when compared to the wealth of information available for index arbitrage. One possible reason for this difference is that index arbitrage acquired its notoriety essentially in the aftermath of October 1987 as a possible culprit, and again in 1989 under similar circumstances, whereas risk arbitrage was never really under the spotlight of public scrutiny.

It is also difficult to take the approach we have taken for index arbitrage, which is based on empirical observations. Following one index and its futures is easy, but it is much more difficult to follow hundreds or thousands of corporate transactions and extract aggregate information from them. Therefore, we will have to take a somewhat less direct path, and accordingly we will have a less robust estimate.

---

[7] For example, in the takeover battle between Société Générale (SG), Banque Nationale de Paris (BNP), and Paribas in France in 1999, risk arbitrageurs holding positions of Paribas because SG had announced its intention to buy it had later the option to tender these shares to BNP when BNP bid for both SG and Paribas. Although their absolute weight was relatively low, the uncertainty as to whether they would favor one tender to the other was considered a sizable part of the uncertainty surrounding the entire battle.

A number of recent studies show that mergers in general are less successful than many CEOs would like to believe. A recent study by KPMG found that more than half destroyed shareholders' value while another third made no discernible difference. See, for example, "How Mergers Go Wrong," *The Economist*, July 22 2000, for an introduction to a series of six articles on the subject.

The idea here is to use data from hedge funds that are involved in risk arbitrage. Performance data from hedge funds in the United States are relatively straightforward to obtain and provide at least a good indication of the aggregate profitability of this family of funds. Naturally, many hedge funds have flexible charters; therefore, they may report risk arbitrage as the primary focus and trade other strategies episodically. Alternatively, many funds enter risk arbitrage situations when they have a chance to do so—that is, when they hold the appropriate position after trading their "natural" strategy. In any case, we will consider the data as good as they get and extract some results from them.

Table 9-2 shows, for example, the yearly performance of risk arbitrage hedge funds from 1990 to 1999. For example, the annual compounded yield of the entire family of risk arbitrage funds was 8.75 percent from 1990 to 1992 or 13.23 percent over the period 1990 to 1996. The purpose of this table is to get a sense of how stable the results are depending on the period over which a risk arbitrage strategy is applied. When considered over a single year, the strategy generated between 5.18 and 23.48 percent, exhibiting an important variability. Over a six-year period, however, it generated between 13.23 and 14.75 percent, a much narrower interval.

Therefore, it is fair to conclude that on average over a reasonable period of time—that is, three to five years—the yield of a diversified portfolio of risk arbitrage hedge funds would have been between 12 and 15 percent. This is not, however, the expected profitability from a typical risk arbitrage desk because hedge funds are generally lever-

TABLE 9-2

Year	1 Y	2 Y	3 Y	4 Y	5 Y	6 Y
1990						
1991	12.45%					
1992	5.18%	8.75%				
1993	19.66%	12.19%	12.27%			
1994	7.15%	13.23%	10.48%	10.97%		
1995	23.48%	15.03%	16.55%	13.60%	13.37%	
1996	12.53%	17.88%	14.19%	15.53%	13.38%	13.23%
1997	17.37%	14.92%	17.71%	14.98%	15.90%	14.04%
1998	9.18%	13.20%	12.98%	15.52%	13.79%	14.75%
1999	12.84%	10.99%	13.08%	12.94%	14.98%	13.63%

(*Source*: Compiled by author from HedgeFund.Net data.)

aged. Suppose we invest $1 in a fund. If the fund is leveraged 10 to 1, the total nominal of the position is $10. Therefore, a return of $0.10, which would amount to 10 percent on our original investment, represents only 1 percent on the nominal of the trading position. A yield of 12 to 15 percent must be divided by the leverage ratio if we want to provide a measure of profitability consistent with the one we used for index arbitrage—that is, a nominal return. This adjustment introduces a new difficulty because we need to estimate the average leverage of hedge funds dedicated to risk arbitrage, and this is a difficult exercise. Assuming a leverage between 2 and 3, which is probably as good as any other figure, the typical profitability of a risk arbitrage strategy can be estimated roughly between 4 and 7 percent. This is a wider range compared to the results we obtained for index arbitrage, but again the methodology is such that we could not hope for much. In fact, the magnitude is really what we are looking for, and this entire discussion shows that risk arbitrage profitability amounts probably to less than 10 percent—that is, significantly more than index arbitrage that would typically be below 1 percent.[8]

Finally, a few words about the organization of a risk arbitrage position. Whereas index arbitrage is usually run on a very small number of indices, a risk arbitrageur will take more positions, each being relatively small. The total nominal can be sizable, several hundred million dollars, but still below the few billion dollars that would normally be dedicated to index arbitrage. The obvious reason for such a fragmented portfolio is the benefit of diversification with respect to the convergence risk.

RISKS

Convergence

Risk arbitrage is dramatically different from index arbitrage because the convergence at expiry is uncertain. The fact that the convergence

---

[8] These figures are gross returns in the sense that they are not adjusted for the level of risk inherent in the strategy. In reality, the decision to allocate resources to one particular type of strategy depends on the risk aversion and cost of capital of a particular financial institution. For example, although there are literally hundreds of hedge funds dedicated to risk arbitrage, there are almost none dedicated to index arbitrage. The reason is probably that risk arbitrage is more profitable under capital constraints, even on a risk-adjusted basis. Large diversified financial institutions are in general less constrained than other institutions in their access to capital and therefore enjoy a competitive advantage that allows them to engage aggressively in index arbitrage.

fails to materialize can be explained by numerous factors. If the proposed transaction is hostile, for example, the takeover target will naturally try to escape the threat with the consequence that the outcome remains highly uncertain for a very long time, typically until the outcome of a tender offer or a proxy fight is known and made public. Even in the case of a friendly transaction, many difficulties and/or delays may appear along the way. Regulators such as the Federal Trade Commission (FTC) in the United States have to give their go-ahead, which can take some time. Shareholders of one of the parties, who may or may not be entirely satisfied with the proposed terms, might want to force their management team to reconsider or renegotiate the deal. Even unexpected delays in the preparatory work to get the deal done might force some adjustments compared to the planned schedule.

There are really two elements in the convergence, its occurrence and its timing. As far as occurrence is concerned, the case of British Telecom (BT) and MCI Communications (MCI) provides a particularly rich illustration of what may go wrong, and that of Staples (SPLS) and Office Depot (ODP), an example of the intervention power of the FTC to block a transaction. Both will help us understand what the nature of the risk is and how to quantify it. With respect to timing, we will take a more formal approach and introduce the notion of theta, a parameter we used several times before to capture a dependence on time.

BT/MCI

The merger of BT and MCI will probably remain in the history of risk arbitrage as the perfect example of a supposedly great deal turned sour. On paper the proposed transaction made perfect sense on every dimension: The industry, telecommunications, was just ripe for a consolidation worldwide and particularly in the United States after the Telecommunications Act of 1996 virtually ended the monopoly of the Baby Bells on local services. BT was a British carrier, already holding 20 percent of MCI, which indicated that both companies had already had the opportunity to get acquainted with each other while their merger offered new opportunities to build a cross-border giant carrier. Finally, the terms were judged very favorable to MCI shareholders, with an offer 43 percent above the last closing price of MCI before the announcement. There were concerns over regulatory issues from the Federal Communications Commission, but this was the first deal of this nature, and there was no real indication that the industry was in any way too concentrated already.

First words of the merger were leaked to the public on November 1, 1996, before the close of the U.S. market. MCI shot up 23 percent before being suspended by the Nasdaq. This original merger was expected to become effective within a year but eventually never took place as Worldcom (WCOM) made—and won—a competing bid for MCI one year later. To set the stage and gain a more detailed understanding, Table 9-3 contains a short chronology of the facts. It is very clear from the individual performances that the market reacts extremely quickly and sometimes with excess to all announcements regarding the likelihood of a given transaction. However, absolute prices in a situation of risk arbitrage do not tell the entire story because what is really important is the spread between the two stocks and its deviation from par.

Indeed, we indicated on several occasions that the ultimate indicator of the certainty of the convergence was the market—in particular, the market spread—and this is essentially why a mark-to-market valuation is absolutely necessary in addition to a theoretical one, which indicates the expected profit *if all goes well*. As an illustration of this point, consider Figure 9-5, which constitutes a visualization of the chain of events from November 1996 to September 1998. The chart shows the spread between MCI and its implied price in the merger, expressed in percentage terms.[9] The continuous line above the x axis therefore indicates that MCI is trading at a discount compared to its parity with BT. Similarly, the dotted line above the x axis indicates that MCI is trading at a discount compared to its parity with WCOM.

During the period from November 1, 1996, to July 11, 1997, a theoretical valuation of a risk arbitrage position between BT and MCI would have been unable to measure the market appreciation of the likelihood of the deal. It is apparent from the chart that the market was indeed more and more comfortable with the merger, and over a period of eight months the spread narrowed steadily, indicating favorable expectations.

On July 11, suddenly MCI announced it was expecting a $800 million loss in its local phone business, more than twice the amount it originally predicted. Its stock tumbled 21.1 percent following the announcement, while BT remained relatively unchanged in comparison, losing only 6.4 percent. As a result, the spread widened from 4.9 to 16.2 percent.[10] In other words, MCI lost 11.3 percent (= 16.2 percent – 4.9 percent) relative to its implied price in the merger agreement. Risk

---

[9] In other words, the quantity plotted is the difference between the market price and the theoretical price of MCI.

[10] Note that the spread does not widen by 14.7 percent (= 21.1 percent – 6.4 percent) because the ratio between BT and MCI is not 1 for 1 and incorporates a cash portion.

TABLE 9-3

Date	Event	BT	MCI	WCOM
Nov. 1, 1996	MCI announces it has entered merger negotiation with BT, which owns 20 percent of its capital. MCI stock price gains 23 percent before being temporarily suspended. BT agrees to pay $6 in cash and 0.54 share of its ADR for each share of MCI.[a]	−3.7%	20.4%	N/S
Jul. 11, 1997	MCI announces it could lose more than $800 million in its local business and even more in 1998 because of delays in penetrating the local market recently deregulated away from the Baby Bells. MCI announces that it has notified BT that the present outlook is worse than expected.	−6.4%	−21.1%	N/S
Aug. 18, 1997	The *Financial Times* announces that terms for the merger between BT and MCI will probably remain unchanged despite complaints from BT shareholders.	−0.2%	3.3%	N/S
Aug. 20, 1997	BT and MCI announce that they are having discussions on the prospects of both companies. There can be no assurance as to the outcome of the discussions, says MCI.	1.9%	6.0%	N/S
Aug. 21, 1997	BT announces it is revising the terms of the proposed merger, cutting the deal by 16 percent. BT will pay $7.75 in cash and 0.375 share of its ADR. In addition, MCI holders will have to wait one more year before getting dividends from the merged entity.	7.1%	−16.7%	N/S
Aug. 26, 1997	One more MCI shareholder files suit against the merger. This occurrence follows at least six other similar actions.	−2.2%	−3.5%	N/S
Oct. 1, 1997	WCOM unveils a $33.88 billion bid for MCI, at $41.50 a share. WCOM agrees to pay 1.2206 share of its stock for each share of MCI.	8.1%	20.2%	−2.8%

TABLE 9-3 (continued)

Date	Event	BT	MCI	WCOM
Oct. 3, 1997	WCOM files a suit against both BT and MCI to remove MCI's "poison pill" and to remove the $450 million termination fee that would be payable to BT if MCI broke the terms of its agreement with BT.	1.67%	−1.2%	0.5%
Oct. 15, 1997	GTE offers to buy MCI for $40 a share, valuing MCI at $32.5 billion.	3.72%	−3.6%	4.4%
Oct. 16, 1997	MCI announces that MCI and BT have mutually waived a provision in their strategic merger agreement that would have restricted discussions with GTE and WCOM.	1.5%	−1.9%	3.4%
Nov. 10, 1997	WCOM announces that it has sweetened the deal for MCI to $51 a share, or 1.2439 shares of WCOM.	3.3%	−6.4%	12.5%
Nov. 11, 1997	MCI agrees to use its poison pill to block any offer competing with WCOM, and BT also agrees to block competing bids through June 30, 1998, when its right to do so expires. WCOM agrees to pay BT $465 million to end BT's competing purchase agreement with MCI. MCI agrees to a $750 million breakup fee and reimbursement of $465 million if it terminates the agreement. WCOM will pay MCI $1.6 billion if the agreement does not get regulatory and shareholder approvals by the end of 1998 and an additional $750 million for canceling the accord.	−0.6%	−2.4%	0.0%
Sep. 15, 1998	MCI merges with WCOM with a ratio of 1.2439 shares of WCOM for each share of MCI. MCI is delisted from Nasdaq.	N/S	N/S	N/S

[a] British Telecom is listed as an American Depository Receipt (ADR) in the United States. Each ADR is equivalent to 10 ordinary shares.

(*Source*: Compiled by author from Bloomberg and miscellaneous news sources.)

arbitrageurs were naturally exposed unfavorably to this shock, and they lost a significant amount of money on this position. It is easy to estimate what this loss must have been. Assuming an arbitrageur entered the position progressively and steadily from the merger

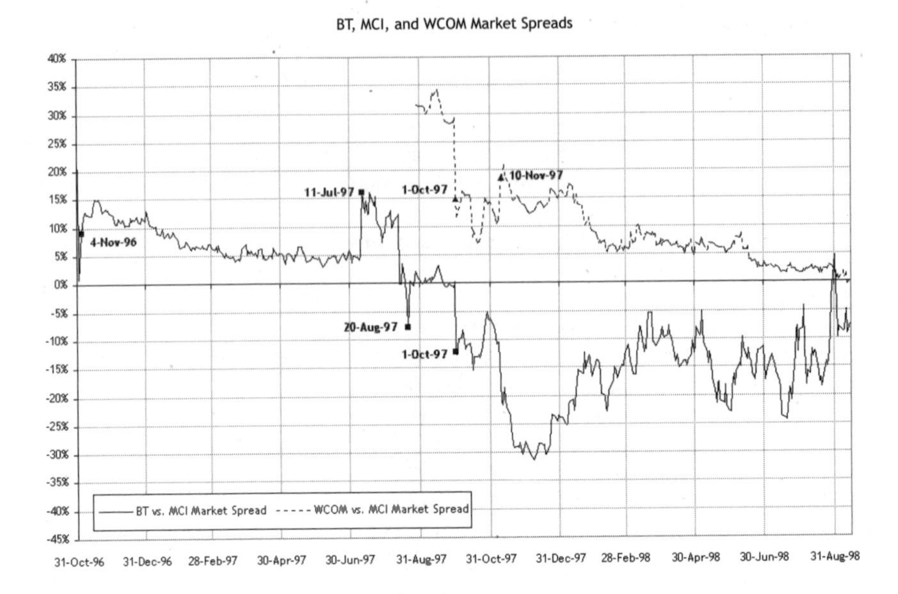

Figure 9-5 BT/MCI
(*Source*: Compiled by author from Bloomberg data.)

announcement onward, the average executed spread in the position is close to the average historical spread between November 1 and July 10. This historical spread is 7.3 percent, which means that a sudden jump to 16.2 percent will generate a loss of 8.8 percent (= 16.2 percent – 7.3 percent) on the entire position. In other words, on a position of $10 million, for example, this move generated a loss of $880,000. Compared to an expected profitability between 4 and 7 percent, a loss of 8.8 percent represents around twice the expected profit.[11]

Naturally, this loss was only a paper loss until the position was actually unwound. In the absence of any change in the terms, arbitrageurs would have been able to make every single dollar back upon completion of the deal. Therefore, by widening the spread, the market indicated very clearly that it believed the merger itself could not proceed as planned. This sentiment grew in amplitude during the following weeks as BT shareholders voiced their concerns very clearly, loud

[11] Note that the loss estimate is probably conservative. In practice, many arbitrageurs could have preferred entering the arbitrage only after it had gained substance, for example, one or two months after the announcement. In that case, the value realized on the arbitrage would have been below 7.3 percent and the loss higher than 8.8 percent.

enough to prompt the two companies to enter additional negotiations about a possible revision of the terms.

The market again gave a very clear indication about the conclusion of these negotiations. During the first week of August, the spread came back remarkably close to 0, which suggested strong expectations that the terms would remain unchanged. In essence, the *Financial Times* only conveyed a very pervasive judgment on August 18 when it ran an article stating exactly that. Strangely enough, however, a relatively conservative joint announcement on August 20 drove both BT and MCI higher, tightening the spread to a negative value. This is somewhat surprising because it indicates that MCI was over its par value in the deal, and this is unusual for such transactions. Clearly, many arbitrageurs were on the sideline at this time and refrained from entering a position before an announcement the next day. Their absence, combined to the uncertainty about possible new terms and speculative buying, led to this situation.

The surprise came on August 21 when BT cut the deal by 16 percent for MCI. This was clearly enough to convince the market of the strength of the deal because the spread remained very close to 0 when corrected for the new terms until the surprise bid of WCOM on October 1. Meanwhile arbitrageurs were now confronted with a situation in which their initial paper loss was being converted to an actual loss. To understand why this is so, consider that we carried a position before August 21 at an executed spread of 7.3 percent. In other words, we bought MCI and sold BT to lock a discount of 7.3 percent in the value of MCI. When MCI lost 16 percent in the new deal, we lost in total 8.7 percent (= 16 percent - 7.3 percent). Because the new deal was most likely final, the market adjusted the spread accordingly, and the 8.7 percent lost on paper was immediately transformed into a pure loss. Arbitrageurs had to adjust the hedge ratio between BT and MCI, effectively taking their loss.

The end of the story is less unusual. WCOM stepped in with a very aggressive bid for MCI, and was joined shortly after by GTE. To secure its bid, WCOM decided to sweeten the deal by almost 20 percent, and finally won the battle and the FCC's approval, merging with MCI on September 15, 1998. Once the situation was cleared and WCOM appeared as the winner, the spread adopted a familiar shape, converging quietly and steadily toward 0.

SPLS/ODP

The failed merger between Staples and Office Depot is also rewarding from a risk management standpoint. More straightforward than BT/

TABLE 9-4

Date	Event	ODP	SPLS
Sep. 4, 1996	Staples announces it will buy rival Office Depot for $3.4 billion in stocks. Holders of Office Depot shares will receive 1.14 shares of SPLS for each of the ODP shares.	28.9%	−3.9%
Sep. 6, 1996	Both parties agree to pay $75 million in breakup fees to the other.	1.9%	0.7%
Nov. 1, 1996	The FTC requests additional information in its examination of the merger.	−3.2%	−4%
Dec. 20, 1996	The *Wall Street Journal* reports that the merger could be delayed or amended because of antitrust questions raised by the FTC.	−1.4%	1.4%
Jan. 13, 1997	The companies announce that they have scheduled simultaneous shareholders' meetings on Feb. 27, 1997 to vote on the merger. The FTC has not informed the companies of any decision regarding the merger.	2%	−3.1%
Feb. 12, 1997	The FTC says it is considering a challenge to the merger unless the companies can convince antitrust enforcers that the combination would not hurt consumers.	−3.1%	2.9%
Feb. 13, 1997	The FTC is talking to companies to see if they are interested in buying superstores that might have to be sold as a condition for the merger. Office Max, number 3 in office supplies, is seen as the most likely buyer.	−1.9%	4.7%
Feb. 17, 1997	Staples and Office Depot said they have agreed with the FTC to extend the antitrust review period from Feb. 25 to Mar. 5.	−2.4%	−4.3%
Feb. 26, 1997	The companies announce that they postponed their shareholder meetings until Mar. 7.	2%	−4%
Feb. 28, 1997	FTC review period extended from Mar. 5 to Mar. 13.	6%	2%
Mar. 4, 1997	"This merger will be completed in one fashion or another," says Staples CEO Thomas Stemberg.	3.1%	4.1%
Mar. 6, 1997	The companies postpone their shareholders' meetings to Mar 14.	1.7%	0%
Mar. 10, 1997	FTC opposes merger by 4-to-1 vote.	−24.3%	−5.4%
Mar. 12, 1997	Staples reaches a tentative agreement with Office Max to sell 63 stores for about $109 million.	19.4%	−5.4%
Apr. 4, 1997	The FTC rejects again the merger proposal, saying that the agreement with Office Max does not resolve antitrust issues. Stemberg says it is "highly likely" that he will fight the FTC's decision in court.	−31.6%	2.9%

TABLE 9-4 (continued)

Date	Event	ODP	SPLS
Apr. 7, 1997	Staples and Office Depot announce they are going to "vigorously contest" the FTC's decision in an expedited court hearing.	12.5%	3.4%
Apr. 9, 1997	FTC files antitrust suit to block the merger.	2.6%	−0.6%
Apr. 14, 1997	U.S. District Judge Thomas Hogan says he will start evidentiary hearing on May 19, hear arguments from lawyers on June 5, and issue a ruling within two weeks.	−2.7%	−0.9%
Apr. 25, 1997	Companies postpone their shareholder meeting again to May 28.	0.9%	−0.3%
May 27, 1997	Companies extend merger agreement until June 30.	−2.2%	−0.6%
May 30, 1997	Merger opposed by eight states, says antitrust official in a court brief.	0%	1.8%
Jun. 18, 1997	Shareholders of both companies approve merger.	0.7%	−1.9%
Jun. 30, 1997	Judge grants order blocking the merger until an antitrust lawsuit can be heard by an FTC administrative law judge. Stemberg admits during hearings that merger was motivated partly by the desire to stop price wars and eliminate competition. "Merger unlikely now," says Office Depot CEO David Fuente.	−19.6%	4.6%
Jul. 2, 1997	Staples and Office Depot formally scrap proposed merger. The *Wall Street Journal* reports estimates of total losses to arbitrageurs around $150 million.	3.2%	−3.7%

(*Source*: Compiled by author from Bloomberg and miscellaneous news sources.)

MCI, it also appeared originally as a very sensible transaction on paper. Staples, the biggest retailer of office supplies, would buy the second largest, Office Depot. The combined entity would benefit from economies of scale, notably in procurement, inventory management, and distribution costs. As with BT/MCI, the market reacted enthusiastically to the announcement before troubles appeared. Table 9-4 is a chronological presentation of the events. Even more than BT/MCI, this merger was a bumpy ride for risk arbitrageurs. To evaluate how bumpy it is again necessary to examine the spread rather than the absolute prices of each party. Figure 9-6 shows the deviation from par in percentage terms for ODP.[12]

---

[12] Again the convention is that if the spread is positive, ODP is trading at a discount.

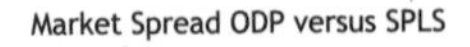

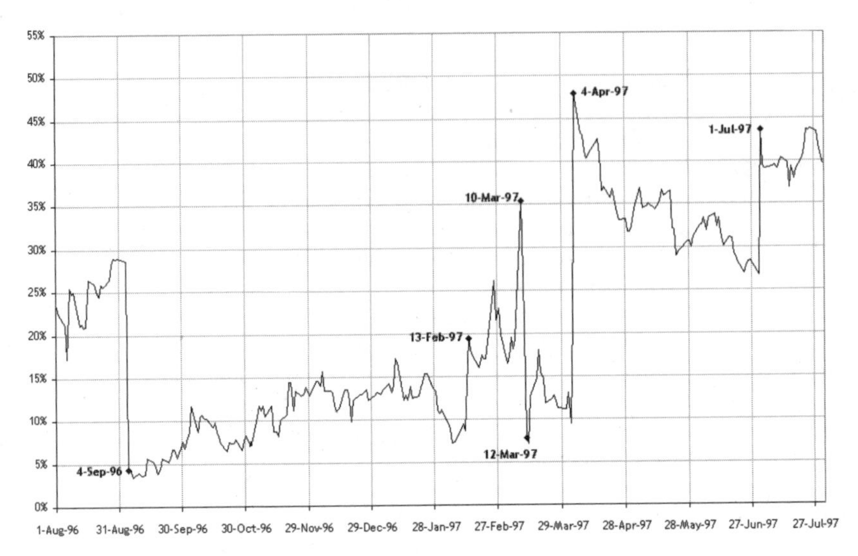

Figure 9-6 SPLS/ODP
(*Source*: Compiled by author from Bloomberg data.)

The chart can be read very easily, and each individual event has a very distinct trace. On September 4, the announcement prompted risk arbitrageurs to aggressively enter the arbitrage. However, instead of narrowing progressively afterward, the spread appears to widen steadily until January 1997, reflecting the ongoing antitrust discussion with the FTC.

The period of March 10 through 12, 1997, is particularly interesting because the spread widened from 20 to 35 percent and came back to 5 percent, all in a matter of days. This type of behavior is even more dramatic than what happened with BT/MCI and illustrates unambiguously an extreme case of "convergence anxiety." Along the same lines, the second rejection by the FTC in April sent the spread 35 percent higher instantly.

Paradoxically, the loss associated to the failed merger is difficult to estimate because a risk arbitrageur had many opportunities to benefit and many more to lose depending on the accuracy of his or her expectations. From September to December 1996, for example, the spread widened steadily, and nothing major happened. Day after day, arbitrageurs, and in fact the market at large, were growing more and more skeptical about the likelihood of the merger's being completed. At this point it was very possible for an arbitrageur to take a position betting on the fact that the merger would be blocked. This is in practice extremely simple to do: Instead of buying Office Depot and selling Staples, an arbitrageur would buy Staples and sell Office Depot.

This type of position, sometimes referred to as *reverse arbitrage*, has potentially a lot of appeal because it is typically a high risk–high reward strategy. Indeed, SPLS/ODP is a brilliant illustration of this point. If toward the end of 1996 an arbitrageur had taken a reverse position, he or she would have executed a spread probably between 10 and 15 percent. If the merger had been approved, this is exactly what he or she would have lost because the spread would have converged back to zero. On the other hand a rejection is likely to widen the spread very suddenly and very significantly, and this is exactly what happened. Playing against the merger therefore had a maximum loss of 10 to 15 percent but an expected profit probably around twice that amount, 25 to 35 percent.

Alternatively, instead of taking a position one way or the other, an arbitrageur could have played the different waves, trying to anticipate the most likely outcome at every juncture. This is naturally a very risky set of bets, and in that situation, judgment, experience, and a solid understanding of the underlying transaction are critical.

Conclusion

These two examples illustrate extremely well all the dangers associated with the convergence hypothesis in a risk arbitrage situation. In both cases the spread jumped all over the place as a result of negative surprises. With respect to our original task, which was to frame the convergence risk and quantify it, they provide a sense of what a "worst case" may look like and how we should look at it.

In essence, we have now an idea of an appropriate way to perform a risk analysis on a risk arbitrage position. If we define $S = P_B - r \cdot P_A$, as the mark-to-market value of the spread on a given time, the convergence risk can be expressed as:

$$R_C = \frac{V(S+\delta) - V(S)}{\delta}$$

This expression is a result of the standard formalism we introduced in the chapter dedicated to risk analysis, except that it is applied to the spread and not to the prices of each stock. In addition, to be representative, δ should be chosen so that the entire spread widens by at least 10 percent *in nominal terms*.

Consider as an example the case of SPLS/ODP. On October 31, 1996, SPLS closed at $18⅝ and ODP at $19⅝. With a ratio of 1.14 SPLS for each ODP, ODP was discounted by 7.6 percent. Its theoretical price in the merger is \$21.23 (= \$18⅝ * 1.14), and its actual price is \$19⅝. The discount is therefore (\$21.23 – \$19.625)/\$21.23 = 7.6 percent.

On this day S was equal to \$1.61 (= 1.14 * \$18⅝ – \$19⅝). To get a realistic evaluation of the divergence risk, we must choose δ so that the spread widens, for example, from 7.6 to 17.6 percent, or more. The 10 percent increase is meant to represent a fair estimation of the possible impact of a negative surprise. We obtain therefore a value of \$3.74 (= 17.6 percent * \$21.23) for S + δ, which implies that $\delta \approx \$2.13$.

To compute R_C, let's assume that we hold a standard position, long 1 share of ODP and short 1.14 share of SPLS. The value of this position is V = 1 * ODP –1.14 * SPLS = -\$1.61 = –S.[13] If the spread widens to \$3.74, V decreases to –\$3.74 and we lost in total \$2.13. Therefore:

$$R_C = \frac{-\$3.74 - (-\$1.61)}{\$2.13} = -1$$

This result comes as no surprise and confirms what we knew before—that is, if we are long ODP, we are exposed to an increase in the spread with the conventions we adopted. Nevertheless, it is an important point to keep in mind that every cent of variation in the spread as quoted by the market gets reflected entirely in the mark-to-market P&L of the position.

Timing

Let's reconsider the expression of CF_1 as the rigorous P&L we expect from a position. If we denote n the number of days to completion when we originally enter the arbitrage, CF_1 can be written as:

$$CF_1 = (r \cdot P_A - P_T) \cdot \left(1 + \frac{n \cdot r_E}{360}\right) - r \cdot \left(\frac{n}{360}\right) \cdot b_A \cdot P_A - r \cdot d_A^* + d_T$$

The next day, we have one day less remaining, so CF_1 naturally becomes:

$$CF_1 = (r \cdot P_A - P_T) \cdot \left[1 + \frac{(n-1) \cdot r_E}{360}\right] - r \cdot \left(\frac{n-1}{360}\right) \cdot b_A \cdot P_A - r \cdot d_A^* + d_T$$

Clearly CF_1 exhibits a dependence on time, precisely on the time remaining to conversion. Consider now that on the day we take the position, a sudden delay appears likely, such that the new number of days to completion is $n' > n$. CF_1 becomes:

[13] Note that this formulation of V is a simplification because, in practice, we would have to compute a rigorous stock valuation, including dividends and borrowing costs. This approximation is innocuous here and allows a much simpler algebra.

$$CF_1' = (r \cdot P_A - P_T) \cdot \left(1 + \frac{n' \cdot r_E}{360}\right) - r \cdot \left(\frac{n'}{360}\right) \cdot b_A \cdot P_A - r \cdot d_A'^{*} + d_T'$$

In all likelihood $CF_1' \neq CF_1$, which means that a profit or a loss is created by the change from n to n'. This P&L is equal to[14]:

$$V_{n \to n'} = CF_1' - CF_1 = (r \cdot P_A - P_T) \cdot \left(\frac{n' - n}{360}\right) \cdot r_E - r \cdot \left(\frac{n' - n}{360}\right) \cdot b_A \cdot P_A$$

which can be written as:

$$V_{n \to n'} = CF_1' - CF_1 = \Theta_C \cdot \left(\frac{n' - n}{360}\right)$$

with:

$$\Theta_C = (r \cdot P_A - P_T) \cdot r_E - r \cdot b_A \cdot P_A$$

The purpose of this exercise is to realize that under most conditions $\Theta_C < 0$, which means that timing is also a parameter to take into consideration when evaluating a convergence risk. The term $(r \cdot P_A - P_T)$ is in general between 2 and 5 percent of $r \cdot P_A$ as we indicated before because this is the market spread, close to the overall level of profitability of a typical position. Therefore, the left part of Θ_C's expression is between 0.12 and 0.30 percent of $r \cdot P_A$ if we take $r_E \approx 6$ percent. This is lower than the right term because A is a scarce resource in an arbitrage situation and borrowing it would probably cost more than 0.30 percent.

Naturally in a period of high interest rates or if the spread $r \cdot P_A - P_T$ is wide, Θ_C may very well turn positive because the benefit of the financing on CF_1 overcomes the added cost associated with carrying the short position in A. However, if the market spread is really wide, we face again a high level of uncertainty, and the possible benefit associated with a change in timing is fairly insignificant with the consequences of a nonconvergence if we expected it. In other words, whenever Θ_C is really meaningful, chances are it is negative, and we don't want to see any delay in the transaction. Consider, as an illustration, SPLS/ODP. In many instances, the spread was so wide that Θ_C would have most likely been positive, but when that happened, the timing was clearly secondary to the antitrust issues and the possibility that the FTC would block the deal entirely.

[14] For simplification purposes we neglect the differences between $d_A'^{*}$, d_A^{*}, $d_T'^{*}$, and d_T^{*}.

Execution

The examples of BT/MCI and SPLS/ODP were used to demonstrate the danger of nonconvergence, but they can also be illustrative of interesting effects in standard merger situations. In particular, a consistent observation in both cases is the fact that the spread is really never equal to zero and always such that the target company is priced at a discount. This is a very frequent situation in practice, even for straightforward mergers completed on time and without any antitrust worry. The merger of Citicorp and Travelers, for example, will confirm the point.

A pervasive positive spread could also be the result of a distortion because we observe only closing prices. It would be very possible to have a spread trading close to zero during the day and closing at a value significantly different from zero. Although there is clearly some of this effect in practice, it does not explain why the spread closes *systematically* positive. The only viable explanation is that the entire market is pricing the spread as systematically positive to account for the noncompletion risk of the merger. Consequently, anybody is in a position to easily execute a positive spread of a few percent at the close, and probably before as well.

In that context it is fair to say that risk arbitrageurs are not under the same pressure to execute their trades as quickly as possible. In contrast to an index arbitrage situation in which opportunities appear and disappear within minutes, a risk arbitrage spread usually exists for months. If a risk arbitrageur has, for example, $10 million to allocate to a particular merger, he or she has the option to trade the spread at any time until the transaction is effective. The typical schedule is to take a reasonable position just after the announcement, trying to benefit from an early adjustment in the market. Afterward there is no need to hurry unless the risk-reward profile of the deal is particularly interesting. Therefore, traders progressively build up their position. In a third phase, typically after shareholders or regulators have approved the merger, there is little to do at interesting prices because the risk is sharply reduced and the spread tends to narrow or disappear.

Naturally this presentation is relatively simplistic. A risk arbitrage is not a money machine in the sense that there is little or no execution skill required. A skilled trader will always make more money than a poor one. However, the nature of the competition between traders is slightly altered. In a situation of absolute convergence, the fastest electronic processing coupled to the fastest order execution system wins the game. In a situation of risk arbitrage, the smartest and most knowledgeable trader has an edge because execution, albeit important, is nevertheless secondary.

Dividends

The dividend risk embedded in a risk arbitrage is by nature different from that associated with index arbitrage. In essence, in an index arbitrage situation each individual stock is diluted within the portfolio. Although there is a clear exposure on each individual component, dividends tend to increase more often than they decrease, which gives some sense of predictability.

In a situation of risk arbitrage, there are really two stocks involved, so the benefit of diversification disappears entirely. If one of the entities decides for some reason to alter its dividend payment after the merger is announced, the arbitrageur will carry an exposure to that change and may have to take a loss. In practice, this situation is not likely to happen because corporations tend to change their dividends only episodically and rarely in the middle of a merger. Nevertheless, the risk exists and should not be ignored. Indeed, BT/MCI offers an example of such a situation. After BT revised the terms of its offer, MCI shareholders had to wait one more year before receiving a dividend from the merged company.

Short Squeezes

Much more important, in contrast, is the risk of short squeeze. The ability of an arbitrageur to build and maintain a position depends entirely on his or her ability to find and sell shares of the acquirer. For this reason in many institutions the activity of risk arbitrage is closely related to the desk in charge of lending and borrowing stocks, and in some instances this is one single trading desk.

A particularly nasty characteristic of a short squeeze is that by nature it happens at the worst moment. We developed this point already, but let's reconsider it for a second. If a trader carries an outright short position in a particular stock, the worst moment for him or her to buy back is when the stock has appreciated sharply. Unfortunately, that is precisely a situation in which a natural holder of the stock would want to sell and in order to do so would have to recall the shares lent out.

For a risk arbitrage position, the risk is very similar. By nature, a merger has usually a very positive impact on the prices of each company. In the case of SPLS or BT, the reaction was minor, but as we will see with Travelers, it can be significant. Furthermore, over the course of the transaction the appreciation is likely to continue if the prospects of the companies are good. Therefore, by virtue of its impact on price, a merger already creates a natural tendency for stock lenders to consider taking their profit. In addition, many investors are naturally looking at the opportunity to arbitrage the deal, which instantaneously transforms the acquirer's stock into a scarce resource, making it more difficult to borrow. As a result, it is certain that if shares are available in the market, they are not cheap, and most probably the original holder will demand the possibility to recall.[15]

From there a short squeeze becomes a very tangible risk. How exactly a squeeze develops is difficult to explain. In general, it gets created by a punctual unbalance in the number of shares available to borrowers and grows very quickly to become a tight squeeze before the situation comes back to normal usually shortly after. Consider, for example, that a strong institutional buyer tries to establish a significant long position in a particular security. If this buyer is legally allowed to lend its portfolio, and if its lending desk is even moderately active, its appearance in the market is absolutely transparent. On the other hand, consider now that this buyer is not allowed to lend these shares. This is the case of certain regulated financial institutions, in the United States as well as elsewhere. The buying could potentially have a strong impact on the stock price, driving it sharply higher. At the same time all the stocks bought by this participant are virtually withdrawn from the loan market. The combination of higher prices and lower supply of shares may create a wave of recall by lenders, which in turn would force short sellers to buy back their positions, driving the price even higher and magnifying the entire loop. The situation comes back to normal when short sellers have closed most of their positions and excess buying pressure disappears. There may naturally be other alternative scenarios. Consider, for example, a stock for which individual investors hold massive short positions. This situation is not frequent but certainly not entirely hypothetical. Individual investors are usually considered less tolerant to risk and losses; therefore, a sharp move up in the stock price could trigger a wave of panic buying driving the price even higher. At a certain point even professionals will get concerned and will want to

[15] Note that in contrast to an outright short, however, a risk arbitrage position is different because the absolute level of price is irrelevant to the arbitrageur. Even if both stocks appreciate sharply, the position will not lose as long as the spread remains close to where it was when the position was initiated.

cut their losses, creating the perfect environment for a squeeze to develop.[16]

How risk arbitrageurs react to a short squeeze is entirely dependent on the ability of their stock loan traders to find and keep a reasonable number of shares through the squeeze because there is really no way to hedge this risk. In turn, this ability is highly dependent on the network of relationships patiently woven between stock loan traders and institutional lenders. Typically these lenders are institutions with large equity portfolios and a very low turnover—for example, pension funds and insurance companies. Therefore, traders most likely to survive a squeeze are those already close to those institutions. In that respect, it is quite certain that large investment banks, notably in the United States, enjoy a clear advantage because of decades of relationship building in the natural conduct of their business.

ILLUSTRATION

CCI/TRV

The merger of Citicorp with Travelers in 1998 is a very straightforward example of a standard situation. On April 6, 1998, Travelers (TRV) announced a merger agreement with Citicorp (CCI), and the news sent the two companies' stocks sharply higher. TRV rose by 18.5 percent from $61\frac{11}{16}$ to $73\frac{1}{16}$, and CCI rose by 26.3 percent from $142\frac{7}{8}$ to $180\frac{1}{2}$. The economic project was to create a giant diversified financial institution, capable of serving the needs of corporate and individual customers covering the entire spectrum. For TRV, traditionally in the insurance market, the merger with CCI came after the acquisition of Salomon Brothers in mid-1997. Salomon brought a culture of proprietary trading and a wealth of expertise in understanding risk and financial markets. The more traditional banking aspect was missing, however, to provide TRV with enough products to offer a one-stop solution to its customers, and this is exactly what CCI brought to the negotiation table.

---

[16] Naturally the probability of a short squeeze is also highly dependent on the maturity of the market at large. In the United States and in other developed markets stock loans are common and well understood, therefore, liquidity is high and squeezes infrequent.

Clearly, the market read the proposed association as extremely beneficial, and the fact that both companies rose indicates that many investors believed the combined entity had significant opportunities to grow. The merger was never questioned by antitrust authorities, and the entire transaction was wrapped up in six months, an impressive achievement considering the size of the contenders.

The deal was an exchange of 2.5 shares of TRV for each share of CCI. Figure 9-7 presents a broad view of the spread before and after the announcement.[17] Not surprisingly, the spread remains very stable and very low immediately after announcement, as we will see in a magnified view shortly. More interesting here is the shape of the chart during the 12 months preceding the announcement. The upward slope indicates that CCI lost around 40 percent of its value compared to TRV from March to December 1997, after which the relative prices of the companies stabilized.

This particular situation offers some insight into the backstage mechanics of the merger. To TRV, probably already focused on the

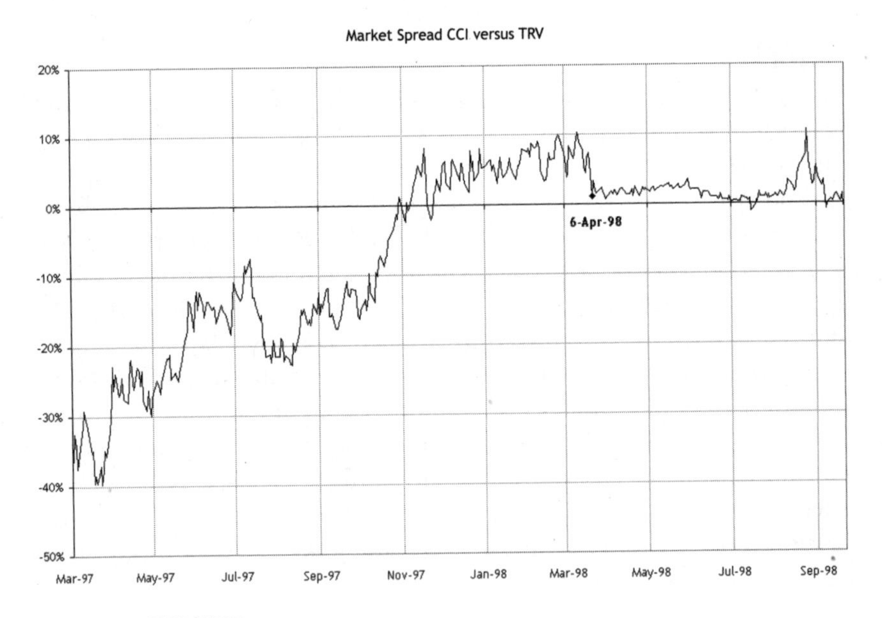

Figure 9-7 CCI/TRV
(*Source*: Compiled by author from Datastream data.)

[17] In agreement with the convention we have adopted so far, the chart plots the discount of CCI compared to its price in the offer. Therefore, the line is above the x axis when CCI is trading below its price in the offer.

next acquisition after Salomon, the depreciation of CCI made it an increasingly interesting target candidate because it was cheaper to finance through a stock swap. At the end of 1997 and well into 1998, it appeared that the spread stabilized, indicating that the market did not have any strong view any more about the prospects of TRV compared to those of CCI. The offer came only a few months after, and this is probably not a pure coincidence. If TRV was aggressively looking to consolidate its position in the banking industry, CCI was considerably cheaper because its own stock had appreciated tremendously. On the day of the announcement, the terms were such that TRV paid a premium close to 10 percent for CCI, as is apparent in the chart. This was still much cheaper than a year before, and it was only possible because the deal was a stock swap, which meant that TRV could enjoy the rich currency provided by its own stock.[18]

After the announcement, the spread remained very close to its par value, providing opportunities only around a few percents. Figure 9-8 is a magnification of the period from April 6 to October 7, 1998. There

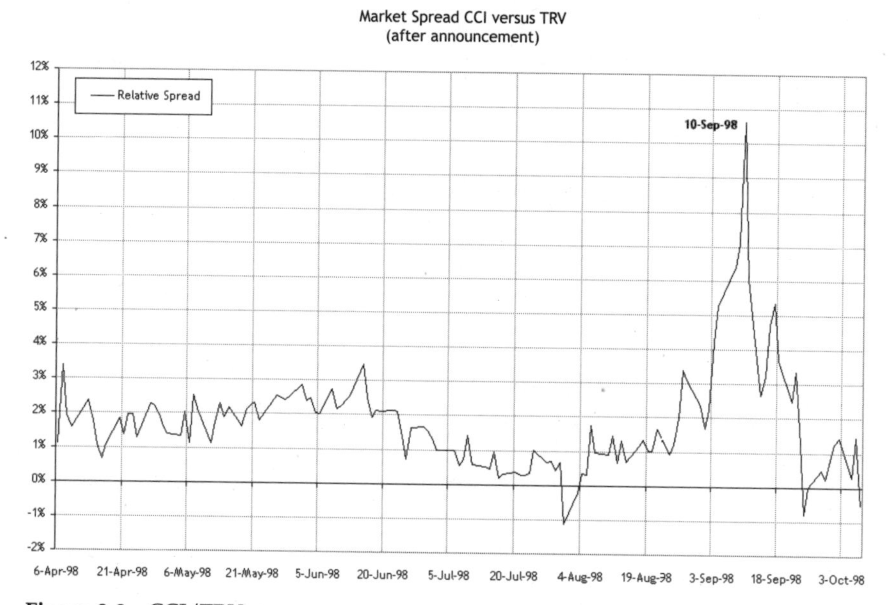

Figure 9-8 CCI/TRV
(*Source*: Compiled by author from Datastream data.)

---

[18] For a variety of reasons, a stock swap is more interesting than a cash tender. For example, in the United States it is usually considered a nontaxable event whereas a tender offer is generally assimilated to an extraordinary dividend and taxed at the income rate.

is a clear narrowing around July because market participants were getting extremely confident that the merger would proceed with the proposed terms. Again this is normally what happens in a fairly standard merger when the deal is proceeding smoothly. Interestingly, however, the later part of 1998 seems to be much more chaotic, and this divergence was the result of the Russian crisis.

In September 1998 Russia virtually defaulted on its sovereign debts and obligations, sending a wave of panic throughout the world. The first targets for massive selling were naturally multinational banking and financial institutions, among which were TRV and CCI. Because CCI was traditionally more involved in banking and lending, the market hammered its stock much more heavily than that of TRV, widening the spread considerably. Consider Figure 9-9, a chart of CCI, TRV, and the S&P 500 during the largest part of the crisis. The market at large suffered, and the S&P lost between 10 and 12 percent before recovering. Banks, however, aggregated much more concern because of the nature of their business, and as a result CCI, for example, lost up to 40 percent in a few weeks. On September 10, when uncertainty about the exact state of Russia's treasury was the highest, CCI lost considerably compared to its price in the merger, probably on worries that TRV

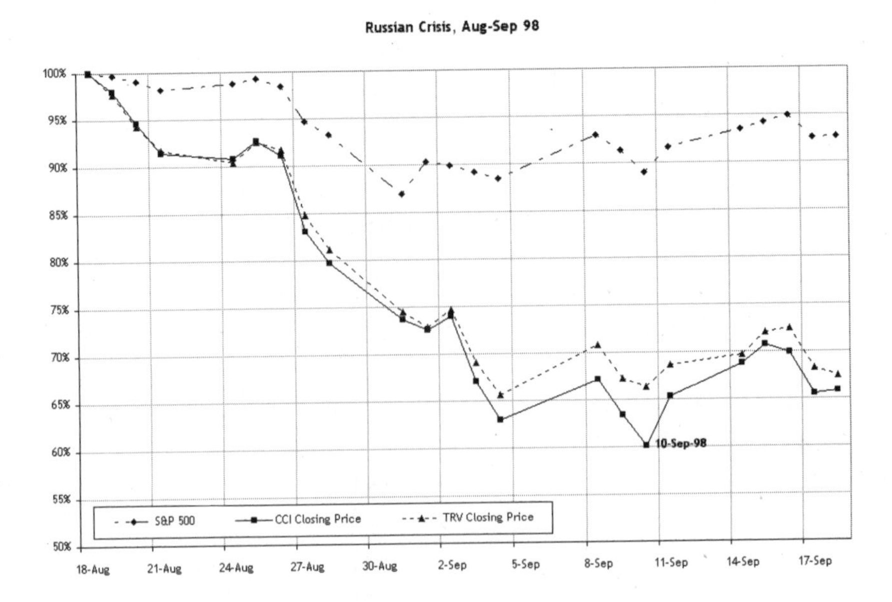

Figure 9-9 CCI/TRV
(*Source*: Compiled by author from Datastream data).

would revise its bid. This appeared to a large extent as a possible replay of BT/MCI one year before.

In contrast to BT/MCI, however, none of the parties really entertained the option of revising the deal, probably because the Russian crisis did not transform itself into a worldwide cataclysm and certainly also because the merger was too advanced. Therefore, arbitrageurs or investors who accepted the risk and entered the merger on September 10 or close to that date ended up with an exceptional reward two months later when the deal effectively closed.

HSBC/CCF

The acquisition of Crédit Commercial de France (CCF) by Hong-Kong and Shanghai Bank (HSBC) in July 2000 was also an example of a fairly straightforward transaction. It proceeded relatively smoothly from the date on the announcement but presented, however, two interesting particularities. First and foremost, the deal implied that one of the last large independent French banks would be acquired by a foreign competitor. Considering the traditional role of the French central bank in monitoring the national banking industry, there was no assurance that the original indication of interest from HSBC could at some point evolve into a clear-cut tender offer. The second point is the fact that CCF was quoted in Paris and HSBC in London, which created a foreign exchange exposure in addition to the particularities associated with the liquidation on the French stock exchange.

The story starts on December 12, 1999, when ING, the biggest Dutch financial-services company, made public a bid it had extended to the CCF board, at €137.5 per share. ING at that time held already 19.2 percent of the bank's capital, and considered the merger as an opportunity to expand its network and business in France. In front of the supposed lack of enthusiasm from CCF's board, ING withdrew its offer the next day. CCF's stock closed at €126 on that day, a gain of 5.2 percent. The prevalent feeling at that time was that the offer was not really dead, but negotiations were being taken away from public scrutiny.

Indeed, ING revived its bid on March 16, 2000, extending the offer until May 30. CCF's shares rose 11.2 percent to close at €124, still fairly low compared to the offer of €137.5. One of the reasons that the gap remained so large is the French regulation that required ING to obtain official approval before increasing its stake in CCF above the threshold of 20 percent. The approval was dependent upon a number of factors, including the fact that the offer should be friendly and therefore agreeable to CCF shareholders.

On April 1, HSBC made a surprise offer for CCF, valued significantly higher the terms proposed by ING. HSBC proposed €150 in cash or 13 shares of its stock, which amounted to €160 considering the price of HSBC and the exchange rate between the British pound and the euro. CCF shares rose 16.2 percent to close at €151.7. ING announced very happily that it was accepting the offer and would tender its share to HSBC. HSBC indicated that it had support from 58 percent of CCF shareholders, and both parties presented the deal as a friendly opportunity to complement each other's line of business. The transaction was cleared by the Banque of France on May 31, and the tender offer was officially extended on June 7 for 25 business days until July 12.

Figure 9-10 illustrates the unfolding of the transaction through the price of CCF shares from December 1999 to July 2000. The two offers from ING are clearly visible, and this is even more true of the HSBC bid on April 3, 2000. Note also the massive increase in trading volume on that particular day and more generally the fact that the volume is definitely higher after the announcement.

A second chart, Figure 9-11, will give us a more detailed view of the spread just after the announcement. The spread is remarkably close to zero until June 23, even though the offer is open until July 12. June 23 is in fact the last trading day of June for which delivery is assured. An

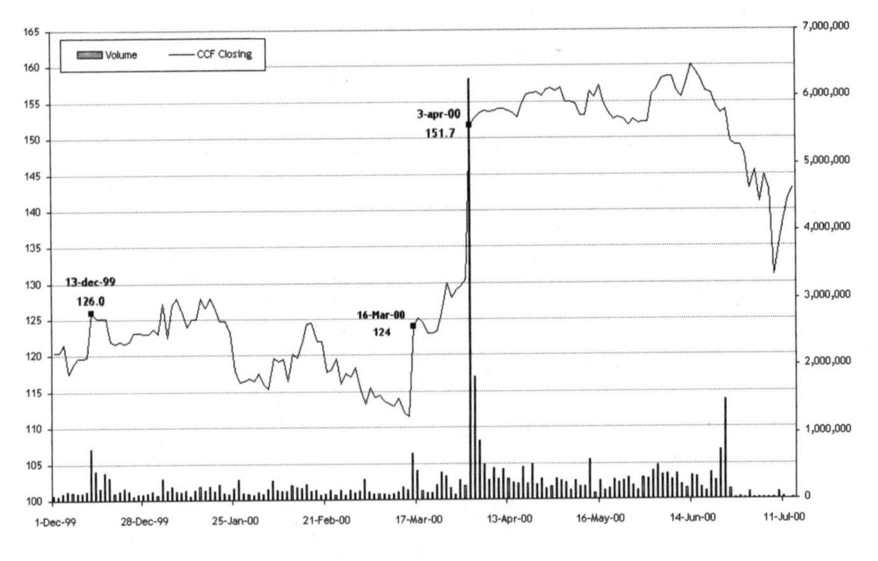

Figure 9-10 HSBC/CCF
(*Source*: Compiled by author from Bloomberg data.)

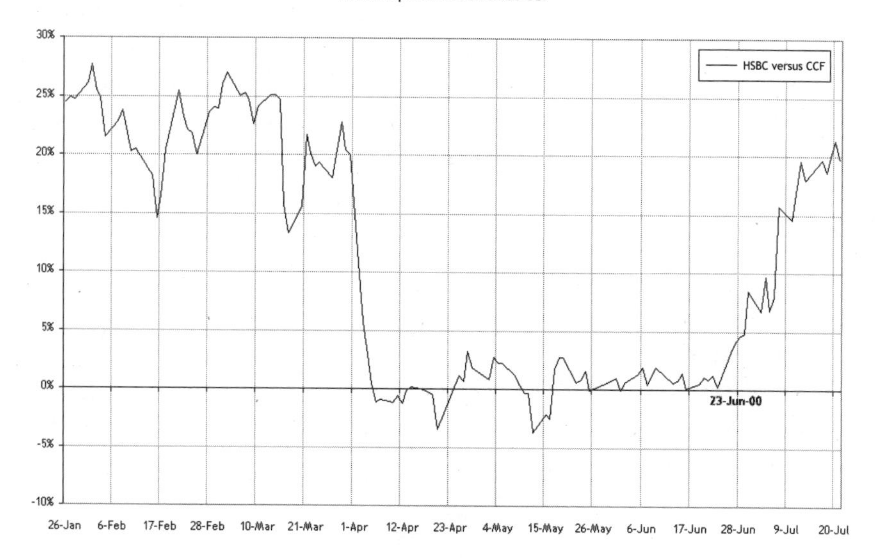

Figure 9-11 HSBC/CCF
(*Source:* Compiled by author from Bloomberg data.)

investor buying CCF on or before June 23 will physically receive the shares on June 30, which is the settlement day for the liquidation of June. Because shares must be physically in the possession of an investor to be tendered to HSBC, June 23 is the last day on which shares can be acquired and delivered. After that day, if the offer is successful, HSBC has full discretion as to the terms of the remaining shares outstanding that it does not own. The results of the offer were made public on July 24, and HSBC successfully tendered 74.6 percent of CCF outstanding shares. Combined with the shares it already owned, HSBC controlled 98.6 percent of CCF's capital.[19]

In addition to the liquidation process, this merger offers an additional curiosity in the sense that it is a cross-border transaction. To enter the arbitrage, traders had to sell HSBC in London and buy CCF in France. Technically speaking, execution presents no particular

[19] Note that the 1.4 percent remaining constitutes an interesting opportunity. To complete its acquisition, HSBC will have to buy these shares. If it does extend terms equal to those of the original offer, then shares acquired after June 23 at a substantial discount could be tendered for a huge profit. There is a chance, however, that HSBC will propose less favorable terms because holders will have no choice but to exchange their shares. The CCF discount after June 23 is the result of this uncertainty.

difficulty, except that the two stocks are not settled in the same currency. To understand how this particular situation affects the arbitrage, let's reconsider the generic diagram in Figure 9-12.

We introduce the second currency through a different interest rate and a foreign exchange rate. $r_E^€$ and $r_E^£$ denote respectively the relevant interest rate for the euro and British pound, and $f_{€/£}$ and $f'_{€/£}$ the spot exchange rate on t_0 and t_1.

On t_0:

- Buy 1 share of T at P_T.
- Secure a borrowing of r shares of A until the expiry at b_A.
- Sell r shares of A at P_A.
- Exchange $r \cdot P_A$ for $r \cdot P_A \cdot f_{€/£}$.

These operations generate a set of cash flows $CF_0^£$ and $CF_0^€$ equal to:

$$CF_0^£ = r \cdot P_A - r \cdot P_A = 0$$
$$CF_0^€ = r \cdot P_A \cdot f_{€/£} - P_T$$

$CF_0^£$ is equal to zero by construction, and $CF_0^€$ will most probably be positive, if P_T is below its par value in the deal.[20] We assume that we lend this amount at $r_E^€$ until the expiry.

On t_1:

- Receive r shares of A from the exchange of T.
- Deliver r shares of A to the original lender.
- Pay borrowing fee $\mathrm{r} \cdot b_A \cdot P_A$.
- Pay accumulated dividends on A to original lender: $r \cdot d_A^* = r \cdot (1 + r_A^£) \cdot d_A$.
- Receive $CF_0^€ \cdot (1 + r_E^€) = (r \cdot P_A \cdot f_{€/£} - P_T) \cdot (1 + r_E^€)$.

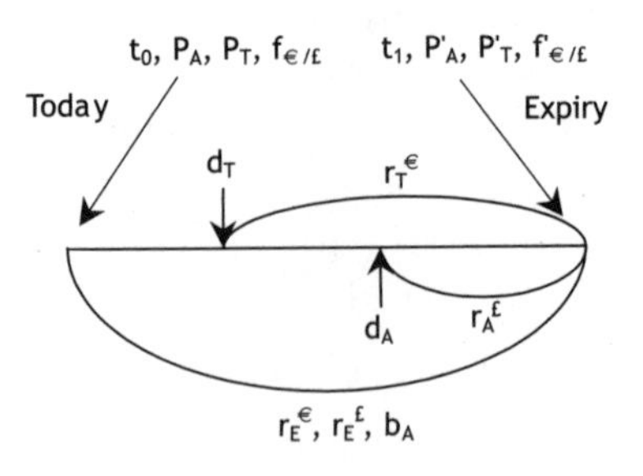

Figure 9-12 ADR

[20] Note that we took implicitly the perspective of a French investor who does not want to carry a position in pounds. Alternatively, a British investor would probably not want to carry a position in euros.

- Receive accumulated dividends on $T : d_T^* = (1 + r_T^€) \cdot d_T$.

The cash flows $CF_1^£$ and $CF_1^€$ are:

$$CF_1^£ = -r \cdot b_A \cdot P_A - r \cdot d_A^*$$
$$CF_1^€ = (r \cdot P_A \cdot f_{€/£} - P_T).(1 + r_E^€) + d_T^*$$

The final P&L is therefore equal to:

$$CF^€ = (r \cdot P_A \cdot f_{€/£} - P_T) \cdot (1 + r_E^€) + d_T^* - (r \cdot b_A \cdot P_A + r \cdot d_A^*) \cdot f'_{€/£}$$

This expression is less simple than the original one, and it has two implications:

- The spread is now $r \cdot P_A \cdot f_{€/£} - P_T$ to reflect the fact that P_A is in British pounds.
- The term $(r \cdot b_A \cdot P_A + r \cdot d_A^*) \cdot f'_{€/£}$ indicates that dividends and the borrowing fee on A are potentially subject to a foreign exchange risk because $f'_{€/£}$ is unknown until the expiry. One way to hedge this risk is to enter a foreign exchange forward transaction for the appropriate amount.

In short, the position is exposed to the foreign exchange through dividends and borrowing fees, not because of the spread itself, which means that the magnitude of the exposure is probably relatively low. To execute the arbitrage, in practice we simply need to exchange an amount equal to $r \cdot P_A$ every time we trade A and T and hedge the future payments of dividends and borrowing fees. A cross-border arbitrage requires a little bit more discipline than a regular situation because of one more variable, the exchange rate, but the general principles hold unchanged.

CONCLUSION

Risk arbitrage is a very active strategy nowadays, and the examination we just performed should give a sense of why this is so. First, returns are higher than index arbitrage, or absolute convergence situations in general, requiring much less capital to start with. Deals are plentiful, and although this may not last forever in the United States, Europe and Asia are only beginning their individual consolidation. Finally, risk is fairly simple to understand and monitor, notably because of the fact that generally only two securities are involved in a given position. It is no surprise, therefore, that more and more capital finds its way to risk arbitrage hedge funds, making the environment more and more competitive and, hopefully, the market more efficient.

10

PAIR TRADING AND TECHNICAL TRADING

INTRODUCTION

Pair trading is a well-known and very simple strategy. It is based on the assumption that a large part of the information affecting stock prices is more related to the industry sector than it is to a particular corporation. In other words, stocks within the same industry group tend to behave in a similar way, and any sudden divergence in their prices is likely to disappear in the very short term. It is then possible to take a position by entering the spread when it is sufficiently wide, expecting a correction. By extension, this strategy can be applied to any pair of companies that are believed to behave in a similar way, even if they are operating in distinct industries. In essence, it is exactly similar to a situation of risk arbitrage without the existence of a corporate event to force convergence.

Therefore, it is no surprise that pair trading in general is considered highly speculative, except in very particular situations like Royal Dutch (RD) and Shell (SC), which we will examine shortly. This type of trading is hardly an arbitrage, although it is sometimes referred to as one. The reason behind the confusion is that pair traders in general have a very strong discipline in monitoring their risks as a consequence of the lack of certitude about the outcome of their day-to-day transactions. Therefore, strictly speaking, the risk of losing very large amounts episodically is relatively low because the traders exercise strict self-discipline, but the illusion is that the strategy is "risk free." On the other hand, the possibility of losing systematically a little bit on every trade—if only because of transaction costs—is extremely real, and being successful at trading pairs is not necessarily easy.

Not surprisingly, pair trading comes in many shapes and forms. If pairs are carefully chosen within identical industry groups and rigorously analyzed with respect to their business models and cost and revenue structures, chances are that a hypothetical convergence will have a lot of substance and as a result will present an attractive risk-reward profile. In that type of situation, a trader will typically follow a small number of pairs, making sure that he or she has backed his or her assumptions with adequate fundamental information about the companies. An alternative procedure is to be more systematic—for example, choosing pairs based on a strictly statistical criterion and trading as often as possible with small positions in order to spread the risk over a large number of convergence patterns. The extreme form of trading in that area is *statistical arbitrage*, a strategy based on trying to take advantage of observed historical patterns, usually for small but numerous positions.

Technical trading is a continuation of the same set of ideas. Traders are typically looking for price patterns in the market, but instead of hedging them with another instrument, which would transform their position in a relative value portfolio, they often keep the position globally unhedged, although they may carry long and short at the same time. In fact, this definition is vague enough to include virtually every strategy based on some sort of pattern analysis, without the explicit knowledge of a convergence, provided the pattern is reasonably stable to give some support to the idea that the strategy is less risky than an outright exposure to the market.

Because trading strategies are so diverse when we move away from traditional forms of convergence, it is naturally more difficult to propose general rules and insights. As a result, the discussion in this chapter will probably appear less focused and less conclusive than before. This is also a reflection of what is happening in real life for new or junior traders. Starting as an index or risk arbitrageur is relatively easy because the market provides some guidance and the techniques are well known. In contrast, traders who want to explore new grounds have to rely above all on their judgment and experience to find new ideas and transform them into profitable trades.

We will give here several relevant examples of common trading strategies, trying to understand what is the general idea behind each of them and what this idea implies in terms of risk. We will start by considering simple and robust examples of pair trading and proceed to more speculative trading.

SPECULATIVE ARBITRAGE

If we refer again to the convergence continuum introduced in the first section, we can infer several characteristics about what a situation of speculative arbitrage would induce in terms of risk and profitability. Table 10-1 presents an overview of a convergence framework applied to both pair trading and technical trading distinctly. It is quite natural that the absence of a convergence behind a particular position virtually voids the meaning of a theoretical valuation. In other words, there is no basis in postulating that the market is actually mispricing a particular set of instruments until the mispricing has been confirmed—that is, it ceases to exist.

For the same exact reason, we cannot consider any hypotheses that a particular trader uses as having any sort of applicability to another market participant. Naturally in a period of rising interest rates, for example, banks will tend to suffer, and obviously all traders quite

TABLE 10-1

Convergence	Absolute	Hypothetical	Pair Trading	Speculative Arbitrage
Valuation	Theoretical	Mark to market	Theoretical meaningless	Theoretical meaningless
Convergence type	Public	Highly proprietary	Proprietary models	Proprietary models
Convergence risk	Low to non-existent	Critical	Critical	Critical
Execution risk	Critical	Low	Medium	Medium to low
Hedge	Fixed quantity	Fixed quantity or delta	Usually fixed quantity	Usually nominal but some-times no hedge at all
Risk of carry	Important	Low	Low	Low
Time horizon	Known or bounded	Unknown	Uncertain, usually short (few weeks)	Uncertain, situation specific
Window of opportunity	Very short	Longer	Reasonably long	Situation specific
Profitability	10×1	1×10	Situation specific, often closer to 1×10	Situation specific, often closer to 10×1 for better risk control
Robustness	Strong	Weak	Medium to weak	Weak
Implications	Pricing	None (Inefficient market?)	None	None

probably share the same view because it is a result of the economic structure of a bank. Therefore, the assumption that rising interest rates will probably cause a decline in banks' share prices is widely shared and certainly not proprietary in any way. Yet the implementation of an idea based on this observation is likely to differ from one participant to the next. One trader will probably take an outright short on the sector, another will take a short but hedge it with a broad-based index, and a third one might want to trade pairs where the long side is expected to be somewhat more resistant to higher interest rates than the short side. Regardless of the specifics, most trading strategies in the area of speculative arbitrage are highly proprietary, and usually the brainchild of one particular trader or group of traders. With pair trading, the proprietary nature is probably less pronounced because common sense supports the idea that similar businesses tend to evolve in a similar way. In fact, many studies of competitiveness have shown that over long periods of time, competitive convergence is a very strong and active force, eventually bringing all competitors within a similar framework characteristic of the economic fundamentals of the particular sector in which they operate. Therefore, a pair trading strategy based on such a fundamental view is likely to produce somewhat similar trades on distinct trading desks.

The most important consequence of a lack of certainty about the outcome of a particular trade is that convergence is really the only risk that matters. *Convergence* here is to be taken in a broad sense. In the case of pair trading, it obviously means that the spread will narrow compared to its value when we originally entered the position.[1] For technical trading, *convergence* means only that the pattern underlying each trade is robust enough to be recurrent. In some cases in which the position is held for a long period of time—that is, several months—borrowing might be an issue and a short squeeze a concern. Along the same lines, the financing of the position may create an additional P&L in some cases—for example, if one leg is a cash instrument and the other a leveraged derivative. Overall, however, convergence is really the most uncertain parameter, and the one that will essentially trigger all decisions, in and out. All other risks, which we termed *risk of carry*, are really secondary.

---

[1] Note that we could also take a reverse position in which we are betting on the spread widening between two different stocks. We will consider this situation in our examples.

As for hedging, the right choice for a speculative arbitrage is dependent on the specific details of that strategy. By and large, pairs are frequently hedged with a fixed quantity method and usually technical positions with a nominal hedge.[2] These are, however, not absolute rules because the underlying pattern dictates the appropriate hedge.

Let's now examine in more detail opportunities and profitability.

OPPORTUNITIES AND PROFITABILITY

Opportunity

For pair or technical trading, it is an understatement to say that opportunities are plentiful. Only in the United States are there more than 5,000 listed companies, and including the five largest markets we concentrate on, the total number is probably close to 10,000. Any combination of these is a candidate for a pair analysis, even if the large majority will probably never lead anywhere. In terms of technical trading, the choice is vast as well. Over the last 20 years, numerous new technical indicators have been proposed, and arguably the ones that have survived and become part of the standard analysis toolkit probably have some value and some interesting informational content. In short, when the assumption of convergence is left behind, imagination is the only limit as to what is possible to try. Nowadays impressive resources, human as well as computational, are dedicated to the specific goal of designing a profitable strategy with an acceptable risk profile.[3] It is no surprise then that the universe to choose from is quite important already and growing every day as new traders experiment with more and more computational power.

To get a sense of what the most classical technical trading strategies are, here is a short list extracted from an academic paper published in

[2] The expression *nominal hedge* in that context means that at a given time, the total nominal long is chosen equal to or close to the total nominal short. The quantities of each individual security may or may not change from one day to the next, or even within the same trading session, but in general, the portfolio is kept relatively balanced to avoid an outright exposure.

[3] For an illustration of this point, consult, for example, the list of the 500 most powerful supercomputers installed in the world, available from www.top500.org. Finance is not the first industrial application, but it appears regularly side by side with telecommunications, automotive, aerospace, chemistry, and the like.

the *Journal of Finance*.[4] The purpose of the paper was to determine if technical trading can beat the market, and we will certainly come back to the results. Meanwhile, the authors studied 7,486 trading rules—an impressive number although a lot of these were obtained by varying parameters without changing the underlying principle of the rule. The rules can be partitioned into the following categories:

- *Filter*: A position is taken if a stock moves up by more than x percent, until a reverse move occurs on the downside with an amplitude above x percent. At that time the position is unwound and an additional short is taken. In essence, the signals are alternatively long or short following the occurrence of a move of amplitude x percent.[5]
- *Moving average*: A position is taken following the crossover of the closing price of a stock with a moving average, or the crossover of two moving averages of different periodicity.[6]
- *Support and resistance*: Buy when the closing price exceeds the maximum price over the past n days, and sell when the closing price is lower than the minimum over the past n days.[7]
- *Channel breakout*: A channel is formed when the high over the previous n days is within x percent of the low over the previous n days. A breakout on the upside is a buy signal, and vice versa for the shorts.[8]
- *On-balance volume averages*: The on-balance indicator is based on the volume traded. Volume is added to the prior value of the

[4] R. Sullivan, A. Timmermann, and H. White, "Data Snooping, Technical Trading Rule Performance, and the Bootstrap," *Journal of Finance*, 54, p. 5. References in footnotes 5, 6, 7, and 8 are extracted from the article. Incidentally, note the years the rules were originally proposed—1966, 1935, 1910, and 1922—which tells a lot about the never-ending effort to outsmart the market. See also W. Brock, J. Lakonishok, and B. LeBaron, "Simple Technical Trading Rules and the Stochastic Properties of Stock Returns," *Journal of Finance*, 47. See also Andrew Lo, Harry Namaysky, and Jiang Wang, "Foundations of Technical Analysis: Computational Algorithms, Statistical Inference and Empirical Implementation," National Bureau of Economic Research, Working Paper N. 7613, March 2000, for other articles on the same subject.

[5] See, for example, E. Fama and M. Blume, "Filter Rules and Stock Market Trading," *Journal of Business*, 39, 1966, for a definition and examination of these rules.

[6] See, for example, H. M. Gartley, *Profits in the Stock Market* (Pomeroy, Wash.: Lambert-Gann Publishing, 1935).

[7] See, for example, R. Wyckoff, *Studies in Tape Reading* (Burlington, Vt.: Fraser Publishing Company, 1910).

[8] See, for example, W. Hamilton, *The Stock Market Barometer* (New York: Harper and Brothers Publishers, 1922).

indicator if the stock closed up, but it is subtracted otherwise. A moving average crossover is then applied to the indicator.

Clearly, these are very classical rules in the sense that even an inexperienced investor is aware of them. To this list should be added the many more that nobody will ever hear about because a trader is actually making a living trading them.

Another illustration of the same idea on the diverse nature of speculative arbitrage can be found in the statistics on hedge funds. Table 10-2 gives a summary of the capital allocated to different relative value strategies. Relative value arbitrage on equity distinct from risk arbitrage accounts for more than half the total capital allocated. Naturally it is difficult to know what is exactly behind the different denominations, but in all likelihood it is either pair trading or some sort of technical trading in its largest sense.

In conclusion, it is fair to say that it is difficult to qualify exactly the opportunities associated with strategies based on some sort of assumed convergence pattern. Overall, however, they probably account for the biggest part of the total capital allocated throughout the world to equity "arbitrage" other than index and risk arbitrage.

Profitability

The academic study we mentioned above was specifically designed to determine if technical trading could beat the market and if so, by what order of magnitude. The study aimed at a rigorous analysis by correcting its results for a common bias in designing and back testing trading

TABLE 10-2

Strategy	Assets ($ millions)	Partition
Convertible arbitrage	$1,865	
Fixed-income arbitrage	$1,584	
Options arbitrage	$778	
	$4,227	27.3%
Market neutral	$4,165	
Statistical arbitrage	$1,440	
Other relative value	$2,627	
	$8,232	53.3%
Risk arbitrage	$3,001	19.4%
Total	$15,460	100%

(*Source*: HedgeFund.net, November 1999, reprinted with permission.)

models: "data-snooping." *Data snooping* refers to the danger of fitting the data to a particular model and then claiming that the model is indeed very profitable. For example, assume you are testing a model over the period 1998 to 2000, and you find out the best value for a given parameter, such that the strategy yields 15 percent over the two-year period. Associating this particular strategy to a yield of 15 percent going forward would be a logical error because 15 percent was obtained by optimizing a parameter today when all historical data are known, something that would have naturally been impossible if the strategy had been traded every day.

Accounting for this bias, the authors make the following two conclusions:

- Applied to the Dow Jones index for the period 1897 to 1996, the best rule given by their selection process yields 17.2 percent in annualized average return, while a buy-and-hold strategy yields 4.3 percent over the same period. This rule is a very simple five-day moving average with a 0.001 band.[9]
- When the best trading rule is determined from the period 1897 to 1986 and applied to the following 10 years 1987 to 1996, the results change entirely and the rule is absolutely not significant anymore.

The first point is interesting because it gives statistical support to the proponents of technical trading, showing that over a large period of time specific trading rules could have been profitable in excess of the market. The second point is also particularly interesting because a possible explanation proposed by the authors is simply that the market has become more efficient and a rule that was profitable in the study sample is simply not significant anymore over the past 10 years. For example, it is very possible that October 1987 might have forced participants to reevaluate their understanding of the market.

For us, the implications of this article are twofold. On one end, we have at least an academic indication of how profitable technical trading may be. Naturally, the particular result of the article should be taken with a grain of salt, if only because in reality the operating mode for a trader would be much more "hands on." For example, it is unlikely that traders would use only one particular rule, even more so consider-

[9] A buy signal is therefore generated if the price of the stock crosses upward a five-day moving average plus 0.1 percent, and a sell signal is generated when the price crosses downward a five-day moving average minus 0.1 percent.

ing that the classical rules included in the sample are relatively "primitive."[10] In fact, the conception of a trading system usually implies several rules and indicators used in combination, and a systematic analysis of the behavior of the system in order to refine it continuously. Therefore, not only would traders use several rules and/or indicators at a given time, including some highly proprietary, they would also probably not use the same ones over a long period. An indication that a single rule would yield 17.2 percent over a 100-year period thus cannot be considered entirely reflective of an intrinsic profitability of technical trading in general.

On the other end, it illustrates very clearly an earlier point: Computational and brain power dedicated to understanding and investigating market efficiency and trading opportunities are more and more significant. The study covered a 100-year period and almost 7,500 different trading configurations. Only 10 years ago such an undertaking would have been impossible, whereas it is extremely reasonable today. Indeed, many trading firms and hedge funds have developed trading systems that monitor virtually thousands of stocks and have the ability to run back-testing simulations for decades or more.

If we use these results as a starting point, we can explore another avenue to get a sense of how profitable pair and technical trading can be. Again hedge funds provide the easiest access to this information by nature of their business. Table 10-3 provides year-to-year performance of four categories of hedge funds. These figures give a sense of the variability of the returns and their average magnitude. As a first approximation, we can place the typical profitability between 10 and 20 percent, in some cases as high as 25 to 30 percent, or as low as 5 to 10 percent. Again these figures have to be adjusted for leverage, which we will take between 1 and 2, lower than before to reflect the fact that the level of risk is higher than risk arbitrage. All in all, we could estimate an average profitability around 10 percent with a reasonable range being 5 to about 15 percent.[11]

Like risk arbitrage, the purpose of the exercise is not to obtain a precise figure; this would naturally be impossible. Rather, we want to demonstrate how public data can help us estimate an order of magnitude with minimal knowledge of what the reality is because we do not

---

[10] By "primitive" we mean to emphasize the fact that these rules have been around for such a long time that they are probably fully "priced" in the marketplace by now.

[11] This result is consistent with quantitative returns found in other studies. See, for example, Evan Gates, William Goetzmann, and K. Gast Rowenhorst, "Pairs Trading: Performance of a Relative Value Arbitrage Rule," National Bureau of Economic Research, Working Paper 7032, March 1999, Cambridge.

TABLE 10-3

Year	Market Neutral	Risk Arbitrage	Statistical Arbitrage	Other Relative Value
1975	37.11%			
1976	23.93%			
1977	−7.15%			
1978	6.56%			
1979	18.61%			
1980	32.50%			
1981	−4.91%			
1982	21.55%			
1983	22.55%			
1984	6.27%			
1985	31.75%			
1986	18.68%			
1987	5.26%			
1988	21.84%			
1989	26.80%			
1990	8.33%			
1991	23.37%	12.45%		
1992	12.61%	5.18%	31.18%	
1993	22.68%	19.66%	37.23%	
1994	4.48%	7.15%	16.86%	
1995	18.11%	23.48%	9.27%	4.83%
1996	19.84%	12.53%	20.61%	13.47%
1997	17.64%	17.37%	12.17%	16.06%
1998	10.53%	9.18%	15.32%	4.68%
1999	12.65%	12.84%	12.20%	20.34%
CAGR	**16.0%**	**13.2%**	**19.0%**	**8.2%**

(*Source*: HedgeFund.net, November 1999, reprinted with permission.)

have access to detailed information. The legitimate conclusion is that technical trading and more generally speculative arbitrage is likely to yield significantly more than risk arbitrage—and naturally much higher than index arbitrage. Again these figures are nominal returns and therefore are not risk adjusted.

RISKS

Convergence

There are not many ways to manage a convergence risk in a technical trading position. Indeed, there is only one, and it is called *discipline*. In virtually every book published by traders or experienced investors trying to explain the basic principles of investing, discipline systematically comes back as a critical requirement, and for good reason. Experience and history show invariably that successful traders are extremely rigorous about the management of their risks—although rigor is certainly not enough to succeed.

Discipline and rigor in that context simply point toward a total elimination of the "human factor" from the trading decision. We mentioned earlier that risk and the perspective of a loss are likely to affect significantly human behavior, all the more if it is one's *own* money involved. Therefore, *being disciplined* simply means applying systematic rules, no matter what. And with respect to risk management and speculative trading, these rules are extremely simple: They are called *stop-profit* and *stop-loss rules*.

Taking a position can then be described as an exercise in applying Boolean logic. A particular position is initiated when a rule is triggered—for example, if two moving averages cross over. At initiation of the position—and not after—a set of risk parameters is fixed, specifically stop profit and stop loss. They are defined according to the expectations associated with the strategy itself and probably to reflect also current market conditions. For example, if we are looking at a moving average crossover trying to capture long-term trends, it does not make any sense to take a profit at 5 percent and cut a loss at −3 percent. A long-term trend by definition is more likely to create moves of wider amplitudes, so thresholds, for example, at 20 percent and −15 percent would probably make more sense. In contrast, a day trader would probably be wise to consider 5 and −3 percent because the nature of his or her business is such that these amplitudes are more reasonable. In any case, both types of investor, will also look, for example, at the overall volatility of the market. In a period of high volatility, it is probably safe to reduce the amplitude between stop-profit and stop-loss triggers. Eventually whenever any of these thresholds is reached or when enough time has lapsed to turn the position into a probable loser, it should be cut immediately, without any consideration—or remorse—whatsoever for its immediate profitability. The thresholds can be variable in many ways, and they do not have to be constant from one position or one day to the next. They could be based, for example, on the success rate of a given strategy in the six months prior to the current opportunity. In any case, they should be rigorously set when the position is effectively taken, and more importantly, *respected*.

Naturally this is a schematic presentation and it should not be taken as a rule that is rigid and absolute. There may be many valid reasons that a particular situation would require a trader to revisit the original assumptions and thereby the original thresholds. This is exactly what judgment and experience are trying to capture: the ability to anticipate when to stick by the rules in a systematic way and when to reevaluate an opportunity. The important point is to realize that the mental process here is fundamentally different from what it was before. In a situation of index arbitrage, the primary concern is to carry the position with the minimum peripheral losses in order to keep the largest part of the original profit, assuming there was an original profit. In risk arbitrage, the original profit is less certain, so the appropriate question is whether a position should be kept at all based on a case-by-case analysis of facts that are absolutely not systematic or statistical in nature but situation specific. In speculative arbitrage the appropriate question is not whether one particular position should be examined more carefully and possibly reevaluated or unwound but rather what are the appropriate risk and reward thresholds that will be applied systematically and will eventually guarantee a positive return on average.

Naturally the appropriateness of a particular stop-profit or stop-loss threshold depends on a number of factors and is not a number created out of thin air. Typically a given strategy can be evaluated for a scenario of maximum loss based on historical simulations, and this analysis would naturally be highly instrumental in determining both the expected and maximum admissible loss from the strategy. This is essentially what we did for risk arbitrage, looking at BT/MCI and SPLS/ODP and extracting an estimate of the impact of a negative event on the spread.

In order to illustrate the basic principles behind the process, let's call p the average success rate of the strategy s_L and s_P the stop loss and stop profit in percentage terms, and P the expected yield from the strategy over a reasonably long period. In other words, out of 100 positions, a number p are profitable and yield a profit s_P percent on average, the remaining losing s_L percent on average. P is then equal to:

$$P = p \cdot s_P - (1 - p) \cdot s_L$$

This equation implies that we can stop every position at its preset stop, which is unlikely in practice.[12] Experience shows that it is much more

[12] The equation also implies that all positions have a similar size, an assumption we consider for the sake of simplicity.

difficult to stop losses than profits because in general, negative responses from the market are associated to higher volatility compared to positive events. Therefore, P is probably an overestimate of the overall profit.

Consider that historical simulations suggest that 10 percent is a reasonable estimate of the loss associated to a failed opportunity and 60 percent an acceptable average success rate. Stated otherwise, when we lose 10 percent, it is very unlikely that the position will turn over and become profitable, so we might as well stop it. P is then equal to:

$$P = 60 \text{ percent} * s_P - 40 \text{ percent} * 10 \text{ percent}$$

If we want a yield of 10 percent on average over a reasonably long period of time, we have to choose s_P such that:

$$60 \text{ percent} * s_P - 40 \text{ percent} * 10 \text{ percent} = 10 \text{ percent} \quad \Rightarrow \quad s_P = 23.3 \text{ percent}$$

This result gives a numerical value to the stop-profit threshold we should use if we want to be consistent with the expectations underlying the model. More importantly, it shows that stop loss, stop profit, success rate, and overall profitability are related, and thus one should not be guessed independently from the others but they should be considered as a coherent set of parameters.

The apparent simplicity behind these results should not occult the fact that there is little in practice directly under a trader's control. Beyond the entry signal—arguably a critical part—and specific values for s_P and s_L, a trader has little influence—which is exactly why stops should be managed very carefully. It is certainly possible to have a reasonably sound strategy give disappointing results because it is not stopped adequately, on either side, profit or loss.

At the same time the above equation should not be considered for more than what it really is: a reality check and one more tool to make better decisions. For example, the following relationship can be used as a back-of-the-envelope proportion:

$$P \geq 0 \quad \Rightarrow \quad \left(\frac{s_P}{s_L}\right) \geq \left(\frac{1-p}{p}\right)$$

Stated clearly, there is a direct dependence between the risk-reward ratio and the success rate of a particular model. The higher the success rate, the lower the required return in terms of expected profit compared to expected loss. For example, a strategy for which $p = 60$ percent could function with $s_P/s_L = 66$ percent at a minimum. This result does not give an indication of the absolute value of s_P and s_L, but if we can extract s_L from a rigorous risk analysis, s_P is automatically fixed. If we realize that the value of s_P we obtain is unrealistic, it might very well indicate that we need to refine the strategy considerably. For example, consider that $s_L = 10$ percent, then s_P should be equal to 6.6 percent. If it turns out that historical profits are below 6.6 percent on average, even with a success rate as high as 60 percent, it is fair to conclude that we are investigating a strategy that is simply not profitable enough for the level of risk it creates. On the other hand, if $p = 40$ percent, we know that we should consider having s_P/s_L above 1.5—that is, $s_P \geq 15$ percent if $s_L = 10$ percent. Again looking at past performance, it is possible to get a sense of whether $s_P \geq 15$ percent is realistic and make a reasonably confident decision about the viability of the system.[13]

In conclusion, it is important to realize how different the thought process can be for a speculative arbitrage compared to situations in which the convergence is more certain, even though the same framework can be used in practice.

Other Risks: Execution, Financing, Dividends, and Short Squeezes

Even more than any other component of a strategy, execution and more generally risks other than convergence are difficult to encapsulate when we move away from absolute convergence. The obvious reason for that is the diversity of opportunities pursued in the marketplace. In terms of execution, for example, a situation of pair trading with a cycle of convergence of a few days will probably present no particular difficulty because like risk arbitrage, the spread is likely to exist for more than a few minutes at a time. At the other extreme, certain forms of statistical arbitrage are trying to capture tiny movements in prices on very frequent trades and therefore are more dependent upon the ability to execute instantaneously at the right price.

Along the same lines, financing and dividends may vary widely from one strategy to another. If, for example, one leg of a strategy is a derivative—futures or options—financing should be monitored with special care because of the leverage on the derivative position and associated margin calls. A futures contract, as we have seen, does

[13] Incidentally, the entire discussion also applies to other forms of arbitrage. The main difference is the magnitude of p. In index arbitrage, p is virtually equal to 100 percent in the sense that a position executed adequately will eventually turn a sure profit. In risk arbitrage, p is high but certainly not close to 100 percent anymore.

not have a major impact on treasury because the financing of margin calls can be hedged. It does however create an exposure to interest rates because of its pricing model. In contrast, a stock position creates an immediate need for cash because it has to be paid for when it is acquired, but it does not create any exposure to interest rates per se. Dividends are another illustration of the same phenomenon. A spread position like risk arbitrage or pair trading creates an exposure to the dividend differential because this differential enters into the P&L formula. Alternatively, a position of statistical arbitrage is mostly immune to dividends, simply because the average holding period of a given stock is in general short enough that dividends are irrelevant.

In the same direction, short squeezes are a threat only when the position is highly dependent on maintaining a short in one particular security for a reasonable period of time and for a decent size. Pair trading, for example, may fall in that category, like risk arbitrage. Statistical arbitrage, on the other hand, considers many stocks as purely random variables, which means that if one is unavailable or expensive to short sell, it can most probably be replaced by another without any difficulty.

Again, it is difficult to offer generic answers here because so many questions can be asked. There are, however, some recurrent themes:

- *Derivatives versus nonderivatives*: The inclusion of a derivative in the strategy may have a significant impact on financing and interest rate exposure, as well as on dividends, for example.
- *Cash flows*: A careful examination of cash flows has allowed us to price futures with the cash-and-carry model and to price a risk arbitrage opportunity. It should be clear by now that a careful flow diagram is a powerful tool to understand the different aspects of a particular implementation, notably in terms of treasury, but not only. This is not an almighty tool, however, because in some cases, in particular when delta hedging and/or options are involved, flow diagrams are almost useless.
- *Time horizons*: A good estimation of what the typical horizon is for a given strategy is also a safe principle. For example, a strategy with a profit cycle of a few days will require an analysis different from a model based on patterns expressed over several months. Stops are naturally different, but execution should also be considered from two different angles, as should probably be risks associated with interest rates, dividends, and so on.
- *Convergences*: If the convergence risk is managed appropriately, the strategy is likely to to be profitable overall. It is, for example, very

unlikely to see a position of pair trading or statistical arbitrage significantly affected by a change in interest rates or dividends, although they may have a second-order effect.

- *Hedging*: Naturally hedging the position appropriately remains a very important part of risk management. Whether the hedge is fixed quantity or nominal, it should be monitored carefully.
- *Short versus long positions*: A short position is always a potential candidate for a short squeeze. If it is kept for a brief period of time, the risk is mitigated, but as a general rule, traders should never exclude the possibility of a short squeeze.

In practice, managing a position requires having every single aspect in check without taking anything for granted. Some risks are more pervasive than others, but the risk analysis engine should be flexible enough to describe and evaluate all of them.

ILLUSTRATION

Royal Dutch and Shell

The arbitrage of Royal Dutch (RD) and Shell (SC) is very popular on Wall Street because it is a pair trading model with characteristic close to those of an absolute convergence. RD and SC are essentially two sides of the same coin, because the two companies are two "shells" deriving their revenues through a fixed partition of the income generated by the Royal Dutch–Shell Group. RD and SC are linked by a corporate charter stipulating that 60 percent of the income received by the Group will be allocated to RD, while the 40 percent remaining is allocated to SC. Therefore, there is a very clear relationship between RD and SC with respect to their respective incomes, and as a result, there should also be a relatively simple relationship between their stock prices.[14]

[14] For more information, see Kenneth Froot and André Perold, *Global Equity Markets: The Case of Royal Dutch and Shell*, Harvard Business School, Case 9-296-077, July 1997.

In order to have a rigorous determination of this ratio, let us call n_{RD} and n_{SC} the number of shares outstanding for RD and SC respectively. For every dollar of income generated by the Group, RD shareholders receive \$0.60—that is, $\$0.60/n_{RD}$ per share whereas SC shareholders receive \$0.40—that is, $\$0.40/n_{SC}$ per share. Therefore, the "exact" ratio between RD and SC should be:

For the purpose of this discussion, let's imagine that we know nothing of the relationship and that we want to trade the pair because there is historically a very high correlation between the two stocks. This correlation manifests itself notably through a relatively stable ratio between the prices of the two companies, a property that we will exploit to generate trading signals. Figure 10-1, for example, shows the ratio between the closing prices of SC and RD over the two-year period from June 1998 to June 2000. The dotted line is a 30-day moving average of the ratio, and it is designed to capture its "stable value." In

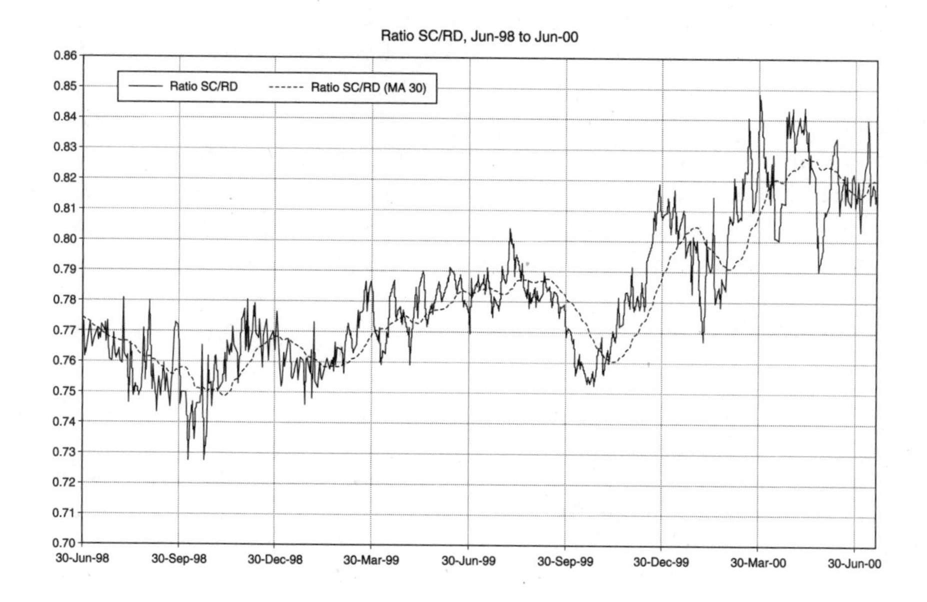

Figure 10-1 SC/RD
(*Source*: Compiled by author from Datastream data.)

(*Footnote continued*)

$$r_{SC/RD} = \left(\frac{0.4/_{n_{SC}}}{0.6/_{n_{RD}}}\right) = \frac{0.4.n_{RD}}{0.6.n_{SC}} = \frac{2}{3}.\frac{n_{RD}}{n_{SC}}$$

In addition, RD and SC are listed on the AMEX as ADRs, with one SC ADR being equivalent to six common shares of SC. Therefore, the ratio between the prices of the ADRs is:

$$r_{SC/RD} = \frac{2}{3}\cdot\left(\frac{n_{RD}}{n_{SC/6}}\right) = 4\frac{n_{RD}}{n_{SC}}$$

Traditionally, this ratio has been around $0.65 \sim 0.85$.

other words, we make the assumption that the observed value of the ratio is the superposition of a fundamental function and market noise, and we chose the moving average as an estimator of the fundamental function.[15] Thirty days is short enough to be reactive to the market and long enough to appear reasonably efficient in stripping noise out. We could have chosen other values, and in reality, we would certainly put other values to the test to determine if 30 is really the best we can find.

Once we have an estimate of this ratio, we can compare the market spread between RD and SC with what we think this spread should be. For example, on July 8, 1998, SC closed at $41¼, RD at $53 15/16, and the 30-day moving average of their ratio was 0.7725. Based on this ratio, SC "should be worth" $41.66 (= $53 15/16 * 0.7725). Because SC closed at $41¼, it is undervalued by $0.4187 (= $41.25 −$41.66). We could at this point use the value of the difference as a trading indicator. For example, if it is below −$1, we could buy SC and sell RD because SC is undervalued, and vice versa. This is not the best way to proceed, however, because an absolute value of $1 does not have any particular meaning for the stocks we are considering. It is smarter to introduce one more step, in which we normalize the value of the difference.[16] If we denote Δ as this difference, we want to compute Δ_{norm} such that:

$$\Delta_{\text{norm}} = \frac{\Delta - MA_{30}(\Delta)}{\sigma_{30}(\Delta)}$$

where $MA_{30}(\Delta)$ is the 30-day moving average of Δ, and $\sigma_{30}(\Delta)$ its 30-day standard deviation. The value of Δ_{norm} then represents the "mispricing" of the spread expressed in terms of standard deviations. The implicit approximation in the process is that Δ is a random variable distributed normally, so that Δ_{norm} is normally distributed with mean 0 and standard deviation 1. The advantage in using Δ_{norm} over Δ is that we know its distribution, and choosing a value for Δ_{norm} has therefore a lot of meaning compared to choosing a value for Δ. For example, there is a 15 percent chance that Δ_{norm} will be above 1 or

[15] Note that what we call a *stable value* is obtained from the market with a moving average and has nothing to do with the rigorous calculation of the ratio $r_{SC/RD}$ we performed earlier by looking at fundamentals of the companies. Along the same lines, we are not trying to explain or understand why the market is pricing the ratio with such variability; we are only taking a very superficial approach by considering purely market prices.

[16] This is exactly what we did already for the mean-reversal strategy in the first part. This procedure is called a *z transform*.

below −1, and a 2.3 percent chance that it will be above 2 or below −2. For our original purpose of creating trading signals, we would then know that trading when Δ_{norm} is above 1 means that we are considering market events that are relatively rare, or even rarer with Δ_{norm} above 2. This is indeed exactly what we want to do because we want to find an indicator that will detect uncommon events, our expectations being that these events will disappear very fast, allowing us to realize a profit.

As an illustration, Figure 10-2 shows the value of Δ_{norm} over the period from June 1998 to June 2000. As we might expect, Δ_{norm} is an oscillator whose values change quite often. The chart confirms that Δ_{norm} is only infrequently above +1 or below −1, and even more rarely above +2 or below −2. To transform this chart into a trading strategy, we need to fix a threshold and implement trading signals whenever Δ_{norm} exits this preset range. We choose here 1.5 standard deviations as the threshold—that is, an occurrence of 6.7 percent if the distribution of Δ_{norm} was perfectly normal. Every time Δ_{norm} is above 1.5, we sell SC and buy RD, and we enter the opposite position if Δ_{norm} is below −1.5. Table 10-4 shows the trading signals over a short period from July 17, 1998, to July 24, 1998.

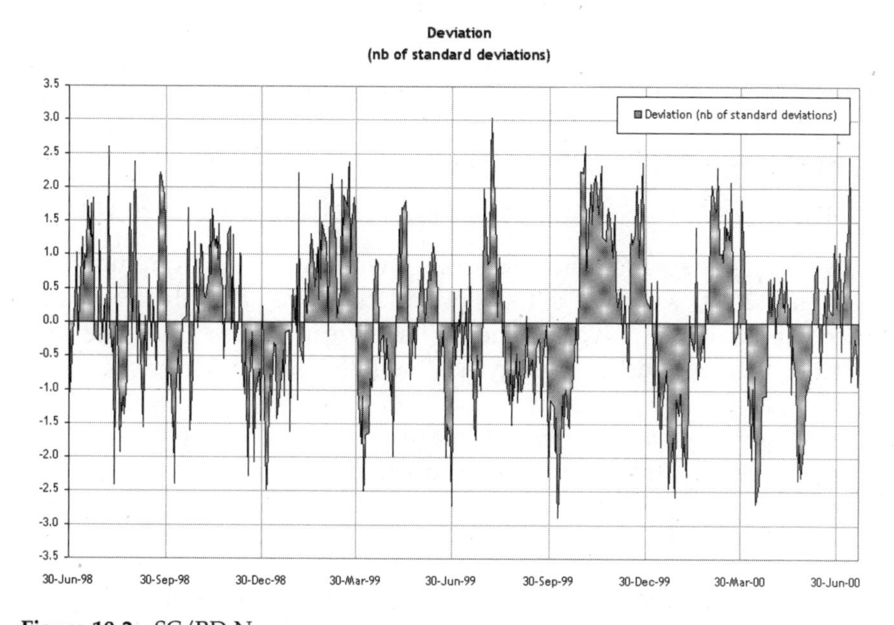

Figure 10-2 SC/RD Norm
(*Source*: Compiled by author from Datastream data.)

TABLE 10-4

Date	SC	RD	$MA_{30}(\Delta)$	Δ	Δ_{norm}	Signal	P&L
July 17, 1998	$41 7/16	$53 5/8	0.7698	0.1594	1.7909	−1	
July 20, 1998	$41 1/16	$53 5/16	0.7695	0.0369	1.2889		$0.13
July 21, 1998	$40 3/8	$52 1/4	0.7692	0.1866	1.7531	−1	
July 22, 1998	$41 1/16	$53 9/16	0.7687	−0.1130	0.7506		$0.33
July 23, 1998	$40 1/8	$51 7/8	0.7685	0.2599	1.8424	−1	
July 24, 1998	$40 1/8	$52 3/4	0.7681	−0.3903	−0.2013		$0.68

On July 17, 1998, for example, Δ_{norm} is 1.7909, indicating that SC is too expensive compared to our model because it is above 1.5 standard deviations; therefore, we sell it and buy RD at the closing price. To keep the position hedged, we choose a fixed-quantity hedge with a ratio equal to $MA_{30}(\Delta)$ because this is our estimator of what the stable value of the ratio should be. In other words, we enter the following deals:[17]

- Sell 1 share of SC at $41 7/16.
- Buy 0.7698 share of RD at $53 5/8.

For the sake of simplicity, we fix a stop in absolute terms on the holding period—that is, we close the position regardless of its profitability the next day at the close. Therefore, on July 20, 1998, we effect the following transactions:

- Buy 1 share of SC at $41 1/16.
- Sell 0.7698 share of RD at $53 5/16

Naturally the P&L for the position is easy to compute:

$$P\&L = 1 * (\$41\tfrac{7}{16} - \$41\tfrac{1}{16}) + 0.7698 * (\$53\tfrac{5}{16} - \$53\tfrac{5}{8}) = \$0.1344$$

If we apply the same principles over a two-year period from June 1998 to June 2000, we have a total of 118 positions, and the daily and accumulated P&L look like the one shown in Figure 10-3. The total P&L is $20.57, and the strategy has the following characteristics:

- *Maximum profit*: 2.6 percent, maximum loss −2 percent
- *P&L on long trades*: $8.74, on short trades $11.83
- *Success rate*: 69.5 percent

---

[17] Note that the position is not hedged in nominal because the residual exposure is 0.7698 * $53 5/8 − 1 * $41 7/16 = −$0.157. We are still appropriately hedged according to our model.

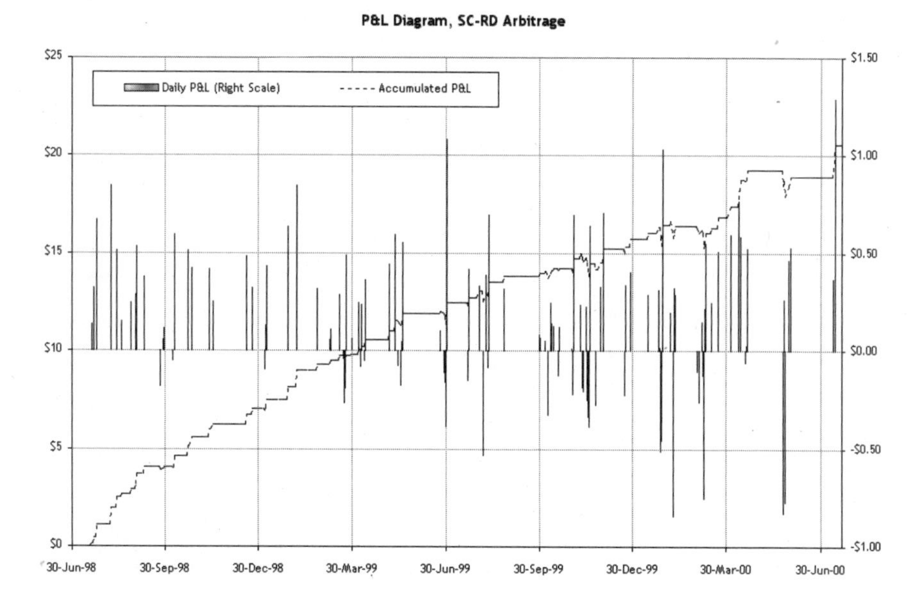

Figure 10-3 SC/RD Arbitrage

Indeed, this is a very successful strategy, for a number of reasons:

- Both long and short trades are equally profitable.
- The overall success rate is better than two in three.
- The accumulated profit is never negative and only rarely decreasing. Even when trades are losing, they are not losing much, which is also visible in the fact that the maximum profit is higher than the maximum loss in percentage terms.

We know in this particular case that the spread is much more predictable than a common pair trading relationship because of the corporate lineage between RD and SC. Our approach also generates losing trades in some cases, however, which is not entirely surprising because we intentionally restrict the information we use.

It is interesting at this point to consider a sensitivity analysis to determine if we were simply lucky in coming up with this model. If, for example, we vary the threshold between 0.25 and 3 standard deviations, Figure 10-4 shows the corresponding accumulated P&L and total success rate.[18] This picture confirms what was already

[18] Note that in reality, we would carry a sensitivity analysis on many more parameters such as the periodicity for the moving averages for $MA_{30}(\Delta)$ and $\sigma_{30}(\Delta)$, the holding periods, the implementation of distinct percentage stops for long and short, or the implementation of distinct thresholds for long and short.

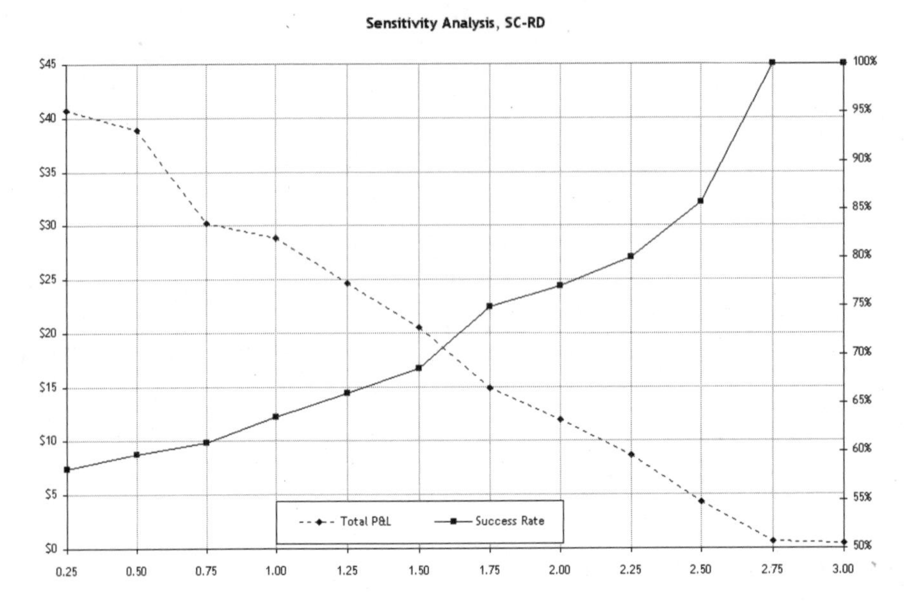

Figure 10-4 SC/RD Sensitivity

apparent: The strategy is *extraordinarily* successful because it is always profitable regardless of the value of the threshold, and its success rate increases steadily to 100 percent. The decreasing P&L might be relatively worrying, but it is simply a result of the lesser number of positions taken because the trading signals are getting sparser and sparser. Indeed, if we ever were to encounter such a diagram for another strategy, it would probably mean that we are in front of a relatively solid convergence without knowing it.

This strategy is relatively peculiar, because we traded pretending we did not know anything about it beforehand. Nevertheless, the basic principles still apply, and in this particular case our primary risk—convergence—was handled by a very strict holding period limited to one trading day. Naturally this procedure does not ensure that we will never incur any loss, simply that these losses are due to the market, not to our inability to cut losing trades early. In addition, this strategy is a perfect example of the relatively benign impact of other traditional risks. With 118 positions a year—that is, 250 open days—we are trading on average every other day, holding a position for 24 hours. In that context, it is unlikely that dividends, interest rates, or borrowing rates for RD or SC will ever be a problem.

DJI Pairs

In this example, we will examine a more systematic approach to pair trading, not relying anymore—even if we did not use it—on any sort of knowledge about the stocks involved. Like RD/SC, this model is widely used in practice but allows many more variations.

The idea is to compute a short-term correlation between a number of stocks typically included in an index. From there we systematically trade the pairs with the highest correlation regardless of any industry representation. As an illustration, Table 10-5 shows the three-month correlation of all pairs of stocks included in the Dow Jones Industrial Average index between August and November 1999. The bold figures represent the extremes:

- Philip Morris (MO) and IBM (IBM): 0.95
- Hewlett Packard (HWP) and IBM: 0.93
- United Technologies (UTX) and Disney (DIS): 0.92
- MO and Goodyear (GT): 0.91
- Exxon (XON) and Chevron (CHV): 0.90[19]

And on the other side:

- Wal-Mart (WMT) and IBM: −0.91
- WMT and MO: −0.89
- IBM and Merck (MRK): −0.88
- WMT and HWP: −0.86
- General Electric (GE) and Goodyear (GT): −0.84

Based on these figures we decide to trade systematically the five first pairs, MO/IBM, HWP/IBM, UTX/DIS, MO/GT, and XON/CHV—the same way we traded SC/RD, using a normalized measure of the deviation from a 30-day moving average of the ratio as a trading signal. For example, the charts in Figures 10-5 and 10-6 show the ratio IBM/HWP, its 30-moving average, and the corresponding normalized deviation Δ_{norm}. Next we trade every pair in a manner identical to the way we traded SC and RD. We fix the threshold at 1.5 standard deviations and enter the arbitrage with a fixed-quantity hedge based on the 30-day moving average of the ratio between the two stocks. The chart in Figure 10-7 plots the results—that is,

[19] Exxon merged in December 1999 with Mobil to form Exxon Mobil (XOM).

TABLE 10-5

	AA	ALD	AXP	BA	C	CAT	CHV	DD	DIS	EK	GE	GM	GT	HWP	IBM	IP	JNJ	JPM	KO	MCD	MMM	MO	MRK	PG	S	T	UK	UTX	WMT	XON
AA		0.75	-0.27	0.49	-0.35	0.73	0.70	0.65	0.73	0.47	-0.59	-0.30	0.80	0.78	0.67	0.27	-0.04	0.29	0.29	-0.19	0.52	-0.67	-0.57	-0.25	0.77	0.37	0.27	0.72	-0.55	0.82
ALD			-0.24	0.24	-0.39	0.76	0.54	0.53	0.76	0.68	-0.52	-0.24	0.78	0.85	0.81	0.17	-0.20	0.26	0.20	-0.03	0.65	0.84	-0.67	-0.20	0.79	0.42	0.05	0.75	-0.64	0.74
AXP				-0.08	0.85	-0.04	-0.02	0.05	-0.19	-0.56	0.77	0.82	-0.48	-0.54	-0.66	0.37	0.71	0.53	0.46	0.22	0.20	-0.58	0.73	0.63	-0.27	0.38	0.52	-0.17	0.76	-0.13
BA					-0.07	0.51	0.56	0.62	0.58	0.24	-0.37	-0.24	0.50	0.43	0.31	0.12	0.28	0.38	0.48	-0.55	0.38	0.29	-0.16	-0.09	0.48	0.28	0.32	0.67	-0.38	0.46
C						-0.14	-0.01	-0.06	-0.25	-0.73	0.83	0.84	-0.65	-0.61	-0.77	0.57	0.74	0.68	0.55	0.35	0.18	-0.72	0.74	0.75	-0.31	0.37	0.67	-0.19	0.80	-0.13
CAT							0.65	0.83	0.82	0.47	-0.51	-0.20	0.75	0.70	0.55	0.36	0.12	0.48	0.53	-0.31	0.62	0.66	-0.47	-0.21	0.86	0.65	0.43	0.86	-0.51	0.76
CHV								0.56	0.71	0.06	-0.30	-0.07	0.50	0.57	0.38	0.53	0.33	0.58	0.60	-0.21	-0.57	0.35	-0.27	0.13	0.57	0.35	0.43	0.69	-0.34	**0.90**
DD									0.64	0.33	-0.47	-0.21	0.67	0.48	0.35	0.27	0.17	0.43	0.48	-0.38	0.42	0.48	-0.31	-0.30	0.79	0.59	0.54	0.72	-0.32	0.63
DIS										0.56	-0.54	-0.30	0.74	0.81	0.69	0.28	0.02	0.43	0.46	-0.39	0.70	0.72	-0.58	-0.14	0.81	0.41	0.26	**0.92**	-0.69	0.82
EK											-0.73	-0.60	0.77	0.75	0.86	-0.38	-0.57	-0.28	-0.26	-0.25	0.23	0.88	-0.74	-0.57	0.62	0.03	-0.37	0.55	-0.80	0.29
GE												0.85	**-0.84**	-0.74	-0.80	0.31	0.56	0.31	0.15	0.51	0.00	-0.82	0.84	0.79	-0.67	0.03	0.26	-0.56	0.89	-0.44
GM													-0.57	-0.52	-0.64	0.45	0.72	0.55	0.45	0.48	0.17	-0.61	0.74	0.82	-0.37	0.35	0.42	-0.23	0.77	-0.17
GT														0.87	0.86	-0.14	-0.28	0.00	0.09	-0.46	0.36	**0.91**	-0.75	-0.56	0.83	0.30	-0.05	0.79	-0.81	0.65
HWP															**0.93**	0.07	-0.30	0.13	0.16	-0.22	0.53	0.92	-0.80	-0.33	0.77	0.25	-0.10	0.79	**-0.86**	0.73
IBM																-0.18	-0.54	-0.14	-0.12	-0.22	0.38	**0.95**	**-0.88**	-0.50	0.69	0.07	-0.32	0.65	**-0.91**	0.57
IP																	0.49	0.75	0.65	0.34	0.48	-0.18	0.18	0.56	0.18	0.49	0.74	0.26	0.25	0.49
JNJ																		0.71	0.75	0.05	0.28	-0.48	0.68	0.71	-0.10	0.42	0.59	0.13	0.55	0.12
JPM																			0.88	0.16	0.67	-0.09	0.20	0.60	0.36	0.64	0.78	0.51	0.19	0.55
KO																				-0.09	0.53	-0.06	0.19	0.50	0.39	0.65	0.70	0.57	0.09	0.52
MCD																					0.01	-0.27	0.20	0.46	-0.24	0.00	0.03	-0.39	0.43	-0.10
MMM																						0.38	-0.23	0.27	0.51	0.49	0.43	0.65	-0.26	0.64
MO																							-0.87	-0.54	0.78	0.21	-0.24	0.71	**-0.89**	0.57
MRK																								0.66	-0.68	0.03	0.27	-0.54	0.90	-0.52
PG																									-0.39	0.24	0.34	-0.12	0.60	-0.01
S																										0.49	0.31	0.86	-0.66	0.78
T																											0.63	0.56	0.04	0.43
UK																												0.33	0.32	0.41
UTX																													-0.64	0.80
WMT																														-0.50
XON																														

(*Source*: Compiled by author from Bloomberg data.)

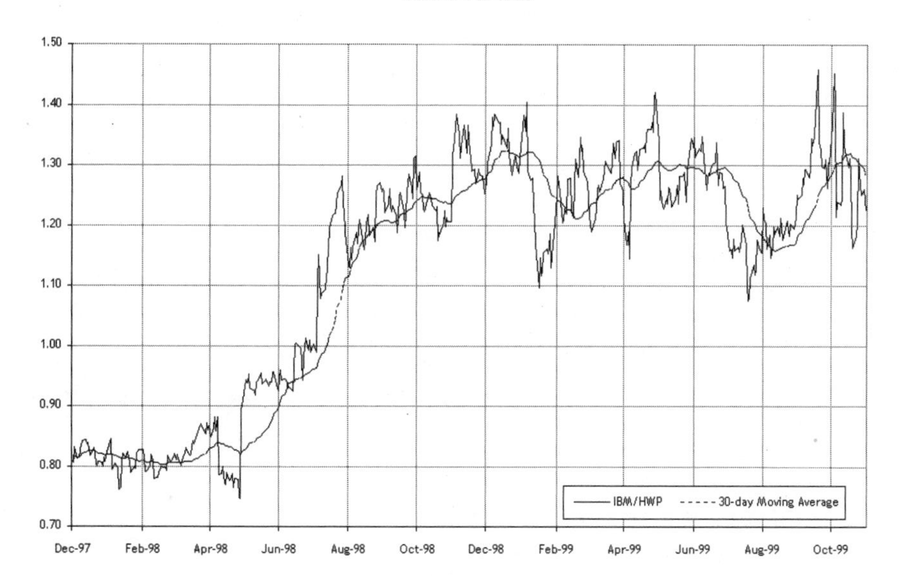

Figure 10-5 IBM/HWP
(*Source*: Compiled by author from Bloomberg data.)

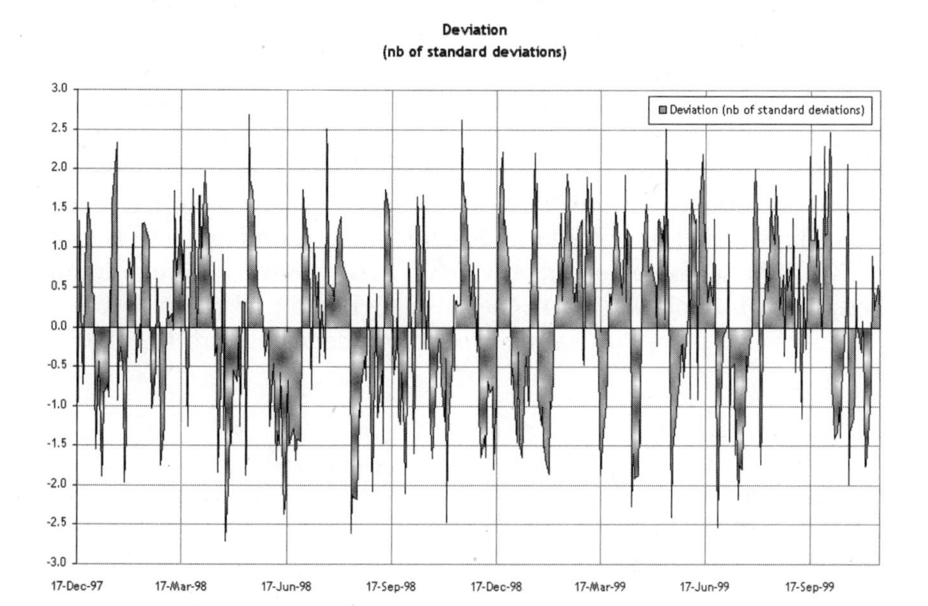

Figure 10-6 IBM/HWP Norm Aligned

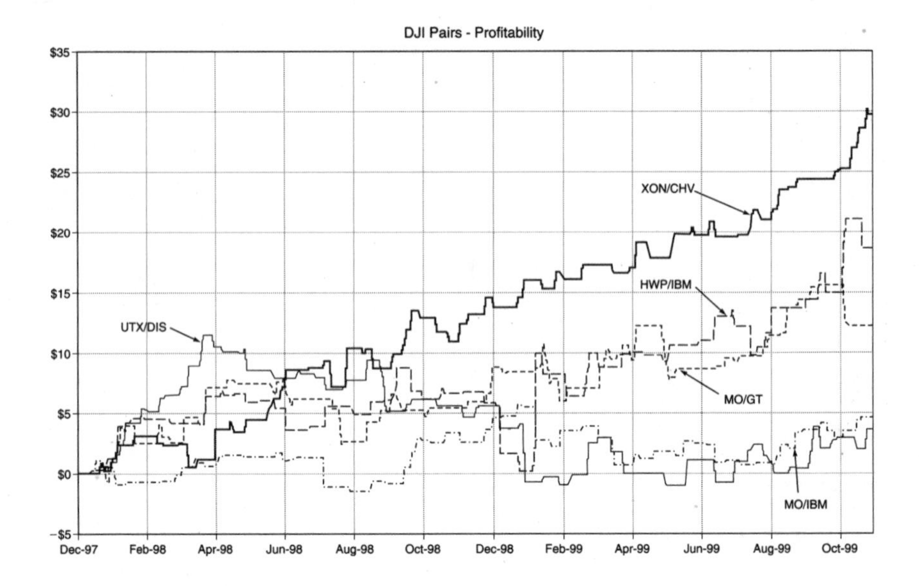

Figure 10-7 DJI Pair Results

the accumulated profit for each pair over the period.[20] Interestingly, the five pairs seem to be profitable, although this may be a result of the methodology because we computed each correlation at the end of the interval. There are, nevertheless, some interesting insights to be gained from this chart and Table 10-6, which is only a summary of the numerical gains for each pair. In particular, it is interesting to note that the magnitude of the profit associated with each pair is unrelated to the correlation of the two stocks. For example, despite a high correlation, MO/IBM and UTX/DIS do not seem to present a significant opportunity, whereas XON/CHV, on the contrary, is the most profitable. In addition, despite being profitable, MO/IBM, UTX/DIS, and to some extent MO/GT, are relatively disappointing because their total P&L never goes very high and is at times negative. The only two pairs that seem to perform adequately are HWP/IBM

[20] Note the fact that our approach is slightly inconsistent. We select pairs based on a three-month correlation from August to November 1999 and trade them from December 1997 to November 1999. In reality, we should have computed the correlation at the beginning of the period—that is, December 1997 to March 1998. This problem is relatively benign here because the purpose of the exercise is to provide a practical illustration of the proposed strategy, and its effect is to show the strategy as more successful than it probably is.

TABLE 10-6

Pair	Correlation	P&L
MO/IBM	0.95	$4.55
HWP/IBM	0.93	$18.66
UTX/DIS	0.92	$5.04
MO/GT	0.91	$12.30
XON/CHV	0.90	$29.79

and XON/CHV. This is hardly surprising because these two pairs are extracted from identical industries. Therefore, there is a common factor in the stock price of each member of the pair, and our trading strategy is only trying to express this particular factor, apparently with some success.

Therefore, it looks like a systematic approach like the one we just implemented is no better than a purely intuitive selection in which we pick stocks based on some common factor, typically their industrial sector. This is not entirely true, however, because such a rapid conclusion overlooks two important elements in what we did.

First, a systematic approach based on a statistical analysis of a large universe of stocks is one more step in the direction of less human intervention. The idea behind the process is that if a given pair has a good reason to be traded, then the statistical process will find it, and indeed this is exactly the case for HWP/IBM and XON/CHV. However, a statistical selection has the added advantage of investigating beyond the obvious. For example, in our case nobody would have proposed to pair Disney with United Technologies, and still the pair is profitable—although barely. Not only did the statistical approach give five pairs instead of two, it also opened new opportunities. If we think it is appropriate to trade stocks that are highly correlated, it may also be appropriate to trade stocks that are highly uncorrelated, taking an opposite position. For example, WMT and IBM have a correlation of –0.91, which suggests that they move in opposite directions quite often. Therefore, when the spread between them gets too thin, we can take a position based on the expectation that it will widen again very quickly. Such a strategy is indeed profitable on IBM/MRK, WMT/MO but loses on the other three pairs. In essence, being systematic offers a number of advantages, if nothing else because it significantly enlarges the available universe. With no need to thoroughly research every stock, a trader can virtually explore thousands of opportunities provided he or she has the adequate computing power.[21]

By far, however, the most important benefit of a systematic approach is diversification. Typically, pair trading based on some sort of correlation analysis is carried out on a large number of pairs, with a clear limit on each individual position. In contrast, a pair trader investigating every pair will carry fewer positions because his or her time becomes a scarce resource. The result of a systematic approach is a portfolio in which the number of sources of uncertainty is higher, but the combination of these sources still reduces the overall uncertainty because they are not behaving identically. If the selection process is sound and the risk procedure rigorously implemented, there is no reason why a systematic pair trading strategy could not offer a steady source of income with a limited downside and relatively low risk overall.

Opening and Closing Gaps

We develop here the two final examples of this chapter dedicated to speculative arbitrage.[22] Whereas we concentrated so far on pair trading in a large sense, we focus here on technical trading. We trade a set of securities based on very simple rules, but we do not hedge the positions in any way, giving rise to an exposure we need to monitor day to day.

The idea behind each strategy is that in the absence of dramatic information, there should be no dramatic move in price. In other words, the market is efficient enough to operate a correction following a move that was not necessarily warranted in the first place. The difficulty here naturally is to define the trading rule such that we capture truly "abnormal" events and leave aside extraordinary moves that may be the result of an earnings announcement, for example. We propose here the first steps in that direction, knowing that there is a number of ways to improve those strategies.

---

[21] In particular, nowadays traders in large institutions have access to virtually every major market in the world. A statistical approach has the advantage of being based—usually—primarily on analysis of market data, which means that it can be readily performed on any market, in contrast to a financial analysis using fundamental corporate data that may or may not be available easily.

[22] These two strategies are inspired by two articles the author published in the magazine *Technical Analysis of Stocks and Commodities*. See "Trading the Opening Gap," November 1999, and "Trading Against the Gap," December 1999.

As an introduction to the concept, consider the histogram in Figure 10-8 for the close-to-open returns for General Electric (GE) between December 1997 and December 1999. A close-to-open return is computed using the following formula:

$$r_t^{\text{close-to-open}} = \frac{P_t^{\text{open}} - P_{t-1}^{\text{close}}}{P_{t-1}^{\text{close}}}$$

where P_t^{open} and P_t^{close} denote respectively the opening and closing prices of GE on date t. In other words, if GE closes today at $73 and opens tomorrow at $73½, the close-to-open return is 0.68 percent (= $0.5/$73).

The histogram shows that the distribution is relatively peaked, the values around 0 being frequently represented in the sample. In other words, the opening price is frequently very close to the last day's closing price. If it is indeed very different, it may be that the market is incorporating new information or simply overreacting without anything fundamentally new. In this latter case, it is probable that the stock will correct at some point, the probability of a correction being most probably proportional to the close-to-open return observed. This correction in turn can be considered an elementary form of convergence, and we can take advantage of it by trading the stock at open and liquidating the position at the close to diminish risk.

This can be done very easily by placing a limit price order before the open around the closing price of the previous day. For example, GE closed on January 21, 1998, at $74 9/16. The next day, January 22, 1998, we could place a buying order at $73 and a selling order at $76 — that is, at 2 percent above and below $74 9/16. If we place these orders "at open" only one, if any, will be executed when the market opens. The threshold of 2 percent means that we consider that any opening move above 2 percent or below −2 percent from the previous day is unlikely to persist and will probably correct by the end of the day, at which time we will close the position regardless of what has happened. Again notice the systematic stop, expressed as a very short holding period, one single trading day. The advantage of choosing this particular value is that we do not carry any risk overnight.

As an illustration, consider Table 10-7 with prices for GE over the period January 20 to January 29, 1998. On January 21, 1998, the close-to-open return is −0.49 percent, which is too small for us to take a position. If we decided to fix the trading threshold at 1 percent, we would place every day a selling order at 1 percent above and a buying order at 1 percent below the last day's close. In doing that, we would trade only on January 26, 1998, placing a sell order for one share at

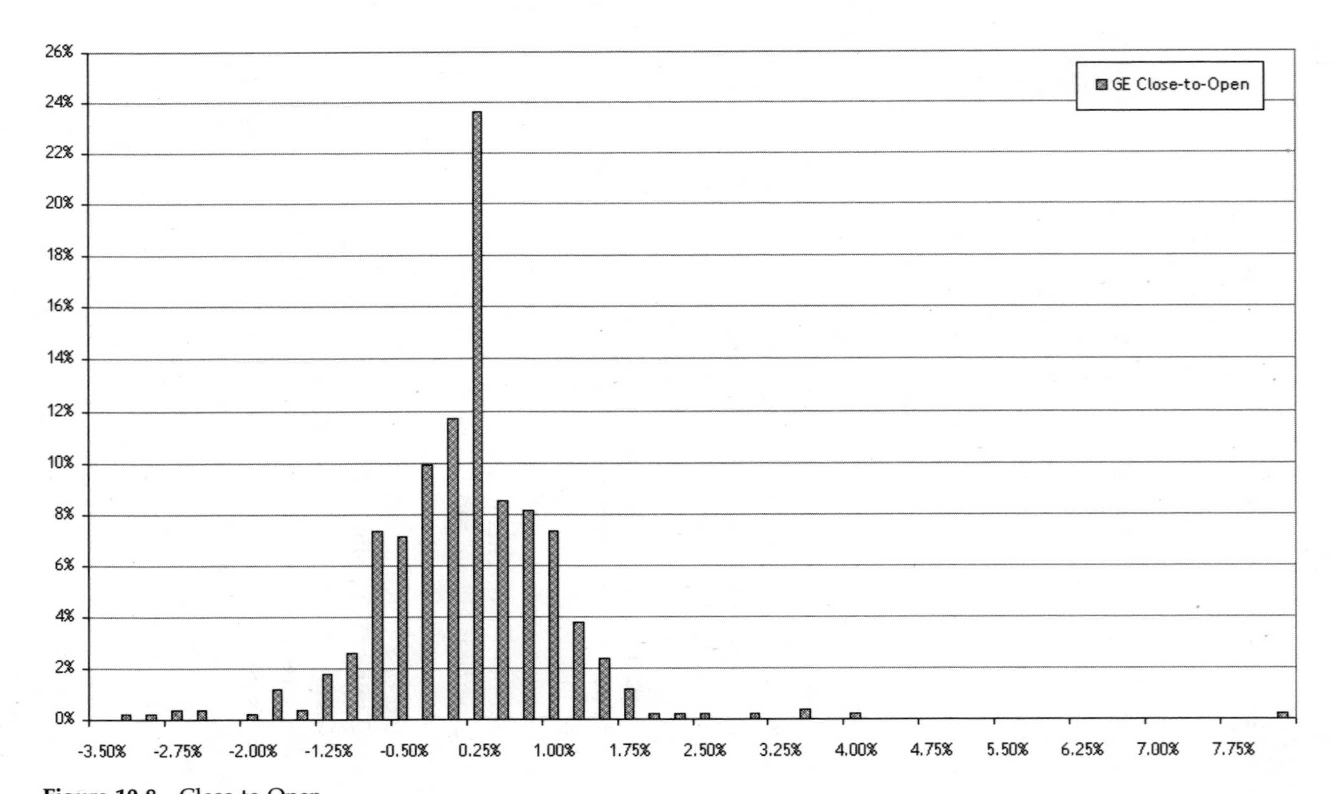

Figure 10-8 Close-to-Open
(*Source*: Compiled by author from Datastream data.)

TABLE 10-7

Date	Open	Close	Return
Jan. 20, 1998	73.38	75.56	0.00%
Jan. 21, 1998	75.19	75.56	−0.49%
Jan. 22, 1998	74.94	75.19	−0.82%
Jan. 23, 1998	75.56	74.06	0.49%
Jan. 26, 1998	74.94	74.69	1.19%
Jan. 27, 1998	74.94	76.25	0.33%
Jan. 28, 1998	76.56	76.25	0.41%
Jan. 29, 1998	76.25	77.13	0.00%

\$74.80 (= \$74.06 * 101 percent) and being executed in reality at \$74.94. We would then buy it back the same day at \$74.69 for a profit of \$0.25.[23]

In fact, we are going to extend the strategy beyond GE to all the stocks of the Dow Jones Industrial index. The idea is similar to the goal we pursued in implementing a systematic pair trading—that is, diversification. If one stock does not correct, for example, chances are that others will, essentially decreasing the overall risk. Table 10-8 shows the results of trading this model from December 1997 to December 1999, on each individual stock, for a threshold set at 2.5 percent.[24] The total P&L for the period is −\$2.59 (+\$31.86 for the long, −\$34.45 for the short), for a total of 602 positions (244 long, 358 short). Obviously this model is much less successful than RD/SC, for example, which is not surprising considering the hypothetical nature of the underlying assumptions. Interestingly, however, it does have some success on certain stocks, so one possible way to refine it is to design a "smart" filter to extract those stocks that are more likely to be profitable on a given day. In addition, despite ending on a small loss, a closer examination shows that is has been profitable for a significant part of the period, as shown in Figure 10-9. This chart is important notably because it gives a more detailed view of the strategy, in terms of potential opportunity as well as risk. As we indicated, a significant

[23] Note that we decided to close the position the same day in this particular example, but in reality, we could choose any other stop—for example, a percentage-based stop. Along the same lines, the threshold of 1 percent is entirely variable and should be experimented with.

[24] Again we keep the position over a single trading day and trade each stock for one single share. Note that the test was run after December 1999—that is, after the recomposition of the index to include Microsoft (MSFT) and Intel (INTC).

TABLE 10-8

Name	No. Long Positions	No. Short Positions	Total Positions	P&L Long	P&L Short	P&L Total
MSFT	9	12	21	14.88	0.96	15.84
HD	12	20	32	4.69	8.6	13.29
GE	6	5	11	7.93	5.06	12.99
HON	11	12	23	3.82	5.15	8.97
KO	6	4	10	3.13	5.19	8.32
IP	11	22	33	3.42	2.53	5.95
UTX	5	12	17	1.33	4.41	5.74
DD	9	10	19	0.38	4.33	4.71
AA	7	13	20	3.51	1.17	4.68
MO	10	8	18	2.54	1.19	3.73
DIS	13	12	25	2.48	−0.15	2.33
JNJ	4	3	7	2.95	−0.75	2.2
XOM	1	2	3	−0.87	2.44	1.57
PG	3	2	5	4.31	−3.07	1.24
MCD	9	7	16	1.13	−1.58	−0.45
GM	4	17	21	1.09	−1.78	−0.69
SBC	4	10	14	−1.51	0.75	−0.76
C	21	27	48	0.75	−1.74	−0.99
WMT	6	15	21	2.01	−3.46	−1.45
BA	13	17	30	0.16	−1.87	−1.71
MMM	2	3	5	1	−3.07	−2.07
CAT	9	21	30	−1.57	−1	−2.57
MRK	3	4	7	−3.19	−0.4	−3.59
HWP	15	19	34	4.39	−11.11	−6.72
T	9	10	19	2.89	−9.91	−7.02
IBM	6	12	18	1.19	−8.45	−7.26
AXP	8	18	26	−5.73	−5.22	−10.95
EK	4	9	13	−6.5	−5.3	−11.8
INTC	13	22	35	1.5	−13.8	−12.3
JPM	11	10	21	−20.25	−3.57	−23.82

part of the period is above the horizontal axis showing that the accumulated profit was positive and for that reason the strategy is certainly worth more investigation. At the same time several elements raise a number of concerns. On two days—September 21, 1998, and January 13, 1998—the strategy is extremely profitable, which at the very least requires a closer look. In addition, from February to December 1999, the P&L is steadily declining, indicating that if the strategy has had some success in the past, it seems inadequate over that particular period, possibly due to changing market conditions. We will not pursue this discussion further here, but clearly there are a number of questions

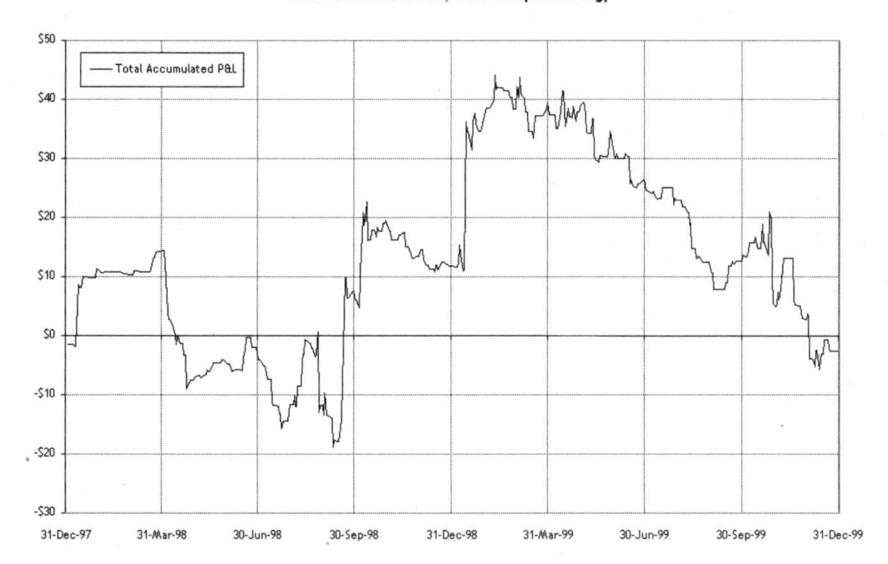

Figure 10-9 Close-to-Open P&L

that should be answered to gain a better understanding of the model and its limitations.

As we did earlier, it is also interesting here to perform a sensitivity analysis to get a better sense of the performance of the model under a wide range of assumptions. Figure 10-10 presents the accumulated P&L over the period for different values of threshold. The strategy is episodically profitable, notably if we increase the threshold. This is a very intuitive result in the sense that a higher amplitude for a close-to-open move is more likely to be considered by the market as "abnormal," giving rise to a correction very early.

In terms of risk management, the strategy presents the advantage of not creating any overnight exposure, but this advantage comes at a price. Because we place orders systematically on every stock in the Dow Jones every morning, we have no control over what will be executed. In other words, if we have a threshold of 2 percent and the entire market opens with a move of 2 percent, we will be executed on all orders at the same time, creating a possibly huge exposure on the same side. To get a sense of the probability of such a worst-case happening, Figure 10-11 gives the nominal exposure through the period with the same threshold of 2.5 percent.[25] There are indeed two days for

[25] This exposure is simply the algebraic sum of all the longs minus all the shorts on a given day.

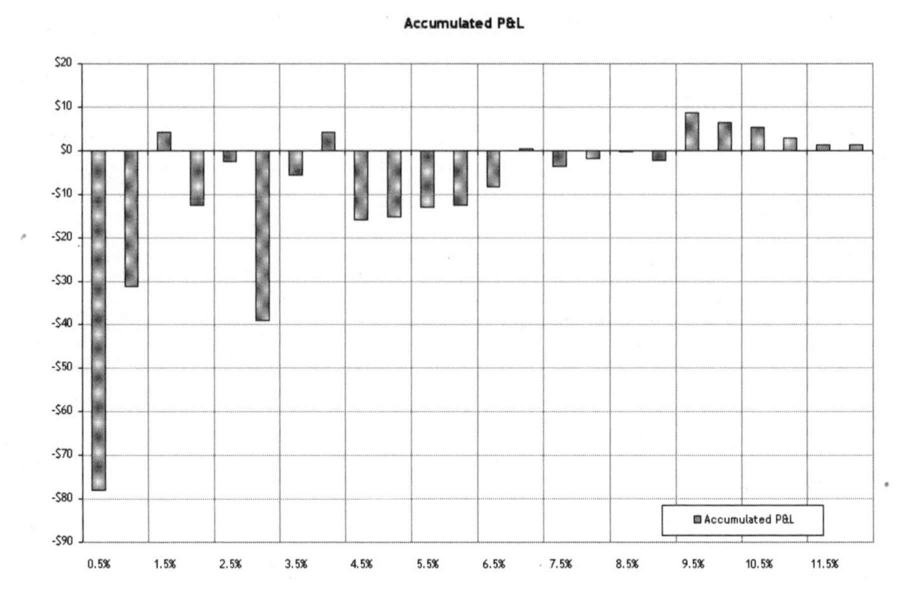

Figure 10-10 Close-to-Open Sensitivity

which the exposure is quite significant: September 8, 1998, and January 13, 1998. On September 8, 1998, in the midst of the Russian crisis, 20 out of 30 stocks opened above +2.5 percent, creating an exposure of $1,017 short. On January 13, 1998, the exact opposite scenario occurred, and 19 stocks opened below −2.5 percent compared to the previous close, generating a long of $1,163.[26] In terms of profit, however, both days ended up being rather reassuring. On September 8, 1998, the strategy lost only $0.52 because of a combination of profits and losses in the 20-stock short. On January 13, 1998, however, the position gained $24.82 because most of the stocks came back from the lows toward the end of the day. This was already one of the days we pinpointed earlier, so we know now what happened and why. In conclusion, even if both occurrences turned out to be nonevents from a risk perspective, they highlight the fragile nature of risk management in this particular model.[27]

---

[26] Note that the risk is not simply that we are executed on all the stocks; rather, that they all open on the same side—that is, there is a major shift in the entire market.

[27] One way to decrease the exposure would be, for example, to hedge it with Dow Jones futures over the course of the day.

Note that this model does not "cost" much in terms of market exposure if we exclude the two extreme days. Generally the level of exposure is remarkably low, notably when compared to the close-to-close arbitrage that we will consider shortly.

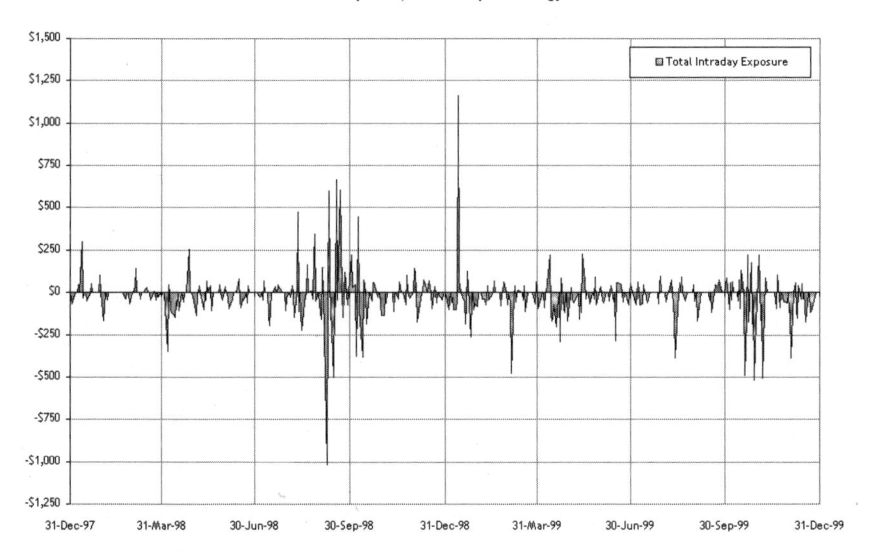

Figure 10-11 Close-to-Open Exposure

As a continuation of the same set of ideas, let's now consider a small variation of the model in which we trade the close-to-close return as opposed to the close-to-open return. This is much more classical and in fact it is also a popular model implemented under many shapes and forms. A quick examination of the histogram in Figure 10-12 of close-to-close returns for GE will give us a sense of what we should expect when comparing it to the close-to-open model. The distribution is much wider, indicating that close-to-close returns are much more volatile than close-to-open returns. For our purpose, which is to trade based on the magnitude of the return, this situation points toward a higher threshold in order to filter out more noise and try to keep only the relevant moves. However, for the sake of comparison, we consider still a 2.5 percent threshold, and Table 10-9 presents the results in a format identical to the close-to-open model. The total accumulated P&L is here +$32.71 ($137.87 for the long, −$105.16 for the short), for 3,395 positions (1,516 long, 1,879 short). Despite the positive result, the time diagram of the P&L as shown in Figure 10-13, reveals that the model is less often profitable on aggregate, and indeed some days it can be quite disturbing. As we recommended before, we would have to look into more details at specific dates, but we probably know the answers to several questions already. The strategy is exposed to a shift in the entire market above the threshold, and indeed this is exactly what happens in

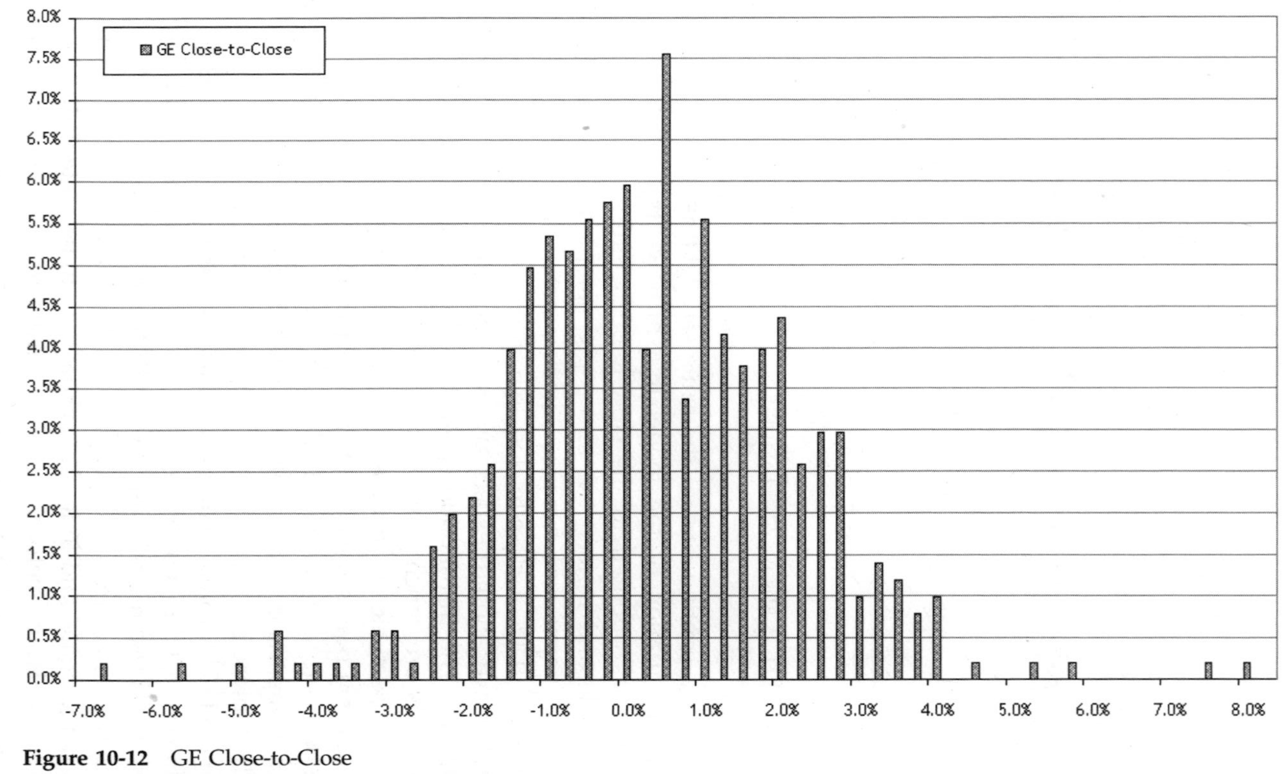

Figure 10-12 GE Close-to-Close
(*Source:* GE Compiled by author from Datastream data.)

TABLE 10-9

Name	No. Long Positions	No. Short Positions	Total Positions	P&L Long	P&L Short	P&L Total
JPM	72	−71	143	27.75	38.75	66.5
INTC	74	−99	173	23.95	9.25	33.2
SBC	56	−63	119	19.88	9.51	29.39
HWP	66	−89	155	7.14	21.55	28.69
PG	38	−47	85	−8.26	22.49	14.23
GM	49	−64	113	12.47	1.44	13.91
CAT	66	−70	136	2.82	9.6	12.42
MO	51	−50	101	−0.57	11.77	11.2
IP	69	−72	141	13.54	−9.02	4.52
HON	46	−59	105	1.3	1.84	3.14
WMT	58	−82	140	6.31	−4.45	1.86
XOM	25	−37	62	2.13	−1.34	0.79
AA	45	−73	118	14.18	−13.61	0.57
AXP	67	−81	148	1.83	−1.94	−0.11
MSFT	66	−90	156	23.26	−25.9	−2.64
IBM	43	−64	107	15.12	−18.48	−3.36
HD	47	−74	121	4.75	−8.92	−4.17
DIS	50	−63	113	5.34	−9.77	−4.43
MCD	43	−51	94	−5.75	−1.73	−7.48
T	51	−58	109	1.15	−8.64	−7.49
BA	53	−50	103	−3.83	−6.25	−10.08
KO	40	−45	85	−7.06	−5.05	−12.11
UTX	44	−58	102	−5.58	−7.89	−13.47
C	74	−80	154	−10.49	−3.33	−13.82
DD	59	−66	125	−1.51	−12.68	−14.19
GE	25	−47	72	5.97	−21.59	−15.62
EK	31	−39	70	4.69	−22.87	−18.18
MRK	40	−50	90	−6.34	−12.42	−18.76
MMM	38	−45	83	−5.87	−13.97	−19.84
JNJ	30	−42	72	−0.45	−21.51	−21.96

September 1998, giving rise to a large loss and an offsetting gain the next day. Similarly, in April 1999, the same type of event occurs, causing the same effects.

In terms of sensibility, the picture is somewhat better, as shown in Figure 10-14. For a large range of threshold values, the system shows profits, and those are somewhat higher than for a close-to-open model, which we know is a result of a higher volatility when considering close-to-close price movements. Interestingly, the above sensibility reveals another effect that is somewhat intuitive. If the threshold is too low, the model is not very successful because we

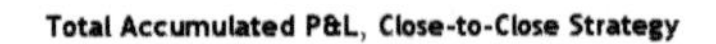

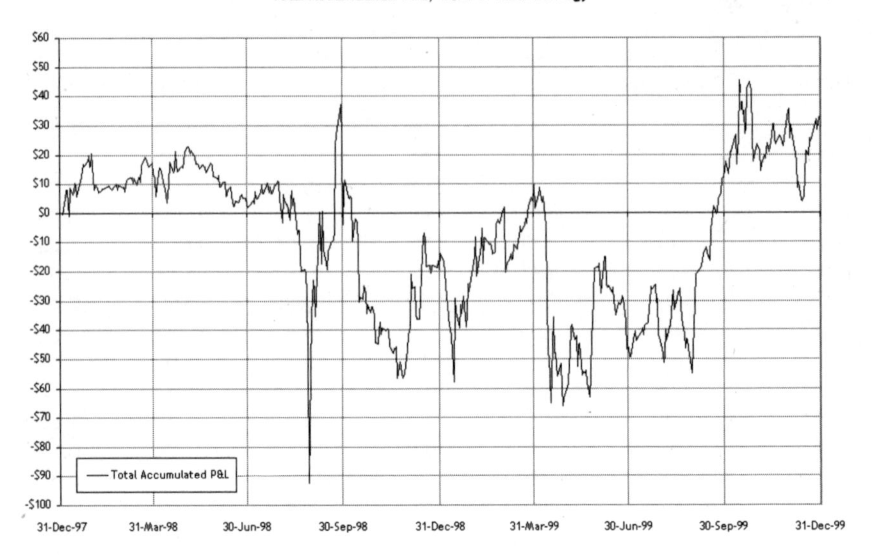

Figure 10-13 Close-to-Close P&L

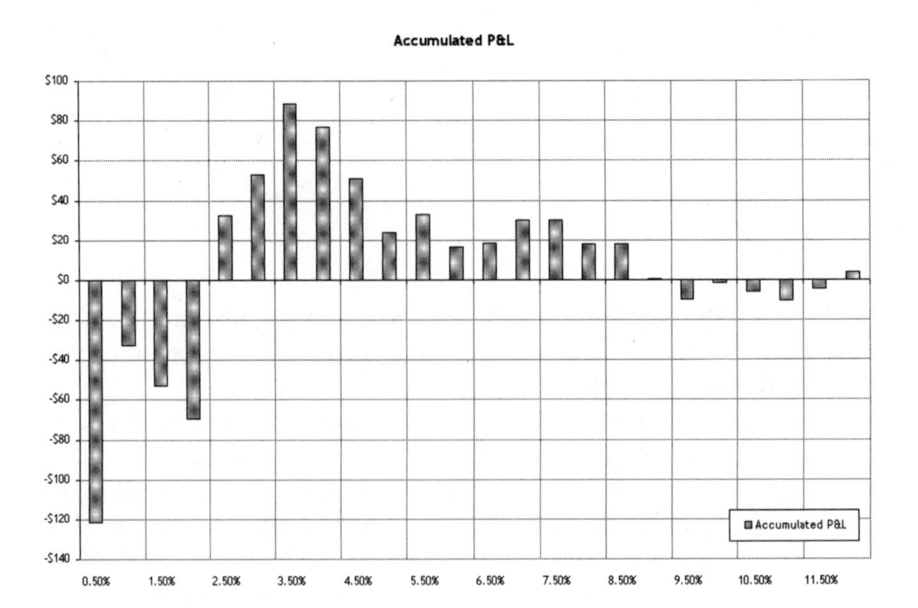

Figure 10-14 Close-to-Close Sensitivity

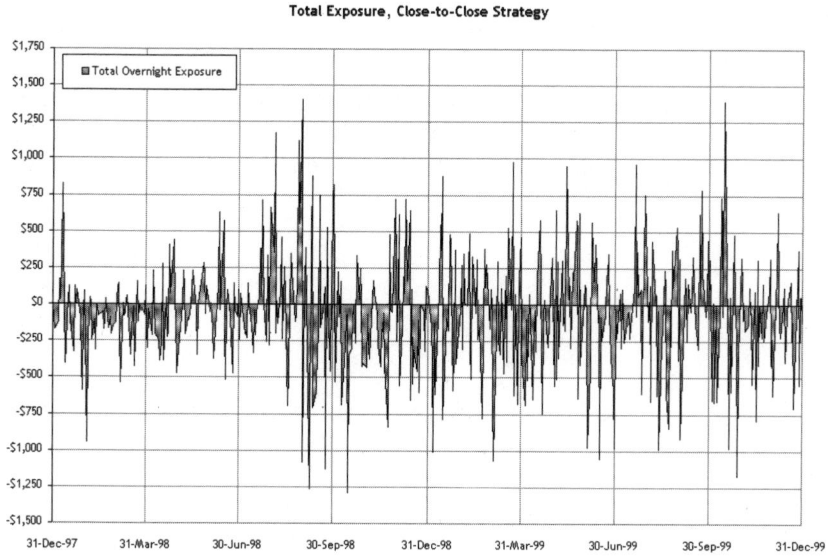

Figure 10-15 Close-to-Close Exposure

are essentially keeping too much "noise" in it. Between 2.5 and 9.5 percent, the model is successful, but it turns negative again above 10 percent. This is probably a result of the fact that we are then taking positions only on moves that have a strong informational content—that is, that will not correct any time soon. Typically, for example, these are the results of very good or bad news on the company. The price moves up or down by 10 percent or more, and it does not come back because the market is actually really pricing new information.

Finally, if we look at the exposure in Figure 10-15, we find a situation somewhat expected. On average, there is always one or more stocks moving by more than 2.5 percent; therefore, we are almost always in the market. Again the most important source of risk is a massive shift in the market whereby all stocks move by more than the threshold, and we see some of it happening around September 1998, for example.

CONCLUSION

It should be apparent after several examples of different nature that the opportunities attached to an uncertain convergence can be quite interesting and potentially very profitable. The management of such positions is in general centered primarily on the convergence exposure, with relatively little worry about traditional risks such as interest rates or dividends. In general, imagination and creativity are key in coming up with new opportunities, whereas experience and discipline are more than ever valuable assets in getting risk under control.

INDEX

About the Author

Stephane Reverre works for Leading Market Technologies, specializing in analytical tools for institutional investors. He is the former head of index arbitrage and quantitative trading for the Tokyo and later New York offices of Société Générale, one of the largest French banks and a leader in the field of equity derivative trading. A graduate of École Central in Paris as well as the Harvard Business School MBA program, Reverre has provided consulting services for software and trading companies and has published numerous articles on equity arbitrage in specialized magazines and publications.